Government and Markets

Toward a New Theory of Regulation

EDWARD J. BALLEISEN

Duke University

DAVID A. MOSS

Harvard Business School

CAMBRIDGE
UNIVERSITY PRESS

CAMBRIDGE UNIVERSITY PRESS
Cambridge, New York, Melbourne, Madrid, Cape Town, Singapore,
São Paulo, Delhi, Dubai, Tokyo

Cambridge University Press
32 Avenue of the Americas, New York, NY 10013-2473, USA

www.cambridge.org
Information on this title: www.cambridge.org/9780521118484

First published 2010

Printed in the United States of America

A catalog record for this publication is available from the British Library.

Library of Congress Cataloging in Publication data

Government and markets : toward a new theory of regulation / [edited by]
Edward Balleisen, David Moss.
p.   cm.
Includes bibliographical references and index.
ISBN 978-0-521-11848-4 (hardback)
1. Trade regulation.   2. Industrial policy.   I. Balleisen, Edward J.   II. Moss, David A., 1964–
HD3612.G68   2010
381.301–dc22   2009037726

ISBN 978-0-521-11848-4 Hardback

After two generations of emphasis on governmental inefficiency and the need for deregulation, we now see growing interest in the possibility of constructive governance, alongside public calls for new, smarter regulation.

Yet there is a real danger that regulatory reforms will be rooted in outdated ideas. As the financial crisis has shown, neither traditional market failure models nor public choice theory, by themselves, sufficiently inform or explain our current regulatory challenges. Regulatory studies, long neglected in an atmosphere focused on deregulatory work, is in critical need of new models and theories that can guide effective policymaking.

This interdisciplinary volume points the way toward the modernization of regulatory theory. Its essays by leading scholars move past predominant approaches, integrating the latest research about the interplay between human behavior, societal needs, and regulatory institutions. The book concludes by setting out a potential research agenda for the social sciences.

Edward J. Balleisen is associate professor of history at Duke University, where he teaches American business history and American legal history. He specializes in the evolving "culture of American capitalism" – the institutions, values, and practices that have both structured and constrained commercial activity. The author of *Navigating Failure: Bankruptcy and Commercial Society in Antebellum America* and *Scenes from a Corporate Makeover: Columbia/HCA and Healthcare Fraud, 1992–2001*, he has also published in numerous journals, including *Business History Review, Australian Journal of Legal History,* and *Reviews in American History*. In 2005, he was awarded the Howard D. Johnson Award for Excellence in Undergraduate Teaching. He received his Ph.D. in history from Yale University. He is currently working on a history of commercial fraud in the United States, focusing on organizational fraud against consumers and investors, from the early nineteenth century to the present.

David A. Moss is the John G. McLean Professor at Harvard Business School, where he teaches in the business, government, and international economy area. Professor Moss's research focuses on economic policy and especially the government's role as a risk manager. He has published three books on these subjects: *Socializing Security: Progressive-Era Economists and the Origins of American Social Policy* (1996), *When All Else Fails: Government as the Ultimate Risk Manager* (2002), and *A Concise Guide to Macroeconomics: What Managers, Executives, and Students Need to Know* (2007). Professor Moss is the founder of the Tobin Project, a nonprofit research organization, and a member of the National Academy of Social Insurance. Recent honors include the Robert F. Greenhill Award, the Editors' Prize from the *American Bankruptcy Law Journal,* the Student Association Faculty Award for outstanding teaching at the Harvard Business School, and the American Risk and Insurance Association's Annual Kulp-Wright Book Award for the "most influential text published on the economics of risk management and insurance." He received his Ph.D. from Yale University in 1992.

Contents

v

Acknowledgments

Named for Nobel laureate James Tobin (1918–2002) and modeled after earlier efforts to link scholars and lawmakers, the Tobin Project seeks to influence public debate by reaching simultaneously outward to connect with the policy community and inward to shape debate within the academic community.

The Tobin Project's Government and Markets Initiative is focused on the economic role of the state and, in particular, on questions of when and how regulation functions best. The Project aims with this work to increase understanding about the role of government in facilitating a healthy economy and society.

This volume is one product of those efforts.

The scholars who contributed the succeeding chapters first met as a group at a 2008 Tobin Project conference with the same title and purpose as this book – to reinvigorate the study of regulation and help foster new theories and strategies for our challenging times. The conference of some sixty scholars and policymakers was held at the White Oak Conference and Residency Center in Florida with the generous support of the Howard Gilman Foundation and the Ford Foundation. White Oak is the centerpiece of the Howard Gilman Foundation's efforts to promote new networks and new thinking on domestic and international issues of current and continuing concern. We gratefully acknowledge the members of the board of the Howard Gilman Foundation and Katherine McFate at the Ford Foundation for their encouragement and participation.

This effort has depended in no small measure on the Tobin Project's Board of Directors, as well as the Tobin Project's financial supporters, whose generosity reflects their faith in the power of ideas. The work of several members of the Tobin Project's staff was indispensable to both the conference and the completion of this volume. Alison Damaskos and Laura Einhorn helped organize the 2008 regulation conference, whereas John Cisternino, Rebecca Chang, and Sage Trombulak assisted greatly with the editorial process. As a research Fellow, Jessica Leight helped us formulate our early regulation efforts. It is wonderful to see her involvement in this volume.

We are grateful to Lewis Bateman and Scott Parris at Cambridge University Press for recognizing the contribution this book could make, to Professor Daniel Carpenter for introducing us to them, and to three anonymous reviewers for their suggestions, which have improved this volume.

Professors David Moss and Edward Balleisen championed this initiative. We are especially grateful to David for founding the Tobin Project and giving shape to this effort and to Ed for his leadership of our regulation team and for working with chapter authors to foster linkages among the contributions.

The network of scholars who have signed on to Tobin efforts has grown from a handful to almost 200. We thank each of them for participating and for bringing their colleagues and graduate students into the fold.

James Tobin noted in *Essays in Economics* that "the most important decisions a scholar makes are what problems to work on." Our deepest acknowledgment is to the spirit of public service that he left to all of us and to the seventeen scholars who took up his call in this book.

Mitchell Weiss
Executive Director, The Tobin Project

Contributors

Edward J. Balleisen is associate professor of history at Duke University, where he teaches American business history and American legal history, as well as a senior Fellow at the Kenan Institute for Ethics and an international Fellow of Oxford University's Centre for Corporate Reputation. He specializes in the evolving "culture of American capitalism" – the institutions, values, and practices that both structured and limited commercial activity. He is the author of *Navigating Failure: Bankruptcy and Commercial Society in Antebellum America* and *Scenes from a Corporate Makeover: Columbia/HCA and Healthcare Fraud, 1992–2001*. His work has been published in numerous journals, including *Business History Review, Australian Journal of Legal History*, and *Reviews in American History*. In 2005, he was awarded the Howard D. Johnson Award for Excellence in Undergraduate Teaching. The recipient of an ACLS Burkhardt Fellowship in 2009–2010, he is currently working on a history of commercial fraud in the United States, and especially organizational fraud against consumers and investors from the early nineteenth century to the present.

Yochai Benkler is the Berkman Professor of Entrepreneurial Legal Studies at Harvard and faculty codirector of the Berkman Center for Internet and Society. Before joining the faculty at Harvard Law School, he was Joseph M. Field '55 Professor of Law at Yale. He writes about the Internet and the emergence of networked economy and society, as well as the organization of infrastructure, such as wireless communications. In the 1990s, he played a role in characterizing the centrality of information commons to innovation, information production, and freedom in both its autonomy and democracy senses. In the 2000s, he worked more on the sources and economic and political significance of radically decentralized individual action and collaboration in the production of information, knowledge, and culture. His books include *The Wealth of Networks: How Social Production Transforms Markets and Freedom* (2006), which received the Don K. Price Award from the American Political Science Association for best book on science, technology, and politics and the Donald McGannon Award for best book on social and ethical relevance in communications policy research and which was named best business book about the future by Strategy & Business. His articles include "Overcoming Agoraphobia" (1997/98, initiating the debate over spectrum commons); "Commons as Neglected Factor of Information Production" (1998); "Free as the Air to Common Use" (1998, characterizing the role of the commons in information production and its relation to freedom); "From Consumers to Users" (2000, characterizing the need to preserve commons as a core policy goal across all layers of the information environment); "Coase's Penguin," or "Linux and the Nature of the Firm" (characterizing peer production as a basic phenomenon of the networked economy); and "Sharing Nicely" (2002, characterizing shareable goods and explaining sharing of material resources online). His work can be freely accessed at benkler.org. Benkler received the Electronic Frontier Foundation's Pioneer Award in 2007 and the Public Knowledge IP3 Award in 2006.

Daniel Carpenter is Allie S. Freed Professor of Government and director of the Center for American Political Studies (CAPS) in the faculty of arts and sciences at Harvard University. He conducts research in political history, regulation, and the history and political economy of pharmaceuticals. He blends historical and mathematical methods in his research, trying to capture the unique contributions of different perspectives. Professor Carpenter's first book – *The Forging of Bureaucratic Autonomy: Culture, Structure and Policy Innovation in Executive Agencies, 1862–1928* (Princeton, 2001) – examined the development of policymaking power by U.S. administrative agencies in the early twentieth-century United States. It received the Harold Lasswell Award and the Gladys Kammerer Award of the American Political Science Association and the Charles Epstein Award of the International Political Science Association. His research and writing has appeared or will appear in *Studies in American Political Development*, the *American Political Science Review*, the *American Journal of Political Science*, the *Journal of Politics*, the *New England Journal of Medicine*, and *Archives of Internal Medicine*, among other professional venues. Professor Carpenter has received a residential fellowship from the Center for Advanced Study in the Behavioral Sciences, Stanford, California (2003–2004); grants from the National Science Foundation (1999–2001, 2004–2008); the National

Endowment for the Humanities (2007–2010); the Robert Wood Johnson Foundation Investigator Award in Health Policy Research (2004–2006); and a fellowship from the Robert Wood Johnson Foundation Scholars in Health Policy Program (1998–2000). At Harvard, Professor Carpenter serves as faculty director of the Harvard College Health Policy Certificate Program. In 2007–2008, Professor Carpenter held a fellowship from the Guggenheim Foundation and is a residential Fellow at the Radcliffe Institute for Advanced Study.

Barry Eichengreen is the George C. Pardee and Helen N. Pardee Professor of Economics and Professor of Political Science at the University of California, Berkeley, where he has taught since 1987. He is also research associate of the National Bureau of Economic Research (Cambridge, Massachusetts) and research Fellow of the Centre for Economic Policy Research (London, England). In 1997–98 he was senior policy advisor at the International Monetary Fund. He is a Fellow of the American Academy of Arts and Sciences (class of 1997). He is the convener of the Bellagio Group of academics and economic officials. He has held Guggenheim and Fulbright Fellowships and has been a Fellow of the Center for Advanced Study in the Behavioral Sciences (Palo Alto) and the Institute for Advanced Study (Berlin). His books include *The European Economy Since 1945: Coordinated Capitalism and Beyond* (Princeton University Press, 2007), *Toward an East Asian Exchange Regime,* coedited with Duck-Koo Chung (Brookings Institution Press, 2007), and *Global Imbalances and the Lessons of Bretton Woods* (MIT Press, 2006). He was awarded the Economic History Association's Jonathan R.T. Hughes Prize for Excellence in Teaching in 2002 and the University of California at Berkeley Social Science Division's Distinguished Teaching Award in 2004. He is also the recipient of a *doctor honoris causa* from the American University in Paris.

Marc Allen Eisner is the Henry Merritt Wriston Chair of Public Policy and Professor of Government at Wesleyan University. Eisner is author or coauthor of six books on topics ranging from the changing role of economic analysis in antitrust policy to the impact of World War I mobilization on interwar state-building. His most recent book is *Governing the Environment* (2007). His current research focuses on the integration of public regulation and association-based and standards-based self-regulation in environmental protection.

Neil Fligstein is the Class of 1939 Chancellor's Professor in the Department of Sociology at the University of California, Berkeley. He is also the director of the Center for Culture, Organization, and Politics at the Institute of Industrial Relations. His main research interests lie in the fields of economic sociology, organizational theory, political sociology, and the sociology of work. He has been interested in developing and using a sociological view of how new social institutions emerge, remain stable, and are transformed to study a wide variety of seemingly disparate phenomena including the history of the large American corporation and the construction of a European legal and political system. He has used this framework to create a more general view of how markets and states are mutually constitutive and has applied this framework to trying to make sense of how global markets work. He is the author of numerous books and papers, *The Architecture of Markets* (Princeton University Press, 2001, winner of the Zelizer Award for the best book in Economic Sociology, Economic Sociology Section, American Sociological Association). He has just finished a book on Europe entitled *Euroclash: The EU, European Identity, and the Future of Europe* (Oxford University Press, 2008). The central theme of the book is to document how European integration in the past twenty years has created a partial integration of European societies along political, economic, but most importantly social lines.

Tony Freyer is University Research Professor of History and Law at the University of Alabama. In 1992 he received the university's Burnum Distinguished Faculty Award. His books include *Forums of Order* (1979), *Harmony and Dissonance: The Swift and Erie Cases in American Federalism* (1981) (Citation of Merit, Wilkes-Barre Law and Library Association and Association of the Bar of the City of New York, 2008), *The Little Rock Crisis* (1984), *Justice Hugo L. Black and the Dilemma of American Liberalism* (1990), *Hugo L. Black and Modern America* (1990), *Regulating Big Business: Antitrust in Great Britain and America, 1880–1990* (1992), *Producers versus Capitalists: Constitutional Conflict in Antebellum America* (1994), (with Timothy Dixon) *Democracy and Judicial Independence: A History of Alabama's Federal Courts* (1995), *Defending Constitutional Rights: Frank M. Johnson* (2001), *Antitrust and Global Capitalism, 1930–2004* (2006), *Little Rock on Trial Cooper v. Aaron and School Desegregation* (2007) (J.G. Ragsdale Book Award 2008 and an "Outstanding Academic Book 2008" from *Choice Magazine*). He has also written numerous articles, including "Cooper v. Aaron (1958): A Hidden Story of Unanimity and Division," winner of the Hughes-Gossett Award, *Journal of Supreme Court History* (2008). Professor Freyer was a

Harvard-Newcomen Postdoctoral Fellow at the Harvard Business School in 1975–76 and a research Fellow at the Charles Warren Center at Harvard in 1981–82. He has been a Senior Fulbright Scholar at the London School of Economics and Political Science (1986) and in Australia (1993). During 1995–96 he held an Abe Fellowship from the Center for Global Partnership and Social Science Research Council to study antitrust in Japan. In spring 2000, he held the Fulbright Distinguished Chair in American Studies at the University of Warsaw, Poland.

Mary O. Furner is professor of history at the University of California, Santa Barbara, where she teaches undergraduate and graduate courses in nineteenth- and twentieth-century United States history, history of social thought, history of public policy, the progressive tradition, and inequality in the United States. Her research examines the ways that social thinkers understand and represent relations between changing the state, society, and market and how social and economic investigation influences public policy; she is also interested in the periodic fracturings and reconstructions of U.S. liberalism, civic culture, and public philosophy. Her first book, *Advocacy and Objectivity: A Crisis in the Professionalization of American Social Science, 1865–1905*, received the Frederick Jackson Turner Prize of the Organization of American Historians and the C. Wright Mills Prize of the Society for the Study of Social Problems. Her work has appeared in various journals and collections, including her chapters in *The State and Social Investigation in Britain and the United States* (coedited with Michael Lacey) and *The State and Economic Knowledge: The American and British Experience* (coedited with Barry Supple). She has held research fellowships from the National Endowment for the Humanities and the Woodrow Wilson International Center for Scholarship. Her article titled, "Structure and Virtue in United States Political Economy," in the *Journal of the History of Economic Thought* (2005) was the Distinguished Lecture for the History of Economics Society in 2004. She held the Fulbright Distinguished Chair in American Studies at the Johann Wolfgang Goethe University in Frankfurt, Germany, in the summer semester, 2007. She is writing a book titled *The Public and Its Limits: Statism and Anti-Statism in the U.S. Political Tradition, 1870–1950*.

Michael Greenstone is the 3M Professor of Environmental Economics in the Department of Economics at the Massachusetts Institute of Technology. He also is a Research Associate at the National Bureau of Economic Research (NBER) and a Nonresident Senior Fellow at Brookings. His research is focused on estimating the costs and benefits of environmental quality. He has worked extensively on the Clean Air Act and examined its impacts on air quality, manufacturing activity, housing prices, and infant mortality to assess its costs and benefits. He is currently engaged in a large-scale project to estimate the economic costs of climate change. Other current projects include examinations of the benefits of the Superfund program; the economic and health impacts of indoor air pollution in Orissa, India; individuals' revealed value of a statistical life; the impact of air pollution on infant mortality in developing countries; and the costs of biodiversity. Greenstone is also interested in the consequences of government regulation, more generally. He is conducting or has conducted research on the effects of federal antidiscrimination laws on black infant mortality rates, the impacts of mandated disclosure laws on equity markets, and the welfare consequences of state and local subsidies given to businesses that locate within their jurisdictions. He is a member of the Environmental Economics Advisory Committee of EPA's Science Advisory Board, and his research has been funded by the NSF, NIH, and EPA. In 2004, Professor Greenstone received the 12th Annual Kenneth J. Arrow Award for Best Paper in the Field of Health Economics. He is currently an editor of the *Review of Economics and Statistics.*

Jessica Leight is a Ph.D. candidate in economics and presidential Fellow at the Massachusetts Institute of Technology and recently received her M.Phil. in economics at Oxford University as a Rhodes Scholar. Her research centers on development economics and political economy; other recent publications focus on trade policy in Latin America and intra-household allocation in China.

David A. Moss is the John G. McLean Professor at Harvard Business School, where he teaches in the business, government, and the international economy unit. Professor Moss's research focuses on economic policy and especially the government's role as a risk manager. He has published three books on these subjects: *Socializing Security: Progressive-Era Economists and the Origins of American Social Policy* (Harvard University Press, 1996), which traces the intellectual and institutional origins of the American welfare state; *When All Else Fails: Government as the Ultimate Risk Manager* (Harvard University Press, 2002), which explores the government's pivotal role as a risk manager in policies ranging from limited liability and bankruptcy law to social insurance and federal disaster relief; and *A Concise Guide to Macroeconomics: What Managers, Executives, and Students Need to Know* (Harvard Business School Press, 2007), a primer on macroeconomics and macroeconomic policy. In addition to these books, Moss has published numerous articles, book chapters, and case studies, mainly in the fields of institutional and policy history, financial history, political economy, and comparative social policy. Professor Moss is the founder of the Tobin Project, a nonprofit research organization, and a member of the National Academy of Social Insurance. Recent honors include the Robert F. Greenhill Award, the Editors' Prize from the *American Bankruptcy Law Journal*, the Student Association Faculty Award for outstanding teaching at the Harvard Business School, and the American Risk and Insurance Association's Annual Kulp-Wright Book Award for the "most influential text published on the economics of risk management and insurance."

Mary Oey is the Lake Conservator for Houghton Library of Harvard College Library and previously served as the Conservator of Music Manuscripts at the Morgan Library & Museum in New York.

Mary A. O'Sullivan is an associate professor in the Department of Management at the Wharton School of the University of Pennsylvania. She has been employed in that capacity since July 2005 and was previously an Associate Professor of Strategy and Management at INSEAD in Fontainebleau, France. Her broad research interests include political economy, business, and economic history as well as international business. In 2000 she published a book entitled *Contests for Corporate Control: Corporate Governance and Economic Performance in the United States and Germany* with Oxford University Press, and she has also written many journal articles on corporate governance. She is currently working on her second book, this one on securities markets and economic development and tentatively entitled *Bonding and Sharing Corporate America: The U.S. Securities Markets, Industrial Dynamics, and Corporate Development, 1885–1930*.

Monica Prasad is associate professor of sociology at Northwestern University and faculty Fellow in the Institute for Policy Research. Her book *The Politics of Free Markets* (University of Chicago Press) won the Barrington Moore Award from the Comparative and Historical Sociology Section of the American Sociological Association.

Joseph E. Stiglitz is University Professor at Columbia University and chair of Columbia University's Committee on Global Thought. He is also the cofounder and executive director of the Initiative for Policy Dialogue at Columbia. In 2001, he was awarded the Nobel Prize in economics for his analyses of markets with asymmetric information. Stiglitz was a member of the Council of Economic Advisers (CEA) from 1993–95, during the Clinton Administration, and served as CEA chairman from 1995–97. He then became chief economist and senior vice president of the World Bank from

1997–2000. Recognized around the world as a leading economic educator, he has written textbooks that have been translated into more than a dozen languages. His most recent book, *The Three Trillion Dollar War*, was published by W. W. Norton in March 2008.

Elizabeth Warren is the Leo Gottlieb Professor of Law at Harvard University. She has written eight books and more than a hundred scholarly articles dealing with credit and economic stress. Her latest two books, *The Two-Income Trap* and *All Your Worth*, were both on national best-seller lists. She has been principal investigator on empirical studies funded by the National Science Foundation and more than a dozen private foundations. Warren was the chief advisor to the National Bankruptcy Review Commission, and she was appointed by Chief Justice Rehnquist as the first academic member of the Federal Judicial Education Committee. She currently serves as a member of the Commission on Economic Inclusion established by the Federal Deposit Insurance Corporation (FDIC), and as the chairwoman of the TARP Congressional Oversight Panel. She also serves on the steering committees of the Tobin Project and the National Bankruptcy Conference. *Time* named her one of the 100 most influential people in the world for 2009. The *National Law Journal* has repeatedly named Professor Warren one of the Fifty Most Influential Women Attorneys in America, and *SmartMoney* magazine recently named her one of the SmartMoney 30 for 2008.

Donald Wittman is a professor of economics at the University of California, Santa Cruz. He uses the tools of economics (competition, equilibrium, optimization, and game theory) to explore a wide variety of subjects, including law (torts, contracts, takings, litigation, and the good Samaritan rule), democratic politics, theocracy, international relations (war, the size of nations, and arms control verification), and purely economic topics (contests and mechanism design). His book, *The Myth of Democratic Failure*, was the winner of the American Political Science Association Best Book in Political Economy Award for 1994–1996. The *Oxford Handbook of Political Economy*, coedited with Barry Weingast, and *Economic Foundations of Law and Organization* were published in 2006. He has published more than fifty journal articles and numerous book chapters.

Introduction

Edward Balleisen and David Moss

After more than a generation of deregulation and a presidential declaration that the "era of big government is over," the political pendulum has apparently begun to swing back toward regulation. Calls for effective government action, long subdued, have grown louder and more numerous. The provocations are not hard to find: the financial crisis first and foremost, but also accounting scandals at some of the nation's largest corporations (Enron, WorldCom, etc.); lead-tainted toys from China; *E. coli* outbreaks in the domestic food supply; collapsing levees and bridges; rising global temperatures and the threat of fundamental climate change.

One might expect that American lawmakers, confronted by these many challenges, could turn to experts in the academy for guidance. Yet to a surprisingly large extent, the academic discussion has remained stuck in a deregulatory mindset, more focused on government failure than on the ingredients of government effectiveness or success. As a result, there is a real danger that the new round of regulation will be rooted not in new research and new thinking, but rather in old ideas that are conveniently dusted off and reused in the absence of anything better.

This book represents an attempt by concerned academics to begin moving beyond old ideas about regulation – very old ones that informed earlier rounds of regulatory activity as well as more recent ones that drove a wave of deregulation beginning in the late 1970s. Now, with interest in regulation again on the rise, it is imperative that we not simply replay the past but move forward based on an improved understanding of the subject. New regulatory initiatives should be informed by past experience to be sure, but also by compelling critiques of the old approaches, as well as new insights about human behavior, regulatory capabilities, and societal needs. Such an ambition constitutes the essential motivation for this volume.

TOUCHSTONES OF THE PREVAILING VIEW

Within the social sciences – and particularly within economics, which as a discipline enjoys the greatest influence over public policy – thinking about regulation often starts with the notion of market failure. In an idealized economic market, individuals maximize the welfare of all simply by pursuing their own self-interest. Sometimes, however, in practice, the invisible hand of the market fails to optimize social welfare. The culprits, economists have taught us, are such things as public goods and externalities, which threaten to drive a wedge between individual and social welfare.

Particularly in the 1950s and 1960s, and even into the 1970s, social scientists often regarded market failure as a sufficient justification for government intervention. Negative externalities such as industrial pollution, for example, had to be regulated or taxed. More generally, regulators were understood to be engaged in an ongoing search and destroy mission, with market failure as the target.

By the late 1970s, social scientists had begun paying more careful attention to the problem of government failure, showing increasing sensitivity to the possibility that even in the presence of market failure policymakers could potentially do more harm than good in their attempts to cure market ills. Policymakers, we learned, were always liable to be captured by special interest groups or otherwise diverted from serving the public interest as a result of weak incentives or ineffective monitoring. And even those policymakers with the best of intentions – and incentives – could fail as a result of inadequate information. So-called command-and-control regulation was seen as particularly vulnerable to information deficiencies because it was thought to run roughshod over the price mechanism, the pivotal purveyor of information in well-functioning markets.

Although market failure remained an important and much-touted concept in the social sciences, government failure increasingly displaced market failure as a dominant subject of study. Article after article in the scholarly literature spotlighted government shortcomings and missteps and the scourge of unintended consequences. Indeed, as skepticism – even cynicism – began to displace optimism in academic thinking about government, pressure mounted in the policy arena for broad-based deregulation. Pushed forward by leading academics, from George Stigler to Alfred Kahn, the movement for deregulation reflected a profound shift in the nation's intellectual climate, a shift that was first evident within the university itself.

By the 1990s, the touchstones of the prevailing academic view of regulation, particularly in economics, included not only the old market failure framework, but also a new economic theory of politics rooted in rational-actor assumptions about individual decision making and interest group models of organized political activity. The term "regulation," meanwhile, had become increasingly associated with words like "heavy handed" and "command and control," a phrase which itself had taken on highly negative connotations, especially during the waning days of the Soviet Union and the collapse of communism.

TOWARD A NEW VIEW

The goal here is not to try to demolish the existing intellectual foundation for academic thinking about regulation, but rather to try to strengthen and add to it, fixing a few cracks and building from there. The essays that follow cut across the social sciences, reflecting the perspectives of economists and political scientists, legal scholars and sociologists, historians and professors of business administration. We have organized them under three broad headings: "Beyond Market Failure," "Beyond the Economic Theory of Politics," and "Beyond Command and Control." Each section aims to enrich our understanding of regulation and to suggest promising directions for research, based in part on new lines of scholarship in related areas.

BEYOND MARKET FAILURE

The concept of market failure, of course, like the possibility that regulatory policies might not achieve their intended goals, remains a powerful framework for thinking about regulation in many contexts, a point reinforced by Joseph Stiglitz's essay. Stiglitz begins by identifying a series of contemporary market failures, but then moves on to highlight two additional rationales for regulation, market irrationality and distributive justice. Implicitly drawing on his extensive experience as a public official, he argues that vigorous regulatory governance – when well conceived and implemented – can effectively redress these shortcomings of the market. Like Stiglitz, the economist Michael Greenstone structures his analysis around the capacity of government to respond effectively to market failure, in this case the Environmental Protection Agency's Superfund program, which seeks to clean up industrial sites contaminated by toxic waste. Greenstone reminds us that the success or failure of particular regulatory work remains an empirical question, insists that social scientists can do a much better job of marshaling an evidentiary basis for their assessments of regulatory outcomes, and encourages policymakers to adopt an experimental mindset when framing regulatory interventions.

For all the conceptual power of market failure, it has never served as the sole justification for regulatory action, even though much recent scholarship has tended to ignore alternative regulatory purposes. As the historian Mary Furner observes in her assessment of key intellectual developments within the American regulatory tradition, Americans have frequently conceived of regulatory policy not simply as a palliative for occasional market weaknesses, but rather as an integral part of a broader social system that encompasses economic institutions and relationships. The sociologist Neil Fligstein pursues a similar line of reasoning as he surveys the European creation of a far more vigorous competition policy since the 1957 Treaty of Rome. In European regulatory politics, moves toward opening up continental markets have worked precisely because European political leaders have carefully linked them to generous social welfare policies, thereby ensuring social legitimacy for the process of economic liberalization.

The political scientist Daniel Carpenter explores yet another crucially important regulatory purpose – that of actually constituting market institutions in the first place. Using the case of post-World War II American pharmaceutical regulation as an evidentiary platform, Carpenter contends that effective regulation is often necessary to lay the groundwork for entire areas of exchange. Without regulatory policy that clearly articulates the rules of the economic game, Carpenter demonstrates, many economic sectors will lack sufficient confidence to drive investment and sustain high levels of consumption.

BEYOND THE ECONOMIC THEORY OF POLITICS

There can be no question that social scientists have made enormous progress applying economic assumptions and tools to the study of politics. The world looks very different once one views it through a prism of unwavering, rational calculation; and the academics who have adopted this prism have shown that political actors at all levels often aim to maximize their own self-interest, rather than the public interest, in their public decision making. The contributions to the second section of the book all grapple with the still-dominant presuppositions of rational/public choice, identifying a number of important conceptual and evidentiary limitations.

The economist Donald Wittman shares many of the key theoretical assumptions of this approach to the study of politics and policy. But his essay maintains that many scholars have poorly applied neoclassical economic theory to politics, substantially understating the power of competition in political markets and, as a result, overstating the frequency with which concentrated interests frustrate the general welfare. In her wide-ranging review of the public choice literature, economist Jessica Leight offers a different critique of the dominant scholarly view of regulation, arguing that many of its leading advocates have overreached, in some cases pushing their conclusions well beyond available supporting evidence. Consistent with Leight's critical assessment, David Moss and Mary Oey highlight three historical cases (passage of the Voting Rights Act, Medicare, and Superfund) in which the general interest actually trumped special interests. In each of these pivotal instances of American policymaking, Moss and Oey note, the power of the press to inform and mobilize a broad electorate substantially blunted the capacity of special interests to dictate policy formulation.

Drawing on social network theory, the legal scholar Yochai Benkler offers a fascinating but quite different perspective, suggesting that traditional economic assumptions – particularly those regarding self-interested rationality – need not be the starting point for all models of political decision making. Cooperative models of social and political behavior, Benkler argues, may prove just as powerful and also far more realistic (i.e., more consistent with evidence on human behavior) than the traditional models that privilege individualistic pursuit of narrowly defined economic gain. Benkler also shifts our attention to questions of institutional design, noting both how policymakers can seek to construct and nurture responsive regulatory mechanisms, and how they might avoid weakening socially useful cooperative ventures that have evolved in recent decades.

BEYOND COMMAND AND CONTROL

Moving from theory to practice, the essays that comprise the third and longest section of the book look beyond the standard caricature of regulation as heavy handed, command-and-control style intervention. Together, these papers highlight the remarkable diversity of regulatory tools available to public officials, while hinting at their comparative advantages and disadvantages as responses to particular kinds of regulatory challenges.

The first four chapters – by the business scholar Mary O'Sullivan, the sociologist Monica Prasad, the legal scholar Elizabeth Warren, and the economist Barry Eichengreen – examine the viability of some well-worn regulatory tools against the backdrop of especially important public policy challenges. O'Sullivan explores the complex task of reworking the regulation of corporate governance, raising searching questions about the utility of shareholder value as a sufficient lodestar for policymaking in this area. Prasad turns our attention to tax-based regulation, a mechanism that governments have long used to constrain disfavored economic activities, and considers its logic, promise, and limits, particularly in the context of pressing environmental challenges. Warren investigates the continuing potential relevance of standard administrative approaches to regulatory rule making and oversight, asking whether the Consumer Product Safety Commission – a traditional regulatory agency of sorts, but with a relatively light touch – should serve as a model for a new commission to regulate retail-level financial services, including both consumer and mortgage lending. Eichengreen identifies several causes of the mortgage debt crisis that began to roil financial markets in the late summer of 2007, and then makes a case for tightened regulation of American banks, which he sees as continuing to serve as linchpins of the new, globalized financial system.

The final set of essays critiques the common impulse to draw excessively stark distinctions between public and private regulatory governance. Drawing on an increasingly rich literature within political science, sociology, and law, the historian Edward Balleisen explores a wide range of rule making and oversight mechanisms that depend on nonstate actors, often from within the business community itself. Generally portrayed as the polar opposite of traditional command and control, these strategies of private regulatory governance can prove to be more powerful and effective than its many critics presume. But Balleisen stresses that such outcomes depend heavily on a framework of coregulation, in which meaningful government monitoring and a credible threat of government regulation stand behind private regulatory efforts. Similarly focused on quasi-private regulation, the legal historian Tony Freyer identifies legal action as a potent regulatory tool, particularly in the area of antitrust and tort. As federal antitrust suits became less frequent and as enforcement of many health and safety regulations weakened during the age of deregulation, he shows that private antitrust and tort actions quickly filled the void. Whereas Freyer's article suggests that widely shared popular support for regulatory action abhors a vacuum, the essay by the political scientist Marc Eisner probes the complicated implications of deregulation as a regulatory strategy. Focusing on the dismantling of many federal regulatory controls in transportation and energy during the 1970s and 1980s, Eisner illustrates how government rule making has continued to powerfully shape these supposedly now unregulated sectors of the economy.

A NEW AGENDA FOR RESEARCH

The essays presented here, then, offer several compelling directions for rethinking overarching approaches to regulatory policy in the United States, alongside numerous concrete suggestions for legislative and administrative policymakers. Initially written for a February 2008 conference on the past, present, and future of the American regulatory state, the volume's contributions also point toward an interdisciplinary research agenda for a new generation of scholarship about regulatory strategies and institutions. The authors by no means agree with each other on every issue about regulatory policy or the best way to conceptualize and study it. Nonetheless, their work collectively suggests the following elements of an emerging new perspective on regulation:

a) Vibrant capitalism is dependent upon, and even constituted by, sensible regulation. There is no market without regulation that defines property rights, sets standards for business practices, and creates widespread confidence in the fairness of the economic rules of the game. To imagine the world in terms of preexisting markets and intrusive government is to conjure up an unhelpful fiction.

b) The still prevailing academic analysis of regulation, rooted in public choice and the economic theory of politics, has some key weaknesses. In particular:

- The public officials charged with making and enforcing regulatory law are not always driven predominantly by a savvy pursuit of self-interest, narrowly defined. Legislators and regulators also seek to protect/enhance their reputations. They at least sometimes focus on what they perceive to be the broader common good. And their perceptions of that public interest are significantly influenced by prevailing narrative frames about the appropriate purposes of government.

- Voters are not always "rationally ignorant" about regulatory issues. Social and political movements can raise public awareness. Voters also do not universally cast their ballots with regard to their self-interest, narrowly conceived. Like policymakers, they also have a deeper sense of the broader common good, shaped not only by their own experience but also by popular ideas about the legitimate roles of government.

- Economic actors – managers, consumers, workers, investors, lenders, insurers, etc. – do not always behave as strictly rational calculators of interest, whether their aims involve narrow self-interest or the broader public good, and whether they possess solid information about economic conditions or face circumstances of uncertainty. Sometimes they act according to the wisdom (or madness) of crowds, and sometimes their choices are powerfully shaped by subtle contextual circumstances that may be beyond their control or even beyond their awareness.

- For many individuals, the pull of social cooperation frequently outweighs selfish impulses. For such cooperatively inclined people, efforts by policymakers to create monetary incentives can backfire, diminishing intrinsic motivations.

c) Achieving greater allocative or productive efficiency is not the only legitimate goal for regulatory initiatives. Concern for distributional outcomes and for the health of democratic political institutions must also have a place in shaping regulatory policy.

d) The institutional matrix of regulation rarely involves only government regulators and regulated businesses. Instead, a broad array of third parties, including commercial counterparties, industry associations, nongovernmental organizations, quasi-public institutions of self-regulation, and even the press, play important roles in the regulatory process with regard to both standard-setting and enforcement.

e) Regulatory policymakers need to appreciate the vast array of regulatory tools available to them. These tools range from taxation, to enforcement of civil liability for tort, to mandates for information disclosure, to the prohibition of particular goods or services, to the detailed rule making and inspection regimes characteristic of "command-and-control," to the delegation of regulatory oversight to self-regulatory bodies. In most regulatory contexts, the key issue is how to select the optimal mix of such tools.

Each of these propositions, of course, leaves crucial questions unanswered, especially from the vantage point of a policymaker struggling to respond to some regulatory dilemma. What circumstances facilitate concern for the public good, rather than the impulse to seize bureaucratic turf or feather one's nest? In which contexts do economic actors predictably act irrationally or prefer social cooperation to self-regarding strategies? How does one sensibly balance regulatory purposes against one another? In what situations do particular regulatory strategies tend to work well or poorly?

The essays that follow only begin to answer these questions while identifying other useful points of departure for additional inquiry. This reality explains the book's subtitle. We see the volume as pointing the way toward a new conceptual framework for regulatory policy. Our hope is that social scientists interested in regulation will pursue the trails – the agenda – laid out in the pages ahead. In a brief conclusion, we flesh out the shape of that agenda, drawing on both the essays themselves and the conference discussions that they prompted, which focused on identifying the most important research questions that social scientists should be pursuing about the regulatory role of the state.

SECTION ONE

BEYOND MARKET FAILURE

ONE

Government Failure vs. Market Failure: Principles of Regulation

Joseph E. Stiglitz

The subject of regulation has been one of the most contentious, with critics arguing that regulations interfere with the efficiency of the market, and advocates arguing that well-designed regulations not only make markets more efficient but also help ensure that market outcomes are more equitable. As the economy plunged into a recession, with more than 3 million Americans already having lost their homes as this chapter goes to press and millions more likely to do so (unless the government intervenes more successfully than it has), and as the government spends hundreds of billions in bailouts to prevent the economic recession from growing worse, there is a growing consensus: There was a need for more government regulation. Even the high priest of laissez faire economics, Alan Greenspan, has admitted that he may have gone too far in believing that markets could be self-regulating.[1]

Responding to these calls – as if to close the barn door after all the horses have gotten out – the Federal Reserve has tightened some regulations. If it is the case that better regulations could have prevented, or even mitigated, the downturn, the country, and the world, will be paying a heavy price for the failure to regulate adequately. And the social costs are no less grave – as hundreds of thousands of Americans will not only have lost their homes but also their lifetime savings. Home ownership has long been thought of as

---

[1] There is a certain irony in all of this: One of the responsibilities of the Federal Reserve is to manage a key price in the economy, the short-term interest rate. Almost no one believes that this should be left totally to the market.

University Professor at Columbia University and chair of its Committee on Global Thought; chairman of the Brooks World Poverty Institute at Manchester University; and president of the Initiative for Policy Dialogue (on the Web at http://www.policydialogue.org). Financial support from the UNDP and Ford, Macarthur, Hewlett, and Rockefeller Brothers foundations is gratefully acknowledged. This article was prepared for the Tobin Project's conference on "Government and Markets: Toward a New Theory of Regulation," held February 1–3, 2008, in Yulee, Florida.

contributing to the strength of communities; with the share of home ownership falling, communities too will be weaker. The foreclosures will exacerbate the decline in housing prices, and property tax bases will erode – a further knock on effect of inadequate regulation.

The systemic effects of banks' bad lending have imposed high costs on our entire society. The collapse of stock market prices has put in jeopardy individual retirement savings. Constraints on credit availability are forcing firms into bankruptcy. Taxpayers are picking up a tab reaching into the hundreds of billions of dollars. Workers are losing their jobs (in the first eight months of 2008, net job loss exceeded 1.2 million), millions more are now worried that they too will be receiving pink slips any day soon, and millions more are working part time because they cannot find full-time work.

There is by now a long list of disasters that have occurred because of inadequate (or poorly designed) regulation. Several of these have been in the financial sector. Milton Friedman, the then high priest of market economics, succeeded in persuading Chile's dictator Augusto Pinochet to try unregulated banking. The ensuing banking crisis led to a deep recession, and it took the country two decades to pay off the bills. At the beginning of this decade, confidence in our financial markets was shaken by a series of scandals involving accounting (the accountants figured out how to apply the tricks they had learned to deceive tax authorities and investors as well) and analysts. Enron became the symbol of everything that was wrong with corporate America.

But though an inadequately regulated financial sector has had more than its fair share of problems, others have suffered as well from inadequate regulation. Failure to regulate air pollution led to London's pea soup smog, a threat to the health and well-being of Londoners. California's deregulation of electricity led Enron to engage in market manipulation, threatening both that state's high-tech industry and budget. The artificially induced scarcity (which advocates of deregulation tried to blame on existing environmental regulations) miraculously disappeared once market regulation was restored.[2]

When Upton Sinclair's novel *The Jungle*[3] depicted the terrible sanitary conditions in America's stockyards, Americans turned away from meat; and

---

[2] The list is not meant to be exhaustive: Houston shows what happens to a city when there is inadequate regulation of land use. Inadequate enforcement of antitrust laws has led to banks that are too big to fail – contributing to their excessive risk taking – and Microsoft's anticompetitive practices that arguably undermine innovative incentives by potential competitors, as they watched Microsoft squelch innovative rivals like Wordperfect, Netscape, and Realnetwork.

[3] Upton Sinclair, *The Jungle*, New York: WW Norton, 2002 (originally published by Doubleday, 1906).

the meat packing industry asked for government food safety regulation to restore confidence. When the Enron/WorldCom scandal eroded confidence in America's financial markets and accounting firms, there was again a demand for stronger regulation to restore confidence. Whether Sarbanes-Oxley, the bill that was passed to try to rectify the problems by improving regulation of accounting firms and strengthening corporate governance, went too far or not far enough may be debated, but what is not debatable is that such regulations were viewed, at least by many Americans, as essential for restoring confidence in America's markets, where scandal had touched every accounting firm, most of the major investment banks, and many of its leading corporations.

Today, America's air and water are cleaner – and Americans are living longer – because of environmental regulations. No one can imagine a world today without food, safety, and environmental regulations. The debate is only whether we have gone too far and whether we could have gotten the desired results at lower costs.

In this chapter, I want to outline the principles underlying the modern theory of regulation. Section I presents the rationale for regulation – why regulation is required. Section II discusses the forms that regulation can and should take. Section III applies these principles to three subjects of current concern: sovereign wealth funds, financial market regulation, and environmental regulations directed at greenhouse gases.

I. The General Theory of Regulation

The general theory of regulation begins with a simple question: Why is regulation needed? This is, in turn, divided into two subquestions: Why do markets by themselves not suffice? And if there is to be government intervention, why does it take the form of regulations?

a. The Need for Government Intervention

i. Conventional Market Failures

Adam Smith (it is widely believed) argued that markets by themselves are efficient.[4] He argued that individuals and firms in the pursuit of self-interest would be led, as if by an invisible hand, to actions that maximized general

---

[4] Actually, his analysis was far more subtle than modern free-market economists would have one believe.

well-being.[5] This argument has been used as the basis for allowing unfettered
free markets. (Smith himself was aware of the limitation of his arguments –
unlike his latter-day followers. For instance, he argued that businessmen
seldom get together without conspiring against the public interest through
the exercise of market power.)[6] Arrow and Debreu established the sense
in which that was true (*Pareto efficiency*, i.e., no one could be made better off without making someone else worse off) and the conditions under
which it was true (perfect competition, no externalities, no public goods).[7]
Subsequently, Greenwald and Stiglitz showed that whenever information is
imperfect or markets incomplete – that is, always – there is a presumption
that markets are not (constrained) pareto efficient.[8] As they put it, one of
the reasons the invisible hand often seems invisible is that it's not there.
Enron's and WorldCom's pursuit of their self-interest (greed) did not maximize societal well-being, nor, more recently, did America's financial sector's
pursuit of its self-interest. Indeed, the latter has led to a global meltdown.

The conclusion of this research is very clear: There are no theoretical
grounds for the belief that unfettered markets will, in general, lead to societal well-being. The notion that markets, by themselves, lead to efficient
outcomes has, in short, no theoretical justification: No one believes that
the conditions under which that statement is true are satisfied. Markets by
themselves produce too much of some things (those that generate pollution) and too little of others (basic research). As mentioned above, the last
experiment with free (unregulated) banking in Pinochet's Chile ended in
disaster. Today's global financial crisis, the result of deregulation and not
adopting new regulations to reflect the changing financial landscape, is far
more grave and longer lasting.

---

[5] "By directing that industry in such a manner as its produce may be of greatest value, he
  intends only his own gain, and he is in this, as in many other cases, led by an invisible
  hand to promote an end which was no part of his intention." A. Smith, *An Inquiry into
  the Nature and Causes of the Wealth of Nations*, Chicago: University of Chicago Press, 1976
  (originally published 1776).

[6] Ibid. "People of the same trade seldom meet together, even for merriment and diversion,
  but the conversation ends in a conspiracy against the public, or in some contrivance to
  raise prices."

[7] See K.J. Arrow, "An Extension of the Basic Theorems of Classical Welfare Economics,"
  Proceedings of the Second Berkeley Symposium on Mathematical Statistics and Probability,
  J. Neyman, ed., Berkeley: University of California Press, 1951, pp. 507–532, and Gerard
  Debreu, *The Theory of Value*, New Haven: Yale University Press, 1959.

[8] See Bruce Greenwald and J. E. Stiglitz, "Externalities in Economies with Imperfect Information and Incomplete Markets," *Quarterly Journal of Economics*, 1986, Vol. 101, No. 2
  (May), pp. 229–64. Reprinted in *Economic Theory and the Welfare State*, Nicholas Barr
  (ed.), Cheltenham, U.K.: Edward Elgar, 2000.

Without adequate regulation, firms like Microsoft would engage in abusive anticompetitive practices, undermining efficiency and incentives to innovate. Without good zoning and environmental regulations, a smelly and noisy factory might move next door to a residential area, depressing house values.

Some advocates of free markets take it as a matter of faith that the magnitude of the inefficiencies are small (though no one has suggested how one might prove that); but more commonly advocates of free markets take it as a matter of faith that government attempts to correct market failures by and large make things worse. To be sure, there are examples of badly designed government regulations, but the disasters associated with unfettered markets at least provide a prima facie case for the desirability of *some* regulation.[9]

Many economists have donned the hat of a political scientist, arguing that political processes are inherently inefficient. But there is no general theorem asserting the inevitability of "government failures" outweighing market failures, and no persuasive "counterfactual" analysis contrasting what a world without regulation might look like as compared to the current regime.

Some advocates of free markets appeal to Ronald Coase's conjecture (sometimes called Coase's theorem). Coase admitted that markets directly could not handle externalities well, but he argued that, even in the presence of externalities, individuals can *bargain* themselves to an efficient outcome as long as there are clearly defined property rights. Those who are harmed by air pollution could bribe the polluters not to pollute. So long as they valued clean air more than the cost that the polluters would bear by not polluting, no pollution would be produced. But such claims cannot be supported as long as there is imperfect information (e.g., concerning an individual's valuation of the external costs) or transaction costs, as there always are. Bargaining is costly. Try to imagine how all consumers in the world could get together, assess the value to each of clean air, collect money, and pay the polluters not to pollute; even ascertaining how much each polluter would require in compensation would be an impossible task. Indeed, one of the standard arguments for regulation (including

---

[9] In addition, in financial markets, where it is the regulated sector (banking) that has so often been the source of the problem, some have argued that it is government regulation that is the source of the problem. What is true is that the interactions between the regulated and unregulated parts of this sector open up opportunities for regulatory arbitrage and present a special set of challenges for regulators.

using taxes as a form of regulation) is that it economizes on transaction costs.[10]

A variant of Coase's argument is that those injured should (be entitled to) sue those who are doing the injury. With a good tort legal system (including class-action suits), in which those who are injured can sue those causing harm, individuals will have appropriate incentives. Interestingly, conservatives (like those in the Bush Administration) argue both for less regulation and reduced capacity to recover damages. They sometimes have a valid argument against the legal system: As currently constituted, in many areas it provides excessive recovery – providing excessive incentives for care, reflected in defensive medicines – at the same time that in other areas it provides insufficient incentives (without class actions, the transactions costs are so large that recovery of damages is impossible). Ensuring that a firm does not pollute is, in fact, a public good. Ensuring that firms do not emit greenhouse gases is a *global* public good; citizens all over the world benefit.

More generally, the sums required to compensate for damage done to individuals may not provide appropriate incentives; by linking the two together, incentives are not in general optimized. Moreover, in many cases, there is no adequate monetary incentive: Someone whose child has died as a result of lead poisoning can never really be adequately compensated. Ex post compensation is not enough. We have to stop the bad behavior ex ante, if we can.

Other forms of market mechanisms, it is now realized, also are insufficient. One is reputation mechanisms. Firms might not cheat their customers even in the absence of regulations prohibiting such behavior, because they know if they do so customers will go elsewhere. Reputation mechanisms do help, but they do not ensure efficiency. Firms are often too shortsighted. A restaurant may reason it can make money today by cutting corners on the quality of food. Present profits are more important than the forgone future profits. This is especially true if it is located in a tourist area, where there are few repeat customers.

Regulations Can Thus Play an Important Role in Addressing Market Failures.

When markets fail to produce efficient outcomes there is a rationale for government intervention. There are several particular categories of market failures to which I want to call attention.

---

[10] There are some limited contexts in which Coase's conjecture might have some validity. One could imagine in a small meeting, assigning the air rights to nonsmokers. The smokers might be able to bribe the nonsmokers to accept the air pollution.

The first relate to externalities, where an individual or firm's actions have consequences for others for which he neither compensates nor is compensated. We have regulations designed to mitigate the extent of *externalities*. These include, for instance, zoning restrictions and environmental regulations.

A second is concerned with competition. We have regulations designed to maintain competition (restrictions on anticompetitive practices) and to ensure that in those situations where competition is not viable (the so-called natural monopolies) firms do not abuse their monopoly position (utilities regulations).

Several categories of regulation are related to problems of information. We have a large set of regulations aimed at protecting consumers (ensuring that the banks where they deposit their money are sufficiently sound, that food and products are safe, or that they are not taken advantage of by unscrupulous merchants, advertising, or lenders). Obviously, if information were perfect, individuals would not deposit their money in a bank that could not repay it; or individuals would not buy food that is unsafe. Disclosure requirements (forcing firms to reveal truthfully information about their products) are important, but the regulations go well beyond disclosure, for reasons that I explain below. There are two broad forms that such regulation takes.

One arises when government provides insurance. Private-sector contractual arrangements often have what would appear to be regulatory structures. A fire insurance firm requires that the insured install sprinklers. Sometimes, insurance companies use the price system, that is, they give a discount if sprinklers are installed. But sometimes they simply will not write the insurance policy if sprinklers are not installed. Many government regulations are similarly motivated: Government absorbs risk, and to reduce its risk exposure, imposes constraints; it provides flood and earthquake insurance – explicitly in some cases and implicitly in others (if an earthquake occurs, it knows that it cannot deny assistance to anyone) – and demands that houses be constructed to reduce the risk of loss. Because of moral hazard (when individuals are insured, they put less effort into reducing the likelihood of the insured against event occurring) – or even because of a failure to perceive accurately the magnitude of the risk[11] – individuals will take insufficient care. Government provides deposit insurance. Indeed, even when governments do not have explicit deposit insurance, they often bail out banks (as we see in the United States today) either because they worry about the

---

[11] See the discussion below.

systemic consequences of a bank failure or because of what are viewed as intolerable adverse effects on ordinary citizens.

The second category concerns what might be called certification. The meatpackers wanted certification that their products were produced in a safe and humane manner. They also knew that the only credible source of such certification was the government – if the meatpackers paid the certifiers directly, there would be a conflict of interest.

Recent troubles in accounting and rating agencies highlight the problems of private certification. The Enron scandal highlighted that the accounting firms' incentives were distorted; and though Sarbanes-Oxley improved matters, it did not fully resolve them.[12] Similarly, with the rating agencies being paid by the financial firms to rate the complex products they were creating, it is perhaps no surprise that they gave AAA ratings to highly risky products.

Information is a public good.[13] All individuals want to be assured that if they put money in a bank, the bank will be there when it comes time to withdraw the money. Government bank regulation is in part certification: it sets certain standards that a bank must satisfy and inspects that it fulfills those standards. It could, of course, stop there, allowing individuals to deposit their money in uncertified banks (and in a sense, it does that – there are many noncertified financial institutions). But it goes beyond that: it does not allow banks to operate unless they satisfy certain conditions. And that, in part, is because it knows that if a bank fails, it may have to be bailed out. As one astute observer put it: There are two kinds of governments – those who provide deposit insurance and know it; and those who do so and don't know it.[14,15]

---

[12] See J. E. Stiglitz, *Roaring Nineties,* New York: WW Norton, 2003.

[13] A public good is a good that benefits all. Knowing that a bank is sound is of benefit to any depositor. This is a theme to which I will return. We have already discussed the incentive problems that arise when the seller pays for certification. In most cases, it is hard to design systems where the buyer pays for certification; others, observing the behavior of those who have purchased the information, can free ride. That is, they can enjoy the benefits of the knowledge without paying for them. Private markets will underprovide public goods.

[14] This is sometimes called implicit insurance. There are good reasons why governments provide such insurance, noted above and elaborated on in J. E. Stiglitz, "The Role of the State in Financial Markets," Proceeding of the World Bank Conference on Development Economics 1993, Washington, D.C.: World Bank, pp. 41–6, and J. E. Stiglitz, "Perspectives on the Role of Government Risk-Bearing within the Financial Sector," in Government Risk-bearing, M. Sniderman (ed.), Norwell, MA: Kluwer Academic Publishers, 1993, pp. 109–30. (Paper prepared for Conference on Government Risk Bearing, Federal Reserve Bank of Cleveland, May 1991.)

[15] Some have argued that deposit insurance gives rise to a moral hazard problem – depositors take less care in inspecting the creditworthiness of the banks in which they put their money. But because information is a public good, it is inefficient for each individual to gather and

This in turn means that to mitigate the moral hazard problem, restrictions on banks have to be imposed.

ii. Irrationality

The market failure approach growing out of an analysis of the standard assumptions required to establish the Pareto efficiency of the economy[16] is, however, only one of at least three strands of analysis underlying the demand for regulation. A second focuses on *market irrationality*. The standard competitive equilibrium model assumed that all individuals were rational; it explained why rational individuals (households) interacting with profit (or value) maximizing firms in a competitive marketplace might not result in Pareto efficient allocations. But individuals may not be rational and may deviate from rationality in systematic ways. Individuals (and even more so societies) have to be saved from themselves. Markets suffer from irrational exuberance and irrational pessimism. Individuals may not save adequately for their retirement.

Until recent work on behavioral economics, economists typically looked askance at such paternalistic arguments for government intervention. Why, it was argued, should there be any presumption that governments are more rational or better informed than individuals? Who are we to impose our beliefs of what is rational on others? Part of the answer was provided by the classic theory of market failure: One might argue that as long as the individual only harms himself, there is no reason for government intervention. But individual actions may adversely affect others (there are, in effect, externalities). Regulation may reduce the likelihood of these adverse effects occurring and their impacts when they do.

There is a special category of externalities that arises in democratic societies. Societies cannot stand idly by when they see someone starving – even if it is a result of the individual's own mistakes, say, not saving enough. Society will bail out the individual (or a bank, which is too big to fail). Knowing that, individuals have an incentive to save too little (or banks to take too much risk). Knowing that, government should impose regulations to ensure that individuals do save enough (or banks do not undertake excessive risk).

---

process this information. Indeed, it is virtually impossible for them to do so. If individuals did that, they would have no time to make money to put into the bank. They can hire services (credit rating agencies) to evaluate the banks in which they deposit their money, but there are well-known market failures in these markets.

[16] This is sometimes referred to as the First Fundamental Theorem.

But the new behavioral economics puts a new perspective on these issues: Individuals may, in some sense, be better off if they are compelled to undertake some actions or are circumscribed from undertaking others. A potential alcoholic or drug addict may realize that he may be tempted to consume these toxic products and then become addicted. He knows *before he becomes addicted* that he will regret getting it, but once he is addicted, he will not be able to change his behavior. He therefore wants the government (or someone else) to make it impossible, or at least more difficult, to become addicted. (Matters are made worse by the fact that there are firms, such as those in the tobacco industry, that profit by taking advantage of addiction. By increasing the addictive properties of their products, they reduce the elasticity of demand and increase profitability.)

Similarly, individuals may know that they can easily be induced to save very little or a great deal simply on the basis of the default set by the employer in choosing the fraction of income to put into a savings account. Accordingly, they might want the government to force the firm to undertake a kind of analysis that sets the default rate in ways that enable the individual to have a reasonably comfortable retirement without excessively sacrificing current levels of consumption.

A formal welfare analysis of such regulations within the traditional welfare economics paradigm is, of course, difficult: Do we evaluate the impacts of the policy intervention using individuals' ex ante expected utility (their incorrect beliefs, for instance, about the consequences of their actions) or using ex post realized (average) utility?

iii. Distributive Justice

There is a third category of rationale for government interventions: The best that can be said for the market economy is that it produces *efficient* outcomes; there is no presumption that it produces outcomes viewed as socially just. Regulations may be an important instrument for achieving distributive objectives, especially when governments face tight budgetary constraints (or other administrative constraints). CRA (Community Reinvestment Act) lending requirements or health insurance mandates may be effective for helping poor individuals when the government cannot afford other ways of helping them.[17]

---

[17] Typically economists argue that a Pareto improvement could be achieved, e.g., by imposing taxes and providing subsidies for health insurance for the poor. But there are deadweight losses associated with raising taxes, and it may be harder to target the subsidies very well. Here we are concerned with the rationale for government intervention. Later, we shall discuss at greater length the relative merits of different forms of intervention.

b. Regulations vs. Other Forms of Intervention

Critics of regulation argue the objectives of regulation can be achieved better at lower costs by using market-based interventions, that is, taxes and subsidies. If smoking gives rise to an externality, tax smoking. If greenhouse gases give rise to global warming, tax greenhouse gas emissions. Price interventions have much to commend them: They are general, simple, and often have low transaction costs. But research over the last quarter century has clarified an important set of limitations. Indeed, the very conditions (such as imperfect and asymmetric information) that imply that markets by themselves do not in general lead to (constrained) Pareto efficient outcomes also imply that price interventions by themselves will not suffice.[18]

i. Imperfect Information and Incomplete Contracting

Most importantly, in the presence of imperfect information and incomplete contracting, optimal incentive schemes typically are highly nonlinear (they do not take the form of a price intervention) and may even impose constraints (like rationing and terminations).[19]

In a sense, most regulations can be recast as (typically simple) forms of nonlinear price schedules. There are, for instance, penalties to be paid if the level of pollution exceeds a certain level. Optimal regulation – and optimal

---

[18] For a broad discussion of this perspective, particularly in the context of regulations for natural monopolies, see D. Sappington and J. E. Stiglitz, "Information and Regulation," in *Public Regulation*, E. Bailey (ed.), London: MIT Press, 1987, pp. 3–43. Greenwald and Stiglitz, *op. cit.* focus on price interventions, but Martin Weitzman ("Prices vs. Quantities," *The Review of Economic Studies*, 41(4), October 1974, pp. 477–91) makes clear that in contexts in which there are imperfect risk markets, quantity interventions may be preferable to price interventions. For a discussion in the context of capital market regulations, see J. E. Stiglitz, José Antonio Ocampo, Shari Spiegel, Ricardo Ffrench-Davis, and Deepak Nayyar, *Stability with Growth: Macroeconomics, Liberalization, and Development*, The Initiative for Policy Dialogue Series, Oxford: Oxford University Press, 2006.

[19] Much of the discussion below views the problem of regulation through the lens of principal-agent problems. The fundamental problem is that the regulator has imperfect information about the firm that it wishes to regulate, e.g., its costs, or even its behavior. It can affect behavior (and thereby outcomes) by controlling or otherwise affecting through incentives those things that are observable, which may include *processes* (what the firm produces and how it produces it), precluding some actions, mandating others, subsidizing some observable inputs or outputs, taxing others, etc. Changing information that is available affects, of course, the nature of the principal-agent problem, including the optimal incentive structures. Many of the problems being considered here may be viewed as "layered" principal-agent problems; the regulator is ultimately interested in the well-being of consumers, but he is simultaneously trying to affect the behavior of firms, directly as well as indirectly, through effects on the behavior of other agents in society (consumers, investors).

incentive structures – typically entail restrictions/payments based not only on output but also on inputs and processes. Environmental regulations may entail standards as well as fines.[20]

Much theoretical literature has focused on designing a regulatory structure for a well-specified environment. Part of the problem, however, is that the economic environment may change rapidly, and there may be disagreement among policymakers about the salient aspects of the economic environment (e.g., how market participants might respond). That is why it is important to identify *robust* regulatory structures, those that work well under a range of conditions.[21]

ii. Prices vs. Quantities

Though there is seldom reason to resort to extremes of a pure price or pure quantity intervention, much of the literature has been couched in exactly these extremes.[22] It has been argued, for instance, that, depending on the nature of the shocks (to the demand and supply curves), quantity interventions (regulations) may lead to a higher level of expected utility than price interventions.[23]

This literature has made one important contribution: it has undermined the presumption among many economists that price interventions are always preferable. If import supply functions are highly variable but domestic demand and supply conditions do not vary, then setting a tariff leads to high variability in price, domestic output, and production; setting a quota eliminates this costly source of "imported" risk. Tariffication (shifting from quotas to tariffs) may, accordingly, not be welfare enhancing.[24]

---

[20] Few price schedules used in the private or public sector are in fact anywhere near the complexities of those that emerge from optimal incentive schemes. Whether a particular regulatory structure is better or worse than a particular simplified nonlinear price system may be hard to ascertain; and in any case, viewed through this lens, the distinction between regulatory systems and (nonlinear) price systems is more a matter of semantics than anything else.

[21] In the context of financial markets, this idea has been developed by P. Honohan and J. E. Stiglitz, "Robust Financial Restraint," in *Financial Liberalization: How Far, How Fast?* G. Caprio, P. Honohan and J. Stiglitz (eds.), Cambridge, U.K.: Cambridge University Press, 2001, pp. 31–63.

[22] Of course, there are some forms of behavior not easily amenable to simple price interventions, e.g., anticompetitive behaviors, though fines and other penalties can be an important part of an incentive scheme to induce firms not to behave in an anticompetitive manner.

[23] See, in particular, M. Weitzman, *op cit.*

[24] See P. Dasgupta and J.E. Stiglitz, "Tariffs Versus Quotas As Revenue Raising Devices Under Uncertainty," *American Economic Review,* 67(5), December 1977, pp. 975–81.

Similarly, it may be preferable to limit the magnitudes of capital inflows or outflows rather than imposing a tax on inflows and outflows.

One has to be careful, however, in applying this analysis. Consider, for instance, the problem of greenhouse gases. Some have suggested that this is a classic case where quantity regulation is preferred. With price interventions, the level of greenhouse gas emissions is uncertain; a change in the demand or supply curve will mean that we will have less or more emissions than desirable.

But the argument is hardly persuasive: Global warming is related to the level of concentration of greenhouse gases in the atmosphere, and what matters for this is not the level of emissions in any particular year. There is, in fact, even some uncertainty about the relationship between emission levels and changes in concentration levels and about the relationship between the level of concentration of greenhouse gases and the (precise) change in climate. There will have to be, in any case, adjustments to the allowable levels of emissions over time. Using prices (emission taxes), there will have to be adjustments too, with one additional factor of uncertainty: The relationship between taxes and emissions. But provided that adjustments are made in a relatively timely way, there is little additional risk in the variables of concern, the level of concentration of greenhouse gases, and climate change.

The use of price interventions has one major advantage – it encourages us to think carefully about the social cost of emissions at different dates. Because what matters is the long run level of concentration of greenhouse gases in the atmosphere, the social cost of emissions at all dates (and at all places) should be the same.

In general, with imperfect information (and incomplete contracting) it is optimal to use a complex set of controls that entail both (generalized) incentives and constraints.

II. Instruments of Regulation

Regulation takes on a number of forms: Information requirements, proscriptions (things firms may not do), or mandates (things firms must do).

a. Disclosure

Recent discussions have favored information requirements. Who can object to more transparency or better information? (Actually, hedge funds, and their representatives in Treasury, have objected: They have argued that those investing in information need to get a return on their investments; if they disclose what they do, they are, in effect, giving this asset away. Some of the same individuals who made this argument in connection with hedge funds are now demanding more transparency for sovereign wealth funds, even when these funds invest heavily in research.)

Recent discussion of disclosure seems predicated on the belief that but for information imperfections, markets would be efficient. Correct this one market failure, and one will have efficient markets. Similarly, the provision of better quality information drove New Deal reconstruction of the securities markets.

Actually, there is little support for this conclusion, as the broader discussion of market failure should have made clear.[25]

Market forces do not necessarily lead to full (or efficient) disclosure of information, so there is a good rationale for disclosure requirements. Markets cannot function well with distorted and imperfect information; hence, requirements that lead to improved information can (by and large) lead to better resource allocations.

The design of disclosure requirements, however, often entails more complex issues than one might have thought. The disclosure of a chemical substance in a product may be interpreted as prima facie evidence that its presence is dangerous, even when there is no scientific evidence that that is the case. Disclosures may be done in ways that in fact do not alert consumers to risks when they are there. That is why the form of cigarette warnings has been tightly regulated. All investment prospectuses describe a large number of risks that the investor may face – they are fully disclosed but in ways that may not be helpful in distinguishing the level of risk.

Disclosures concerning stock options, which dilute shareholder value, are still done in a manner that does not convey relevant information to most shareholders in an effective way. Those companies (and those that work with them) have lobbied strongly and so far successfully against such disclosure requirements. There are technical details in calculating the value of the dilution, but what is clear is that assigning a zero value is incorrect.

Disclosure of potential conflicts of interest, ownership, or remuneration may help market participants interpret the actions of others. For instance, knowing that a salesman gets a higher commission from selling one product than another may shed some light on his praise of the product generating higher commissions; knowing that analysts' pay is not related to the accuracy of their prediction of stock performance but to the investment deals they

---

[25] Indeed, in a second best world in which there is imperfect risk markets, better information can lead to more volatility and lower expected utility.

bring in sheds some light on the reliability of their forecasts; knowing that CEOs are remunerated on the basis of *reported* earnings may affect judgments about the reliability of those reports; and knowing the structure of remuneration of hedge fund managers should lead to an expectation that they will engage in excessive risk taking.

Disclosure requirements seem less invasive than other regulations, such as the restrictions and mandates to be described below, but it should be clear that in many areas disclosure itself does not fully address the market failures discussed earlier. This is partly because market participants do not know how to process fully the information that has been disclosed and partly because even if market participants *know* what firms are doing, firms may still not behave appropriately. Citizens may put pressure on firms that have been disclosed to be polluting the atmosphere – disclosure has been shown to have some effects on some firms – but some firms continue to pollute excessively. And there are some firms willing to take advantage of individuals who remain uninformed – even when the information is potentially available – for instance, by producing unsafe products. That is why regulations entail restrictions and mandates.

b. Restrictions

The most direct restrictions are proscriptions on behaviors: Firms are not allowed to collude in price setting or to engage in other anticompetitive practices, and banks are not allowed to engage in insider lending.

(There is a peculiar variant of regulation that has become popular in the United States, self-regulation, which I view as an oxymoron. Banks are told to have good risk management systems, to regulate their own risks. But what else would one expect a bank to do? In fact, such self-regulation proved totally ineffective. And such regulation does not identify systemic and external effects that should in fact be a focus of real regulation.)

One would like to be able to tell banks only to give "good loans." But regulators cannot tell what is a good or a bad loan. They can tell when there might be distorted incentives. Regulation thus often focuses not on behaviors so much as on factors that might affect behaviors. It attempts to proscribe conflicts of interest (e.g., recent restrictions on accounting firms) or to ensure that the firm has enough wealth not to act in a reckless way[26] (e.g., capital requirements on banks and airlines).

---

[26] Bankruptcy means in effect that even risk-averse owners/managers may behave in a risk-loving way.

Some forms of behavior are easy to identify and restrict. Insider lending is prohibited, even though one might have better information about relatives than others. The temptation to provide a risky loan is simply too great.

Rapid expansion of lending portfolios, it has been suggested, is very risky.

A critical issue is the specificity of the restrictions. The economy is constantly changing; this is particularly so in the financial sector. Financial innovators will figure out a way of getting around any set of regulations – and, in what has come to be called regulatory arbitrage, make a great deal of profits in doing so. In some states, laws and regulations have been passed (like the Martin Act) that have a broad target, recognizing that the specific means by which these "antisocial" objectives can be achieved will change. The Martin Act also provides extensive investigatory powers. In return for the lack of specificity in actions, the punishments are more muted: Fines that will recapture the ill-gotten gains rather than prison terms. It was these laws that were among the most effective in addressing the series of scandals in which financial firms were involved in the late '90s and early years of this decade, including those involving analysts, stock options, the investment banks, and CEOs.

Similar issues have arisen in antitrust. Firms have been extraordinarily clever in devising ways of reducing competition. Microsoft bundled its Internet browser with its operating system in a successful attempt to crush Netscape. AT&T was told that it had to provide interconnection with other providers, but it did so in ways that gave it a competitive advantage. If regulators impose restrictions on particular behaviors, monopolies will innovate to find new ways of acting anticompetitively that are consistent with the rules (but obviously against the spirit of the rules). The only way to reduce the scope for such anticompetitive behavior is to affect incentives, that is, structural remedies, such as breaking up the firm or limiting the scope of intellectual property protections.[27]

c. Mandates

Mandates have increased in popularity because they enable the accomplishment of public purposes without the expenditure of money. But as critics point out, they are often a hidden form of taxation, though the incidence

[27] See, e.g., Jason Furman and J. E. Stiglitz, "U.S. versus Microsoft, Declaration as Part of The Tunney Act Proceeding," commissioned by the Computer & Communications Industry Association, Jan. 28, 2002.

of the tax is often difficult to assess, and the tax/expenditure programs that are implicit are often inefficient and inequitable.

Yet some mandates may be viewed as efficient ways of addressing complex societal problems involving externalities. The CRA requirements (that banks provide certain levels of funding to underserved communities) have arguably expanded access to finance for minorities, and many banks today claim that – after paying the initial costs of entering these markets – their returns are just as high as elsewhere. Granting a license to a bank is a privilege, with market value. Governments do not typically auction off licenses to the highest bidder (doing so might not be the best way to get the best bankers[28]). So society engages in a kind of barter: Rights (e.g., access to the Fed discount window) are exchanged for responsibilities (e.g., to lend in underserved communities). This kind of exchange has become particularly common as a part of zoning – restrictions on land usage. The lack of transparency is disturbing, offset in part by how effective it often is, particularly in the presence of budgetary constraints.

Mandates related to interconnectivity in networks represent another category, related in part to anticompetitive behavior. Consider Microsoft's control of the PC operating system. From a social perspective, the more users and the more applications written for the operating system, the better and more valuable the network. If there were many networks competing with each other, the owner of each would try to maximize these network benefits. But Microsoft, as a monopolist, must weigh these benefits from the monopoly profits that it can extract by, say, undermining competition in applications. Mandates (regulations) that establish protocols that enhance interconnectivity may thus be welfare enhancing.

The health insurance mandate proposed by several candidates in the 2008 election illustrates the advantages and disadvantages of mandates. America has an employer-based system for the provision of health insurance. But there are some 50 million Americans without health insurance. In many cases, when these uninsured individuals require major medical care, they are not able to pay fully the costs. The burden is shifted to others. Often they postpone receiving needed care, and this raises the costs further. Firms that do not provide such health insurance may have a competitive advantage over those that do. The market is thus distorted. A mandate would thus increase coverage and reduce cost shifting. But the mandate can be viewed as a

---

[28] This is a standard problem of adverse selection. See, e.g., J.E. Stiglitz and A. Weiss, "Credit Rationing in Markets with Imperfect Information," *American Economic Review*, 71(3), June 1981, pp. 393–410.

hidden health insurance tax, with complicated incidence, imposing higher costs on some firms than on others. It distorts behavior – encouraging firms to hire young and healthy workers. It would be better to finance health insurance through a tax. But increased taxes in the current environment are politically unpopular, and there is some preference for incremental changes, the consequences of which can be more easily assessed than large systemic changes.

d. Ownership Restrictions

The previous subsections have described how regulations force disclosure of information (which firms might not otherwise disclose), restrict some actions, and mandate others. However, we go beyond restricting actions – partly because we often cannot easily observe actions; we observe them, or their consequences, only with a lag. Thus, we not only restrict anticompetitive actions, but we also break up monopolies because we believe it is impossible to stop them from acting in an anticompetitive way. Before the break-up of AT&T, there was an attempt to restrict its anticompetitive actions, but when those attempts failed, it was broken up. Microsoft was not broken up, and even after it agreed not to continue acting anticompetitively, it could not resist taking advantage of its monopoly power. This was the predictable, and predicted, consequence of the failure to alter incentives (e.g., by breaking up Microsoft).

Owners of banks are not allowed to make loans to themselves. It may be because their *motives* are wrong: They gain even if the government (as the insurer of deposits) is put at greater risk. But even apart from these distorted incentives, they are likely to have distorted judgments – to think that they are a better risk than they really are.

Bank regulators also regulate ownership out of fear that the "wrong" owners might have perverse incentives. Thus racketeers are not allowed to own banks. Proposed restrictions on sovereign wealth funds fall in this category (see the discussion below).

The Glass-Steagall Act of 1933 restricted commercial banks from owning investment banks and vice versa, again partially because of the potential for conflicts of interest. In discussions of the repeal of this act in the 1990s, advocates of the repeal said not to worry, they would construct Chinese Walls. But that raised the question: If these Chinese Walls were really constructed, where were the economies of scope that provided the rationale for the elimination of the restrictions? In the end, lobbying by the banks (and undoubtedly the links between Treasury and financial markets) succeeded in getting the repeal, and worries about conflicts of interest proved justified, evidenced in the ensuing Enron/WorldCom scandals.[29]

We may feel better knowing that a company that is selling blood is doing it not-for-profit; a profit-maximizing firm seeks to minimize costs and in doing so may buy blood from those who are desperate and unhealthy, with diseases that may not be detected.[30] Many governments restrict ownership of certain key assets (such as airlines) to citizens of their country. Others recognize that there is an inevitable conflict of interest in certain areas between private owners' interests and the public interest – contrary to Adam Smith. Private firms wish to minimize what they pay for natural resources on publicly owned lands; the government wishes to maximize the return. The two interests are diametrically opposed. In a world with robust competition for resources, with perfect information, the two interests can be aligned, provided that the resources are sold in an appropriate way with the right regulations. But mining and oil interests will work hard to make sure that that does not occur. In these instances, public ownership may be desirable. Regulations to ensure that the private owners act in the public interest may not suffice. Indeed, more generally, social objectives can be achieved through privatization only under highly restrictive assumptions – akin to the assumptions required to ensure that competitive markets are efficient.[31]

The Council of Economic Advisers opposed privatization of the United States Enrichment Corporation (USEC), the government corporation charged with enriching uranium (low enriched uranium is used in nuclear power plants; highly enriched uranium is the key ingredient in nuclear bombs). We believed that private incentives for the sale of enriched uranium (and the importation of the material from deactivated warheads from Russia, to be deenriched) did not coincide with national interests in nonproliferation, *and* we could not perfectly monitor their activities. The advocates

---

[29] The repeal may have played a part in the current financial problems in quite a different way. Commercial banking, lending other people's money with an implicit government guarantee, should be conservative. Investment banks, investing the assets of wealthy individuals, typically pursue riskier strategies. When the two were merged, the latter culture dominated, with serious consequences to the country's financial system.

[30] Richard Morris Titmuss, *The Gift Relationship: From Human Blood to Social Policy*, New Press: New York, 1997 (reissue of 1970 book); Joel Schwartz, "Blood and Altruism – Richard M. Titmuss' Criticism on the Commercialization of Blood," *Public Interest*, Summer 1999.

[31] David Sappington and J. E. Stiglitz, "Privatization, Information and Incentives," *Journal of Policy Analysis and Management*, 6(4), 1987, pp. 567–82. Reprinted in *The Political Economy of Privatization and Deregulation*, E. Baily and J. Hower (eds.), Edward Elgar, 1993.

of privatization (at least one of whom has now, ironically, expressed worries about the risks of Sovereign Wealth Funds) believed that we could. In the end, these anxieties turned out to be fully warranted.[32]

For the most part, however, we do not impose ownership restrictions, partially because we typically do not have information about ownership – some worry that gathering such information might invade individuals' rights to privacy. We do not know who owns hedge funds and private equity firms, and in fact, with many owners of corporations registered abroad, ascertaining who the ultimate beneficial owner is might not be that easy. But there is another reason we do not impose ownership restrictions: Though ownership may alert us to an increased risk of behavior contrary to societal interests, whenever there is scope for such behavior, it needs to be restricted, *whatever the motivation.*

e. Regulatory Takings

As we have noted, regulations (whether restrictions or mandates) can also sometimes be viewed as hidden tax/expenditure programs. The Endangered Species Act can be viewed as requiring private property owners to provide a public good – the protection of endangered species. At the time it was passed, it represented a change in property rights. Today, a repeal of the act, or providing compensation to those whose use of property is encumbered, would also represent a grant of an additional property right.

All regulations affect property values (as does anything else the government does, such as the construction of a road). Presumably, the fact that a regulation forces a firm to do something it would not otherwise have done means that (normally) it will reduce profits.[33] When property values are enhanced, no one offers to give back the increased value to the government, and those enjoying these capital gains often lobby strongly for lower tax rates. But when property values are decreased, many want compensation. Providing compensation for regulatory takings in a world with strong budgetary constraints greatly constrains regulation, and indeed, that is the intent of many in the regulatory takings movement. It is not just a matter of equity (say, fair compensation for the loss in value) or efficiency (say, ensuring that only regulations the value of which exceeds the costs are

---

[32] For a discussion of this episode, see J.E. Stiglitz, *Globalization and its Discontents,* New York: W.W. Norton, 2002.

[33] There are some important exceptions: Some regulations are designed to prevent managers of corporations from taking actions that benefit themselves at the expense of shareholders.

adopted). Courts have consistently rejected the view that regulatory takings require compensation, and with few exceptions, so have legislatures. A possible important exception is Chapter 11 of NAFTA; whether it does so remains in dispute, but wording in subsequent investment agreements has changed in response to the fear that it might.[34]

The debate over regulatory takings highlights the complexity of regulatory control. As in any area of public policy, there are efficiency and distributive consequences. Economists sometimes distinguish between the Endangered Species Act, which required private parties to provide a public good, and a zoning restriction, which prevents a factory from imposing a negative externality on neighboring houses. The nature of the distributive consequences (and who bears them) depends too on the extent to which the regulation was anticipated.[35]

f. Laws and Regulations

Though we typically think of regulations in areas of environment, safety, banking, and utilities, many of the other laws affecting economic activity can be looked at through a regulatory lens. Bankruptcy laws restrict the set of contracts that parties can draw up with each other – no matter what the contract says about what happens in the event a debtor cannot meet his obligations, bankruptcy law will prevail if those provisions are in conflict. Similarly, corporate governance laws restrict how corporations may govern themselves.

i. Regulatory Processes

Much of the difference between regulation and these areas relates to the processes by which regulations get adopted. Typically, in the case of regulations, there is some delegation: The legislature delegates authority to a regulatory agency, which is assumed to have greater expertise in addressing complex technical issues. The delegation raises concerns about democratic accountability, particularly given the frequency with which regulatory agencies are

---

[34] For a more extensive discussion of some of the legal and economic issues, see J. E. Stiglitz, "Regulating Multinational Corporations: Towards Principles of Cross-border Legal Frameworks in a Globalized World Balancing Rights with Responsibilities," *American University International Law Review*, 23(3), 2008, pp. 451–558, Grotius Lecture presented at the 101st Annual Meeting of the American Society for International Law, Washington, D.C., March 28, 2007.

[35] Underlying this debate is a debate over the nature of property rights, implicit and explicit.

captured by special interests.[36] These concerns may not be fully obviated by legislative review processes. Regulations on how regulatory agencies design regulations (e.g., on the regulatory process) are designed to enhance democratic accountability (including transparency), but there is concern that these too have not been fully effective.

Related issues are raised by central banks, where recent doctrines have held that independent central banks lead to better performance. The evidence on that is less than compelling; what it shows is that independent central banks focusing on inflation do achieve lower rates of inflation – it would be really surprising if that were not the case – but do not succeed in achieving economically significant or even statistically significant better performance in more relevant metrics, like growth, unemployment, or real wages. Central banks effectively control a critical price in the market, the interest rate, not so much by price regulation but by intervention. In many economies, they control a second critical price, the exchange rate. There are many doctrinal disputes over whether government should control the exchange rate, but ironically, almost none about whether government should control the interest rate (though there are many disputes about *how* it should control the interest rate).

The controversy over central bank independence is part of a broader debate of democratic accountability.[37] One can have an independent central bank that is more broadly representative – some countries insist that there be representation of labor (which is likely to be more concerned with unemployment and less with inflation), others impose restrictions that limit participation of financial sector representatives, viewed as a special interest. In the United Kingdom, the government sets the inflation target; the Bank of England then has independence in how it fulfills that mandate. Independence does not necessarily mean that it has the right to operate in the nontransparent way that it traditionally has; the Bank of England has, for instance, led the way in greater transparency. The U.S. Federal Reserve has, in the recent financial crisis, undertaken actions that are almost identical to those the Treasury might have undertaken. It has lent massive amounts

---

[36] G. Stigler, 1971, "The Theory of Economic Regulation," *Bell Journal of Economics*, 2(1), Spring 1971, pp. 3–21; J.J. Laffont and J. Tirole, "The Politics of Government Decision Making: a Theory of Regulatory Capture," *Quarterly Journal of Economics*, 106(4) November 1991, pp. 1089–127; and M.E. Levine and J.L. Forrence, "Regulatory Capture, Public Interest, and the Public Agenda: Toward a Synthesis," *Journal of Law, Economics, and Organization*, 6, April 1990, pp. 167–98.

[37] See J. E. Stiglitz, "Central Banking in a Democratic Society," *De Economist* (Netherlands), 146(2), 1998, pp. 199–226. (Originally presented as 1997 Tinbergen Lecture, Amsterdam, October).

of money to the private sector and accepted as collateral very risky assets, putting the taxpayer at risk. In doing so, it has put into question constitutional presumptions that Congress should control spending.[38] In addition, the Fed has denied that basic democratic protections, reflected in the Freedom of Information Act, are applicable to it.[39]

ii. Implementation of Regulations

In the current crisis, the concern is not just that regulations were inadequate but that the regulations that existed were inadequately implemented. We had regulators who did not believe in regulations, with predictable consequences. It is not just that the process of designing the regulation gets captured, but so too the process of implementation. And it is not just capture by vested interests; it is capture by ideologies.

That raises deep issues concerning regulatory design and transparency in regulatory implementation. In some cases, the benefits of duplication – of multiple regulators, making regulatory capture more difficult – far outweigh the costs. The savings from avoiding the current crisis would have been millions of times greater than the costs of regulatory duplication. Some systems of regulation may be easier to monitor. That is the case, for instance, for "speed limits," ownership restrictions, and restrictions on incentive structures.

g. Government Failures

We noted the compelling case for regulation based on the fact that markets often fail and that *in principle* there are government interventions that would be welfare enhancing; we noted too that *in principle* more than just price interventions are required. There is a need for *regulation.*

But we also noted that many of those who object argue that such an analysis underestimates the scope for government failure. It is all well and good to argue that government could in principle improve welfare. But what happens in practice?

Anyone who has watched the U.S. government in the last seven years is well aware not only of the possibility of government failure but also of its

---

[38] I am not addressing here the technical legality of their actions. That is a matter for legal experts. I am questioning the congruence between their actions and basic democratic principles.

[39] Bloomberg LP v. Federal Reserve, U.S. District Court, Southern District of New York (Manhattan), Case number 1:2008cv09595.

reality. In some cases it is a matter of incompetence, in others of corruption, in still others it is a result of ideological commitments that preclude taking appropriate actions. In some cases it may be hard to distinguish the relative role played by each. Government programs can be subverted.

The analytic questions are, first, are these problems *inevitable*? Secondly, when they occur, are there corrective processes? Thirdly, are there some regulatory measures (and some regulatory processes) that are less likely to be subverted? Just as much of recent economic research has been directed at the question of how we mitigate the consequences of economic failure, we can ask, what can we do to mitigate the likelihood and consequences of government failure?

Government failure – at least on the scale that we have seen it in recent years – is not inevitable. Indeed, the Reinventing Government initiative undertaken by Vice President Gore showed that concerted efforts to improve the efficiency and responsiveness of government could succeed. Beyond that, some of the same reforms that work in the private sector are relevant in the public sector: Increasing competitiveness and transparency and improving incentive structures, where outputs can be reasonably well defined and attributed to particular individuals.

As long as there is sufficient transparency and competition, there are corrective processes. Governments that fail will be replaced; they lose their credibility and legitimacy. To be sure, those in the political process try to reduce competitiveness (e.g., by gerrymandering) and to hide failures (through a lack of transparency), just as do those in markets.

Finally, some regulatory processes are more subject to public failure than others, and part of the art of the design of regulatory regimes is to identify those that are less likely to be captured or abused. One of the arguments for disclosure requirements is that they are less subject to abuse, and one of the arguments against barter arrangements (zoning variances in return for providing certain public goods) is that they are never perfectly transparent and are therefore subject to abuse.

One reason for having multiple oversight (e.g., of banks or securities markets) is that it reduces the scope for capture. It means that even if there is a failure in one part of the regulatory system, there will not be in others. The SEC failed to take appropriate action in the case of many of the abuses earlier in the decade, but fortunately New York state did (using the flexibility provided by the Martin Act). In some ways, our antitrust framework provides a model for combating government failure (and it was designed with an awareness of the political pressures put on government *not* to take action): There are both civil and criminal actions; there is oversight by more than one federal agency and at both the federal and state levels. The larger the consequences of government failure and the larger the probability of government failure, the greater the value of multiple oversight.[40]

This argument for multiple oversight seems to run contrary to the conventional wisdom of unifying regulatory structures. There is a simple reason for the difference. The conventional wisdom is based on a simplistic model that does not recognize the risk of regulatory capture and the limitations in information of the regulatory structure and consequent risk of regulatory failure. In such a world, of course, duplication represents a waste of resources (both on the side of government and on the part of the regulated party, in terms of compliance costs). There are further problems: There is a risk of lack of congruence of the regulations. But this lack of congruence makes the point that if all regulators had exactly the same objective and the same information, they would presumably impose the same regulations. It is differences in objectives and information that lead to differences in regulations and different emphases in enforcement. As we noted, the current crisis makes clear that the costs of duplication pale in comparison to the costs of regulatory failure.

III. Applications

In this section, we apply these general principles to three areas of regulations that are the subject of extensive current discussion. They are chosen both because of the importance of these issues in current public policy debate and because they nicely illustrate the principles and issues raised previously in this chapter.

a. Sovereign Wealth Funds: Does Ownership Matter?

Sovereign Wealth Funds are the funds of government assets being invested abroad. Oil exporters have accumulated hundreds of billions of dollars. They have been advised not to spend their money – to manage their wealth to take account of the variability of international prices and to mitigate Dutch

---

[40] The general theory is set forth in a series of papers with R. Sah: "Human Fallibility and Economic Organization," *American Economic Review*, 75(2), May 1985, pp. 292–6; "The Architecture of Economic Systems: Hierarchies and Polyarchies," *American Economic Review*, 76(4), September 1986, pp. 716–27; "Committees, Hierarchies and Polyarchies," *The Economic Journal*, 98(391), June 1988, pp. 451–70; and "Qualitative Properties of Profit-Maximizing K-out-of-N Systems Subject to Two Kinds of Failure," *IEEE Transactions on Reliability*, 37(5), December 1988, pp. 515–20.

disease problems. With oil prices soaring to $100 a barrel, the magnitude of these funds has soared too.

The other group of countries with large sovereign funds is developing countries that have had high savings rates, that have bought dollars to avoid currency appreciation, and that have built up large reserves to buffer them against shocks posed by global volatility. China has more than $1.9 trillion in reserves and a national savings rate of 5 percent. The amount in the reserves of various other Asian countries is now in the trillions. Singapore's Provident Fund has been built up with workers contributing 42 percent of their salaries.

It was only a matter of time before these countries figured out that holding dollar T-bills was a bad store of value – especially with the declining dollar.

These funds grabbed public attention when they bailed out Citibank and Merrill Lynch.[41] They had billions in liquid assets and could act quickly. According to some Wall Street rumors, had they not bailed out these financial institutions, they would have gone under – or required a government bailout. But not only did existing shareholders have to give up a significant fraction of their ownership share, collectively the sovereign funds' ownership shares may have given them effective control. Some began to fret: Should the American government (or more generally, "host governments") regulate these funds?

The G-8 and the International Monetary Fund (IMF) called for more transparency. They wanted to be sure that these funds had strictly commercial objectives. Norway's highly transparent funds were evidently unobjectionable – even though as a shareholder, Norway had often expressed its views about corporate governance, human rights, and the environment (views that went beyond strictly commercial concerns).

There was a certain naiveté – and hypocrisy – in these stances. Evidently, nontransparent hedge funds were permissible. No one knows who owns these hedge funds. They could even be owned by a secret Cayman Islands corporation whose owners were the sovereign fund. Were the IMF and the G-8 simply asking the sovereign funds to act more obscurely indirectly through hedge funds? With the close connections of some in Western financial markets to these hedge funds, one could understand the rationale: Increased fees for the hedge funds. But this was hardly a compelling basis of

---

[41] Since then, of course, Merrill Lynch has been acquired by Bank of America, and Citibank has had two massive bailouts from the federal government. The sovereign wealth funds have suffered large losses.

public policy.[42] Defenders of hedge funds say they know that hedge funds are commercially oriented. We don't know what motivates sovereign funds. They might have political objectives – that would be contrary to America's best interests. But if that worries one, one should be equally worried about the hedge funds. We don't know who owns them, and so we don't know what motivates them.

Most of the debate is motivated by fear. It is not that the sovereign funds have taken actions that are objectionable, which are motivated by anything other than profit maximization. It is only that they *might* do so, and we need to take preventive action. Of course, no one wants to stop the funds. If the funds had not bailed out Citibank and Merrill, America's economic problems might have been even worse. Today's buzzword is transparency. What is demanded is more transparency.

What kind of transparency would make a difference? Should we take comfort that they *say* they are pursuing just commercial objectives? How can we be sure that they do what they say? If a bank says that it will not lend to a country because such lending is too risky, how do we know whether those economic judgments have been tainted by political perspectives? What information would a disclosure of balance sheets make? We normally don't require such disclosures. Why here?[43]

Moreover, the pursuit of commercial objectives has never been a requirement for ownership in the past. Many a newspaper and TV station have been bought not for commercial reasons but as a basis to advance a political perspective.

What is clear is that the brouhaha over the sovereign funds is partly a fairly transparent form of new American protectionism and partly an attempt to shift attention from the failures of America: If America had saved more, and if its financial institutions had behaved better, it wouldn't have had to turn to these sovereign funds.

Nonetheless, the debate has served a salutary purpose: It has opened up the question, does ownership matter? For years, the IMF and the U.S. Treasury have been telling developing countries to privatize their assets

---

[42] One ex-Secretary of Treasury who has been among the most vociferous in calling for greater transparency of sovereign funds had resisted calls for greater transparency for hedge funds. In making his arguments, he has not usually disclosed that he has himself been working for a hedge fund.

[43] Market advocates would argue further that disclosure of the portfolio would make public the fruits of their research, undermining incentives to gather information, thereby decreasing the informational efficiency of the market. (These are the arguments put forward in defense of hedge fund secrecy.)

and to remove restrictions on foreign ownership. Many within the country were anxious about selling national assets. They were told: Don't worry. *The nationality of the owner doesn't matter.* No objection was made even when a firm owned by a foreign government bought an enterprise.

But of course there can be a conflict of interest, between the interests of the nation as a whole and the interests of the owner, as we have already noted, but they can arise whether the owner is domestic or foreign. For instance, private firms managing a country's natural resource seek to minimize payments made to the government, though it is in the nation's interest to have these payments maximized.

Underlying the objections to sovereign funds is a simple fallacy. It is based on the hypothesis that (a) rational owners will desire firms to maximize the value of their firms, and (b) value maximization leads to social welfare maximization. Each of these hypotheses has been the subject of extensive research and has been shown to be true only under certain limiting conditions (e.g., a complete set of risk markets, no information asymmetries, perfectly competitive markets).[44] Some have argued that competitive markets *force* firms to maximize value; if they do not, they will be taken over. But this too has been shown not to be true in general.[45] Interestingly, many takeovers do not result in an increase in the value of the firm(s); they seem motivated by the hubris of the CEO of the taking over firm, who is willing to sacrifice the value of his firm for personal gratification.[46]

There are certain circumstances when there are systematic conflicts between, say, what firms might do (whether a result of value maximization or not) and societal welfare that we impose regulations to constrain the behavior of firms. We restrict, for instance, their pollution.

Ownership matters, as we noted earlier, because it affects incentives for behaviors that are not in the social interest *and* because we cannot adequately control behavior. But this is true whether the owner is a private American or a foreign government. In the one case, it is profit motives; in the other because there *may* be political motives. If there is scope for behavior that is adverse

---

[44] See, for instance, Sanford Grossman and J. E. Stiglitz, "On Value Maximization and Alternative Objectives of the Firm," *Journal of Finance*, 32(2), May 1977, pp. 389–402, and "Stockholder Unanimity in the Making of Production and Financial Decisions," *Quarterly Journal of Economics*, 94(3), May 1980, pp. 543–66.

[45] See, for instance, Sanford Grossman and Oliver Hart, and O. Hart, 1980. "Takeover Bids, the Free-rider Problem and the Theory of the Corporation," *Bell Journal of Economics*, 11(1), pp. 42–64; and "The Allocational Role of Takeover Bids in Situations of Asymmetric Information," *Journal of Finance*, 36(2), 1981, pp. 253–70.

[46] This reinforces the conclusion: Noneconomic motives often play an important role in market economies.

to public interest, even well-motivated people may take adverse actions: Those engaged in subprime mortgage activities had ordinary motives of profit maximizing; some were not explicitly engaged in predatory lending but simply had very bad judgment – they didn't understand the nature of risk. There may, nonetheless, be severe consequences for our economy. Such behavior should be proscribed.

In short, the debate about sovereign wealth funds highlights the limitations of our regulatory systems. If a sovereign wealth fund were to buy a pencil company, and, motivated by politics, decided to give away pencils as an act of friendship, no one would be concerned. If the firm is mismanaged and goes bankrupt, no one would be much concerned – antitrust laws would have ensured that the firm is small, and if the economy is functioning well, those who lose their jobs would quickly find others. If a sovereign fund bought a bank and decided not to lend to a particular country (whether it thought it a bad risk or a rogue state), it would have little economic consequence (though we might socially disapprove of this discrimination and pass antidiscrimination laws), as long as there was a competitive banking system. Even if it shut down a plant and moved it overseas to create jobs in its own country, there would be little concern: New jobs would quickly be created here at home. But if our competition laws or other regulatory systems are not working well, a firm owned by a sovereign fund – or a private firm – might take actions adverse to the public interest. Ownership conveys information; it may tell us about the likelihood of such actions being undertaken. In some circumstances, it may provide an additional rationale for regulatory scrutiny. But in only limited circumstances, such as those described earlier – where regulatory oversight is so impaired that appropriate actions cannot be taken *in a timely way* and where consequences of the adverse actions cannot be easily repaired – is there a compelling case for ownership restrictions. When ownership restrictions are warranted, though, they should be nondiscriminatory. Sovereign funds might be restricted, but if so, hedge fund ownership should be as well unless there is full transparency of the true owners of the hedge fund.

b. Financial Sector Regulation

During the Clinton Administration, I led a review of the federal government's regulation of the financial sector as part of Vice President Gore's "Reinventing Government" initiative. Our objective was to identify the objectives of regulation and to assess whether current regulations achieved those objectives in the most effective way. As a result of the review, we eliminated some regulations – such as those requiring notification of every installed ATM – but supported the continuation of others.

We identified five interrelated reasons for government intervention: (a) ensuring competition, (b) protecting consumers, (c) ensuring the safety and soundness of financial institutions and the financial system, (d) ensuring access, and (e) promoting macroeconomic stability and growth. The list included concerns both about efficiency – market failures – and equity (without government regulation, certain groups may not have access to finance and may be exploited).

Competition is largely the responsibility of the Department of Justice, but there are distinctive characteristics of this market that require special attention or more specialized knowledge.[47] The market is complex; though there may be a large number of banks, the number providing particular financial services – say, loans to small businesses in the state of Washington – may be very limited. There may also be complicated questions balancing out competition with other objectives (such as safety and soundness).[48]

i. Consumer Protection

One of the concerns about the subprime mortgage crisis is that it would have been less severe had legislation or regulations to restrict predatory lending been adopted. At the time, some argued that loose lending standards would enable more individuals to become homeowners. But it should have been clear that giving a loan to someone beyond their capacity to pay is not doing a favor. The main beneficiaries were those making the loans – there was even opposition to regulations requiring that lenders demonstrate that refinancing be in the interests of the borrower. But the debate surrounding these restrictions highlights the complexities of regulation: Under the hypothesis that house prices would continue to go up, denying the poor the right to participate in this economic giveaway would have been unfair. Though the Ponzi scheme was working, some did benefit. Like any pyramid scheme, those who get in and out earlier can win. But government has the responsibility to see through the hype – it is arithmetically impossible for house prices to continue to rise while the incomes of most Americans are falling, unless the cost of capital continues to fall.

---

[47] This is one of those instances, noted earlier, where there is especial value to multiple oversights.

[48] Enhanced competition reduces profitability, making banks more vulnerable.

Consumer protection begins with disclosure – individuals should, for instance, know what interest rate they are paying on loans. It is clear that there are strong market forces moving in the opposite direction. Ensuring the safety and soundness of financial systems – so individuals know that when they put money into a bank they will be able to get it out – and ensuring competition can also be thought of as part of consumer protection. Even with regulation, of course, banks may go under, which is why deposit insurance is required. As I noted earlier, the argument that deposit insurance leads to moral hazard is largely (but not totally) misguided. Individuals do not have the capacity to inspect the books of the banks in which they are depositing, and it would be inefficient for each of them to do so. But the existence of deposit insurance necessitates stronger bank regulation: The S & L debacle arose in part because banks offered high interest rates. Depositors may have known that those high interest rates could only have been paid on the basis of risky loans, but because of deposit insurance they did not have to worry.

Restrictions on high interest rates have been opposed by advocates of liberalization; they point out that such interventions in the market deny access to loans by risky borrowers who would not otherwise have access to credit. But high interest rates can also arise as a result of exploitation of borrowers, especially ill-informed poor borrowers in noncompetitive markets, and the higher risk associated with higher interest rates has a cost to the public, with either implicit or explicit deposit insurance. (High interest rates lead to riskier behavior and have adverse selection effects.) There is a balance of concerns in which by and large I think such interest rate restrictions are desirable.

ii. Safety and Soundness

Regulations directed at ensuring the safety and soundness of the banking system illustrate many of the instruments discussed earlier in this chapter. There are ownership restrictions – industrial firms cannot, in general, own banks (though in many other countries they can), nor can certain individuals of ill repute. There are capital adequacy requirements – in effect ensuring that the bank has sufficient capital *at risk* that it would not undertake excessive risk, and so the probability of bankruptcy is sufficiently low. But governments often forget these objectives when the economy faces a downturn and losses mount, and there is a need for an equity injection. With no other sources available, governments often provide the requisite equity. Unless they take over control of the bank, the *incentive* effects are nil or may even be perverse. The original owners only worry about the loss of their own capital, not the capital provided by the bank. All the government is doing is providing up front some of the money it would have provided in the event of a crisis.

Capital adequacy standards that are appropriately risk adjusted can help undo the distortions associated with government deposit insurance and provide incentives for banks to undertake less risk, thus reducing the likelihood of a bank failure. The problem in the past is that the risk adjustments actually distorted bank behavior and even contributed to the contraction of credit availability. A key error, for instance, made by the Fed in the 1980s was to treat long-term government bonds as if they were safe; there might not have been any credit risk (the risk of bankruptcy of the issuer of the bond), but there was still market risk (interest rates could change, resulting in a change in the market value of bonds). This encouraged banks to buy long-term government bonds and to make fewer loans. Accounting failures also contributed – the banks were not forced to set aside a reserve to reflect the risk of a fall in price. They could book the entire gap between the long-term interest rate and the short-term interest rate at which they borrowed as profit, even though the reason for this gap was market expectation of a fall in the bond price.

In many countries, restrictions on bank portfolios have played an important role. Speculative real estate lending has been the basis of many an economic downturn, and some regulatory authorities have accordingly restricted such lending (and insisted on high collateral standards). (In the case of Thailand, they were concerned both with development and stability; they hoped that by restricting speculative real estate lending, more funds would go into more productive investments, generating employment.) Ironically, the IMF (supported by the United States) was highly critical of such restrictions. If the market demanded the construction of empty office buildings rather than investments in productive factories generating employment, one should not interfere with the market. Under pressure, Thailand abandoned some of these prudential regulations, and this contributed to the crisis that the country faced a few years later.

One of the many problems with earlier standard bank regulations was that they focused on risk, asset by asset, but didn't take into account correlations.[49] That was why there was hope that a more sophisticated form

---

[49] This earlier system of bank regulation, formulated by the Basel Committee on Bank Supervision of the Bank of International Settlements (BIS) in Basel was called Basel I.

of regulation based on banks' own risk management systems and credit rating agencies, taking into account asset correlations, would be a major improvement. This new system, called Basel II, is in the process of being adopted in advanced industrial countries. After the current crisis, it is clear that Basel II is dead. The banks' risk management systems were badly flawed – evidently, the banks did not understand correlated risks, let alone fat-tailed distributions. The rating agencies (once again) were even worse, though this time there is evidence not only of ordinary incompetence but also of a serious problem with incentives.

An important part of any regulatory system is information disclosures and accounting standards: Regulations requiring banks to mark their assets to market are viewed as important for providing depositors (and others dealing with the bank) with better information about the bank's financial position. It can also avoid the perverse effects of not marking to market, which can encourage excessive risk taking. Banks can buy a set of risky assets, knowing that it can sell those that do well – reflecting the profits in its accounts – but hold on to the assets making a loss. Yet marking to market can also have other real and adverse effects. If markets exhibit irrational pessimism, marking to market may in a downturn force banks to acquire new equity injections – or force them to reduce outstanding loans. Poorly designed regulation can be procyclical, exacerbating economic fluctuations. As we noted above, the decision of the Fed under Greenspan to treat long-term government bonds as safe and not requiring them to set aside reserves played a large role in *creating* the recession of 1991.

There has been a natural tendency for those who would prefer to have no regulation to suggest that the optimal regulation is minimum regulation. Some have argued that disclosure is all that is required. Some have argued that all that is required is to eliminate deposit insurance. For the government to provide deposit insurance contributes to moral hazard, because depositors will not take due care in deciding where to put their money. But as noted earlier, all countries have, in effect, deposit insurance: When a crisis hits, depositors will be bailed out. Moreover, information is a public good. It makes no sense for all individuals to evaluate for themselves the creditworthiness of each bank – even if it were possible for them to do so; and as we explained, there are real problems in market-based certification. Still others have argued that all that is required is forceful implementation of capital adequacy standards. Each of these simplistic arguments is flawed. Effective regulation is more complex. Given the ability of those in the financial markets to engage in regulatory arbitrage, some discretionary regulation will inevitably be required to innovate around regulations.

iii. Ensuring Access

These include regulations against discrimination and redlining[50] and the Community Reinvestment Act, requiring banks to lend a certain fraction of their portfolio to underserved communities.[51] Earlier laws restricting interstate banking had a similar motivation: There was a worry that New York banks would garner all the deposits but then divert the money back to East Coast money centers. (In many developing countries, similar concerns are raised today: Foreign banks are more likely to lend to multinationals and large domestic firms than to domestic small and medium-sized enterprises. Modern banking theory, which sees banks as processing information, assessing creditworthiness, and monitoring, provides an explanation for these lending patterns.) CRA lending requirements have been successful in extending access to credit.

Many developing countries face a more general problem: Banks prefer to lend to the government or to hold money abroad (speculating on a capital gain) rather than to lend money at home, especially to small and medium-sized enterprises. In short, banks are not performing the role they ought to perform. Several policies have been proposed for addressing the problem. One is to change incentives, for example, by taxing at a high rate capital gains on foreign exchange speculation. Governments typically have large deposits and can link where they hold deposits to bank performance, so that banks that lend to small and medium-sized enterprises at low margins will get more government deposits. A second policy is regulatory: Not allowing banks to hold government paper. If they wish to provide money to the government, they can do so, but they would get only a small service fee for providing depository services. (Government can, alternatively, provide direct competition to the private sector.) Generalized CRA requirements requiring banks to lend minimal fractions to small and medium-sized enterprises or to the rural sector may also help.

The argument for these lending mandates is that the private sector is more able to make risk judgments, untainted by political connections, than a development bank or government agency. Within the rural sector, they will be able to find good borrowers. Such mandates and restrictions may lower short run returns (though not necessarily long run returns, as banks learn how to lend in each of these markets). Obviously, if excessive, these

---

[50] A practice in which banks exclude from lending properties lying within particular areas.

[51] Underlying these (and some of the other restrictions described earlier) is a simple notion: There is a discrepancy between private and social returns to lending.

mandates will lower profitability to the point that there will be an exit from the industry, but it appears in most cases that the value of a bank franchise (including the right to access the funds of the Central Bank) are sufficiently great that this has not occurred.

iv. Macrostability

Many of the regulations discussed so far have macroeconomic implications. Safety and soundness focuse on the ability of individual banks to repay amounts deposited. But when risks are correlated, if many banks have a problem, the economy risks slipping into a recession. Without access to credit, it is hard for an economy to function.

Policies that make sense if an individual bank faces a problem do not make sense if all banks face problems. If only one bank is in trouble, regulators can be tough and refuse forbearance; if many banks face difficulties, such an approach may force the economy into a deep downturn.

Similarly, regulatory rules have to be sensitive to cyclical implications. There is worry, for instance, that strict enforcement of high (and non-cyclically adjusted) capital adequacy requirements can act as an automatic *destabilizer*. That is why it may be important to develop cyclically adjusted capital adequacy requirements or provisioning requirements.

c. Greenhouse Gas Emissions

The third example concerns greenhouse gas emissions that contribute to global warming. The policy debate has centered on emission taxes versus cap and trade systems. When the caps (the targets) are auctioned, the two systems are almost equivalent. In one case, the government is setting a quantity and letting the price adjust; in the other it is setting a price and letting the quantity adjust. If the government had good information about the demand curve, the two would be perfectly equivalent. In practice, either price or quantity will adjust over time (as we have noted earlier) in response to success in achieving the objective of ultimate interest, overall concentration of atmospheric greenhouse gases (or even more directly, change in temperature). One widely discussed proposal is the safety valve, a mixture of a price and quantity system: A quantity constraint, provided the price does not exceed a particular level, after which it becomes a price intervention. This has the short run advantage of limiting risk – firms know the maximum price they will have to pay for emissions. It also provides the basis of a political agreement based on different perceptions: Many environmentalists claim the cost of mitigation is low, and at the same time they want strict emission constraints. If they are correct, the safety valve will never have to be used.

Different systems have different distributive consequences. When the international community grants a particular cap to a country, it is as though it is granting a cash-equivalent endowment (assuming emission permits are tradable). This is one of the reasons the debate is so contentious. The Kyoto system gave more emission rights to those countries that were emitting more; those who had polluted more in the past were, in effect, given more cash, a peculiar policy, to say the least. The developing countries argue that, if anything, those who have polluted more in the past should have less pollution rights going forward. They have already used up their share of the global atmosphere.

The international distributive consequences of an agreement of a common tax rate, with the proceeds kept within each country, are likely to be small. There are small distortions associated with any tax. The replacement of, say, a labor tax with a pollution tax reduces one distortion and increases another. The net impact is simply the difference between the two distortions, and the difference in the net impacts is likely to be relatively small.[52]

There are, of course, large distributive consequences for different sectors. The cap and trade system offsets these by providing emission rights to past polluters. But the same equity concerns raised earlier arise. Moreover, it sets the stage for high levels of corruption, as private actors seek more emission rights: In some countries, it will be outright; in more advanced industrial countries, it will be more subtle, with campaign contributions designed to affect the *rules* by which targets are set in ways that favor some (obviously, at the expense of others).[53]

Though there is a consensus that, setting aside the distributive consequences, both cap and trade and a carbon tax, if universally applied, could lead to efficient outcomes, there remains strong support behind additional regulatory measures. The EU has imposed renewable energy mandates, the U.S. CAFE standards, and everywhere there is discussion of imposing other controls, such as on coal-fired generating plants. Why, one might ask, should we resort to these "distorting" regulations when we have at hand an efficient mechanism for reducing emissions? The regulatory interventions create, in

---

[52] Technically, we say that the welfare loss is (roughly) just the difference between the difference in the two Harberger triangles (that associated with the emissions tax, and that associated with the taxes that it replaces).

[53] This is an example of how the form of government intervention may affect the likelihood of government failure.

effect, a system that taxes emissions at different rates in different sectors. Part of the reason is concern about the distributive consequences of the large reductions required in emissions. To elicit the required behavioral changes, explicit or implicit taxes on emissions will be very high – beyond levels likely to be politically acceptable. This in part may be because market participants are myopic. They see upfront costs more clearly than they do costs down the line; their implicit discount rate seems "irrationally" high. A more fuel efficient car that, at reasonable discount rates, is less expensive will not be bought because its upfront price is higher. Many firms similarly respond to current patterns of consumption. In the 1990s, American automobile firms did not diversify their portfolio but rather concentrated their attention on the SUVs then in fashion. If one forces large behavioral changes through regulation in certain key sectors, the burden on the remaining sectors – changes that have to be accomplished through taxes – is reduced. The *seeming* cost of mitigation,[54] and probably the actual cost as well, would appear to be lower. There is a more general point: Typically optimal tax systems (designed either to raise a fixed revenue or to achieve a given reduction in emissions) are differentiated and nonlinear.

IV. Elements of a Research Agenda

The case for regulation is compelling. There are important market failures and important arenas for addressing distributive concerns. Regulation often fails to achieve the ambitions we hold for it, but it is still the case that, at least in many instances, matters are better *with* regulation than *without* it.

At a theoretical level, and ignoring issues of political economy, regulation can be viewed, as we noted, as part of a system of indirect societal control. Even simple models suggest that optimal control systems are highly complex. Once the fallibility of control systems is taken into account, the complexity grows further, and in most social contexts, there are multiple objectives, contributing further to the complexity.

Yet complexity itself gives rise to problems. It is the complex financial products that have generated so many problems in financial markets – even more than transparency. We have no simple way of characterizing complexity.

Moreover, there are, as we have noted, complex trade-offs among objectives. Economic theory has focused on the design of optimal regulatory

---

[54] To critics of these regulatory approaches, the lack of transparency is itself one of the main criticisms.

schemes for simple, well-defined problems typically in contexts in which there are limited problems of information asymmetries.

More attention should be paid to designing principles of *robust regulation*, which works reasonably well under a variety of circumstances.

The world is always changing, and that means regulations need to change. And that means the regulatory system needs to be *flexible*.

A second major set of issues concerns capture – which entails not only capture by special interests but also by particular ideologies. How can we design regulatory structures that are resistant to capture? We have suggested duplicative regulation may be desirable, systems of checks and balances. But what are good systems of checks and balances? And are some systems more amenable to multiple oversight because they are simpler and more transparent, with failures to exercise oversight or compliance failures easier to detect?

A third related set of issues concerns democratic accountability. We delegate regulation in part because we believe designing good regulatory systems is too complex to be left to relatively uninformed legislators. But formal compliance with rule making and formal enforcement procedures do not suffice. In terms of emergencies, democratic protections may be further weakened. As I have noted, what the Federal Reserve didn't do prior to the crisis and what it has now done both strain democratic principles.

Some of the principles and objectives may come into conflict. It may be harder to change a regulatory system when there are multiple regulators.

We have a wealth of information about how regulatory processes have worked in particular contexts. We have some general theories of optimal incentive structures and institutional design in the presence of human fallibility. The research challenge going forward is to combine these bodies of knowledge to provide guidelines for the construction of robust regulatory frameworks.

CONCLUDING REMARKS

The Arrow-Debreu model set forth a set of conditions under which Adam Smith's invisible hand worked perfectly with no government intervention required. However, the conditions required – not just the absence of externalities, public goods, and perfect competition, but also perfect information, a complete set of markets, including markets for risk, and no (endogenous) innovation – have meant that the model has been most useful in providing a taxonomy for why government intervention is required. Many economists, still in love with the price system, leapt to the conclusion that the government should only intervene through simple, linear taxes and subsidies. But, alas, for many of the same reasons that markets fail, so too simple price interventions are, in general, not optimal. More complicated *regulatory* interventions are, in general, required. In this chapter, I have tried to outline some of the critical issues in the design of regulatory systems. The question today is not *whether* to regulate, or even *whether we have overregulated* – the subprime mortgage crisis suggests a problem of underregulation – but rather, whether we have designed a regulatory system that is as efficient and equitable as it could be.

## TWO

Effective Regulation through Credible Cost–Benefit Analysis: The Opportunity Costs of Superfund[1]

Michael Greenstone

I. Introduction

American government, at every level, regulates a dizzyingly broad swath of social and economic life. Regulatory policy determines the drugs we can buy, the pollutants in the air we breathe and the water we drink, the speed we can drive, the materials builders use to construct our homes, the cars we buy, and so much more.

In making decisions about regulations, public officials must choose which areas of our lives merit government rules, as well as how stringent those rules should be. For example, the federal government first decided to regulate airborne particulate matter in 1970 and has tightened these regulations twice since then. Simultaneously, the government has had to decide whether and how to regulate hundreds of other air pollutants and other hazards. These choices have been further complicated by the fact the distributional impacts of some pollutants are spread unevenly across the population (e.g., they may differ by region, income, or race). At the same time, policymakers have had to grapple with the economic impacts of proposed environmental rules on manufacturers and other polluters. The essence of regulation is that it requires the regulated to take actions that they would not otherwise take, actions that often increase their costs, reduce their utility, or in some other way harm them.

When faced with this incredible array of complex and often uncertain trade-offs, what is a well-intentioned government to do?

The only humane solution to this enduring dilemma lies with careful and rigorous cost-benefit analysis. This approach's fundamental goal is to

[1] I am grateful to Edward Balleisen, David Moss, and Katherine Ozment for insightful comments and encouragement. I thank the Tobin Project for financial support. This paper was prepared for the Tobin Project's Conference, "Toward a New Theory of Regulation."

analyze regulatory decisions rationally and quantitatively, with the goal of maximizing societal welfare. Specifically, regulators should seek to maximize the expected net benefits of regulation, which is just the difference between the expected benefits (e.g., lives saved, illnesses prevented) and the costs (e.g., investments required to scrub smokestacks, expenditures on monitoring pollution emissions).

Cost-benefit analysis requires that regulators convert both the costs and the benefits of a proposed policy initiative into a common unit, money. Some critics of the practice consider such quantitative translation cold-hearted and impossible (Ackerman and Heinzerling 2004; Kelman 1981), but it is in fact the most humane approach to regulation we have.[2] By converting all costs and benefits to the same unit, government can avoid setting irrational regulatory policies that harm human welfare. A failure to use cost-benefit analysis could lead to irrational policies across pollutants. For example, it might lead to strict regulation on airborne particulate matter that prevents all deaths due to this pollutant at a tremendous cost to business; while arsenic pollution is regulated very lightly such that hundreds of people die annually, even though tougher rules would require only a minor burden on firms. Cost-benefit analysis is a transparent method to help policymakers determine which pollutants they should regulate and to what degree.

The current regulatory problem does not involve cost-benefit analysis per se, but rather the poor quality of the evidence underlying many cost-benefit decisions. At its core, regulatory policy aims to alter the world so that the lives of at least some members of society are improved. But in so doing, regulations generally restrict or regulate the behavior of other members of society. The goal of a beneficent government is to implement regulations where the benefits outweigh the costs, accounting for costs and benefits to all members of society.

But without a well-developed strategy for evaluating regulation policies, it is impossible to know what would have happened in the absence of the policy. The fundamental issue is that we would like to observe the world with and without a regulation. Then we could determine whether society gains or is harmed by a regulatory policy. Of course, it is impossible to observe both states of the world simultaneously.

---

[2] There are several standard criticisms of cost-benefit analysis. They include that it immorally commodifies objects (e.g., human life) that are beyond valuation, gives a false sense of scientific certainty, and unfairly benefits the rich. Several commentators, including Revesz and Livermore (2007) and Sunstein (2004), provide powerful responses to these criticisms. Interestingly, these criticisms have done little to dislodge cost-benefit analysis as the major lens through which government agencies and legislators assess regulations.

What can be done to improve the quality of evidence on regulations' causal impact on social welfare? The ideal solution is to use the same experimental techniques used in "hard sciences" such as chemistry and medicine. Classical experimental design incorporates the random assignment of the population into a treatment group, those affected by a given treatment, and a control group, those who are not. The random assignment of the treatment means that there is no *a priori* reason to believe that in the absence of the regulation the average behavior of the two groups would have differed. Thus, a comparison of outcomes among the treatment and control populations yields a causal estimate of the treatment.

Although the random assignment of regulation may seem like a radical idea, it should not. Randomized trials are the primary tool to learn about the efficacy of drugs and medical devices. Further, there is increasing acceptance of this approach in many areas of social science, including educational policy and interventions in developing countries.[3]

Despite their evident appeal, randomized evaluations of regulations may not be possible in some instances. In these cases, quasi-experiments and natural experiments provide an appealing alternative approach. In analyzing regulations with quasi-experiments, one measures the differences in outcomes between the treatment and control groups just as in a classical experiment. In these cases, however, "treatment" (or in a regulatory context, "policy") status is determined by politics, public pressure, or some other action beyond the researcher's control. Despite the nonrandom nature of treatment status, it is still possible to draw valid inferences on the effects of regulation from the differences in outcomes between the treatment and control groups, provided that the quasi-experiment meets certain, potentially testable, assumptions.

Another important feature of evidence-based regulation is to use economic theory to guide the experiment or quasi-experiment. Theory provides the framework for identifying the people and firms that may be affected by a given regulation. Consequently, it is crucial to use economic theory to structure the empirical analysis so that the results can be used to determine

---

[3] See Ioannidis et al. (2001) on the central role of randomized experiments in medicine and epidemiology. Angrist (2004) describes a sea change in research on education policy that has led to a growing consensus that randomized trials are the only way to determine the causal effect of alternative educational interventions. Notably, the U.S. Department of Education has enfranchised this view with the creation of the Institute of Education Science, whose mission is to "provide rigorous evidence on which to ground education practice and policy" (U.S. Department of Education 2006). See Duflo, Glennerster, and Kremer (2008) for a discussion of the increasing use of randomized experiments in assessments of interventions in developing countries.

the impact of the regulation on societal welfare. Further, economic theory can help assess the generality of any findings (e.g., whether the findings are likely to apply in other settings).

A government that fails to rely on credible cost-benefit analyses is rolling the dice with its citizens' welfare because implementing regulations whose impacts are unknown is often equivalent to gambling with tens of billions of dollars and unknown numbers of human lives. Poorly informed regulatory choices can lead to a nation's citizens being exposed to lethal concentrations of pollutants. Or conversely, the imposition of regulations with little benefit can burden citizens and firms with expensive compliance efforts that reduce incomes and the quality of citizens' lives. Indeed, regulations' costs can even shorten individuals' lives as income is an important determinant of longevity. As the costs of regulation in the United States amount to many hundreds of billions of dollars, calling the stakes high is an understatement.

The remainder of this essay conducts an abridged cost-benefit analysis based on research by Greenstone and Gallagher (2008) and Currie, Moretti, and Greenstone (2007) of the federal Superfund program that cleans up hazardous waste sites. Through 2005, the federal government has spent approximately $35 billion (2005$) on Superfund clean-ups, and firms have expended considerable additional funds. The program continues to grow, with remediations ongoing at roughly 800 sites and regulators continually adding new sites to the list of those slated for clean-up.

This essay focuses on Superfund for several reasons. First, it demonstrates that it is possible to conduct a credible empirical analysis in a setting where it might not have seemed feasible. Second, the cost-benefit analysis is guided by economic theory, so in principle the connection between the results and social welfare is immediate. In short, this abridged cost-benefit exercise demonstrates that opportunities for sophisticated, credible cost-benefit analyses are more readily available than widely believed.

Third, the analysis of the Superfund program suggests that its benefits to people living near these hazardous waste sites are likely to be smaller than its costs. This finding holds whether one allows for the possibility that the benefits are evident in housing prices and/or infant health (although the health results are based on a subset of sites and consequently must be considered preliminary and incomplete). This is an uncomfortable finding, akin to conclusions that people do not like ice cream or sunshine. However, it helps to underscore that, though cost-benefit analyses may not fit our prior expectations, they can lead to an improvement in social welfare by directing resources to the projects that produce the largest social benefits.

The remainder of the chapter examines the costs and benefits of the Superfund program. It then concludes with a brief discussion of why the best and most humane path forward for regulation is to implement a culture of experimentation and evaluation and provides some directions on how to jump start such a culture.

II. An Abridged Cost-Benefit Analysis of the Superfund Program

This section of the chapter is divided into five subsections. The first provides a history of the Superfund program and the outline of the research design that, along with my collaborator Justin Gallagher, I have used to test for impacts of clean-ups on house prices (see Greenstone and Gallagher 2008). The second briefly outlines an economic model that guides the empirical analysis. The third derives estimates of the costs of Superfund clean-ups and provides some other statistics about them. The fourth subsection derives estimates of the benefits of Superfund clean-ups as measured in the housing market. In principle, the full benefits (i.e., aesthetic and health) of clean-ups will be capitalized into housing prices. The fifth subsection estimates the impacts of Superfund clean-ups on infant health. Though this is an incomplete measure of the potential health benefits, fetuses and infants are a population that is likely to be especially sensitive to exposure to the contaminants found at Superfund sites.

A. The Superfund Program and a New Research Design

1. History and Broad Program Goals

Before the regulation of disposal of hazardous wastes by the Toxic Substances Control and Resource Conservation and Recovery Acts of 1976, industrial firms frequently disposed of wastes by burying them in the ground. Love Canal, New York, offers perhaps the most infamous example of these disposal practices. Throughout the 1940s and 1950s, this area served as a landfill for industrial waste, receiving more than 21,000 tons of chemical wastes. After New York state investigators found high concentrations of dangerous chemicals in the air and soil at Love Canal, concerns about the safety of this area prompted President Carter to declare a state of emergency in 1978, an action that led to the relocation of the area's 900 residents. As David Moss and Mary Oey make clear in their essay on the impact of the Love Canal crisis on regulatory politics (Moss and Oey 2009), this incident helped galvanize support for addressing the legacy of industrial waste, a movement that culminated in the creation of the Superfund program in 1980.

The centerpiece of the Superfund program, and this chapter's focus, is the long-run remediation of hazardous waste sites.[4] These multiyear remediation efforts aim to reduce permanently the serious but not imminently life-threatening dangers caused by hazardous substances. By the end of 2005, the Environmental Protection Agency had placed 1,552 sites on the National Priorities List (NPL), thereby slating them for long-run clean-ups. The next subsection describes the selection process, which forms the basis of our research design.

2. Site Assessment & Superfund Clean-Ups Processes

As of 1996, environmental activities, neighborhood groups, and other interested parties had referred more than 40,000 hazardous waste sites to the EPA for possible inclusion on the NPL. Because there are limited resources available for these clean-ups, the EPA follows a multistep process to identify the most dangerous sites.

The final step of the assessment process involves the application of a Hazardous Ranking System (HRS), a rating system reserved for the most dangerous sites. The EPA developed the HRS in 1982 as a standardized approach to identify the sites that pose the greatest threat to humans and the environment. The original HRS evaluated the risk for exposure to chemical pollutants along three migration "pathways": groundwater, surface water, and air. The major determinants of risk along each pathway for a site are the toxicity and concentration of chemicals present, the likelihood of exposure and proximity to humans, and the size of the potentially affected population. EPA officials also consider nonhuman impacts, but they play a relatively minor role in determining the HRS score.

The HRS produces a score that ranges from 0 to 100, with 100 being the highest level of risk. From 1982–1995, the EPA assigned all hazardous waste sites with a HRS score of 28.5 or greater to the NPL. Only these sites become eligible for Superfund remedial clean-up. The Data Appendix provides further details on the determination of HRS test scores and their role in assignment to the NPL.

Once a site moves onto the NPL, it generally takes many years until clean-up firms complete their work. The first step is a further study of the extent of the environmental problem and how best to remedy it, an assessment that regulators summarize in the Record of Decision (ROD), which also

---

[4] The Superfund program also funds immediate removals, which are short-term responses to environmental emergencies aimed at diminishing an immediate threat. These actions are not intended to remediate the underlying environmental problem and are not exclusive to hazardous waste sites on the NPL.

outlines recommended clean-up actions for the site. After workers finish physical construction of all clean-up remedies, removing immediate threats to health, and putting long-run threats "under control," the EPA gives a site a "construction complete" designation. The final step is the agency's deletion of the site from the NPL.

3. 1982 HRS Scores as the Basis of a New Research Design

This chapter's goal is to obtain reliable estimates of the effect of Superfund-sponsored clean-ups of hazardous waste sites on housing market outcomes in areas surrounding the sites. The empirical challenge is that NPL sites are the most polluted in the United States, so it is likely that there are unobserved factors that co-vary with both proximity to hazardous waste sites and housing prices. Although this possibility cannot be tested directly, it is notable that proximity to a hazardous waste site is associated with lower population densities, lower household incomes, higher percentages of high school dropouts, and a higher fraction of mobile homes among the housing stock.

Consequently, cross-sectional estimates of the association between housing prices and proximity to a hazardous waste site may be severely biased due to omitted variables.[5] In fact, economists have long noted that the possibility of confounding due to unobserved variables is a threat to the validity of the results from efforts to develop reliable estimates of individuals' willingness to pay for environmental amenities (Small 1975). This chapter's challenge is to develop a valid counterfactual for the housing market outcomes near Superfund sites in the absence of their placement on the NPL and clean-up.

A feature of the initial NPL assignment process that has not been noted previously by researchers may provide a credible solution to the likely omitted variables problem. In the first year after the legislation's passage, groups and individuals referred 14,697 sites to the EPA, which then investigated them as potential candidates for remedial action. Through an initial assessment process, the EPA winnowed this list to the 690 most dangerous sites.

---

[5] Cross-sectional models for housing prices have exhibited signs of misspecification in a number of other settings, including the relationships between land prices and school quality, air pollution, and climate variables (Black 1999; Chay and Greenstone 2005; Deschenes and Greenstone 2006). Incorrect choice of functional form is an alternative source of misspecification (Halvorsen and Pollakowski 1981; Cropper et al. 1988). Other potential sources of biases of published hedonic estimates include measurement error and publication bias (Black and Kneisner 2003; Ashenfelter and Greenstone 2004).

Although the Superfund legislation directed the EPA to develop an NPL of at least 400 sites (Section 105(8)(B) of CERCLA), budgetary considerations caused the EPA to set a goal of placing exactly 400 sites on the NPL.

The EPA developed the HRS to provide a scientific basis for determining the 400 out of 690 sites that posed the greatest risk. Pressured to initiate the clean-ups quickly, the EPA developed the HRS in about a year, applied the test to the 690 worst sites, and ranked their scores from highest to lowest. A score of 28.5 divided numbers 400 and 401, so the initial NPL published in September 1983 was limited to sites with HRS scores exceeding 28.5. See the Data Appendix for further details.

The central role of the HRS score provides a compelling basis for a research design that compares housing market outcomes near sites with initial scores above and below the 28.5 cutoff for at least three reasons. First, it is unlikely that sites' HRS scores were manipulated to affect their placement on the NPL, because the 28.5 threshold was established *after* the testing of the 690 sites was completed. The HRS scores therefore reflected the EPA's assessment of the risks posed by each site *rather* than the expected costs or benefits of clean-up.

Second, the HRS scores are noisy measures of risk, so it is possible that true risks are similar above and below the threshold. This noisiness results from the scientific uncertainty about the health consequences of exposure to the tens of thousands of chemicals present at these sites.[6] Further, there was no evidence that sites with HRS scores below 28.5 posed little risk to health. The Federal Register specifically reported that the "EPA has not made a determination that sites scoring less than 28.50 do not present a significant risk to human health, welfare, or the environment" and that a more informative test would require "greater time and funds" (U.S. Environmental Protection Agency 1984).[7]

---

[6] A recent history of Superfund makes this point. "At the inception of EPA's Superfund program, there was much to be learned about industrial wastes and their potential for causing public health problems. Before this problem could be addressed on the program level, the types of wastes most often found at sites needed to be determined, and their health effects studied. Identifying and quantifying risks to health and the environment for the extremely broad range of conditions, chemicals, and threats at uncontrolled hazardous wastes sites posed formidable problems. Many of these problems stemmed from the lack of information concerning the toxicities of the more than 65,000 different industrial chemicals listed as having been in commercial production since 1945" (U.S. Environmental Protection Agency 2000, p. 3–2).

[7] One way to measure the crude nature of the initial HRS test is by the detail of the guidelines used for determining the HRS score. The guidelines used to develop the initial HRS sites were collected in a thirty-page manual. Today, the analogous manual is more than 500 pages.

Third, the selection rule that determined placement on the NPL is a highly nonlinear function of the HRS score. This allows for a quasi-experimental regression discontinuity design. Specifically, we will compare outcomes at sites near the 28.5 cutoff. If the unobservables are similar or changing smoothly around the regulatory threshold, then one can make causal inferences on the impact of Superfund clean-ups on housing markets.[8]

An additional key feature of this data set is that an initial score above 28.5 is highly correlated with eventual NPL status but is not a perfect predictor of it. The EPA rescored some sites, with the later scores determining whether they ended up on the NPL.[9] The subsequent analysis uses an indicator variable for whether a site's initial (i.e., 1982) HRS score was above 28.5 as an instrumental variable for whether a site was on the NPL to purge the potentially endogenous variation in NPL status.

Finally, it is important to emphasize that sites that failed to qualify for the NPL were ineligible for Superfund remediations. My collaborators and I investigated whether these sites were cleaned up under state or local programs and found that they were frequently left untouched. Among the sites that the EPA targeted through these programs, a typical solution was to put a fence around the site and place signs indicating the presence of health hazards. The point is that the remediation activities at NPL sites dramatically exceeded the clean-up activities at non-NPL sites in scope and cost.

B. Economic Theory as a Guide

As an alternative to the health effects approach, we use the housing market to infer individuals' valuations of clean-ups. Economists have estimated the association between housing prices and environmental amenities at least since Ridker (1967) and Ridker and Henning (1967). However, Rosen (1974) and Freeman (1974) were the first to give this correlation an economic interpretation. In the Rosen formulation, a differentiated good can be described by a vector of its characteristics, $Q = (q_1, q_2, \ldots, q_n)$. In the case of a house,

---

[8] The research design of comparing sites with HRS scores "near" the 28.5 is unlikely to be valid for sites that received an initial HRS score after 1982. This is because once the 28.5 cutoff was set, the HRS testers were encouraged to minimize testing costs and simply determine whether a site exceeded the threshold. Consequently, testers generally stop scoring pathways once enough pathways are scored to produce a score above the threshold.

[9] As an example, 144 sites with initial scores above 28.5 were rescored, and this led to seven sites receiving revised scores below the cutoff. Further, complaints by citizens and others led to rescoring at a number of sites below the cutoff. Although there has been substantial research on the question of which sites on the NPL are cleaned up first (see, e.g., Sigman 2001), we are unaware of any research on the determinants of a site being rescored.

these characteristics may include structural attributes (e.g., number of bedrooms), neighborhood public services (e.g., local school quality), and local
environmental amenities (e.g., distance from a hazardous waste site). Thus,
the price of the ith house can be written as:

$$P_i = P(q_1, q_2, \ldots, q_n). \tag{1}$$

The partial derivative of $P(\bullet)$ with respect to the nth characteristic, $\partial P/\partial q_n$,
is referred to as the marginal implicit price. It is the marginal price of the
n^{th} characteristic implicit in the overall price of the house.

Locations close to hazardous waste sites must have lower housing prices
to attract potential homeowners, so $\partial P/\partial q_n$ reveals the price that allocates
individuals across locations. Thus, it can be used to infer the welfare effects
of a marginal change in a characteristic.[10] In principle, the price differential reflects both individuals' valuations of the health risk associated with
proximity to a site *and* the site's damage to a neighborhood's aesthetics.
In this respect, the use of housing markets to value an amenity provides a
fuller examination of the valuation than an exclusive focus on the health
risks.[11]

The consistent estimation of (1) is the foundation for accurate welfare
calculations of both marginal and nonmarginal changes. However, consistent estimation may be difficult because it is likely that there are unobserved
factors that co-vary with, for example, both distance from a hazardous waste
site and housing prices.[12] Although this possibility cannot be directly tested,
it is notable that proximity to a hazardous waste site is associated with a
number of important observable predictors of housing prices. For example,
areas with hazardous waste sites tend to have lower population densities
and a higher proportion of mobile homes and are more likely to be in the
Northeast.

Consequently, cross-sectional estimates of the association between housing prices and proximity to a hazardous waste site may be severely biased

[10] See Rosen (1974), Freeman (1993), and Palmquist (1991) for fuller explanations of the
hedonic method and in particular that $P(\bullet)$ represents the equilibrium interactions of
consumers and producers. Further, they describe the necessary conditions to use the
hedonic method to recover individuals' demand functions, which allow for the valuation
of nonmarginal or large change in the amenity. Also see Ekeland, Heckman, and Nesheim
(2004).

[11] Generally, the hedonic approach cannot account for aesthetic benefits that accrue to
nonresidents that, for example, engage in recreational activities near the site. The health
effects approach has this same limitation.

[12] Additionally, the estimation of equation (1) may be misspecified due to incorrect choice
of functional form for observed covariates (Halvorsen and Pollakowski 1981; Cropper
et al. 1988).

due to omitted variables. In fact, the cross-sectional estimation of equation (1) has exhibited signs of misspecification in a number of other settings, including the relationships between land prices and school quality, total suspended particulates air pollution, and climate variables (Black 1999; Chay and Greenstone 2005; Deschenes and Greenstone 2007).[13] Small (1975) recognized the consequences of the misspecification of equation (1) just one year after publication of the Rosen and Freeman papers:

> I have entirely avoided . . . the important question of whether the empirical difficulties, especially correlation between pollution and unmeasured neighborhood characteristics, are so overwhelming as to render the entire method useless. I hope that . . . future work can proceed to solving these practical problems. . . . The degree of attention devoted to this [problem] . . . is what will really determine whether the method stands or falls . . . [p. 107].

In the intervening years, this problem of misspecification has received little attention from empirical researchers, even though Rosen himself recognized it.[14]

A key assumption underlying the use of housing markets to value proximity to a Superfund site is that the individuals living near a site are aware of when clean-ups have occurred. If this assumption is invalid, it is possible that there are substantial benefits to Superfund clean-ups not reflected in housing prices. Rather than blindly accepting this assumption, this chapter will also report on tests of whether Superfund clean-ups led to improvements in measures of infant health. A finding of substantial health benefits but little increase in housing prices might still lead to Superfund's benefits exceeding its costs.

C. Costs and Other Background Information on Superfund Clean-Ups

The housing price analysis that follows emerged from two samples of hazardous waste sites. The first is called the "All NPL Sample" and includes the 1,398 hazardous waste sites in the fifty U.S. states and the District of

---

[13] Similar problems arise when estimating compensating wage differentials for job characteristics, such as the risk of injury or death. The regression-adjusted association between wages and many job amenities is weak and often has a counterintuitive sign (Smith 1979; Black and Kneisner 2003).

[14] Rosen (1986) wrote, "It is clear that nothing can be learned about the structure of preferences in a single cross-section . . . " (p. 658), and "On the empirical side of these questions, the greatest potential for further progress rests in developing more suitable sources of data on the nature of selection and matching . . . " (p. 688).

Columbia that were placed on the NPL by January 1, 2000. The second is the "1982 HRS Sample," comprising the 690 hazardous waste sites tested for inclusion on the initial NPL. As I will explain below, the infant health component of the analysis is based on Superfund sites in Michigan and Pennsylvania.

Table 2.1 presents summary statistics on the hazardous waste sites in these samples. The entries in column (1) are from the All NPL Sample and are limited to sites in a Census tract for which there is nonmissing housing price data in 1980, 1990, and 2000. After these sample restrictions, there are 985 sites – more than 70 percent of the sites ever placed on the NPL by 2000. Columns (2) and (3) report data from the 1982 HRS Sample. The column (2) entries are based on the 487 sites located in a Census tract with complete housing price data. Column (3) reports on the remaining 189 sites located in Census tracts with incomplete housing price data (generally due to missing 1980 data). Fourteen sites are located outside of the continental United States and were dropped from the sample.

Panel A reports on the timing of the sites' placement on the NPL. Column (1) reveals that about 75 percent of all NPL sites received this designation in the 1980s. Together, columns (2) and (3) demonstrate that the EPA eventually placed 443 of the 676 sites in the 1982 HRS Sample on the NPL. This number exceeds the 400 sites that Congress set as an explicit goal, because, as we have discussed, the agency rescored some sites with initial scores below 28.5, resulting in new scores above the threshold, thus qualifying them for the NPL.

Panel B reports on the size of the hazardous waste sites measured in acres, which is available for NPL sites only. The median site size ranges between twenty-five and thirty-five acres across the samples. The means are substantially larger due to a few very large sites. The modest size of most sites suggests that any expected effects on property values might well be confined to relatively small geographic areas around the sites.

Panel C reveals that the clean-up process is slow. We report the median time until the achievement of different milestones rather than the mean, because many sites have not reached all of the milestones yet. One hundred ninety-eight (16) of the NPL sites in column (2) received either the construction complete or deleted designation by 2000 (1990). For this reason, we focus on changes in housing prices, rental rates, and quantities between 1980 and 2000.

Panel D reports the expected costs of clean-up for NPL sites, and E details expected and actual costs among sites that are construction complete or deleted. The EPA estimates the expected costs before any remediation

Table 2.1. *Summary statistics on the superfund program*

	All NPL sites w/ nonmissing house price data (1)	1982 HRS sites w/nonmissing house price data (2)	1982 HRS sites w/ missing house price data (3)
Number of Sites	985	487	189
1982 HRS Score Above 28.5	–	306	95
A. Timing of Placement on NPL			
Total	985	332	111
# 1981–1985	406	312	97
# 1986–1989	340	14	9
# 1990–1994	166	4	3
# 1995–1999	73	2	2
B. Size of Site (in acres)			
Number of Sites with Size Data	920	310	97
Mean (Median)	1,187 (29)	334 (25)	10,507 (35)
Maximum	195,200	42,560	405,760
C. Stages of Clean-Up for NPL Sites Median Years from NPL Listing Until:			
ROD Issued	–	4.3	4.3
Clean-Up Initiated	–	5.8	6.8
Construction Complete	–	12.1	11.5
Deleted from NPL	–	12.8	12.5
D. Expected Costs of Remediation (Millions of 2000 $s)			
# Sites with Nonmissing Costs	753	293	95
Mean (Median)	$28.3 ($11.0)	$27.5 ($15.0)	$29.6 ($11.5)
95th Percentile	$89.6	$95.3	$146.0
E. Actual and Expected Costs Conditional on Construction Complete (Millions of 2000 $s)			
Sites w/Both Costs Nonmissing	477	203	69
Mean (Median) Expected Costs	$15.5 ($7.8)	$20.6 ($9.7)	$17.3 ($7.3)
Mean (Median) Actual Costs	$21.6 ($11.6)	$32.0 ($16.2)	$23.3 ($8.9)

Notes: All dollar figures are in 2000 $s. Column (1) includes information for sites placed on the NPL before 12/31/99. The estimated cost information is calculated as the sum across the first Record of Decisions for each operating unit associated with a site. See the Data Appendix for further details.

activities have begun, whereas actual costs are our best estimates of total remediation-related expenditures assessed after the site achieves the construction complete designation. We believe this is the first time these variables have been reported for the same sites. In the 1982 HRS Sample that we focus on (i.e., column (2)), the mean and median expected costs are $27.5 million and $15.0 million.

Among the construction complete sites in the 1982 HRS Sample, the mean actual costs exceed the expected costs by about 55 percent. We multiply the overall mean expected cost of $27.5 million by 1.55 to obtain an estimate of

Figure 2.1. Geographic distribution of NPL hazardous waste sites in the All NPL sample. Notes: The All NPL sample consists of the 985 hazardous waste sites assigned to the NPL by January 1, 2000, that we placed in a Census tract with nonmissing housing price data in 1980, 1990, and 2000.

the mean actual costs of clean-up in the 1982 HRS Sample of $43 million (the analogous figure in the All NPL sample is $39 million). This estimate of costs understates the true costs, because it does not include the legal costs or deadweight loss associated with the collection of funds from private parties or taxes, nor does it include the site's share of the EPA's costs of administering Superfund. Nevertheless, it is contrasted with the estimated benefits of Superfund clean-ups in the remainder of the chapter.[15]

Figure 2.1 displays the geographic distribution of the 985 hazardous waste sites with complete housing data in the All NPL Sample. There are NPL sites in forty-five of the forty-eight continental states, demonstrating that Superfund is genuinely a national program. The highest proportion of sites is in the Northeast and Midwest (i.e., the "Rust Belt"), reflecting the historical concentration of heavy industry in these regions.

Figure 2.2 presents a histogram of the initial HRS scores, so it depicts the number of sites with HRS scores in relatively small ranges. The ranges, or bins, are four HRS points wide, because the EPA considered HRS scores within four points to be statistically indistinguishable and to reflect comparable risks to human health (U.S. Environmental Protection Agency 1991).

---

[15] The similarity of the column (1) sites with the other sites suggests that it may be reasonable to assume that the results from the application of the HRS research design to the 1982 HRS Sample are informative about the effects of the other Superfund clean-ups.

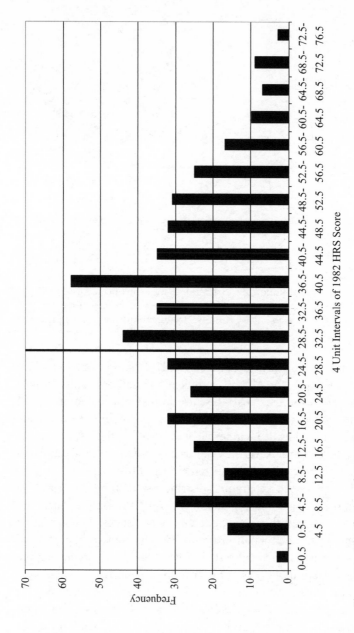

Figure 2.2. Distribution of 1982 HRS scores.

Notes: The figure displays the distribution of 1982 HRS scores among the 487 hazardous waste sites that were tested for placement on the NPL after the passage of the Superfund legislation but before the announcement of the first NPL in 1983. The 188 sites with missing housing data in 1980, 1990, or 2000 are not included in the subsequent analysis and hence are excluded from this figure. The vertical line at 28.5 represents the cutoff that determined eligibility for placement on the NPL.

The distribution looks approximately normal, with the modal bin covering the 36.5–40.5 range. Further, there is no obvious bunching just above or below the threshold, which supports the scientific validity of the HRS scores and suggests that they were not manipulated. Importantly, 227 sites have HRS scores between 16.5 and 40.5. This set is centered on the regulatory threshold of 28.5 that determines placement on the NPL and constitutes the regression discontinuity sample we exploit in the subsequent analysis.

D. The Impact of Superfund Clean-Ups on Housing Prices

This subsection examines the benefits of Superfund clean-ups as measured through the housing market. It begins by reviewing the econometric or statistical approach, then presents the results and interprets the findings.

1. Econometric Approach

The goal of the empirical exercise is to measure the impact of Superfund clean-ups on the prices of homes located near the remediated hazardous waste sites. There are two key features of the exercise. First, its basis is an examination of the growth of house prices in these areas between 1980 and 2000 using decennial Census price data. The beginning year (1980) is the starting point because it precedes the start of the Superfund program. 2000 is useful as an ending point because remediation was complete at nearly 65 percent of the sites originally placed on the NPL by then.

Second, the chief threat is the possibility of unobserved variables that affect the growth of housing prices between 1980 and 2000 near these sites. For example, the fraction of the population living in cities where many Superfund sites are located increased during the 1990s (presumably for reasons unrelated to Superfund). Plus, proximity to a hazardous waste site is associated with lower household incomes, higher percentages of high school dropouts, and a higher fraction of mobile homes among the housing stock. Thus, valid inference on the impact of Superfund requires the identification of an empirical strategy that avoids confounding the direct impact of the clean-ups with these types of unobserved variables.

Greenstone and Gallagher's (2008) potentially valid solution is to restrict the analysis to the neighborhoods around the 690 hazardous waste sites that the EPA deemed to be the most dangerous in the United States when deciding which 400 sites to place on the initial NPL. The basic idea is to compare the growth of housing prices near the 400 hazardous waste sites with initial HRS scores exceeding 28.5 that qualified for a Superfund clean-up to housing price growth near the 290 sites with HRS scores below 28.5 that narrowly missed placement on the NPL. The necessary assumption for valid inference is that in the absence of the Superfund clean-ups, the growth in house prices would have been equal in the areas near sites with 1982 HRS scores just above and below the 28.5 cutoff for clean-ups.

I now briefly describe the technical details involved in implementing what at its core is simply a comparison of housing price growth near sites with HRS scores above and below the 28.5 cutoff. The basis of the econometric approach is a two-stage least squares (2SLS) strategy that accounts for the possibility that some sites received a second score if it was thought that the initial score was too high or low. Because this decision about rescoring might be related to future house price growth, we rely on the variation in NPL status based on the *initial* HRS score. Specifically, we fit the following system of equations:

$$y_{c2000} = \theta(1NPL_{c2000}) + X_{c1980'}\beta + \varepsilon_{c2000}, \qquad (2)$$

$$(1NPL_{c2000}) = X_{c2980'}\Pi + \delta 1(HRS_{c1982} > 28.5) + \eta_{c2000}, \qquad (3)$$

where c references a Census tract. The year (1980, 1982, or 2000) that the variable is measured is also denoted in the subscripts. In practice, the sample is limited to Census tracts containing the 487 sites in the 1982 HRS Sample with housing price data in 1980 and 2000.

The indicator variable $1(NPL_{c2000})$ equals 1 if the observation is from a tract that contains a site placed on the NPL by 2000. The vector X_{c1980} includes a wide set of Census tract-level variables available in the Census files. These are detailed in the Data Appendix. X_{c1980} also includes the natural log of the mean housing price in 1980. Consequently, the parameter of interest, θ, measures the growth in housing prices in Census tracts with an NPL site, relative to Census tracts with hazardous waste sites that narrowly avoided placement on the NPL (after adjustment for the X vector).

The indicator variable $1(HRS_{c1982} > 28.5)$ in equation (3) serves as an instrumental variable. It equals 1 for Census tracts with a site that has a 1982 HRS score exceeding the 28.5 threshold. We then substitute the predicted value of $1(NPL_{c2000})$ from the estimation of equation (3) in the fitting of (2) to obtain an estimate of θ_{2SLS}. In this 2SLS framework, θ_{2SLS} is identified from the variation in NPL status that is due to a site having a 1982 HRS score exceeding 28.5.

For θ_{2SLS} to provide a consistent estimate of the HRS gradient, the instrumental variable must affect the probability of NPL listing without having a direct effect on housing prices. The next section will demonstrate that the first condition clearly holds. The second condition requires that the unobserved determinants of 2000 housing prices are orthogonal to the portion of the nonlinear function of the 1982 HRS score that is not explained by X_{c1980}. In the simplest case, the 2SLS estimator is consistent if $E[1(HRS_{c82} > 28.5) \, \varepsilon_{c2000}] = 0$.

More informally, the aim of this approach is to compare the growth of housing prices in tracts with NPL sites to tracts with hazardous waste sites that narrowly missed a Superfund clean-up. The instrumental variables strategy purges any bias associated with rescoring sites where clean-ups are expected to have large benefits.

We also exploit the regression discontinuity design implicit in the $1(\bullet)$ function that determines NPL eligibility in three separate ways to obtain 2SLS estimates that allow for the possibility that $E[HRS_{c82} > 28.5) \, \varepsilon_{c2000}] \neq 0$ over the entire 1982 HRS Sample. This approach focuses the regression so that it compares housing price growth among tracts with NPL sites and with non-NPL hazardous waste sites when the sites have very similar HRS scores. Intuitively, the idea is to compare tracts with HRS scores of 28.6 to those with sites with scores of 28.4. Practically, we actually use a somewhat wider range of HRS scores to avoid small sample problems. But, the intuition is that this approach further refines the comparisons so that apples are being compared to apples (rather than to oranges).

In the first regression discontinuity approach, a quadratic in the 1982 HRS score is included in X_{c1980} to partial out any correlation between residual housing prices and the indicator for a 1982 HRS score exceeding 28.5. This approach relies on the plausible assumption that residual determinants of housing price growth do not change discontinuously at the regulatory threshold. The second regression discontinuity approach involves implementing our 2SLS estimator on the regression discontinuity sample of 227 sites with 1982 HRS scores between 16.5 and 40.5. Here, the identifying assumption is that all else is held equal in the "neighborhood" of the regulatory threshold (or that all tracts are apples in this range of HRS scores). More formally, it is $E[1(HRS_{c82} > 28.5) \, \varepsilon_{c2000}|16.5 < 1982 \text{ HRS} < 40.5] = 0$.

Recall, the HRS score is a nonlinear function of the ground water, surface water, and air migration pathway scores. The third regression discontinuity method exploits knowledge of this function by including the individual pathway scores in the vector X_{c1980}. All three regression discontinuity approaches are demanding of the data, so the resulting estimates are less well determined than is ideal.

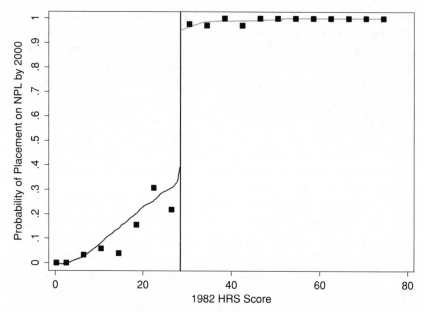

Figure 2.3. Probability of placement on the NPL by 1982 HRS score.
Notes: The figure plots the bivariate relation between the probability of 2000 NPL status
and the 1982 HRS score among the 487 sites in the 1982 HRS sample. These plots are
done separately for sites below (dark colored line) and above (light colored line) the
28.5 threshold. They come from the estimation of nonparametric regressions that use
Cleveland's (1979) tricube weighting function and a bandwidth of 0.5. The data points
present the mean probabilities in the same four-unit intervals of the HRS score as in
Figure 2.2. See the text for further details.

2. Results

I now turn to the preferred quasi-experimental approach, assessing the
relationship between 1982 HRS scores and NPL status. Figure 2.3 plots the
bivariate relation between the probability that a site was placed on the NPL
by 2000 and its initial HRS score among the 487 sites in the 1982 HRS Sample. The plots are done separately for sites above and below the 28.5 threshold
and come from the estimation of nonparametric regressions that use Cleveland's (1979) tricube weighting function and a bandwidth of 0.5.[16] Thus,
they represent a moving average of the probability of NPL status across 1982

[16] The smoothed scatterplots are qualitatively similar with a rectangular weighting function
(i.e., equal weighting) and alternative bandwidths.

HRS scores. The data points represent the mean probabilities in the same four-unit intervals of the HRS score as in Figure 2.2.

The figure presents dramatic evidence that an initial HRS score above 28.5 is a strong predictor of NPL status. The EPA placed virtually all sites with initial scores greater than 28.5 on the NPL by 2000. Again, rescoring explains the nonzero probability of placement on the NPL by 2000 among sites with an initial score below 28.5. A statistical version of the figure reveals that an HRS score above 28.5 is associated with an 83 percent increase in the probability of placement on the NPL (Greenstone and Gallagher 2005). It is evident that there is a powerful relationship between HRS scores above 28.5 and NPL status.

Table 2.2 presents 2SLS estimates of the effect of NPL status on housing prices in 2000. In Panel A, the observations are from the Census tracts containing the 487 hazardous waste sites in the 1982 HRS Sample. In Panel B, each observation is comprised of the average of all variables across tracts that share a border with these tracts. In Panels C and D, the sample is comprised of the land area within circles with radii of two and three miles centered at each site's longitude and latitude. The means of the 1980 values of the total housing stock in the four samples are $71 million, $525 million, $349 million, and $796 million, respectively. The exact covariates in each specification are noted in the row headings at the bottom of the table and are described in more detail in the Data Appendix.

The regression discontinuity approach is implemented by altering the column (2) specification in three different ways. In the column (3) specification, the 1982 HRS score and its square are added. In column (4), the separate pathway scores are included. Finally, the column (5) sample is the regression discontinuity sample comprised of the 227 sites with 1982 HRS scores between 16.5 and 40.5.

The Panel A results suggest that a site's placement on the NPL has little impact on the growth of property values in its own Census tract, relative to tracts with sites that narrowly missed placement on the NPL. The point estimates indicate an increase in prices that ranges from 0.7 percent to 4.7 percent, but they all have associated t-statistics less than two. The regression discontinuity specifications in columns (3) through (5) may be the most credible, so it is notable that they produce the smallest point estimates (although they are also the least precise).

Panel B presents the adjacent tract results. The point estimates from the regression discontinuity estimators range between −0.6 percent and 0.1 percent, and zero cannot be rejected at conventional levels for any of

Michael Greenstone

Table 2.2. *Two-stage least squares (2SLS) estimates of the effect of NPL status on house prices*

	(1)	(2)	(3)	(4)	(5)
A. Own Census Tract					
1(NPL Status by 2000)	0.037	0.047	0.007	0.022	0.027
	(0.035)	(0.027)	(0.063)	(0.042)	(0.038)
B. Adjacent Census Tract					
1(NPL Status by 2000)	0.066	0.015	−0.006	−0.002	0.001
	(0.035)	(0.022)	(0.056)	(0.035)	(0.035)
C. Two-Mile Radius from Hazardous Waste Sites					
1(NPL Status by 2000)	0.019	0.001	0.023	−0.018	−0.007
	(0.032)	(0.023)	(0.054)	(0.035)	(0.034)
Ho: > 0.138, P-Value	0.000	0.000	0.018	0.000	0.000
D. Three-Mile Radius from Hazardous Waste Site					
1(NPL Status by 2000)	0.055	−0.004	−0.027	−0.024	−0.006
	(0.038)	(0.022)	(0.051)	(0.034)	(0.034)
Ho: > 0.058, P-Value	0.467	0.003	0.048	0.007	0.031
1980 Ln House Price	Yes	Yes	Yes	Yes	Yes
1980 Housing Characteristics	No	Yes	Yes	Yes	Yes
1980 Economic & Demographic Vars	No	Yes	Yes	Yes	Yes
State Fixed Effects	No	Yes	Yes	Yes	Yes
Quadratic in 1982 HRS Score	No	No	Yes	No	No
Control for Pathway Scores	No	No	No	Yes	No
Regression Discontinuity Sample	No	No	No	No	Yes

Notes: The entries report the results from twenty-four separate instrumental variables regressions. The ln (2000 median house price) is the dependent variable throughout the table. The units of observation are the Census tract that contains the site (Panel A), tracts that share a border with the site (Panel B), the areas within a circle of two-mile radius from the site (Panel C), and the areas within a circle of three-mile radius from the site (Panel D). In Panels B–D where the unit of observation is comprised of multiple Census tracts, the dependent and independent variables are calculated as weighted means across the relevant Census tracts where the weight is the fraction of the tract that fits the panel's sample selection rule multiplied by the tract's 1980 population. The variable of interest is an indicator for NPL status, and this variable is instrumented with an indicator for whether the tract had a hazardous waste site with a 1982 HRS score exceeding 28.5. The entries are the regression coefficients and heteroskedastic consistent standard errors (in parentheses) associated with the NPL indicator. In Panel A (B–D) the sample sizes are 487 (483) in columns (1) through (4) and 227 (226) in column (5). Panels C and D also report p-values from tests of whether the NPL parameters multiplied by the value of the housing stock in 1980 exceeds $43 million, which is our best estimate of the cost of the average clean-up. The values of the housing stocks in 1980 in the four panels are roughly $75 million, $552 million, $311 million, and $736 million (2000 $s), respectively. See Greenstone and Gallagher (2008) for further details.

them. Thus, there is little evidence of meaningful gains in housing prices outside the site's own Census tract.

Panels C and D summarize the total gain in housing prices associated with a site's placement on the NPL by using the two- and three-mile radius circle samples. They also report whether the clean-ups pass cost-benefit tests analogous to those in Table 2.3. The threshold housing price gains are 13.8 percent and 5.8 percent.

The circle sample results provide further evidence that the NPL designation has little effect on housing prices. In the columns (3)–(5) specifications, only one of the six point estimates is positive. Further, in the eight specifications that adjust for characteristics, the null that the gain in housing prices exceeds the break-even threshold is rejected at conventional significance levels. Overall, these quasi-experimental estimates suggest that Superfund clean-ups fail to pass this cost-benefit test.

Figure 2.4 provides an opportunity to better understand the source of these regression results. It plots the nonparametric regressions of 2000 residual housing prices (after adjustment for the Table 2.2 column (2) covariates) against the 1982 HRS score in the two-mile radius sample.[17] The nonparametric regression is estimated separately below (dark line) and above (light line) the 28.5 threshold. The graph confirms that there is little association between 2000 residual housing prices and the 1982 HRS score. A comparison of the plots at the regulatory threshold is of special interest in light of the large jump in the probability of placement on the NPL there. It is apparent that the moving averages from the left and right are virtually equal at the threshold.

3. Interpretation

These results have failed to find evidence that Superfund clean-ups increase social welfare substantially.[18] In light of the significant resources devoted

---

[17] Figure 2.4 provides a qualitative graphical exploration of the regression results. The relationship between housing prices and 1982 HRS scores cannot be exactly inferred from this graph because the HRS score has not been adjusted for the Table 2.2 column (2) covariates. However, the meaningfulness of this graph is supported by the finding that the covariates are well balanced among sites with 1982 HRS scores above and below the regulatory threshold, especially near the regulatory threshold (Greenstone and Gallagher 2008).

[18] Greenstone and Gallagher (2008) also find little impact of the clean-ups on rental prices for rental units, new home construction, or migration into the area surrounding the site. Additionally, Greenstone and Gallagher test for whether the absence of substantial price increases reflects a stigma that remains even after Superfund clean-ups. In particular,

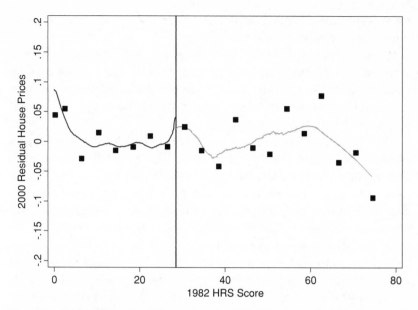

Figure 2.4. Year-2000 Residual House Price by 1982 HRS Score, Sample of Two-Mile Radius Circles around 1982 HRS Sites.

Notes: The figure plots the results from nonparametric regressions between 2000 residual housing prices from the two-mile radius sample after adjustment for the covariates in the column (2) specification of Table 2.2 (except the indicator for a HRS score above 28.5) and the 1982 HRS scores. The nonparametric regressions use Cleveland's (1979) tricube weighting function and a bandwidth of 0.5. These plots are done separately for sites below (dark colored line) and above (light colored line) the 28.5 regulatory threshold. The data points are based on the same four-unit intervals of the HRS score as in Figures 2.2 and 2.3. See the text for further details.

to these clean-ups and the claims of large health benefits, this finding is surprising. This section reviews three possible explanations.

First, the individuals that choose to live near these sites before and after the clean-ups may have a low willingness to pay to avoid exposure to hazardous waste sites. In this case, society provides these individuals a good that they do not value highly. It is possible (and perhaps likely) that there are segments of the population with a high willingness to pay (WTP) to avoid exposure to hazardous waste sites. It may even be the case that the population average WTP is substantial. However, the policy relevant parameter is the WTP of

they found that a site's placement on the NPL has little immediate impact on housing rental prices in areas near the sites. This suggests that the Superfund designation fails to stigmatize these neighborhoods.

the population that lives near these sites, and this is the parameter that this chapter has estimated.[19]

Second, the sites with initial HRS scores less than 28.5 may have also received complete remediations under state or local land reclamation programs. In this case, a zero result is to be expected because both the above and below 28.5 sites would have received the same treatment. Along with Gallagher, I investigated this possibility by conducting an extensive search for information on remediation activities at these sites. From these investigations, we concluded that the clean-up activities were dramatically more ambitious and costly at sites with initial scores exceeding 28.5. For example, we were unable to find evidence of any remediation activities by 2000 at roughly 60 percent of the sites with scores below 28.5. Further, among the 40 percent of the sites where there was evidence of clean-up efforts, the average expenditure was roughly $3 million. This is about $40 million less than the estimate of the average cost of a Superfund clean-up. This difference is not surprising, because the state and local clean-ups were often limited to restricting access to the site or containing the toxics rather than trying to achieve Superfund's goal of returning the site to its natural state. Nevertheless, some remediation took place at these sites, so it may be appropriate to interpret the results as the impact of the extra $40 million that a Superfund clean-up costs.

Third, there could be substantial health benefits from the clean-ups, but the local residents may be unaware of them. Although there is usually substantial newspaper coverage about Superfund clean-ups, this nevertheless remains a possibility, striking at the housing market approach's key assumption that people have perfect information. If this assumption is invalid, then it is necessary to use alternative methods to identify the benefits of Superfund clean-ups.

E. The Impact of Superfund Clean-Ups on Infant Health

This subsection examines the impacts of Superfund clean-ups on infant health. It is part of a larger project on this topic that I am undertaking with my colleagues Janet Currie and Enrico Moretti (Currie, Greenstone, and Moretti 2008). The full project will analyze data from Florida, Michigan, New Jersey, Pennsylvania, and Texas. The results here are based on data

---

[19] A popular theory is that sites become permanently stigmatized when they are placed on the NPL. As Greenstone and Gallagher (2008) demonstrate, the data contradict this explanation in important ways.

from just two of these states (Michigan and Pennsylvania), so they can only provide a preliminary and incomplete picture of the infant health benefits of Superfund clean-ups.

1. Why Focus on Infants?

It is possible that Superfund clean-ups affect many dimensions of human health. A thorough investigation of this issue would require an individual-level data file with detailed information on the respondents' health status (including mortality) and the location of their residences throughout their lifetimes. Such a data file would allow for an examination of whether exposure to Superfund sites leads to poor health outcomes. For example, it would be possible to test whether living near a Superfund site for an extended period of time increases the probability of being stricken by cancer. This type of data file does not exist in the United States. Some available data files report individuals' current residence, but with the high degree of mobility in the United States the assumption that individuals have never moved is unappealing.

It is possible to match infants to particular locations through their mother's place of residence on birth certificate forms. In practice, the analysis utilizes a data file constructed by merging data on the location of Superfund sites, the progression of their clean-ups, and detailed infant health records from the universe of births in Pennsylvania and Michigan for the years 1989–2003. Importantly, the infant health information contains the street address of the mother's residence, so it is possible to focus on births that occur within one mile of Superfund sites. The infant health data were obtained by reaching agreements with these two states' Departments of Vital Statistics to gain access to the confidential versions of these data files.

A key advantage of focusing on infants is that it seems reasonable to presume that their mother's residence is their place of residence during the entire fetal period and the first year of their lives. Further, the fetal and infant periods are especially vulnerable ones, so the results from tests of exposure to Superfund sites on infant health may be informative about the possibility of health impacts in the broader population.

2. Econometric Approach

The goal of this empirical exercise is to measure the impact of Superfund clean-ups on a series of health outcomes for infants born near these sites.

Since data are only available for Pennsylvania and Michigan, it is not feasible to implement the research design based on 1982 HRS scores. As an alternative, Currie, Greenstone, and Moretti (2008) implement an econometric approach that at its core compares birth outcomes before clean-ups with those after clean-ups have been completed. Because the most dangerous toxics may be removed during the clean-up process (i.e., not just at the end), the analysis also compares birth outcomes from before the remediation's initiation to those that occurred during the clean-up process. This section briefly summarizes the Currie, Greenstone, and Moretti approach and results for Pennsylvania and Michigan.

I now briefly describe the technical details of the statistical model. Specifically, the analysis is based on the fitting of the following equation for births that occur in Michigan and Pennsylvania:

Health Outcome$_{icst}$

$$
\begin{aligned}
= {} & \alpha_0 + \alpha_1 \, 1(\text{Clean-Up Active at Nearest Site})_{st} \\
& + \alpha_2 1(\text{Clean-Up Completed at Nearest Site})_{st} \\
& + \alpha_3 1(\text{Nearest Site} < 1\text{Mile})_{st} \\
& + \alpha_{41} X_{icst} \\
& + \beta_1 \, 1(\text{Clean-Up Active at Nearest Site})_{st} \cdot 1(\text{Nearest Site} < 1 \text{ Mile})_{st} \\
& + \beta_2 \, 1(\text{Clean-Up Completed at Nearest Site})_{st} \\
& \quad \cdot 1(\text{Nearest Site} < 1 \text{ Mile})_{st} \\
& + \mu_s + \theta_{ct} + \eta_m + \varepsilon_{icst}
\end{aligned}
\tag{4}
$$

where i represents an infant, c denotes the county of her mother's residence at the time of birth, s indicates the closest hazardous waste site, and t references the year. Additionally, m references her mother. The health outcomes or dependent variables are whether the infant dies within the first year of life, the presence of a congenital abnormality, whether the birth weight was less than 2,500 grams (i.e., classified as low birth weight), birth weight, whether the birth was premature, and the one-minute APGAR score (a measure of the infant's health immediately after birth).

The indicator variable $1(\text{Clean-Up Active at Nearest Site})_{st}$ equals 1 for births where a clean-up has been initiated but has not been completed at the nearest hazardous waste site, regardless of the distance from the mother's home to the site. The indicator $1(\text{Clean-Up Completed at Nearest Site})_{st}$ equals 1 for births when the clean-up has been completed at the nearest hazardous waste site, again regardless of the distance. The third main effect,

Figure 2.5a. Geographic distribution of hazardous waste sites in Michigan. Notes: National Priorities List sites are in red and non-National Priorities List sites are in blue.

1(Nearest Site < 1 Mile)$_{st}$, equals 1 for births to mothers that live within one mile of the nearest hazardous waste site.

The X vector includes a set of covariates describing the parents that may affect infant health. It includes indicator variables for their age, education, race, and Hispanic origin, all interacted with year indicators. When the mother's or father's information is missing, a new category is created for age, education, race, and Hispanic origin so that these observations are not dropped.

The two parameters of interest are β_1 and β_2. The first captures the variation in outcomes specific to births to mothers that live within one mile of a site during the period while the clean-up is ongoing. It measures whether birth outcomes among those living near a site improve during the clean-up relative to before remediation was initiated. The second parameter of interest, β_2, tests for a mean difference in outcomes among births to mothers living within one mile of a site after remediation has been completed (again relative to the period before the clean-up was initiated). Thus, this model allows for the possibility that birth outcomes are differentially affected during the clean-up and after it is completed.

The richness of the data allows for the inclusion of a series of fixed effects that adjust for several forms of unobserved heterogeneity that might otherwise bias the estimates of β_1 and β_2. They include ones for the closest hazardous waste site (μ_s) and county by year (θ_{ct}).

Because the clean-ups can take many years to complete, it is possible that individual mothers gave birth in different stages of the clean-up. For example, clean-up could cause a reshuffling of people in the area near a Superfund site so that the composition of mothers has changed in a way that affects the outcomes. This type of behavioral response would undermine the validity of the analysis. The mother fixed effects, η_m, are an important

Figure 2.5b. Geographic distribution of hazardous waste sites in Pennsylvania. Notes: National Priorities List sites are in red and non-National Priorities List sites are in blue.

way to adjust for this unobserved form of heterogeneity, because they ensure that the regression compares the birth outcomes of two children from the same mother where one occurs before the clean-up and the other occurs during remediation or after completion.

3. Results

Figures 2.5a and 2.5b graphically depict the locations of the hazardous waste sites in Michigan and Pennsylvania, respectively. Although the sites are concentrated in the most heavily industrialized parts of the state, there is substantial variation in their locations within these states.

Table 2.3 presents the results of the estimation of equation (4) for six different dependent variables and four separate specifications. The column (1) specification is the most parsimonious as it only includes site fixed effects and year fixed effects. Column (2) adds the mother and father characteristics, while column (3) then adds county by year fixed effects. Finally, the column (4) specification includes site, county by year, and mother fixed effects. This specification is very demanding of the data.

The entries are the estimates of the parameters β_1 and β_2 and below them their estimated standard errors in parentheses. To gain intuition, consider the panel on birth weight, which has a mean of 3,297 grams.[20] The estimates in the first row indicate that the weight of infants was 5.1 to 12.9 grams greater during the clean-up among nearby births, relative to before. These are small effects. Further, the null of a zero effect cannot be rejected at conventional levels for any of the specifications.

The next row reports on β_2, which measures the effect on birth weight in the period after the clean-up is completed, again relative to the period before the clean-up was initiated. The estimates of β_2 range from -5.9 to 38.3. Again, none of these would be judged statistically significant by

---

[20] Recent research indicates that lower birth weights are associated with negative long-run outcomes, including educational attainment and wages (Black, Devereux, and Salvanes 2007).

Michael Greenstone

Table 2.3. *Association between superfund clean-ups and birth outcomes births within one mile of NPL site*

	(1)	(2)	(3)	(4)
Probability of Infant Mortality (Mean = 0.0067)				
1(< 1 Mile) * 1(After Clean-Up Starts)	.0001	.0001	−.0004	−.0007
	(.0009)	(.0009)	(.0009)	(.0119)
1(< 1 Mile) * 1(After Clean-Up Ends)	−.0006	−.0006	−.0011	.0073
	(.0010)	(.0010)	(.0009)	(.0176)
Probability of Congenital Abnormality (Mean = 0.0196)				
1(< 1 Mile) * 1(After Clean-Up Starts)	−.0024	−.0007	−.0001	−.0072
	(.0021)	(.0020)	(.0017)	(.0138)
1(< 1 Mile) * 1(After Clean-Up Ends)	−.0017	−.0015	.0001	.0038
	(.0015)	(.0015)	(.0019)	(.0196)
Probability of Low Birth Weight (Mean = 0.089)				
1(< 1 Mile) * 1(After Clean-Up Starts)	−.0030	−.0044	−.0001	−.0063
	(.0033)	(.0033)	(.0027)	(.0302)
1(< 1 Mile) * 1(After Clean-Up Ends)	.0026	.0012	**.0063**	.0030
	(.0029)	(.0027)	(.0027)	(.0384)
Birth Weight (Mean = 3,297)				
1(< 1 Mile) * 1(After Clean-Up Starts)	8.38	11.59	2.10	38.08
	(8.47)	(7.63)	(6.73)	(76.25)
1(< 1 Mile) * 1(After Clean-Up Ends)	−14.13	−13.68	**−26.63**	−41.11
	(8.47)	(8.03)	(7.99)	(74.36)
Probability of Premature Birth (Mean = 0.073)				
1(< 1 Mile) * 1(After Clean-Up Starts)	−.0008	−.0018	**.0092**	.0107
	(.0032)	(.0037)	(.0028)	(.0271)
1(< 1 Mile) * 1(After Clean-Up Ends)	−.0047	−.0041	.0056	.0132
	(.0038)	(.0039)	(.0040)	(.0398)
APGAR 1-Minute Score (8.4)				
1(< 1 Mile) * 1(After Clean-Up Starts)	.0462	.0610	−.0176	−.2344
	(.0547)	(.0553)	(.0546)	(.6812)
1(< 1 Mile) * 1(After Clean-Up Ends)	−.1139	−.1161	**−.1553**	.1205
	(.0885)	(.0880)	(.0698)	(.7403)
Site Fixed Effects	Yes	Yes	Yes	Yes
Year Fixed Effects	Yes	Yes	No	No
Mother, Father Characteristics x Year	No	Yes	Yes	No
County by Year Fixed Effects	No	No	Yes	Yes
Mother Fixed Effects	No	No	No	Yes

Notes: Standard errors clustered at the county-year level in parenthesis. The sample includes mothers 15 to 45 in PA and MI. Mother and father characteristics include dummies for age, education, race, Hispanic origin, all interacted with year. Observations for which the father information is missing are included in the analysis. When father is missing, a new category is created for father age, education, race, and Hispanic origin. In columns 1 to 4, sample sizes for rows 1 to 6 are 122,471, 122,471, 122,063, 122,485, 122,485, and 121,793.

conventional criteria. My conclusion is that there is little evidence that Superfund clean-ups led to increases in the birth weight of infants born within one mile of the sites.

The remaining panels provide an opportunity to assess the impact on other measures of infant health, including infant mortality. In general, there is little evidence that Superfund clean-ups have a meaningful impact on infant health outcomes. Some of them suggest improvements in these outcomes, whereas others indicate declines. However, the null of a zero effect cannot be rejected for any of the twenty estimates for the five remaining outcome variables. It is noteworthy that the mother fixed effect specifications frequently produce the largest point estimates, but they are quite poorly determined so their empirical content is not especially meaningful. Overall, these results fail to provide substantial evidence that Superfund clean-ups cause an improvement in the health of infants born within one mile of these sites.

F. Does Superfund Pass a Cost-Benefit Test?

This chapter has provided the material necessary to conduct a cost-benefit analysis of Superfund clean-ups. On the cost side, the best estimate of the cost of current Superfund clean-ups is roughly $43 million.

As subsection B highlighted, an appeal of the housing market approach is that in principle it captures *all* of the benefits of Superfund clean-ups to local residents. For example, the value of any aesthetic improvements, as well as reductions in rates of morbidities and mortality, should be reflected in housing prices. The largest estimated gain in housing prices comes from the two-mile radius sample and the column (3) specification; this estimate implies that the value of the housing stock increased by roughly $7 million between 1980 and 2000. However, this estimate is statistically indistinguishable from zero and the null hypothesis that the gain in housing prices exceeds the costs of the clean-ups is rejected at conventional significance levels. The clear conclusion is that the benefits to local residents of Superfund clean-ups are substantially smaller than the costs.

As I have emphasized, the validity of this conclusion rests on the assumption that local residents are aware of the clean-ups and their health benefits. Rather than let the cost-benefit calculations rest on this unverifiable assumption, I present new evidence on whether Superfund clean-ups affect infant health. This exercise also fails to find that Superfund clean-ups led to meaningful benefits.

There are at least two important caveats to this health analysis. First, it has only been conducted on Superfund sites in Michigan and Pennsylvania.

These sites may be unrepresentative of Superfund sites. Further, a larger sample is likely to improve the precision of the estimates. The next version of Currie, Greenstone, and Moretti's paper will expand the sample to also include data from Florida, Michigan, and Texas. Consequently, these results must be considered preliminary and incomplete. Second, although it seems plausible that infant health would be especially sensitive to the contamination at Superfund sites, it is possible that other health outcomes are affected. For example, it is possible that exposure leads to developmental and learning disorders or chronic health conditions, such as cancer. The absence of large panel data sets with precise information on respondents' addresses poses what is likely to be an insurmountable challenge to fully exploring these possibilities.

Overall, the available evidence suggests that the benefits from Superfund clean-ups to the people living near these sites are small, at least relative to the costs of these clean-ups (again noting the preliminary and incomplete nature of the health results). To the extent that the aim of the policy is to improve the lives of individuals living near these sites, Superfund is not an effective policy; the most optimistic calculation suggests that it costs $1 to get sixteen cents in the hands of the targeted group. The current version of Superfund appears to fail a cost-benefit test.

What are the policy implications of this finding? The above analysis cannot reject that there are positive benefits, so one solution is to scale back the cost of Superfund remediations. After all, Superfund remediations aim to return the site to its natural state. In the United States where land is so plentiful, this may not be very valuable. Thus, it may be cost effective to cap the areas where pollution is concentrated and/or fence off the entire site or even just the part that is considered the most dangerous.

III. Implications

This chapter's primary message is that humane regulatory policies require the persistent application of credible cost-benefit analysis to assess the regulations that govern a dizzyingly broad swath of social and economic life. This is the best and only hope to develop a system of regulation that maximizes our well-being.

There are four concrete steps that can be taken to achieve this goal. The first is that government must adopt a culture of experimentation in assessing regulations. In practice, this means that government should, whenever possible, implement proposed regulations on a small scale and undertake rigorous evaluations. This may mean allowing state or local governments to implement different policies for a specified period of time to infer the impacts of alternative forms of regulation; this has been carried out in several policy arenas already (e.g., welfare policy). In many instances, it is possible to implement genuine randomized trials. In other settings, the structure of the regulations can be used to evaluate them (as the above Superfund example illustrates). In other cases, it is only possible to evaluate a regulation *ex post*, and in these cases the results can be used to strengthen, reform, or even remove the regulation. For example, Greenstone, Oyer, and Vissing-Jorgensen (2006) analyze the consequences of mandatory disclosure laws in U.S. equity markets. The key theme is that quantitative evidence should trump qualitative evidence and rhetorical appeal whenever possible.

Critical to implementing a norm of experimental evaluation is the acceptance that not all studies are of equal value. The most compelling evidence comes from randomized trials. In cases where such evidence is unavailable, quasi-experimental evidence can be a good substitute.

Because in many instances studies look similar to the untrained eye and results can be manipulated, governments must invest in attracting the best talent available to form review boards. This has been successfully accomplished in the case of drug trials. However, the same commitment to professional assessment is absent in the assessment of regulatory interventions. (My own experiences as an advisor to the EPA have left me certain there is room for improvement in environmental policy.) I find it inhumane to treat economic regulation differently from the regulation of drugs sold to the public.

On a related note, there may be instances where political and other considerations trump insights from credible cost-benefit analyses. My own personal view is that these instances are rarer than widely believed. But even in these cases, it is still imperative to engage in credible cost-benefit evaluations. If politics is going to trump cost-benefit analysis, then politics' cost to society should be transparent.

The second step is to fund credible evaluations. Evaluations can be expensive, but their cost is generally small compared to the costs of implementing regulations that harm social welfare. The Department of Education's recently established "Institute of Education Sciences" and the related "What Works Clearinghouse" demonstrate that scientific analysis can be used to improve our nation's schools. Indeed, education once seemed to be immune to credible evaluations, but this is changing rapidly.

The third step is to be forthright about cases where the evidence is unclear or of insufficient quality to conduct a credible cost-benefit analysis. Because deciding not to take action is also making a choice, there may still be good reasons to enact a regulation in these cases. However, the absence of credible evidence should be noted and research funded so that future decisions in such areas are on firmer ground.

The fourth step is to recognize and become comfortable with the inevitability that cost-benefit analyses will lead to controversial implications in some instances. Indeed, I chose to focus on Superfund precisely because the results make me, and I suspect many others, uncomfortable. However, the power of credible cost-benefit analysis is that it provides a framework for making these tough judgments. After all, is it more humane to devote our scarce resources to cleaning up Superfund sites instead of devoting them to environmental problems where social payoffs are high? As just one example, my previous research has found large payoffs via higher housing prices and lower infant mortality rates from regulations that reduce total suspended particulate air pollution (Chay and Greenstone 2003a, 2003b, and 2005). The resources currently devoted to Superfund could be spent on the regulation of suspended particulate matter or regulations that mitigate other environmental problems.

There will always be decisions between regulations that *must* be beneficial or make us feel good and regulations that improve our lives. Credible cost-benefit analysis helps us make the right choices.

DATA APPENDIX

This data appendix provides information on a number of aspects of the data set that we compiled to conduct the analysis for this paper. This is an abridged version of the data appendix that is available in Greenstone and Gallagher (2005). The longer data appendix includes details on the variables on: the size of the hazardous waste sites; whether a site has achieved the construction complete designation; and the determination of expected and actual remediation costs. It also includes a discussion of how we placed hazardous waste sites in 2000 Census tracts and a lengthier discussion on the 1982 HRS sample.

I. Covariates in Housing Price and Rental Rate Regressions

The following are the control variables used in the housing price regressions. They are listed by the categories indicated in the row headings at the bottom of these tables. All of the variables are measured in 1980 and are measured at the census tract level (or are the mean across sets of census tracts, for example tracts that share a border with a tract containing a hazardous waste site).

1980 Ln House Price

ln mean value of owner occupied housing units in 1980 (note: the median is unavailable in 1980)

1980 Housing Characteristics

total housing units (rental and owner occupied)
% of total housing units (rental and owner occupied) that are occupied
total housing units owner occupied
% of owner occupied housing units with 0 bedrooms
% of owner occupied housing units with 1 bedroom
% of owner occupied housing units with 2 bedrooms
% of owner occupied housing units with 3 bedrooms
% of owner occupied housing units with 4 bedrooms
% of owner occupied housing units with 5 or more bedrooms
% of owner occupied housing units that are detached
% of owner occupied housing units that are attached
% of owner occupied housing units that are mobile homes
% of owner occupied housing units built within last year
% of owner occupied housing units built 2 to 5 years ago
% of owner occupied housing units built 6 to 10 years ago
% of owner occupied housing units built 10 to 20 years ago
% of owner occupied housing units built 20 to 30 years ago
% of owner occupied housing units built 30 to 40 years ago
% of owner occupied housing units built more than 40 years ago
% of all housing units without a full kitchen
% of all housing units that have no heating or rely on a fire, stove, or portable heater
% of all housing units without air conditioning
% of all housing units without a full bathroom

1980 Economic Conditions

mean household income
% of households with income below poverty line
unemployment rate
% of households that receive some form of public assistance

1980 Demographics

population density

% of population Black

% of population Hispanic

% of population under age 18

% of population 65 or older

% of population foreign born

% of households headed by females

% of households residing in same house as 5 years ago

% of individuals aged 16–19 that are high school drop outs

% of population over 25 that failed to complete high school

% of population over 25 that have a BA or better (i.e., at least 16 years of education)

II. Assignment of HRS Scores and their Role in the Determination of the NPL

The HRS test scores each pathway from 0 to 100, where higher scores indicate greater risk.[21] The individual pathway scores are calculated using a method that considers characteristics of the site as being included in one of three categories: waste characteristics, likelihood of release, and target characteristics. The final pathway score is a multiplicative function of the scores in these three categories. The logic is, for example, that if twice as many people are thought to be affected via a pathway then the pathway score should be twice as large.

The final HRS score is calculated using the following equation:

$$\text{HRS Score} = \left[(S_{gw}^2 + S_{sw}^2 + S_a^2)/3 \right]^{1/2} \tag{1}$$

where S_{gw}, S_{sw}, and S_a, denote the ground water migration, surface water migration, and air migration pathway scores, respectively.[22] As equation (1) indicates, the final score is the square root of the average of the squared individual pathway scores. It is evident that the effect of an individual pathway on the total HRS score is proportional to the pathway score.

It is important to note that HRS scores can't be interpreted as strict cardinal measures of risk. A number of EPA studies have tested how well the

---

[21] The capping of individual pathways and of attributes within each pathway is one limiting characteristic of the test. There is a maximum value for most scores within each pathway category. Also, if the final pathway score is greater than 100 then this score is reduced to 100. The capping of individual pathways creates a loss of precision of the test since all pathway scores of 100 have the same effect on the final HRS score but may represent different magnitudes of risk. See the EPA's *Hazard Ranking System Guidance Manual* for further details on the determination of the HRS score.

[22] In 1990, the EPA revised the HRS test so that it also considers soil as an additional pathway.

HRS represents the underlying risk levels based on cancer and non-cancer risks.[23] The EPA has concluded that the HRS test (at least from the late 1980s version) is an ordinal test but sites with scores within 4 points of each pose roughly comparable risks to human health (EPA 1991).[24]

From 1982–1995, the EPA assigned all hazardous waste sites with a HRS score of 28.5 or greater to the NPL. Additionally, the original legislation gave every state the right to place one site on the NPL without the site having to score at or above 28.5 on the HRS test. As of 2003, 38 states have used their exception. It is unknown whether these sites would have received a HRS score above 28.5. Six of these "state priority sites" were included on the original NPL released in 1983, but due to their missing HRS scores these six sites are excluded from this paper's analysis.

In 1995 the criteria for placement on the NPL were altered so that a site must have a HRS score greater than 28.5 <u>and</u> the governor of the state in which the site is located must approve the placement. There are currently a number of potential NPL sites with HRS scores greater than 28.5 that have not been proposed for NPL placement due to known state political opposition. We do not know the precise number of these sites because our Freedom of Information Act request for information about these sites was denied by the EPA.

III. Primary Samples of Hazardous Waste Sites

The paper relies on two primary samples of hazardous waste sites, which we label the "All NPL Sample" and the "1982 HRS Sample."

A. All NPL Sample

The All NPL sample includes NPL sites located in the 50 US states and the District of Columbia that were placed on the NPL before January 1, 2000. Although there are NPL sites located in US territories such as Puerto Rico, they are not included in the sample because the census data from these areas differs from the data for the remainder of the country. Further, the sample is limited to sites that were listed on the NPL before January 1, 2000

---

[23] See Brody (1998) for a list of EPA studies that have examined this issue.

[24] The EPA states that the early 1980s version of the HRS test should not be viewed as a measure of "absolute risk", but that "the HRS does distinguish relative risks among sites and does identify sites that appear to present a significant risk to public health, welfare, or the environment" (Federal Register 1984).

to ensure that site listing occurred before any data collection for the 2000 census. There are 1,398 sites in this sample.

B. 1982 HRS Sample

The second sample consists of the 690 sites that were tested between 1980 and 1982 for inclusion on the initial National Priority List announced on September 8, 1983. In this sample, sites that received a HRS scored exceeding 28.5 were placed on the NPL. See Greenstone and Gallagher (2005) for a more extensive discussion about some of the details surrounding the first NPL and this sample, more generally.

IV. Matching of 2000 Census Tracts to 1980 and 1990 Censuses

The census tract is used as the unit of analysis, because it is the smallest aggregation of data that is available in the 1980, 1990 and 2000 US Census. As noted in the text, year 2000 census tract boundaries are fixed so that the size and location of the census tract is the same for the 1980 and 1990 census data. The fixed census tract data boundaries were provided by Geolytics, a private company. Information on how the 1980 and 1990 census tracts were adjusted to fit the 2000 census tract boundaries can be found on their website at: www.geolytics.com.

An outline of their approach is as follows. Geolytics mapped 1990 census tracts into 2000 census tracts using block level data. Their documentation states, "The basic methodology was to use the smaller blocks to determine the population-weighted proportion of a 1990 tract that was later redefined as part of a 2000 tract."[25] A 1990 street coverage file was used to weight populations of 1990 blocks included in 2000 census tracts when the 1990 blocks were split among multiple census tracts. The assumption is that local streets and roads served as a proxy for where populations were located. Block level data for 1980 were unavailable. This complicated the mapping of 1980 tracts into 1990 tracts. However, the correspondence between 1980 tracts and 1990 blocks is "very good." As such "splitting a 1980 tract into 1990 tracts had to be done spatially, meaning based solely on the 1990 block to 1980 tract correspondence."[26]

---

[25] Appendix J: Description of Tract Remapping Methodology of Geolytics Data Users' Guide for Neighborhood Change Database (1970–2000), page J3.
[26] Ibid., page J4.

V. Neighbor Samples

We use two approaches to define the set of houses outside each site's tract that may be affected by the clean-up. We refer to these sets of houses as "neighbors."

The first approach defines the neighbors as all census tracts that share a border with the tract that contains the site. GIS software was used to find each primary census tract and extract the identity of its adjacent neighbors. In the 1982 HRS sample, the maximum number of neighboring census tracts is 21 and the median is 7. The population of each adjacent census tract was used to weight the housing price, housing characteristics, and demographic variables for each tract when calculating the mean adjacent neighbor values.

The second approach defines neighbors based on circles of varying radii around the exact location of the site. GIS software is used to draw a circle around the point representing the site (generally the center of the site, but sometimes the point associated with the street address). For example in the 1 mile sample, the GIS program draws circles with radii of 1 mile around each of the sites. For a given site, data from all census tracts that fall within its 1-mile radius circle (including the tract containing the site) are used to calculate the mean housing values, housing and demographic characteristics, and economic variables. To calculate these weighted means, each census tract within the circle is weighted by the product of its population and the portion of its total area that falls within the circle. The maximum number of census tracts included in the 1 mile ring for a site is 37 and the mean and median are 3.9 and 3. For the 2 (3) mile ring the maximum number of neighbor sites is 80 (163), with a mean and median of 9.9 and 8 (18.2 and 12).

References

Ackerman, Frank and Lisa Heinzerling. 2004. *Priceless: On Knowing the Price of Everything and the Value of Nothing.* New York: The New Press.

Angrist, Joshua D. 2004. "American Education Research Changes Tack." *Oxford Review of Economic Policy*, 20 (2): 198–212.

Ashenfelter, Orley and Michael Greenstone, 2004. "Estimating the Value of a Statistical Life: The Importance of Omitted Variables and Publication Bias." *American Economic Review: Papers and Proceedings*, 94 (2): 454–60.

Black, Dan A. and Thomas J. Kneisner. 2003. "On the Measurement of Job Risk in Hedonic Wage Models." *Journal of Risk and Uncertainty*, 27 (3): 205–220.

Black, Sandra E. 1999. "Do Better Schools Matter? Parental Valuation of Elementary Education." *The Quarterly Journal of Economics*, 114 (2): 577–99.

Black, Sandra E., Paul J. Devereux, and Kjell G. Salvanes. 2007. "From the Cradle to the Labor Market? The Effect of Birth Weight on Adult Outcomes." Quarterly Journal of Economics, 122 (1): 409–439.

Chay, Kenneth Y. and Michael Greenstone. 2003a. "Air Quality, Infant Mortality, and the Clean Air Act of 1970." NBER Working Paper No. 10053.

Chay, Kenneth Y. and Michael Greenstone. 2003b. "The Impact of Air Pollution on Infant Mortality: Evidence from Geographic Variation in Pollution Shocks Induced by a Recession." *Quarterly Journal of Economics*, CXVIII: 1121–1167.

Chay, Kenneth and Michael Greenstone. 2005. "Does Air Quality Matter? Evidence from the Housing Market," *Journal of Political Economy*, 113(2): 376–424.

Cleveland, William S. 1979. "Robust Locally Weighted Regression and Smoothing Scatterplots," *Journal of the American Statistical Association*, 74 (368):829–836.

Cropper, Maureen L., Leland B. Deck, and Kenneth E. McConnell. 1988. "On the Choice of Functional Form for Hedonic Price Functions." *Review of Economics and Statistics*, 70 (4): 668–75.

Currie, Janet, Michael Greenstone, and Enrico Moretti. 2007. "Are Hazardous Waste Sites Hazardous to Human Health? Evidence from Superfund Clean-Ups and Infant Health." Mimeograph.

Deschenes, Olivier and Michael Greenstone. 2007. "The Economic Impacts of Climate Change: Evidence from Agricultural Output and Random Fluctuations in Weather," *The American Economic Review*, 97 (1): 354–385.

Duflo, Esther, Rachel Glennerster, Michael Kremer. 2008. "Using Randomization in Development Economics Research: A Toolkit," in T. Paul Schultz and John A. Strauss (Eds.) Handbook of Development Economics, Volume 4. Amsterdam: Elsevier, North Holland, pp. 3895–3962.

Ekeland, Ivar, James J. Heckman, and Lars Nesheim (2004): "Identification and Estimation of Hedonic Models," *Journal of Political Economy*, 112 (1): S60 S190.

Freeman, A. Myrick, III. 1974. "On Estimating Air Pollution Control Benefits from Land Value Studies." *Journal of Environmental Economics and Management*, 1 (1): 74–83.

Freeman, A. Myrick, III. 2003. *The Measurement of Environmental and Resource Values: Theory and Methods. 2 ed.* Washington, DC: Resources for the Future.

Greenstone, Michael and Justin Gallagher. 2005. "Does Hazardous Waste Matter? Evidence from the Housing Market and the Superfund Program," NBER Working Paper No. W11790.

Greenstone, Michael, and Justin Gallagher. 2008. "Does Hazardous Waste Matter? Evidence from the Housing Market and the Superfund Program," *Quarterly Journal of Economics*, 123 (3): 951–1003.

Greenstone, Michael, Paul Oyer and Annette Vissing-Jorgensen. 2006. "Mandated Disclosure, Stock Returns, and the 1964 Securities Act." *Quarterly Journal of Economics* 121(2): 399–460.

Halvorsen, Robert and Henry O. Pollakowski. 1981. "Choice of Functional Form for Hedonic Price Equations," *Journal of Urban Economics*, 10(1): 37–49.

Ioannidis, John P. A., Anna-Bettina Haidich, Maroudia Pappa, Nikos Pantazis, Styliani I. Kokori, Maria G. Tektonidou, Despina G. Contopoulos-Ioannidis, and Joseph Lau. 2001. "Comparison of evidence of treatment effects in randomized and non-randomized studies." *Journal of the American Medical Association*, 286: 821–30.

Kelman, Steven. 1981. "Cost-Benefit Analysis: An Ethical Critique," *Regulation*, 5(1): 33–40.

Moss, David and Mary Oey. 2009. "The Paranoid Style in the Study of American Politics," in Ed Balleisen and David Moss (eds.), *Toward A New Theory of Regulation*. Cambridge University Press.

Palmquist, Raymond B. 1991. "Hedonic Methods," in John Braden and Charles Kolstad (eds.), *Environmental Benefit Measurement*. Amsterdam: North Holland.

Revesz, Richard and Michael Livermore 2008. *Retaking Rationality: How Cost Benefit Analysis Can Better Protect the Environment and Our Health*. Oxford University Press.

Ridker, Ronald G. 1967. *Economic Costs of Air Pollution: Studies in Measurement*. New York: Frederick A. Praeger, Publishers: 1967.

Ridker, Ronald G. and John A. Henning. 1967. "The Determinants of Residential Property Values with Special Reference to Air Pollution," *The Review of Economics and Statistics*, 49 (2): 246–257.

Rosen, Sherwin. 1974. "Hedonic Prices and Implicit Markets: Product Differentiation in Pure Competition" *Journal of Political Economy*, 82 (1): 34–55.

Rosen, Sherwin. 1986. "The Theory of Equalizing Differences." In: *Handbook of Labor Economics*, 1, Orley C. Ashenfelter and Richard Layard (eds.), 641–692. (New York: North-Holland).

Sigman, Hilary A. 2001. "The Pace of Progress at Superfund Sites: Policy Goals and Interest Group Influence," *Journal of Law and Economics*, 44 (1): 315–344.

Small, Kenneth A. 1975. "Air Pollution and Property Values: Further Comment." *Review of Economics and Statistics*, 57 (1): 105–7.

Smith, Robert S. 1979. "Compensating Wage Differentials and Public Policy: A Review." *Industrial and Labor Relations Review*, 32 (3): 339–52.

Sunstein, Cass R. 2004. "Your Money or Your Life." *The New Republic*, March 15.

U.S. Department of Education. 2006. "Institute of Education Sciences." *ED.Gov.* <http://www.ed.gov/about/offices/list/ies/index.html>.

U.S. Environmental Protection Agency. 2000. "A Series of Firsts (continued)." *Superfund 20th Anniversary Report.* <http://www.epa.gov/superfund/20years/ch3pg1.htm>.

U.S. Environmental Protection Agency. 1984. "Federal Register Notice: Final 49 FR 37070, 09/21/1984" *National Priorities List (NPL).* <http://www.epa.gov/superfund/sites/npl/f840921.htm#SUMMARY>.

THREE

From "State Interference" to the "Return of the Market": The Rhetoric of Economic Regulation from the Old Gilded Age to the New

Mary O. Furner

Democracies have perennially faced questions regarding whether, what, when, why, and how to regulate. Fruitful reflection on the subject of economic regulation falls squarely within the larger context of longstanding conversations in the United States and the Atlantic world about the optimal relationship between market and state, economy and polity, individual and society. In such discussions, social thinkers have never conceived of their ideal constructions of these relations as matters involving considerations of economic efficiency alone, though some discourses have certainly pushed the conversation in that direction. In the U.S. case, discussions along these lines have questioned what arrangements of these boundaries and what particular forms of regulation were most likely to sustain virtue in politics, to reduce inequality of income and wealth, to enable full development of individual talents, and to promote realization of aspirations toward fuller democracy. The state-society boundary – and thus our thinking about economic regulation – has a history. Conceptions of "the best" social arrangements, approaches to political economy, and visions of individual liberty have diverged from one era to the next.[1]

This essay assumes that the rich and diverse traditions of thought and practice regarding regulation in the United States have been formed in relation to five major factors: theoretical developments in relevant fields of political, social, and economic knowledge; popular beliefs – often formulated

[1] James Farr, "Understanding Conceptual Change Politically," *Political Innovation and Conceptual Change*, eds. Terence Ball, et al. (New York: Cambridge University Press, 1989), 24–49.

I am grateful to David Moss and the Tobin Project for their generous support of this research, to Edward Balleisen for his wise editorial counsel on earlier versions, and to Michael Lacey, William Leach, Joseph McCartin, Kenneth Mouré, and Alice O'Connor for helpful suggestions. Earlier research on the subject was generously supported by the Woodrow Wilson International Center for Scholars.

and expressed in social and political movements; previous regulatory policy decisions that have defined specific paths and foreclosed others; prevailing and emergent structures of political power and cultural authority; and the evolution of U.S. liberalism in relation to alternatives to the right and left on the ideological spectrum.[2] Although each of these sources of regulatory innovation and tradition deserves careful attention, this chapter attends mainly to the first two – expert knowledge and popular beliefs – and to the traffic, interaction, agreement, or opposition between them. Even while acknowledging other influences (power relationships between social classes, interest group lobbying, and political partisanship, for example), it can be taken as given that the politics of regulation and the regulation policies adopted or displaced have been in significant part conceptually constituted. That is, at any given point in time, the way that policy makers frame conditions in the economy as "problems" that require government attention, and the solutions that they fashion to those problems, reflect prominently, among other considerations, ideas that have standing among intellectual elites and informed citizens.

My central point is not that specific experts are forever whispering from behind the scenes into the shell-pink ears of specific policymakers, though such whispering has certainly happened. I rather wish to recall a powerful Enlightenment principle still given much credence in democracies – that governments should base policy on knowledge, on careful analysis of socioeconomic conditions, on historical experience, and on forecasts based on the best available theory of the likely consequences for the general welfare of various possible alternative actions. However much this premise has withered in the face of modern-day cynicism and postmodernist assaults on the "objectivity" of "truth," it retains tremendous influence in the political and policy realms. Leaders still need to justify their actions, and they need to justify them with a decent regard for both the popular sense(s) of what "makes sense" and the various theories on offer, especially those embraced by thinkers considered expert on the subject at hand who are held to be sufficiently removed from narrow partisanship to merit attention. By the same token, knowledge makers/intellectuals/experts must have a care for the needs of the public, lest their sciences be dismissed as unresponsive or irrelevant.[3]

---

[2] Mary O. Furner & Barry Supple, "Ideas and Institutions in the United States and Britain," *The State and Economic Knowledge: The American and British Experiences* (New York: Cambridge University Press, 1990), 3–39, discusses this subject and provides a brief typology of three kinds of policy knowledge.

[3] The literature on relations between power and expertise is vast. One could begin with Leon Fink, et al., eds., *Intellectuals and Public Life* (Ithaca: Cornell University Press, 1996);

U.S. historians have approached the history of economic regulation in various ways. For some, both in the early twentieth-century Progressive Era and in the mid-twentieth century ascendancy of pluralism and heightened ideological consensus, economic regulation (e.g., involving railroad rates, food and drug quality, industrial safety, child labor, the money supply, international trade and investment) was thought to result from one-directional struggles by those who stood to gain from controlling state policy. For progressive historians, it was an unequal struggle of the people against the monied interests who frequently dominated politics as usual. For the pluralists, the conflicting claims of an array of organized interest groups were arbitrated by a black-box broker state, and the resulting policy matrix reflected a compromise of those brokered interests. These days, policy historians typically reject the naked versions of these interest-driven approaches in favor of one in which ideas matter. In most historical policy contexts, and especially in past contexts riven by considerable controversy, ideology and values provided the foundation, along with empirical findings, for moral or ethical assessment as well as for efficiency claims, and thus for political change.[4]

But not all policy-relevant ideas are created equal. One factor in the purchase that ideas achieve in policy deliberations is timing; crises, wars, and "watershed" historical moments often permit or even seem to require new and different approaches to regulation. Seen in this light, the various regulatory strategies that Joseph Stiglitz catalogues in his essay emerged at such moments, in response to particular policy dilemmas and in light of prevailing concepts of governmental capacity and authority. But the framing of situations matters enormously as well. The rhetoric that political leaders use to package policy-relevant ideas for dissemination both to the inner circles of intellectuals and experts and to a broader public has influenced their ability to win converts. In the longer run we can identify the innovations

---

Thomas Haskell, *The Authority of Experts* (Bloomington, Ind.: Indiana University Press, 1984); Stephen Brint, *In an Age of Experts: The Changing Role of Professionals in Politics and Public Life* (Princeton, N.J.: Princeton University Press, 1994); Philippe Nonet and Philip Selznick, *Toward Responsive Law* (New York: Harper and Row, 1978).

[4] Farr, "Understanding Conceptual Change"; Clifford Geertz, "Ideology as a Cultural System," *The Interpretation of Cultures* (New York: Basic Books, 1973). It may be true – as Daniel Rodgers has argued regarding policy making during the U.S. New Deal – that a number of the solutions to what Americans in the Great Depression recognized as problems that a democratic state must help to solve came "off the shelf." But these solutions – ideas about mass unemployment, overproduction, underconsumption, securities regulation, labor market regulation, and the like – were on the shelf because they had been recognized in earlier depressions, research was happening, discourses about them were ongoing – as they had been on these subjects in professional, political, and reform circles since the Old Gilded Age.

that have generated sufficient rhetorical power to shape the creation of turning points in the realm of theory and practical politics.

Leaders who seek to bring about political change by deploying compelling new rhetorics often look for authority to creditable theory and – in the case of economic and social policy issues – to the social sciences. Arguments for new departures in public policy such as Theodore Roosevelt's New Nationalism or Franklin Roosevelt's New Deal are often delivered in highly simplified or popularized language; yet they typically draw upon and are fleshed out using innovative analyses that have been suggested by serious students of political economy and other social disciplines. Thus the ways that scholars in these fields create knowledge, the critical practices they use in judging its credibility, and the standing they grant to long and well established general theories, or paradigms, become matters of considerable interest – as do changes in all of these. Since the 1960s, a profusion of studies of the work habits of scientists has highlighted sociological determinants for the formation and defense, and even the occasional collapse, of hegemonic scholarly paradigms. This work has pointed tellingly to matters such as well warranted respect for the eminent founders of powerfully persuasive general theories such as Einstein's theory of relativity, close ties among those who seek to refine and extend them, and the benefits – both honorific and material – of belonging to such a "school" of practitioners. It has also exposed the contrary, liberating effect of being one of those – not infrequently outsiders to the discipline involved – who are most likely to challenge the reigning paradigm and nominate a replacement for it. [5]

The best cases for viewing the growth of knowledge as a succession of reigning paradigms in this vein have come from the so-called "natural" or "exact" sciences, particularly physics, whereas for the social sciences the fit has not been so good. Unlike some literally earth-shaking discoveries in natural science, such as the irrefutable fossil evidence that Darwin offered for evolution or the crustal evidence of plate tectonics, new paradigms in social thought seldom have totally vanquished previous ones, and they may even have eluded detection in the initial moments of their occurrence, except by the most astute observers. Yet in retrospect careful historians can recover those moments when new ways of framing events in the economy, structuring causal explanations for economic changes, and announcing

---

[5] Thomas Kuhn's seminal *The Structure of Scientific Revolutions* (1962: 2d. ed., Chicago: University of Chicago Press, 1972) set off a wide-ranging discussion of the paradigm concept in the history and philosophy of science.

innovative ways of thinking about their implications for regulation arrived on the scene, offering compelling new vocabularies for naming and understanding economic and social phenomena that became potent alternatives to previously respected ones. The adoption of "rational choice" or "public choice" language described by Jessica Leight in this volume is an excellent recent example.

In the century under scrutiny here, the rhetorics of economic regulation that most conspicuously won traction as alternative frames for policymaking between the Gilded Age and the New Deal typically ran against the laissez faire principle that privileged "free market" competition over any form of state intervention. These new rhetorical framings of market dysfunction named, and specified policy implications for, the limits of competition, the problem of social costs, the negative consequences of administered prices, and the case for national planning. Subsequently, between the 1940s and the 1980s, opponents of state action responded to these regulation-affirming discourses with new, market-affirming rhetorics that denied the beneficence of regulation and called for re-examination of the concept of the public interest. These new rhetorical approaches included most prominently the rhetoric of a 'new serfdom' that Friedrich von Hayek warned was certain to accompany the rise and extension of welfare states. Among them also were major theoretical movements in economics and law, labeled 'rational choice' or 'public choice', which, their adherents argued, supported the inferences that government was not demonstrably better at maximizing the general utility than the market was, and the further claim that no genuinely democratic method existed for ascertaining what could be counted as the public good. Following the oil shocks and stagflation of the 1970s, but also in response to extensive efforts by conservative intellectual elites and their foundation backers toward conversion of popular opinion regarding the proper roles of government, the experts' case for deregulation entered the vernacular when Ronald Reagan, speaking as the political head of a neoconservative movement, declared government regulation "the problem" and a "return to the market" the essential solution.

LIMITS OF COMPETITION RHETORIC IN THE MAKING OF STATIST NEW LIBERALISM

Expert and popular thinking took a new turn in the early post-Civil War decades, as Republican economic policies once again embraced state-sponsored economic development initiatives such as tariff protection and national banking in the hopes of accelerating America's industrial transformation.[6] Among the policies that spurred capital deepening, none was more salient than the rapid proliferation of the corporate form of business organization into the manufacturing sector. This development fueled elite and popular discussions of the nature of the business corporation, the impact of the corporate reorganization of U.S. capitalism on public life, and the need for regulating the new economic behemoths. In the early republic, ingrained suspicions of concentrated economic power, along with the fearful legacy of the South Sea Bubble and other such schemes, had confined the corporate form to large-scale ventures in transportation and finance. Corporations required special chartering by elected legislatures that closely limited them to public purposes, with the broad public viewing them as arms of the state, entirely subject to this test. In public discourse, as Louis Hartz discovered by tracking debates in Pennsylvania in the early republic, entirely private corporations were suspect; most political commentators expected corporate investors to be motivated by greed and thus to bear close watching. They could safely be granted a measure of control over the public's business only in the context of mixed public and private enterprises, in which state agents remained on hand to look out for the public interest.[7]

Yet by the 1830s public opinion grew decidedly skeptical about government intervention. A general democratization of American life, a carefully cultivated fear of elites, the failure of numerous state-bonded enterprises, the growing influence of imported *laissez faire* principles, and intensifying concerns about the power of monopolies in a liberalized republic that enshrined competition all counseled that the states should withdraw – and in some cases even bar themselves – from engaging in business ventures. These same developments encouraged the adoption of state-level general incorporation laws, which converted the corporate form to nothing more than an enforceable agreement among freely contracting, rights-bearing, free-willing, stock-owning individuals. The device's name remained the same, but the rhetoric surrounding corporate enterprise was new. So too was the impact of corporations upon the shape of a U.S. economy in which technological innovations, expanding population, protection for manufactured goods, and disallowance by the courts of state laws protecting individual states'

---

[6] On the "return to the market" that undid policies designed to promote economic development during the early republic, see Charles Sellers, *The Market Revolution: Jacksonian America, 1815–1846* (New York: Oxford University Press, 1991); Harry Watson, *Liberty and Power: The Politics of Jacksonian America* (1st rev. ed., New York: Hill and Wang, 2006).

[7] Louis Hartz, *Economic Policy and Democratic Thought, 1776–1860* (Cambridge: Harvard University Press, 1948).

domestic producers created the basis for a national market in producers'
and consumers' goods. Such national economic integration made it conceivable, and feasible, for business elites to attempt to dominate markets.[8]

As the waning of competition in the era of the trusts undermined a
Smithian vision for achieving the public good, political and economic theorists of what became known as the Gilded Age began crafting a "new
liberalism" to replace it. An exemplary American "new liberal" and master
rhetorician among the early academic economists, Henry Carter Adams of
the University of Michigan, looked back upon the Jackson-era withdrawal
of the states from internal improvements as an unmitigated disaster. This
withdrawal, he argued, had hollowed out state governments and left hapless
citizens prey to monopolistic corporations, whose business now extended
to provision of "the necessaries of life." The Jacksonian regime that oversaw this transformation had justified its policies of general incorporation
through liberal-democratic ideology and a free market rhetoric that naturalized the market, competition, and contract. By the 1880s, Adams lamented,
this new political economy had produced, in the hands of an investor class
enriched by war, economic policy, and control of new technology, a profoundly unintended consequence – large-scale corporate enterprises in core
manufacturing, distilling, refining, transport, and communication industries that either could or sought to administer prices for the highest gain.

In a classic, widely circulated, discourse-generating piece titled *The Relation of the State to Industrial Action* (1887), Adams viewed these events from
a perspective that blended his native heartland republicanism and evan-
gelical Christianity with lessons learned through exposure to bloody class
conflict in Baltimore during the Great Railroad Strike of 1877. For Adams,
this episode required more enlightened state interference than that provided
by strike-breaking federal troops. His analysis was also informed by a hefty
dose of historicist contempt for appeals to universal and timeless natural
laws that were believed by the English Manchester School to govern economic policy. Adams's German mentors in the late 1870s had been liberal
statists such as Berlin's Adolph Wagner, who explicitly rejected socialism
but were intensely critical of the English classical economists' celebration of
a night-watchman state.[9]

---

[8] Morton Horwitz, *The Transformation of the Law, 1780–1860* (New York: Cambridge Uni-
versity Press, 1977). For a different interpretation of the direction of changes in the law, see
William Novak, *The People's Welfare: Law and Regulation in Nineteenth-Century America*
(Chapel Hill: University of North Carolina Press, 1996).

[9] *Publications of the American Economic Association* 1(1887): 465–549. Adams delivered
substantially this same paper to the New York Constitution Club in 1885 as "Principles

In 1885–86, in the early stages of the corporate reorganization of U.S. capitalism and shortly before being named to head the professional staff of the first national regulatory body, the Interstate Commerce Commission, Adams self-consciously fashioned a new rhetoric of regulation. For fellow economists, he grounded this new rhetoric in empirical observation and robust theory regarding economies of scale. He also tailored it rhetorically to convey new political meanings to U.S. policy elites and to capture the imaginations of ordinary citizens. Americans were accustomed to thinking about regulation within an unstable blend of older categories: civic republicanism, which feared concentrated power, prized equality, and subordinated private gain to the public good; individualist liberalism, which prized economic freedom and counted on Adam Smith's invisible hand to maximize welfare; and Protestant moralism, which subjected competition to the demands of religious teaching. In the post-Reconstruction years, a resurgent republicanism voiced by the Knights of Labor and the Farmers Alliances and an emerging social gospel ignited a swelling demand for economic regulation through state-level railroad rate commissions and antitrust laws designed to restore competition, and through factory laws framed to moralize it. Sympathetic to these impulses but rejecting some of their key premises, Adams obligingly recounted the dangers of relying exclusively on the regulatory action of competition to protect the public good. This approach allowed him to make an important distinction between businesses engaged in what he detected as "natural monopolies," which the state ought not to force into competition lest it bring about enormous economic waste, and businesses of the ordinary type that did not enjoy such economies of scale. Just as classical theorists had effectively naturalized competition, Adams now managed to historicize competition as a system appropriate for quite general application to a specific economic period, and simultaneously to naturalize the disappearance of it in a certain class of industries at a later time. Attending adroitly to inherited republican prejudices, he carefully distinguished natural and thus potentially beneficial monopolies from the artificial ones created by force or fraud, which had been demonized in U.S. political culture since the Declaration of Independence recited the abuses of that inveterate granter of monopolies, King George III.

That Should Guide the Interference of the State in Business." Indicating the transatlantic nature of this discourse, his title was similar to T. H. Farrar, *The State in Relation to Trade* (London: Macmillan and Co., 1883). On Adams's career, see Mary O. Furner, *Advocacy and Objectivity: The Professionalization of American Social Science, 1865–1905* (Lexington: University Press of Kentucky, 1975).

Having established this new category, Adams insisted that wherever natural monopoly appeared the public interest – a general or consumer interest in this instance – required "state interference," the quaint term of art in that decade for economic regulation. Whether through state ownership or regulatory control, in this instance state interference meant controlling the rate of profit and the level of performance, and it demanded development of talents that barely existed in the United States, for "public financiering." Evoking cultural memories constantly renewed in patriotic oratory, Adams equated the monopoly pricing power of increasing returns industries with the power to tax, an aspect of sovereignty that, in the republican discourse so pervasive in the nineteenth century, simply could not be left in private hands.[10]

Adams also launched in this piece a second rhetorical strategy aimed at reconciling tensions in the consideration of labor standards then under way. On the one hand, the Supreme Court had recently articulated an influential expression of legal individualism in the precedent setting case *In re Jacobs* (1885), which insulated employers against protective legislation for workers by guaranteeing individual workers the freedom to contract their labor under any conditions – however onerous or debilitating – that they might choose. On the other, a broad segment of urban Americans had begun to demand a higher ethical standard from employers, a view aroused by the evils of child labor and by unsafe or unduly arduous working conditions in many industries. Drawing upon concrete examples from every-day business practice, Adams explained how especially during recurrent periods of capitalist crisis, when wages and standards were among the few variable costs that owners of capital intensive industries could cut, a lack of labor-standards regulation fueled what is today called a race to the bottom. Adams's rhetorical strategy here suggested that the state – specifically its legislative arm – should have the power to enact the labor standards that were accepted as reflecting the best moral sense of the community. The state should establish "a moral plane of competition" by placing a floor under labor standards, at a level that he expected to rise along with an evolving collective judgment of what standards for various groups of workers and industries were fair and just and in the general interest.[11]

---

[10] Richard T. Ely's popularization of these ideas is in "Social Studies. – I. The Nature and Significance of Corporations"; Social Studies. – II. "The Growth of Corporations"; "Social Studies. – III. The Future of Corporations," *Harper's Weekly* (1887).

[11] Adams, "Relation of the State." See also Richard T. Ely, "Ethics and Economics," *Science 1886*. Comparing corporation ethics with those of "private management," Adams taught that the moral element in corporate practice was "at a minimum," whereas it was "at

These two intellectual devices – natural monopoly and the moral plane – filtered quickly into both professional and civic conversation, embodied in a two-way traffic with important consequences for American public policy. Within the professionalizing discipline of economics, they provided a language for alternatives (reasonable regulation or state ownership) to the ban on state interference that had mingled for decades with party politics and liberal jurisprudence to enshrine classical liberalism as a kind of American creed, and thereby weakened the dominant republican idea of the state as an agency empowered through representative government to promote the public interest. Something of the older republican meaning for the term public interest was captured in Chief Justice Morrison Waite's famous ruling in *Munn v. Illinois* (1877) that the recently ratified Fourteenth Amendment to the U.S. constitution did not prevent regulation by the states of railroad or elevator storage rates. Waite's opinion stressed that the placement of one's property in the service of the public justified its regulation in the public interest, a goal related to the general welfare that would not be achieved by the action of an unseen hand, but only through positive action and as a consequence of deliberate intention. Thus embraced by participants in political and legal controversies, the concept of a public interest that transcended even the sum of individual private interests was well established in U.S. civic discourse long before it came in for criticism at the hands of scholars identifying themselves with public choice theory, which from this earlier standpoint seems anomalously named.

In the wider civic discourse, detection of natural monopoly and concerns about economic and social justice embodied in the idea of a moral plane of competition also shaped an array of reform proposals put forward in the 1880s and 1890s by aroused farmers, rebellious workers, and middle-class activists appalled by urban poverty and the threat of mass unemployment. Two "evils of competition" – ill-considered attempts to break up natural monopolies along with all the others, and a vicious race to the bottom in labor practices – could, according to Adams's philosophy, safely be remedied by, and only by, public policy. The federal government could put a stop to these evils through actions justifiable through economic theory, grounded to some extent in state-level regulatory practice, and intrinsic to a "new liberalism," by then being shaped by many hands, that envisaged

its maximum in business organized on a private basis." Cited in Richard T. Ely, "I. The Nature and Significance of Corporations," *Harper's New Monthly Magazine* 74 (May 1877): 970–77. Ely argued that "an effort should be made to replace the conscience of the natural man by some contrivance which will render artificial persons amenable to the moral law." (977)

much enhanced functions for a smarter, more capable, better informed government.[12]

But Adams's reconceptualization of political economy had still more significant ramifications. By infusing his analysis with the biblical image of one ruthless competitor (clearly a sinner) who, by using child labor for example, forced nine more scrupulous employers to do the same, Adams affirmed the necessity of an ethical test for the beneficence of competition. This rhetorical maneuver deeply complicated the metaphor of the unseen hand, questioning the morality of a policy that privileged price competition in all circumstances. By showing how regulatory limits might be necessary to ensure that economic rivalry did not create social injustice, he endorsed a broad-based movement for a social or a Christian economics. At the time, Richard Ely, John R. Commons, settlement house folk largely of Protestant background, a segment of the Protestant clergy, social feminists, and important figures in the emerging field of social journalism saw no hard boundary between Christian sociology and Christian socialism.[13]

Drawing out the implications of his image of a "moral plane," Adams urged citizens, employers, and lawmakers toward considering the impact of the arduous new conditions of mechanized production on workers who no longer, as they had in artisan production, possessed the means to protect themselves. The following year, New York City garment workers called upon middle-class Americans to take responsibility for the welfare of employees by buying only from retail stores that sold clothing made under fair conditions and granted fair working conditions to their sales clerks, setting in motion a movement that blossomed into city and state consumers leagues. A classic example of a nonstatist effort to raise the moral plane, the National Consumers League that emerged from these efforts in 1899/ eventually coordinated a particularly effective consumer-action campaign, based once again upon the principle that working conditions should reflect the aroused moral sense of the community, and framed in a language of human rights, not economic efficiency. Endeavors as diverse as those of housing reformers Jacob Riis and Lawrence Veiller, seekers after safety legislation in the wake of mine disasters, and industrial safety activists who succeeded in outlawing phosphorus match production drew upon a similar rhetoric and

---

[12] Ely reproduced Adams's definition of three classes of industries, among them natural monopolies blessed with increasing returns to scale, in a large-circulation weekly. See "III. The Future of Corporations," ibid., 75 (July 1887): 259–66. His classification was taken up by historical and institutional economists more generally.

[13] On the social outlook of these groups, an excellent recent source is John Recchiuti, *Civic Engagement: Social Science and Progressive Era Reform in New York City* (University of Pennsylvania Press, 2007).

rationale. When Theodore Roosevelt accompanied Riis on his nighttime rambles through New York City tenements in the 1880s, he was taking the first steps in an ethical apprenticeship that showed up later in the Progressive Party platform of 1912.[14]

Adams's critique of the legislated state incapacity of the Jackson era, of cutthroat competition, and of the sorry state of capitalist ethics in the Gilded Age was in essence a deep probe into the price-making process at the heart of industrial capitalism – a process that classical economists viewed as legitimately determining the going price of labor, land, and capital, as well as goods, all in accordance with natural economic laws. A kind of answer to this question had been building among economic writers since the 1870s, in the form of an elaboration of Ricardian rent theory from the rent of land to the other factors of production. Henry George had shown how land speculation stripped away as rent much of the wealth that urban capital and labor – not natural enemies, in his view – cooperated in producing. Developing a keen understanding of the appeal of rent-seeking behavior in uncertain times, economist John R. Commons expressed sympathy for essentially similar methods used by skilled workers to sustain decent earnings by controlling their numbers. Elaborating the device further, government statistician and economist Francis Amasa Walker even justified profit as a "rent of ability."[15]

Adams's innovations, and their further elaboration by like-minded social thinkers and political economists, elicited a contrary, antistatist response from more conservative-minded intellectuals. At the century's end, economists among this latter group fashioned the first American statement of a productivity theory of factor shares in distribution. This new theory, presented most fully in economist John Bates Clark's *The Distribution of Wealth* (1899), took aim at competing supply-side, cost-of-production theories featured in both classical liberalism and Marxian socialism that posited embodied labor as the measure of value. In this American version of neoclassical theory, the value (price) in wages, interest, or rent of a specific input to production was based on the utility supplied by the final increment of each that could be profitably employed. Assuming that in modern production all these units were interchangeable, the value of the final increment became the price of all preceding units.[16]

---

[14] See, as an example of publicity for these efforts, "What the National Consumers League Has Done for Saleswomen," *New York Times Magazine Supplement* (August 25, 1901).

[15] Francis A. Walker's rent of entrepreneurial ability as a source of business profit provoked a reply from John Hobson that outlined a theory of three rents.

[16] Thorstein Veblen ridiculed Clark's logic regarding interchangeability of all the units of factors by pointing out that workers hired earlier worked with better machines and produced more that those last hired, who were also likely to be less competent than

Clark's *Distribution of Wealth* defined monopoly – to the extent he granted
that it existed at all in any industry – as a temporary "friction," similar to the
wave produced by a transient disturbance of the water in a tub. So long as
an element of monopoly did not have legal protection, the natural mobility
of capital to points of highest return (utility) that prevailed in a free capital
market, a beneficial force that constituted the natural regulatory regime
of what Clark termed potential competition, would eradicate such strictly
temporary gains, smoothing the surface of the water in the tub. Clark's static
equilibrium model of the economy suggested that the Sherman Antitrust
Act of 1890, not applied as yet by the courts to monopolies in manufacturing
in any event, had been unnecessary. For Clark, the more dramatic the short-
term gains of a monopoly such as Standard Oil, the greater the willingness
of would-be competitors to invest in potential substitutes for kerosene, or
to seek out alternative sources of petroleum, or to develop novel means of
transporting the new black gold. Yet Clark's homely metaphor had trouble
standing against the barrage of contrary evidence provided by the Great
Merger Movement of 1898–1902. During that brief period, roughly 300
industrial firms a year disappeared into mergers, including the nation's first
billion dollar deal, the U.S. Steel Corporation, which swallowed three of
the country's largest steel producers and several major fabricators, and then
proceeded to impose the basing point system that standardized prices of
steel shipped from any point of production.[17]

Even as defenders of bigness in industry proclaimed the regulatory effect
of potential competition, Clark's neoclassical language and imagery provoked a sharp rhetorical response from economist Thorstein Veblen, who
scorned the view that a reified free market operated according to fixed natural laws. Turning to anthropology for his theoretical inspiration, Veblen
described human social evolution as a passage from savagery, a state he
thought to have been largely peaceful, through an era of barbarism, dominated by predatory warriors, in which private property had originated,

the earlier hires. Veblen, "Professor Clark's Economics," *Quarterly Journal of Economics* 22:2 (1908): 147–95.

[17] Thomas K. McCraw and Forest Reinhardt, "Losing to Win: U.S. Steel's Pricing, Investment Decisions, and Market Share, 1901–1938," *The Journal of Economic History* 49:3 (Sept. 1989): 593–619. For the impact of the steel merger on industry prices, see Naomi R. Lamoreaux, *The Great Merger Movement in American Business, 1895–1904* (1985), 134–38. Not all of these mergers were successful, of course, as defenders of bigness seeking to justify concentration of ownership by extending the argument for economies of scale to manufacturing as well as public utilities pointed out. On the case for economies of scale in manufacturing, see Jeremiah Jenks, "Industrial Combinations and Prices," United States Industrial Commission, *Report*, 19 vols. (1900–1902) Vol. 1: 39–57.

to modern industrial society. In the latter, elements of the two previous stages survived in the form of two horizontal layers, a pecuniary upper class devoted to accumulating wealth and an industrial laboring class that made things. In this modern phase, industrial workers were still driven by an instinct of workmanship, hanging over from earlier times, to produce abundantly for use, whereas among capitalists the barbaric urge to conquer and exploit still flourished.

Veblen's deliberately picturesque account of the vastly different lifeways of these two modern social classes provided powerful languages of class and price down through the New Deal. In the tough, unsteady business climate of the Gilded Age, he explained, the profitability of capitalist enterprise, which was the source of the pecuniary class's position and power, required limiting production. Uncaring that they threw employees out of work, capitalists engaged in a form of private regulation, contriving a scarcity of vital goods in order to sustain their prices and protect the price and profit systems. Collusion toward this end – and not, by implication, a desire for greater efficiency – explained "the urge to merge." Because pecuniary society and its wealthy elites – what we might think of as the networks of financial capitalism – owned the factories and tools of industrial society, workers were powerless against this intentional sabotage of production that cost them their jobs. In addition, the pervasive tendency of the lower social orders to engage in pecuniary emulation of elite conspicuous consumption made it unlikely that even the most educated skilled workers, those regularly exposed to the cause and effect relations of modern industry, would rebel against the hegemonic economic and cultural power of capital to reform or overthrow the new industrial order.[18]

FROM THE MORAL PLANE TO SOCIAL COSTS

Among Gilded Age intellectuals, Veblen was among the first to probe and expose the forms of private market regulation that controlled supply, limiting marginal production to the point of optimal return.[19] Equally intent on understanding the sources of fluctuations in prices, he produced insights

[18] Veblen, "Industrial and Pecuniary Employments," *Publications of the American Economic Association* (1901); idem, *The Theory of the Leisure Class* (New York: Charles Scribner's Sons, 1899). Robert and Helen Lynd reframed pecuniary emulation as keeping up with the Joneses in their classic *Middletown: A Study in Modern American Culture* (New York: Harcourt, Brace and company, 1929), which was clearly influenced by the rhetoric devised by Veblen.

[19] In addition to this, Veblen's major theoretical contribution to economics was an astute analysis of the increasing role of borrowed capital in the business cycle, as it created the

that highlighted a different aspect of price making than H. C. Adams had decried. Whereas Adams explained debilitating *downward* pressure on prices as the source of declining labor standards under the conditions of keen industrial competition, Veblen explained how the new industrial magnates, at least in those parts of the economy that supported creation of sustainable barriers to entry, crafted strategies of combination that effectively held prices *up*. Significantly, for Veblen, the purpose animating formation of the new trusts was more than just another form of elite rent-seeking. Much of the capital used in modern industry was no longer savings but loan credit. Knowing this, and recognizing the corresponding power of the investor class to determine the pace of the economy, the Schwabs and Carnegies and especially Wall Street bankers such as J. P. Morgan understood that repeated overproduction crises would undermine the ability of the modern capitalist system to reproduce itself. These crises – often worsened by a drastic contraction of available credit – might even spark another American Revolution.[20]

Following a line closer to Adams's, Columbia University economist John Maurice Clark highlighted the pricing function in unregulated capitalism as the source of morally unacceptable social costs. Along with Veblen, Commons, Walton Hamilton, and Wesley Mitchell, Clark helped to found the institutionalist strand of political economy in the early years of the twentieth century. During World War I, the patriotic response of working Americans to the demands of the war economy had let Clark see how much American society could actually accomplish if it collectively concentrated its full attention on production while attempting to enlist the complete cooperation of workers by promoting good wages and working conditions. Clark noticed two main differences between this dynamic and the normal peacetime economy. In wartime, there had been more unity of purpose, more pressure from government for democracy in the workplace, higher employment and earnings, and more willingness among policy makers to deal responsibly with the problem of social costs. In the midst of the return to normalcy, Clark feared that the country would quickly slip back into business as usual.[21]

Also known for later innovative work on the multiplier principle, in this crucial rhetorical moment of postwar reconstruction Clark appropriated from Adams, and renamed, the issue of the "moral plane of competition."

---

circumstances in which the tightening of bank credit could trigger recession or depression. See Veblen, *Theory of Business Enterprise* (New York: Charles Scribner's Sons, 1904).

[20] Ibid.

[21] J. M. Clark, "The Basis of War-Time Collectivism," *American Economic Review* 7 (1917): 772–90.

He secularized and socialized the problem and related it to the absence of a social component in the making of prices, a situation that permitted firms to make and sell goods at prices well below the real cost to society of their production. Here we see the younger Clark pointing to the costs of foregone education, bad housing and unsanitary slums, sick and crippled working-class children, ruined adult workers' health, wage loss through accident or unemployment, early old age and death – costs that modern capitalist enterprise shifted from the price system of the marketplace onto the shoulders of workers' families and communities. These were costs that in some other countries were partially met through social insurance provided by the state. In the U.S. trade unions, through mutual benefit associations of various kinds, provided cooperative methods for meeting some of these costs, but the unorganized who were the vast majority of workers were unprotected.

Across the Atlantic, a similar emphasis known as welfare economics led into being by English economist Alfred C. Pigou posited, on the basis of a differential theory of individual utility functions, that income transfers from the wealthier to the poorer segments of the population would increase total utility, and thus total social welfare. Although this Pigouvian analysis and its general-welfare rhetoric became a major policy influence in the rise of the British welfare state, J. M. Clark's repeated emphasis on the need for businesses to internalize or governments to regulate social costs failed to achieve realization in U.S. policy beyond the minimal mothers' pension and workers' compensation programs already enacted during the Progressive Era to address (minimally) the costs of workplace injury or early death of a breadwinner. After the turn of the century, when industrial unions had been driven from the scene, only skilled craft unions survived to bear, along with charitable organizations and the generally more tepid initiatives associated with professional social work and welfare capitalism, other unmet burdens faced by the wage-earning class.[22]

Between the Gilded Age and the Progressive Era, authority over price-making became a formative issue in U.S. political economy and politics. The prices for industrial goods, farm produce, raw materials, industrial

---

[22] John Maurice Clark, *Social Control of Business* (Chicago: University of Chicago Press, 1926); Luca Fiorito, "John Maurice Clark's Contribution to the Genesis of the Multiplier Analysis," *Quaderni* (Università degli Studi di Siena, Dipartimento Di Economia Politica, Maggio, 2001): 1–16. On Clark's analysis of social costs, see Mary O. Furner, "Structure and Virtue in United States Political Economy," *Journal of the History of Economic Thought* 27:1 (2005): 1–27. The classic work in the British school of welfare economics is A. C. Pigou, *The Economics of Welfare* (London: Macmillan and Co., Ltd., 1932).

labor, freight transport, credit, and insurance, as well as the inequalities of power and wealth that they implicitly represented, figured not only in expert discourses but also centrally in the rhetoric of popular reform. This characterization holds for the Granger movement of the 1870s, in which perceived inequities in pricing the shipping or storage of grains were the main grievance of rural communities. It holds with regard to the Farmers Alliance and Populist movements, which intensely scrutinized monopoly pricing of shipping, storage, crop insurance, and above all rural credit, and which prominently voiced demands for the nationalization of natural monopolies, the running of them on public accounting and civil service principles that kept prices close to production costs, government currency, and an end to private local monopolies in the provision of credit. It holds for the movement for municipal ownership of public utilities in communities victimized by private monopolies in essential services that families must buy. It further holds for urban movements such as child protection, the consumers' leagues, and the social settlements, which sought to address environmental causes of poverty by legislating public health, housing, education, and labor standards, or by lifting standards and wages through organized voluntary action. It holds for much of a U.S. male labor movement from the 1880s forward that – sadly – discriminated in its own struggles on the basis of race and gender and for union organizing crusades in occupations open to women. And it certainly holds for the massive post-World War I strike wave that protested coordinated efforts by employers to roll back representation rights, improved working conditions, and better wages that workers had won during the war.

In these episodes, as well as in formal theory where research agendas registered the concerns of social movements, the rhetoric of economic regulation aimed, as it typically did prior to the 1950s, at exploitation of workers and inequities of the pricing process in U.S. capitalism. As more and more Americans produced nothing that they ate or wore, the prices of these things and how to pay them became constant preoccupations, filtering into works of fiction as well as into scholarly treatises. Regulatory reformers, whether in the halls of academe, legislative corridors, organized social movements, or the streets, generally believed that the new industrial behemoths all too often skimped on wages, ruined smaller competitors, and gouged consumers by denying them a fair share of the benefits created by technological innovations, improved skill, and scale economies. Furthermore, the advocates of economic regulation wished to discredit a price-making function for labor and goods that failed to contribute in a socially beneficial way either to the just distribution of income and wealth or to stabilization at the fullest possible level of production and employment.[23]

Even in periods of relative prosperity, incomes that determined the ability to buy varied widely. As the 1920s wore on, the pretax income share of the top 1 percent of the population reached nearly 25 percent, a level not reached again until the turn of the twenty-first century.[24] Nonetheless, wage workers' real wages did advance by about 1 percent a year in that same decade, growth was strong, and employment relatively full after the early postwar depression. These factors, along with the American Federation of Labor's continuing commitment to voluntarism, occasional concessions by employers to persuasive research-based arguments for the efficiency of shorter hours and better working conditions, and experiments in welfare capitalism that offered benefits in exchange for workers' loyalty to the firms that employed them limited the audience for more vigorous public regulation until the 1930s. Antistatist "new liberals" of the "New Era" placed their faith in the burgeoning capacity to analyze market conditions, a capacity greatly expanded by economic initiatives of Herbert Hoover's Commerce Department that were intended to inform microlevel production and price decisions in socially beneficial ways.[25]

Yet when the economy sank into yet another severe depression in the 1930s, harsher even than those of the 1870s and 1890s, events belied the confidence that Hooverian corporate liberals and social conservatives expressed in the prevailing economic order. As late as 1932, Adolph Berle and Gardiner Means could find considerable support for their seminal and mildly procorporate assessment of the separation of ownership from control that had come to characterize so much of corporate America. With the

---

[23] Evidence of the preoccupation with prices is everywhere and cut in many directions, viz., the Clayton Antitrust Act's strictures on underselling, future Supreme Court Justice Louis Brandeis's crusade against chain stores, and myriad references to the ubiquitous and exploitive company store.

[24] Emmanuel Saez and Thomas Piketty, "Income Inequality in the United States, 1913–1998," *Quarterly Journal of Economics* 118:1 (2003): 1–39. A data series updated to 2002 is available at http://elsa.berkeley.edu/~saez/TabFig2004prel.xls and http://emlab.berkeley.edu/users/saez/piketty-saezOUP04US.pdf.

[25] On U.S. Steel's reluctant abandonment of the twelve-hour day in the face of foundation-sponsored research on the effects of fatigue, see G. Mark Hendrickson, "Labor Knowledge and the Building of Modern Industrial Relations, 1918–1929" (Ph.D. diss.: University of California, Santa Barbara, 2004). See also Stuart Brandes, *American Welfare Capitalism: 1880-1940* (Chicago: University of Chicago Press, 1976); Sanford M. Jacoby, *Modern Manors: Welfare Capitalism since the New Deal* (Princeton, Princeton University Press, 1997).

marketing of industrial stocks to Main Street and the emergence of a class
of professional managers who apparently possessed authority over corporate decision making, Berle and Means envisioned a day when the fiduciary
responsibility of the corporation might extend beyond the benefit of shareholders to the welfare of the community. In some respects, this impulse had
a good deal in common with Hooverian associationalism, and a resurgence
of it helped to shape post-World War II corporate culture; but it would not
offer the most influential guidance for the coming New Deal. Disagreement
between institutionalists and neoclassicists in economics over the nature of
economic knowledge and of the market persisted, as did differences in the
images and metaphors employed to represent the social relations of U.S.
capitalism. Yet the New Deal should be seen as an enactment of sorts of the
public interest rhetoric that leading progressive economists had been shaping since the 1880s and as a partial realization of the dreams and designs of
a wider circle of statist new liberal publics with whom they had been closely
in touch.[26]

FROM ADMINISTERED PRICES TO NATIONAL PLANNING

The Great Depression provided the occasion for experimentation with new
ways of understanding and expressing rhetorically the limitations and vulnerabilities of a privately administered market, even as the hardships it
imposed generated new arguments in favor of public economic regulation.
Initially, as historians of the New Deal have long noted, the New Deal was
friendly to pricing agreements and other forms of commercial associationalism that the Clayton Anti-Trust Act had ostensibly prohibited. Under
the mantle of the Roosevelt administration's Re-employment Agreement,
the National Recovery Administration (NRA) announced by posting its
famous Blue Eagle in its front window a cooperating business firm's "We
Do Our Part" commitment to the maintenance of a code of fair competition.

---

[26] I intend here to reject characterizations of the New Deal as any of the following: a ruling-
class based rescue operation for capitalism, a failure rooted in insufficiencies of U.S. state
structure and capacities, a hodgepodge of pragmatic experiments that were nonideolog-
ical in character, and – conversely – a coherent set of visionary left-liberal reforms that
degenerated after 1937 into "commercial Keynesianism." For an assessment of Berle and
Means that makes *The Modern Corporation* a generative text in the formation of a vision
of a coming postcapitalist era, see Howard Brick, *Transcending Capitalism: Visions of a
New Society in Modern American Thought* (Ithaca and London: Cornell University Press,
2006). On the active involvement of one prominent set of academic economists with settlement houses, charitable and philanthropic societies, labor activists, and urban government
reform groups, see Recchiuti, *Civic Engagement,* passim.

Carrying over from the Hoover years a faith in industry-wide cooperation as an economic stabilization mechanism, New Dealers experimented initially with the proposition that industry-based code-writing authorities composed of capitalist managers, labor leaders, and consumer representatives might coordinate prices and wages to expand production, reemploy workers, and heal the depression.

During the NRA's brief tenure, the voices of workers and consumers turned out to have little if any influence. The acronym read for many of the dispossessed as the National Run Around, No Recovery Allowed, Negro Removal Act, or No Relief Anywhere; and most New Dealers had turned their backs on the NRA before the Supreme Court ruled it unconstitutional. From the perspective of statist liberals, including those in the working class, NRA codes represented little more than rent-seeking attempts to maintain prices by restricting production; as such, they were living proof of Veblen's telling distinction between the pecuniary and industrial economies. The objective of achieving a measure of social regulation of the pricing power migrated, along with some of the NRA's personnel, into other New Deal agencies, there to pursue similar efforts toward economic stabilization and fuller employment, for the moment without effective resistance from proponents of voluntarism.[27]

The clearest example of the continuity of this effort surfaced in the National Resources Committee and its successor agency, the National Resources Planning Board (NRPB), headed by FDR's uncle, Frederic Delano, and Charles Merriam, a leading University of Chicago political scientist. A well-published advocate of centralized planning as both an antidote to depression and a means for extending economic democracy, Merriam was perhaps the key figure in these agencies.[28] Able to reach the president and his

---

[27] Robert F. Himmelberg, *The Origins of the National Recovery Administration: Business, Government, and the Trade Association Issue, 1921–1933* (New York: Fordham University Press, 1976); Donald Brand, *Corporatism and the Rule of Law: A Study of the National Recovery Administration* (Ithaca, N.Y.: Cornell University Press, 1988); Alan Brinkley, *The End of Reform: New Deal Liberalism in Recession and War* (New York: Random House, 1996).

[28] Phillip W. Warken, *A History of the National Resources Planning Board* (New York: Garland Publishing, 1979); Marion Clawson, *New Deal Planning: The National Resources Planning Board* (Baltimore, JHU Press, 1981); Patrick Reagan, *Designing a New America* (Amherst: University of Massachusetts Press, 1999). In addition to Delano and Merriam, the NRPB was led by Columbia University and National Bureau of Economic Research economist Wesley Clair Mitchell, who was later replaced by regional planner George Yantis. The at sequence of planning agencies that culminated with the National Resources Planning Board goes like this: the National Planning Board, 1933–34, in the PWA, under NIRA and Ickes, and intended to inventory and help to schedule public works in part as a way of

top advisors, he promoted a strategic shift of emphasis from more efficiently deploying natural resources to attacking mass unemployment directly. Although Merriam's defense of democratic planning did not directly address issues of class and distribution, it emphatically rejected the Hooverian premise that the enlightened corporate interest was the equivalent of the public interest.[29]

Under Merriam's direction, moreover, a research group led by economist Gardiner Means, the author during this era of the term "administered prices," focused more directly on fundamental problems of income inequality. Means had proposed the title the agency bore between 1935 and 1939, the National Resources Committee (NRC), which signified the way that New Deal planners conceptualized industries in private hands as essentially national resources, underutilized and needing leadership that only government could provide in the quest for economic security and greater democracy. At this moment, Means' Industrial Section of NRC spearheaded efforts within the New Deal to democratize and even nationalize America's new, postclassical version of liberalism.[30]

Like H. C. Adams, Means was the son of a progressive Congregationalist minister. He also shared Adams's expectation that a genuine movement from political toward economic democracy – which Adams had styled as a fuller extension of liberty – would require some degree of socialization of critical decisions regarding production and price levels. These arenas, in Means's opinion, effectively determined whether the great mass of the people would have a job, earn wages, and even, as the depths of the Depression made all too clear, survive. Struck, as were many, by the incongruous picture

deflecting pork-barrel demands from Congress; the National Resources Board, 1934–35, made directly responsible to FDR; the National Resources Committee,1935–39, detached from NRA after it was declared unconstitutional; and the National Resources Planning Board, 1939–43, created as part of an executive reorganization, which Merriam and NRC helped to instigate, a part of Executive Office of the President reporting directly to FDR, but dependent directly for the first time on Congress for appropriations, which were cut off after a battle that closed down the agency in 1943.

[29] Merriam to Ickes, October 2, 1933, Box 50; Ruml to Merriam, October 27, 1937, Box 56; Ruml to Merriam, April 25, 1938, Box 56, Merriam MSS; Alan Brinkley, "The National Resources Planning Board and the Reconstruction of Planning," 173–91, in Fishman, ed., *American Planning Tradition.* On the planning dimension more generally, see Ellis Hawley, *New Deal and the Problem of Monopoly,* 282–403; Herbert Stein, *The Fiscal Revolution in America* (Chicago: University of Chicago Press, 1969), 91–130; Brinkley, *End of Reform;* Albert V. Romasco, *The Politics of Recovery: Roosevelt's New Deal* (New York: Oxford University Press), 216–40; Reagan, *Designing a New America,* 196–223.

[30] In addition to Means, Thomas Blaisdell and Hildegarde Kneeland joined the Industrial Section of the NRC in 1935, and Isador Lubin, Leon Henderson, Lauchlan Currie, Herbert Feis, and Mordecai Ezekiel worked closely with the National Resources Committee.

of idle plants and idle men, Means transformed his program at NRC/NRPB from studies of productive capacity in single industries to multi-industry studies, and then enhanced these analyses with initiatives to improve on the consumption studies underway at the federal Bureau of Labor Statistics.[31]

The NRC's emphasis on consumption followed from Means's perception that redistribution of income would be an essential element in forcing strategic shifts in the core manufacturing industries that administered their prices and that employed key segments of the American work force. In justifying this conclusion, Means considered that it was "only necessary for a state to know its productive capacity when it proposes to institute a social control over the productive facilities of its citizens, or when it proposes to build some plants of its own." The necessity for such actions arose in his view from the failure of existing forms of wage bargaining to apportion income fairly and effectively between the poor, who would consume every bit they received, and rich savers, who actually invested only under favorable conditions and had currently gone on a spending strike. Means argued that "the increasing intensity of each subsequent depression seems to indicate that the percentage of national buying power that society diverts to owners and which these owners are in a position to defer using, is continually increasing." Yet "the combination of working rules and property rights which we have supported in our American bargaining economy have been and are such that industrial activity has fallen off to where millions of people are unemployed and some twenty millions are on relief."[32]

For Means, the business policy of administered prices had in recent decades become by default what passed in the United States for an industrial policy, with precisely the result that had also sparked Upton Sinclair's End Poverty In California (EPIC) campaign in 1934 aimed at taking over idle plants and farms for production for use. Means believed, given the malfunction of the market controls that were supposed to maintain equilibrium in a "bargaining" or market economy, that the time had come for the

---

[31] I draw much of this material on Gardiner Means from Mary O. Furner, "New Deal Planning as a Discourse of Democracy and Nation," unpublished paper presented at the 2002 Conference on Policy History, St. Louis Missouri, in the author's possession.

[32] Means, *Industrial Prices and Their Relative Inflexibility.* Senate Document No. 13, 74th Cong., 1st. Sess. (Washington: GPO, 1935). See also Allan G. Gruchy, "The Economics of the National Resources Committee," *American Economic Review* 29 (1939): 60–73; Frederic S. Lee, "From Multi-Industry Planning to Keynesian Planning: Gardiner Means, the American Keynesians, and National Economic Planning at the National Resources Committee," *Journal of Policy History* 2 (1990): 186–212. The influence of Veblenian thinking regarding the relations of the pecuniary and industrial economies is obvious.

state – temporarily at least – to adopt the principles of a "rationing economy." This would not likely mean nationalization, but rather some degree
of political control, by methods as yet unspecified, over decisions on construction, types and volumes of production, prices, wages, hours, and other
details of production "in order to sustain our people." Small wonder – even
though the approach Means advocated initially received a strong endorsement from the NRC, that someone in the administration later marked his
analysis, an unmistakably collectivist justification of a strong government
role in determining the level of economic activity, as "suppressed."[33]

The NRC released its most far-reaching study of industry structure in
1939. Its conclusions, based on detailed statistical studies of the behavior
of prices in the 1920s and 1930s, represented a considerable advance over
the classification of industries by returns to scale that H. C. Adams had
put forth fifty years earlier. Influenced by the work of Edwin Chamberlain
and Joan Robinson on oligopoly, Means no longer erected a bright line
that defined monopoly power absolutely, as a situation in which a business
could take monopoly profits without inviting new competition. He believed
the typical situation contained elements of both monopoly and competition that could be discerned through careful study. But, more important,
administered prices did not necessarily yield monopoly profits; in many
cases of price administration during the depression, there were no profits
at all. Even so, in administered industries, the adjustment of prices (and
wages for that matter) to changing demand turned out to be slower, stickier,
and less quickly correcting than prices in industries such as furniture-
making and textiles that still faced more traditional forms of price competition.

These findings led Means to focus on the potentially destructive impacts
of market dynamics within modern industrial society. "This differential sensitivity of prices to depression influences," he observed, "tends to introduce
serious distortions in the price structure and appears to reflect a disorga-
nizing rather than an organizing role that the market can play." Prices were
one method for controlling industry, but the often hidden and little-studied

---

[33] "National Survey of Productive Capacity: Justification," RG 187, P. I. 50, National Resources
Planning Board MSS, NARA (n.d., but just prior to the September 5, 1934, meeting of the
NPB Council). Means hoped to improve on a recent Brookings Institution study by Edwin
Nourse, future chief of the Council of Economic Advisers, *America's Capacity to Produce*
(Washington: Brookings Institution, 1934), which was followed soon by Maurice Leven,
Harold G. Moulton, and Clark Warburton, *America's Capacity to Consume* (Washington,
D.C., The Brookings Institution, 1934). Means's mature analysis of the impact of admin-
istered prices is reported in National Resources Committee, *The Structure of the American
Economy. Part I* (Washington: GPO, 1939).

controls that large corporations, trade associations, labor unions, farmers' organizations, and consumers' organizations exerted on prices constituted another. Equally important, the nonprice methods of control available to corporations (control of credit by banks, control of individual firm policies by major buyers, influence through intercorporate major share holding or interlocking boards of directors) tended to outweigh all others. The exceptions to this pattern involved the areas where governments already were shaping the legal terrain for economic activity, which Means referred to, in a historical reference to the first great American work of public infrastructure, as "canalizing rules" – the protection of property, enforcement of contracts, rules for incorporation, rules governing the legal rights of corporations and claims of creditors, regulation of various kinds, and – only recently – protection for collective bargaining.[34]

Here, Means was making a point similar to one emphasized by Marc Eisner in his essay for this volume. In a host of ways, law and regulatory frameworks give form and identity to the economic institutions of the market. The Means team at NRC conducted studies of current consumption, with the aim of helping an envisioned new government agency to project what changes in the distribution of income the economy would require in order to raise effective demand, thereby pulling the country out of depression, and then sustaining production and employment. Bringing the production and consumption studies together, Means and his crew gave some of the basic insights of Keynesianism a solidly empirical base, even as they disagreed with Keynes on points of theory.

Their analysis and proposals served as a vital part of the intellectual foundation for the Full Employment Bill of 1946. The preparation of production and consumption budgets would show what level of employment private investment would generate, allowing the government to develop a supplementary budget with sufficient government spending for construction programs capable, along with automatic stimulators of consumption such as Social Security payments, to bring the economy up to full employment of capital and labor. Yet when the Means Report was vetted by the full committee following the so-called Roosevelt recession of 1937, with rival theories on offer and the political ground shifting as business and congressional conservatives mobilized against the New Deal, other members forced Means to lower his sights. In essence, he had to scale down his blueprint for direct government intervention to ease the imbalances between prices

---

[34] *Structure*, 122–72; Blaisdell, "The Industrial Structure and the Problem of Strategic Controls," (n. d., [early 1938]), Blaisdell files, Box 1, NRPB Mss., NARA.

in the competitive and the price-administered sectors and thus, putatively, to reallocate private investment.[35]

In these deliberations among the experts, some skeptics evinced doubts about the ability of the existing government bureaucracy to handle such a sizeable planning task and, if it could, whether unfixing prices would deal effectively with the depression. Means continued with studies aimed at specifying more precisely the control points where government intervention and democratic pressures would alter the structure and operation of industry. But dissenters such as Leon Henderson, New Deal economic adviser and subsequently head of the Office of Price Administration, and U.S. Labor Statistics Commissioner Isador Lubin became involved in a competing investigation by the Temporary National Economic Committee (TNEC) into the role of monopoly in retarding recovery. The goal of TNEC, at least for the experts involved, could be stated in a Veblenian rhetoric that pitted production for profit against production for use. Supportive of the Means approach to pricing questions, TNEC poured much of its energy into exposing strategies, such as the basing point system in steel, through which concentrated industries administered prices, perpetuating the imbalances that the structure report had documented.

For the TNEC economists, then, Means's diagnosis proved more convincing than his bureaucratic remedy. Henderson, Lubin, and Thurman Arnold from the Justice Department's Antitrust Division envisaged policing pricing policies largely through antitrust enforcement, which would not require construction of so much new state capacity. What H. C. Adams had hoped to achieve through regulation, what advocates of permissive combination had hoped to achieve through intrafirm planning, what Hooverians had hoped to achieve by enriching the climate of information for private, firm-level decisions on production and pricing, what TNEC hoped to achieve through forcing competition, Gardiner Means had hoped to achieve through a developed planning capacity, continuous bureaucratic monitoring, and informed pressure from government for adjustment of price imbalances that did not accurately reflect actual utilities. Such efforts might help to redirect investment to industries capable of contributing more to sustained higher consumption and full employment.[36]

---

[35] On the emerging division within the committee, see William Barber, *Designs within Disorder: Franklin D. Roosevelt, the Economists, and the Shaping of American Economic Policy, 1933–1945* (New York and Cambridge: Cambridge University Press, 1996), Chs. 4 & 5, "Rethinking the Structuralist Agenda."

[36] For the cross-fertilization of ideas among the economists in these agencies, see the testimony of Thurman Arnold, Mordecai Ezekiel, and Isador Lubin, among others, in

What Means had hoped to accomplish through the rhetoric of administered prices, and most particularly the creation of a more permanent role for the state in directing private and public investment, of course, ran afoul of intellectual currents and political realities. After the Roosevelt recession of 1937, which weakened him and key New Deal planners, the weight of expert opinion and business thinking shifted decisively toward less directly interventionist methods. Instead of a second volume of argument and statistical evidence locating potential control points that regulators could use to affect prices, the NRC produced a slim volume full of polite and not quite so polite disagreement on how to define the public interest. Means restated his case for targeting the problem of administered prices as the place where the government could most effectively exert leverage to redress imbalances in the economy that prolonged the depression. In reply, John Maurice Clark cautioned against forcing reductions in prices that might result in even more unemployment. To replace Means's approach, Clark introduced the two main themes that would appear in the powerful 1942 NRPB report on *Security, Work, and Relief* – full employment of manpower and "policies directed toward mitigating the incidence of the burden of inadequate utilization on those on whom it falls most heavily." Once again, he was identifying as a primary concern the problem of unmet social costs, created this time through a failure of the entire economy. Although Clark still wrestled with the problem of defining what would be considered employment and how the government should finance its augmentation, he rejected relief as an unjust and undignified policy for employing people eager to and capable of doing real work.[37]

At the other extreme from Means, Alvin Hansen, who had come into planning initially riding an economic stagnation thesis, adopted a "Curried Keynesian" approach to mass unemployment of capital and labor. In his consideration of rigid prices as an issue, he distinguished between structural and cyclical price inflexibilities. Structural ones were normally traceable to efficiency gains from technological innovations that cheapened production but were not quickly passed on to consumers because of "institutional

---

Temporary National Economic Committee, *Investigation of Concentration of Economic Power: Final Report and Recommendations*, Senate Document 35, 77th Cong., 1st Sess. (Washington: GPO, 1941), 517–57.

[37] Gerber, "National Industrial Recovery Act," identifies J. M. Clark as a major supporter of the movement for creation of a national economic council that led to LaFollette's introduction of a bill in 1931 and hearings. He identifies Clark as one of the "technocratic witnesses." Instead of a corporatist-type structure that NRA eventually had, Clark favored creating a small council with special expertise to serve as "an economic general staff," with a larger advisory council of functional representatives called in as needed.

controls, corporate, trade union, agricultural, and governmental" – in short, institutional rigidities that conferred at least temporary rents. These rigidities harmed consumers, but most of them would be self-correcting, he thought, much as the ripples in John Bates Clark's metaphorical tub would eventually subside.[38]

As for cyclical price inflexibility, Hansen simply denied the Means hypothesis, which gave a causal role in bringing on and sustaining depressions to imbalances between competitive and monopoly prices that kept capital from moving to newer industries with greater potential for employment growth. Hansen turned the equation on its head; most cyclical price imbalances were the result, rather than the cause of depressions, he argued. If, as he now believed, depressions were caused by insufficient investment overall, rather than in specific sectors, then draconian public measures to force prices down even more would worsen an already parlous situation, and would further dampen private investment. Within Hansen's critique of Means, in a nutshell, was the case for government intervention of an altogether different stripe. Hansen's logic led to moves like opening the Federal Reserve's credit window wider and embracing countercyclical deficit spending by government for productive public works as well as compensatory payments of various kinds to support consumption.[39]

Between 1941 and 1943, at FDR's direction, the NRPB shifted its attention to planning for postwar reconversion and specifically to avoiding a postwar recession. To accomplish these goals, the board shifted strategies, from the rather covert operating style that had earlier aimed its advice toward a small circle within the administration to a pamphleteering crusade aimed at reaching a wider public with promises that the war against tyranny would be worth winning, and thus, implicitly, with assurances that all the wartime sacrifices were worth making.[40] In these appeals, the emphasis was on the

[38] This analysis was by now forty years old; it had first appeared in Jeremiah Jenks contribution to the report of the United States Industrial Commission in 1902. See Furner, "The Republican Tradition and the New Liberalism: Social Investigation, State Building, and Social Learning in the Gilded Age," *The State and Social Investigation in the Britain and the United States*, eds. Michael J. Lacey and Mary O. Furner (New York: Cambridge University Press, 1993), 171–241.

[39] Means, "The Controversy over Full Employment," Clark, "The Attack on the Problem of Full Use," and Hansen, "Price Flexibility and the Full Employment of Resources," in *Structure of the American Economy, II: Toward Full Use of Resources* (Washington: GPO, 1940). Also Barber, *Design*, pp. 116–31. Means's ambition for the operation study is in a memo to Merriam, January 23, 1937; Means to Delano, June 3, 1938, NRPB Mss, RG 187, Box 1733.

[40] Samples of the NRPB pamphlets issued in 1941–42 include *After Defense What?*, *After the War – Full Employment*, *Building America – Better Cities*, *Building America – The Role of*

nation's obligation to ensure security. NRPB laid out in general terms a program for maintaining full employment through extensive reliance on deficit financing of public expenditures as a supplement to private investment, primarily in the form of worthwhile civil works projects and additions to social spending for health, housing, transportation, and education programs, alongside the various New Deal social insurance programs. Among the most advanced elaborations of this New Deal statism, *Security, Work, and Relief Policies* conveyed NRPB's synthesis of three related but discrete government roles: guaranteeing work – through supplementary government spending for public works jobs as needed – for the segment of the population securely attached to the labor market; financing and extending social insurance to care for those unable to participate in the work economy; and underwriting a still highly contested version of industrial democracy through the National Labor Relations Board and the self-organization of labor. Here, articulated in a classic statement of the primary goals of New Deal liberals, was a blueprint for realization of the promise, running back in "new liberalism" to the 1880s, of the "right to a job."[41]

The NRPB furnished some of FDR's most memorable rhetoric during the transitional phase between Dr. New Deal and Dr. Win the War – the proclamation in 1941 of the Four Freedoms as universal goals for the world after the war, and the Economic Bill of Rights for Americans, submitted to Roosevelt in 1941 by Merriam and Delano as "the 10 promises of American life," and contained in the NRPB report that the administration submitted to Congress in 1943. The first of the ten promises was the right to work, and among the others were the right to security, freedom from fear of old age, want, dependency, sickness, unemployment, and accident, and the

---

the *Housebulding Industry, Post-war Planning, After the War – Toward Security. Freedom from Want,* and *A Post-war Agenda.*

[41] *Security, Work, and Relief Policies: Report of the Committee on Long-Range Work and Relief Policies to the National Resources Planning Board* (Washington: GPO, 1942). The Urbanism Committee of the NRPB under Charles Dykstra made the first major national study of cities in the United States, which was quite self-consciously an analogue to Teddy Roosevelt's County Life Commission. A disproportionate number – one of five in 1935 – of the nation's unemployed were located in the ten largest cities. The Urbanism Committee cited economic insecurity traceable to structural factors – the uncontrolled business cycle and "drastic inequalities of income and wealth" found most acutely in the cities – as the basis for recommending a major collaborative effort between the national and urban governments to expand capacity for countercyclical public works as an automatic stabilizer of employment, and to address the tragic insufficiency of affordable urban housing. The NRPB played a significant role in making the right to adequate housing a part of the Economic Bill of Rights. Regarding "right to a job" rhetoric, H.C. Adams had actually framed it in the 1880s as a "proprietary right" on the part of workers to a degree of ownership in the firm to which they had given their time and strength.

right to equality before the law, if not explicitly social and economic equality. Although neither racial nor gender equality was among them, these promises extended the functions of government well beyond the traditional ones achieved in earlier decades of minimal economic regulation and minimal social provision. They asserted a primary government responsibility for reemploying at least (largely white, male) industrial workers, improving health and housing, stabilizing the climate for private investment, and in general facilitating the balanced economic and civic development of the commonwealth.[42]

These goals, which – depending on one's perspective – were either essential to genuine freedom and democracy or corrosive of liberty, provoked serious opposition. A coalition of Republicans and conservative Democrats shut down the NRPB in 1943, prohibiting the board even from bequeathing its papers to a successor agency. The Full Employment Bill became the watered-down Employment Act of 1946, lacking the requirement for regular projections of national output and employment in the private economy that would be supplemented by necessary public works, and lacking a guarantee of measures designed to ensure full employment. The postwar Congress also purged the leftists in the first National Labor Relations Board, shut down the agency's economic research arm, and passed the Taft-Hartley Act over President Harry Truman's veto, weakening the redistributive potential of collective bargaining. As a result of coverage limitations that excluded many women, domestic and farm workers, and most Blacks, neither the hallmark social insurance programs of the New Deal, nor the Fair Labor Standards Act, nor the Fair Employment Practices Commission set a very high or inclusive standard, for what H. C. Adams had called with stronger ethical overtones "the moral plane of competition."[43]

---

[42] On the ten promises, see Barry Karl, *Charles Merriam and the Study of Politics* (Chicago: University of Chicago Press, 1974), 276. The shift to spending did not cut off work on coordinating production. Means kept the NEC staff working on how redistribution would contribute to recovery, as in Hildegarde Kneeland, "To what extent would a redistribution of national income contribute to the attainment and maintenance of a higher national income?" (May 16, 1939); Blaisdell to Delano, April 1, 1940, NRPB MSS, Box 1733.

[43] On the backlash against planning, see Alan Brinkley, *End of Reform*; Reagan, *Designing a New America*. On the continuation of elements of a democratic statist agenda in the postwar era, see Robert Griffith, "Forging America's postwar order: domestic politics and political economy in the Age of Truman," 57–88; Craufurd D. Goodwin, "Attitudes toward industry in the Truman administration: the macroeconomic origins of microeconomic policy," 89–127, in Michael J. Lacey, ed., *The Truman Presidency* (New York: Cambridge University Press, 1989); Meg Jacobs, *Pocketbook Politics: Economic Citizenship in Twentieth Century America* (Princeton: Princeton University Press, 2005).

Nonetheless, from the Old Gilded Age through the New Deal, a certain unity of perception and broad purpose linked the leading theoretical justifications of, and rhetorical appeals for, far-reaching economic regulation. Raise the moral plane. Extend democracy from the suffrage to the economy. Permit the efficiencies that certain monopolies can provide, but keep them from turning pricing power into the power to tax consumers. Absorb more social costs into prices, so that these costs do not fall most heavily on the least advantaged. Identify and assist those of the community who lose their livelihoods through no fault of their own. Ensure that the system of private investment provides adequate employment, or supplement it from public funds. See to it that the social relations of capitalism are "fair."

Collectively, these rhetorical and programmatic planks constituted more than the sum of their parts, offering a normative vision of modern industrial society, as well as an integrated set of policies to realize that vision. Confronting the ingrained individualism of nineteenth century liberalism, their language of a *moral* plane, *social* costs, and *national* planning proclaimed – even while bracketing gender and race – a new sense of collective responsibility as defining the public good. It also conveyed a sense that capitalism as a going concern could not proceed as it had previously and yet continue to fulfill what a progressive adviser to Theodore Roosevelt, Herbert Croly, had termed the promise of American life, defined as abundance within the framework of political democracy and rough economic equality. This constellation of ideas circulated from the world views of leading economic thinkers into the perspectives of reformers, social activists, and progressive politicians and back again.

The key channels of intellectual exchange lay in direct interactions among members of these groups. Policy intellectuals visited social settlements, spoke and taught courses for labor groups, served on the governing boards of philanthropic foundations and advocacy groups such as American Association for Labor Legislation, and worked as researchers for public agencies, from the Bureau of Labor and the United States Industrial Commission to the Department of Labor Women's Bureau, the Division of Negro Economics during World War I, FDR's Committee on Economic Security, and the NRPB. At the same time, there were more indirect methods of popularization. Their ideas reached wider audiences through a highly diverse multi-language press and political journals such as the *Forum, Arena, Dial, Appeal to Reason,* and *New Republic* that proliferated from the 1880s onward, in response to – but also helping to fuel – a rising demand from an engaged populace for serious attention to economic subjects. For women attending college in increasing numbers in the first Gilded Age, courses on social issues taught by professional social scientists were available, as was graduate study in the social sciences. Educated women became activists and organizers who carried women's and families' economic issues into the public sphere, contributing through their support of women wage workers to the rejection of the "pin money" fallacy suggesting that women worked not out of necessity but rather to engage in frivolous consumption, and to the popularization of rhetorical strategies aimed at greater distributive equity such as the "living wage." Professional women joined their wage-working counterparts in demanding increased knowledge of working conditions, even as investors, entrepreneurs, laborers, and public officials pressed for better understanding of the business cycle and how to deal with it. The presence of hundreds of thousands of socialists, radicals, and communists in the United States between the 1880s and World War II created a climate in which liberal reformers faced the necessity of competing with and – more than has been recognized – cooperating with ideological rivals who had their own ardent followings in the working and thinking classes. Not merely active nationally, leading progressive economists, among them many who had studied in and frequently traveled to Europe, participated in international reform organizations. They served, for example, in the International Association for Labor Legislation founded in 1900, helped to establish the International Labor Organization in 1919 to lead the drive for international regulation of labor standards, and pressed for U.S. membership until the nation finally joined the ILO in 1934.[44]

In all these venues, the ranks of statist-leaning regulatory reformers in this period, with fits and starts to be sure, increasingly pushed back against the inherited traditions of individualism, antistatism, and *laissez faire* and the invented tradition of private intercorporate rule making. They convinced the courts to refrain from further expanding corporate property rights, advocated a reinterpretation of the U.S. Constitution's commerce clause that permitted effective national regulation, and animated the adoption of a political economy that decreased income inequality over three subsequent decades, redistributing not only income and wealth but also political and economic power between the 1930s and the 1960s. In all these discourses about the pricing function, the significance of competition and monopoly, the salience of social externalities, and the disproportionate influence of financial and corporate elites, the rhetoric of economic regulation

---

[44] Recchiuti, *Civic Engagement*, provides a marvelously textured account of the remarkable degree of participation by New York City's academic social and economic knowledge creators in its infrastructure of reform organizations and political journalism.

encouraged collective action. In some cases, that collective action took the form of new government roles and capacities; in others, it translated into encouragement for private entities to pursue initiatives for the benefit of the public interest. Consider John L. Lewis's "Mr. Roosevelt wants you to join a union," or Robert Wagner's idea that promoting collective bargaining helped not only workers but all classes by underwriting the expanded buying power needed to stabilize the economy, or the Keynesian message that governments must engage in deficit spending to compensate for the paradox of thrift and offset the liquidity preference of private investors, which together confined economic output to a level far below the full productive employment of labor and capital.[45]

FROM NEW DEAL PLANNING TO THE NEW SERFDOM

This reformist rhetoric of a "more statist and more democratic liberalism" that culminated in the New Deal planning ideal had all along attracted substantial criticism – both among experts and in more popular venues. In retrospect, certainly, the New Deal liberals' decision to adopt a language of planning to describe their liberal statist vision of democratic capitalism was a strategic error. The rise of fascism in Europe and the consolidation of Soviet communism under Joseph Stalin in the 1930s cast a negative aura over the idea of government command and control. Yet planning was "in the air," in no small part due to the discourses and rhetoric of New Deal economists. For Brains Truster Rexford Tugwell and Department of Agriculture economist Mordecai Ezekiel, the failure of the NRA to cure the depression by contriving scarcity fueled a desire to adopt aspects of the idea of production for use, also popular with members of the Farmer-Labor Party. Thinking along lines even more advanced than those of Means at NRC, they proposed experimenting with planning for full production, with a government super-agency in charge of setting quotas and prices not only for farm produce but throughout the manufacturing sector as well. Representing the League for Progressive Political Action founded by Senator Paul Douglas and John Dewey, staunchly anti-communist Wisconsin farmer-laborite Thomas Amlie introduced measures in Congress calling for expropriation of absentee-owned property, which an elected government

---

[45] On continued disagreement among Keynes, Means, and Hansen over what policies would most effectively end a recession, see Theodore Rosenof, *Economics in the Long Run: New Deal Theorists and Their Legacies, 1933–1993* (Chapel Hill and London: University of North Carolina Press, 1997).

could use to shift the economy away from production for profit and toward production for use.[46]

Yet even as these ideas and slogans found wide audiences in the cities and rural America, opposing movements were afoot to rebrand them—from latterday republican or new liberal to un-American. The U.S. House of Representatives began investigating organizations thought to be communist fronts, including the American Civil Liberties Union, as early as 1930, and by 1938 the House Un-American Activities Committee (HUAC) was up and running as a permanent, roving investigative authority with broad powers to compel testimony regarding infiltration into the country of agents bent on subverting the institutions of democratic government. Reaction to the Nazi-Soviet Pact of 1939-41 strained previously amicable relations between many liberals and the left. Anti-communism gained adherents with every high-profile exposé of alleged or actual Soviet agents, and as the war drew to a close many in policy circles and in the wider public had concluded – contrary to former Vice-President Henry Wallace, and along with Democrats such as Harry Truman – that patriotic Americans simply could no longer work cooperatively with communists.

Strategically timed in relation to the fracturing of the liberal-left alliance and the growth of business conservatism around the country, the most important single moment in the rhetorical counterthrust against the new liberal economists' more than half-century assault on *laissez faire* surely occurred in 1944, almost precisely at the moment when FDR dropped Henry Wallace from the Democratic ticket. The key event was the publication of Austrian émigré economist Friedrich von Hayek's broadside against the welfare state, *The Road to Serfdom.* Together with Russian-American author and publicist Ayn Rand, Hayek set in motion the coinage of a potent rhetoric *against* economic regulation that helped to convert business reaction to the New Deal and the growing fear of communism into a more cohesive antistatist, promarket, libertarian philosophical and political movement. Unwilling to distinguish between state socialists and central planners in liberal polities, Hayek dedicated *Road to Serfdom* to "The Socialists of All Parties," whom he hoped to help see the error of their ways. Although the

[46] Arthur Schlesinger, Jr., *The Politics of Upheaval* (Boston: Houghton Mifflin Company, 1960); Mordecai Ezekiel, *Jobs for All Through Industrial Expansion* (New York: Alfred A. Knopf, 1939). On the liberal-left alliance in the New Deal era and its plans for restructuring capitalism, see Douglas Rossinow, *Visions of Progress: The Left-Liberal Tradition in America* (Philadelphia: University of Pennsylvania Press, 2008), 103-142; William J. Barber, *Design within Disorder: Franklin D. Roosevelt, the Economists, and the Shaping of American Economic Policy, 1933-1945* (New York: Cambridge University Press, 1996).

book grew out of long reflection on the evils of European fascism and its sources, Hayek made it clear that he considered the rise of welfare states throughout the West every bit as dangerous to individual liberty and free institutions as he did "hot socialism." Both of these variants of centrally directed economies placed societies on slippery slopes to fascism.[47]

British and U.S. critics of Hayek – economists prominently among them – insisted that the distinctive historical traditions, state structures, and political cultures of their two countries provided ample protection against the rise of autocratic rule. Even so, the image of a new serfdom successfully captured the attention of a wide Western (and an especially large American) audience. In the decades since the rise of steel and electricity, much of that audience had become accustomed to viewing modernity, which included new forms of rational, bureaucratic rule making based on specialized knowledge, as the road to escape from all things feudal. Instead, Hayek portrayed many such aspects of modernity as a troubling reinvention of an age-old paternalism, in which populations increasingly dependent on government largesse traded liberty for security. (By way of contrast, H.C. Adams had compared favorably the rude security of peasants during the Middle Ages to the increasingly precarious liberty of the propertyless industrial working class.) For Hayek, society could safely and legitimately provide minimal security against only a modest insurable class of hurts that inevitably befell certain individuals. But any provision of security for specific classes – beyond what individuals could provide by their own free choices of occupation and effort – would necessarily subtract from rewards sought and deserved by others. Like Adam Smith and other Scottish Enlightenment figures, Hayek believed that the character of a people was shaped by the consequences they saw arising from their fellow citizens' actions. In time, with liberty slowly giving way before a relentlessly subsidized and enervating security, fewer individuals would be willing or would even feel the need to take the risks that gave concrete meaning to liberty, which in turn sustained both freedom and the innovations that fueled long-term economic progress.[48]

Planning was if anything an even greater threat to liberty than was social security, in Hayek's much publicized view. Hayek attacked the liberal

---

[47] Friedrich A. Hayek, *The Road to Serfdom* (Chicago: University of Chicago Press, 1944). English philosopher Michael Oakeshott's essay "Rationalism in Politics," first published in *The Cambridge Journal* in 1947 and reprinted in Oakeshott's *Rationalism in Politics and Other Essays* (1962), struck similarly critical notes toward social engineering, left liberalism, and socialism.

[48] Contrast Hayek, *Road,* Ch. 9, "Security and Freedom" with the definition of liberty supplied by John Stuart Mill's, *On Liberty.*

rhetoric of the Charles Merriams of the world by denying the inevitability they claimed for planning, a claim he considered nothing more than
a rhetorical ploy, in the sense intended in the phrase "mere rhetoric."
Merriam had held that in modern, complex economies the choice was not
between planning and no planning, "regimentation or no regimentation,
but between public control and private regimentation, between two systems
of regulation, one in public and one in private hands." Merriam described
"the planning program of democracy" as one that would respond to specific needs and situations, experiment, and evolve in the "determination of
broad national policies commanding the consent of the governed." Operating pragmatically, the democratic state would foster health, educational,
and cultural programs; it would "encourage science, technology, and social
arrangements to expand production progressively, with the assumption that
the gains of production are essentially mass gains."[49]

Against the argument for the necessity of increased regulation in the face
of modern tendencies to concentration of ownership and control, Hayek
quoted approvingly from the Final Report of the U.S. Temporary National
Economic Committee as follows:

The superior efficiency of large establishments has not been demonstrated; the
advantages that are supposed to destroy competition have failed to manifest themselves. Nor do the economies of size, where they exist, invariably necessitate
monopoly.... The size or sizes of optimum efficiency may be reached long before
the major part of a supply is subjected to such control.... [M]onopoly is frequently
the product of factors other than the lower costs of greater size. It is attained through
collusive agreements and promoted by public policies.

Hayek offered as confirming evidence the German case, in which suppres-
sion of competition and state promotion of cartelization had been public
policy, whereas large-scale firms had not appeared until much later in earlier
industrializing England.[50]

---

[49] Merriam laid out his thinking on the clash of systems in *The New Democracy and the New
Despotism* (New York and London: McGraw-Hill, 1939), 145–90. His reasoning showed
the influence of the "cultural lag" theorizing that had gone into *Recent Social Trends*: the
rapid pace of change both increased the need for more intelligent control and made it
more difficult to adjust traditional values and ideologies to the needs of the new system.
See also Reagan, *Designing a New America*, 214. Cf., F. A. Hayek, et al., *Collectivist Economic
Planning* (London: Routledge, 1935). Merriam wrote a great deal about democracy during
the life of NRPB. See also his *What is Democracy?* (Chicago: University of Chicago Press,
1941) and *On the Agenda of Democracy* (Cambridge, Mass.: Harvard University Press,
1941).
[50] Hayek, *Road*, Ch. IV, "The 'Inevitability' of Planning." See 45 for the quotation from *Final
Report and Recommendation of the Temporary National Economic Committee* (77th Cong.,
1st sess.; Senate Doc. No. 35 [1941], 89).

For conservative economists, business conservatives, and anti-New Deal Republican and southern Democratic politicians, Hayek's greatest contribution was his vigorous defense of the superiority of the price system of which New Deal statists had been so critical. Proponents of planning typically argued that individual actors could never have enough information to understand the workings of a modern, complex economy, and thus modern societies needed to rely on a centralized agency with access to sufficient information to coordinate the various functions of the economy. Without a steady public hand on the economic tiller, society might well descend into chaos, or at least into sustained underdeployment of economic resources. Hayek argued, conversely, that the more complex the economy, the more decentralized scrutiny and effective oversight of it would have to be. Yet given the rapidity of changes in the economy, he continued, the receipt of information would always come too late for the central planner, whose guidance would always be lagging behind the intelligence that an individual needed to adjust her actions to those of other actors in the economy. But lo and behold, Hayek argued, a superb mechanism both for registering information and for coordinating segments of the economy already existed. "That is what the price mechanism does under competition," he insisted, "and what no other system even promises to accomplish." And, he claimed, flying – some certainly must have thought – in the face of the on-the-ground reality of imperfect competition, "the price system will fulfill this function only if competition prevails, that is, if the individual producer has to adapt himself to price changes and cannot control them."[51]

Hayek, then, unambiguously depicted the market and competition as natural and naturally efficient but often in need of protection from misguided interference. If, as he asserted, German fascism had resulted from an excess of social provision and economic regulation, then the already decades-old welfare states of England and much of continental Europe and the only recently accomplished welfare state in the United States were on the same historical trajectory. The book (also serialized in *Reader's Digest*) struck a chord in the United States, as business groups – especially the National Association of Manufacturers, the U.S. Chamber of Commerce, and their state and local branches – had adopted a postwar strategy of obstructing the growth of unionization and opposing further government efforts to continue price controls, construct public housing, provide health

---

[51] Hayek, *Road*, 48–50. Hayek was not bothered by theories of imperfect or monopolistic competition from the 1930s nor apparently by the extent of economic regulation it would have required to restore a self-regulating market in which all private producers were "busted back" to the status of price-takers.

insurance, and promote full and fair employment. Meanwhile, Congress was investigating alleged "subversives" in colleges, the social sciences, and foundations; and Churchill's "Iron Curtain" speech along with Truman's "Containment" doctrine had framed long-lasting metaphors for Cold War relations with the Soviets.[52]

The economics journals and the popular political magazines were full of reviews of Hayek, both pro and con. A number of economists who had been associated with the New Deal – among them J. M. Clark, with his provocative *Alternative to Serfdom* (1948) – confronted Hayek's bleak rendition of the dangers of active government directly. Intriguingly, the most notable contrast with Hayek's dark assessment of the fate of Western liberalism was the very different interpretation of the rise and meaning of social provision offered by another Austrian émigré, Karl Polanyi, whose *Great Transformation: The Political and Economic Origins of Our Time* also appeared in 1944, in the midst of the attempted rhetorical turn against planning in the United States following World War II.

Hayek's story was a one-directional one, in which the true liberalism of the nineteenth century had been misnamed "conservatism" by thinkers who had allowed opponents of *laissez faire* to capture the cherished title for a revolutionary new liberalism that disastrously dismembered the old orthodoxy. Polanyi's narrative, reaching even further back to the origins of the first English Poor Laws, rather described a two-directional "Double Movement." One direction had been that taken by English economic and political elites who, seeing the disastrous consequences of the system of parish relief for the English poor in the early nineteenth century, had concluded that all welfare measures led to degrading results. Only outright repeal of the poor laws would throw rural paupers into a modern labor market, stemming their degradation and allowing them to develop a healthy economic individualism, spurred by the need continuously to sell their labor to the highest bidder. Fervently convinced of the need to remove paternalism from economic policy, these powerful political and intellectual elites further adopted, in a brief span of years centering on the 1830s, a stunning range of "liberal" policies. Thus they repealed the Corn Laws, throwing England on the world's grain markets for subsistence; they

---

[52] On the U.S. reception of Hayek's book, see his foreword to the 1972 edition. See also Juliet Williams, "The Road Less Traveled: Reconsidering the Political Writings of Friedrich von Hayek," *American Capitalism: Social Thought and Political Economy in the Twentieth Century*, ed. Nelson Lichtenstein (Philadelphia: University of Pennsylvania Press, 2006), 213–27.

subscribed with the other nations of Europe to a balance of power system in which all weaker states would band together to restrain the most powerful; and they swore allegiance to the gold standard as the indispensable medium of stable finance and international exchange.

Against this radical movement toward *laissez faire*, according to Polanyi's account, a number of soon devastated social groups rejected the utopian idea that the self-regulating market would deliver the common good. In England and elsewhere, these groups formed voluntary social protection movements, not only of farmers and workers but eventually of bankers and industrialists, whose fortunes sometimes rose, but often drastically fell, amidst the insecurities of the self-regulating market. Unlike Hayek, who believed the economy created by English liberals had energized the highest human dispositions and created the indispensable setting for realizing individual freedom, Polanyi argued that the "great transformation" had been a revolutionary movement against human nature and contrary to most of human history. He had learned from the burgeoning field of cultural anthropology that most of the world's economies had run since time immemorial according to systems of either reciprocity or redistribution, in which such markets as existed remained embedded in society and subordinated to communal norms and needs. (This insight dovetails nicely with the emphasis on the long history of social structures of mutuality and interdependence described in Yochai Benkler's essay for this volume. As Benkler notes, drawing upon empirical evidence from both the natural and social sciences, cooperation is at least as prevalent in human behavior as egoistic competition, particularly when it is reinforced rather than obstructed by supporting institutions.)

A similar insight led Polanyi to emphasize the havoc wreaked by the modern emergence – actually the deliberate creation, in his telling – of the disembedded markets that for many Western political and economic thinkers had come to represent all there was or could be to advanced society. Community and society had been reduced to economy. This worldview, he insisted, had dragged the West and with it the world into a First and then a Second World War. Precisely because the first war ended with a punitive peace rather than the extension of social protections against the ravages of international *laissez faire*, Polanyi insisted, central Europe became the seedbed of fascism. Reactions to market failure and geopolitical conflict in the early twentieth century could have taken a softer, liberal, and democratic course, he argued. They could have led to the creation of viable social liberal welfare states that abandoned the ruinously deflationary gold standard

sooner, empowered workers for their own protection, and set about constructing a new, peace-oriented internationalism to replace the old, and
dangerous, balance of power.[53]

FROM THE GREAT SOCIETY TO DEREGULATION
AND THE RETURN TO THE MARKET

After Western liberal states and societies experienced the twin shocks of
depression and war in the 1930s and 1940s, they embarked not only on
political, economic, and social reconstruction, but on a dramatic ideological
reconstruction as well. The ideological dimension of postwar reconstruction in the West proved especially difficult,, as it necessarily confronted the
hardening opposition between the capitalist and communist blocs, which
in some degree set the terms for all other reform ideas and projects. The
rhetorical juxtaposition of communism and democracy – seldom communism and capitalism – became common in the United States in those years.
In line with this, U.S. policymakers were heavily pressured to see to it that
they lived up to the country's stated democratic ideals, which demanded
visible and convincing efforts to eradicate racial discrimination, reform
capitalism, address poverty, eliminate colonialism, and elevate formerly
colonized peoples around the world, while calling concurrently for a degree
of denial about the actual shortcomings of the 1960s War on Poverty.

   In such a climate, questions with powerful implications for economic policy reverberated through American society and politics. What should be the
goal of such far-reaching efforts to remake Western and postcolonial societies in a bipolar world? Was it stability – much to be treasured after the long
prewar years of capitalist crisis? Was it development – in line with the depic-
tion by modernization theorists of what was lacking in the economies and
cultures of newly independent nations? Or was it justice – so often threatened on the homefront by curtailment of civil liberties during the war, and
yet enjoyed in new ways then as well, as doors opened for women, people
of color were able to gain manufacturing jobs, and many industrial workers
won representation and collective bargaining rights for the first time? Was
it security? The word had resonated across the United States for decades
by the time FDR's Committee on Economic Security had debated how to

---

[53] Karl Polanyi, *The Great Transformation: The Political and Economic Origins of Our Time*
(Boston: Beacon Press, 1944). See also, on both Hayek and Polanyi and on the reversal of
thinking on economy and state in the 1960s, Mark Blyth, *Great Transformation: Economic
Ideas and Institutional Change in the Twentieth Century* (New York: Cambridge University
Press, 2002.)

insure Americans against old age and childhood indigence, unemployment, and disability, and as Harry Truman's Fair Deal sought to provide increased access to affordable housing and health care. Was it – reaching back to the Gilded Age concern to regulate the moral plane of competition and to discussions by A. C. Pigou, J. M. Clark, Frank Knight,[54] and others in the 1920s – a way to ensure that social costs did not fall upon those least able to bear them? Was it an expansion of the idea of the public interest, which – as John Dewey had argued in the 1920s, echoing the concern about social costs – came into play when the consequences of agreements between freely contracting parties spilled over to affect unprotected third parties? Did sound policy include not only Keynesian fine tuning of the economy but also a real war on poverty, affirmative action against all forms of discrimination, and even efforts to secure environmental justice?

In ways too numerous and diverse to evoke even briefly here, the era of sustained economic growth in the 1950s and 1960s was also an era of government growth that purported to address a number of these questions. "State interference" was significantly extended into the spheres of public health and safety, environmental protection, reduction of poverty, control of corporations, and protection for civil rights, while simultaneously – after a period of inevitable U.S. economic dominance – postwar U.S. governments worked through the General Agreements on Tariffs and Trade to withdraw government protection for U.S.markets. Historians have painted several of these new positive regulatory demands as quality of life movements arising from the aspirations of an affluent middle class for greater security, aesthetic pleasure, and comfort. Yet we can not ignore new forms of political mobilization among previously disfranchised Americans who were most likely to suffer the consequences of environmental pollution (e.g., the Love Canals), unequal schooling, job and housing discrimination, and actual violence against those who dared to challenge the system of racial apartheid so poignantly described in Gunnar Myrdal's 1944 exposé of The American Dilemma. The mobilizations of Blacks and others of color, women, environmentalists, and opponents of the Vietnam War, all perceived in one way or other as antiestablishment, anticorporate movements, challenged hegemonic ideas and structures of power in the name of democracy, equality, participation, and popular – often preferably local – control. These movements envisaged an end to pernicious forms of private economic and

---

[54] There were striking similarities in the views of University of Chicago economist Frank Knight at this time to those of Veblen and J.M. Clark. See Knight, "The Ethics of Competition," *Quarterly Journal of Economics* 37 (1923):579-624.

social regulation such as redlining in real estate markets, discrimination in hiring and access to credit, frustration of union organizing drives, and glass ceilings. They demanded extensive use of new forms of public regulation employing methods such as racial quotas in hiring, school busing, mandatory clean-up of dangerous industrial sites, environmental impact studies, scattered siting of public housing, and the like.[55]

The proliferation of state and national agencies endowed with regulatory powers was clear evidence that both liberal policymakers and popular majorities in those postwar years (as pollsters confirmed) possessed a high level of confidence that government would do the right thing. For all their shortcomings, and they were many, postwar American local, state, and national governments generally moved, in Polanyi's terms, to "re-embed" the market in society. Yet several historical currents also worked to dislodge popular faith in a government that remained in the hands of liberals. These ranged from radical (including antiwar, anticolonial, subaltern, feminist, and LGBT) movements on the left that spread across the globe to, on the right, social and political formations of conservative evangelicals, defenders of traditional marriage, working class and suburban whites who turned sometimes violently against public programs seen to empower the poor and racial minorities at their expense, and talk radio entrepreneurs who fueled antagonism to liberal programs and values. In the realm of ideas, the emergence of postmodern critical theory fostered an intellectual climate skeptical of both truth and power. For postmodernists, Enlightenment universalism was a sham belief system that had cynically masked racial, gender, and class inequities behind false premises regarding human rationality, the value neutrality of scientific method, and the inevitability of progress. New ways of studying institutions revealed the constructed nature of law, even as new theories of modern state formation offered a vision of the modern state and its rational-bureaucratic teaching and regulatory functions as ingenious

---

[55] The literature here is incredibly vast. Some useful beginning sources are Samuel Hays, *Beauty, Health, and Permanence: Environmental Politics in the United States, 1955–1985* (New York: Cambridge University Press, 1987); Todd Gitlin, *The Sixties: Years of Hope, Days of Rage* (New York: Bantam Books, 1987); Thomas Sugrue, *The Origins of the Urban Crisis: Race and Inequality in Postwar Detroit* (Princeton, N.J.: Princeton University Press, 1996); Maurice Isserman, *If I Had a Hammer: The Death of the Old Left and the Birth of the New Left* (New York: Basic Books, 1987); Harvard Sitkoff, *The Struggle for Black Equality, 1954–1992* (New York: Hill and Wang, 1993); Alice Kessler-Harris, *In Pursuit of Equity: Women, Men, and the Quest for Economic Citizenship in 20th-Century America* (Oxford and New York: Oxford University Press, 2001); Nancy Maclean, *Freedom is not Enough: The Opening of the American Workplace* (New York: Russell Sage Foundation, 2006).

if often covert ways to discipline and punish, disguised by public interest rhetoric, but actually authoritarian in intent.[56]

Despite the appearance of radical ideas and movements in these decades, historian Howard Brick has recently argued for an ideological convergence in which midcentury U.S. intellectuals believed that modern capitalism was already well advanced toward transcending its single-minded allegiance to the profit motive, turning instead into a service- and abundance-oriented system that had much in common with socialism.[57] Yet during these same prosperous decades, conservative intellectuals with no intention of transcending capitalism were already laying the groundwork in social thought and in the organizational infrastructure of knowledge production for wide-ranging campaigns intended to liberate the capitalist market from so much regulation and restore the market economy to its youthful vigor. As Ronald Reagan smilingly put it, first as California governor in the 1960s and later as president, the conservative mission for America was to "get the government off the people's backs."

The return of a Republican majority had been anticipated since Kevin Phillips announced the arrival of a new Southern strategy for the party in 1969, following the election of Richard Nixon. Scholars have traced the strongly antigovernment trend in public opinion since the 1970s to the conservative social movements mentioned above as well as to tax revolts, fear of crime, opposition to new immigration policies, an energy crisis, stagflation, and the fracturing of the liberal center. Business conservatism was also a factor in the growth of strongly pro-market popular ideology, as New South and Sunbelt business elites competed aggressively to attract industry by promising nonunion wages, extensive subsidies for infrastructure, and a business-friendly regulatory climate that would boost local employment.

But none of these movements provided the sophisticated intellectual rationales for smaller, less active government, reduced regulation, and a return to the "free market" that arrived in timely fashion from conservative intellectuals recruited by think tanks such as the venerable American Enterprise Institute, the Heritage Foundation (1973), the Cato Institute (1977),

---

[56] Good examples of this critical turn are criticisms of Jurgen Habermas's conception of the rise of the public sphere by Nancy Fraser and Geoff Ely in Craig Calhoun, ed., *Habermas and the Public Sphere* (MIT Press, 1992); the work of Robert Gordon and Mark Tushnet in critical legal theory; and the enormous influence in this period of works by Michel Foucault. Michael B. Katz, *The Undeserving Poor: From the War on Poverty to the War on Welfare* (New York: Pantheon, 1989) reviews the "demonization" of the poor.

[57] Brick, *Transcending Capitalism*. For a contrasting account, see Rossinow, *Visions of Progress*.

and the Manhattan Institute (1978), and also – most authoritatively – from academic economists and legal scholars.[58] From these disciplines, new theories challenged the liberal conviction that law and politics were the most effective and ethically defensible methods for achieving the public good, providing arguments that others could mobilize politically to promote deregulation. Some of these theories merely evoked the familiar language of efficient markets or the need to keep government spending from crowding out private saving and investment. But others, more original, inserted into the debate about the roles of government and market a catchy, democratic-sounding rhetoric of "social choice" or "public choice." These rhetoricians linked to a language of the social and the public a reference to choice that resonated with and reinforced the high regard for individual freedom against illegitimate authority that had long been hallowed in U.S. political culture, even as they opened up in economics, law, and political science entire new lines of inquiry into the workings of politics and government.

Ronald Coase's 1960 essay on "The Problem of Social Costs" provides an instructive example of the latter type. Coase offered a reassessment of assumptions regarding the need for what he saw as a presumption often in play in favor of intrusive, costly, inefficient government regulation of harms to persons and property, as against smoothing the way for private bargaining in the marketplace to resolve and prevent them. This reinterpretation, as Joseph Stiglitz's essay points out, has proved quite influential in later twentieth-century regulatory policy debates. Coase, a law professor at the University of Chicago and founder of the law and economics movement, took a fresh look at ways of addressing the kinds of costs whose displacement onto the community had so troubled J. M. Clark and A. C. Pigou. Pigou had argued for recovering these socialized costs for the community by outlawing the offending acts, fining or taxing the perpetrators of the harms and, through compensatory measures and public works, redistributing that revenue from the wealthier to the poorer members of the community. His theory rested on the intuitively reasonable proposition that the relative utility of the redistributed funds would be much greater for those with the least income, and thus this method would not only curtail the harms inflicted upon innocent victims but enhance total social welfare.

---

[58] On the roles of business and foundations in the turn to the right, see Alice O'Connor, "The Politics of Rich and Rich: Postwar Investigations of Foundations and the Rise of the Philanthropic Right," in Nelson Lichtenstein, ed., *American Capitalism: Social Thought and Political Economy in the Twentieth Century* (Philadelphia: University of Pennsylvania Press, 2006); Elizabeth Tandy Shermer, "Origins of the Conservative Ascendancy: Barry Goldwater's Early Senate Career and the De-Legitimization of Organized Labor," *Journal of American History* 95:3 (2008): 678–709.

Coase's analysis of business firms, which viewed them as mechanisms for internalizing and thus reducing the costs to society of a multitude of individual transactions, led him to jettison the Pigouvian theory. Coase reimagined harms to bystanders as two-way rather than one-way propositions, in which the person who had habitually been considered the passive recipient of an injury was in reality also a perpetrator, by virtue of being in the way of the other actor. One of Coase's homely examples involved a grain farmer whose crops were in the way of a rancher whose cattle would inevitably break through the fence and trample the farmer's field. Given the potential for loss on both sides through the injury, the costly litigation to recover for it, and the penalty for causing it, Coase reasoned, the parties involved would happily bargain their way to the solution, involving direct payment by one to the other, that contributed the most to the total value output – in beef and grain – of the ranch and farm.

His larger argument, and one that contributed greatly to the justifications for the public choice or rational choice theories so well described by Jessica Leight's essay in this volume, was that in a regime of definite property rights and low or no transaction costs, government regulation was neither the only nor typically the best remedy for dealing with externalities, even egregious ones such as pollution. From the standpoint of efficient use of resources, the way was also open for arriving at a socially optimal solution through the market. By extension, in the case of nuisances such as environmental pollution that were incidental to production of desirable goods, bargaining could again provide an alternative to taxation or fines, through the making of a market in rights to pollute, as against command and control type regulation. This line of argument led Coase to question a presumption in favor of government regulation, even in the face of stark negative externalities.[59]

Other key figures in the postwar social sciences raised additional critiques of the "new liberal"/New Deal liberal rationales for social and economic regulation, reinforcing a pro-market rhetoric they named social choice. This new language worked against the pro-regulation discourses that valued majoritarian democratic politics for choosing between social policy alternatives designed to empower government to apply the chosen methods for

---

[59] R. H. Coase, "The Problem of Social Cost," *Journal of Law and Economics* 3 (1960): 1–44. See also D. W. Pearce and S. G. Sturmey, "Private and Social Costs and Benefits: A Note on Terminology," *The Economic Journal* 76:301 (1966): 152–58; Elizabeth Hoffman and Matthew L. Spitzer, "The Coase Theorem: Some Experimental Tests," *Journal of Law and Economics* 25:1 (1982): 73–98; Steven B. Medema, "Legal Fiction: The Place of the Coase Theorem in Law and Economics," *Economics and Philosophy* 15 (1999): 209–33; Daniel A. Farber, "Parody Lost/Pragmatism Regained: The Ironic History of the Coase Theorem," *Virginia Law Review* 83:2 (1997): 397–428.

meeting the problem of social costs. Kenneth Arrow's *Social Choice and Individual Values* (1951) stands as a pivotal work in this regard. Arrow offered a mathematical analysis of voting that struck numerous conservative theorists as a definitive refutation of the idea that democratic elections could actually achieve what could rightly be defined as the "social" choice, or what could be defended logically as the collective good. In hypothetical situations in which two or more individuals ranked three or more options in the order of their individual preferences, Arrow's analysis showed that it was impossible to achieve a single collective ranking that fairly aggregated the individuals' votes into a clear hierarchy of choices. There was no certainty that the majority or collective choice in election situations would accurately "collect" the preference rankings of all individual voters. Thus election situations (standing in for the entire policy making process) would typically violate one or more of the conditions of fairness that most observers would consider necessary.[60]

Working somewhat in the same vein as Arrow, Mancur Olson, a political scientist also interested in the sources of collective action, argued in an influential 1965 book, *The Logic of Collective Action: Public Goods and the Theory of Groups*, that policy outcomes were not the products of an informed public acting in the general interest. They reflected rather the greater commitment and political clout of well organized groups whose members stood to benefit greatly from a specific policy choice, as against the less pressing interests of a wider, less informed, poorly organized general public whose members individually had little of an economic character to gain or to lose from the outcome. Emphasizing organizational problems in democracies and variations in incentives to action, this line of investigation claimed also to upset conventional assumptions about the wisdom of looking to either individual or collective rationality in the making and implementing of policy – except, of course, for the selfish, maximizing kind of rationality related to expectations of pleasure and pain that utilitarian philosophy placed at the center of individual human behavior.

---

[60] For a detailed summary and critical assessment of reactions to what Arrow considered the reasonable requirements for a fair voting method, see Duncan Black, "On Arrow's Impossibility Theorem," *Journal of Law and Economics* 12:2 (1969):227-48. Arrow simplified some of the requirements in *Social Choice and Individual Values* (1951; 2nd ed.; New Haven: Yale University Press, 1963), which established Pareto efficiency, a situation in which the social ordering of preferences must give the same ranking to a given preference that all of the individual preferences do, as an overarching criterion of fairness. See also, for a contemporary, highly influential treatment from political science of relations between individual volition, governmental structures, voting, and public choice, James M. Buchanan and Gordon Tullock, *The Calculus of Consent: Logical Foundations of Constitutional Democracy* (Indianapolis: Liberty Fund, Inc., 1958).

Following Arrow, critics of Pigouvian economics assumed that interpersonal comparisons of utilities among individuals of different incomes were not valid, as it was impossible to determine exactly how much pleasure any given individual derived in a given situation. As a result, rational choice economists and political scientists questioned whether policy makers could ever be confident that redistribution of income and wealth was actually welfare enhancing, as it necessarily took from one person or group to give to another. Or, in the technical language of this discourse, redistribution inevitably defied Pareto optimality by making someone worse off than before. If accurate, this supposition would leave the judgment as to what would maximize collective utility, or promote the greatest satisfaction, in the eye of the beholder.[61]

For the scholars who found such arguments compelling, welfare economists and economic and social regulators tended to look like paternalistic busy-bodies, imposing their own ideologically driven values upon society. Although Arrow addressed himself narrowly to the arguments of recent "welfare economists," his work, again for many social scientists, also constituted a rebuke to the progressive worldview that had grown in influence since the 1880s and come to fruition in the New Deal order, extending from the 1930s down through the civil rights and early environmental movements. At the beginning of that intellectual journey, H. C. Adams had contended that governments should enact as the legal plane of competition the standards set by a collective judgment, based on observation and due deliberation, of what constituted the good and fair, which, in a manner reminiscent of Adam Smith's *Theory of Moral Sentiments*, he termed the best moral sense of the community.

Around the time that Coase and Arrow were undermining previously accepted theories of regulation and seemingly devaluing the possibility of demonstrably valid collective choice, a resounding affirmation of an Enlightenment version of collective rationality also captured the imagination of political theorists and social thinkers. The German public philosopher Jürgen Habermas, in his *Structural Transformation of the Public Sphere* (1966) and in later works on the philosophy of communication, described the historical development of the public sphere constructed initially by bourgeois males interested in influencing the affairs of early modern states. Habermas wished to respond critically to postmodernists who debunked

---

[61] For detailed and conflicting recent accounts of the rational choice and rational expectations movements, see S. M. Amadae, *Rationalizing Capitalist Democracy: The Cold War Origins of Rational Choice Liberalism* (Chicago: University of Chicago Press, 2003); David F. Prindle, *Democratic Capitalism: Politics and Economics in American Thought* (Baltimore: The Johns Hopkins University Press, 2006), as well as Jessica Leight's essay in this volume.

liberal claims for the efficacy of reason such as Theodor Adorno, Max Horkheimer, and Michel Foucault. He conceived the bourgeois public sphere (and in a later revision the multiple ones created by sub-altern, female, and working class publics) as a space – indeed as actual sites, such as coffee houses and salons in the eighteenth century, or in the present era internet chat rooms – located in civil society. Situated between the market and the state, these sites offered citizens who wished to understand and influence events forums where they might (and historically had) set aside their selfish interests, come together as equals, and deliberate as moral and thinking beings about what would serve the public good. In this rendering, the citizen's capacity for rationality would not be defined quantitatively, as agility in calculating individual pleasure or gain, detecting the economically efficient measure, or determining whether majority rule violated some individual preferences. Rather, public policy choices would arise ideally from collective, evidence- and value-based deliberation regarding what courses of action would best accord with ethical purpose and social aspiration.

Yet according to the precepts of post-Coase and post-Arrow conservative political economy, political determinations of what constituted the public good had often sent governments down a deeply regrettable path. From this perspective efficiency in the allocation of scarce resources, as a quantity that could be calculated with accuracy at least after the fact, once again became the gold standard against which scholars, legislators, administrators, and judges ought to measure economic institutions. The same approach shaped appraisals of political institutions, to the extent that regulation interfered with efficiency. Weighed down by a series of political, economic, and foreign policy failures in the 1970s, American liberals increasingly encountered a steady drumbeat from a resurgent New Right, animated by abiding faith in the incompetence of government, the incapacity of citizens, the waste of regulation, the beneficence of competition, and the efficiency of the unregulated market. For acolytes of Hayek and Coase, the solution to both domestic policy problems and Cold War competition with communist economies rested in the same basic credo of political economy. At home and abroad, Americans needed to defend, sustain, and export the free market.

Buffeted by the pressures of energy crises, stagflation, rising third-world nationalism, and ever more powerful global economic competition, consecutive presidential administrations from Jimmy Carter onward sought ways of measuring the costs of regulation – economic rather than social – against its benefits. At the same time, conservative thinkers and activists built an extremely effective political movement around the themes of reducing the size and influence of government as a way of redirecting resources to better uses, restoring traditional individualism, reinvigorating entrepreneurship, and "ending welfare as we know it." At no point in the last thirty years did the resulting dismantling of regulation, the elimination or destaffing of regulatory agencies, and the repudiation of related policy interventions to redress inequalities of wealth and power proceed as far as conservatives and neoliberals who invoked the rhetoric of the efficient market called for in their various platforms for American revival. Inequality of income and wealth did begin growing rapidly in the 1970s, after three decades of decline, and by the early twenty-first century reached levels not seen since the 1920s.

The United States is now struggling to come to terms with an era of disconcertingly rapid transition in the economic base, characterized by a rapid decline in manufacturing and tremendous growth in the value added to GDP by a highly leveraged and lightly regulated financial sector. Americans need to recognize that ideas about political economy can have profound consequences, confining, or opening up, our political imaginations. In this vein, it appears that the competing rhetorics of economic regulation and the policy regimes they depict have come full circle, between the Old Gilded Age and the New.

In the final years of the twenty-first century's first decade, the devastating consequences of deregulation of the financial markets are unfolding in a cascade of home mortgage defaults, bank and brokerage failures, and credit crises. At a time when the people of the United States are interested as seldom before in what is going on in the troubled national and global economy, they would do well to reconsider the reconstruction of U.S. political economy in the final quarter of the twentieth century, placing that reconstruction in the longer historical frame that began in first Gilded Age. The representation of U.S. capitalism has always turned on a complex set of relationships between owners and non-owners, knowledge and governance, expertise and democratic self-rule. Policy makers should resist the temptation to approach their task by assessing the options solely in terms of the muscle of conflicting interest groups; they need to give at least equal consideration to the power of ideas, and especially to the power of those ideas that generate powerful discourses of reform, shaping the very perception of what counts as a problem of the public that demands a policy solution, as well as the character and range of political solutions on offer.

The shifting ground of American ideas about political economy since the professionalization of the social sciences in the late nineteenth century clearly suggests that the changing structure of U.S. capitalism has periodically provoked fresh thinking regarding the optimal relation of government to the market and to economic actors, and that it will again. But this history of competition among different ways of modeling the state-market relationship also suggests that the persistence of tensions between constitutive traditions in American public philosophy – between a democraticized republican tradition in which the public good would be defined through civic deliberation and achieved through politics, as against a nineteenth-century liberal tradition holding that the governing of the economy was better left to the working of an unseen hand. Even as – in business historian Alfred Chandler's apt phrase – the "visible hand" of corporation management came prominently into play in the first Gilded Age, a strong preference persisted among capitalist interests and in certain intellectual and policy circles for forms of voluntary industrial self-regulation that did not require extensive government involvement, and indeed might require moving aspects of the law – notably the Sherman Antitrust Act – out of the way.

Yet for others at that troubled time the logical path forward was a revision of liberalism that looked to government to sustain democratic social relations that the newly constituted corporate order did not protect. Just as "the market," in fact, has never managed to shake loose its moorings in actual social relationships, so too economics has never truly escaped its deep connections to democratic political culture, nor has economic policy been able to avoid being judged by a republican sense of what constitutes a good society and a virtuous polity. In this country, no less than in others across the Atlantic or Pacific or below the Rio Grande, the scholarly study of the economy has never shed its normative character and function.

To the extent that the consequences of any particular configuration of the state-market relationship undermines social and political democracy, moreover, it must answer to those large numbers of people who simply do not privilege allocational efficiency ahead of equality, democracy, and social justice. As they have in the past, popular movements as well as objections from dissenting social thinkers will surely continue to challenge the naturalization of the market, though in new ways, drawing on the rapidly changing technologies for exchanging information to draw converts to their causes.

In the present context of economic crisis and apparently deeply felt longing for political renewal, Americans need to know more and to think more deeply about several issues:

- the meaning and consequences – for better and worse – of the dramatically increased politicization of knowledge and intellect under way in the era of polarized "think-tanks" that, despite their strong ideological foundations, tend to clothe the arguments of their partisans in the Enlightenment rhetoric of objectivity while attacking their opponents for partisanship;

- the consequences for democracy of the highly mathematized, reality-abstracting, model-building, positivistic economic science of the post-World War II era, which has become inaccessible not only to the public at large, but also to highly educated policy makers and a great many academics;

- the dominance of economic policy prescriptions that have, since the 1970s, increased rather than ameliorated harsh living and working conditions in the United States and in the societies of its low-wage suppliers, frequently through undemocratic governance structures;

- the acquiescence of legislators up and down the governmental hierarchy in the financing of election campaigns by donors who place implicit limits on policy innovation, censor political talk, and establish boundaries of permissible dissent

- the possibility that democracies do, after all, have the capability to define, through deliberative processes open to all comers, those forms of collective rationality and cooperative action that are both morally and politically more compelling as guides to rule making than the individual rationalities of private actors.

In the years ahead we must think hard about the goals and strategies of regulation we should be building for a globalized economy that seems increasingly to have transcended the ability of either national sovereignties or central bankers to control. Amid global supply chains and shadow financial systems that span the planet, who, really, is in charge of the twenty-first century? We as yet lack a convenient label or intellectual shorthand for the key causes of the current financial crisis, which surely include insufficient standards of economic behavior, a lack of sufficient oversight, and a failure on the part of legions of supposed experts to anticipate and take steps to prevent a crisis that has been extremely costly in terms of financial loss and human misery. The time has come for candidly recognizing the economic and social costs of deregulation and admitting the insufficiency of oversight– indeed the overwhelming temptation to excessive risk encouraged in certain crucial market sectors by regimes of voluntary, unsupervised self-regulation. An incessant, decades-long demonization of government and its companion mythologizing of the "free market" – those twin hallmarks of far-Right American media – have seriously damaged the capacity for effective citizenship. At the present moment, when the New Gilded Age has finally drawn ignominiously to a close, when policy failure and ideological fracturing will be followed by some kind of ideological and policy reconstruction, when it remains to be seen whether the economic stimulus packages provided by the U.S. and a few other governments will be robust enough to ignite recovery, we can certainly use new techniques for smart, effective regulation. What the United States even more desperately needs is a set of fresh, probing, expert and popular discourses of economic regulation that are both responsive to the current need and faithful to democratic and republican values. These discussions must be framed in vocabularies of reform that are more moral, more civic, and more muscular in their descriptions of citizens' rights and government responsibilities than the language of "write downs" and "bailouts." At this historic juncture, leaders at all government levels and social locations must recognize the existence of an intelligent public, even as they perform the teaching function of continuously engaging and creating one. Thus the urgent need for new theories – and for convincing new scholarly and popular rhetorics – of regulation.

FOUR

Lessons from Europe: Some Reflections on the European Union and the Regulation of Business

Neil Fligstein

Before the mid-1970s, the United States pioneered the regulation of product markets, labor markets, and the environment. But the intellectual and political assaults on social and economic regulation over the past thirty years, a process whose intellectual basis receives careful attention in Jessica Leicht's contribution for this volume, have left American regulators with neither the inclination to enforce the law, or in the case where such inclination persists, the staff to do so. So, for example, competition laws like the Sherman Act, the Federal Trade Commission Act, and the Celler-Kefauver Act no longer have much bite, having given way to the idea that market concentration, mergers, and anticompetitive acts do not undermine competition as long as the antitrust division can see a glimmer of potentially contestable markets. Congressional appropriations bills have stripped regulatory bodies like the Occupational Safety and Health Administration and the Securities and Exchange Commission of personnel and their ability to monitor infractions of the law.[1]

At this historical moment, the main source of market and environmental regulation in the developed world has moved across the Atlantic, to Europe. Indeed, large American multinational corporations that have significant activities in Europe increasingly find themselves having to embed European rules and standards into their practices. So, for example, American firms that engage in anticompetitive behavior or mergers that might erode competition find themselves confronting European competition authorities who are skeptical of their claims that such activities are procompetitive.

---

[1] See, for example, a recent article in *The New York Times*, "Quick, Call Tech Support for the S.E.C.," on Dec. 16, 2007, which cites a GAO report that the SEC lacks the manpower and wherewithal to monitor insider trading.

Perhaps the two most famous cases in this regard are the Microsoft case and the attempt by General Electric (GE) to merge with Honeywell in 2001. The Microsoft case in Europe paralleled the U.S. lawsuit against the company. In 2004, the European antitrust authorities ruled that Microsoft needed to open its operating system to allow rival products onto the platform. In 2006, they began to fine Microsoft for not moving quickly enough or fully enough in revealing the source code. In fall of 2007, Microsoft agreed to pay all of the fines and to fully comply. In the Microsoft case, both U.S. and European authorities agreed that Microsoft had broken antitrust laws. But European authorities have been more aggressive than American authorities in making sure that Microsoft complied with its antitrust agreement.

The General Electric-Honeywell merger was valued at more than $41 billion. U.S. antitrust authorities signed off on the deal without any restrictions. Meanwhile, European authorities were worried that the jet engine businesses of Honeywell and GE overlapped sufficiently and that this would allow the merged firm to raise prices. They negotiated with General Electric to sell some assets. In the end, European antitrust authorities forced General Electric to call off the merger because they were not satisfied that General Electric had adequately satisfied their conditions. These developments have placed Americans in the odd position of having effectively delegated many forms of market regulation to the European Union (EU).

One interesting question raised by this curious state of affairs is why the Europeans have been able to keep up and even expand their market regulatory project while the United States has not. One answer is, of course, politics. Over the past three decades, as the United States has undergone its age of deregulation, the member states of the EU, and by inference the citizens of Europe, have been amenable to market opening. At the same time, however, they have created a body of rules that enforce market competition yet offer protection for both jobs and the environment. Indeed, the market opening projects would not have been possible in isolation from continuing efforts to protect consumer safety, the environment, and labor market regimes. The political reason for this linkage is that there are strong labor unions and social democratic parties across Europe that have kept the pressure on the EU to make sure that in exchange for market opening projects, citizens continue to have social protection. In a host of contexts, the European regulatory impulses of extending competition across the continent and maintaining social protection have been joined at the political hip.

But though politics have been important, ideas have mattered as well. The member state governments of the EU have rejected the main deregulatory idea that removing rules on all forms of market activity is the main way to induce competition, economic growth, and the creation of jobs. Since its inception, the EU has viewed this form of market opening as "negative integration." It has viewed the removal of tariff and nontariff barriers to trade across Europe as a first step to creating a single market in Europe. But its philosophy has emphasized that market creating projects require a system of rules to guide and constrain newly created zones of continental competition, an approach that Europeans refer to as "positive integration." There are two aspects to a positive integration market opening project that require regulation. First, to facilitate competition, this approach needs to ensure market access to any competitor. Second, market rules must be set in place to protect product safety, labor, and the environment. Such rules ensure that competitive processes do not produce a race to the bottom that degrades products, working conditions, and the environment. This concern with positive integration has motivated the regulatory philosophy of the EU.[2]

I do not want to suggest that this process has been planned out or is without controversy. The countries that compose the EU have been engaged in a fifty-year open-ended project oriented toward economic and political integration, a project that has attracted considerable opposition. On more than one occasion, the EU has appeared to be stalled and dead in the water. To date, governments have found ways to cover up their differences and move forward. As a result, the continent now possesses a set of agreements to create a single market for goods and services across Europe, a monetary union, and standards ensuring the free movement of labor and capital (albeit with some temporary restrictions on labor for new member states), all in the context of a continuous expansion of the number of members of the club from seven to twelve to fifteen to twenty-seven and now twenty-nine.

This chapter probes how the European theory of regulation evolved and how it helped ameliorate many of the difficult dilemmas that regulation tends to create in modern industrialized economies. It considers

- the political and legal process by which the EU has created positive integration;
- pivotal regulatory goals/aspirations;
- the generally cooperative nature of relations between regulators and regulated industries, and the best explanations for that culture of cooperation;

---

[2] This distinction is explicated in J. Tinbergen. 1965. *International Economic Integration.* Amsterdam: Elsevier. Fritz Scharpf uses the concept in the context of the EU in *Governing in Europe*, Oxford: Oxford University Press, 1999, ch. 2.

- the dominant regulatory strategies prevalent in Europe and the continuing significance of national styles of enforcement;
- the interplay of regulatory policy and other compensatory policies, especially with regard to deregulation and social welfare provision.

I will end with some potential research agendas that may be applied to the American context.

THE EVOLUTION OF THE EU

One cannot make sense of the current regulatory scene in Europe without a grasp of the EU's complicated evolution. The Treaty of Rome, which set up the institutional framework for the EU in 1957, was premised on the idea of setting up some form of single market in Europe. The exact meaning of that market emerged through both contention and negotiation. Initially, the EU aimed at a customs union – a zone in which member nations would stop discriminating against goods across national borders through differential tariffs – a goal the organization attained by the 1970s. The Treaty of Rome further created a set of organizations with the job of continuing to promote economic and political integration.

Social scientists remain divided about whether the member state governments of the EU actually realized what they had done by creating the European Commission, the Council of Ministers, the European Court of Justice, and later the directly elected Parliament. Some scholars have argued that the member state governments assumed all along that they would be able to control the EU, and so they would be able to sidestep any form of economic integration they found too onerous; these analysts tend to argue that no countries have ever agreed to anything that was not in their national interest.[3] Other scholars have insisted that these organizations began to function like a quasi-state, pooling the sovereignty of the nations and operating not like intergovernmental organizations, like the United Nations or the World Trade Organization, but rather as supranational organizations that gave the EU a political and legal identity of its own.[4]

During the 1960s, the most important organization in the EU was the European Court of Justice (ECJ).[5] Almost from the day it opened, the

---

[3] See A. Moravcsik. 1998. *The Choice for Europe: Social Purpose and State Power from Massina to Maastricht*. Ithaca, NY: Cornell University Press.

[4] J. H. H. Weiler. 1991. "The Transformation of Europe." *Yale Law Review* 100(8): 2403–483.

[5] The process of European economic and political integration bears more than a casual resemblance to what happened to the United States in the nineteenth century. The Supreme Court came to interpret the Constitution of the United States as a set of arguments that separated the powers between the federal government and the state governments.

ECJ began to consider lawsuits from both government and private citizens. These lawsuits used the provisions in the Treaty of Rome that guaranteed the freedom of movement of goods, capital, and labor to make it difficult for national governments to use national laws to protect local business and labor and keep foreign nationals out. The Treaty of Rome provided that these lawsuits would begin in the courts of the member states, with potential appeals to the ECJ. During the 1960s, national judges and courts, not quite knowing what to do with these cases, used Article 177 of the Treaty of Rome to turn them over to the ECJ. The ECJ made two landmark rulings during the 1960s that established crucial precedents. It first held that private citizens could bring cases against national governments that violated the Treaty of Rome, creating the doctrine of direct effect. It also ruled that EU law (and the Treaty of Rome itself) took precedence over conflicting national law, the doctrine of EU "supremacy."[6]

These and other ECJ rulings transformed the institution into a kind of Supreme Court and the Treaty of Rome and all other EU legislation into a kind of constitution. Almost overnight, the EU became a kind of federal system in which EU rules trumped national rules in the policy domains specified by the Treaty of Rome. This shift raised the stakes for any actions collectively agreed to by the member state governments. Governments could no longer easily engage in rear guard actions to forestall the effects of the Treaty of Rome and EU rules.

The actions of the ECJ created the first political crisis of the EU, the so-called empty chair crisis. In 1965, French President de Gaulle threatened to boycott the EU until everyone agreed that there would have to be unanimity in any decisions taken by the EU. Six months later, all of the member state governments agreed to acquiesce to de Gaulle's demands. But the constitutionalization of the treaty by the ECJ already had opened the door for the EU to become a quasi-federalist structure, because the court would enforce the Treaty of Rome and any new EU rules in such a way that would decide private lawsuits in favor of those rules and against national law.

The Commerce Clause of the constitution gave the federal government wide authority to regulate interstate commerce and prevented state governments from passing laws to prevent out-of-state businesses from investing and selling goods in any state. The court continuously struck down attempts on the part of state governments to pass laws that favored local economic elites and tried to keep national firms out. In this, way, federal law on interstate commerce came to dominate and an integrated market economy emerged in the United States.

[6] See A. Stone Sweet and T. Brunell. 1998. "Constructing a Supranational Constitution: Dispute Resolution and Governance in the European Community," *American Political Science Review* 92: 63–81.

One by-product of the EU's consolidation of authority involved the emergence of vibrant continental politics in Brussels. Corporations, industries, and representatives of labor began to flock to Brussels to influence the adoption rules that would govern market activities, lobbying the European Commission and national governments about which policies they supported and which ones they opposed. The cases decided by the ECJ clearly pushed forward the negative integration project of removing national barriers to trade.[7]

At home, national governments soon encountered serious pressure from their national firms to adopt various kinds of trade barriers, and those governments frequently acceded to the requests, enacting standards that defined products to favor national firms. One tactic was to argue that local products like pasta could only be called pasta if they contained wheat from national farmers. European parliaments also invoked health and safety standards that would make it prohibitively expensive for foreign competitors to refit their products to sell them abroad. So, for example, by specifying national standards for automobile parts like headlights and bumper strength, the Bundestag or French National Assembly could protect national producers, much as late nineteenth-century American states sought to protect their local industries and merchants through meat inspection requirements or license fees for sales representatives of out-of-state businesses.[8]

During the 1970s, attempts to extend continental rules to govern European markets more adequately bogged down, a result of the need for every piece of legislation to have unanimous approval of the member state governments. One politically connected firm could get its government to object to new proposals in Brussels and thereby forestall any progress at creating new rules. The ramifications of this classic bargaining trap, in which any one player could block any agreement, led many observers in the late 1970s to view the EU as an organization that had reached a dead end.

Predictions of the EU's impending demise, however, proved ill judged. In 1978, the ECJ ruled in a pivotal case called Cassis de Dijon[9] that governments could not use rules to prevent foreign products from being sold across borders by specifying product definitions based on different national

---

[7] See N. Fligstein and A. Stone Sweet. 2002. "Creating markets and politics: the case of the European Union," *American Journal of Sociology.*

[8] See C. McCurdy, "American Law and the Marketing Structure of the Large Corporation," *Journal of Economic History* (Sept. 1978), 631–49.

[9] See K. J. Alter and S. Meunier-Aitshalia. 1994. "Judicial Politics in the European Community: European Integration and the Path breaking Cassis de Dijon Decision," *Comparative Political Studies* 26: 535–61.

standards. They articulated unambiguous hostility to the use of product definitions as trade barriers, arguing that the member state governments had to mutually recognize the validity of products if foreign governments accepted them as valid. In addition, longstanding negotiations finally culminated in a proposal to change voting rules to allow for some form of majority voting. Finally, one of the European Commission's leaders, a man named Heinz Karl Narjes, began to put together a proposal to complete the single market.

But it would require the member state governments agreeing to a new round of political and economic integration to renew the EU. In the end, the main cause for relaunching the EU was the relatively poor performance of the European economies during the late 1970s and early 1980s.[10] Governments were grappling everywhere with slow economic growth, high inflation, and high unemployment. The governments of the largest countries, France, Great Britain, and Germany, found that they were unable to use the traditional Keynesian tools of loose monetary policy and deficit spending to jump start their economies. In 1985, the member state governments agreed to relaunch the EU by agreeing to complete the single market.

That undertaking entailed the passage of around 290 directives (laws or rules) that had been languishing because of unanimous voting rules.[11] The member state governments agreed to use a qualified majority scheme to pass these directives. They also agreed to increase their cooperation on issues of the environment. The single market program enshrined in the Single European Act in 1987 began the new era of cooperation among EU member state governments. In 1991, the member state governments agreed to the monetary union. They also agreed to several rounds of enlargement and eventually extension of qualified majority voting to all issues. Most recently, they have begun to cooperate on common foreign, security, and immigration policies as well as agree in the summer of 2007 on a wide-reaching reorganization of the EU that would streamline decision making and for the first time elect a president of the EU and create a post for a foreign minister.

The single market project was less about the opening of new markets and more about making sure that firms could easily ship their goods, secure payment, and not encounter barriers to trade. One partially symbolic gesture (though it was practical as well) was to take down the customs stations at national borders. This action meant that trucks and cars could travel

[10] See W. Sandholtz and J. Zysman. 1989. "1992: Recasting the European Bargain," *World Politics* 42: 95–128.

[11] See N. Fligstein and I. Mara-Drita. 1996. "How to Make a Market," *American Journal of Sociology* 102: 1–33.

unimpeded across the core of Europe, ending long delays at border crossings and making it easier to ship goods across Europe.

The only markets that the EU liberalized in the single market program were those in transportation, communication, and banking. The single market streamlined rules for freight carrying, the interrelationships between telecommunications systems, and allowed banks to operate anywhere in Europe. Not surprisingly, in the wake of the single market initiative, there was a large merger wave as national firms merged with their counterparts in their own countries but also across borders.[12]

The turning point in EU cooperation came when governments began to realize that if done properly, the opening of markets was a win-win situation. Firms would rationalize their production processes, be able to take advantage of economies of scale and scope, and find new markets for goods and services, thereby increasing economic growth and raising employment. Governments during the 1990s continued this cooperation. Many European countries privatized government-owned firms and opened markets to wireless phone service, utilities, airlines, many services, and even defense procurement. The goal of EU market opening projects was to allow firms to reorganize themselves on a European basis. In return, governments agreed to enforce product competition and use EU competition policy to police potentially anticompetitive behavior, such as mergers and forms of predatory price competition.

It is useful to briefly consider one case of government-led market deregulation, that of the telecommunications companies.[13] In the early 1980s, the largest firms were government-owned bureaucracies. But the member state governments began to liberalize the industry. There were four key elements to making these changes: 1) the single market initiative being negotiated in Brussels, 2) the general perception among EU governments that their high-technology industries were in danger of being shut out of world markets by virtue of being behind in product innovation, 3) the support and lobbying of large technology industries that wanted new and growing markets and found themselves in conflict with government-owned phone companies, and 4) the European Commission, which was able to begin the process of market deregulation in telecommunications, and as it picked up steam, to get governments to agree to privatize their telephone companies.

European governments played a pivotal role in the creation of the telecommunications market. They decided that creating a single market for

---

[12] See Fligstein and Mara-Drita, op cit.
[13] See N. Fligstein, ch. 4, Oxford, England: Oxford University Press, 2008.

telecommunications services across Europe was a good way to spur innovation, increase competition, and give consumers more for their money. In the mid-1990s, the member state governments agreed to privatize their telecommunications companies and open all of their markets to competition. The European governments freed up their telecommunications markets in the past fifteen years, a period of the convergence of telephones, television, and computers, and gave their leading firms the opportunity to pioneer these technologies. So, for example, the EU pioneered third-generation wireless telephone standards. EU firms were the primary innovators of wireless phones and created new products such as text messaging, ring tones, and video downloads.

The Internet bust and simultaneous downturn in telecommunications markets in 2001 caused a shake-out in the industry. The survivors of this shake-out, not surprisingly, are mainly the heirs to the companies of the national telecommunications champions. British Telephone, France Telecom, and Deutsche Telecom continue to dominate their national fixed-line markets and play a large role in wireless services. These companies also have pursued joint ventures and mergers with firms in America and from the rest of the world. Several large freestanding wireless companies have emerged, notably ATT (U.S.), Sprint (U.S.), Vodaphone (U.K.), and Verizon (U.S.). The new European wireless companies like Orange (now owned by France Telecom), Bouygues (owned partially by France Telecom and the Belgian government), T-Mobile (owned by Deutsche Telecom), and E-plus (owned by KPN, the Netherlands phone company) are either the offspring of existing large telecommunications companies or joint ventures between companies in different countries.

RELATIONSHIPS BETWEEN REGULATORS AND REGULATED INDUSTRIES

Readers following my story might wonder how it is that firms, which in the 1970s were working with their governments to protect national markets, changed their tactics and began to embrace competition. My story about telecommunications gives a brief answer to this question. First, the poor economic conditions of the 1970s were not good for business people in mature industrial economies, all of which faced slow growing markets. Second, governments wanted to respond to economic stagnation by stimulating their economies and they decided, sometimes unilaterally, to engage in market opening projects. So, for example, the large European telephone and utility companies were all run as state-owned monopolies until the

1990s. The managers of these firms often actively resisted their governments' attempts to open these markets. But, at a certain point, governments forced their state-owned firms to become more competitive by privatizing them and pushing them to modernize.

Finally, a political gap emerged between the most international European corporations, which generally saw market opening as a good thing for their business, and firms that generally operated in a national market. Increasingly enmeshed in global economic networks, these firms became more vocal in their support for European-wide economic integration. At the same time, extensive mergers by smaller firms into larger international firms convinced their managers that participation in European markets was an opportunity, not a disaster. In the case of telecommunications firms, for example, the hardware and software producers found themselves at odds with government-owned phone companies that were trying to keep control over patents, equipment, and new markets. Once the market was freed up, joint ventures and alliances between companies across national borders became common.

Most European corporations, moreover, saw positive integration as a way to create a level playing field for all firms. If national governments could no longer favor national firms in procurement, government contracts, or keeping foreign goods and services away from consumers, all firms stood to benefit. In this situation, European corporations interested in doing business across state borders saw European-wide rules as ensuring the same conditions of doing business for everyone. Although many firms might have preferred rules that kept competitors out of the home market but let them into other countries' markets, geopolitical realities blocked such alternatives. The only real option was to continue protection or to give everyone the chance to compete everywhere. Corporations, particularly large corporations, supported positive integration.

For example, when European governments agreed to open retail banking to firms across Europe, they did so with a minimum of rules. One important rule was to put a minimum on depositor insurance so that banks would not be tempted to offer high interest rates on deposits when they did not have to worry about paying depositors back if they failed. At the same time, continental banking rules also left regulation of any given bank up to home country authorities. This strategy meant that there was no need to set up a new international banking agency and that national bank regulators no longer possessed the ability to keep foreign banks out, policies that enabled foreign banks to set up shop wherever it made sense.

Firms continue to lobby their national governments directly on issues that matter in the national context. But they also lobby their governments in Brussels and cooperate with European counterparts on issues of mutual concern. Firms that oppose continued market opening projects have sought protection from their national governments. One common feature of European policymaking is that member state governments are allowed to make side payments to national level actors (both firms, but also workers) who might be negatively impacted by European market opening projects. These side payments help buy off dissent and ensure that firms have an opportunity to adjust to changed market conditions.

DOMINANT REGULATORY STRATEGIES IN EUROPE

The EU has created what some scholars have termed a "multilevel polity,"[14] an inelegant phrase that refers to the division of authority for governing across levels of government. The member state governments have delegated to the EU the task of making market rules that facilitate free movement of products and services, labor, and capital in Europe. For those countries in the Euro, there is a single monetary policy that sets interest rates across Europe and ensures that currency fluctuations do not undermine trading. But the member state governments have kept almost all other important governmental functions to themselves. Taxation, health care, pensions, social welfare, education, and labor market policies are all decided by national or regional parliaments. Though the EU has moved cautiously to more cooperation in foreign and security policy, governments maintain veto rights over whether they agree with EU initiatives or participation in military arrangements. This division of labor is enshrined in the treaties.

Scholars have wondered for a long time why more aspects of governing have not migrated to Brussels. I propose an easy explanation: The citizens of Europe are happy with the current division of labor between their governments and the EU.[15] They support the framing of key economic rules written in Brussels, but they are skeptical that a Brussels regime would sufficiently respond to their concerns about social policies. In countries like Great Britain, the great worry is that the rest of Europe would force higher

---

[14] See G. Marks, L. Hooghe, and K. Blank. 1996. "European Integration from the 1980s: State-Centric v. Multilevel Governance," *Journal of Common Market Studies* 34/3: 341–78.

[15] See R. Eichenberg and R. Dalton. 1993. "Europeans and the European Community: The Dynamics of Public Support for European Integration," *International Organization* 47: 507–34.

levels of taxes on British citizens and put into place less liberal labor market regimes. In countries like France, the worry is that the privileges of highly organized social groups like professionals, state workers, and some unionized workers would be threatened by a Brussels-run government. Though there is evidence that most center-left and center-right parties in Europe support the current configuration of European integration, there is little evidence that many of these parties favor more European political integration to include issues of social welfare.[16]

A final point to make about the division of labor between the EU and member state governments concerns enforcement of EU policies. The EU is a relatively small organization employing about 20,000 people, only about 2,000 of whom are in any policymaking position. Standard analyses of the EU view most of what the employees of the European Commission do is to try and find ways to produce agreement on directives by negotiating between the governments and lobbying groups.[17] The small numbers of EU employees means that there is very little direct regulation going on in Brussels. So, for example, in 1994, after the banking directives passed, there was one person in the EU Financial Directorate whose job it was to monitor whether the directives were being obeyed.

How can the EU know if its directives are being followed? The answer is that EU member state governments have the legal obligation to turn EU agreements into national laws. In the past few decades, more than half of the laws passed by the parliaments in EU countries may well involve such obligatory transpositions of EU law into national law.[18] These laws are then enforced by national regulators and in national courts. Thus, the enforcement of EU rules is controlled by member state governments.

There has been a great deal of concern across Europe that some national governments might be less likely to enforce rules than others. One theory is that even if governments pass EU rules into law, national bureaucracies will just not enforce those rules. The legitimacy of EU politics obviously is related to the degree that EU rules are translated into national law, and more importantly, are put into force by national government bureaucracies. There are several mechanisms in place to ensure that EU rules get enforced. The European Commission follows the transposition of EU rules into national law on a yearly basis. It publishes a report that brings attention to governments

---

[16] See N. Fligstein, *Euroclash*, ch. 5, op cit.

[17] See S. Mazey and J. Richardson. 1993. *Lobbying in the European Union.* Oxford: Oxford University Press.

[18] See J. Lodge. 1992. *European Community and the Challenge of the Future.* London: Palgrave.

that fall too far behind in passing EU rules. This report shows over time that there is a high level of compliance in putting EU rules into law.

A second problem is the degree to which national regulatory agencies enforce EU rules. Here, too, EU regularly undertakes studies of the degree to which national officials have incorporated such rules into their practices. Academic studies have consistently shown that nation states enforce EU rules in much the same way as national law. This is not a very comforting thought for many critics of the EU. There is a concern across Europe that the bureaucratic capacity of southern and eastern European member state governments to actually enforce any rules, including their own, varies greatly. But there is one final check against member state government intransigence in passing or enforcing an EU rule. If a private party, usually a foreign firm, feels that EU rules are not being followed by national governments, it can sue in national courts. These courts will follow European rules, subject to appeal to the ECJ. So, in the last instance, failure to apply EU rules will result in governments being embarrassed by ECJ decisions.

At the beginning of this article, I mentioned that the EU regulatory style was to try to create positive market integration. The EU has a wide berth to consider issues that might be relevant to ensuring markets are open and competitive. The bulk of market rules deal with making sure that foreign firms have fair and equal access to home markets. They are the most explicit about making sure national governments do not unduly protect or prefer national firms. They also specify competitive and anticompetitive practices that might favor one firm over others. The EU has an active antitrust authority that considers mergers and other forms of potentially anticompetitive tactics such as selling goods under cost and price fixing. It has been active in enforcing those standards. So, for example, after the Bush Administration decided not to pursue Microsoft even though it had clearly been convicted of violating American antitrust law, the European authorities continued their intention to force Microsoft to stop engaging in predatory behavior.

Even more importantly, part of creating positive integration in European markets is to use EU-wide policy to make sure there are not incentives in place to create a race to the bottom in product safety, health, labor, and environmental standards among member state governments. These issues, which in America are seen as tangential to regulatory practice, are seen in EU politics as important to creating markets. If governments can provide incentives to firms to locate facilities in their country by having lower environmental standards, this is viewed as a kind of unfair competitive advantage. The EU has tended to produce high standards for product safety, health, labor, and environmental issues. Eichener and Heretier review the process by which a number of these rules were constructed. Both conclude that in the negotiations, the tendency was for governments to search for best practices and high standards.[19] In Europe, firms now have to compete on products, quality, and price and not on finding ways to avoid costs by passing them onto the citizens of a given country.

THE INTERPLAY OF REGULATORY POLICY
AND SOCIAL WELFARE POLICIES

In the opening section, I suggested that politics were important to how regulation has proceeded. I would like to make this argument more explicit. One can certainly make the case that in spite of agreeing to the Treaty of Rome, circa 1975, most European governments had a kind of neomercantilist policy toward trade. Governments concentrated on protecting the jobs of their workers and toward that end sought to protect national markets from encroachments by foreign firms. They were very interested in having market access to other countries' markets and thereby allowing their national champion firms to prosper, but they were less interested in allowing firms and products from foreign firms to enter their countries. If they had to choose, many governments would have preferred the certainty of protecting the national market over opening it up to some uncertain future, particularly in sensitive sectors of the economy. These policies were driven by electorates that saw their jobs and social protection as the main engine of economic welfare.

To say the least, this attitude on the part of governments was not conducive to market integration projects. During the 1970s, the member state governments of the EU were ambivalent about the continuous expansion of market privileges for other countries' firms. They had a zero sum view of markets and felt that if someone came into their country and took over a particular market, their country would lose jobs and economic growth would slow. What is really astounding is that continental European governments eventually came to embrace market opening projects. This shift meant that politicians needed to persuade citizens that such changes would be good for everybody and that liberalization of trade would not undermine social protections. If citizens felt that such changes would produce

---

[19] See, for example, A. Héretier. 1999. *Policymaking and Diversity in Europe.* Cambridge, U.K.: Cambridge University Press, and V. Eichener. 1997. "Effective European Problem-Solving: Lessons from the Regulation of Occupational Safety and Environmental Protection," *Journal of European Public Policy* 4: 591–608.

more insecurity and economic instability, they would immediately vote any government who supported such changes out of power.

The main source of this shift was the bad economic times of the 1980s. It is interesting to compare the experiences in Europe with the experiences of the United States. Both parts of the world experienced the 1973 and 1979 oil price shocks. Both parts of the world found themselves with high inflation, slow economic growth, and relatively high employment throughout the 1970s.

In the United States, as Marc Eisner shows in his essay for this volume, the government began to experiment with product and labor market deregulation. The Carter Administration removed rules governing the trucking and airlines industries to stimulate competition and economic growth. It also initiated a discourse that suggested that workers were partially to blame for persistent inflation, arguing that because union contracts were indexed for inflation, inflationary expectations triggered a self-reinforcing and vicious cycle. The Reagan Administration embarked on a series of policies to undermine labor (most prominently through the breaking of the air traffic controllers' unions) and to promote corporations making new investments (as by granting large tax credits). These policy shifts, along with a much more lenient antitrust policy toward large American corporations that faced international competition, the emergence of financial engineering as a key element of corporate strategy, and a relentless focus on shareholder value, helped bring about a significant restructuring of large American corporations during the 1980s. This process deindustrialized the economy and significantly merged the assets of many of the largest corporations.

Through this period, there was little or no concern for issues of social welfare and income inequality. Indeed, these issues were intentionally kept separate from economic growth issues. The basic argument that won the day in American political circles was that firms should be left alone to pursue profit any way possible. Government should not try to make market rules because in doing so they would tend to either protect inefficient producers or anachronistic workers' jobs. Left to their own devices, the managers of the most innovative enterprises would deploy their assets to earn the highest rate of return, and in doing so would provide new jobs. By the early 1990s, this argument had largely persuaded most influential Democrats along with the country's conservatives.

The economic crisis of the 1970s found European governments operating with more protectionist sentiments. Many citizens and the social democratic parties that represented them saw the economy as a means to an end. Economic growth and jobs were a way to provide adequate living standards and opportunities for everyone. In the European model (with the notable exception of Great Britain), all citizens were entitled to a good life and an extensive social safety net. Though the nature of those safety nets differed across countries, the underlying principle was the same.[20]

During the economic crisis of the 1970s, the first instinct of political parties was to operate to protect jobs and social safety nets. The jockeying in the EU and the national elections across Europe in this period was mostly oriented toward preserving the status quo. The election of Margaret Thatcher in Great Britain was viewed by many political scientists as a watershed event. But Thatcher's attempts to impose U.S. style product and labor market policies to Great Britain never inspired politicians in the rest of Europe to follow suit.

So, the question to raise is why did many member state governments agree to what amounted to a deregulatory project to complete the single market across Europe? The key development here was the failure of protectionist policies undertaken by several European countries, tactics that, far from stimulating economic growth, made matters worse. This was particularly true in France when Francois Mitterand came to power in 1981 and nationalized the banks. As a result, France experienced a massive capital flight and the economy sank into a recession. Mitterand and his colleagues began to realize that they needed different tactics to promote economic growth.

When British, German, and French governments agreed to complete the single market, they did not see the project as a huge risk. The directives that made up the single market were relatively modest, and even the most optimistic economic projections envisioned that the largest gains that could be made were GDP growth of 5–7 percent.[21] Instead, the leaders of these countries undertook this project to appear to be trying something to break out of the economic crisis. As it turns out, the single market worked and was very popular with corporations, executives, and the people who gained from the increases in trade. Indeed, one EU report shows that literally all of the gains in private sector employment between 1985 and 1995 in Europe were due to the single market.[22] This success emboldened governments to continue cooperating and undertake even more ambitious collective projects like the reconfiguring of European telecommunications and utilities industries.

[20] G. Anderson, *The Three Worlds of Welfare Capitalism.* Princeton, N.J.: Princeton University Press, 1990.

[21] See P. Cecchini, 1988. *Benefits of a Single Market.* London: Glower.

[22] See European Commission, 2001, "Ten Years Without Frontiers: The Single Markets Effects on Income and Employment." Brussels, Belgium: Publication of the European Communities.

But vocal parts of the European citizenry remain skeptical of what they saw as the creeping American-style deregulation into their economies. Calling something "neoliberal" is a political epithet in most of continental Europe today. So, for example, during the campaign on the referendum of the EU constitution in France, the French left consistently branded the EU a "neoliberal organization" and the EU constitution a "neoliberal document." As a result, governmental leaders who wanted to stay in power needed to find a balance between freeing up markets to promote economic growth and protecting the losers from such economic projects. As I suggested earlier, this tension has forced governments to do two things. First, they continue to keep issues around social welfare out of European discussions. Citizens are afraid that a European social policy will not favor ordinary citizens but instead will work to undermine the substantial privileges citizens across Europe enjoy. The existing European labor market and political institutions across Europe operate to monitor and mitigate increases in income inequality. Where such changes have occurred, they have generally been met with changes in policies that work to lessen the effect of those changes (again, with the exception of Great Britain).[23]

Second, European political elites have explicitly agreed to tie market changes to increases in the social safety net. European countries have experimented with a series of labor market and welfare reforms that offer flexibility to firms but high levels of social protection to workers. Firms in Europe can relatively easily lay workers off (contrary to much opinion in the United States). But, to do so, corporations must pay many of the real costs associated with doing so, that is, costs of unemployment and, in some countries, costs of job retraining. So, for example, in Germany firms that want to lay off workers have to announce their plans in advance and have to consult with both workers and local governments. They also have to provide adequate severance compensation and pay high unemployment benefits. In Germany unemployment benefits replace 70 percent of previous earnings and last up to thirty-six months.[24] Given this high cost, German firms tend to reduce hours of work before laying workers off permanently. Workers are allowed to go on partial unemployment to compensate for lost hours of work. As a result, Houseman and Abraham argue that American corporations tend

---

[23] See, for example, the review by P. Gottschalk and T. Smeeding (1997) "Cross National Comparisons of Earnings and Income Inequality," *Journal of Economic Literature* 35: 633–87, and more recently D. Acemoglu (2003), "Cross Country Inequality Trends," *Economic Journal* 113: 121–49.

[24] If workers have not found jobs, they are moved to the welfare rolls. Here, they make less in benefits, but the benefits can be paid for an unlimited period.

to use layoffs too liberally, whereas German firms tend to reduce hours first and only lay off workers under more drastic circumstances.[25]

Governments pursue these explicit trade-offs to gain the benefits of having markets be more open and competitive while at the same time making sure that workers are protected. It is not only the case that governments view market creation as needing positive integration. It is the case that the construction of markets can only be done when the rights of all stakeholders are protected. This is the core difference between market regulation in the United States and Europe.

IMPLICATIONS FOR FUTURE REGULATION IN THE UNITED STATES

Trying to draw some lessons from the experience of the EU to the situation of the United States is fraught with difficulties. The political evolution of Europe and the United States in the past twenty-five years could not have diverged in a more dramatic fashion. At its base, the decision to undertake any kind of market regulation involves the most passionate and entrenched politics. The ideas of market liberalism are so deeply woven into our debates that it is hard to imagine how one might even begin to engage them. Jodi Short has shown that the discourse in the legal literature about regulation is now less about economics and more about freedom.[26] Even with the prospect of a Democratic president and Congress and the current economic crisis, it is hard to imagine that the U.S. Congress is about to tackle issues such as changing labor market policies to make social protection more extensive and increasing union power more generally.

I do, however, think that there are some parallels in the European situation that might push forward both a political and a research agenda. I would like to return to the conceptual distinction between a negative and a positive integration project as a wedge into thinking about how regulation might be brought more reasonably into the fore in the United States. The debate in America among policymakers in the past twenty-five years has generally been that globalization, defined as mainly a negative integration project, and its domestic cousin, deregulation, have been good for U.S. corporations and consumers even if they cause some workers to lose their jobs permanently. There is a persistent voice on the liberal Democratic side that argues for

---

[25] See K. Houseman and S. Abraham. 1993. *Job Security in America: The Lessons from Germany.* Washington, D.C.: Brookings.

[26] J. Short. "From Command-and-Control to Corporate Self-Regulation: Legal Discourse and the Changing Regulatory Paradigm." Paper presented at the annual meeting of the Law and Society Association, July 6, 2006.

more positive integration that would provide more social protection on the product safety, employment, and environment fronts. There is also a rising tide of protectionism on the left and right that seeks to sanction developing countries, particularly China, for engaging in varying kinds of unfair trade practices.

The Europeans have been through these debates intensely for the past fifty years. They have hit on the solution of high levels of social protection coupled with high levels of trade openness. The purpose of my chapter has been to argue that by and large the Europeans have managed to find their way to what I would view as a positive integration project that was a win-win situation along both lines. The experience of Europeans is that the quality of life that we all share together is only possible in market society if we engage in *both* forms of positive integration projects. Market rules that guarantee firms access to markets (what might be called rules of exchange), regulate competition, and create and enforce property rights are necessary to making markets work. With no rules, the possibility for firms to engage in forms of predatory competition, work with local politicians to keep out their competitors, and create conditions where products are unsafe, working conditions dangerous, and the environment is spoiled is the end result.

How do we know this is true? In American economic history, one can argue that forms of positive integration first came to protect the integrity of markets and later to ensure that market actors could not exploit consumers, workers, and the environment. The history of American capitalism from the Civil War until the Great Depression is a story of the search for ways to regulate exactly these problems of unbridled capitalism. The emergence of the large corporation was met by a long political period that created new forms of regulation: the Sherman Antitrust Act, the Federal Trade Commission Act, the Federal Reserve Act, and the Securities and Exchange Act, to mention a few.

Over the course of the twentieth century, there has been a rise and fall in concern over workers' rights and workplace health and safety issues. Issues of product safety and environmental degradation were taken up. As Joseph Stiglitz carefully catalogs in his essay "Market Failure and Government Failure," these myriad efforts reflect an increasingly broad range of regulatory purposes and strategies, many of which have proved successful. The agencies these acts created worked on and off to regulate and alter the behavior of the largest corporations. As a result, many of the collusive and predatory behaviors of large firms declined, market transactions were made safer, and the financial system was made more stable (until the deregulation of the past twenty years!). For at least part of American economic history, firms found they could not compete by making unsafe products and to a lesser degree by producing under unsafe working conditions and degrading the environment. Far from undermining the possibility of economic growth, one could argue that the American economy did pretty well for the first eighty years of the twentieth century.

What has happened in the United States, I would argue, is that we have undermined both forms of positive integration and severed the link between recognizing that the two forms are reinforcing. The economic crisis of the 1970s produced a discourse that claimed that neither form of positive integration was necessary to produce economic growth. Indeed, the argument was made that both could be used to stifle competition, push firms to underinvest in new products, plant, and equipment, and thereby slow future economic growth. This argument has won out.

The most important research agenda that this suggests to me for the United States is to look more closely at the claims of those who oppose both forms of positive integration about the alleged negative economic effects of regulation. It is my belief that if we look carefully at most new industries where economic growth and innovation have flourished, we will not discover a negative integration project promoting such growth but instead the deep involvement of government. The computer, biotechnology, nanotechnology, and even securitization of housing mortgage industries all have relied on government regulation, money, and yes, protection. We know, for example, that the emergence of the modern computer hardware and software industry would not have been possible without the federal government.[27] Government made laws and rules that determined the enforcement of patents and property rights that evolved to support the industry. The Defense Department was a provider of research and development funds to firms and was the main customer for many of its early products. Government facilitated the use of foreign engineers in Silicon Valley labor markets. It is difficult to imagine how the computer industry would have developed in a purely negative integration world.

---

[27] For the real history of Silicon Valley, see T. Breshahan. 1999. "Computing." In D. Mowery (ed.), *U.S. Industry in 2000: Studies in Comparative Performance.* Washington, D.C.: National Academy Press; D. Henton. 2000. "A Profile of Silicon Valley's Evolving Structure." In C. Lee, W. Miller, M. Hancock, and H. Rowen (eds.), *The Silicon Valley Edge.* Stanford, Calif.: Stanford University Press; C. Lecuyer. 2000. "Fairchild Semiconductor and its Influence." In C. Lee, W. Miller, M. Hancock, and H. Rowen (eds.), *The Silicon Valley Edge.* Stanford, Calif.: Stanford University Press; and S. Leslie. 2000. "The Biggest Angel of Them All: The Military and the Making of Silicon Valley." In M. Kenney (ed.), *Understanding Silicon Valley.* Stanford, Calif.: Stanford University Press.

There is a large and exciting literature in the field of comparative political economy that shows that positive integration is important to economic growth. It is now conventional wisdom that societies that lack market rules and the rule of law suffer from various forms of rent-seeking on the part of politicians and firms and that this effects long-term economic growth.[28] There is more controversy about the role of unions and laws about product safety, working conditions and labor market rules, and environmental law in economic growth. But the degree to which a consensus has emerged suggests that societies make different kinds of trade-offs in terms of the distribution of income, but this does not affect economic growth very much.

The time is right to look more closely in the United States at how regulation and deregulation have historically affected real economic growth in regions, industries, and corporations.

CONCLUSION

There are two sorts of lessons we can take from the experience of regulators in Europe. First, market creation projects do not just involve the tearing down of regulations. By building positive rules of integration, market regulators can work to ensure that markets remain open to competition and that all firms have to worry about producing products safely and in accordance with rules of environmental best practices. These practices do not have to impose such high costs on firms that they choose to close down facilities and locate them offshore. One proof of this is that in Europe, where labor costs are allegedly too high, manufacturing employment is still close to 30 percent of the labor force as America's has shrunk to under 20 percent.

Second, ensuring that citizens do not bear all of the costs of capitalism's turbulence increases economic security, lowers poverty rates, and produces a better life for everyone. It also increases the legitimacy of such changes and makes society more stable. European societies generally experience a much higher rate of social organization. As a result, there are fewer social problems like crime and poverty. The trick is to see that economic growth and regulation are not trade-offs but lead to more positive outcomes for all members of society.

---

[28] For a review see N. Fligstein and J. Choo. (2005). "Corporate Governance and Economic Performance," *Annual Review of Law and Social Science.*

FIVE

Confidence Games: How Does Regulation Constitute Markets?[1]

Daniel Carpenter

We live in an information-rich, highly networked world, one saturated
with information and choice alternatives – some trustworthy, some not. In
such a society, the confidence of citizens in the marketplace is a key goal
of any economic and political institution. Increasingly, our entire political
system, our society, and our economy are built upon expectations – expectations of fairness, of safe and fraud-free transactions, of known risks (but
also transparent, finite, and reasonable risks), of reasonable and equitable
treatment (the absence of pervasive price discrimination and ethnic and
racial discrimination). Effective regulation helps to maintain a structure
of beliefs that make prosperity and liberty possible (or appreciably more
likely). Regulation, in other words, in some sense creates the very possibility
of marketplaces.[2]

In this chapter I advance a particular version of this argument, focusing on institutions of entry regulation and approval regulation. I define
approval regulation as that form of regulation in which the state must confer
particular rights upon a producer or a consumer for an economic transaction to take place, where the rights are conferred at the discretion of the
state and only upon the completion of a submission process in which
the producer may test the product. Various forms of entry regulation can
be considered as special cases of this genre. The emblematic case I have in
mind is that of national pharmaceutical regulation, as carried out by the

[1] This paper was first presented at the Tobin Project Conference at White Oak, February
1–3, 2008. For helpful conversations and comments I am greatly indebted to Jerry Avorn,
Edward Balleisen, J. Richard Crout, David Cutler, Jeremy Greene, Michael Greenstone,
Marc Law, Harry Marks, David Moss, Susan Moffitt, Mary Olson, Ariel Pakes, Charles
Rosenberg, and Michael Ting. I retain full responsibility for all arguments, characterizations, errors, and omissions.
[2] Related arguments about the market-making capacities of regulation appear in the essays
of Neil Fligstein and Joseph Stiglitz in this volume.

U.S. Food and Drug Administration (FDA) and the European Medicines Evaluation Agency (EMEA). In these institutions, firms can market pharmaceutical products and other therapeutic commodities (medical devices, vaccines, diagnostics) only after express registration of the product by a national agency. Approval occurs at the discretion of this regulator (the FDA, the EMEA), and only after the completion of required experimentation with the drug. This discretionary feature of approval regulation, combined with experimentation hurdles, renders its institutions quite different from those of "fee for entry" licensure, which is practiced by many national and local governments worldwide (Djankov et al. 2002). Fee for entry licensure does not often compel research and development benchmarks for initiation of the approval process, and approval is discretionary in the sense that a firm's fee payment does not compel the regulator to allow market entry. In addition to therapeutic commodities, this model of governance applies to many forms of grant-making, wetlands, and some construction permitting, and professional and occupational licensure (where the state mandates educational requirements and examinations).

Other forms of health and safety regulation such as occupational safety regimes (Kelman 1981, Huber 2007) and public health regulations are related but do not contain the experimentation and veto properties of approval regulation. The arguments expressed here may or may not apply to these areas. I focus here upon approval regulation because it represents a case of strong state power, namely the veto capacity of a government agency over research and development, and the related requirement for private actors to engage in greater R&D than they would otherwise in order to gain marketing rights.

In this chapter I advance four arguments that lie at the interstices of social science disciplines.

- Institutions of approval regulation have been chosen worldwide by republican polities through democratic processes and have been continually legitimated by societies with embedded rule of law. The emergence of these institutions continually defies capture-based explanations.
- Evidence from the most rigorous and historically contextual studies suggests that institutions of entry and approval regulation have arisen in markets characterized by learning constraints, including credence good markets and markets with appreciable information asymmetries. In the absence of regulation, as well as in the presence of weak regulation, these markets are characterized by equilibrium fraud and "lemons

problems" (Akerlof 1970) – consumers will repeatedly purchase and use inferior commodities, human agents will repeatedly choose products that reduce their welfare relative to lesser known alternatives, and more cheaply developed "bad" products will drive out more expensively developed "good" ones.

- Institutions of approval regulation may serve to produce more information, and higher-quality information, than would be provided in their absence. By raising the returns to research and development, institutions of approval regulation also induce the production of superior and lower-variance commodities. In this way, the markets constituted by approval and entry regulation are fundamentally different from those that would appear in the absence of these institutions, and the products in these markets are qualitatively different from those that would appear in the absence of these institutions. *Approval regulation actually makes new and more sophisticated markets.*

- The restrictions of institutions of approval regulation and entry regulation, combined with this information provision, can and often do materially improve human welfare in the setting of advanced republican polities, where the occasional drawbacks of these regulatory policies can be detected and reformed through legislation and other mechanisms of revision.

The chapter's initial section advances these four arguments as theoretical claims, drawing on mathematical, philosophical, and historical considerations where appropriate.

I. The Republican Origins of Regulatory Institutions

A proper theoretical account of any political or economic institution begins with the institution itself. Many theories of regulation start not with institutions but with an institutional vacuum (an unregulated market) and then proceed to deduce the set of market failures that would justify their creation. Although this approach can foster illuminating thinking about regulation, it cannot serve alone as a theoretical or policy guide. It commits first the fallacy of assuming that institutions of governance arise for reasons primarily related to our normative theories used to rationalize them. Unless accompanied by a careful analysis of the institutions themselves (and their development and variance), such market failure thinking often generates unscientific, functionalist accounts of institutions that have more complex and nuanced histories. It further presupposes, as the essays in this volume by

Table 5.1. *Institutions of approval regulation for pharmaceuticals, by government and year of appearance*

Nation/State	Year of first state regulatory body for drugs	Year of compulsory premarket review (approval regulation)
Norway	1928	1928
Sweden	1934	1934
United States	1906/1927	1938
United Kingdom	1963/1971	1963
France	1978	1945
Germany/W. Germany	1961	1961
Japan	1962	1948
India	1940	
Canada	n/a	1963
Australia	1963	1963
European Union	1995	1995
China	1979	1985
South Korea	1953	

Marc Eisner and Joseph Stiglitz both observe, that societies could somehow generate vibrant markets in the absence of webs of supporting institutions.

In this treatment, then, I start with the regulatory institutions themselves, not as an add-on to the market but as a basic institution whose institutions need better understanding.

The institutions of pharmaceutical approval furnish a useful place to begin. Table 5.1 displays the year that twelve nation states and the European Union first created regulatory bodies for pharmaceuticals and the year in which those same bodies instituted a compulsory premarket approval process. Most other nations did not create such formal processes until the 1980s. In general, these moves occurred only under conditions of general democratization. Thus Germany under National Socialism did not possess a system of premarket approval, whereas the United States and several Scandinavian nations already did. The Nazi *Stopverordnung* in fact prohibited the production of and research into many therapeutic medicines. South Korea created institutions of approval regulation in 1953; North Korea still has yet to do so. The Soviet Union never created a system of drug approval regulation, despite a nontrivial level of pharmaceutical production. India began a system of pharmaceutical regulation in 1940 and is now home to a large clinical trials industry; Communist China, meanwhile, has yet to nationalize its system of regulation, and as its export sector has grown, the global press has recently highlighted the weaknesses of its food and drug regulations.

The lesson of these data, I would argue, is that institutions of approval regulation appear in the context of mature republican (representative) and constitutional democracies. Authoritarian regimes, communist nations, and otherwise "institutionally backward" countries are not likely to generate such institutions, even though they may have large state sectors, heavy government intrusion into national and regional economies, and rather robust scientific programs.[3]

Of equal importance, the democratic legislative processes that generated bureaucratic approval regulation of food and drugs do not offer evidence of industry control over political decision making. Capture, in other words, did not drive the creation of agencies like the FDA. Carpenter (2001), Law (2002), and Law and Libecap (2005) examine the Progressive Era creation of food and drug regulation in the United States. In all three quantitative studies, tests of producer capture hypothesis produce null or negative (evidence contradicting the producer capture hypothesis) results. More recently, Carpenter and Sin (2007) have examined the passage of the Food, Drug and Cosmetic Act of 1938 and have adduced evidence from roll calls and legislative histories that directly contradicts the predictions of producer capture theory. Table 5.2 displays relevant evidence from Carpenter and Sin (2007). The votes for S.5 reconsideration were votes to strengthen the FDA's power over pharmaceuticals; a gatekeeping provision did not appear until after the sulfanilamide tragedy of 1937, after these votes took place. In particular, legislators representing those firms that stood most to gain from stronger government regulation (representatives of the United Medicine Manufacturers' Association) were less likely, not more likely, to vote for FDA-strengthening legislation in the middle 1930s (see the coefficient estimates for the variable entitled "Number of UMMA firms in state," the last row of coefficient estimates). This legislation remained unaltered until the 1937 sulfanilamide tragedy, in which a drug suspended in a diethylene glycol solution caused more than one hundred deaths. In the months following that episode, the FDA's parent bureaucracy, the U.S. Department of Agriculture, responded immediately by introducing legislation with a premarket approval requirement. Congress enacted the USDA's proposal into a law a few months later (Jackson 1970, Carpenter and Sin 2007).

---

[3] One could make the point statistically by regressing the existence or duration of such institutions upon some numerical indicator of democratization and/or representation. I would regard such an exercise as having little value-added, because it would simply reproduce what one can view from the table and from examining the data with intuition. (Most nations do not possess independent institutions of approval regulation for pharmaceuticals, so most of the data would be null observations.) From a statistical vantage, there is also massive cross-unit dependence in the data, as most countries have copied American (and to a lesser extent, European) arrangements in the genesis of their national institutions.

Table 5.2. *Probit analyses of three votes on S. 5 (Senate votes, 74th congress)*

Variable	[Senate votes, 74th congress]		
	S. 5 Amendment reconsideration [4/1/1935]	S. 5 Amendment reconsideration [4/2/1935]	Bailey amendment [4/8/1935]
Consent	1.8371 (1.5636)	3.8839 (1.8262)	−1.7690 (1.4917)
D-NOMINATE 1-D	−2.0944 (0.8531))	2.6960 (1.0643)	1.8166 (0.8019)
D-NOMINATE 2-D	−1.3916 (0.8194)	0.3583 (1.1096)	0.3844 (0.8613)
Party {Democrat = 1)	−0.7572 (0.6857)	1.3627 (0.8369)	1.0947 (0.6750))
Percentage of State Vote for FDR, 1932	−0.0041 (0.0206)	0.0169 (0.0250)	0.0081 (0.0185)
Change in % of State for FDR, 1932–1936	−0.0103(0.0321)	−0.0471 (0.0386)	−0.0177 (0.0250)
% of State Population African-American	0.0 445 (0. 0396)	−0.0429 (0.0492)	0.0153 (0.0377)
% of State Population Illiterate	−0.1166 (0.0790)	−0.2109 (0.0924)	0.1061 (0.0818)
% of State Population Educated	−0.0879 (0.0494)	0.2119 (0.0683)	0.0370 (0.0469)
% of State "Gainful Workers" Unemployed	0.4181 (0.1327)	0.5893(0.1736)	−0.0815 (0.1134)
Retail Sales as % of Wholesale	−0.0010 (0.0026)	−0.0009 (0.0028)	−0.0007 (0.0025)
South	2.1259 (0.9639)	1.1556 (1.5649)	−0.8767 (0.8770)
Number of Proprietary Association Firms in State	0.0375 (0.0215)	0.0311 (0.0245)	0.0179 (0.0178)
Number of UMMA Firms in State	0.2596 (0.0829)	−0.2888 (0.0929)	0.0882 (0.0541)
N(df)	83 (69)	75(61)	81 (67)
LLF	−43.512	−33.796	−49.307
Pseudo-R^2	0.2417	0.3396	0.1139

Notes: Asymptotic standard errors in parentheses. Bold coefficient estimate implies statistical significance at $p < 0.05$ (two-tailed test). UMMA firms and PA firms variables correlated at 0.5598. Removal of UMMA firms variable results in negative but insignificant coefficient estimate for PA firms variable.

The sulfanilamide tragedy, then, crystallized common public opinion about two facts: (1) the capacity of an administrative and regulatory agency to protect consumers and impose minimal order and standardization upon a therapeutic market, and (2) the perils of an unregulated market for therapeutics. The public character of the deliberation reduced (although it did not eliminate) the influence of particularistic interest organizations. Here one sees a powerful example of a crisis situation reducing the capacity of even well-connected interest groups to influence legislative decision making, much as David Moss and Mary Oey's essay describes for the Voting Rights Act, the passage of Medicare, and the creation of the EPA's Superfund program.

Whether in cross-national perspective or in the details of particular statutes, then, institutions of drug approval regulation have arisen by legislative choice in republican and constitutional democracies, in a manner inconsistent with rent-seeking accounts. This conclusion, of course, is not equivalent to the claim that such laws always reflect the public interest in all of their details. It is the correlation of market-constituting regulation with core political and philosophical concerns of the republican political tradition that concerns me here. These concerns animated the American founding, not least as voiced by Alexander Hamilton, but also by other scholars of political economy such as Montesquieu and John Adams. Although appreciable differences separate the sorts of institutions created in modern pharmaceutical regulation from the regulatory institutions of early and mid-modern republican governments, there is also considerable overlap, not least in public health regulations, hazard regulations, the regulation of finance and other policies (Novak 2000; Balleisen 2001; Wood 1967).[4]

The Debility of Capture Theory and its Rules of Evidence. It is worth pausing at this point to note that the account presented here starkly diverges from capture and rent-seeking theories that have long held sway in economics and political science. Despite capture theory's successes in the academy, the account leaves some very large holes, a point also emphasized by Jessica Leight and Donald Wittman in their contributions to this collection. Perhaps the most enduring problem in modern capture theory is that it relies on a set of rules of evidence that fall well short of rigor. The core empirical method of the theory of economic regulation was elaborated by Stigler in the 1970s. "The theory tells us to look," Stigler then explained, "as precisely and carefully as we can, at who gains and who loses, and how much, when we seek to explain a regulatory policy." Thus if regulation is inefficient and its benefits flow to large producers, analysts should assume it to have been designed with these effects in mind. Stigler's moral is lucid and he rehearses it unapologetically: protection implies capture. "The announced goals of a policy," he insisted, "are sometimes unrelated or perversely related to its actual effects, and the truly intended effects should be deduced from the actual effects." If a given regulation bestows advantages on a specific firm of industry, scholars ought to infer producer capture regardless of the stated purposes of the law.[5]

An entire cottage industry in the economic analysis of regulation has adopted Stigler's logic as something of a universal method. At its core,

---

[4] See for instance Novak, *The People's Welfare*; Wood, *The Creation of the American Republic*; Pettit, *Republicanism: A Philosophy of Freedom and Government.*

[5] Stigler, *The Citizen and the State,* 140.

the rules of inference in the modern economic theory of regulation are simple. If econometricians can demonstrate the incidence of a regulation or measures of its effects to be partially associated with the presence or strength of an organized interest, then they reject a public interest account in favor of a capture or rent-seeking explanation. Thus if weight limits on four- and six-wheel trucks were less severe (higher) in those states where the share of trucks in farming and the average length of a railroad haul were higher, Stigler inferred capture and rent-seeking from these associations, even though farming and freight haul length both connote less urbanization and infrastructure development. Urbanization (population density) and infrastructure (bridges, tunnels) create conditions that may induce safety-conscious legislators to place weight limits on trucks. Hence the associations observed by Stigler could easily and probably have arisen for reasons having nothing to do with capture or interest group politics at all. In other studies, adherents of capture theory have observed that the arrival of occupational safety regulation, environmental regulation, and pharmaceutical regulation all coincide with retarded entry and reduced product innovation by small firms. These scholars cite such reductions in firm entry as evidence for capture, despite the fact that they might have happened even if the regulation had never emerged, and despite the fact that even a legally neutral scheme of regulation would impose heavier costs upon smaller and newer firms in an industry. More generally, numerous statistical studies have shown evidence of a correlation between measures of regulatory policy or agency behavior and indicators of the presence or strength of a certain interest, which their authors then interpret as evidence for capture and rent-seeking accounts, implicitly discounting the possibility that such correlations might have arisen under a regulatory regime that was neutral or designed with noncapture purposes in mind.[6]

The fundamental flaw of capture and rent-seeking accounts concerns causality and the rules for establishing and inferring it. Capture accounts using the Stigler method generally fail to consider other explanations that may account for the patterns observed. The problem in statistics is known

---

[6] The statistical analyses of trucking weight limits are undertaken in Stigler, "The Theory of Economic Regulation"; *The Citizen and the State*, 120–24. Despite obvious flaws in Stigler's research design and his inferences, it would seem that few if any scholars in economics or related disciplines have revisited his assertions. On environmental regulation, see Peter Pashigian, "Environmental Regulation: Whose Self-Interests Are Being Protected?" *Economic Inquiry* 23 (4) 551–84. For other examples, see Bartel and Thomas, "Predation through Regulation"; Lacy Glenn Thomas, "Regulation and Firm Size: FDA Impacts on Innovation," *RAND Journal of Economics* 21 (4) (Winter 1990) 497–517.

as one of "observational equivalence." If two theories or causal mechanisms potentially lead to the same pattern of evidence, then the evidence in question cannot be used to distinguish between the theories. If a scholar conducting a statistical analysis finds that regulation is more stringent where certain interest groups are more prevalent, or where government is more autocratic, what exactly does this prove? The presence of an interest group and the autocracy of government may be correlated with other factors such as urbanization, education, a legacy of colonialism and slavery, and other factors that capture-based analyses fail to consider.

The influence of capture theory in academic scholarship, I am convinced, has resulted in part from the weakness of its dominant alternative: public interest theory. Indeed, it would appear that "the public interest theory" of regulation persists in part as an artificial alternative to capture theory. The simple dichotomy between "public interest" and "public choice" persists for several reasons. One is the simplicity of the world it presents. Another is the rhetorical skills of some of capture theory's innovators and votaries, in particular George Stigler. Yet a crucial and disturbing feature of the public-interest versus public-choice dichotomy is that it often stacks the deck in favor of capture. At their extremes, capture arguments prop up public interest as a sort of straw man competitor. The slightest empirical departure from the public interest model ostensibly justifies the capture or rent-seeking view. In a world with just two theories, one response to evidence that is inconsistent with one theory is to favor its alternative. But a more compelling path may be to admit that there are still other possible theories and to look for them.[7]

An oft-cited cross-country study published by Simeon Djankov and colleagues in 2002 ("The Regulation of Entry") exemplifies this tendency, committing the all-too-common errors of assuming that protection implies capture and otherwise stacking the deck in favor of capture-based accounts of regulatory action. The authors report that entry regulation (measured

---

[7] Numerous papers in economics, history, political science, and sociology make this inference. In the study of pharmaceutical regulation, scholars have taken business involvement in the writing of regulatory statutes and rules as prima facie evidence of rent-seeking. See Harry Marks, "'The Origins of Compulsory Prescriptions' Revisited," *American Journal of Public Health*, 85 (1) (1995) 109. Clayton A. Coppin and Jack High make a similar inference, concluding that Harvey Wiley's involvement with business interests in the writing of the 1906 Pure Food and Drug Act is evidence for a form of rent-seeking. *The Politics of Purity: Harvey Washington Wiley and the Origins of Federal Food Policy* (Ann Arbor: University of Michigan Press, 1999). In fact the evidence suggests that Wiley was consulting with business interests for information on how to write and specify more appropriate and effective regulations, and in part to build a broad and credible coalition behind his reforms. James Harvey Young, *Pure Food* (Princeton: Princeton University Press, 1990); Carpenter, *The Forging of Bureaucratic Autonomy*, Chapter 8.

as the number of procedures required to start a business in a country) is not associated with superior social outcomes (reduced pollution, reduced accidental deaths, a smaller unofficial economy). Instead, they find that entry regulation is higher where countries are poorer and governments are less transparent and more autocratic. These associations, the authors claim, are "inconsistent with public interest theories of regulation, but support the public choice view that entry regulation benefits politicians and bureaucrats." In this instance, the study's findings are skewed by a heavy presence of African countries in the sample, and (probably) by the lack of a control for education; if these researchers had restricted their analysis to countries in Europe and North America, the findings would disappear. Moreover, certain forms of regulation that decidedly affect entry and that are more common in wealthier countries – such as environmental regulation and occupational safety regulation undertaken by national governments – are excluded entirely from the authors' measure. This exclusion almost certainly inflates the authors' findings and creates an odd situation in which well-known social democratic governments such as Sweden, Germany, Norway, and Canada appear far less stringent than countries such as Singapore, Taiwan, and South Korea. Finally, the inference that poorer countries with more severe health and environmental problems adopt more entry regulation may well suggest that countries with more traditional religious and social cultures regulate entry more heavily (as in, for example, countries governed by more conservative versions of religious law such as Islamic *sharia*). Hence the incidence of entry regulation may have little to do with grabbing hands and much more to do with features of national, ethnic, and religious culture.

Besides its lack of rigor, the deeper problem with the Djankov study (and others like it) is its lack of institutional depth. All sorts of regulations create barriers to entry, but this fact does not imply the restrictions lend themselves to a common scale or metric. If poor and unstable African countries have institutions that smell of rent-seeking and also have high "fee for entry" barriers, does this fact tell us much – does it tell us *anything* – about entry regulation in other settings? Probably not. A superior approach would be to examine the incidence of the regulations themselves, where researchers can draw meaning and inferences directly from particular statutes or administrative/legal institutions.

II. Credence Goods and Placebo Economies

A second consideration in examining institutions of approval regulation involves the sorts of commodities typically governed by such arrangements.

Here I claim that approval regulation institutions govern commodities that are characterized by severe learning problems for those using the product. As a result of self-remitting disease patterns and placebo effects, as well as the interaction between these dynamics (Carpenter 2005b), drugs are types of credence goods, whose quality consumers can assess neither through inspection (as for "inspection goods" like a tomato) nor experience (as for experience goods like a job). Such goods, social scientists have demonstrated both theoretically and empirically, create "lemons problems." Because of informational shortcomings, consumers will continually purchase or consume inferior products when superior alternatives are available, whereas the presence of more cheaply produced inferior goods leads to a "crowd out" of superior products with greater development costs.

Before I partially elaborate this claim, a caveat is in order. To say that institutions of approval regulation help to solve particular problems is not to say that they were created for this purpose. Nor is it to render the regulation in question consistent with a public interest account. It is instead to say that the many (possibly unintentional) purposes served by such institutions possibly include the creation of better access to good information, and hence the manufacture of public confidence.

The argument that information asymmetry between producer and consumer can create "lemons problems" to the benefit of inferior goods, which drive out good ones, has been a staple conclusion of informational economics for several decades (Akerlof 1970, Leland 1974). These models are powerful but also limited by the *a priori* status of credence goods. What makes quality unknowable, and what makes information about quality asymmetric? Mathematical models of lemons and credence good markets do not provide a theoretical answer.

In the therapeutic marketplace, several mechanisms exist to confound proper learning, mechanisms that may or may not be applicable to other markets. In the pharmaceutical example, Carpenter (2005a) considers a model of dynamic utilization (a "multi-armed bandit" model) where the human agent uses Bayes's rule to update on drug quality from a history that is (unknowingly) affected by the agent's own expectations. As a rolling example, consider the influenza patient who learns about the quality of a therapeutic product ("Dr. Cure's Magic Thera-Pee") by conducting a simple "before-versus-after" comparison of his experience with it. If the consumer purchases and takes the product and his condition improves, he infers that the product worked. If the consumer takes the product and his condition does not improve, then he infers that the product did not work and begins a search for another therapy.

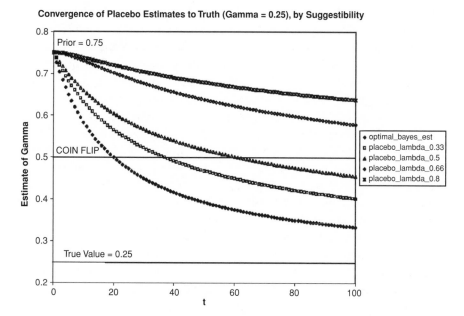

Figure 5.1. Convergence of placebo estimates to truth (Gamma = 0.25), by suggestibility.

In many ways, this hypothetical consumer is behaving rationally, even somewhat scientifically, comparing his experience with the product (after) with his experience without the product (before). The problem is that the "evidence" in this scenario (the consumer's felt health state) is influenced by his own expectations about the quality of the product. It is well known from a half-century of research in medicine, psychology, and neuroscience that patients' mere expectations of a product's healing power will influence their own physiological reaction to it. To magnify problems, the patient's condition – influenza in this example, but also true with migrane or depression – would have subsided anyway. The human agent conflates improvements that are generated pharmacologically and improvements that are generated by placebo effects. Under very simple assumptions, a minimal amount of suggestibility (the enhancement of experienced health by the agent's own prior expectations of the quality of the therapy) will lead to inefficient Bayesian estimation of product quality, exacerbated by the dynamics of word-of-mouth advertising, in turn generating patterns of equilibrium fraud whereby consumers durably opt for an inferior product when a cheaper one (or no treatment at all) would serve them as well.

Figure 5.1 is taken from a simulation in which the true curing probability associated with a drug is 0.25 but the patient starts with optimistic prior beliefs of 0.75. Under regular Bayesian estimation (the lowest curve), the human agent's estimate follows the law of large numbers and returns appropriately to the true value. But wherever the agent's experienced health is contaminated by his own expectations, the human estimate converges progressively more slowly to the truth. In the example above, a medium level of suggestibility (0.5, where the parameter lies on the unit interval 0–1) leads to a tripling of the time required for the Bayes estimate to cross the "coin-flip" threshold.

This point is interesting enough, but when one adds the fact that many health conditions (as well as other utility states such as mood and health-affected utility) are cyclic, the problem gets worse, not better. When self-remitting conditions (mood, hypertension, stress, muscle injury, influenza) are added to the model, the agent can conflate the pharmacological power of the drug, the probability of self-healing, and the curing power of the patient's own expectations. The following figure shows that a medium amount of remission (probability = 0.5) can lead to asymptotically inconsistent estimates of the curing probability of the treatment (continuing the previous example, the prior is 0.75 and the "truth" is 0.25) (Figure 5.2 and 5.3).

A second simulation from the Carpenter model, shown in the following, suggests that different levels of self-remission can generate more optimistic estimates of treatment efficacy that are retained asymptotically.[8]

The upshot of these models is that otherwise rational consumers will, under placebo learning from diseases with self-remission or other forms of cyclicity, consistently overestimate the therapeutic effect of the treatments they try first. They will either fail to rationally abandon a bad medicine, or they will abandon the therapy eventually, but too slowly. This serves as a brute but effective metaphor for the continued profitability of quack treatments and methods in therapeutic markets, particularly unregulated and less regulated therapeutic markets. As shown in many historical examinations of the subject, the market for patent medicines in the United States was immensely profitable, especially among well-educated and literate sectors of the population. Although it is far short of an empirical demonstration of the theory, it is worth noting that similar patterns hold for many nutritional supplements today. The enduring marketing strategies pursued by the purveyors of health scams further bear out these theoretical ruminations, dependent as they often are on heartfelt personal testimonials.

---

[8] Thanks to Justin Grimmer, a graduate student in the Department of Government, for the necessary programming and the code. I harbor full responsibility for use and misuse of the demonstration here.

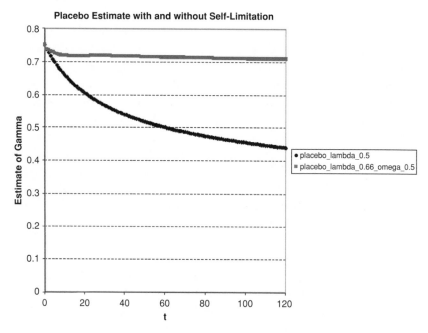

Figure 5.2. Placebo estimate with and without self-limitation.

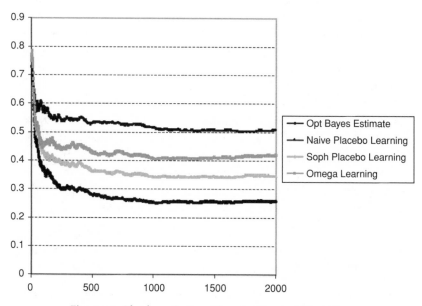

Figure 5.3. Placebo estimate with and without self-limitation.

Theoretically, it is but a brief step from these results – which essentially endogenize the credence good properties of drugs and other therapeutic commodities (that is, explained through assumptions internal to the nature of those goods) – to the analyses of Akerlof (1970) and Leland (1979). When consumers consistently choose inferior products, then cheaply developed bad products drive out good alternatives, and the induced distribution of product quality is less than would be the case in the absence of placebo- and remission-based learning constraints.

Speaking more practically, learning constraints in therapeutic markets generate at least two additional thorny problems. First, therapeutic sponsors no longer invest in areas where the bad drugs take up space. This is the Akerlof "crowd out" hypothesis, and it is directly testable in the pharmaceutical arena. Second, consumers (patients) get stuck on the bad drugs and suffer worse health outcomes. Evidence for this claim comes from Jishnu Das's study of the market for physicians in India (2001).

A more detailed logic of this model essentially elaborates upon the difficulty of decentralized, market-based learning about efficacy. When medical conditions are either self-remitting or cyclic (following a natural history), the impact of placebo effects upon human learning is multiplied. Such situations frustrate decentralized learning about product quality in therapeutic markets; even markets characterized by many consumers and many products will end up with long-term (asymptotic) bias. In other words, no matter how many people take the products, and no matter how long they take them, the true quality of the products will never be accurately revealed to anyone, much less to the whole of society. This general pattern underscores the factual nature of the kind of "economic irrationality" discussed by Joseph Stiglitz in his essay for this volume, and its strong presence in the pharmaceutical and therapeutic marketplace.

From this point the standard "lemons" arguments of Akerlof and others apply. Either uncertain consumers will not sign up for the pharmaceutical "lottery" and will forgo superior treatments that would have been good for them, or they will continually choose inferior treatments that will drive more expensive and superior alternatives out of the market.

III. Approval Regulation Institutions Induce Markets with Higher Rates of Experimentation and Superior Product Quality

Given the previous portrait of "credence good" marketplaces, or placebo economies, we can now consider some of the effects and possible desirability of regulation. Approval regulation sharply truncates the array of products that the consumer faces. Speaking in mathematical concepts, if a consumer (a patient, or that patient's physician) is uncertain about a product, such that she faces a nondegenerate distribution of efficacy (a range of potential outcomes), then an entry restriction can be welfare improving if it dampens the "lower tail" of the distribution (or restricts the especially problematic cases). In even more precise mathematical language, entry regulation must induce a product quality distribution that first-order stochastically dominates the original distribution, in which the likelihood of getting a product that works dramatically improves over the situation prior to the introduction of regulation. In other words, the regulator must be able to separate good from bad products, even if brutally and inefficiently. Notice that this argument is about welfare; nothing about the preceding argument implies that regulation is efficient or the best way of obtaining improvements in patient welfare.

How exactly does approval regulation bring about this improvement in quality? Until recently, students of regulatory institutions were without models to account for this process. In a recent chapter devoted to the study of regulatory error in political science, Carpenter and Ting (2007) advance a model that can be used as a metaphor for approval regulation institutions. Their model posits two-sided uncertainty – both the firm and the regulator (both singular in the model) are uncertain about product quality, but the firm's estimates are more precise than those of the regulator. The regulator, in addition, has a higher quality standard for market admissibility than does the firm for product launching. The essential logic of the model is that the regulator's higher standards, combined with the firm's incentives in bringing the drug to market, induce the firm to engage in more experimentation than it would otherwise. Figure 5.4 shows the stages of play for the firm and the regulator, given that the firm's product is of a given type. In each of the first two periods, the firm can submit (S) its product to the regulator for possible approval (A) or rejection (R), can experiment (E) further (in the sense of taking a draw from a Bernoulli distribution with Beta-distributed priors or it can withdraw (W) the product entirely.[9] The most compelling

---

[9] For a rolling example, suppose I was handed a bent or warped coin and wanted to know whether it was "fair" in the sense that it returned "heads" with the same probability that it returned "tails." One way of testing the assumption of fairness would be to toss the bent coin ten times. If the coin returned five heads and five tails after ten tosses, I would have some evidence that the hypothesis of fairness (heads probability $= 0.5$) was supported. If I tossed the coin one hundred times and saw fifty tails and fifty heads I would have even better evidence. If on the other hand I tossed the coin ten times (or one hundred times) and saw "all tails" then I would begin to wonder. In my wondering, I would be updating on a Beta distribution (deciding where between 0 and 1 to place my probability estimate) using Bernoulli trials (coin tosses, or "experiments" where the outcome is of two sorts).

Stages of Approval Regulation Game

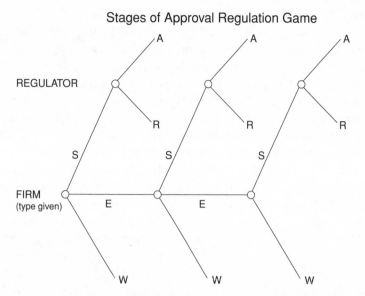

Figure 5.4. Stages of approval regulation game.

equilibria of the model are those in which the regulator adopts the mixed strategy that deters firms from submitting poor products, encourages information acquisition for (and then submission of) "good" products, and leaves firms indifferent between submitting and withdrawing "just-below-standard" products (Carpenter and Ting 2007, Figure 5.1, p. 841).

This approval regulation model and its associated veto metaphor, of course, shoehorn a nuanced and complicated bureaucratic process into a simpler, binary set of outcomes. The model nonetheless conveys important intuition about how these institutions function. Even though the government does not conduct most experiments with therapeutic products – testing is largely funded by private industry, with government science agencies and academia also playing an appreciable role – its veto power over market entry induces greater experimentation than would otherwise prevail. My point is not that more experimentation always redounds to the benefit of society, but that a simple veto power of the government over therapeutic product development has wide-ranging impacts on corporate behavior.

The model also suggests that depictions of approval regulation as "intervention" into the market are seriously misleading. Approval regulation institutions do not intervene in existing marketplaces but create new markets altogether. This characterization much more sensibly fits the evidence about developments in the post-World War II European and American pharmaceutical industries, especially if one conceives of governmental action broadly. The randomized, placebo-controlled trial did not originate in industry, but rather in academic and government science (Marks 1997). By the same token, the requirement for controlled studies of therapeutic products did not emerge as a market-based mechanism – instead, governments imposed that requirement upon the pharmaceutical industry, responding to the findings of academic and government scientists, and their bureaucratic and legislative allies. These requirements brought forth a new commercial world. They created a "scientific" demand for new instrumentation and new research capacity. More importantly, they generated a far broader and deeper demand for pharmaceutical goods, in part because of the way that government certification then triggered insurance coverage. A similar story can be told for the American market for "generic" drugs, which took off only after the FDA and Congress established common standards for the "bioequivalence" of generic drugs to the pioneer molecules they were trying to copy.[10]

IV. Improvements in Human Welfare and Liberty

Institutions of approval regulation not only create new markets, they create markets that are plausibly superior in many respects to those that were (historically) and are (counterfactually) displaced by these institutions. There are many dimensions on which one can compare institutions of approval regulation with other arrangements, but I am concerned here with three especially trenchant comparisons. First, effective approval regulations create a market with better products, in part through the direct effect of screening, in part through by indirectly encouraging private abandonment and "crowd out" of quack products. Second, even if the characteristics of the products in the market do not change, approval regulation may generate better information about the products that exist. Third, in a particular way, approval regulation may protect a vital form of liberty, emancipating citizens from unjust subjection to the whims and capricious decisions of producers.

---

[10] This argument has some relation to Professor Yohai Benkler's paper in this volume. Benkler's claim is that in many contexts, the dynamics of social cooperation can produce significant innovations, and that these innovations in turn can create platforms and networks for new kinds of commercial activity. The point here is that in some contexts, like clinical trials for drugs, governmental action can create a reputational mechanism that extends the impact of those socially produced innovations.

Formally and conceptually, a minimum quality standard can create a market with higher average quality, where the quality effects are sufficient to outweigh the changes in equilibrium price (Leland 1979). This result can occur either because the standard is sufficiently high as to induce a higher quality distribution (Leland), or because its existence deters the one-time makers of low-quality products from even attempting to pass the necessary hurdles for market entry (which is akin to a costly signaling mechanism) (Carpenter and Ting 2007). Hence even with the possible price rises that entry restrictions might entail, equilibrium consumption might rise under such a scenario.[11]

Studies of markets with quality standards suggest that such effects are plausible. In a skillful analysis of state pure food laws in the late nineteenth and early twentieth century, Law (2003) shows that capture mechanisms poorly account for those laws, whereas increases in food consumption did correlate with passage of such legislation. Zhin and Leslie (2003) show that disclosure regulation, related to though distinct from approval regulation, induced superior health outcomes at Los Angeles restaurants, and Hsu, Roberts and Swaminathan (2007) have demonstrated that markets with quality standards generally experience reduced commodity price variability.[12]

In part because the confidence effects of pharmaceutical regulation have been so little theorized academically, no empirical studies of these phenomena exist. Yet there is suggestive evidence from the decades before and after the 1962 Kefauver-Harris Drug Amendments. Those amendments mandated that all new drugs demonstrate effectiveness for their treated conditions as well as safety, and they charged the FDA with creating a new system of experimentation in which the best evidence of safety and effectiveness would be produced through controlled clinical trials that were prospectively designed (in other words, where the hypotheses and research design were established before the start of the experiment). As is well known among social scientists who study the FDA, those amendments coincided with a decline in the introduction of New Molecular Entities (NMEs – essentially newly concocted chemical compounds that have some medicinal value) to the marketplace, as the FDA began to siphon good from bad products and

---

[11] More formally, one would wish to prove that the imposition of regulation induces a quality distribution that has first-order stochastic dominance (FOSD) and possibly second-order stochastic dominance (SOSD) over that of no approval regulation. This result emerges quite readily from the Carpenter and Ting (2007) model.

[12] This may speak to the second-order stochastic dominance criterion discussed in notes 8 and 10.

as the costs of pharmaceutical R&D increased. As Temin and Hilts have noticed, however, this decline began precipitously at least five years before Congress enacted the 1962 amendments. Most of the statistical studies have involved very brute annual time-series regressions (and hence very small N), so the evidence here is not good for causal inference as to the effects of the 1962 law.

Other intriguing post-1962 changes in the drug markets have attracted much less scholarly attention. A full empirical examination of the effects of FDA regulation on consumer confidence and pharmaceutical consumption and confidence effects lies beyond the scope of this chapter. But I will note some key dimensions of that apparent impact.

One key point is that the decline in the number of new drugs was not accompanied by a rise in pharmaceutical prices. Instead, prices actually fell in the decade following the Kefauver-Harris Amendments, and those price declines look even more substantial once total CPI is taken into account.[13] The substantial fall in the cost of prescription pharmaceuticals in the 1960s and 1970s remains an anomaly in the policy literature on the 1962 amendments (Carpenter 2005b). If regulation restricted entry but had no other effects upon consumption, we should have witnessed a substantial rise in equilibrium price. Yet precisely at the time when inflation elsewhere in the U.S. economy was raging, prescription drug prices stayed flat. This finding suggests that either other unmeasured factors contributed to the price decline, or that the regulatory reforms had effects beyond simply reducing the number of NMEs entering the market. All of this deserves much more investigation than we can give it here.[14]

At the same time that drug prices fell, per-NCE (new chemical entity) sales rose significantly. Furthermore, the pharmaceutical markets became much more predictable, at least in prices, consistent with the idea that regulation created greater certainty in patient and physician utilization of pharmaceuticals. It is possible – and the hypothesis deserves further investigation – that federal regulation accomplished these effects through standardization pathways. The dissemination of drug trial findings, combined with their interpretation upon common metrics that were scientifically established,

---

[13] Statistics taken from Bureau of Labor Statistics industry-specific CPI aggregates, also the *Drug Development and Marketing* volume. There are other possible sources for this argument.

[14] I realize that all of this falls a light-year short of an empirical demonstration that FDA regulation enhances consumer and physician confidence in drugs by reducing uncertainty about the efficacy and safety. Again, a genuine investigation would require a book-length treatment. Yet this hypothesis has been maintained, and brute price and sales statistics from the decades before and after the 1962 amendments are consistent with the account.

plausibly permitted the establishment of insurance formularies in which physicians and insurers had greater confidence.[15]

These correlations and inferences, of course, do not establish causation; but they do suggest causal possibilities that deserve rigorous academic investigation. This evidence is certainly consistent with the hypothesis that pharmaceutical markets (particularly prescription and utilization) were characterized by greater stability and certainty after the 1962 amendments.

Second, it is plausible (though perhaps hard to assess empirically) that institutions of approval regulation produce superior information about the products in the marketplace, and that this additional information can have desirable effects as well. In the case of national pharmaceutical markets, one might look for evidence that drugs in existence before the 1962 amendments were prescribed by doctors and used by patients more often and more effectively after the amendments relative to their use before the transformation in the regulatory process.

Third, approval regulation may actually generate more republican liberty – or "freedom from domination" – in the sense that modern theorists of republicanism have used the term (Pettit 1997, 2005). As Pettit and others have argued, one of the tasks of modern democratic government is to impose institutional constraints upon centers of power. From the colonial period through the nineteenth century, a great deal of regulatory activity by American governments reflected this republican approach to politics and political economy (Novak 2000, Balleisen 2001). The underlying mechanisms linking approval regulation to personal liberty have at least two dimensions. By reducing the ability of producers to defraud consumers, approval regulation dramatically improves the capacity of individuals to

---

[15] For evidence on increasing per-drug sales, see Balter (1975: 37–43) and Schwartzman (1975: 68–69). Per-drug data on prescription patterns are unavailable, but the variance of prescription pharmaceutical prices dropped heavily after the 1962 regulations. In the twelve years before the 1962 amendments the variance of the pharmaceutical CPI was 18.7 CPI points, whereas the variance in the twelve years following the Amendments was 6.1, less than one-third of its pre-1962 value. The level of the prescription pharmaceutical CPI also fell continuously during the 1960s, from 51.4 in 1961 to 46.9 in 1970, and reached its preregulation peak only in 1976. All data are from Consumer Price Indices as calculated by the Bureau of Labor Statistics, U.S. Department of Labor. The decline of prescription pharmaceutical prices in the decades following the 1962 amendments is something of an anomaly in the study of pharmaceutical regulation, one that deserves continued study. If the 1962 regulations increased the cost of entry and had no other effects upon the market, we would expect to witness a sharp increase in prices as entry and supply were restricted. The long-term decline in pharmaceutical prices during this very period, at the same time that inflation was raging, suggests either that other factors were driving the price of drugs or that the new regulatory regime had impacts on more than innovation alone.

make informed decisions about crucial dimensions of their lives. Compared to a similar individual living in 1960, an individual living in 1975 with a chronic fungal infection or with heart disease had a much enhanced capacity to choose among treatment options. She and her physician could refer to clinical trials in which the different drugs available to her had been tested, and many of the results of these trials were now readily in the medical literature, in patient package brochures, and even in physician advertisements. Moreover, many inefficacious treatments for this patient's diseases had been removed from the market by 1975, either voluntarily or by virtue of the DESI review. In addition, by constraining the ability of powerful producers unilaterally to set the terms of market interactions (as in antitrust), institutions of approval regulation may serve as a countervailing force to concentrations of economic power. The dependence of companies such as Pfizer or Merck on the FDA – these companies must, if they are to remain profitable, continually introduce new products and gain the FDA's clearance of their marketability – and this dependence functions as a partial constraint on their behavior. Current firm behavior must anticipate the necessity of appearing and reappearing before the regulator in the future for purposes of drug approval.[16]

V. Research Agendas

The argument here, although speculative, rests upon a broader and emerging literature on the effects of regulatory institutions. It rests upon formal theories of market operations (Akerlof 1970, Leland 1979, Das 2001, Carpenter 2005a), formal theories of regulatory dynamics (Carpenter 2004, Carpenter and Ting 2007), and historical and empirical accounts of regulatory operation (Law 2003, Hilts 2003, Law and Libecap 2006, Carpenter and Sin 2007). In concluding I sketch several research agendas that would expand our grasp of the larger concepts and theories discussed here.

A. Formal and Mathematical Research Agendas

I direct the remarks in this section to those who are interested in the mathematical modeling of regulation, regulatory behavior, and regulated industries. The mathematical theory of regulation has concentrated heavily for three decades on the issue of information asymmetry, but almost entirely

---

[16] This argument is currently rather opaque.

with respect to cost information and price regulation. The related literatures on mechanism design and cost revelation (Baron and Myerson 1982, Baron and Besanko 1984a, 1984b) are well known. Yet in thinking about empirical and historical forms of regulation – occupational licensing and pharmaceutical and medical technology regulation, to name two common forms – mathematical theorists have until recently (Carpenter 2004, Carpenter and Ting 2007) made little progress in the analysis of these institutions.

Laffont and Tirole (1993) have provided the most comprehensive investigation of these forays into the mathematical conceptualization of regulation. Yet even they lack a model where both the firm (or firms) *and* the regulator are uninformed, much less models that incorporate explicit experimentation. These conditions – dual (possibly asymmetric) uncertainty and experimentation – would seem to characterize a large number of markets, so there is no empirical basis for the exclusion of these components from further formal models. One set of research agendas, then, would be the formal development of models that analyze credence good economies, regulations for credence good and placebo economies, and institutions of approval regulation.[17]

B. Empirical and Policy Research Agendas – the Case of the Drug Efficacy Study

One obvious context to explore the more tangible impact of regulation on expectations is pharmaceutical policy. For institutions of approval regulation, like the FDA, I would wager that cost-benefit analysis of major regulatory changes should focus on the very long term (as in Greenstone's work on the impact of environmental initiatives (Chay and Greenstone 2005), rather than Peltzman's work on pharmaceutical regulation (1973).[18]

More particularly, the analysis of pharmaceutical regulation in the United States has been complicated by issues of multiple simultaneous causes of the outcomes one would wish to examine and the very blunt nature of the data used. Numerous scholars (starting with Peltzman 1972) have attempted to

---

[17] Another area deserving of attention concerns how regulation affects beliefs. At the core of markets lies a set of expectations. The mathematical theory of expectations (e.g., Billingsley 1979, 1999) relies upon integrals, which rely upon probability measures and in turn, upon countable and co-countable spaces. As a conjecture, consider: Does regulation render essential outcomes in certain markets more countable, more integrable, more measurable, furnishing more people access to credible and relevant information that otherwise might not exist?

[18] A related point concerns the statistical quantity of interest in empirical studies of regulation. Scholars should examine not only the mean effects of government regulation but the variance effects (see Hsu et al. 2007 for a recent exception).

examine the "effects" of the 1962 drug amendments upon different measurable policy outcomes, but all of these attempts have incorporated fatal flaws, usually related to the fact that the "intervention" or "treatment" in question was a highly aggregated and time-dependent change in institutions. Put differently, a great many changes occurred simultaneously at the time of the 1938 and 1962 statutes, significantly complicating efforts to link consequences to causes.

Although I am very skeptical of the existence of informative "natural experiments," I do think that a move toward more finely grained data is in order, and that the Drug Efficacy Study Initiative (DESI) of the 1960s and the 1970s may provide a quasi-experiment that merits close analysis. The DESI project was occasioned by the 1962 law's requirement that the FDA examine the effectiveness of drugs approved from 1938 to 1962. Where a national advisory panel concluded that a previously approved drug lacked evidence of efficacy, the FDA was charged with removal of the drug by substantive administrative rule making. Scholars have assessed this episode in regulatory history largely for its influence upon administrative law and for its effect upon clinical trial standards – it was here where the FDA began to mandate randomized, controlled clinical studies as the "gold standard" of evidence for drug efficacy – but its larger social, economic, and health effects have so far escaped careful examination.

Using data from the National Archives, one can examine the exact timing of market withdrawals for hundreds of medications from 1969 to 1975. A (possibly asymmetric) panel data set can then be created that uses Federal Register listings as a proxy for market withdrawals in a therapeutic class. If we can trust the DESI process, then the timing of the market removal would constitute a quasi-experimental treatment in approval regulation that varied by therapeutic class, by disease, and over time. Although the overall "exogeneity" of this intervention may be difficult to establish (I am generally dubious of such claims), it would be useful to estimate the association between these removals and subsequent economic and health outcomes, including (in all cases for therapeutic classes in which the FDA revoked licenses to make and sell particular drugs (a) subsequent levels of pharmaceutical use, (b) subsequent prices and price variability, (c) subsequent research and development and pharmaceutical innovation,[19] and (d) and subsequent health outcomes. After this statistical analysis is complete, we would then be in a position to ask important questions such as: Did investment in new therapies increase in those areas where DESI pulled drugs off the market? Did therapeutic outcomes improve?

---

[19] A brute test of Akerlof ("bad products crowd out good ones") may be possible here.

The upshot of these empirical hypotheses is that DESI and its associated institutions – the randomized, controlled trial (RCT) as a technology for quality assessment in pharmaceuticals – did not merely intervene into an existing market, but created a new market altogether. It is difficult to imagine therapeutic markets today without the presence of an RCT standard, not to mention other, less well-known regulatory standards such as bioavailability, bioequivalence, and others.

C. Historical Research Agendas

Other research agendas suggest themselves for historians and other social scientists interested in the temporal development and evolution of regulatory institutions and markets. Inquiries into the confidence mechanisms of regulation points toward a larger need for all social scientists to examine the origins and patterns of consumer and citizen beliefs about markets, and in particular the effect of regulation upon these beliefs. So too, social scientists such as sociologists, political scientists, and historians should examine the variable credibility of regulatory institutions. Insofar as the confidence and market-constituting effects of regulation depend in some respects on the confidence that citizens and consumers have in regulatory arrangements themselves, this area beckons as a central subject of inquiry. It matters greatly whether citizens trust what the bureaucratic agencies operating in their name are doing. Again, though, beyond broad analyses of "institutional trust," "trust in government," and "trust in physicians," there is little or no empirical or historical scholarship on these vital questions.

CONCLUSION

By imposing a rigorous entry structure upon the pharmaceutical industry, regulation has generated a technological future, kept bad products from the marketplace, stabilized expectations in the pharmaceutical market, and, ultimately, supported liberty. Libertarian theorists view this sort of entry restriction as inevitably destructive. The standard view of pharmaceutical regulation sees exactly this debilitating dynamic, as the 1962 amendments ostensibly produced a steep decline in the number of "new chemical entities." But "the Tobin view" sees something else going on: the FDA was wedding bad products from the marketplace, buttressing "consumer" (physician, pharmacist, and patient) beliefs in the quality of available drugs. This essay considers the pharmaceutical example as a metaphor for a whole host of related institutions. My hunch is that these institutions can be approached through common theoretical lenses, common strategies of empirical and historical research, and ultimately through renewed normative appreciation of their presence in American and global society.

References

Akerlof, George A. 1970. "The Market for 'Lemons': Quality Uncertainty and the Market Mechanism." *Quarterly Journal of Economics* 84: 488–500.

Balleisen, Edward. 2001. *Navigating Failure: Bankruptcy and Commercial Society in Antebellum America.* Chapel Hill: University of North Carolina Press.

Baron, David P., and David A. Besanko. 1984a. "Regulation, Asymmetric Information, and Auditing." *RAND Journal of Economics* 15 (4): 447–70.

Baron, David P., and David A. Besanko. 1984b. "Regulation and Information in a Continuing Relationship." *Information Economics and Policy* 1: 267–302.

Baron, David P., and Daniel Diermeier. 2007. "Strategic Activism and Nonmarket Strategy." *Journal of Economics and Management Strategy* 16 (3): 599–634.

Baron, David P., and Roger Myerson. 1982. Regulating a Monopolist with Unknown Costs." *Econometrica* 50 (4): 911–30.

Billingsley, Patrick. 1979. *Probability and Measure.* New York: Wiley.

Billingsley, Patrick. 1999. *Convergence of Probability Measures,* Second Edition. New York: Wiley.

Carpenter, Daniel. 2004. "Protection without Capture: Product Approval by a Politically Responsive, Learning Regulator." *American Political Science Review* 98 (4): 613–31.

Carpenter, Daniel. 2005a. "A Simple Model of Placebo Learning with Self-Remitting Diseases." Unpublished manuscript, Harvard University.

Carpenter, Daniel. 2005b. "A Modest Proposal for Financing Postmarketing Drug Safety Studies by Augmenting FDA User Fees." *Health Affairs – Web Exclusive* W5–469.

Carpenter, Daniel, and Gisela Sin. 2007. "Policy Tragedy and the Emergence of Regulation: The Food, Drug and Cosmetic Act of 1938." *Studies in American Political Development* 21 (2): 149–80.

Carpenter, Daniel, and Michael M. Ting. 2005. "Regulatory Errors with Endogenous Agendas." *American Journal of Political Science* 51 (4): 835–53.

Chay, Kenneth Y., and Michael Greenstone. 2005. Does Air Quality Matter? Evidence from the Housing Market." *Journal of Political Economy* 113: 376–424.

Das, Jishnu. "Three Essays on the Provision and Use of Services in Low Income Countries." Ph.D. dissertation, Harvard University, 2001.

Djankov, Simeon, Rafael La Porta, Lopes-de-Silanes, and Andrei Shleifer. 2002. "The Regulation of Entry." *Quarterly Journal of Economics,* Vol. CXVII, Issue 1, 2002.

Feddersen, Timothy J., and Thomas W. Gilligan. 2001. "Saints and Markets: Activists and the Supply of Credence Goods." *Journal of Economics and Management Strategy* 10 (1): 149–71.

Gordon, Sanford, and Catherine Hafer. 2005. "Flexing Muscle: Corporate Political Expenditures as Signals to the Bureaucracy." *American Political Science Review* 99: 245–61.

Gordon, Sanford, and Catherine Hafer. 2007. "Corporate Influence and the Regulatory Mandate." *Journal of Politics* 69: 298–317.

Gorton, Gary, and Donald J. Mullineaux. 1987. "The Joint Production of Confidence: Endogenous Regulation and Nineteenth-Century Commercial Bank Clearinghouses." *Journal of Money, Credit and Banking* 19 (4): 457–68.

Hilts, Philip. 2003. *Protecting America's Health: The FDA, Business, and One Hundred Years of Regulation.* New York: Knopf.

Hsu, Greta, Peter W. Roberts, and Anand Swaminathan. 2007. "Standards for Quality and the Coordinating Role of Critics." Unpublished manuscript, Department of Economics, UC-Davis.

Huber, Gregory A. 2007. *The Craft of Bureaucratic Neutrality.* New York: Cambridge University Press.

Kelman, Steven. 1981. *Regulating America, Regulating Sweden: A Comparative Study of Occupational Safety and Health Policy.* Cambridge, Mass.: MIT Press.

Laffont, Jean-Jacques, and Jean Tirole. 1993. *A Theory of Incentives in Procurement and Regulation.* Cambridge, Mass.: MIT Press.

Law, Marc. 2003. "The Origins of State Pure Food Regulation." *Journal of Economic History* 63 (4): 1103–30.

Law, Marc, and Gary D. Libecap. 2006. "The Determinants of Progressive Era Reform: The Pure Food and Drugs Act of 1906," in *Corruption and Reform: Lessons from America's Economic History*, eds. Edward L. Glaeser and Claudia Goldin (Chicago: University of Chicago Press), 319–42.

Law, Marc, and Mindy S. Marks. 2007. "The Effects of Occupational Licensing Laws on Minorities: Evidence from the Progressive Era." SSRN Working Paper No. 943765.

Leland, Hayne. 1979. "Quacks, Lemons and Licensing: A Theory of Minimum Quality Standards." *Journal of Political Economy* 87 (6): 128–46.

Novak, William. 1996. *The People's Welfare: Law and Regulation in Nineteenth-Century America.* Chapel Hill: University of North Carolina Press.

Peltzman, Sam. 1973. "An Evaluation of Consumer Protection Legislation: The 1962 Drug Amendments." *Journal of Political Economy* 81: 1049–91.

Pettit, Philip. 1997. *Republicanism: A Theory of Freedom and Government.* New York: Oxford University Press.

Pettit, Philip. 2005. "Freedom and Probability." Unpublished manuscript, Department of Politics, Princeton University.

Skowronek, Stephen. 1982. *Building a New American State: The Construction of National Administrative Capacities, 1877–1920.* New York: Cambridge University Press.

Zhin, Ginger Zhe, and Philip Leslie. 2003. "The Effect of Information on Product Quality: Evidence from Restaurant Hygiene Grade Cards." *Quarterly Journal of Economics* 118 (2): 409–51.

SECTION TWO

BEYOND THE ECONOMIC THEORY
OF POLITICS

SIX

The End of Special Interests Theory and the Beginning of a More Positive View of Democratic Politics

Donald Wittman

Public choice (sometimes known as rational choice) assumes that individuals act to promote their own interests. From this simple assumption, a large body of theoretical and empirical work has been spawned. Much of this research shows that bureaucrats, politicians, and pressure groups get their way at the expense of the voters and that regulation reflects the desires of these concentrated interests rather than the appropriate balancing of all the costs and benefits. But if one really believes in the economic model of behavior, then one should be skeptical of such results. After all, it was Adam Smith who showed that the self-interest of the baker and the candle-stick maker leads them to provide what consumers desire. So by the same economic logic, one should expect that the invisible hand works for the democratic political system, as well. Now there are counter arguments to this last statement, but in this chapter I counter these counter arguments by using standard economic theory and methodology. Along the way, I show that many of the negative results arise because the authors (1) have incorrectly assumed that the political system is characterized by monopoly rather than by competition, and (2) have implicitly assumed that voters are irrational, which, of course, is contrary to the rational choice paradigm. The arguments that I use against the theory of special interests can also serve as the foundation for a theory that democratic markets are well served by the invisible hand. In the final section, I outline this positive theory of regulation.

By far, the majority of papers on political economy emphasize the power of special interests in the political process. This argument takes several forms: (1) In comparison to the typical voter with diffuse interests, it is more worthwhile for concentrated special interests, who have much to gain, to organize and influence the political outcome. (2) Legislators are re-elected by representing the interests of their constituents (which tend to be local) rather than the interests of the nation as a whole. Therefore, Congress enacts costly pork-barrel projects. (3) Congress is controlled by special-interest committees (such as the agricultural committee) that institutionalize the power of special interests. And (4) candidates for office cater to special interests to finance their campaigns.

All of these arguments appear to provide plausible explanations for the power of special interests. However, as I will show, these arguments have logical gaps, and the conclusions can only be reached by assuming that voters are irrational and/or that competition for political office is absent.

I. Rationality

Because rationality plays such an important role in public choice, it is useful to digress and discuss the meaning of rationality. The following is how economists define rationality: If a person can rank order her preferences (e.g., Tom prefers Obama to Clinton to Romney), these preference rankings are transitive (that is, if Tom prefers Obama to Clinton and Clinton to Romney, then Tom prefers Obama to Romney) and reflexive (that is Tom does not strictly prefer Obama to Obama, whatever that would mean), and the person chooses her most preferred *feasible* alternative, then the person is rational. Rationality is a plausible assumption regarding human behavior. Isn't it a better theory of human behavior that people do what they prefer to do rather than that people behave randomly (they are arational) or that they consistently act against their own preferences (they are irrational)?[1]

In this chapter, we explain *aggregate*, rather than a particular individual's, behavior. Because we are interested in aggregates, our predictions are not undermined if some people do not act rationally. While one might argue that a particular voter is irrational, it is much harder to claim this to be the case for voters in general. Note that there is no need to assume that individuals are perfectly informed. Rational people can be misinformed and

---

[1] Presumably, individuals at different times are characterized by one of the three (rationality, irrationality, and arationality). The problem is that we cannot predict which characterization is operative (which would be the case if we could detect which part of the brain is being used or how much alcohol was consumed, for example). Under such circumstances, to predict behavior rather than merely define behavior ex post, we need to go with the characterization that works the best on average. The argument here is that rationality works best.

make mistakes. However, voters on average will not persist in their mistakes over a long period of time if the evidence is to the contrary and a mistake is costly.[2]

Note that being rational does not mean that voters are selfish. Rational people may be altruistic; but being rational, they will try to achieve their altruistic ends in the best way possible. Note also that being rational does not mean that voters have nice preferences. Voters may be homophobic, racist, and xenophobic. And if this is the case, a democratic electorate will elect representatives who are homophobic, racist, and xenophobic.

It is common to view emotional responses as being contrary to rational behavior; indeed, emotional is often used as a synonym for irrational. For example, someone might say that he got angry and did something that he regrets. I have a different view. Emotions are what shape our preferences and rationality is the handmaiden to these emotions. Consider our emotional attachment to our children. Because of this attachment, we rationally try to figure out ways of making our children successful and happy adults. And in a similar way, we rationally figure out ways to defeat those that we hate. "Appealing to the voters' emotions" is generally considered pejorative and implies that the candidate is manipulating the voters; but translating the phrase into "appealing to the voters' preferences" produces a less negative connotation. It is my view that when we don't like the preferences of the majority of voters, we are inclined to use the word "emotions" and claim that the voters are manipulated.[3] We will come back to the issue of voter irrationality in Section VII.

II. Empirics

In this essay, I concentrate on the theory of special-interest politics. But before doing so, it is worthwhile to undertake a brief discussion of the "evidence" demonstrating the power of special interests. There are, no doubt, numerous government policies that are inefficient. I will not be arguing that inefficiencies do not exist. However, I am skeptical about the methodology used to demonstrate the power of special interests.

---

[2] This holds when the information is available contemporaneously. Obviously, in the eighteenth century doctors did not know that penicillin killed bacteria and voters and consumers might have been against its use.

[3] Even if candidates could manipulate voters, remember that there are two candidates running so that their ability to manipulate in their own favor is diluted when both candidates engage in such tactics.

My first methodological concern is the way that examples are counted. To illustrate, let us consider rent control in New York City. Some would treat this example as demonstrating the power of special interests (in this case, the power of the existing renters). I agree that rent control is a costly and inefficient regulation. I would therefore argue that this explains why rent control is relatively rare, at least in the United States. While others see the existence of rent control as proof of the power of pressure groups, I see its rarity as proof that pressure-group explanations for policy outcomes are not that powerful in this domain.[4] In a similar fashion, while some might point to the existence of any tariff as illustrating the power of pressure groups, I would find the relatively low tariffs that we now have in the United States as illustrating the weakness of pressure groups in getting their way. The Moss-Oey chapter considers numerous instances where some of the most powerful special-interest groups give way before political coalitions that claim to speak for a more expansive common good.

Related to this issue is the choice of areas to study. We are shocked and awed when government behaves inappropriately, but not when it acts appropriately. It is the former that grabs our attention when maybe it should be the latter. Why do we see more signals in cities than in rural areas? Is it because the signal producers have less political clout in rural areas or is it because economic efficiency suggests that there should be more signals in urban settings? We don't even ask the question in the first place, and no academic journal would bother publishing a study that showed that efficiency, rather than special-interest politics, explained why there are fewer signals on interstate highways than on urban streets.

There are plenty of examples where efficiency rather than special-interests politics explains policy differences. The normative (efficiency) theory of government predicts that the government will subsidize the production of public goods when the market is likely to fail in that endeavor. And by and large, the evidence conforms to the normative expectations. Governments subsidize vaccinations more than plastic surgeries, rather than vice versa. Governments subsidize a greater percentage of the cost of building streets than the cost of building cars, rather than vice versa. And the role of government relative to the private market is much greater in national defense than in consumption, rather than vice versa. None of these statements is very new or exciting to a public finance economist. But they are puzzling

---

[4] In various jurisdictions there is rent control for people living in mobile home parks. I doubt that rent control would exist in these jurisdictions if the average voter did not have some warm spot for low-income families. So attributing outcomes to special interests may be misleading even in this case.

Table 6.1. *Shares of U.S. cash receipts and program payments for crop year 2002–05*

	Share of total value of production	Share of individual commodity payments in total outlays
Upland Cotton	1.9	22.3
Rice	0.6	7.3
Wheat	3.0	9.5
Corn	8.7	43.5
Soybeans	7.2	5.5
Other Grains/Oilseeds	1.3	4.2
Horticultural Crops	21.3	∼0.0
Meat Animals	37.8	∼0.0
Dairy	10.8	5.1
Other Commodities	7.4	2.5
Total	100.0	100.0

facts to those who believe in rent-seeking theory and the power of special interests. Are those who build streets more organized and politically savvy than those who build automobiles?

So the first problem I have with the evidence in favor of the special-interests theory of politics is that it is very selective. There are plenty of exceptions to the normative theory. But selectively choosing exceptions and then "testing" them is not really good science. Either the sample needs to be random or one needs a compelling theory as to when special interests trumps normative public finance (and vice versa).

Another major methodological concern is that special-interest explanations tend to be ad hoc and contradictory across subject matter. A quick look at Table 6.1 reproduced from Sumner (2007) should raise a number of questions about the extant theories. Do we really have a good explanation for why U.S. agricultural program payments for rice, wheat, and corn are large while meat animals and nuts are not? In each case there is a special interest.[5]

We should keep in mind that all kinds of special interests are interested in any particular government policy. With regard to sugar, whose domestic producers are protected by tariffs, the users of sugar, including jam producers, baking companies, soft-drink producers, the Sweetener Users Association (a lobby group for food companies that use sugar), and consumers would be against restrictions on sugar imports, while the American

---

[5] Special interests may use different venues besides government support payments to accomplish their goals.

Sugar Cane League (a lobby representing sugar cane growers), the Colorado Sugar Beet Growers Association, and manufacturers of sugar cane equipment would be in favor. Wheat producers also have to face bakers (more concentrated than wheat farmers) and consumers (less concentrated). Stories that favor one concentrated interest over a diffuse interest are just stories as these stories leave out some of the players (e.g., manufacturers are left out of the sugar growers vs. consumers story).[6] At a minimum, one should have a comparative static story. For example, one industry became more concentrated and as a result the equilibrium changed in its favor.

Finally, I am always fascinated by the contradictory special-interests explanations. Consider the following statements: Environmental regulation is too weak because of the power of special interests (mining and industry). Environmental regulation is too strong because of the power of special interests (lawyers and wealthy people who don't care about jobs). Both sides adhere to the special-interest story, but the stories are inconsistent. The standard excuses for being on the losing side of a political battle are that voters are biased and ignorant and special interests (always on the other side) have their way in the political process. So maybe special interests are an excuse rather than a reality.

III. Diffuse Versus Concentrated Interests

What happens in other forms of government – namely that an organized minority imposes its will on the disorganized majority – happens also to perfection whatever the appearance to the contrary under the representative system.... This is because the only candidates who have any chance of succeeding are those who are championed by organized minorities. Mosca (1939, 154)

The steel industry and its workers... are willing to act because the benefits from protection are concentrated on the relatively few who invest and work in the industry. Their incomes are significantly affected. The larger costs of their protection are borne in dispersed fashion by the much more numerous population of taxpayers and consumers. The dilution of costs renders its bearers politically ineffective. Demsetz (1982)

[A democratic] system tends to give undue political power to small groups that have highly concentrated interests.... Consider the government program of favoring the

---

[6] One might argue that the benefit of lower sugar tariffs to the more concentrated bakers is less than the cost to sugar beet and sugar cane growers, and therefore the sugar growers win out. But such an argument violates the theory of concentrated interests that they get their way despite the cost to others being greater than their own benefit. I note that a nonmonotonic relationship between concentration and political power cannot be constructed under reasonable assumptions; so this is not a way out of the contradictory results (see Wittman 1989).

merchant marine by subsidies for shipbuilding.... The estimated cost ... is 15,000 dollars per year for each of the 40,000 people actively engaged in the industry. Ship owners, operators and their employees have a strong incentive to get and keep these measures.... On the other hand [these subsidies] only come to about 3 dollars a person per year. Which of us will vote against a candidate because he imposed that cost on us? Friedman and Friedman (1980)

Politically successful groups tend to be small relative to the size of the groups taxed to pay their subsidies. Becker (1983)

These quotes represent only a small subset of the numerous authors who have argued that those who have concentrated benefits (e.g., the defense industry) will have an upper hand in the political process over those who face diffuse costs (the taxpayer). The logic is that it does not pay to enter the political arena when only small amounts are involved. There are two strands to this argument. The first is that it does not pay for diffuse interests to organize and lobby Washington, the state capital, city hall, or wherever lobbying takes place. The second strand argues that diffuse interests will not even know about special-interest legislation and therefore will not vote against those representatives who have voted for the legislation. However, both strands of the argument confuse individual motivation on one issue with overall political effect. In fact, quite plausible arguments can be made that concentrated interests are at a great disadvantage in majority rule systems; after all, majority rule is about the majority not the minority.

Let us start with the second strand, which depends on the diffuse interests not being aware of the special-interest legislation. Consider the case in which a candidate's policy would result in taking a dollar from a million voters and distributing the proceeds to 1,000 members of a pressure group. This could be done directly or indirectly through some kind of legislation (e.g., imposing tariffs on the importation of sugar). Obviously, the probability that each of the thousand members of the pressure group vote for the candidate is a lot greater than the probability that each of the 1 million voters (most of whom may not even be aware of the policy) vote against the candidate. But even if this policy reduces the probability of each of the million voters voting for the candidate by only .005, such a redistribution will not take place, for it involves a loss of 5,000 votes from the diffuse majority in return for a thousand more from the pressure group. Indeed, given these stylized facts, we would observe the diffuse majority taxing the concentrated minority.[7] Despite the widespread arguments claiming that

---

[7] But, as we will argue later, candidates always have the incentive to provide efficient policies over inefficient ones.

the concentrated interests of a minority will override the diffuse interests of the majority, the contrary theoretical results presented here should not be surprising. As in other areas of economics, some people are at the margin, and thus very small changes will have an effect. This effect multiplied times the very large number of voters with diffuse interests may be very substantial.[8]

Furthermore, one might expect that the other candidate would inform the voters that the first candidate was in favor of special interests. In this regard, Kingdon's (1989) book on congressmen's voting decisions is insightful. He interviewed congressmen after roll-call votes and discovered that they regularly adjusted their votes in ways designed to forestall electoral problems. When one congressman was asked whether anyone in his district would notice his vote, the congressman replied: "No, I know that nobody will notice it right now. People never do. But it may be used against you in the next campaign. I learned that lesson in my first campaign for re-election. About 5 days before election-day, they hauled out [some charge against me] because I cast a vote against some ridiculous District [of Columbia] bill. You see, most people don't notice it. But your opponent will comb down through every aspect of your record, every vote you've ever cast, looking for dirt and using it." (Kingdon 1989, 60)

Even if voters are not particularly interested in any particular government regulation, a candidate might run on a policy of abolishing a whole slew of regulations as Reagan did. While one might argue that the monetary loss to a consumer-voter from any particular regulation was small, the overall effect could be quite large.

Turning to the second strand of the argument, it is true that consumers are unlikely to go to Washington to lobby their representatives against some form of legislation that hurts them only in a very minor way. But they don't have to go to Washington to influence policy. All they have to do is vote against the incumbent who has voted against their interests. And while virtually no voter pays attention to what his/her representative has been doing in Washington, there is one very important person who has – the challenger. And, as the Kingdon quote shows, the challenger will bring out every misdeed (real or imagined) to the attention of the voters.[9]

---

[8] There is also an inherent logical problem that occurs if minorities have a natural advantage over larger groups – it is easy to make a group smaller, and everyone is a concentrated-interest minority of one.

[9] Even if the monetary effect on a particular voter were small, the voter could be outraged by government waste and read websites that were devoted to discovering government waste. See the Leight chapter for further arguments against voter ignorance.

In a nutshell, the authors quoted above have only a very partial model of the political process. Their major omission is considering the competitive process of elections, which is rather strange if you are trying to analyze democratic politics.[10] We will come back to the issue of competition later.

IV. Pork-Barrel Politics and Special Interest Committees

One does not have to search far to find complaints about Congress. Scholars have placed the blame on two interrelated structural aspects: Congressmen represent individual districts and committees represent special interests. The result is pork-barrel politics and special-interest legislation. In this section, I consider each of these in turn.

Special interests may form along geographical lines. Voters in corn-producing states (even if they are not farmers) will be interested in promoting the use of ethanol, either through direct subsidies or through regulation. And in general, voters in each state will be interested in promoting pork-barrel projects within their state. Representatives will want to promote those expenditures that benefit their constituents and are paid for by voters in other legislative districts, even if the benefit to their district does not outweigh the cost to other districts. So we have a rational choice explanation for the demand for pork-barrel projects. But what about the supply-side explanation – why would other districts want to pay for these wasteful pork-barrel policies?

Let us see how the rational choice literature answers this question. Shepsle and Weingast (1981) assume that voters in a congressional district respond positively to pork-barrel expenditures in their own district but not negatively to wasteful pork in other districts. As a result, Congress funds wasteful projects in a majority of districts. The reason Shepsle and Weingast give for voters not responding negatively to pork spent in other districts is that voters are unaware of what is going on in other districts. Their model implicitly assumes that voters underestimate rather than overestimate the amount of wasteful expenditures in other districts. That is, their model assumes that lack of information leads to biased beliefs in one direction. But Shepsle and Weingast present neither a theoretical explanation nor

---

[10] This omission is not confined to economists (as the inclusion of Mosca suggests). Political sociologists have been known to ignore elections also. See how much discussion of elections you can find in Alford and Friedland (1985), Domhoff (2005), and other tomes in political sociology.

empirical evidence to justify this claim. So their model implicitly violates the assumption that individuals have rational expectations. Without this irrationality assumption, their model would not predict wasteful pork-barrel expenditures.

We now turn our attention to the committee structure. An extensive literature views congressional committees as centers of power and the prime source for political-market failure. The logic proceeds as follows: Many committees represent special interests. The senate agricultural committee has members from agricultural states and generally represents the interests of agriculture; the armed services committee is often composed of senators from states where large defense expenditures take place, and in general these senators are supporters of the armed services. And the same goes for other specialized committees. So it is not at all surprising that these committees would send to the floor special-interest legislation.[11]

In general, blaming the congressional structure for wasteful policies seems to be misguided for the following reasons: It is Congress that decides the structure of Congress. We would not expect its members to design a harmful committee structure. And given the committee structure, one would expect its members to bargain over policy to exclude negative-sum outcomes.[12] This is just a public sector application of Coase (1960), who showed that when transaction costs are low, bargaining could overcome wasteful activity and achieve an efficient outcome in the private sector. Furthermore, political parties are organized to increase the likelihood of election and re-election of their candidates. Political parties do not win elections by implementing inefficient policies that make those who voted for the party worse off. Indeed, inefficient policies never make sense, because by definition of inefficiency there exists another policy that makes someone better off without making anyone worse off. Because each party wants to get as many votes as possible, the parties will strive for the most efficient policies possible.

---

[11] For McConnell (1970) and Lowi (1979) committees are part of the "iron triangle" of interest group liberalism, pork-barrel politics, and policy reciprocity. See Shepsle and Weingast (1991) for a more positive view.

[12] Logrolling is a common method of exchanging rights in legislatures. Although logrolling is often seen in a negative light, it in fact allows for Pareto improving trades. Politicians create efficiency-enhancing bundles of policies. Without trades (either in the legislature or in the private sector), resources would not go to their highest use. Hillman's 1989 book on the political economy of trade protection *explicitly* assumes away the possibility of such efficiency-enhancing trades. So it should not be at all surprising that he finds that trade policy will be inefficient. He should be commended for being explicit in this regard.

I will now show how political parties exert control over the special-interest committees. An important method of party control is to make transfers to major committees partially dependent on past behavior on minor committees. Those who have voted with the leadership on key votes in the past are rewarded with choice reassignments.[13] More important committees also have a greater percentage of members from the majority party, thereby controlling for the possibility of defection. While Congress has a committee structure that could be seen as representing special interests, it also has control committees such as Budget and Appropriations that oversee the more specialized committees. Parties are very careful in choosing members on control committees to reflect the preferences of the median congressperson in the party, there being less potential for opportunism when the goals of the agent and the principal coincide.[14] Even after committees have been set up, Congress has considerable power over them. The House can shift jurisdictions of committees, refer certain bills to several committees, and impose procedural rules (e.g., minority members can choose witnesses). In the Senate, each senator has the right to propose riders for most legislation under an open-amendment rule, thereby undermining the power of special committees to influence legislation.

In a nutshell, the power of special-interest committees has been exaggerated because Congress and the majority party design the committee system, influence the staffing of committees, make the special-interest committees subservient to the gate-keeping committees, and allow for changes to legislation from the floor.

Understanding of committee structure is enhanced by looking at the analogous structure for firms. Firms are not unorganized amorphous blobs. Rather, divisions are created within firms to deal with specific issues. A structure, not ad hoc arrangements, is imposed. The structure facilitates comparative advantage and reduces transaction costs. The upper layers of management provide general direction to the lower levels and deal with the occasional conflicts between departments. Congress is structured in the same way. Specialized committees deal with specialized concerns, which

---

[13] Empirical support is found in Coker and Crain (1992), who show that House members who have demonstrated more loyalty to the party leaders by voting in agreement with their positions in the past are more likely to obtain assignments on important committees (see also Cox and McCubbins 1990).

[14] See Cox and McCubbins (1989), who show that these control committees (universal, in their terms) are more representative of Congress than special committees, such as agriculture.

facilitate trades among the people within the committee and even between committees. Overall direction is given by the party leadership. It is hard to imagine an effective Congress without a committee structure very similar to the existing one.

V. Politicians Trade Off Good Policy for Campaign Donations

We now turn to the most controversial part of this essay and argue that pressure groups aid the political process.[15]

Just about everyone "knows" that candidates grant favors to special interests in return for campaign donations that in turn are used for political advertising. And presumably, the more that special interests donate, the more that candidates will bend to their wishes if elected to office (Grossman and Helpman, 1996, have the most carefully delineated model along these lines). But this standard explanation for the power of special interests makes no sense if voters are rational. If everyone *knows* that politicians trade off good policy in return for advertising money, then rational voters will vote against the candidate doing the most advertising (which is easy to monitor – just see which candidate has the most campaign adds on TV). So either voters are irrational and they respond positively to political advertising or voters are rational and the view that candidates trade off good policy for donations from special interest groups is wrong.[16]

To show how campaign donations and endorsements by special interests aid the political process, we start with the standard Downsian model. Downs (1956) postulated that the most preferred positions of the voters can be arrayed along a single continuum and that voters have single-peaked preferences – the closer a position is to a voter's preferred position, the happier the voter is. Downs also assumed that each candidate wants to maximize the expected number of votes that the candidate will receive. Under such conditions, candidates R and D will choose policies at the median voter's most preferred position (position M in Figure 6.1). The logic is as follows. If both candidates are at position M, then both candidates will expect to gain

---

[15] For a more formal analysis, see Wittman (forthcoming); for the role of pressure groups when candidates differ in quality, see Wittman (2007).

[16] It is conceivable (especially if you are not an economist) that uninformed voters are irrational and respond positively to political advertising even though it makes them worse off. But the evidence seems to be to the contrary. As we will show later in this section, political advertising and endorsements provide valuable information that results in voters making choices more congruent with their pre-existing preferences.

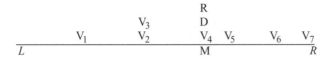

There are 7 voters arranged on a left-right continuum. For convenience, the voters are numbered from left to right. Note voters 2 and 3 have the same preferred position. Candidates R and D will be at M, the median position.

Figure 6.1. Both candidates will be at the median.

3.5 votes and have a 50 percent chance of winning. If one of the candidates moves to the left, then a majority of voters will prefer the candidate who has stayed at the median (all of those voters at the median or to the right of the median). So, the candidate moving left will have three or fewer votes and lose with certainty. Because the candidate wants to maximize the expected number of voters, this will not happen. By the same logic, neither candidate will want to move to the right of the median. This is the essence of the median voter theorem.[17]

Now this is a model of how informed voters vote. But how do uninformed voters behave under these circumstances? Uninformed voters do not know the relative positions of the candidates. So they either vote randomly for one candidate or the other or, more likely, abstain. So the outcome is again at the median of the informed voter.

Let us now consider the role of pressure groups when voters are rational. A pressure group will provide money for political advertising in return for the candidate moving closer to the pressure group's own position. Realistically, the information provided in political campaigns is likely to be sparse. The information is often limited to identifying that the candidate is endorsed by a particular pressure group, say the NRA, NAACP, AARP, etc. As long as the uninformed voter knows where the pressure group stands, this will be enough information for the uninformed voter to determine the relative positions of the candidates and to vote effectively. Essentially uninformed voters who are closer to the NRA than what they perceive as the average voter's preference will vote for the candidate endorsed by the NRA, and those farther away from the NRA than the average voter will vote against

---

[17] Political issues may be multidimensional rather than unidimensional. Unfortunately, dealing with multidimensionality requires a much more technical presentation. For surveys of the research on spatial models, see Enelow and Hinich (1984) and Duggan (2006).

the candidate endorsed by the NRA. Hence, if the uninformed voters are on average closer to the NRA than the informed voters are and there are enough uninformed voters, then the candidate will willingly be endorsed by the NRA and win the election. So the pressure group endorsement and donations help shift the outcome from the median informed voter to the median voter overall. Of course, if uninformed voters on average prefer gun control, then the NRA will want to avoid the election and turn its resources elsewhere. In a nutshell, donations by pressure groups are used to provide political information to uninformed voters who are, on average, closer to the pressure group's position than informed voters are. So pressure groups aid the political process rather than hinder it.

Statistical evidence corroborating the use of endorsements is found in Lupia (1994), who showed that voter choice on five ballot measures to reform insurance in California was strongly dependent on knowledge of the positions of various interest groups on the measures. Lupia identified fifteen organizations that took positions on one or more of the five measures. These organizations included the California Trial Lawyers Association, the insurance industry, Ralph Nader, and the Friends of Motorcycling. The first two organizations tried to hide their sponsorship and advertised themselves as pro-consumer or pro-citizen, as did all the other organizations. Despite the fact that there were five complex measures on the ballot and that some organizations tried to hide their true identity, many of those who were otherwise *very poorly informed about the substance of the ballot measures were able to correctly identify the positions of the various interest groups and then make the same choice that they would have made if they had been fully informed.*

Other studies have come to similar conclusions. Looking at more than 1,400 voters in the U.S. 2000 election, Freedman et al. (2004) showed that political advertising increased political knowledge of the candidates. Gelman and King (1993), Finkel (1993), and Iyengar and Simon (2000) showed that campaigns, by increasing the amount of relevant political information available to voters, help citizens cast votes in line with their *pre-existing attitudes and proclivities.* Arceneaux (2005), using cross-national survey data, showed that campaigns enlighten voters as the election draws near. This effect was particularly noticeable for politically unsophisticated individuals (uninformed voters) who used campaigns to learn which party matched them ideologically. Rather than persuading voters to change their minds, as a model of voter irrationality would predict, this research suggests that campaigns help voters (particularly uninformed voters) gain information for making up their minds.

VI. Competition

Economists believe in competition in the marketplace much more than other social scientists do. But when it comes to the political sphere, many economists, particularly those who believe very strongly in the competitive nature of economic markets and their good effects, see only monopoly power.[18] In economic markets, monopolies (without potential competitors and without the ability to engage in multiple pricing) are inefficient. It is therefore not surprising that monopoly models of government also lead to bad results. Some of the most influential papers in political economy ignore the fact that in democracies there is competition for electoral office. For example Brennan and Buchanan (1980) have a model where government behavior is not at all constrained by the need to be elected or re-elected to office. Democratic politics is missing – the government just maximizes tax revenue. Along the same lines, neither Tullock's 1967 paper nor Krueger's 1974 paper on political rent-seeking incorporates electoral competition. And the same holds true for Peltzman's 1976 paper on the political economy of regulation.

Competition is not restricted to candidates running in elections. In federal systems, competition takes place within and across government levels. There is competition between cities and between states. People and businesses choose to locate where their consumer and producer surpluses are maximized. Those cities and states that provide better government will attract more residents (Tiebout 1956). There is also competition between city, state, and federal governments (Breton 1996). Citizens choose the arenas where their preferences can be best satisfied. Often one sector has a clear comparative advantage: cities are better at deciding school location, and federal governments are better at deciding defense expenditures. But there are many times when the appropriate arena is not so obvious and the various levels of government are in competition with each other. Finally, there is competition between these governments and other institutions, such as religious organizations, unions, corporations, and families in trying to satisfy consumer demands.

Competition is like water held in a sieve. To argue that competition does not exist because it is absent somewhere is like saying water is not leaking because one of the holes in the sieve is plugged. So beware of monopoly models of government; they are likely to be highly misleading.

---

[18] Examples include Friedman and Friedman (quoted earlier) and some of the people cited in the remainder of this paragraph.

VII. Irrationality

Could voters be irrational? Psychologists, sociologists, and even some behavioral economists suggest that people are irrational. Caplan (2006) compares voters' beliefs to economist beliefs and argues that when there is a disagreement, this is evidence that voters are not rational. As a social scientist, I must allow for the possibility that voters are irrational. I cannot just assume it away. Nevertheless, I am very skeptical regarding its use in answering political issues. There are just too many ways that people can be irrational. We have covered two ways of being irrational here: (1) Voters may systematically underestimate the cost of pork-barrel projects; and (2) uninformed voters may respond positively to political advertising even if the candidate's policy is expected to be worse for the voter than the other candidate's policy. Caplan highlights three other sources of voter irrationality: (3) antimarket bias; (4) antiforeign bias; and (5) pessimistic bias. While those in psychology highlight still other biases such as (6) confirmatory bias, and (7) bias in favor of tall candidates. The list is endless (perhaps some people even have an irrational fear of pressure groups) and who knows under what conditions which set of biases are the most influential or how they would actually operate in an election. There are just too many degrees of freedom, and neither evolutionary psychology nor empirical studies has been able to narrow the list sufficiently.[19] As a consequence, irrationality serves either as an ad hoc explanation for the unexplained variation in rational explanations of voter behavior or as an easy excuse for why the majority does not agree with me (whoever the me is).

And most important, we have plenty of results demonstrating rational behavior. People who are pro-abortion are more likely than people who are anti-abortion to vote for pro-abortion candidates; African-Americans, who have a larger proportion of people on welfare, tend to be in favor of more liberal welfare policies than European-Americans are; and individuals from corn-growing states, in comparison to those in other states, are more likely to support legislation in favor of ethanol.[20] The list could go on and on.

---

[19] I believe that there is strong evidence for antiforeign bias, but I am not sure whether this bias should be considered irrational rather than merely reflecting individual preference. In any event, this antiforeign bias or some other mistaken understanding of economics may explain why tariffs have popular support even among the majority who are hurt by such policies.

[20] This is not to imply that all voters vote their pocketbook, but rather to demonstrate that assuming that voters are rational yields predictable results. And as the tariff argument in the previous footnote suggests, I would not argue that voters are never irrational.

VIII. Toward a More Positive Positive Theory of Regulation[21]

Public choice has provided a number of explanations for political market failure. This chapter has been a long exercise in dispelling the intellectual foundations for such explanations. All of these criticisms have been undertaken within the paradigm of rational choice – voters like consumers make rational choices within a competitive market.

Having torn down the special-interest theory of regulation, how do we explain democratic politics? The answer is implicit in my earlier criticisms. In a nutshell, competition for office leads candidates to provide the policies that voters want. To expand on this idea, let us first start with the underlying rationale for the *efficiency* of economic markets, where efficiency means that you cannot make someone better off without making someone worse off. Competition forces producers to provide what consumers want at the lowest price. To do otherwise is to be driven from the market when consumers go elsewhere for their purchases. Now this scenario only works in the absence of both externalities (such as pollution where the firm does not implicitly or explicitly pay for the harm to others) and economies of scale that undermine the possibility of competition. And, of course, there is no guarantee that economic markets provide a "just" distribution of income.[22]

The argument for efficiency is more straightforward in democratic markets. Candidates try to create platforms that are efficient. To do otherwise would mean that someone could be made better off without making anyone worse off; a candidate for office would not want to lose a vote by engaging in such an inefficient strategy. So the race for office involves finding a set

---

[21] I use the word positive twice to connote two different meanings. The first meaning is the common use of the word and is roughly equivalent to a more optimistic view of regulation. In contrast, in economics, a positive theory means a realistic theory. So the theory that I present in this section is both more descriptive of reality and less cynical about regulation. Note that I use the word "regulation" in a general way to mean government policy. It does not mean, for example, that government would use quantity regulation rather than cap and trade to reduce carbon emissions. Indeed, one would expect the latter if it is a more efficient method of reducing carbon emissions.

[22] Economists are concerned with both efficiency and the distribution of wealth. Economic markets distribute wealth to those with marketable resources, such as human capital and land. Democratic markets may distribute or redistribute wealth according to different criteria. If people were purely selfish, then wealth might be redistributed to the median voter (see Londregan 2006). But it appears that the median voter is less selfish than the self-interested caricature as middle-income voters are more generous to those who are poor and less rapacious towards those who are wealthy (see Caplan 2007). But in any event, regulation (in its narrow meaning) is a very inefficient method of redistribution. And, if the arguments in this chapter are correct, we would expect the redistribution explanation for regulation to hold only on very rare occasions.

of policies that appeal to a majority of voters over the other candidate's set of policies. And because policy encompasses the whole society, externalities and economies of scale are internalized in the policy platform. In the absence of a fine, a firm can ignore the cost of pollution to the surrounding area, but a politician cannot ignore such costs in his/her calculations because some votes will be lost. As I argued earlier, Coasean bargaining in legislatures produces efficient outcome even when legislative districts represent diverse districts. Note well that government policy may include a hands-off policy toward business. In trying to win office, politicians will want to provide the most efficient policies – politicians will leave the market alone where the market is superior to government intervention and undertake regulation when the outcome is superior to the market solution. So democratic politics tends toward efficient regulation.

Just as economics markets are imperfect (for example, consider the recent economic meltdown, where among other things, bank CEOs clearly were not maximizing stockholder wealth), democratic markets make mistakes. But the key is ex ante expectations. The argument here is that given the dynamics of the democratic system, one would expect regulations to be efficiency enhancing. And if ex post shows otherwise, one would expect a diminishment of the regulation.

Anthony Down's classic book, *An Economic Theory of Democracy* (1957) argued that two-party elections would produce policy near the median voter's most preferred preference. This is a positive view of democracy (unless you believe that the median voter is irrational or poorly informed). But those in public choice who came afterward tended to drop competition from the analysis and exaggerated voter lack of information. Not surprisingly, this yielded a negative view of democratic politics in general and regulation in particular. At the same time, the virtues of the economic market were extolled. This chapter suggests a more balanced view. Government regulation is innocent until proven guilty, rather than guilty until proven innocent.

Bibliography

Alford, Robert R., and Roger Friedland. 1985. *Powers of Theory: Capitalism, the State and Democracy*. Cambridge: Cambridge University Press.

Arceneaux, Kevin. 2005. "Do Campaigns Help Voters Learn? A Cross-National Analysis." *British Journal of Political Science* 36: 159–73.

Becker, Gary S. 1985. "Public Policies, Pressure Groups and Deadweight Costs." *Journal of Public Economics* 28: 329–47.

Breton, Albert. 1996. *Competitive Governments*. Cambridge: Cambridge University Press.

Caplan, Bryan. 2007. *The Myth of the Rational Voter: Why Democracies Choose Bad Policies*. Princeton, N.J.: Princeton University Press.

Congleton, Roger. 1996. *The Political Economy of Environmental Protection*. Ann Arbor: University of Michigan Press.

Demsetz, Harold. 1982. *Economic, Legal and Political Dimensions of Competition*. Amsterdam: North-Holland.

Downs, Anthony. 1957. *An Economic Theory of Democracy*. New York: Harper & Row.

Duggan, John. 2006. "Candidate Objectives and Electoral Equilibrium." in *Oxford Handbook of Political Economy*, eds. Barry Weingast and Donald Wittman (Oxford: Oxford University Press).

Domhoff, William G. 2005. *Who Rules America? Power, Politics and Social Change*. New York: McGraw-Hill.

Enelow, James M., and Melvin Hinich. 1984. *The Spatial Theory of Voting*. Cambridge: Cambridge University Press.

Finkel, Steven E. 1993. "Re-examining the 'Minimal Effects' Model in Recent Presidential Campaigns." *Journal of Politics* **55**: 1–21.

Freedman, Paul, Michael Franz, and Kenneth Goldstein. 2004. "Campaign Advertising and Democratic Citizenship." *American Journal of Political Science* **48**: 723–41.

Friedman, Milton, and Rose Friedman. 1980. *Free to Choose*. New York: Harcourt Brace Jovanovich.

Gelman, Andrew, and Gary King. 1993. "Why Are American Presidential Election Campaign Polls So Variable When Votes Are So Predictable?" *British Journal of Political Science* **23**: 409–51.

Grossman, G. M., and E. Helpman. 1996. "Electoral Competition and Special Interest Politics." *Review of Economic Studies* **63**: 265–86.

Hillman, Arye L. 1989. *The Political Economy of Protection*. Chur: Harwood Academic Publishers.

Iyengar, Shanto, and Adam F. Simon. 2000. "New Perspective and Evidence on Political Communication and Campaign Effects." *Annual Review of Pscyhology* **51**: 149–69.

Keohane, Nathaniel O., Richard L. Revesz, and Robert N. Stavins. 1998. "The Choice of Regulatory Instruments in Environmental Policy." *Harvard Environmental Law Review* **22**: 313–354.

Kingdon, John. 1989. *Congressmen's Voting Decision*. Ann Arbor: University of Michigan Press.

Kreuger, Anne O. 1974. "The Political Economy of the Rent-Seeking Society." *American Economic Review* **64**: 291–303.

Londregan, John. 2006. "Political Income Redistribution," in *Oxford Handbook of Political Economy*, eds. Barry Weingast and Donald Wittman (Oxford: Oxford University Press).

Lupia, Arthur. 1994. "Shortcuts versus Encyclopedias: Information and Voting Behavior in California Insurance Reform Elections." *American Political Science Review* **88**: 63–76.

Mosca, Gaetano. 1939. *The Ruling Class*. Translated by H.D. Kahn. New York: McGraw-Hill.

Oates, Wallace E. 2001. "The Political Economy of Environmental Policy." *Resources for the Future Discussion Paper* 01–55.

Peltzman, Sam. 1984. "Toward a More General Theory of Regulation." *Journal of Law and Economics* **19**: 211–40.

Posner, Richard A. 1974. "Theories of Economic Regulation." *Bell Journal of Economics* **5**: 335–58.

Shepsle, Kenneth A., and Barry R. Weingast. 1981. "Political Preferences for the Pork Barrel: A Generalization." *American Journal of Political Science* **25**: 96–112.

Shepsle, Kenneth A., and Barry R. Weingast. 1994. "Positive Theories of Congressional Institutions." *Legislative Studies Quarterly* **19**: 149–79.

Stavins, Robert N. 2004. *The Political Economy of Environmental Regulation.* Cheltenham: Edward Elgar.

Sumner, Daniel. 2007. "Farm Subsidy Tradition and Modern Agricultural Realities." Paper prepared for American Enterprise Institute project on Agricultural Policy for the 2007 Farm Bill and Beyond.

Tiebout, Charles M. 1956. "A Pure Theory of Local Expenditures." *Journal of Political Economy* **64**: 416–24.

Tullock, Gordon. 1967. "The Welfare Costs of Tariffs, Monopolies and Theft." *Western Economic Journal* **5**: 224–32.

Wittman, Donald A. 1989. "Pressure Group Size and the Politics of Income Redistribution." *Social Choice and Welfare* **6**: 275–86.

Wittman, Donald A. 1995. *The Myth of Democratic Failure: Why Democracies are Efficient.* Chicago: University of Chicago Press.

Wittman, Donald. 2007. "Candidate Quality, Pressure Group Endorsements and the Nature of Political Advertising." *European Journal of Political Economy* **23**: 360–78.

Wittman, Donald. Forthcoming. "How Campaign Endorsements Activate Uninformed Voters." *Economic Journal.*

SEVEN

Public Choice: A Critical Reassessment

Jessica Leight

INTRODUCTION

The school of thought broadly known as public choice, emphasizing the pervasiveness of self-interested behavior in government, the capture of the state by private interests, and thus the pernicious influence of the government's role in the economy, has now been ascendant in academia for several decades. Arguments emphasizing the failures of government dominate the majority of both theoretical and empirical work undertaken in a variety of fields. On the other hand, studies that analyze or even define cases of policymaking success, or offer a theoretical rationale for government action, particularly in the economic realm, are rare and receive relatively little attention.

Accordingly, the dominant impression gleaned by the layman and the specialist alike is that a fairly wide consensus has been reached and the debate concluded: scholars have a clear and accurate understanding of the fundamental mechanisms of the operation of government and its intervention in the economy, as well as the consequences of that intervention. It is the contention of this chapter that, on the contrary, the dominant literature has ignored important critiques of the public choice theory of policymaking that highlight major weaknesses of the theory. Taken together, these critiques deserve far more attention than they have received.

Far from being a minor academic controversy, the validity or lack thereof of public choice is centrally important, shaping our views about the most fundamental of questions: not what the government should do to correct a perceived deficiency in the polity or economy, but whether the government has a role in resolving collective dilemmas at all. Thus rigorously theorizing and testing models of policymaking and the economic role of the state remains a crucial unfinished research agenda.

ORIGINS OF PUBLIC CHOICE

The debate over the economic potential of government began as a debate over the failings of the market, as a significant body of research into its flaws emerged for the first time in late-nineteenth century continental Europe. The first major conceptual innovation was the idea of "public goods," originally developed by economists Ugo Mazzola, Knut Wicksell, and Eric Lindahl. This paved the way for the landmark article by Paul Samuelson (Samuelson 1954) arguing that in the case of goods – such as clean air or national defense – that are jointly consumed by all without exclusion, the market level of provision will be inefficiently low. In the 1920s, A. C. Pigou launched a related strand of analysis, defining the economic importance of externalities and arguing that government taxes or subsidies could be used to correct divergences between the public and private rates of return. Subsequently, scholars analyzing the sources of potential market failures increasingly turned their attention to the role of government in regulating natural monopolies and the implications of informational imperfections for the operation of markets.

Broadly speaking, these theories identified various circumstances in which the market might prove inadequate to achieve collective goals – the provision of public goods, the existence of externalities, the presence of natural monopolies and an absence of adequate information – and argued that the government could effectively play a role in correcting these failures. However, these various strands of analysis never constituted a coherent or self-identified school of thought or intellectual movement. As Michael Hantke-Domas points out, "no author has claimed intellectual ascendancy over the public interest theory, nor have they mentioned any author or supporter of it... the Public Interest Theory does not have any known origin" (Hantke-Domas 2003, 166). "Public interest" was a term that originally had deep roots in political and legal discourse, particularly among reformers. In its new incarnation, however, it became a label that public choice theorists retrospectively, and critically, bestowed on this collection of approaches to market failure and government intervention. This is not to suggest that theories of regulation as a mechanism to correct market failure did not exist. In the aftermath of the New Deal, such theories were influential and arguably dominant, both in economics and in political science, sociology, and law. Yet public interest as we now refer to it only became a significant and recognizable school within the social sciences after a new wave of academic analysis took the initiative to name its conceptual forerunners.

Public choice, by contrast, emerged as a coherent, self-conscious intellectual movement and so has grown into maturity with a significant complement of intellectual historians who chronicle its origins and growth. Such historians generally highlight the founding theoretical contributions as those of Duncan Black (1948), Anthony Downs (1957), and James Buchanan and George Tullock (1962). Equally important, however, were a series of empirical works published in the same period that analyzed the impact of existing regulatory policies and found them to be inefficient, oblivious to the impact of ongoing technological change, and welfare-decreasing.[1] Rather than enhancing the public welfare, existing forms of regulation appeared only to reinforce the power of existing cartels or oligopolies. These research findings presented researchers with an obvious question: If regulation was not serving the public interest, whose interest was it serving, and why? This became a central preoccupation of public choice theory.

The two key early lodes of public choice work were the Center for Study of Public Choice, now at George Mason University, and the University of Chicago economics department, with notable outposts also to be found at the University of Rochester and Indiana University-Bloomington (Mitchell 1988). Chicago and Virginia continue to be principal centers of public choice work and the intellectual homes of its most distinguished proponents, though the work of scholars at the two universities reflects different emphases. Primarily trained in political science, with the notable exception of Buchanan, public choice scholars at Virginia have developed a detailed theory of political motivation, mechanisms of collective decision making and the potential flaws of those mechanisms, while devoting less attention to particular policies that the political process might generate (Romer 1988). By contrast, the Chicago school is composed principally of economists, focused on identifying socioeconomic inputs of interests or demands and evaluating the form and impact of government intervention in the economy (outputs), without emphasizing the conversion process by which interest groups obtain the policies they seek (Mitchell 1989).

As a rule, the Chicago scholars do not emphasize their intellectual ties to earlier public choice theorists and the Virginia school. However, their account of politics as an economic marketplace, essential to their theories of regulation, reflects their connections to the work of the Virginians. Moreover, the two groups have been united by a certain self-conscious spirit of

---

[1] These include Meyer et al. (1959) on railroads, buses and trucking, Caves (1962) on airlines, MacAvoy (1965) and Kolko (1965) on railroads, and MacAvoy and Sloss (1967), Friedlaender (1969) and Harbeson (1969) again on transportation.

rebellion against the perceived dominance, both in the academy and in government, of what they contemptuously deemed public interest analysis. In 1965, Stigler declared that "Pigou's views of the competence of the state were, like his predecessors' views, a tolerably random selection of the immediately previous views, warmed by hope" (Stigler 1965). James Buchanan was no less sweeping in his characterizations, arguing that the prevailing mindset in the 1950s "was socialist in its underlying presupposition that the government offered the solution to social problems" and that inevitably led to the overreaching and failure of governments in the 1960s and '70s (Buchanan 2003). In the following analysis, I will note at some points a divergence in the analytical approaches adopted by what are frequently considered to be the "classic" public choice theorists, and the Chicago scholars and their successors, many of whom are more frequently associated with the economic theory of regulation. Despite these differences, considering them together is appropriate for two reasons. First, public choice as a school clearly considers the work of Stigler and his successors to be part of their canon, even if Stigler et al. do not explicitly identify themselves in this manner;[2] and second, these authors share many of the same fundamental assumptions about politics, market failure, and government failure that I wish to analyze here.

THE DOMINANCE OF PUBLIC CHOICE

One can see the profoundly deep imprint of public choice as a framework for analysis of the modern state in three areas that public choice has devoted itself assiduously to exploring: mechanisms of collective choice; the behavior of voters; and the causes and consequences of government intervention in the market. In each case, the direction of current academic writing embraces the key assumption that government frequently acts as a perverse mechanism for wealth transfers, yielding policies that benefit select interest groups but are detrimental to the public welfare. The following three sections will outline the current state of research in each of these areas. Subsequently, I will consider criticisms of public choice. A final section evaluates the state of the field as a whole, offering an initial hypothesis as to why public choice has

---

[2] Robert Tollison, a leading public choice researcher based at the center at George Mason, characterizes the work of the Chicago political economists as "the Chicago version of the modern development of public choice theory." He argues that the principal theory of economic regulation at the time of Stigler's first paper, the Pigovian or public interest theory, was "already under heavy assault from earlier contributions to public choice theory by Buchanan, Tullock and others" and now has been virtually discredited, while the interest group theory "has accumulated widespread recognition" (Tollison 1989, 295).

remained so clearly dominant, despite the profusion of largely unanswered criticisms.

MECHANISMS OF COLLECTIVE CHOICE

Anthony Downs launched public choice as a coherent school with his *An Economic Theory of Democracy*, published in 1957, thereby becoming the first scholar to articulate three central postulates of public choice political analysis. First, voters making political decisions seek to maximize the utility they glean from the political process. Second, lawmakers seek to maximize the votes they obtain, and thus carry out "those acts of spending which gain the most votes by means of those acts of financing which lose the fewest votes" (Downs 1957, 52). Third, given that voting and informing oneself about policy are both costly, and the benefit derived from an individual vote is virtually zero, it is rational for voters to remain ignorant about public policy. All of these postulates were, at the time, relatively new in political analysis, and they were at least partially inspired by Kenneth Arrow's then-recently established "impossibility theorem." These two works served to launch a research agenda that reexamined the operation of mechanisms of collective choice, applying techniques for analyzing the behavior of individuals in markets to the study of politics. Also important in this period was the pioneering work done by Ronald Coase reanalyzing Pigou's problem of externalities, which concludes that establishing property rights and creating a market for such rights would more efficiently address externalities than direct intervention by the government (Coase 1959; Coase 1960). Coase's work served to introduce the question of whether and in what circumstances the unanticipated costs associated with regulatory action might be worse than the socioeconomic problem it sought to correct.

The true bible of public choice, James Buchanan and Gordon Tullock's *The Calculus of Consent*, was published later in the decade. Buchanan and Tullock highlighted the congruence between the individual as "economic actor," a trope that has long been the preoccupation of economic theory, and the individual as a political actor participating in collective decision-making processes. "No one seems to have explored carefully," they pointed out,

... the implicit assumption that the individual must somehow shift his psychological and moral gears when he moves between the private and social aspects of life. We are, therefore, placed in the somewhat singular position of having to defend the simple assumption that the same individual participates in both processes against the almost certain onslaught of the moralists. (Buchanan and Tullock 1962, 20)

Despite this call to equate political and economic man, Buchanan and Tullock did note that it was not necessary to conclude that exactly the same imperatives governed individuals in social choice as in individual choice. A similar point had been made by Buchanan even earlier (Buchanan, 1954), when he outlined a series of differences between economic and political behavior. Nonetheless, subsequent scholarship frequently ignored these qualifications.

Following Buchanan and Tullock, George Stigler furnished the next notable advance in public choice and the first volley in the Chicago school's contribution to it. In his foundational article on the theory of economic regulation in 1971, Stigler applied the political economy framework of Buchanan and Tullock to the analysis of the formation of regulatory policy via the interaction of those groups that desire (and pay for) regulatory policy and the legislators who supply it. Stigler contended that "the problem of regulation is the problem of discovering when and why an industry (or other group of like-minded people) is able to use the state for its purposes," and defined the terms of the exchange to be such that an industry receives one of four things – direct subsidies, control over entry, control over substitutes and complements, or price-fixing – in return for providing a political party what it wants, namely money and votes (Stigler 1971, 4). This basic model was then further elaborated, refined, and formalized by Peltzman (1976) and Becker (1983). Peltzman focused on the relationship between the size of an interest group, its informational and organizational costs, and the gains it obtained from the political process, arguing that smaller groups would be more likely to win rents from the government since they face a less severe collective action problem in organizing their members (an insight originally articulated by Mancur Olson). Subsequently, Becker's analysis modeled the policymaking process as one of competition for policies between interest groups with opposing policy goals and differential abilities to capture policymakers.

INTEREST GROUPS, LEGISLATORS, AND REGULATORS

Drawing on the conceptual framework of these seminal scholars, a number of other authors developed somewhat more specific or detailed accounts of the intervention of interest groups in economic policymaking (McKenzie and Macaulay 1980; Barke and Riker 1982; Becker 1985; Ellig 1991). A second strand of the literature examined the role of legislators as the nexus of the political marketplace (Kalt and Zupan 1984; Maloney, McCormick, and Tollison 1984; Crain, Tollison, and Leavens 1988; Tollison 1988). Subsequent work on the executive and judicial branches argued that both of these institutions serve to provide more durable forms of protection to interest groups, for which they are willing to pay a higher price (Landes and Posner 1975; Crain and Tollison 1979a, 1979b). In addition, the preoccupation with assessing the legislative supply and demand process suggested the importance of examining campaign contributions, given that they are the analogue to the price paid for the policy desired, and this generated a robust literature that sought to model the determinants and the impact of both campaign contributions and lobbying expenditures.[3]

Scholars remained divided, however, as to whether it was legislators, bureaucrats, or some other agent who were the targets of interest group blandishments and thus the pivotal actors in shaping the state's intervention in the economy. Stigler suggested that industries seeking regulatory action of some kind must pay tribute to the political party in power, whereas Peltzman noted the problem of separation of agency between elected officials and bureaucrats but concluded that the two could reasonably be considered to be equivalent, given the political dynamics of appointments. Weingast and Moran (1983) and Weingast (1984) argued there was systematic congressional influence over regulatory commission decisions, but McCubbins, Noll, and Weingast (1987, 1989) contended that there exists a principal–agent problem between legislators and bureaucrats, and the former does not have a perfect ability to control the latter.

Subsequent empirical work divided between efforts to demonstrate interest group influence over legislators and attempts to document influence over bureaucrats. Becker (1983) cited as evidence for the contention that interest groups purchase policies two studies[4] analyzing the funding of political campaigns, which he presumably views as a mechanism for establishing control over legislators. Becker (1986) likewise applied the analysis of the influence of competing interest groups to legislators, and the theme of legislative self-interest was echoed by Abrams and Settle in their studies of campaign finance reform (1978, 2004). At the same time, there is a strain of literature that instead attempted to provide evidence of the capture of unelected regulators, suggesting that the object of analytical focus should be bureaucrats rather than – or in addition to – elected officials.[5] A final strand

---

[3] See for example Austen-Smith 1987 and 1997; Baron 1989; Ben-Zion and Eytan 1974; Besley and Coate 2001; Lohmann 1995; Snyder 1990; Welch 1974 and 1980.

[4] Jacobson 1979; Palda 1975.

[5] See for example Besley and Coate (2003); Caudill et al. (1993); Eckert (1973); Hazlett (1990); Hilton (1972); Kaserman et al. (1984); Olson (1995); Russell and Shelton (1974); Toma (1983).

of literature directly modeled the interaction between interest groups, a regulatory agency, and a political principal (Baron 1988; Spiller 1990; Laffont and Tirole 1991; Martimort 1999). Most recently, there has been a new wave of scholarly interest in the formal modeling of capture, drawing on game theory and often using mathematical frameworks far more sophisticated than those employed in the earlier scholarship on the subject. This work includes Grossman and Helpman (1994), Martimort (1996), Martimort (1999), Laffont and Martimort (1999), Bardhan and Mookherjee (2000), and Willenborg (2000).

In all of this large and diverse set of works analyzing policymaking processes and their implications for government economic interventions, the focus remains interest groups and their interactions with legislators; public choice scholars generally, though not uniformly, exclude voters from the frame of analysis. In fact, this is entirely logical, given that the dominant theory of voter behavior within public choice has hypothesized that voters will rationally remove themselves from an influential role in the policymaking process, thus making possible the brazen operation of interest groups. I will analyze this literature on voting in the next section.

VOTERS AND RATIONAL IGNORANCE

One of the pillars of the political analysis of public choice is the rationally ignorant voter: interest groups can exert an outsized influence on the operation of government because voters know nothing about their depredations and have no incentives to attempt to stop them given the high cost of informed participation. Without this assumption, the conceptual architecture of the public choice account of the policymaking process would be seriously weakened. Accordingly, the motif of the rationally ignorant or rationally abstaining voter, which scholars often refer to as the rational choice model of voter behavior, frequently recurs in public choice research.

The basic principle of the voter as a rational, strategic decisionmaker was first advanced by Downs, who argued that given the high cost of information and the low expected return, the rational decision for voters is to remain uninformed. The problem, of course, is that a voter's level of relevant information is virtually impossible to observe. Analysts soon realized, however, that a virtually identical collective action argument could be applied to the decision to vote itself, characterized by high costs and a low expected return given the minimal incidence of an individual voter's decision in the overall voting process.

Riker and Ordeshook (1968) formalized this insight into a simple model. Voters will vote if the gain is greater than the cost, where the gain is defined as a postulated consumption benefit from voting C, plus the expected benefit from casting the decisive vote for a winning candidate. However, other scholars pointed out that the probability of casting the decisive vote in most elections is tiny (Beck 1975; Chamberlain and Rothschild 1981; Margolis 1977) and the potential costs diverse, including the opportunity cost of time required, transportation expenses, the transaction costs of registering, and a number of other potential inconveniences (Knack 1993; Rosenstone and Wolfinger 1978; Tollison and Willett 1973). Given these assumptions, a low-turnout voter equilibrium appears to be the only reasonable prediction, although it clearly contradicted available evidence. Accordingly, public choice scholars acknowledged the low-turnout equilibrium predicted by their models of voter decision to be an empirical failure (Brennan and Buchanan 1984; Hardin 1982; and Tullock 1967).

This problem of explaining the behavior of the voter – particularly the stubborn fact of reasonably high turnout – generated a vast literature from scholars of many persuasions across several disciplines, principally seeking to tweak the Rider-Ordeshook model by redefining the various terms, and to evaluate empirically what factors are the most accurate predictors of turnout.[6] The rather dispiriting mismatch between the Downsian-derived theory of voter behavior and the everyday fact of voting in elections served to generate an entire subfield within political science devoted to attempting to develop a cogent explanation of turnout, a debate that still continues. Yet at the same time the broader field has pursued a variety of different analytical and empirical strategies to explain turnover, public choice scholars continue

---

[6] Downs and Stigler (1972) argued that the probability that a vote was influential was higher than infinitesimal. Niemi (1976); Uhlaner (1989); Hinich (1981); Brunk (1980); Blais et al. (2000); and Feddersen and Sandroni (2001) focused on redefining the consuption term. Ledyard (1981, 1984), Owen and Grofman (1984), Palfrey and Rosenthal (1983, 1985) and Myerson (1988) sought to endogenize the probability a vote was decisive using game-theoretic models. Morton (1981, 1991), Shachar and Nalebuff (1999) and Feddersen (2004) developed group-based theories of turnout. A vast array of studies empirically test for a relationship between the perceived closeness of an election and turnout, or between cost and benefit and turnout: See for example Barzel and Silberberg (1973); Ashenfelter and Kelley (1975); Silberman and Durden (1975); Smith (1975); Tollison et al. (1975); Settle and Abrams (1976); Frohlich et al. (1978); Rosenstone and Wolfinger (1978); Powell (1980); Filer and Kenny (1980); Rubinfeld and Thomas (1980); Sanders (1980); Crewe (1981); Thompson (1982); Bennett and Orzechowski (1983); Foster (1984); Darvish and Rosenberg (1988); Colomer (1991); Knack (1993, 1994); Heckelman (1995); Matsumaka (1995); and Blais (2000).

to use the theory of rationally ignorant voters to buttress conclusions about the operation of the policymaking process.

THE STATE AND THE MARKET

A third substantial body of literature in the broader public choice canon seeks to analyze the causes and consequences of government intervention in the economy. This work rounds out the earlier, more theoretical contributions by providing an overview of the potential consequences of the perversions of policymaking by interest groups. Within this family of empirical articles on regulation, the first wave focused largely on linking public choice theory to specific case studies, providing a descriptive account of existing regulatory regimes that, as predicted by the theory, largely benefited the industries they were designed to control; the most commonly cited case studies assessed regulatory policy in trucking, airlines, railroads, taxis, and telecommunications.[7] These articles generally lacked formal empirical testing and failed to engage in any systematic search for disconfirming evidence. At times, the historical analysis seemed strongly guided by, if not dictated by, the expectations of the theory, as demonstrated in one recent analysis that criticizes Hazlett's argument regarding the determinants of the decisions of the Federal Radio Commission and presents a range of contrasting evidence (Moss and Lackow 2007). This strain of analysis was also challenged by several additional case studies that detailed instances in which commissions were not dominated by the industries they regulated.[8]

A second set of studies analyzed the operation of regulation in given industries in order to demonstrate prejudicial impact to consumers or the public welfare, usually in the form of higher prices, higher profits, or more limited competition, again largely focusing on the same handful of industries. Joskow and Rose (1989) furnish an excellent overview of these studies, including their methodological approaches and the various questions they addressed. As they note, Bernstein (1952) was the first to publish a general study of regulatory commissions, arguing that they were subservient to the regulated industries. This was the starting gun for an

---

[7] This includes Adams (1982); Benson (2002); Ellig (1991); Hammond and Knott (1988); Hazlett (1990); Hilton (1972); Huntington (1952); Kitch, Isaacson and Kasper (1971).

[8] Berry (1984) cites numerous studies in this regard, including Anderson (1981); Culhane (1981); Katzman (1980); Meier and Plumlee (1978); Sanders (1981); Welborn and Brown (1979); Wilson (1980).

enormous literature that examined in detail utilities,[9] banking,[10] trucking and freight,[11] railroads,[12] airlines,[13] and pharmaceuticals.[14] There was also a substantial body of work examining regulation of a range of lesser-known industries.[15] In this enormous literature, the vast majority of studies confirmed the Stiglerian public choice hypothesis of regulation as a mechanism to distribute rents to powerful interest groups, with only a handful of dissenters.[16] The conclusion was similar to that drawn above: the negative welfare consequences of regulation, whatever their manifestation, are presented as evidence of the flaws inherent in, and particularly the interest-group dominance of, the policymaking process.

A third important area of empirical work examined regulation at the state (or provincial) level. Here, researchers sought to take advantage of the natural experiment that states can provide. Given that they frequently face similar regulatory dilemmas, comparing fifty responses in fifty different institutional contexts offers considerable scope for analytical advances. In contrast to the previously cited studies that generally inferred conclusions about the nature of the policymaking process from an observation of the

---

[9] See for example Demsetz (1968); Gerwig (1962); MacAvoy (1971); MacAvoy and Pindyck (1973).

[10] See for example Black and Strahan (2001); Edwards and Edwards (1974); Peltzman (1965).

[11] See for example Annable (1973); Daniel and Kleit (1995); Farris (1969); Frew (1981); Gellman (1971); Kim (1984); Moore (1978); Noll (1971); Jordan (1972); Prager (1989); Rose (1985, 1987); Sloss (1970).

[12] See for example Boyer (1987); Braeutigam and Noll (1984); Golbe (1983); Keeler (1983); Spann and Erickson (1970); Zerbe (1980).

[13] See for example Hendricks et al. (1980); Keeler (1972); Olson and Trapani (1981); Graham et al. (1983).

[14] See for example Danzon and Chao (2000); Grabowski, Vernon and Thomas (1978).

[15] Other industries studied include milk (Brinegar 1957; Carter 1957; Ippolito and Masson 1978; Kessel 1967; Masson and DeBrock 1980), automobile safety regulation (Peltzman 1975), electricity (Jarrell 1978; Joskow et al. 1989; Sampson 1958; White et al. 1996), motor carriers (Carter 1958; Maxwell 1960), automobile distribution (Smith 1982), insurance (Frech and Samprone 1980; Ippolito 1979), dry-cleaning (Plott 1965), hospitals (Sloan and Steinwald 1980), television (Comanor and Mitchell 1972; Crandall 1972; Crawford 2000; Fournier and Martin 1983; Krattenmaker and Powe 1994; Webbink 1973), mining (Kalt 1983), and medicine and its various subspecialties (DeVany, Gramm, Saving, and Smithson 1982; Haas-Wilson 1987; Kleiner and Kudrle 2000; Paul 1982; Shepard 1978). Similar analyses were extended to the realm of nonindustry-specific "social regulation." Ackerman and Hassler 1981, Crandall 1983, and Magat et al. 1986 analyzed environmental regulation, Bartel and Thomas (1987) examined occupational safety and environmental regulations, and Morrison et al. (1999) evaluated airplane noise controls.

[16] These are Edwards and Edwards (1974) on banking, Schwert (1977) on securities regulation, Leffler (1978) on medicine, Levin (1978) on surface freight regulation, Ippolito (1979) on insurance, Zerbe (1980) on the regulation of short-haul rail freight, Mayo and Otsuka (1991) on cable television, and Kridel et al. (1996) on telecommunications.

policies it generates and their economic impact, these articles attempted to examine directly those factors relevant to the formation of regulatory policy, particularly the role of interest groups.

Cross-state analyses performed along these lines have yielded mixed results as to the determinants of regulatory policy. In his seminal 1971 article, Stigler found the relative political influence of different professions to be positively correlated to the stringency of licensing laws. A number of subsequent articles similarly found that the strength of interest groups predicted regulatory outcomes.[17] On the other hand, a second group of studies found that institutional variables (such as government autonomy, resources, and ideology) as well as the power of interest groups determine regulatory outcomes in electricity, labor disputes, and telecommunications, respectively.[18] Most usefully, Gerber and Teske (2000) and Teske (2003) provided exhaustive overviews of a massive literature on regulatory outcomes in states that categorize a wide variety of studies (forty-eight in the first article and ten in the second) according to the explanatory variables they consider, which include the strength of interest groups, the characteristics of the elected legislators, bureaucratic or institutional characteristics, and economic and demographic variables. Their findings demonstrate that a wide variety of factors have been identified as significant in explaining regulatory outcomes, including variables in each of the broad categories cited above.

In a sense, such a conclusion may be so general as to seem not particularly illuminating. It does, however, suggest that a theory of some complexity may be needed in order to accurately match the richness of the empirical data, and raises some questions as to whether one that hypothesizes interest groups as the sole (or dominant) determinant of political decision making has sufficient predictive capacity, given the abundance of studies that identify other variables as significant in explaining political outcomes.

CRITICISMS OF PUBLIC CHOICE

As public choice theory has matured and increased in influence, it has attracted a number of important criticisms, both in terms of its theoretical

---

[17] See for example Caudill et al. (1993); Howard (1998); Kaserman et al. (1993); Kroszner and Strahan (1999); Teske et al. (1994); Williams and Matheny (1984). Becker (1986) found professionals less successful at winning stringent licensing laws when overall voter participation was higher.

[18] See for example Anderson (1981); Berry (1979); Berry (1984); Moe (1985); Teske (1991); Welborn and Brown (1979).

conceptualization and its empirical support. These objections center on three central points. First, the claim that utility maximization is the central motivation of political actors lacks coherence. Second, the meaning of capture, clearly a crucial analytical element of the public choice account of collective decision making, remains unclear. Third, the theory has weak empirical foundations and little predictive power.

MAXIMIZING WHAT?

The public choice theory of politics manifests a fundamental ambiguity about the definition of utility and the utility-maximizing impulse that supposedly underlies all political motivations, a flaw that Green and Shapiro analyze as the competition between "thin" and "thick" accounts of individual rationality. Thin rational accounts of political actors suggest only that they should "efficiently employ the means available to achieve their ends" or maximize their utility. Thick-rational accounts make more specific assumptions about the content of that utility, and, in the context of models of political behavior, typically emphasize money, reelection, and the holding of political office. Green and Shapiro note that rational choice theorists vary in the type of rationality they assume, and there is frequently ambiguity about the type of rationality that is required to support a given conclusion (Green and Shapiro 1994).

I would suggest, however, that this critique is only part of the story. The analytical flaw, and rhetorical advantage, of public choice theory is that it claims to require only utility maximization – a definition of individual behavior so flexible and capacious that it remains impervious to contravening evidence – but invokes various forms of thick rationality in practice. As Kelman puts it, "the general public choice notion that public leaders (whether elected or appointed) seek to maximize anything resembling a narrowly specified wealth function is likewise hard to defend unless put in nonfalsifiable form (i.e., incorporating all ideological and desire-for-service variables within the selfish utility function)" (Kelman 1988, 217–18). In fact, when outlining their theory of political motivation, public choice theorists do employ precisely such "nonfalsifiable" formulations, and they defend them easily. In their empirical analysis, however, they routinely equate utility with votes, reelection, or money, an elision that receives no defense and frequently not even any explicit acknowledgment. The ambiguity on this point is not incidental, but central to the theory's appeal: it serves to obscure a major, and potentially unresolvable, contradiction.

In their original works, Downs and Buchanan-Tullock appear to advocate a thin-rational account of human behavior, arguing that a model of individuals interacting in accordance with their specific preferences is useful to analyze exchange in both the political and economic realms, but specifically noting that they do not assume identical preferences in economic and political decision making. These carefully parsed statements offer considerable room for analytical flexibility. However, the implicit assumptions used to sustain the central conclusions of public choice theory are in fact far stronger than these statements would suggest and more difficult to defend in analyses of both political actors and voters. Here, I will outline the operation of differing concepts of utility in each separately.

First, consider the analysis of political actors within the government, whether legislators or regulators. Stigler does not even address the conundrum of defining utility, simply asserting that industries pay political parties with votes and resources (Stigler 1971, 12). Becker, on the other hand, employs the same general formulation favored by Buchanan and Tullock, stating that "political choices are determined by the efforts of individuals and groups to further their own interests" (Becker 1983, 371). Such a statement seems unimpeachably plausible, yet it is also vague. Clearly, a more specific account of political motivation underpins the analysis that follows. Interest groups undertake expenditures on "maintaining a lobby, attracting favorable votes, issuing pamphlets, contributing to campaign expenditures, cultivating bureaucrats and politicians," and all of this activity somehow increases the utility of the policymaker and induces his or her cooperation (Becker 1983, 377). There is no obvious reason to rule out the presumption that some interest groups or legislators view emotional commitments, or ideology, or the considered recommendations of policy experts, as one element of their motivational calculation. However, public choice scholars routinely ignore this possibility. As Croley puts it, "the legislator motivation claim is similarly indispensable to the interest group theory's capture vision. Were legislators by and large immune to interest groups' regulatory preferences, it would not matter much how lopsided interest-group activity was" (Croley 1988, 16).

There are, of course, works that do apply a more sophisticated theory of political motivation. Niskanen in his classic work on bureaucracy argues that bureaucrats' core objective is the maximization of their budget (Niskanen 1971), and the budgetary-maximizing objective was subsequently employed by, among others, Laffont and Tirole (1991). De Alessi (1974), Russell and Shelton (1974), Evans and Gerber (1988), and Grossman and Helpman (1996) likewise employ more complex objective functions for the regulator that balance interest group interests and consumer interests, or the demand of multiple interest groups.

However, most public choice analyses follow the example of Stigler, Becker, Tollison, and other "founders" of public choice, employing a certain degree of analytical subterfuge. The most common maneuver is to assert the broadest and most unobjectionable theory of political behavior – utility maximization – while implicitly assuming a much more specific, and questionable, account without any explicit justification. Eckert, for example, argues that the regulator is a utility-maximizer, which he defines as "a function of numerous items such as his personal prestige, wealth, convenience, and working conditions"; however, he then tests the validity of his theory by conflating utility with money – an assumption likewise employed without any justification by McChesney (1987). This assertion appears problematic: it is only logical that individuals seeking solely to maximize their lifetime earnings might reasonably be expected to select a field other than politics initially (Kelman 1988). Brock and Magee (1978), Barke and Riker (1982), and Abrams and Settle (1986, 2004), on the other hand, equate utility with reelection in their analysis without even noting the potential implausibility of this assumption. First, it is contradicted by the evidence of voluntary retirement, and second, it begs the question of some more fundamental motivation. It is difficult to assert that politicians seek political office only to continually attempt to maximize their utility by remaining in office without specifying what exactly is to be gained from this status in the first place.[19]

The problem is neatly summarized by Wilson, who notes that theorizing that politicians' or regulators' behavior serves "personal interests" represents a trivial and "nearly useless" interpretation of the theory (Wilson 1980, 361). In this sense, everyone's behavior serves his or her perceived personal interests, somehow defined, all the time. The theory may be true, but it is of little interest and has no predictive power. However, the various attempts by public choice scholars to narrow their analytical focus to money or reelection have serious limitations. A more realistic account of political behavior, more specific than utility maximization, must inevitably concede that political actors are driven by a spectrum of often changing motivations, personal, ideological, and pecuniary.

Even public choice theorists themselves appear at times not to find this account of political motivation particularly convincing. The most frequent

---

[19] As already noted, Stigler simply defines parties to be seeking money and votes, an assumption echoed by Peltzman (1976) and applied to all "regulators," not merely parties. Although implicitly suggesting that political actors are motivated by money and reelection, the two authors seem to be open to both sets of criticisms, in that neither half of their utility formulation is particularly cogent.

stumbling block, somewhat ironically, is their own policy success. The legislative embrace of deregulation after the economic shocks of the 1970s largely followed the policymaking dynamics that David Moss and Mary Oey discuss in their essay on "The Paranoid Style in the Study of American Politics." Together, a widely perceived crisis, a set of ideas that offered plausible solutions to that crisis – public choice – and the presence of effective political entrepreneurs overcame the political power of established interests. However, public choice theory itself offers little room for this type of intellectual influence over policymakers, given that their presumed sources of utility admit of no mechanism by which theory might shape policy. As Tollison stated bluntly in his analysis of Chicago political economy, "another strand of argument... mostly associated with Stigler is that ideas do not matter" (Tollison 1989, 295). In 1978, Buchanan had likewise rather dourly suggested that "government failure against standard efficiency norms may be demonstrated, analytically and empirically, but I see no basis for the faith that such demonstrations will magically produce institutional reform" (Buchanan 1978, 368).

Yet the triumph of deregulation, proudly claimed by Tullock, among others, as a public choice achievement and acknowledged as pivotal by a number of analysts of the deregulation movement, demonstrates that ideas can indeed make a difference (Crew and Rowley 1988; Derthick and Quirk 1985; Joskow and Noll 1981; Pasour 1992; Tullock 1988). Michael Levine, Roger Noll, and Peltzman himself noted that deregulation was a heavy blow to public choice (Levine 1981; Peltzman et al. 1989). Many other theorists, however, seemed to remain blithely unaware of their predicament.

The example of deregulation effectively encapsulates the central criticism of the public choice theory of political motivation. Politicians may gain utility from monetary advantage or reelection, to be sure, but any assertion that these goals exhaust their objectives immediately runs up against major conceptual challenges. If we wish to follow the summons of the public choice or rational choice theorists and treat political behavior like economic behavior and political actors like economic actors, we should acknowledge the obvious. Individuals operating in the market gain utility from a variety of different sources beyond the purely pecuniary, and it is perfectly reasonable to conclude that individuals as politicians will be driven by a similarly diverse range of motivations.

The public choice account of the voter's utility-maximization calculus similarly manifests a divergence between the capaciously broad models of the voter's rationality, and the very specific (and again, often acknowledged) assumptions about voter behavior that sustain public choice accounts of policymaking. As has already been outlined, theorists' responses to the empirical failings of the Rider-Ordeshook cost–benefit account of the voting decision have been to stretch the definitions of the costs and benefits in every possible direction so as to match the available evidence that many people vote, but not all. As Aldrich put it, "There is a genuine danger that interpreting cost and benefit terms broadly will make the rational choice explanation tautological. If everything is a cost or benefit, then the theory predicts everything, which is the same as predicting nothing" (Aldrich 1993, 275). Green and Shapiro likewise argue that public choice scholars stretch the theory of strategic voting to such an extent that it becomes impossible to falsify, noting that any observation could be consistent with "a theoretical framework that allows for post hoc insertion of idiosyncratic tastes, beliefs and probability assessments as explanatory devices" (Green and Shapiro 1994, 69). Ultimately, rational choice voting theory seems to argue that those who perceive the benefits to be greater than the costs vote – not a particularly illuminating insight.

For all the power of these criticisms, yet another important dimension of public choice's conceptual fuzziness has not been sufficiently acknowledged. The literature on voter behavior has continued to alter, and at times painfully twist, its basic model to fit the empirical evidence. However, the account that underlies the enormously influential public choice analyses of the policymaking process remains the original Downsian collective-action theory that predicts rational ignorance on the basis of a simple cost–benefit analysis. This analytical framework, applied to the decision of whether to vote, has already been deemed inadequate to explain the phenomenon of turnout at any level above an extremely low one; indeed, this predictive failure is precisely what motivated the subsequent research. Voters, at least some of them, do vote, and thus disprove the collective action dilemma account of turnout – thus suggesting the need for a much more nuanced understanding of the psychological impulse toward cooperation evidenced in voting, as argued in Benkler's contribution to this volume. In the meantime, however, noting the failure of the cost–benefit collective action argument in the case of explaining voter turnout, there seems to be no reason to conclude on the basis of the hypothesized existence of a similar dilemma that they must necessarily be rationally ignorant.

Nonetheless, public choice continues to rely on the rational ignorance assumption either explicitly (recall Becker's assertion of the irrelevance of voters for his analysis) or implicitly, when an analysis of voters is frequently excluded from an account of the interaction of interest groups and legislators that yields policy outcomes. This assumption is visible in much of the theoretical work already cited,[20] including as well as an enormous empirical literature that seeks to evaluate interest group influence over legislators' votes. As Shughart et al. state, "The discussion of the political process tends to be carried out in terms of the interests of groups within the polity that either demand or supply wealth, and those of the legislators who broker the transfers" (Shughart et al. 1986, 962). In a sense, then, the body of public choice literature on rational voting is not only flawed in itself. It also appears to serve as a screen of sorts for the fact that the essential theory of voter behavior relied on by the field has not changed since Downs – and that theory rests on extremely shaky empirical foundations.

DECONSTRUCTING CAPTURE

"Capture" is a pervasive, if sometimes implicit, concept in public choice theories of regulation, a conceptual summary of all things perverse in economic policymaking. Why is regulation bad? In a word, capture. However, the economic theory regarding the influence of interest groups over the formation of government policy – a school of thought variously called capture theory, primarily with reference to Stigler, or the interest group theory of government, primarily with reference to Peltzman and Becker, or the economic theory of regulation – has two principal flaws. First, despite the development of models of interest group operation broad enough to account for an abundance of influences on government decisions and a wide range of regulatory outcomes, the assumptions underlying the bulk of both theoretical and empirical work on this topic clearly, and often explicitly, reflect Stigler's original 1971 conclusion: the dominance of a single interest group of producers, with negative welfare implications for government intervention in the economy.[21] This is an assumption that is somewhat outmoded, if not discredited, and has been so virtually since Peltzman disowned it in 1976. Yet there is a disjuncture between the increasing sophistication of the modeling framework, broad enough to be difficult to criticize, and the persistent assumptions – highly specific, and certainly open to criticism – that nonetheless remain widely in evidence in the broader literature. Even as the capacity to predict has grown, there persists a strong tendency to

[20] See for example Barke and Riker (1982); Crain and Tollison (1979a, 1979b); Landes and Posner (1975); Peltzman (1976); Stigler (1971); Tollison (1988).

[21] See for example Abrams and Settle 2004; Bardhan and Mookherjee 2000; Barke and Riker 1982; Benson 2002; Coates 1995; Crew and Rowley 1988; Faure-Grimaud and Martimort 2003; Howard 1998; Jordan 1972; Krosner and Strahan 1999; Laffont and Martimot 1999; Martimort 1996; Martimort 1999; Teske 1991; Teske 2003; Williams and Matheny 1984.

presume the outcome of regulatory analyses based on widely shared, but not explicitly defended, assumptions.

Second, the fundamental concept that there is a mechanism by which interest groups establish influence over legislators or regulators rests on empirical foundations that, at this point, are still relatively weak. Every model in this field, from Stigler forward, relies on the postulation of some sort of relationship between an interest group and a regulator that impacts policy decisions in some specific way. However, a strong and comprehensive case outlining the type of evidence that would serve to confirm or disconfirm this hypothesis has not yet to emerge, and the existing literature addressing these questions suffers from some serious weaknesses. This point will be considered in the subsequent section on the empirical literature.

To begin with, consider the evolution of the concept of "capture."[22] Stigler provided a clear starting point in his analysis, with an unmistakable conclusion about the presence and negative implications of capture. Despite his endorsement elsewhere of the view that all observed economic phenomena are the outcome of the behavior of utility-maximizing individuals and therefore must be efficient (Stigler 1976), in this case he unequivocally maintains that the fundamental incentives embodied in the process of regulation make it welfare-decreasing. "The idealistic view of public regulation," Stigler argues,

is deeply imbedded in professional economic thought. So many economists, for example, have denounced the ICC for its pro-railroad policies that this has become a cliché of the literature. This criticism seems to me exactly as appropriate as a criticism of the Great Atlantic and Pacific Tea Company for selling groceries, or as a criticism of a politician for currying popular support... Until the basic logic of political life is developed, reformers will be ill-equipped to use the state for their reforms, and victims of the pervasive use of the state's support of special groups will be helpless to protect themselves. (Stigler 1971, 17–18)

Peltzman and Becker's theories of multiple interest group interaction, on the other hand, do not suggest any particularly obvious conclusion regarding the nature of regulatory policy generated by this process, the identity of its beneficiaries, or its welfare implications. Thus Becker observed that interest group competition could be efficient or nearly so, arguing that "policies that

---

[22] I will employ the term "capture theory" throughout the subsequent analysis to refer to Stigler, Peltzman, Becker and the later analyses of the operation of regulation cited here. Clearly, I recognize that some of these authors do not employ the concept or the term capture in the same way that Stigler does. However, I hope to make the case that this cluster of work has shared conceptual underpinnings justifying a common rubric.

raise efficiency are likely to win out in the competition for influence because they produce gains rather than deadweight costs, so that groups benefited have the intrinsic advantage compared to groups harmed" (Becker 1983, 396). In fact, this agnosticism about the efficiency implications of regulation has attracted criticism from scholars disposed toward a more robust condemnation of government interference (Benson 2002, Crew and Rowley 1988). Moreover, with the caveat that larger groups, such as various classes of consumers, may find it more difficult and expensive to organize, this analytical framework suggests a genuine indeterminacy regarding regulatory outcomes. Influence will be exerted by a variety of interest groups, including a range of different consumer and producer groups differentially affected by various proposals (including, for example, other sectors that supply or consume the inputs or outputs of the industry in question), and any one of them could potentially "win" depending on a host of organizational and political variables that scholars must specify and then measure. Such an account is broad enough to encompass many accounts of policymaking, and virtually any outcome: hence, perhaps, its appeal.

Yet the majority of subsequent work in this area, both theoretical and empirical, ignores this indeterminacy and take as preordained Stigler's conclusion about business "using" the state. Through thirty years of analytical work on this topic, the basic assumption that regulation will inevitably serve as an instrument for the most powerful interest group in the sector it administers remains pervasive, permeating both the empirical and the theoretical literature. Consider the following examples. Williams and Matheny argue that "the work of Stigler (1975), Bernstein (1955), Huntington (1952), Wilson (1980), and others has produced a consensus that, when regulation bestows concentrated benefits on a group and its costs are dispersed . . . organized representatives of the regulated 'capture' regulatory agencies" (Williams and Matheny 1984, 430). Similarly categorical statements can be found in Barke and Riker (1988), Crew and Rowley (1988), Teske (1991), Howard (1998), Krosner and Strahan (1999), and Martimort (1996). Martimort (1999) states bluntly in the first sentence that "following Stigler (1971), it is now accepted that regulatory capture shapes policy outcomes" (Martimort 1999, 929).

Even as Stigler's landmark article approached its thirtieth anniversary, it appeared to remain as dominant as ever. Analyses focusing on the relationships between Congress and regulatory authorities note that "nonbenevolent regulators may use their power to pursue personal agendas, for example by colluding with the regulated firm" (Laffont and Martimort 1999, 233), and "independence increases the scope for capture by the interest group that he [the regulator] is supposed to regulate" (Faure-Grimaud and Martimort 2003, 413). Teske (2003) perhaps sums it up best, and most concisely: "The dominant view about much economic regulation over the past 25 years is that it was either a bad idea from the start or a practice that failed over time." He cites as evidence for this observation Stigler (1971) and unnamed "subsequent Chicago-school arguments about regulation."

This vast literature, then, crucially rests on an inconsistency that parallels the difference between the "thick" rationality that many public choice theorists concede and the "thin" rationality that they actually rely on to generate their most important conclusions. Stigler's simple model of capture has since been broadened by many theorists into a far more flexible model that accommodates a complex interaction of interest groups and can explain a variety of outcomes. As such, the model is relatively easy to defend. Yet the majority of the time, the reigning presumption seems to be the same. Regulatory capture by a small group of producers, and the search for its presence, reigns supreme. In some cases, moreover, belief in the theory of capture powerfully shapes interpretation of evidence (Moss and Lackow 2007).

Despite having largely moved beyond a model that considered the operation of only a single interest group and its dominance over regulatory decision making, public choice does not appear to have moved far beyond its conclusions. If the field wishes to demonstrate its theoretical sophistication by pointing out the many more complex models it has generated, its theorists should take seriously the indeterminacy inherent in these theories, use them to generate predictions, and rigorously test those predictions. If it wishes to employ the conclusions reached by the earliest, and simplest, models in the field, its reliance on those conclusions should be explicit and explicitly defended. An ambiguous middle ground is not a viable option.

EMPIRICAL WEAKNESSES

Writings in public choice have long cited an abundance of regulatory studies that justify their theories and the policy conclusions that grow out of them. According to intellectual historians of the discipline, Stigler's 1971 article was itself inspired by earlier, empirical work published in the *Journal of Law and Economics* analyzing the operation of New Deal-era utilities regulation, particularly Stigler's joint work with Claire Friedland and the work of Harold Demsetz (Priest 1993). The wide range of the literature in this area has contributed to the impression that the weight of evidence overwhelmingly supports the theory.

In fact, a substantial number of the empirical studies in this area either suffer from methodological weaknesses or are relatively limited in scope, insufficient to support the weight of their conclusions. As Williams and Matheny noted, "Scholars have asserted rather than empirically tested their beliefs about several critical political and economic processes underlying the politics of social regulation" (Williams and Matheny 1984, 429). More bluntly, Barke and Riker contended that "most of the discussion consists of biased, ad hoc explanations of particular cases, with little effort to formulate and test alternative generalizations. We have, therefore, nothing but unresolved and unresolvable disputes about a more or less random collection of stories and some contradictory recipes about cause and effect" (Barke and Riker 1982, 73).

The majority of case studies cited in this chapter fall into this category. Only rarely do these studies consider examples beyond the industries mentioned, or compare more than one possible explanation for the regulatory result observed, whereas the focus on industry-level studies allows for the invocation of idiosyncratic explanations for features of the regulatory process that prove difficult to explain. In the words of Richard Posner, a judge and law scholar highly sympathetic to public choice, "[I]t is, of course, a weakness rather than a strength in a theory that it is so elastic as to fit any body of data with which it is likely to be confronted... Exceptions to the general rule that regulatory agencies are captured by the regulated firms are explained away by facile references to the personality of the legislators, public opinion, ignorance, folk wisdom, etc." (Posner 1974, 343–44). Although this critique, along with those of Williams and Matheny and Barke and Riker, emerged quite early in the evolution of the field, their core criticism remains valid. Public choice is characterized by an excessive reliance on case studies tailored to meet the requirements of the theory, and a paucity of careful and systematic testing of a meaningfully formulated, and clearly falsifiable, null hypothesis.

The more formal empirical studies that public choice has generated also suffer from analogous flaws. Despite the persistent analytical importance of the concept of capture, a compelling account of how to identify it or its milder variants, such as interest group influence, remains elusive. The answers provided by the enormous literature to the three most important questions – how does capture occur, how do we know it has occurred, and what type of evidence would show that capture has *not* occurred – are varied, at times contradictory, and subject to serious challenge.

In general, the most common answers in the literature are that capture occurs via campaign contributions (Becker 1983; Jacobson 1980; Palda

1975), and proof that it occurs is found in the evidence that legislators vote for initiatives favored by interest groups that are strong in their constituencies, long a popular topic for study.[23] A second strand of analysis directly addresses the role of contributions, finding a statistically significant relationship between contributions received from an interest group or lobbying contacts and votes cast in accordance with the group's policy preferences.[24]

However, no studies have firmly established that interest groups are the only or even the principal determinant of legislators' decisions. Kau and Rubin state that at the beginning of their research they were convinced that Stigler's hypothesis that "voting could be explained entirely on the basis of economic interests" was correct (Kau and Rubin 1979, 381–82). Their empirical results, however, indicate that ideology (or potentially some unobserved economic variable) is significant in legislative decision making, and a number of other studies also find that ideology is significant and interest group influence limited.[25] The already cited literature comparing regulatory policies enacted across states – rather than different votes across legislators – also frequently identifies significant ideological variables.[26] This body of work together appears to pose a significant challenge to the assumption that that legislators or regulators are exclusively self-interested rent-seekers, driven in their decision making by purely pecuniary incentives within the constraints of the offers provided by interest groups.

As previously noted, there is also a persistent ambiguity regarding the question of whether interest groups capture legislators or bureaucratic regulators. Though the dominant strand of empirical work analyzes the role of interest groups in capturing legislators, another set of articles instead attempts to demonstrate the way in which largely unelected regulators make

[23] See for example Bailey (1985); Coates (1995); Crandall (1983); Danielsen and Rubin (1977); Gilligan, Marshall, and Weingast (1987); Jackson (1974); Jarrell (1978); Kalt (1981, 1982); Kau and Rubin (1979); Kingdon (1973); Leone and Jackson (1981); Oster (1980); Peltzman (1984); Pashigian (1985); Peltzman (1985); Riddlesperger and King (1982); Silberman and Durden (1976).

[24] See for example Hall and Wayman (1990); Langbein and Lotwis (1990); Steagall and Jennings (1996); Stratmann (1991, 1995); Wilhite and Theilman (1987); Wright (1990).

[25] These include Bernstein and Anthony (1974); Bernstein and Horn (1981); Chappell (1982); Davis and Porter (1989); Fleisher (1985); Lindsay (1990); Levitt (1996); McCormick and Black (1983); Kau, Keenan, and Rubin (1982); Miller and Stokes (1963); Nelson and Silberberg (1987); Poole and Daniels (1985); Poole and Rosenthal (1985); Wright (1985).

[26] In these studies, ideology is generally measured by the ratings given to legislators on the basis of their voting record by nongovernmental organizations that advocate and lobby for a particular broad policy agenda, such as the American Civil Liberties Union, the National Rifle Association, etc. Thus "ideology" does not refer to an overarching theory of politics, as the term is generally used in more theoretical work, but rather the endorsement of various sets of policy goals, clearly identified with the left or the right in American politics.

their decisions according to material or tenure incentives, suggesting that the object of analytical focus should be bureaucrats (Caudill et al. 1993; Eckert 1973; Hazlett 1990; Kaserman et al. 1984). In light of these two different sets of analyses, one might reasonably wonder if both legislators and regulators are available for interest group purchase, and if so, what happens if one interest group purchases the legislators and another, the bureaucrats. Imposing an identity of interest, one potential solution, seems no better. The ambiguity opens the door to a certain empirical opportunism: by not specifying the identity of the appropriate target of capture analysis, scholars can cite a diverse range of evidence as proof that regulation serves the ends of interest groups without ever making clear what theoretical account of the political process underlies these conclusions.

Perhaps most important, studies that seek to establish the relationship between interest groups and legislative decision making by analyzing roll-call votes – or the relationship between interest groups and bureaucratic processes by analyzing commission rulings or the like – invite two fundamental methodological criticisms. First, a pattern of correlations between interest groups and votes does not, in and of itself, demonstrate a causal relationship between interest group influence and political decision making; social science has long attempted to guard against such fallacious conflation of correlation and causation. Legislators cast many votes, they have many constituents, they receive many contributions, and they presumably have some opinions of their own. Inferring capture on a wide scale from voting patterns alone requires a risky, and arguably indefensible, analytical leap. In any given policy dispute, someone has to win and someone has to vote for the winner. Given that most legislators, if not all, have conflicting interest groups represented in their constituency and among their contributors, does voting in accordance with the preferences of any one of them constitute evidence of capture? Is it plausible to suppose that a legislator could last a term without casting some votes that line up with the interests or opinions of some subgroup of his constituents?

This weakness suggests that Peltzman and Becker's key insight – that there may be a relationship between the characteristics of interest groups, their size and organizational costs, and their political influence – is rarely tested adequately. In order to empirically validate this theory, it is not sufficient to show that legislators' votes are correlated with the policy preferences of one or two or more interest groups. Any model that took such a correlation as a confirmation of its predictions would be virtually nonfalsifiable, and thus of little interest. A more realistic test of Peltzman-Becker requires developing an empirical framework that identifies how interest group characteristics affect their quotient of political influence, measures groups along those dimensions, generates predictions regarding which interest groups should be more influential, and tests those predictions against the data regarding the relationship between different groups' policy preferences and the outcomes. Yet attempts to implement such a strategy are rare. Jordan (1972) proposed a test based on one element of industry structure (an oligopoly vs. a natural monopoly) but did not implement it systematically. Caudill and his colleagues, after noting the inadequacy of most empirical studies seeking to show the influence of interest groups in regulatory outcomes involving rate-setting, nonetheless test a simple model that incorporates as characteristics of the industry only the rate of return requested and expenditures on lobbying the commission (Caudill et al. 1993). Such basic tests may not be sufficient.

A second key methodological flaw in the existing literature on the empirical foundations of capture concerns the fact that many analyses of roll-call votes for evidence of capture utilize a set of observations – individual votes cast by legislators – that are clearly endogenous. Tullock himself highlighted the importance of log-rolling or vote-trading in one of his earliest articles (Tullock 1959). A single legislator's different votes may be related to each other because they represent elements in some broader trade such as those that Tullock hypothesizes, because they are cast on similar issues, or because (very plausibly) the legislator's opinions on a diverse set of topics are interrelated. Votes cast by different legislators could also be correlated if they are elements of a vote trade, or if they are jointly determined (or partially determined) by a common external force. A typical analysis of roll-call votes considers a certain number of votes cast over a given period or on a given topic, and thus bias will be introduced by the presence of correlations between a given observation (legislator–vote) and the unobserved error term for another vote cast by the same legislator or any other. Given this, any analysis of causality based on such a regression is questionable, if not unjustifiable.

To sum up. the evidence that interest groups are a primary determinant of government regulatory decisions is mixed at best and open to some potentially serious methodological criticisms. Moreover, the empirical strategy implemented by the proponents of capture theory is, in general, characterized by the troubling absence of a search for disconfirming evidence. Public choice theorists point to correlations between various measures of interest group activity and decisions of government actors of various types as evidence of capture, often without a systematic attempt to examine and test other hypotheses. In some cases, the definition of "interest group influence" has been made so broad that it is not clear that the theory is even falsifiable. Given these weaknesses, a more promising avenue of exploration in the field may be the studies already cited that compare regulatory outcomes and causal factors across states and enable the formulation of systematic theories of the determinants of regulatory policy that can be tested.

At the same time, it bears mentioning that surveys of work in this area provided an extensive taxonomy of ideological, demographic, and structural variables that have been deemed significant, along with measures of interest group strength, in explaining regulatory outcomes in various contexts. In order to be empirically validated, purist capture and interest group theorists must be able to show in some way that a more precise formulation would demonstrate all of these variables to be insignificant. This is a formidable hurdle.

A RESPONSE TO SKEPTICS

Before concluding, it seems appropriate to preemptively address two major critiques that can potentially be made of the argument I have presented here: first, that public choice is no longer an important school of thought in social science, and second, that I inappropriately characterize its membership, subsuming under the public choice label scholars who would not define themselves as such.

First, some will argue that public choice is, for all intents and purposes, outmoded and discredited, and that the most current work in academia has moved on. No part of my argument should be construed as an assertion that public choice is the only current school of thought in economics, political science, or law that analyzes the formation and impact of economic policy. On the contrary, there has been a profusion of new work in a variety of different fields over the last decades in this area, some grouped under political economy, some under the new institutional economics, and some under positive political theory. My intention is not to minimize the significance of this work or to criticize the general methodological framework of applying techniques of formal analysis traditionally associated with economics to the consideration of political processes; on the contrary, my critique addresses a very specific set of ancillary assumptions that have been imposed within this methodological framework.

Nonetheless, any serious consideration of the state of social science and particularly economics today must concede that the public choice view of regulation remains an enormously influential one. The textbook on regulation by Jean-Jacques Laffont and Jean Tirole identifies public choice as one of two major extant theories explaining the pattern of government intervention in industry (Laffont and Tirole 1993). Djankov, La Porta, Lopez-de-Silanes, and Shleifer (2002) likewise declare that there are two theories of regulation, public interest and public choice, and argue that a comparative study of regulations governing business start-ups favors a public choice theory. Moreover, they perhaps unintentionally highlight the recent dominance of public choice by citing only a single reference for the public interest theory of regulation, Pigou's seventy-year-old work from 1938. Public choice is not the only scholarly school analyzing regulation; yet it seems equally clear that it remains important and influential and is widely acknowledged to be so among practitioners of the discipline, surveying their own field. This alone seems sufficient to indicate that it is a worthy object of analytical consideration.

A second potential objection holds that I inappropriately characterize scholars as "public choice." Clearly, there are no public choice membership cards; academic schools are flexible constructions, and there is disagreement about their boundaries. Some of the work cited here may not have been explicitly identified as public choice by its authors, and they may object to that identification. My preoccupation is not with particular labels, but with a certain set of analytical assumptions and practices that generate a body of work that has been widely characterized as "public choice." These are the assumptions I have sought to analyze here, and my argument should be evaluated on this basis.

CONCLUSION

If one traces public choice back to the work of Duncan Black and Anthony Downs, it has already passed its fiftieth anniversary. If one likewise considers Posner's 1974 article to be the first articulation of the major flaws of public choice – perhaps somewhat surprisingly, given that his general intellectual sympathies certainly lay with the project – it has now been more than thirty years since the first critiques. Yet despite the existence of a significant body of criticism, the public choice account of policymaking still remains enormously influential both inside and outside the academy. In the words of one analyst, "Governmental efforts are viewed as inevitably flawed . . . all things 'public' have become suspect. For some, the only public purpose worthy of respect seems to be the elimination of the public sector" (Mashaw 1997, 23). This view, dominant in both politics and the academy, has been crucial in sustaining the wave of privatization and deregulation evident in the American economy over the last two decades.

This panorama raises further questions. Why does public choice continue to be so successful despite its many weaknesses, why are its critics so ineffective, and why are they so few in number? Public choice theorists themselves might be sympathetic to the argument that their would-be academic critics face a collective action problem. Although theorists of public choice have clustered at recognizable academic homes, rely on *Public Choice* and *The Journal of Law and Economics* to provide a receptive outlet for their work, credit the inspiration provided by a few respected founding scholars, and steadily add to their ever-expanding corpus of work, public choice skeptics appear to be scattered and without any institutional focal point. The dispersion of authors across disciplines exacerbates the lack of coordination. Most of the authors who have addressed the flaws of public choice have published on the subject only once or twice, and their critiques exist largely in isolation, without extensive cross-citations. There have been no attempts to synthesize the existing literature and use it to generate a coherent research agenda that could begin to generate an alternative to public choice – likely the most important reason for its continued dominance. Equally important, few scholars have attempted to illuminate this debate by engaging in cross-country comparisons and testing the ability of public choice as well as competing theories to explain differences in regulatory regimes between polities.

Beyond such organizational problems, however, one can imagine that public choice theory's tenacity is due partly to the fact that it resonates with a widespread sense that American legislative and regulatory processes lack adequate transparency and equality of access. Frequent cases of legislator misconduct, the influence of lobbyists, and the often incestuous relationships between the two all appear to lend weight to the argument that some narrowly defined groups, whose interests do not coincide with those of the majority of voters, wield excessive control over policy. These apprehensions are legitimate, and in many cases rooted in abuses that may require a remedy. However, this alone is not adequate support for a *general* theory of the political process and the economic role of the state. The sense that public choice addresses aspects of the operation of the political system that we find troubling may have served as a shield for the many flaws in the way in which it addresses those challenges.

Regardless of the explanation for public choice's continuing appeal, our understanding of legislative and regulatory decision making (and of democracy itself) remains far from complete. The existing theories lack both internal coherence and strong empirical foundations. Further work in this area – particularly coordinated and sustained work across the social sciences – is urgently needed if we are to move beyond the current flawed consensus.

References

Abrams, Burton A., and Russell F. Settle. 1978. "The Economic Theory of Regulation and Public Financing of Presidential Elections." *The Journal of Political Economy* 82 (2): 245–57.

———. 2004. "Campaign-Finance Reform: A Public Choice Perspective." *Public Choice* 120: 379–400.

Abrams, Burton A., and Kenneth Lewis. 1987. "A Median-Voter Model of Economic Regulation." *Public Choice* 52 (2): 125–42.

Ackerman, Bruce, and William Hassler. 1981. *Clean Coal/Dirty Air*. New Haven, Conn.: Yale University Press.

Adams, Walter. 1982. "The Rocky Road Toward Deregulation," in *Deregulation: An Appraisal Before the Fact*, eds. Thomas G. Gies and Werner Sichel (Ann Arbor: University of Michigan), 119–27.

Aldrich, John. 1993. "Rational Choice and Turnout." *American Journal of Political Science* 37 (1): 246–78.

Anderson, Douglas. 1981. *Regulatory Politics and Electric Utilities*. Boston: Auburn House.

Annable, James. 1973. "The ICC, the IBT, and the Cartelization of the American Trucking Industry." *Quarterly Review of Economics and Business* 13: 33–47.

Ashenfelter, Orley, and Stanley Kelley, Jr. 1975. "Determinants of Participation in Presidential Elections." *Journal of Law and Economics* 18 (3): 675–733.

Austen-Smith, David. 1987. "Interest Groups, Campaign Contributions and Probabilistic Voting." *Public Choice* 54 (2): 123–39.

———. 1997. "Interest Groups: Money, Information and Influence," in *Perspectives on Public Choice: A Handbook*, ed. Dennis Mueller (Cambridge: Cambridge University Press), 296–322.

Bardhan, Pranab, and Dilip Mookherjee. 2000. "Capture and Governance at Local and National Levels." *The American Economic Review* 90 (2): 135–39.

Barke, Richard, and William Riker. 1982. "A Political Theory of Regulation with Some Observations on Railway Abandonments." *Public Choice* 39 (1): 73–106.

Baron, David. 1988. Regulation and Legislative Choice." *RAND Journal of Economics* 19 (3): 467–77.

———. 1989. "Service-Induced Campaign Contributions and the Electoral Equilibrium." *Quarterly Journal of Economics* 101 (1): 45–72.

Bartel, Ann, and Lacy Glenn Thomas. 1987. "Predation through Regulation: The Wage and Profit Impacts of OSHA and EPA." *Journal of Law and Economics* 30 (2): 239–364.

Barzel, Yoram, and Eugene Silberberg. 1973. "Is the Act of Voting Rational?" *Public Choice* 16 (1): 51–58.

Beck, Nathaniel. 1975. "The Paradox of Minimax Regret." *American Political Science Review* 69 (3): 918.

Becker, Gary. 1958. "Competition and Democracy." *Journal of Law and Economics* 1: 105–9.

———. 1983. "A Theory of Competition among Pressure Groups for Political Influence." *Quarterly Journal of Economics* 98 (3): 371–400.

———. 1985. "Public Policies, Pressure Groups and Dead Weight Costs." *Journal of Public Economics* 28 (3): 329–47.

Becker, Gilbert. 1986. "Public Interest Hypothesis Revisited: A New Test of Peltzman's Theory of Regulation." *Public Choice* 49 (3): 223–34.

Ben-Zion, Uri, and Zeev Eytan. 1974. "On Money, Votes and Policy in a Democratic Society." *Public Choice* 17 (1): 1–10.

Bennett, James, and William Orzechowski. 1983. "The Voting Behavior of Bureaucrats: Some Empirical Evidence." *Public Choice* 41 (2): 271–83.

Benson, Bruce. 2002. "Regulatory Disequilibrium and Inefficiency: The Case of Interstate Trucking." *The Review of Austrian Economics* 15 (2–3): 229–55.

Bernstein, Marver. 1955. *Regulating Business by Independent Commission.* Princeton, N.J.: Princeton University Press.

Bernstein, Robert, and William Anthony. 1974. "The ABM Issue in the Senate, 1967–1970: The Importance of Ideology." *American Political Science Review* 68 (3): 1198–206.

Bernstein, Robert, and Stephen Horn. 1981. "Explaining House Voting on Energy Policy: Ideology and the Conditional Effects of Party and District Economic Interests." *Western Political Quarterly* 34: 235–45.

Berry, William. 1979. "Utility Regulation in the States: The Policy Effects of Professionalism and Salience to the Consumer." *American Journal of Political Science* 23 (3): 263–77.

———. 1984. "An Alternative to the Capture Theory of Regulation: The Case of State Public Utility Commissions." *American Journal of Political Science* 28 (3): 524–58.

Besley, Timothy, and Stephen Coate. 2001. "Lobbying and Welfare in a Representative Democracy." *Review of Economics Studies* 68: 67–82.

———. 2003. "Elected versus Appointed Regulators: Theory and Evidence." *Journal of the European Economic Association* 1 (5): 1176–206.

Black, Sandra, and Philip Strahan. 2001. "The Division of Spoils: Rent-Sharing and Discrimination in a Regulated Industry." *American Economic Review* 91 (4): 814–31.

Blais, Andre. 2000. *To Vote or Not to Vote? The Merits and Limits of Rational Choice Theory.* Pittsburgh: University of Pittsburgh Press.

Blais, Andre, and Robert Young. 1999. "Why Do People Vote? An Experiment in Rationality." *Public Choice* 99 (1–2): 39–55.

Blais, Andre, Robert Young, and Miriam Lapp. 2000. "The Calculus of Voting: An Empirical Test." *European Journal of Political Research* 37 (2): 181–201.

Boyer, Kenneth. 1987. "The Costs of Price Regulation: Lessons from Railroad Deregulation." *The RAND Journal of Economics* 18 (3): 408–16.

Braeutigam, Ronald, and Roger Noll. 1984. "The Regulation of Surface Freight Transportation: The Welfare Effects Revisited." *The Review of Economics and Statistics* 66 (1): 80–87.

Brennan, Geoffrey, and James Buchanan. 1981. "The Normative Purpose of Economic Science." *International Review of Law and Economics* 1 (2): 155–66.

Brinegar, George. 1957. "Economic Effects of Regulation and Price Fixing in the Milk Industry." *Journal of Farm Economics* 39 (5): 1173–85.

Brock, William, and Stephen Magee. 1978. "The Economics of Special Interest Politics: The Case of the Tariff." *American Economic Review* 68 (2): 246–50.

Brunk, Gregory. 1980. "The Impact of Rational Participation Models on Voting Attitudes." *Public Choice* 35: 549–64.

Buchanan, James. 1954. "Individual Choice in Voting and the Market." *Journal of Political Economy* 62 (4): 334–43.

———. 1978. "Markets, States and the Extent of Morals." *American Economic Review* 68 (2): 364–68.

———. 1988. "Is Public Choice Immoral?" *Virginia Law Review* 74 (2): 179–89.

———. 2003. "Public Choice: Politics without Romance." *Policy* 19 (3): 13–18.

Buchanan, James, and Gordon Tullock. 1962. *The Calculus of Consent.* Michigan: University of Michigan Press.

Caplan, Bryan. 2005. "From Friedman to Wittman: The Transformation of Chicago Political Economy." *Economic Journal Watch* 2 (1): 1–21.

Carter, Clyde. 1957. "State Regulation of Milk in the Southeast." *Southern Economic Journal* 24 (1): 63–74.

———. 1958. "State Regulation of Commercial Motor Carriers in the Southeast." *Southern Economic Journal* 24 (4): 434–46.

Caudill, Steven, Bae-Gun Im, and David Kaserman. 1993. "Modeling Regulatory Behavior: The Economic Theory of Regulation versus Alternative Theories and Simple Rules of Thumb." *Journal of Regulatory Economics* 5 (3): 251–62.

Caves, Richard. 1962. *Air Transport and its Regulators.* Cambridge: Harvard University Press.

Caves, Douglas, Laurits Christensen, and Joseph Swanson. 1981. "Economic Performance in Regulated and Unregulated Environments: A Comparison of U.S. and Canadian Railroads." *The Quarterly Journal of Economics* 96 (4): 559–81.

Chamberlain, Gary, and Michael Rothschild. 1981. "A Note on the Probability of Casting a Decisive Vote." *Journal of Economic Theory* 25 (1): 152–62.

Chappell, Henry W., Jr. 1982. "Campaign Contributions and Congressional Voting: A Simultaneous Probit-Tobit Model." *The Review of Economics and Statistics* 64 (1): 77–83.

Coase, Ronald. 1969. "The Federal Communications Commission." *Journal of Law and Economics* 2: 1–40.

———. 1960. "The Problem of Social Cost." *Journal of Law and Economics* 3: 1–44.

Coates, Dennis. 1995. "Electoral Support and the Capture of Legislators: Evidence from North Carolina's Vote on Radioactive Waste Disposal." *RAND Journal of Economics* 23 (3): 502–18.

Colomer, Josep. 1991. "Benefits and Costs of Voting." *Electoral Studies* 10 (4): 313–25.

Comanor, William, and Bridger Mitchell. 1972. "The Costs of Planning: The FCC and Cable Television." *Journal of Law and Economics* 15 (1): 177–206.

Courville, Léon. 1974. "Regulation and Efficiency in the Electric Utility Industry." *Bell Journal of Economics and Management Science* 5 (1): 38–52.

Crain, W. Mark, Donald Leavens, and Lynn Abbot. 1987. "Voting and Not Voting at the Same Time." *Public Choice* 53 (3): 221–29.

Crain, W. Mark, and Robert Tollison. 1976. "Campaign Expenditures and Political Competition." *Journal of Law and Economics* 19 (1): 177–88.

———. 1979a. "Constitutional Change in an Interest-Group Perspective." *Journal of Legal Studies* 8 (1): 165–75.

———. 1979b. "The Executive Branch in the Interest-Group Theory of Government." *Journal of Legal Studies* 8 (1): 165–75.

Crain, W. Mark, Robert Tollison, and Donald Leavens. 1988. "Laissez-faire in Campaign Finance." *Public Choice* 56: 201–12.

Crandall, Robert. 1972. "FCC Regulation, Monopsony and Network Television Program Costs." *Bell Journal of Economics and Management Science* 3 (2): 483–508.

———. 1983. *Controlling Industrial Pollution: The Economics and Politics of Clean Air.* Washington, D.C.: Brookings Institution.

Crawford, Gregory. 2000. "The Impact of the 1992 Cable Act on Consumer Demand and Welfare." *Rand Journal of Economics* 31 (3): 422–49.

Crew, Michael, and Charles Rowley. 1988. "Towards a Public Choice Theory of Monopoly Regulation." *Public Choice* 57 (1): 49–67.

Crewe, Ivor. 1981. "Electoral Participation," in *Democracy at the Polls: A Comparative Study of Competitive National Elections*, eds. D. Butler, H. R. Penniman, and A. Ranney (Washington, D.C.: American Enterprise Institute).

Croley, Steven. 1998. "Theories of Regulation: Incorporating the Administrative Process." *Columbia Law Review* 98 (1): 1–168.

———. 2000. "Public Interested Regulation." *Florida State University Law Review* 28 (7): 7–107.

Culhane, Paul. 1981. *Public Lands Politics: Interest Group Influence on the Forest Service and the Bureau of Land Management.* Baltimore: Johns Hopkins University Press.

Daniel, Timothy, and Andrew Kleit. 1995. "Disentangling Regulatory Policy: The Effects of State Regulation on Trucking Rates." *Journal of Regulatory Economics* 8 (3): 267–84.

Danielsen, Albert, and Paul Rubin. 1977. "An Empirical Investigation of Voting on Energy Issues." *Public Choice* 31 (1): 121–28.

Danzon, Patricia, and Li-Wei Chao. 2000. "Does Regulation Drive Out Competition in Pharmaceutical Markets?" *Journal of Law and Economics* 43 (2): 311–57.

Darvish, Tikva, and Jacob Rosenberg. 1988. "The Economic Model of Voter Participation." *Public Choice* 56 (2): 185–92.

Davis, Michael, and Philip Porter. 1989. "A Test for Pure or Apparent Ideology in Congressional Voting." *Public Choice* 60 (2): 101–11.

De Alessi, Louis. 1974. "An Economic Analysis of Government Ownership and Regulation: Theory and the Evidence from the Electric Power Industry." *Public Choice* 19: 1–42.

Demsetz, Harold. 1968. "Why Regulate Utilities?" *Journal of Law and Economics* 11 (1): 55–65.

Derthick, Martha, and Paul Quirk. 1985. *The Politics of Deregulation.* Washington, D.C.: The Brookings Institution.

DeVany, Arthur, Wendy Gramm, Thomas Saving, and Charles Smithson. 1982. "The Impact of Input Regulation: The Case of the U.S. Dental Industry." *Journal of Law and Economics* 25 (2): 367–81.

Dhillon, Amrita, and Susana Peralta. 2002. "Economic Theories of Voter Turnout." *The Economic Journal* 112: 332–52.

Djankov, Simeon, Rafael La Porta, Florencio Lopez-de-Silanes, and Andrei Shleifer. 2002. "The Regulation of Entry." *Quarterly Journal of Economics* 117 (1): 1–36.

Dowding, Keith. 2005. "Is It Rational to Vote? Five Types of Answer and a Suggestion." *The British Journal of Politics and International Relations* 7 (3): 442–59.

Downs, Anthony. 1957. *An Economic Theory of Democracy.* New York: Harper & Brothers.

Eckert, Ross. 1973. "On the Incentives of Regulators: The Case of Taxicabs." *Public Choice* 14 (1): 83–99.

Edwards, Linda, and Franklin Edwards. 1974. "Measuring the Effectiveness of Regulation: The Case of Bank Entry Regulation." *Journal of Law and Economics* 17 (2): 445–60.

Ellig, Jerome. 1991. "Endogenous Change and the Economic Theory of Regulation. *Journal of Regulatory Economics* 3 (3): 265–74.

Evans, Lewis, and Steven Garber. 1988. "Public-Utility Regulators Are Only Human: A Positive Theory of Rational Constraints." *The American Economic Review* 78 (3): 444–62.

Farris, Martin. 1969. "Transportation Regulation and Economic Efficiency." *American Economic Review* 59 (2): 244–50.

Faure-Grimaud, Antoine, and David Martimort. 2003. "Regulatory Inertia." *The RAND Journal of Economics* 34 (4): 413–37.

Feddersen, Timothy. 2004. "Rational Choice Theory and the Paradox of Not Voting." *Journal of Economic Perspectives* 18 (1): 99–112.

Feddersen, Timothy, and Alvaro Sandroni. 2001. *A Theory of Ethics and Participation in Elections.* Mimeo.

Filer, John, and Lawrence Kenny. 1980. "Voter Turnout and the Benefits of Voting." *Public Choice* 35 (5): 575–85.

Fiorina, Morris. 1982. "Legislative Choice of Regulatory Forms: Legal Process or Administrative Process?" *Public Choice* 39: 33–66.

Fleisher, Richard. 1985. "Economic Benefit, Ideology and Senate Voting on the B-1 Bomber." *American Politics Quarterly* 13: 200–11.

Foster, Carroll. 1984. "Performance of Rational Voter Models in Recent Presidential Elections." *American Political Science Review* 78 (3): 678–90.

Fournier, Gary, and Donald Martin. 1983. "Does Government-Restricted Entry Produce Market Power? New Evidence from the Market for Television Advertising." *Bell Journal of Economics* 14 (1): 44–56.

Frech, H. E., and Joseph Samprone, Jr. 1980. "The Welfare Loss of Excess Nonprice Competition: The Case of Property-Liability Insurance Regulation." *Journal of Law and Economics* 23 (3): 429–40.

Frew, James. 1981. "The Existence of Monopoly Profits in the Motor Carrier Industry." *Journal of Law and Economics* 24 (2): 289–315.

Friedlaender, Ann. 1969. *The Dilemma of Freight Transport Regulation.* Washington, D.C.: Brookings Institution.

Frohlich, Norman, Joe Oppenheimer, Jeffrey Smith, and Oran Young. 1978. "A Test of Downsian Voter Rationality: 1964 Presidential Voting." *The American Political Science Review* 72 (1): 178–97.

Gellman, Aaron. "Surface Freight Transportation," in *Technological Change in Regulated Industries,* ed. William Capron (Washington, D.C.: Brookings Institution), pp. 166–97.

Gerber, Alan. 1998. "Estimating the Effect of Campaign Spending on Senate Election Outcomes." *The American Political Science Review* 92 (2): 401–11.

Gerber, Brian, and Paul Teske. 2000. "Regulatory Policymaking in the American States: A Review of Theories and Evidence." *Political Research Quarterly* 53 (4): 849–87.

Gerwig, Robert. 1962. "Natural Gas Production: A Study of Costs of Regulation." *Journal of Law and Economics* 5: 69–92.

Gilligan, Thomas, William Marshall, and Barry Weingast. 1978. "Regulation and the Theory of Legislative Choice: The Interstate Commerce Act of 1887." *Journal of Law and Economics* 32 (1): 35–61.

Golbe, Devra. 1983. "Product Safety in a Regulated Industry: Evidence from the Railroads. *Economic Inquiry* 21 (1): 39–52.

Grabowski, Henry, John Vernon, and Lacy Glenn Thomas. 1978. "Estimating the Effects of Regulation on Innovation: An International Comparative Analysis of the Pharmaceutical Industry." *Journal of Law and Economics* 21 (1): 133–63.

Graham, David, Daniel Kaplan, and David Sibley. 1983. "Efficiency and Competition in the Airline Industry." *Bell Journal of Economics* 14 (1): 118–38.

Green, Donald, and Ian Shapiro. 1994. *Pathologies of Rational Choice Theory: A Critique of Applications in Political Science.* New Haven, Conn.: Yale University Press.

Grossman, Gene, and Elhanan Helpman. 1994. "Protection for Sale." *The American Economic Review* 84 (4): 833–50.

———. 1996. "Electoral Competition and Special Interest Politics." *Review of Economic Studies* 63 (2): 265–86.

Haas-Wilson, Deborah. 1987. "The Effect of Commercial Practice Regulations: The Case of Optometry." *Journal of Law and Economics* 29 (1): 165–86.

Hägg, P. Göran. 1997. "Theories on the Economics of Regulation: A Survey of the Literature from a European Perspective." *European Journal of Law and Economics* 4: 337–70.

Hall, Richard, and Frank Wayman. 1990. "Buying Time: Moneyed Interests and the Mobilization of Bias in Congressional Committees." *American Political Science Review* 84 (3): 797–820.

Hammond, Thomas, and Jack Knott. 1988. "The Deregulatory Snowball: Explaining Deregulation in the Financial Industry." *The Journal of Politics* 50 (1): 3–30.

Hanks, Christopher, and Bernhard Grofman. 1998. "Turnout in Gubernatorial and Senatorial Primary and General Elections in the South, 1922–90: A Rational Choice Model of the Effects of Short-Run and Long-Run Electoral Competition on Relative Turnout. *Public Choice* 94: 3–4: 407–21.

Hantke-Domas, Michael. 2003. "The Public Interest Theory of Regulation: Non-Existence or Misinterpretation?" *European Journal of Law and Economics* 15 (2): 165–94.

Harbeson, Robert. 1969. "Toward Better Resource Allocation in Transport." *Journal of Law and Economics* 12 (2): 321–38.

Hardin, Russell. 1982. *Collective Action.* Baltimore: Johns Hopkins University Press.

Hazlett, Thomas. 1990. "The Rationality of U.S. Regulation of the Broadcast Spectrum." *Journal of Law and Economics* 33 (1): 133–75.

Heckelman, Jac. 1995. "The Effect of the Secret Ballot on Voter Turnout Rates." *Public Choice* 82 (1–2): 107–24.

Hendricks, Wallace, Peter Feuille, and Carol Szerszen. 1980. "Regulation, Deregulation and Collective Bargaining in Airlines." *Industrial and Labor Relations Review* 34 (1): 67–81.

Hilton, George. 1972. "The Basic Behavior of Regulatory Commissions." *American Economic Review* 62: 47–54.

Hinich, Melvin. 1981. "Voting as an Act of Contribution." *Public Choice* 36 (1): 135–40.

Howard, Robert. 1998. "Wealth, Power and Attorney Regulation in the U.S. States." *Publius: The Journal of Federalism* 28 (4): 22–42.

Huntington, Samuel. 1952. "The Marasmus of the ICC: The Commission, the Railroads, and the Public Interest." *Yale Law Journal* 61 (4): 467–509.

Ippolito, Richard. 1979. "The Effects of Price Regulation in the Automobile Insurance Industry." *Journal of Law and Economics* 22 (1): 55–89.

Ippolito, Richard, and Robert Masson. 1978. "The Social Cost of Government Regulation of Milk." *Journal of Law and Economics* 21 (1): 33–54.

Jackson, John. 1974. *Constituencies and Leaders in Congress*. Cambridge, Mass.: Harvard University Press.

Jackson, John, and John Kingdon. 1992. "Ideology, Interest Group Scores and Legislative Votes." *American Journal of Political Science* 36 (3): 805–23.

Jackson, Raymond. 1969. "Regulation and Electric Utility Rate Levels." *Land Economics* 45 (3): 372–76.

Jacobson, Gary. 1978. "The Effects of Campaign Spending in Congressional Elections." *The American Political Science Review* 72 (2): 469–91.

———. 1979. "Public Funds for Congressional Campaigns: Who Would Benefit?" in *Political Finance*, ed. Herbert Alexander (Beverly Hills, Calif.: Sage), 99–129.

———. 1980. *Money in Congressional Elections*. New Haven, Conn.: Yale University Press.

———. 1985. "Money and Votes Reconsidered: Congressional Elections, 1972–1982." *Public Choice* 47 (1): 7–62.

Jarrell, Gregg. 1978. "The Demand for State Regulation of the Electric Utility Industry." *Journal of Law and Economics* 21 (2): 269–95.

Jordan, William. 1972. "Producer Protection, Prior Market Structure and the Effects of Government Regulation." *Journal of Law and Economics* 15 (1): 151–76.

Joskow, Paul, and Roger Noll. "Regulation in Theory and Practice: An Overview," in *Studies in Public Regulation*, ed. Gary Fromm (Cambridge, Mass.: MIT Press), 1–65.

Joskow, Paul, and Nancy Rose. 1989. "The Effects of Economic Regulation." *Handbook of Industrial Organization II* (Amsterdam: Elsevier), 1449–504.

Joskow, Paul, Douglas Bohi, and Frank Gollop. 1989. "Regulatory Failure, Regulatory Reform and Structural Change in the Electrical Power Industry." *Brookings Papers on Economic Reform: Microeconomics*, 125–208.

Kalt, Joseph. 1981. *The Economics and Politics of Oil Price Regulation*. Cambridge: MIT Press.

———. 1982. "Oil and Ideology in the United States Senate." *Energy Journal* 3: 141–66.

———. 1983. "The Costs and Benefits of Federal Regulation of Cal Strip Mining." *Natural Resources Journal* 23 (4): 893–915.

Kalt, Joseph, and Mark Zupan. 1984. "Capture and Ideology in the Economic Theory of Politics." *American Economic Review* 64 (3): 279–300.

Kaserman, David, L. Roy Kavanaugh, and Richard Tepel. 1984. "To Which Fiddle Does the Regulator Dance?" *Review of Industrial Organization* 1 (4): 246–58.

Kaserman, David, John Mayo, and Patricia Pacey. 1993. "The Political Economy of Deregulation." *Journal of Regulatory Economics* 5 (1): 49–63.

Katzman, Robert. 1980. *Regulatory Bureaucracy: The FTC and Antitrust Policy.* Cambridge, Mass.: MIT Press.

Kau, James, and Paul Rubin. 1979. "Self-interest, Ideology, and Logrolling in Congressional Voting." *Journal of Law and Economics* 22 (2): 365–84.

Kau, James, Donald Keenan, and Paul Rubin. 1982. "A General Equilibrium Model of Congressional Voting." *The Quarterly Journal of Economics* 97 (2): 271–93.

Keeler, Theodore. 1972. "Airline Regulation and Market Performance." *The Bell Journal of Economics and Management Science* 3 (2): 399–424.

———. 1983. *Railroads, Freight and Public Policy.* Washington, D.C.: Brookings Institution.

Kelman, Mark. 1988. "On Democracy-Bashing: A Skeptical Look at the Theoretical and 'Empirical' Practice of the Public Choice Movement." *Virginia Law Review* 74 (2): 199–273.

Kessel, Reuben. 1967. "Economic Effects of Federal Regulation of Milk Markets." *Journal of Law and Economics* 10: 51–78.

Kim, Moshe. 1984. "The Beneficiaries of Trucking Regulation, Revisited." *Journal of Law and Economics* 27 (1): 227–41.

Kingdon, John. 1973. *Congressmen's Voting Decisions.* New York: Harper and Row.

Kitch, Edmund, Marc Isaacson, and Daniel Kasper. 1971. "The Regulation of Taxicabs in Chicago." *Journal of Law and Economics* 14 (2): 285–350.

Kleiner, Morris, and Robert Kudrle. 2000. "Does Regulation Affect Economic Outcomes? The case of Dentistry." *Journal of Law and Economics* 42 (3): 547–82.

Knack, Stephen. 1993. "The Voter Participation Effects of Selecting Jurors from Registration Lists." *Journal of Law and Economics* 36 (1): 99–114.

———. 1994. "Does Rain Help the Republicans? Theory and Evidence on Turnout and the Vote." *Public Choice* 79 (1–2): 187–209.

Kolko, Gabriel. 1965. *Railroads and Regulators, 1977–1916.* New York: Norton.

Krattenmaker, Thomas, and Lucas Powe, Jr. 1994. *Regulating Broadcast Programming.* Cambridge, Mass.: MIT Press.

Kridel, Donald, David Sappington, and Dennis Weisman. 1996. "The Effects of Incentive Regulation in the Telecommunications Industry: A Survey." *Journal of Regulatory Economics* 9 (3): 269–306.

Kroszner, Randall, and Philip Strahan. 1999. "What Drives Deregulation? Economics and Politics of the Relaxation of Bank Branching Restrictions." *Quarterly Journal of Economics* 114 (4): 1437–67.

Laffont, Jean-Jacques, and David Martimort. 1999. "Separation of Regulators against Collusive Behavior." *The RAND Journal of Economics* 30 (2): 232–62.

Laffont, Jean-Jacques, and Jean Tirole. 1991. "The Politics of Government Decision-Making: A Theory of Regulatory Capture." *Quarterly Journal of Economics* 106 (4): 1089–127.

———. 1993. *A Theory of Incentives in Procurement and Regulation.* Cambridge, Mass.: MIT Press.

Landes, William, and Richard Posner. 1975. "The Independent Judiciary in an Interest-Group Perspective." *Journal of Law and Economics* 18 (3): 875–901.

Langbein, Laura, and Mark Lotwis. 1990. "The Political Efficacy of Lobbying and Money: Gun Control in the U.S. House, 1987." *Legislative Studies Quarterly* 15 (3): 413–40.

Ledyard, John. 1981. "The Paradox of Voting and Candidate Competition: A General Equilibrium Analysis," in *Essays in Contemporary Fields of Economics*, eds. G. Horwich and J. Quirk (West Lafayette, Ind.: Purdue University Press).

———. 1984. "The Pure Theory of Large Two-Candidate Elections." *Public Choice* 44 (1): 7–41.

Leffler, Keith. 1978. "Physician Licensure: Competition and Monopoly in American Medicine." *Journal of Law and Economics* 21 (2): 165–86.

Leone, Robert, and John Jackson. 1981. "The Political Economy of Federal Regulatory Activity: The Case of Water-Pollution Controls," in *Studies in Public Regulation*, ed. Gary Fromm (Cambridge, Mass.: MIT Press).

Levin, Richard. 1978. "Allocation in Surface Freight Transportation: Does Rate Regulation Matter?" *The Bell Journal of Economics* 9 (1): 18–45.

Levine, Michael. 1981. "Revisionism Revised? Airline Deregulation and the Public Interest." *Law and Contemporary Problems* 44 (1): 179–95.

Levine, Michael, and Jennifer Forrence. 1990. "Regulatory Capture, Public Interest and the Public Agenda: Toward a Synthesis." *Journal of Law, Economics & Organization* 6: 167–98.

Levitt, Steven. 1996. "How Do Senators Vote? Disentangling the Role of Voter Preferences, Party Affiliation, and Senator Ideology." *The American Economic Review* 86 (3): 425–41.

Lindsay, James. 1990. "Parochialism, Policy and Constituency Constraints: Congressional Voting on Strategic Weapons Systems." *American Journal of Political Science* 34 (4): 936–60.

Lohmann, Suzanne. 1995. "Information, Access and Contributions: A Signaling Model of Lobbying." *Public Choice* 85 (3–4): 267–84.

MacAvoy, Paul. 1965. *The Economic Effects of Regulation: The Trunkline Railroad Cartels and the ICC Before 1900*. Cambridge: MIT Press.

———. 1971. "Regulation-Induced Shortage of Natural Gas." *Journal of Law and Economics* 41 (1): 167–99.

MacAvoy, Paul, and Robert Pindyck. 1973. "Alternative Regulatory Policies for Dealing with the Natural Gas Shortage. *Bell Journal of Economics and Management Science* 4 (2): 454–98.

MacAvoy, Paul, and James Sloss. 1967. *Regulation of Transport Innovation*. New York: Random House.

McChesney, Fred. 1987. "Rent Extraction and Rent Creation in the Economic Theory of Regulation." *The Journal of Legal Studies* 16 (1): 101–18.

McCormick, James, and Michael Black. 1983. "Ideology and Senate Voting on the Panama Canal Treaties." *Legislative Studies Quarterly* 8 (1): 45–63.

McCormick, Robert, and Robert Tollison. 1978. "Legislatures as Unions." *Journal of Political Economy* 86 (1): 63–78.

McCubbins, Matthew. 1985. "The Legislative Design of Regulatory Structure." *American Journal of Political Science* 29 (4): 721–48.

McCubbins, Matthew, Roger Noll, and Barry Weingast. 1987. "Administrative Procedures as Instruments of Political Control." *Journal of Law, Economics, & Organization*
3 (2): 243–77.

_____. 1989. "Structure and Process, Politics and Policy: Administrative Arrangements
and the Political Control of Agencies." *Virginia Law Review* 75 (2): 413–82.

McKenzie, Richard, and Hugh Macaulay. 1980. "A Bureaucratic Theory of Regulation."
Public Choice 35 (3): 297–315.

Macey, Jonathan. 1988. "Transaction Costs and the Normative Elements of the Public
Choice Model." *Virginia Law Review* 74 (2): 471–518.

Magat, Wesley, Alan Kruppington, and Wesley Harrington. 1986. *Rules in the Making:
A Statistical Analysis of Regulatory Agency Behavior.* Washington, D.C.: Resources for
the Future.

Maloney, Michael, Robert McCormick, and Robert Tollison. 1984. "Economic Regulation, Competitive Governments and Specialized Resources." *Journal of Law and
Economics* 27 (2): 329–38.

Margolis, Howard. "Probability of a Tie Election." *Public Choice* 31 (1): 134–37.

Martimort, David. 1996. "The Multiprincipal Nature of Government." *European Economic Review* 40: 673–85.

_____. 1999. "The Life Cycle of Regulatory Agencies: Dynamic Capture and Transaction
Costs." *Review of Economic Studies* 66 (4): 929–47.

Mashaw, Jerry. 1997. *Greed, Chaos and Governance: Using Public Choice to Improve Public
Law.* New Haven, Conn.: Yale University Press.

Masson, Robert, and Lawrence DeBrock. 1980. "The Structural Effects of State Regulation of Retail Fluid Milk Prices." *Review of Economics and Statistics* 62 (2): 254–
62.

Matsusaka, John. 1995. "Explaining Voter Turnout: An Information Theory." *Public
Choice* 84 (1–2): 91–117.

Maxwell, W. David. 1960. "The Regulation of Motor-Carrier Rates by the Interstate
Commerce Commission." *Land Economics* 36 (1): 79–91.

Maxwell, John, Thomas Lyon, and Steven Hackert. 2000. "Self-Regulation and Social
Welfare: The Political Economy of Corporate Environmentalism." *Journal of Law and
Economics* 43 (2): 583–617.

Mayo, John, and Yatsuji Otsuka. 2001. "Demand, Pricing and Regulation: Evidence from
the Cable TV Industry." *The RAND Journal of Economics* 22 (3): 396–410.

Meehl, Paul. 1977. "The Selfish Citizen Paradox and the Throw Away Vote Argument."
American Journal of Political Science 71 (1): 11–30.

Meier, Kenneth, and John Plumlee. 1978. "Regulatory Administration and Organizational Rigidity." *Western Political Quarterly* 3 (1): 80–95.

Meyer, John, Merton Peck, John Stenason, and Charles Zwick. 1959. *The Economics of
Competition in the Transportation Industries.* Cambridge, Mass.: Harvard University
Press.

Miller, Warren, and Donald Stokes. 1963. "Constituency Influence in Congress." *American Political Science Review* 57: 45–63.

Mitchell, William. 1988. "Virginia, Rochester and Bloomington." *Public Choice* 56 (2):
101–19.

_____. 1989. "Chicago Political Economy: A Public Choice Perspective." *Public Choice*
63 (3): 283–92.

Mitchell, William, and Michael Munger. 1991. "Economic Models of Interest Groups: An Introductory Survey." *American Journal of Political Science* 35 (2): 512–46.

Moe, Terry. 1985. "Control and Feedback in Economic Regulation: The Case of the NLRB." *The American Political Science Review* 79 (4): 1094–116.

―――. 1987. "An Assessment of the Positive Theory of 'Congressional Dominance.'" *Legislative Studies Quarterly* 12 (4): 475–520.

Moore, Thomas Gale. 1961. "The Purpose of Licensing." *Journal of Law and Economics* 4: 93–117.

―――. 1978. "The Beneficiaries of Trucking Regulation." *Journal of Law and Economics* 21 (2): 327–43.

Morrison, Steven, Clifford Winston, and Tara Watson. 1999. "Fundamental Flaws of Social Regulation: The Case of Airplane Noise. *Journal of Law and Economics* 42 (2): 723–43.

Morton, Rebecca. 1987. "A Group Majority Model of Voting." *Social Choice and Welfare* 4 (2): 117–31.

―――. 1991. "Groups in Rational Turnout Models." *American Journal of Political Science* 35 (3): 758–76.

Moss, David, and Jonathan Lackow. 2007. "Rethinking the Role of History in Law & Economics: The Case of the Federal Radio Commission in 1927." Unpublished draft paper.

Myerson, Roger. 1988. "Population Uncertainty and Poisson Games." *International Journal of Game Theory* 27 (3): 375–92.

Nelson, Douglas, and Eugene Silberberg. 1987. "Ideology and Legislator Shirking." *Economic Inquiry* 25: 15–26.

Niemi, Richard. 1976. "Costs of Voting and Nonvoting." *Public Choice* 27 (1): 115–19.

Niskanen, William, Jr. 1971. *Bureaucracy and Representative Government.* Chicago: Aldine Publishing Company.

Noll, Roger. 1971. "The Economics and Politics of Regulation." *Virginia Law Review* 57: 1016–32.

―――. 1985. *Regulatory Policy and the Social Sciences* (ed.). Berkeley: University of California Press.

Noll, Roger, Merton Peck, and John McGowan. 1973. *Economic Aspects of Television Regulation.* Washington, D.C.: Brookings Institution.

Olson, C. Vincent, and John M. Trapani III. 1981. "Who Has Benefited from Regulation of the Airline Industry?" *Journal of Law and Economics* 24 (1): 75–93.

Olson, Mancur. 1965. *The Logic of Collective Action.* Cambridge, Mass.: Harvard University Press.

Olson, Mary. 1995. "Regulatory Agency Discretion among Competing Industries: Inside the FDA." *Journal of Law, Economics & Organization* 11 (2): 379–405.

Ordeshook, Peter, and Langche Zeng. 1997. "Rational Voters and Strategic Voting: Evidence from the 1968, 1980 and 1992 Elections." *Journal of Theoretical Politics* 9 (2): 167–87.

Oster, Sharon. 1980. "An Analysis of Some Causes of Interstate Differences in Consumer Regulations." *Economic Inquiry* 18: 39–54.

Owen, Guillermo, and Bernard Grofman. 1984. "To Vote or Not to Vote; the Paradox of Nonvoting." *Public Choice* 42 (3): 311–25.

Palda, Kristian. 1975. "The Effect of Expenditure on Political Success." *Journal of Law and Economics* 18 (3): 745–71.

Palfrey, Thomas, and Howard Rosenthal. 1983. "A Strategic Calculus of Voting." *Public Choice* 41 (1): 7–53.

———. 1985. "Voter Participation and Strategic Uncertainty." *American Political Science Review* 79 (1): 62–78.

Pashigian, B. Peter. 1985. "Environmental Regulation: Whose Self-Interests Are Being Protected?" *Economic Inquiry* 23: 551–84.

Pasour, E. C. 1992. "Economics and Public Policy: Chicago Political Economy versus Conventional Views." *Public Choice* 74 (2): 153–67.

Paul, Chris. 1982. "Competition in the Medical Profession: An Application of the Economic Theory of Regulation." *Southern Economic Journal* 48 (3): 559–69.

Peltzman, Samuel. 1965. "Entry in Commercial Banking." *Journal of Law and Economics* 8: 11–50.

———. "The Effects of Automobile Safety Regulation." *The Journal of Political Economy* 83 (4): 677–726.

———. 1976. "Toward a More General Theory of Regulation." *Journal of Law and Economics* 19 (2): 211–40.

———. 1984. "Constituent Interest and Congressional Voting." *Journal of Law and Economics* 27 (1): 181–210.

———. 1985. "An Economic Interpretation of the History of Congressional Voting in the Twentieth Century." *American Economic Review* 75 (4): 656–75.

Peltzman, Samuel, Michael Levine, and Roger Noll. 1989. "The Economic Theory of Regulation after a Decade of Deregulation." *Brookings Papers on Economic Activity: Microeconomics*, 1–59.

Plott, Charles. 1965. "Occupational Self-Regulation: A Case Study of the Oklahoma Dry Cleaners." *Journal of Law and Economics* 8: 195–222.

Poole, Keith, and R. Steven Daniels. 1985. "Ideology, Party, and Voting in the U.S. Congress, 1959–1980." *The American Political Science Review* 79 (2): 373–99.

Poole, Keith, and Howard Rosenthal. 1985. "The Political Economy of Roll-Call Voting in the 'Multi-Party' Congress of the U.S." *European Journal of Political Economy* 1 (1): 45–58.

Posner, Richard. 1971. "Taxation by Regulation." *Bell Journal of Economics and Management Science* 2 (1): 22–50.

———. 1974. "Theories of Economic Regulation." *Bell Journal of Economics and Management Science* 5 (2): 335–58.

Powell, G. Bingham. 1980. "Voting Turnout in Thirty Democracies.," in *Electoral Participation*, ed. R. Rose (Beverly Hills, Calif.: Sage).

Prager, Robin. 1989. "Using Stock Price Data to Measure the Effects of Regulation: The Interstate Commerce Act and the Railroad Industry." *The RAND Journal of Economics* 20 (2): 280–90.

Priest, George. 1993. "The Origins of Utility Regulation and the 'Theories of Regulation' Debate." *Journal of Law and Economics* 36 (1): 289–323.

Rasmusen, Eric, and Mark Zupan. 1991. "Extending the Economic Theory of Regulation to the Form of Policy." *Public Choice* 72 (2–3): 167–91.

Riddlesperger, James, and James King. 1982. "Energy Votes in the U.S. Senate." *Journal of Politics* 44 (3): 838–47.

Riker, William, and Peter Ordeshook. 1968. "A Theory of the Calculus of Voting." *American Political Science Review* 61 (1): 25–42.

Romer, Thomas. 1988. "On James Buchanan's Contributions to Public Economics." *Journal of Economic Perspectives* 2 (4): 165–79.

Rose, Nancy. 1985. "The Incidence of Regulatory Rents in the Motor Carrier Industry." *The RAND Journal of Economics* 16 (3): 299–318.

———. 1987. "Labor Rent Sharing and Regulation: Evidence from the Trucking Industry." *The Journal of Political Economy* 95 (6): 1146–78.

Rosenstone, Steven, and Raymond Wolfinger. 1978. "The Effect of Registration Laws on Voter Turnout." *American Political Science Review* 71 (2): 22–45.

Rowley, Charles. 1997. "Donald Wittman's 'The myth of democratic failure.'" *Public Choice* 92 (1–2): 15–26.

Rubinfeld, Daniel, and Randall Thomas. 1980. "On the Economics of Voter Turnout in Local School Elections." *Public Choice* 35 (3): 315–31.

Russell, Milton, and Robert Shelton. 1974. "A Model of Regulatory Agency Behavior." *Public Choice* 20: 47–62.

Sampson, Roy. 1958 "Comparative Performance of Electric Utilities under State and under Local Rate Regulation." *Land Economics* 34 (2): 174–78.

Samuelson, Paul. 1954. "The Pure Theory of Public Expenditure." *The Review of Economics and Statistics* 36 (4): 387–89.

Sanders, Elizabeth. 1980. "On the Costs, Utility and Simple Joys of Voting." *The Journal of Politics* 42 (3): 854–63.

Sanders, M. Elizabeth. 1981. *The Regulation of Natural Gas: Policy and Politics, 1938–1978*. Philadelphia: Temple University Press.

Schwert, G. William. 1977. "Public Regulation of National Securities Exchanges: A Test of the Capture Hypothesis." *The Bell Journal of Economics* 8 (1): 128–50.

Shachar, Ron, and Barry Nalebuff. 1999. "Follow the Leader: Theory and Evidence on Political Participation." *American Economic Review* 89 (3): 525–47.

Shaviro, Daniel. 1990. "Beyond Public Choice and Public Interest: A Study of the Legislative Process as Illustrated by Tax Legislation in the 1980s." *University of Pennsylvania Law Review* 139 (1): 1–123.

Shephard, Lawrence. 1978. "Licensing Restrictions and the Cost of Dental Care." *Journal of Law and Economics* 21 (1): 187–201.

Shughart, William, Robert Tollison, and Brian Goff. 1986. "Bureaucratic Structure and Congressional Control." *Southern Economic Review* 52 (4): 962–72.

Silberman, Jonathan, and Garey Durden. 1976. "The Rational Behavior Theory of Voter Participation." *Public Choice* 23 (1): 101–8.

Sloan, Frank, and Bruce Steinwald. 1980. "Effects of Regulation on Hospital Costs and Input Use." *Journal of Law and Economics* 23 (1): 81–109.

Sloss, James. 1970. "Regulation of Motor Freight Transportation: A Quantitative Evaluation of Policy." *The Bell Journal of Economics and Management Science* 1 (2): 327–66.

Smith, Jeffrey. 1975. "A Clear Test of Rational Voting." *Public Choice* 23 (1): 55–67.

Smith, Richard. 1982. "Franchise Regulation: An Economic Analysis of State Restrictions on Automobile Distribution." *Journal of Law and Economics* 25 (1): 125–57.

Snyder, James. 1990. "Campaign Contributions as Investments: The U.S. House of Representatives 1980–86." *Journal of Political Economy* 98 (6): 1195–227.

Spann, Robert, and Edward Erickson. 1970. "The Economics of Railroading: The Begin-
    ning of Cartelization and Regulation." *The Bell Journal of Economics and Management
    Science* 1 (2): 227–44.
Spiller, Pablo. 1990. "Politicians, Interest Groups and Regulators: A Multiple-Principals
    Agency Theory of Regulation, or 'Let Them Be Bribed.'" *Journal of Law and Economics*
    33 (1): 65–101.
Steagall, Jeffrey, and Ken Jennings. 1996. "Unions, PAC Contributions and the NAFTA
    Vote." *Public Choice* 17 (3): 515–21.
Stigler, George. 1965. "The Economist and the State." *American Economic Review* 65 (1):
    1–18.
———. 1971. "The Theory of Economic Regulation." *The Bell Journal of Economics and
    Management Science* 2 (1): 3–21.
———. 1972. "Economic Competition and Political Competition." *Public Choice* 13
    (1): 91–106.
———. 1976. "Xistence of X-efficiency." *American Economic Review* 66 (1): 213–16.
Stratmann, Thomas. 1991. "What Do Campaign Contributions Buy? Deciphering Causal
    Effects of Money and Votes." *Southern Economic Journal* 57 (3): 606–20.
———. 1995. "Campaign Contributions and Congressional Voting: Does the Timing
    of Contributions Matter?" *The Review of Economics and Statistics* 77 (1): 127–36.
Teske, Paul. 1991. "Interests and Institutions in State Regulation." *American Journal of
    Political Science* 35 (1): 139–54.
———. 2003. "State Regulation: Captured Victorian-era Anachronism or 'Re-enforcing'
    Autonomous Structure?" *American Political Science Association* 1 (2): 291–306.
Paul Teske, Samuel Best, and Michael Mintrom. 1994. "The Economic Theory of Reg-
    ulation and Trucking Deregulation: Shifting to the State Level." *Public Choice* 79:
    247–56.
Thompson, Fred. 1982. "Closeness Counts in Horseshoes and Dancing ... and Elec-
    tions." *Public Choice* 38 (3): 305–16.
Tollison, Robert. 1982. "Rent Seeking: A Survey." *Kyklos* 35: 575–602.
———. 1988. "Public Choice and Legislation." *Virginia Law Review* 74 (2): 339–71.
———. 1989. "Chicago Political Economy." *Public Choice* 63 (3): 293–97.
Tollison, Robert, Mark Crain, and Paul Pautler. 1975. "Information and Voting: An
    Empirical Note." *Public Choice* 24 (1): 43–50.
Tollison, Robert, and T. D. Willett. 1973. "Some Simple Economics of Voting and Not
    Voting." *Public Choice* 16 (1): 59–71.
Toma, Eugenia. 1983. "Institutional Structures, Regulation and Producer Gains in the
    Education Industry." *Journal of Law and Economics* 26 (1): 103–16.
Tullock, Gordon. 1959. "Problems of Majority Voting." *Journal of Political Economy* 67
    (6): 571–79.
———. 1967. "The General Irrelevance of the General Impossibility Theorem." *Quar-
    terly Journal of Economics* 81 (2): 256–70.
———. 1984. "A (Partial) Rehabilitation of the Public Interest Theory." *Public Choice*
    41 (1): 89–99.
———. 1988. *Wealth, Poverty and Politics.* Oxford: Basil Blackwell.
Uhlaner, Carole. 1989. "Rational Turnout: The Neglected Role of Groups." *American
    Journal of Political Science* 33 (2): 390–422.

Vestal, Allan. 1993. "Public Choice, Public Interest and the Soft Drink Interbrand Competition Act: Time to Derail the 'Root Beer Express?'" *William & Mary Law Review* 34: 338 (Winter).

Webbink, Douglas. 1973. "Regulation, Profits and Entry in the Television Broadcasting Industry." *The Journal of Industrial Economics* 21 (2): 167–76.

Weingast, Barry. 1984. "The Congressional-Bureaucratic System: A Principal-Agent Perspective." *Public Choice* 44 (1): 147–91.

Weingast, Barry, and Mark Moran. 1983. "Bureaucratic Discretion or Congressional Control? Regulatory Policymaking by the Federal Trade Commission." *The Journal of Political Economy* 91 (5): 765–800.

Welbom, David, and Anthony Brown. 1979. "State Public Service Commissions in Political Perspective: Illustrations from Georgia, Kentucky and Tennessee." Paper presented at the annual meeting of the Southern Political Science Association, Gatlinburg, Tenn. (Nov.)

Welch, W. P. 1974. "The Economics of Campaign Funds." *Public Choice* 20 (1): 83–97.

―――. 1980. "The Allocation of Political Monies: Economic Interest Groups." *Public Choice* 35 (1): 97–120.

White, Matthew, Paul Joskow, and Jerry Hausman. 1996. "Power Struggles: Explaining Deregulatory Reforms in Electricity Markets." *Brooking Papers on Economic Activity: Microeconomics*, 201–67.

Wilhite, Allen, and John Theilmann. 1987. "Labor PAC Contributions and Labor Legislation: A Simultaneous Logit Approach." *Public Choice* 53 (3): 267–76.

Willenborg, Michael. 2000. "Regulatory Separation as a Mechanism to Curb Capture: A Study of the Decision to Act against Distressed Insurers." *The Journal of Risk and Insurance* 67 (4): 593–616.

Williams, Bruce, and Albert Matheny. 1984. "Testing Theories of Social Regulation: Hazardous Waste Regulation in the American States." *The Journal of Politics* 46 (2): 428–58.

Wilson, James Q. 1980. "The Politics of Regulation," in *The Politics of Regulation*, ed. James Wilson (New York: Basic Books), 357–95.

Winson, Clifford. 1993. "Economic Deregulation: Days of Reckoning for Microeconomists." *Journal of Economic Literature* 31 (3): 1263–89.

Winston, Clifford, and Robert Crandall. 1994. "Explaining Regulatory Policy." *Brookings Papers on Economic Activity: Microeconomics*, 1–49.

Wittman, Donald. 1989. "Why Democracies Produce Efficient Results." *The Journal of Political Economy* 97 (6): 1395–424.

―――. 1995. *The Myth of Democratic Failure: Why Political Institutions Are Efficient.* Chicago: University of Chicago Press.

Wright, John. 1985. "PACs, Contributions and Roll Calls: An Organizational Perspective." *American Political Science Review* 79 (2): 400–14.

―――. 1989. "PAC Contributions, Lobbying and Representation." *Journal of Politics* 51 (3): 713–29.

―――. 1990. "Contributions, Lobbying and Committee Voting in the U.S. House of Representatives." *American Political Science Review* 84 (2): 417–38.

Zerbe, Richard, Jr. 1980. "The Costs and Benefits of Early Regulation of the Railroads." *Bell Journal of Economics* 11 (1): 343–50.

## EIGHT

The Paranoid Style in the Study of American Politics

David A. Moss and Mary Oey

What drives policymaking in a democracy? Is it our lawmakers' desire to serve the public interest or their desire to serve themselves through the accumulation of money, power, and votes? Most social scientists have long since concluded it is the latter – or, to put it another way, that the old public interest theory is dead. The central behavioral assumption of modern *economic* analysis, that individuals act in their own self-interest, has become the reigning behavioral assumption of modern *political* analysis as well.

Partly as a result, a large subset of social scientists – perhaps the vast majority in some fields – has come to assume that special interest groups dominate, or capture, the policymaking process by satisfying the policymakers' need for money and other forms of political support. "The preferences of the 'majority,'" writes Jonathan Macey, "are virtually irrelevant in determining legislative outcomes. Instead, law is made by legislators whose primary goal is to aggregate the political support they receive from competing special interest coalitions. Legal rules are generated by a process that conforms to standard microeconomic models of rationally self-interested behaviour."[1]

What makes this economic theory of regulation at once so powerful and so peculiar is its portrayal of representative democracy as profoundly unrepresentative – a tool of organized minority interests rather than of the majority interest. To arrive at this result, it is not enough to assume that lawmakers behave as rationally self-interested actors. It would, after all, be entirely rational for an elected official interested in reelection to try to serve the majority when facing an informed electorate. One must also assume, following Anthony Downs, that the voters themselves are ill-informed,

---

[1] Jonathan R. Macey, "Public Choice and the Law," in Peter Newman, ed., *The New Palgrave Dictionary of Economics and the Law* (New York: Stockton Press, 1998), vol. 3, 177.

presumably because of the high cost of obtaining useful information on any particular issue.[2]

Ironically, this pivotal assumption ends up inverting the connection between self-interested behavior and social-welfare maximization that lies at the heart of economic analysis, from which the economic theory of regulation is derived. Whereas social scientists generally accept the idea that self-interest is transformed into public interest (via an invisible hand) in *economic* markets, proponents of the economic theory of regulation reject this notion for *political* markets. Instead, they maintain that in the political realm, self-interest is typically inscribed directly into law, subverting the public interest in most, if not all, cases.[3] When applied to the study of politics, the rosy economic model of Adam Smith somehow turns depressingly dark.

But does this characterization of democratic politics accurately describe reality? George Stigler, widely regarded as the father of the economic theory of regulation, acknowledged that the theory "would be contradicted if, for a given regulatory policy, we found the group with larger benefits and lower costs of political action being dominated by another group with lesser benefits and higher cost of political action." He insisted, however, that "[t]emporary accidents aside, such cases simply will not arise: our extensive experience with the general theory in economics gives us the confidence that this is so. Indeed there is no alternative hypothesis."[4]

In this chapter, we suggest that such cases – including major cases – have arisen in the past. We focus on three historical episodes in which special interests appear to have given way to the general interest in the policymaking process: the enactment of the Voting Rights Act in 1965, Medicare that same year, and the Comprehensive Environmental Response, Compensation and Liability Act (CERCLA, or Superfund) fifteen years later. In all three cases, and especially in the first and last, the proposed legislation

---

[2] Anthony Downs, *An Economic Theory of Democracy* (New York: Harper & Row, 1957).

[3] In this chapter, we use the terms "public interest" and "general interest" almost interchangeably. Michael Levine, however, has astutely distinguished the "public interest" (which he characterizes as a normative notion "that is largely expressive of the preferences of the commentator rather than the polity") from the "general interest" (which "refers to an outcome that would be approved by a fully informed polity according to its accepted aggregation principles and procedures"). See Michael E. Levine, "Why Weren't the Airlines Reregulated?" New York University Law and Economics Working Papers, 54 (2006), 4. Here, we mainly have the second definition in mind in our use of both terms.

[4] George Stigler, Supplementary Note on Economic Theories of Regulation, in *The Citizen and the State* (1975), 140.

became unstoppable in the aftermath of a relevant "horror" story that received extensive coverage in the press – for example, Selma in the case of the Voting Rights Act, and Love Canal in the case of Superfund.

Defenders of the traditional Stiglerian position might argue that we focus solely on high-profile cases, and that the economic theory of regulation applies more cleanly to policies that slip under the public's radar. Almost by definition, a highly visible legislative process would be difficult for special interests to capture. Although this caveat is sometimes acknowledged in the literature, we have never seen the economic theory of regulation advertised as "a theory of minor legislative events."

Ultimately, the challenge for scholars is to identify the *conditions* under which special interests dominate (or capture) public policy and the conditions under which they do not. Although such a task lies far beyond the scope of this chapter, the three cases surveyed here suggest at least one potentially important dynamic – namely, that in the presence of a free press, real-life horror stories with bearing on policy issues may serve to blunt the power of special interests by informing and catalyzing public opinion.

WRESTLING WITH GHOSTS?

The earliest articulation of the economic theory of regulation is generally (and appropriately) credited to George Stigler,[5] although Stigler himself no doubt owed a significant intellectual debt to a number of social and public choice theorists – including Duncan Black, Kenneth Arrow, Anthony Downs, James Buchanan, and Gordon Tullock – who had already begun applying the tools of economic analysis to the study of politics in earlier years.[6]

In his classic paper, "The Theory of Economic Regulation," Stigler observes that regulation "may be actively sought by an industry, or it may be thrust upon it. A central thesis of this chapter is that, as a rule,

---

[5] George Stigler, "The Theory of Economic Regulation," Bell Journal of Economics and Management Science, vol. 2, no. 1 (Spring 1971), 3–21.

[6] See Duncan Black, "On the Rationale of Group Decision Making," *Journal of Political Economy*, vol. 56, no. 1. (Feb. 1948), 23–34; Kenneth J. Arrow, "A Difficulty in the Concept of Social Welfare," *Journal of Political Economy*, vol. 58, no. 4 (August 1950), 328–46; Anthony Downs, *An Economic Theory of Democracy* (New York: Harper & Row, 1957); James Buchanan and Gordon Tullock, *The Calculus of Consent: Logical Foundations of Constitutional Democracy* (Ann Arbor: University of Michigan Press, 1962); Gordon Tullock, "The Welfare Costs of Tariffs, Monopolies, and Theft," *Western Economic Journal* [now: *Economic Inquiry*], vol. 5, no. 3 (June 1967), 224–32.

regulation is acquired by the industry and is designed and operated primarily for its benefit."[7] He then identifies four essential benefits that the state can provide to an industry: (1) direct subsidies, (2) control over entry into the industry by rivals, (3) limitations on substitute goods and support for complements, and (4) price-fixing to facilitate "more than competitive rates of return."[8] According to Stigler, an industry will obtain these benefits when their value (to the industry) exceeds the industry's cost of acquiring them. "The industry which seeks regulation," he suggests, "must be prepared to pay with the two things a party needs: votes and resources."[9]

As Stigler readily points out, the acquisition of such benefits by industry may well undercut the public interest. "When an industry receives a grant of power from the state," he writes, "the benefit to the industry will fall short of the damage to the rest of the community." The question, then, is why a democratic political system will not prevent such adverse results. "Even if there were no deadweight losses from acquired regulation . . . one might expect a democratic society to reject such industry requests unless the industry controlled a majority of the votes." As an example, Stigler suggests that a "direct and informed vote on oil import quotas would reject the scheme," and he adds parenthetically: "If it did not, our theory of rational political processes would be contradicted."[10]

Why, then, are many industries, in Stigler's words, "able to employ the political machinery to their own ends"?[11] The answer, in a phrase, is voter ignorance:

The costs of comprehensive information are higher in the political arena [than in the private marketplace] because information must be sought on many issues of little or no direct concern to the individual, and accordingly he will know little about most matters before the legislature. The expressions of preferences in voting will be less precise than the expressions of preferences in the marketplace because many uninformed people will be voting and affecting the decision.

The channels of political decision making can thus be described as gross or filtered or noisy.

Particularly in cases where the costs of an industry-acquired policy are widely diffused across the citizenry and relatively small on a per capita

---

[7] Stigler, "Theory of Economic Regulation," 3.
[8] Stigler, "Theory of Economic Regulation," 4–6.
[9] Stigler, "Theory of Economic Regulation," 12.
[10] Stigler, "Theory of Economic Regulation," 10.
[11] Stigler, "Theory of Economic Regulation," 10.

basis, voters are likely to remain passive. "If voter group X wants a policy that injures non-X by a small amount, it will not pay non-X to discover this and act against the policy."[12]

Much of the rest of this chapter is devoted to three prominent examples from American policy history that seem to run contrary to Stigler's theory of politics. The critical reader, however, may wonder whether we are in effect wrestling with ghosts, since Stigler published his seminal paper on the topic more than a quarter century ago and economic models of interest group politics have matured significantly since then. Indeed, the relevant models have been formalized (starting with Peltzman in 1976) and have become considerably more nuanced – allowing for the interplay of multiple interest groups in shaping regulatory decision making, for a range of possible avenues through which special interest groups could influence regulators (from bribes to threats to information provision), and even for the explicit inclusion of concerns for voter welfare in politicians' utility functions.[13] Even so, a great deal has remained the same since Stigler's original foray, including – in most cases – the assumption of rational voter ignorance and, partly as a result, the characterization of politicians as available for purchase by interest groups. As Dal Bó and Di Tella acknowledge, "In virtually every model that we know of, politicians voluntarily trade policies for money, either for themselves (bribes) or for the party (campaign contributions)."[14]

Despite the emergence of more nuanced models since Stigler, relatively simple notions of capture remain deeply embedded in the psyche of the social sciences and often are taken as shorthand for the broader economic theory of regulation. As Jessica Leight shows in her contribution to this volume, these simple notions of capture show up in many guises throughout the literature.[15] Social scientists are often quick

---

[12] Stigler, "Theory of Economic Regulation," 12.

[13] Sam Peltzman, "Toward a More General Theory of Regulation," *Journal of Law and Economics*, vol. 19, no. 2 (August 1976), 211–40; Gary S. Becker, "A Theory of Competition Among Pressure Groups for Political Influence," *Quarterly Journal of Economics*, vol. 98, no. 3 (August 1983), 371–400; Gene M. Grossman and Elhanan Helpman, "Protection for Sale," *American Economic Review*, vol. 84, no. 4 (September 1994), 833–50; Ernesto Dal Bó and Rafael Di Tella, "Capture by Threat," *Journal of Political Economy*, vol. 111, no. 5 (2003), 1123–54; Ernesto Dal Bó, "Regulatory Capture: A Review," *Oxford Review of Economic Policy*, vol. 22, no. 2 (2006), 203–25.

[14] Dal Bó and Di Tella, "Capture by Threat," 1124.

[15] See Jessica Leight, "Public Choice: A Critical Reassessment," in Edward Balleisen and David Moss, eds., Government and Markets: Toward a New Theory of Regulation (Cambridge: Cambridge University Press, 2009).

to assume that because X benefited from a public policy, X must have captured the policy.[16] Some even engage in circular reasoning, using inferences about who acquired a policy (based on who benefited from it) as supporting evidence for the theory that generated those inferences in the first place.[17]

Presumptions and tautologies of this sort are typical of conspiracy theories. As a character of novelist P. D. James once observed, "Every death was a suspicious death if one looked only at motive."[18] And every policy is a suspicious policy (a captured policy) if one looks only at motive. Recalling Richard Hofstadter's famous essay, "The Paranoid Style in American Politics," we characterize this cynical approach as reflecting a "paranoid style" in the *study* of American politics.[19] In order to help move beyond it, we review three prominent cases in which this paranoid style of political analysis seems demonstrably to fail.

THREE MAJOR CASES

The three cases we have chosen to highlight – the Voting Rights Act, Medicare, and Superfund – by no means constitute a random or representative sample of possible cases. We selected all three because their legislative histories seem difficult to square with the economic theory of regulation. Devotees of capture theory are sure to point out many reasons why these cases are less than ideal subjects of study, including, in particular, their prominence in the public eye. But if history had gone the other way – if the doctors and insurance companies had defeated Medicare, or if the chemical

---

[16] Stigler himself maintained that the economic theory of regulation "tells us to look, as precisely and carefully as we can, at who gains and who loses, and how much, when we seek to explain a regulatory policy.... The first purpose of the empirical studies is to identify the purpose of the legislation! The announced goals of a policy are sometimes unrelated or perversely related to its actual effects, and the *truly intended effects should be deduced from the actual effects*" (Stigler, Supplementary Note, 140 (emphasis in original)).

[17] See e.g., David Moss and Jonathan Lackow, "Rethinking the Role of History in Law & Economics: The Case of the Federal Radio Commission in 1927," Harvard Business School Working Paper No. 09-008 (August 2008), which dissects one such case in the law and economics literature.

[18] P. D. James, *The Black Tower* (New York: Scribner, 1975), 196. We are indebted to Jim Wooten for bringing this passage to our attention.

[19] Although there have been some powerful critiques of this approach, they remain voices in the wilderness. See e.g., Donald Wittman, *The Myth of Democratic Failure: Why Political Institutions Are Efficient* (Chicago: University of Chicago Press, 1995). The original Hofstadter essay can be found in Richard Hofstadter, *The Paranoid Style in American Politics, and Other Essays* (New York: Knopf, 1965).

and oil industries had defeated Superfund (or, even better from their perspective, had diffused the costs of environmental clean-up broadly across
the citizenry) – can there be any doubt that these cases would have been
heralded as supporting evidence for a capture model?

Over the past several decades, social scientists have identified or alleged
numerous examples of capture from the Interstate Commerce Commission
to the Civil Aeronautics Board. Yet little systematic attention has been
devoted to identifying examples that might run the other way. We hope the
three legislative histories that follow will not only broaden the available case
library, but also facilitate the identification of distinguishing conditions and
characteristics on *both* sides of the capture divide.

The Voting Rights Act of 1965

Passage of the Voting Rights Act presents an intriguing puzzle for social
scientists. The direct beneficiaries of the act, disenfranchised blacks, had
precious little political clout, at least in a traditional sense, since they were
poor in both money and (by definition) voting power. Nor can it be said
that the promise of a solid black vote in the future was sufficient to make the
legislation politically attractive to most lawmakers. Southern members of
Congress largely voted against the bill and many of its most vocal Northern
supporters hailed from districts with disproportionately small black populations (i.e., smaller than the non-Southern national average).[20] In fact,
just one year earlier, after signing the Civil Rights Act of 1964, President
Johnson had conceded privately (and presciently), "I think we just delivered
the South to the Republican party for a long time to come."[21]

How, then, can we explain that the Voting Rights bill passed overwhelmingly in Congress (79–18 in the Senate and 328–74 in the House) and that
President Johnson ultimately signed it into law? The most succinct answer
is "Selma."

[20] David J. Garrow, *Protest at Selma: Martin Luther King, Jr., and the Voting Rights Act of 1965*
(New Haven, Conn.: Yale University Press, 1978), 171–74.
[21] Bill Moyers as quoted in Robert Dallek, *Flawed Giant: Lyndon Johnson and His Times, 1961–
1973* (New York: Oxford Univeristy Press, 1998), 120. Another version of the statement
has Johnson saying, "I think we've just delivered the South to the Republican Party for
the rest of my life and yours" [Bill Moyers in Robert L. Hardesty, ed., *The Johnson Years:
The Difference He Made* (Austin: University of Texas at Austin Edie and Lew Wasserman
Public Affairs Library, 1993), 32]. According to students of the subject, "White support
for the Democratic party peaked in 1964 and has since steadily deteriorated" [Edward G.
Carmines and Robert Huckfeldt, "Party Politics in the Wake of the Voting Rights Act,"
in *Controversies in Minority Voing: The Voting Rights Act in Perspective*, Bernard Grofman
and Chandler Davidson, eds. (Washington D.C.: The Brookings Institution, 1992), 129].

Selma and its Consequences

Increasingly impatient with existing civil rights laws that "had conspicuously failed to end the systematic exclusion of blacks from the polling stations," Martin Luther King, Jr. and the Southern Christian Leadership Conference (SCLC) began a massive voter registration drive in Selma, Alabama, in January 1965.[22] Across the South, just 43 percent of eligible blacks were registered to vote.[23] In Alabama, Georgia, Louisiana, Mississippi, and South Carolina, the figure was only 22 percent.[24] In Dallas County, where Selma was located, it was a mere 2 percent and "[i]n the adjacent counties of Lowndes and Wilcox, where blacks outnumbered whites more than two to one, there were no black voters at all."[25]

Although the SCLC's mass registration rallies were organized and peaceful, local law enforcement officials arrested thousands of those participating in a span of two weeks – including 500 schoolchildren and King himself – prompting intense national media coverage.[26] "The choice of Selma," writes Chandler Davidson, "was strategically sound.... Its sheriff, James G. Clark, Jr., much like Police Commissioner Eugene 'Bull' Connor in Birmingham two years earlier, could be counted on to overreact to peaceful civil rights demonstrations."[27]

Senator Jacob Javits (R-NY) was the first on Capitol Hill to react publicly to the events in Selma. On February 3, he suggested that the situation "be watched closely to see whether additional law is now necessary...."[28] The following day, Representative Augustus Hawkins (D-CA) announced that a bipartisan group of fifteen members of Congress would visit Selma to assess the need for voting rights legislation.[29]

---

[22] Adam Fairclough, *To Redeem the Soul of America: The Southern Christian Leadership Conference and Martin Luther King, Jr.* (Athens, Georgia: University of Georgia Press, 1987), 208.

[23] Chandler Davidson, "The Voting Rights Act: A Brief History," in *Controversies*, 13; James E. Alt, "The Impact of the Voting Rights Act on Black and White Voter Registration in the South," in *Quiet Revolution in the South: The Impact of the Voting Rights Act, 1965–1990*, Chandler Davidson and Bernard Grofman, eds. (Princeton: Princeton University Press, 1994), 374.

[24] Davidson, "The Voting Rights Act: A Brief History" in *Controversies*, 13.

[25] "In ... Dallas County, where slightly more than half the 30,000 persons of voting age were black, only 335 were registered in the fall of 1964 ... " (Davidson, "The Voting Rights Act: A Brief History" in *Controversies*: 15); Fairclough, 210.

[26] Fairclough, 230–33.

[27] Davidson, "The Voting Rights Act: A Brief History" in *Controversies*, p. 15.

[28] Javits as quoted in Garrow, 49.

[29] Garrow: 49. The fifteen congressmen were: Don Edwards (D-CA), Jeffrey Cohelan (D-CA), Ken Dyal (D-CA), Weston Vivian (D-MI), Augustus Hawkins (D-CA), William

On the afternoon of Hawkins's announcement, Johnson held a press conference in which he decried voting discrimination and the recent events in Alabama. Although his administration had already begun developing plans for new voting rights legislation in late 1964, at this point Johnson promised little more than more aggressive enforcement of existing legislation.[30] In addition, Johnson indicated that he would not send federal troops to Alabama.[31]

On February 6, however, the White House changed course and announced that President Johnson would send a "strong recommendation" to Congress for a new voting rights bill, although the administration offered neither a timeline nor legislative details.[32] Over the previous two days, pressure from the events unfolding in Selma had mounted rapidly, with reports emerging that local police had been using electric cattle prods in addition to nightsticks and guns on peaceful demonstrators. King, moreover, had announced that upon his release from jail, he intended to visit the president personally to press for voting rights legislation.[33] Finally, two Republican representatives who had visited Selma told reporters that they were now convinced that "there is a clear need for new civil rights legislation, particularly in regard to federal registrars."[34]

On the morning of Monday, February 8, New York representatives John Lindsay (R) and Joseph Resnick (D) introduced separate voting rights bills, both of which were supported by at least a half-dozen colleagues.[35] Over the following month, both Democratic and Republican members of Congress continued to vocalize strong support for new voting rights legislation and an interest in eliciting a formal proposal from the executive branch. Although Vice President Humphrey finally conceded on February 21 that the

Ryan (D-NY), James Scheuer (D-NY), Charles Diggs (D-MI), Jonathan Bingham (D-NY), John Conyers, Jr. (D-MI), John Dow (D-NY), Joseph Resnick (D-NY), Charles Mathias, Jr. (R-MD), Bradford Morse (R-MA), and Ogden Reid (R-NY) (Garrow, 268, n. 46).

30 John D. Morris, "Johnson Pledges Alabama Action," *New York Times,* February 5, 1965, 17; Garrow, 37–40; Howard Ball, Dale Krane, and Thomas P. Lauth, *Compromised Compliance: Implementation of the 1965 Voting Rights Act* (Westport, Conn.: Greenwood Press, 1982), 44–45; Dallek, 213–14.

31 Morris, "Johnson Pledges Alabama Action," 17; Dallek, 213–14. Johnson wanted to avoid "vindictive or punitive" actions against the South – he believed that this approach would only further alienate the nation's "moral, economic, and political outsider" (Johnson as quoted in Dallek, 211; Dallek, 113).

32 Garrow, 54.

33 Fairclough, 236.

34 Ogden Reid as quoted in Garrow, 54. The other representative was Charles Mathias.

35 Garrow, 56.

administration had decided a new law directly addressing voting discrimination was necessary, the White House remained vague about the schedule and legal details. As late as March 5, when President Johnson received King for over an hour at the White House, he still refused to divulge the language of the Justice Department's draft or to commit to any specifics, despite a formal criticism of the administration by thirty-one Republican politicians one week earlier for such extended ambiguity.[36]

Events in Alabama, and the national reaction to their extensive coverage in the press, soon forced the administration's hand. On Sunday, March 7, about 600 passively resisting demonstrators were teargassed and attacked by state troopers and local police in riot gear just outside Selma. That evening, ABC television broadcast a "long film report of the assault on Highway 80."[37] The following day, the *Washington Post* ran a banner headline story and the *New York Times* put a four-column photo of the event on the top of the front page.[38]

On March 9 alone, forty-three representatives and seven senators called for voting rights legislation, a response mirrored by mounting expressions of public outrage at the grass roots. "Bloody Sunday," one historian observed, "triggered a wave of sympathy demonstrations, including a march of ten thousand in Detroit led by the mayor and the governor, one of fifteen thousand in Harlem, and a rally in Washington that attracted a similar number."[39] Within a week of Bloody Sunday, President Johnson held a press conference and announced that he would present his voting rights proposal in a speech to Congress on March 15. In this address – the first presidential message on a domestic piece of legislation in nineteen years – Johnson asked for passage without delay or compromise.[40] The speech was broadcast live on all three major networks and drew more than 70 million viewers.[41]

The bill arrived on Capitol Hill two days later. It passed both houses of Congress after several months of legislative wrangling and was finally signed by President Johnson on August 6, 1965.

---

[36] Statement issued by thirty-one Republicans on February 23, 1965, as quoted in Garrow, 63.

[37] Garrow, 78.

[38] Leon Daniel, "Tear Gas, Clubs Halt 600 in Selma March: State Troopers Beat and Injure Many Negroes," *Washington Post*, March 8, 1965, A1; Roy Reed, "Alabama Police Use Gas and Clubs to Rout Negroes," *New York Times*, March 8, 1965, 1. The photo caption began: "Crushing Voter Demonstration."

[39] Fairclough, 247.

[40] Fairclough, 249.

[41] Davidson, "The Voting Rights Act: A Brief History" in *Controversies*, 16.

Capturing the Public

A cynical reading of the record might lead one to suspect that Johnson wanted the Voting Rights Act as an electoral counterweight to the Civil Rights Act. If the Democratic Party was going to alienate whites in the South with civil rights legislation, it might as well make sure that the blacks it was trying to protect could vote. By some accounts, such reasoning did come into play before Selma, when administration officials were quietly considering whether to put forward a modest voting rights bill. As Davidson suggests, "Johnson's motives were probably a mixture of genuine concern for voting rights and a fear that the Civil Rights Act of 1964 had so alienated white southerners from the Democratic party that only a vastly increased black vote could offset the party's losses."[42]

But even if this political context helps to explain Johnson's logic prior to Selma, it hardly stands as a sufficient explanation afterward. Once Selma hit the news, public pressure became so intense that most lawmakers, including the president himself, quickly concluded that there was little alternative to sweeping voting rights legislation. As Senator Walter Mondale put it after Bloody Sunday, "Sunday's outrage in Selma, Alabama, makes passage of legislation to guarantee Southern Negroes the right to vote an absolute imperative for Congress this year."[43]

Such a result was certainly no accident. King had learned from his experience with Bull Connor in Birmingham two years before that official violence against peaceful demonstrators could exert a powerful effect on public opinion. As David Garrow explains, Birmingham helped mark a shift in SCLC strategy from one of "nonviolent persuasion" to one of "nonviolent coercion" – a shift that was solidified in Selma:

While by late 1964 there may well still have been a "philosophy" of nonviolence within the SCLC leadership, the choice of Clark and Selma, and the SCLC's tactical decisions once there, both served to indicate that it was a philosophy based not upon a moral commitment to nonviolence or upon a desire to reform the hearts and minds of the likes of Jim Clark, but upon the pragmatic knowledge that nonviolence, coupled with violent opponents, would best serve the movement in its effort to gain active support from the American populace.... This shift from nonviolent persuasion to a more aggressive nonviolent coercion was based upon a very shrewd ... understanding of the dynamics of protest and of what would most aid the movement in its attempt to secure the enactment of a new federal voting rights law.[44]

[42] Davidson, "The Voting Rights Act: A Brief History" in *Controversies*, n. 33, 14.
[43] Walter Mondale (D-MN) as quoted in Garrow, 82.
[44] Garrow, 222–23. See also n. 27; Ball, Krane, and Lauth, 46 ("SCLC leaders expected that Sheriff Jim Clark would prove to be a violent law enforcement officer and that this

In a sense, therefore, a special interest group – the SCLC – *had* "captured" the legislative process. Yet its influence was not the result of financial contributions to politicians. Nor can we attribute its success to its ability to guarantee a solid block of votes for the Democratic Party. In the North, the black vote was already solidly Democratic, having gone at least 90 percent for Johnson in 1964; and, as we have seen, the strongest supporters of voting rights legislation in Congress often came from districts with disproportionately small black populations.[45] In the South, where a new block of black votes was a realistic expectation, most lawmakers voted against the bill, apparently fearing an even larger white backlash.

The secret of the SCLC's success lies elsewhere. Instead of capturing the lawmakers directly (through promises of money or votes), the civil rights movement succeeded in capturing the conscience of the nation. And it was only in this way – indirectly – that it ended up capturing the votes of the lawmakers themselves. It is impossible to know whether members of Congress who favored the Voting Rights Act voted their consciences (in support of what they viewed as the "public interest") or, alternatively, simply wished to satisfy their constituents and thus maximize their chances for reelection. The point is that once King and the SCLC captured the conscience of the nation, these two potential motivations came into alignment. Self-interest and public interest, significantly, both pointed in the same direction.

Medicare, 1965

Unlike the campaign for the Voting Rights Act, the battle over Medicare attracted a great deal of special interest money. The American Medical Association (AMA) likely spent more than any other interest group and conceivably more than all the others combined. The curious thing, though, is that the doctors lost. Despite the fierce opposition of the AMA, which involved what was probably the most intense and well-financed publicity and lobbying campaign of any up to that time, the House and Senate passed

violence against defenseless blacks would incur the wrath of the general public and lead to the demand for more effective voting rights legislation.")

[45] The proportion of black registered voters whose party identification was Democrat reached 74 percent in 1964 (up from 48 percent in 1960). See Pearl T. Robinson, "Whither the Future of Blacks in the Republican Party?" *Political Science Quarterly*, vol. 97, no. 2 (Summer 1982), 211, table 1. Although estimates of President Johnson's share of the black vote in the 1964 election vary, most estimates are 90 percent or higher. Immediately after the 1964 election, for example, a Johnson advisor informed the President that he had won 96 percent of the black vote. Always quick with a comeback, Johnson asked, "What about the other 4 percent?" (Johnson as quoted in Neil A. Lewis, "Louis E. Martin, 84, Aide to 3 Democratic Presidents," *New York Times*, January 30, 1997, D21).

the Medicare bill over the association's objections (by votes of 313–155 in
the House and 68–21 in the Senate), and President Johnson signed it into
law on July 30, 1965.

Background: Failed Campaigns for Public
Health Insurance, 1915–1950

By the 1960s, reforms calling for compulsory public health insurance in the
United States had been cycling in and out of favor for about half a century.
But they had all been defeated.

In the 1910s, numerous state legislatures took up proposals for public
health insurance, only to see them widely attacked by a curious coalition of
"commercial insurance carriers, physicians, labor leaders, prominent capitalists, druggists, employers, fraternal societies, and Christian Scientists."
Critics dismissed the proposals as un-American, socialistic, and "Born in
Germany." In the end, these well-organized opponents succeeded in swaying
not only lawmakers, but the public more generally. In California, a proposed
constitutional amendment that would have permitted compulsory health
insurance in the state went down to a crushing defeat at the polls, rejected
by a popular vote of nearly 3 to 1.[46]

After a series of further defeats in the late 1910s and a sharp political turn
to the right after World War I, the campaign for public health insurance
reemerged about a generation later. Although President Franklin Roosevelt
was unwilling to include health insurance in his Social Security bill in 1935,
for fear of undermining support for the unemployment and old-age insurance components, the Social Security Board ultimately endorsed a "unified
and comprehensive social insurance system" that included health insurance
in 1942.[47] Based in large part on the board's proposal, the Wagner-Murray-
Dingell bill (first introduced in 1943) promised comprehensive health insurance for nearly every American citizen. Despite strong public support from
President Truman, a national health insurance bill was introduced without
success year after year into the early 1950s.

An extraordinarily successful "National Education Campaign" conducted
by the American Medical Association (AMA) during these years, combined
with the spread of voluntary employer-based health plans, had broken what

---

[46] David Moss, *Socializing Security: Progressive-Era Economists and the Origins of American
Social Policy* (Cambridge, Mass.: Harvard University Press, 1996), 136–57.

[47] Peter A. Corning, *The Evolution of Medicare . . . from idea to law,* U.S. Department of Health,
Education, and Welfare, Social Security Administration, Office of Research and Statistics,
Research Report No. 29 (Washington: U.S. Government Printing Office, 1969), 54.

appeared to be an emerging national consensus in favor of a federal solution. "In the first year of the 'national education campaign,'" writes Peter Corning,

> several million pieces of literature were distributed by the AMA, and endorsements were won from no fewer than 1,829 organizations.... Perhaps the biggest coup, though, was the reversal by the social welfare arm of the Catholic Church of its long-standing support of National Health Insurance. Editorial opinion also turned against the program, and by late 1949 a Gallup poll showed that support for Government health insurance had dropped to a bare 51 percent. Meanwhile, private health insurance continued to make progress.[48]

The doctors ran an aggressive campaign. As Theodore Marmor describes it, "[T]heir crusade was conducted on a note of hysteria, holding out horrific visions of a socialized America ruled by an autocratic federal government."[49] Long fearful of centralized power and government ownership, and newly attuned to the supposed dangers of communism as a result of the early conflicts of the Cold War, many Americans proved instinctively sympathetic to the AMA's case.

Targeting Public Health Insurance for the Elderly

Proponents of a public system refused to give up, however. Seeing little prospect of securing national health insurance at this time, they instead set their sights on the more modest goal of enacting public health insurance for Social Security recipients. After considering proposals to cover various types of medical costs under Social Security for almost ten years, in 1960 Congress settled on a less controversial bill (Kerr-Mills) that provided funds to the states for "medically indigent" senior citizens.

Meanwhile, momentum began to build for a broader program of public health insurance for the elderly, particularly after the Senate Subcommittee on Problems of the Aged and Aging launched hearings in 1959. Although the subcommittee initially failed to attract much attention in Washington, it drew significant media coverage once the senators took their show on the road, hitting cities from Boston to San Francisco. "We knew we had a popular issue," a Senate staffer later reported,

> but we didn't realize it would be *that* popular.... [T]he old folks lined up by the dozen everyplace we went. And they didn't talk much about housing or recreational

---

[48] Corning, 66–67.
[49] Theodore R. Marmor, *The Politics of Medicare* (Chicago: Aldine Publishing Company, 1973), 13.

centers or retirement problems or part-time work. They talked about medical care.... [W]e had these people telling what life was like for them.... The upshot was that the hearings got headlines and front-page stories everyplace we went. This gave the movement its first big push forward on the national scene.[50]

Many of the stories that the subcommittee heard were tragic. Particularly poignant was an elderly couple's suicide note, written by the husband to the couple's doctor: "I am sorry that it had to end this way but I see no other way.... If you will look over the drug bills you can see that what little money we have could not last long.... Pray for us that God in his great mercy will forgive us for our act."[51]

Moved by stories like these and energized by a surge in public support (a Gallup poll at the time showed 67 percent of the public favoring federal health insurance for the elderly), reformers introduced in 1961 a new, more ambitious bill, known as Anderson-King.[52] Originally designed to cover only Social Security beneficiaries who were at least sixty-five years old, the bill was amended in 1963 to cover all Americans sixty-five and over (rather than just Social Security beneficiaries). Not long after the assassination of President Kennedy, his successor, Lyndon Johnson, said of Anderson-King, "I can think of no piece of legislation that I would be happier to approve than that bill."[53]

After the bill narrowly failed to gain legislative approval in 1964, congressional leaders made it their first order of business in January 1965, reintroducing the legislation as H.R. 1 and S. 1. The Democrats' landslide election victory in November had not only left Johnson in control of the White House, but also "brought 42 new Northern Democrats into the House, almost all of them medicare supporters."[54] In addition, general public

---

[50] Quoted in Richard Harris, "Medicare [part] II – More Than A Lot of Statistics," *New Yorker*, July 9, 1966, 62, emphasis in original.

[51] Quoted in Harris, "More Than A Lot of Statistics," 64. Ironically, in its final form, Medicare did not cover prescription drugs.

[52] See "Old-Age Medical Insurance," Survey #645-K, June 9, 1961, in *The Gallup Poll Public Opinion, 1935–1971* (New York: Random House, 1972), Volume Three: 1959–1971, p. 1721. In Gallup polls where respondents were asked which plan they favored, government health insurance for the elderly (compulsory) or private health insurance for the elderly (voluntary), government insurance was preferred 55 percent to 34 percent in a March 1962 poll, 48 percent to 41 percent in a May–June 1962 poll, and 44 percent to 40 percent in a July 1962 poll ("Health Care for the Aged," Survey #656-K, April 1, 1962, 1759; "Health Care for the Aged," Survey #659-T, July 1 1962, 1774; "Medicare," Survey #661-K, August 22 1962, 1781; all in *Gallup Poll*, Volume Three).

[53] Richard Harris, "Medicare [part] III – We Do Not Compromise," *New Yorker*, July 16, 1966, 74–76.

[54] Carmen D. Solomon, "Major Decisions in the House and Senate Chambers on Social Security: 1935–1985," CRS Report for Congress (Congressional Research Service, December 29, 1986), 54.

support remained above 60 percent. According to a Gallup poll, the public rated "[m]edical care to the aged" as the second most important problem (after Vietnam and just before civil rights) that respondents "[would] most like to have President Johnson deal with now that he has won the election."[55]

Cognizant of the rapidly emerging consensus, opponents of Medicare quickly proposed noncompulsory alternatives, essentially as defensive measures. "Eldercare," offered by the AMA, and "Bettercare," proposed by the ranking Republican on the House Ways and Means Committee, John Byrnes, both called for federal funds to subsidize health insurance policies for senior citizens. Advocates of Eldercare and Bettercare also promised that their plans would provide better coverage than the main bill in Congress (now called King-Anderson) by including doctors' fees and drugs as well as hospitalization costs. Although both proposals promised no government coercion, the two plans were in fact quite different from one another. Under Eldercare, the states would receive federal grants (as in Kerr-Mills) to help needy senior citizens buy private health coverage. Under Bettercare, the federal government would create a voluntary health insurance program for the elderly, financed through a combination of individual premiums and a federal contribution drawn from general revenues.[56]

The bill that finally became law in July 1965 was the brainchild of House Ways and Means Committee Chairman Wilbur Mills. Until Johnson's landslide victory in November, Chairman Mills – well known for his fiscal conservatism – had continually frustrated the White House by dragging his feet on Medicare. But now he surprised everyone with a masterful political maneuver that made passage all but certain.[57] Known as the "three

[55] "Medicare Program," Survey #703-K, January 3, 1965, 1915 and "Most Important Problem," Survey #701-K, November 18, 1964, 1908, in *Gallup Poll*, Volume Three.

[56] See Marmor, *Politics of Medicare*, 61–65; Eric Patashnik and Julian Zelizer, "Paying for Medicare: Benefits, Budgets, and Wilbur Mills's Policy Legacy," *Journal of Health Politics, Policy and Law*, vol. 26, no. 1 (February 2001), 17–18. With respect to Bettercare, Marmor writes, "The Byrnes bill was ready for discussion because the Republicans on the committee, in the wake of the 1964 election, wanted to prevent Democrats from taking exclusive credit for a Medicare law. The Republican staff counsel, William Quealy, had explained this point in a confidential memorandum in January, reminding the Republican committeemen that they had to 'face political realities'" (63). Similarly, at the time, the *New York Times* reporter covering the AMA characterized the introduction of Eldercare as representing "a major tactical shift" for the organization (Austin C. Wehrwein, "A.M.A. Opens Bid to Kill Medicare," *New York Times*, January 27, 1965, 14).

[57] Representative Byrnes commented at the time, "I assume Wilbur saw the election returns and he could see he was being left behind. The troops were charging right past him. He figured he'd better give his horse some oats and get up there in front where a leader belonged." Quoted in Harold B. Meyers, "Mr. Mills's Elder-medi-bettercare," *Fortune*, June 1965, 166.

layer cake," Mills's Medicare bill covered the medically indigent through an adaptation of Eldercare and Kerr-Mills (now called Medicaid); covered hospital and related expenses for Social Security beneficiaries through King-Anderson (Part A of Medicare); and offered Bettercare benefits as a voluntary supplement covering those expenses not included in the first two layers, such as doctors' fees (Part B of Medicare). Although the addition of Part B represented a dramatic expansion of what was originally contemplated in King-Anderson, it was widely characterized as a political compromise with Republicans.

The House and Senate versions of the new bill passed by large margins, and the House-Senate Joint Conference Committee took just fourteen days to resolve differences between the two. The conference report was approved by a vote of 307 to 116 in the House and 70 to 24 in the Senate. By this point, of course, the President's signature was a foregone conclusion.

Well-Organized Opposition from the American Medical Association

Whereas reformers were understandably jubilant about the passage of Medicare, leaders of the AMA were left in a state of shock. Even after the legislation passed, the AMA continued trying to drum up opponents for several more months and flirted with the idea of a boycott.[58]

Over the years, the AMA had opposed every major proposal for coverage of the elderly other than its own Eldercare proposal.[59] In fact, between 1935 and 1965, the AMA publicly opposed nearly every health-related measure introduced in Congress, including "compulsory vaccination against smallpox and compulsory inoculation against diphtheria, the mandatory reporting of tuberculosis cases to public-health agencies, the establishment of public venereal-disease clinics and of Red Cross blood banks, federal grants for medical school construction and for scholarships for medical students, Blue Cross and other private health-insurance programs, and free centers for cancer diagnosis."[60] Its opposition to public insurance measures – which it repeatedly characterized as "socialist" schemes[61] – proved particularly fierce.

---

[58] Richard Harris, "Medicare [part] IV – A Sacred Trust," 56, 63; "A.M.A. Head Predicts Medicare Boycott," *New York Times*, August 18, 1965, 35; "A.M.A. Plans Special Session on Problems of Medicine," *New York Times*, September 11, 1965, 28.

[59] Another possible exception is Kerr-Mills, which the association opposed until it was signed into law, and then supported in an effort to kill King-Anderson.

[60] Richard Harris, "Medicare [part] I – All Very Hegelian," *New Yorker*, July 2, 1966, 29.

[61] Harris, "We Do Not Compromise," 37, 56.

For about thirty years after the AMA first published a resolution in 1920 "declar[ing] its opposition to . . . any plan . . . of compulsory [medical] insurance . . . provided, controlled, or regulated by any state or the federal government," its strategy for influencing public policy was based mainly on legislative testimony and public education campaigns to sway popular opinion.[62] It is unclear whether the association relied in any substantial way on lobbying during the early part of this period. By 1949, however, the AMA had begun to align itself publicly with politicians who opposed federal health insurance, and it had already emerged as "the biggest spender among Washington lobbies."[63] Between 1948 and 1952, the AMA devoted approximately $4.5 million to its "National Education Campaign" against national health insurance.[64]

As a tax-exempt corporation, the AMA was legally barred from making direct political contributions, but several historians have suggested that it nevertheless may have engaged in this sort of activity.[65] Either way, by 1961 the AMA's political activities had reached a scale that led it to create a separate entity called the American Medical Political Action Committee (AMPAC), which was authorized to make campaign contributions.[66]

In 1964, AMPAC spent $402,000 "to bring about the election of candidates who . . . are sympathetic towards conservative government, free enterprise, and private practice of medicine."[67] Of 164 organizations that reported contributions exceeding $10,000 to the House of Representatives that year, AMPAC was number seventeen.[68] Moreover, according to AMPAC's first executive director, the "national office handled only one out of every six dollars . . . the remaining five were raised and spent locally, and were not reported."[69]

---

[62] AMA as quoted in Elton Rayack, *Professional Power and American Medicine: The Economics of the American Medical Association* (Cleveland: The World Publishing Company, 1967), 145.

[63] Rayack, 11.

[64] Harris, "More Than A Lot of Statistics," 31.

[65] In 1925, a federal law was passed "forbid[ding] . . . corporation[s] from making contributions to or expenditures on behalf of candidates for federal office" [Frank D. Campion, *The AMA and U.S. Health Policy Since 1940* (Chicago: Chicago Review Press, 1984), 210]. See Harris, "More Than a Lot of Statistics," 57–58 and "We Do Not Compromise," 49–50.

[66] Harris, "We Do Not Compromise," 49.

[67] Dr. Malcolm C. Todd, AMPAC National Board of Directors, as quoted in Rayack, 12. Campion, 271 (see n. 78).

[68] Rayack, 12, citing *Congressional Quarterly Weekly Report*, No. 3, Part I of II Parts, January 21, 1966, 72–78.

[69] Harris, "We Do Not Compromise," 65.

The AMA's political operations, already formidable in 1964, exploded the following year. As Elton Rayack observed, "The A.M.A.'s 1965 campaign against medicare broke all . . . records for expenditures by lobbyists. In the *first quarter* of 1965 the A.M.A. spent more than $950,000. [Between 1945 and 1965] there have been only two occasions when lobby spending by any organization for any *full year* reached or exceeded $900,000 – and on both those occasions, as in 1965, the A.M.A. was the group involved."[70] Richard Harris has suggested that the AMA's campaign contributions sometimes may have come with strings attached:

According to several members of Congress who have been on the receiving end, opponents of Medicare have employed all the usual tactics at one time or another. A couple of years ago, one member of the House was overheard saying that a representative of his state's medical society had approached his assistant and offered to make a campaign contribution of ten thousand dollars if the congressman would come out publicly against government health insurance. "That's a good bit of money, especially when I'm not even on Ways and Means," he said. "And a colleague of mine who isn't on the committee, either, but has a few years' seniority on me in the House told me he was offered twenty thousand."[71]

Organized Support for Medicare

The lobbying on Medicare, of course, was not entirely one-sided. Organized labor had long had an interest in compulsory health insurance. In particular, the American Federation of Labor and Congress of Industrial Organizations (AFL-CIO) played a substantial role helping to draft key bills and lobbying for them. The political arm of the AFL-CIO, the Committee on Political Education (COPE), had a reputation for "keeping an alert eye on congressmen's voting records, endorsing candidates, marking others for defeat, purchasing pre-election air time, and coordinating the work of local organizations, which rang the doorbells, furnished the campaign workers, and got the right-minded people to the polls on election day."[72] One indication of the AFL-CIO's influence in the passage of Medicare is that the organization's chief lobbyist, Andrew Biemiller, attended the signing ceremony in Independence, Missouri, and received – as a token of the

---

[70] Rayack, 11, emphasis in original. According to the *New York Times*, "Officials of the association noted that $829,484 had been spent on newspaper, television and radio advertising and $113,080 on pamphlets and related matter. The rest, $9,005, was spent for person-to-person lobbying" (Austin C. Wehrwein, "Lobby Expenses of A.M.A. at Peak," *New York Times*, June 23, 1965, 63).

[71] Harris, "More Than a Lot of Statistics," 57–58.

[72] Campion, 211.

president's appreciation – one of the seventy-two pens Johnson used to sign the legislation.[73]

The AFL-CIO also played a significant role in establishing and funding the National Council of Senior Citizens for Health Care through Social Security (NCSC). The NCSC grew out of Senior Citizens for Kennedy, which in turn fell under an umbrella organization – Citizens for Kennedy – that was "controlled, funded, and supported logistically by the DNC [Democratic National Committee]."[74] Established as an independent entity (with the help of several labor leaders) in 1961, the NCSC attracted 500,000 members within its first few months of operation and boasted a membership five times that by 1964.[75] According to William Hutton, the executive director of NCSC, the organization's budget between 1961 and 1965 totaled a half-million dollars, obtained "in more or less equal parts" from the DNC and the AFL-CIO and including voluntary membership dues of one dollar a year.[76] Although other senior-citizen organizations existed at the time, including the American Association of Retired Persons (AARP), the NCSC was a leading one – and arguably the only major senior-citizen group that actively promoted Medicare in the years leading up to its passage.[77]

---

[73] John D. Morris, "President Signs Medicare Bill; Praises Truman," *New York Times*, July 31, 1965, 1, 8.

[74] Henry J. Pratt, *The Gray Lobby* (Chicago: University of Chicago Press, 1976), 63. "In the case of Senior Citizens for Kennedy, the staff consisted of fourteen people, headed by [Blue] Carstenson from the DNC staff, and including two other DNC staff members, two people on loan from organized labor, one Senate and one House staffer, four volunteers, and secretarial help" (Pratt, 63–64).

[75] Harris, "We Do Not Compromise," 50–51, 70; Harris, "A Sacred Trust," 35. These figures include direct (dues-paying) as well as indirect members: Existing senior organizations (especially so-called "Golden Age" social clubs) could join the NCSC as chartered affiliates. Under this arrangement, the NCSC would extend (indirect) membership to all club members so long as a minimum of ten club members paid NCSC dues (interview with Betty Cooper, former director of communications at NCSC, June 2002). See also Pratt, 89, 44. In 1971, the number of directly contributing, dues-paying members ("Gold Card members") was about 71,000 (Pratt, 89).

[76] Harris, "We Do Not Compromise," 51. Harris, however, does not use citations. Dan Schulder, one of the original staff members of the NCSC, believes that anyone who would be able to verify these figures is no longer living (interview June 2002). See also Pratt, 96.

[77] NCSC documents suggest that "other seniors' groups ... fought vigorously to stop [Medicare]" (NCSC, "About Us: A Brief History" [text online], accessed June 2002, available at http://www.ncscinc.org/about/ history.htm). While this assertion is somewhat exaggerated, it is by no means entirely false. In 1955, the eight-year old National Retired Teachers Association (NRTA) began offering life insurance policies – and later travel, pharmacy, and training services – to its members. "So great was the interest [among] retirees outside the teaching profession" that the NRTA spun off a new organization, the American Association of Retired Persons, to offer the plan to "a far broader constituency." "AARP ... prospered, not only through its ever-expanding membership, but also by virtue of the fact that the

Sorting Out the Evidence on Influence: Special Interests or General Interest?

Given Medicare's long and complex legislative history, one can naturally find pieces of evidence to support many different interpretations of what drove its passage, including interpretations consistent with political capture.

Perhaps the strongest argument of this sort is that organized labor and the NCSC "captured" Medicare. Both of these special interests fought for the legislation, claimed to represent large numbers of voters, spent large sums of money, and ultimately got most of what they wanted. Organized labor played an especially large role supporting candidates during the 1964 election, apparently outspending the AMA by a significant margin.[78] For its part, the NCSC became increasingly visible during the battle over Medicare the following year. As he signed the legislation in 1965, President Johnson announced that "[w]ithout the National Council of Senior Citizens, there would have been no Medicare."[79]

Although such evidence is indeed suggestive, the argument that organized labor and senior citizens captured Medicare also faces significant evidentiary problems. First, the constituencies that the AFL-CIO and the NCSC represented were already heavily Democratic, and it was arguably the

insurance operation... returned a fixed percentage of premiums and fees to help meet NRTA-AARP operating expenses." For this reason, it has been suggested that NRTA-AARP had an interest in not supporting government health insurance. During the 1959 Forand hearings, NRTA-AARP submitted to the Ways and Means Committee its own health care proposal that, "while not identical to that being offered by the American Medical Association, was not inconsistent with it." Additionally, students of the subject have observed that the NRTA-AARP has historically remained rather distant from organized labor (Pratt, 90–91). "NRTA-AARP... did not voice grievances of the aged but rather served to market a service – insurance. In fact, the AARP conducted no government lobbying until 1967 because [its founder] was committed to free-enterprise solutions to social problems" (Stephen P. Wallace and John B. Williamson, *The Senior Movement: References and Resources* (New York: G.K. Hall & Co., 1992), xii. On the (limited) political influence of senior citizen groups at this time, see Wallace and Williamson, xxxiv; Pratt, 117.

[78] "According to its chairman, AMPAC was 'outgunned,'" writes a historian of the AMA. "In comparison with the $402,050 spent by AMPAC (and about $125,000 by other medical organizations), the AFL-CIO's COPE disbursed $988,810 to support its candidates, with over $1 million from other labor-affiliated political action committees and $44,788 from an organization called Senior Citizens for Johnson and Humphrey. Democratic candidates for federal offices declared $5,735,555 in campaign expenses for 1964, Republican candidates, $3,368,568" (Campion, 271).

[79] President Johnson as quoted by the NCSC, "About Us: A Brief History: A History of Accomplishments" [text online], accessed June 2002, available at http://www.ncscinc.org/about/history.htm.

Democratic landslide of 1964 that made Medicare inevitable.[80] Unless one maintains that the AFL-CIO and the NCSC actually delivered that landslide, it would be hard to argue that they captured the lawmakers who enacted Medicare, particularly since the legislation passed by such large margins in both houses of Congress.

Moreover, although good data on lobbying expenses are scarce, it appears that the AMA was essentially in a league of its own in 1965. When the *New York Times* reported that the AMA had devoted over $950,000 to lobbying in the first quarter of 1965, it also noted that this was "nearly 20 times the amount reported by the group that ranked second in the first quarter of 1965...."[81] In fact, the AMA's first-quarter lobbying expenditures were nearly twice as much as the NCSC's *total budget* for the years 1961–65.[82] What's more, roughly half of the NCSC's budget apparently came from the Democratic National Committee, which means that money was flowing *from* the politicians *to* the special interest group, raising questions about exactly who influenced whom.

An encounter at the Medicare signing ceremony between the AFL-CIO's lobbying chief, Andrew Biemiller, and former President Harry Truman offers an additional piece of anecdotal evidence about how the AMA's lobbying muscle was perceived at the time. Truman greeted Biemiller by telling him, "You're the guy that had guts enough to take on the doctors. You're one of the few people I know that had the kind of guts I had to take on the doctors. And God bless you, Andy Biemiller, I hope you last a long time."[83] There was little doubt about who represented David and who Goliath in this political drama – at least in the eyes of the winners.

A second possible argument – which again would be consistent with capture – is that the AMA actually won the debate, since its broader goal was to defeat national health insurance covering all citizens, not just the elderly. The reason President Truman expressed such hostility toward "the doctors" in his interchange with Biemiller was that the AMA had defeated him when he threw his support behind national health insurance in the

---

[80] See Marmor, *The Politics of Medicare*, 59 ("The electoral outcome of 1964 guaranteed the passage of legislation on medical care for the aged").

[81] Wehrwein, "Lobby Expenses of A.M.A. at Peak."

[82] Pratt has noted that "the NCSC was handicapped by limited funds and staff resources," (Pratt, 88).

[83] Truman as quoted by Biemiller in "Oral History Interview with Andrew J. Biemiller," Washington, D.C., July 29, 1977, conducted by James R. Fuchs, Truman Presidential Museum and Library, 35–36 [text online], accessed December 2008, available at http://www.trumanlibrary.org/oralhist/biemiller.htm.

1940s. The AMA spent over $1.5 million on its campaign in 1949 and a similar amount in 1950 as part of a successful drive to defeat the president's proposal.[84] In fact, the results of the battle proved so decisive that national health insurance was barely considered again in the United States for more than a decade.[85]

A closer look at the evidence from the 1949–50 contest, however, suggests that the AMA's real victory, like the civil rights movement's later victories in the mid-1960s, lay in capturing public opinion itself. The AMA appears to have devoted the vast majority of its expenditures in 1949–50 to public relations efforts. Although there are scattered indications that the AMA may have violated rules barring tax-exempt corporations from making direct political contributions during these years, the AMA did not officially establish a political action committee until 1961. Instead, it devoted considerable resources to its National Education Campaign, designed to influence public opinion; and the available polling data suggest that this campaign may have been effective. Back in the early 1940s, polls showed support for government health insurance ranging from 59 to 74 percent.[86] Yet when asked as part of a Gallup poll in March 1949 whether they supported the Truman plan (national health insurance financed through a payroll tax) or the AMA plan (voluntary private health insurance combined with federal funds for the poor), only 33 percent of respondents supported Truman whereas 47 percent supported the AMA.[87]

By 1965, however, both the issue and the surrounding political context had changed. The public proved far more sympathetic to the notion of government health insurance for the elderly than it had to government health insurance for all. This, at root, explains why the AMA lost so decisively in 1965, despite having prevailed over a similar array of interests fifteen years earlier.

One final argument that has been advanced to suggest Medicare was "captured" focuses on the unusually generous reimbursement of doctors

[84] Harris, "More Than A Lot of Statistics," 36, 31.
[85] Paul Starr, *The Social Transformation of American Medicine* (New York: Basic Books, 1982), 382.
[86] Corning, 57.
[87] "Government Health Insurance," Survey #438-K, April 6, 1949, *Gallup Poll*, Volume Two: 1949–1958, 802. The results were more favorable to Truman in a November poll limited to New York state residents, in which 51 percent of respondents supported the idea of a federal compulsory health insurance program ("Government Health Insurance," Special Survey, November 4, 1949, *Gallup Poll*, Volume Two, 862–63). Yet even this measure of public sentiment – a bare majority favoring Truman's plan in Franklin Roosevelt's home state – could hardly have been very reassuring to proponents of national health insurance.

in the early years of the program. As enacted, the Medicare statute spec-ified that reimbursements to hospitals and doctors for medical services would have to cover the "reasonable cost of such services."[88] The statute also prohibited payment to "any Federal provider of services," except under special circumstances; it asserted that nothing in the health insurance title "shall be construed to authorize any Federal officer or employee to exercise any supervision or control over the practice of medicine;" and it guaran-teed that patients would have "free choice" to "obtain health services from any institution, agency, or person qualified to participate" and willing to "provide... such services."[89] Wilbur Cohen, one of the architects of the Medicare law and a top official at the Department of Health, Education, and Welfare, later said that he

was required to promise before the final vote in the Executive Session of the House Ways and Means Committee that the Federal Agency would exercise no control.... There was no voice in Congress for effecting constraints on physicians' incomes, hospital costs... or for any basic change in the health delivery system. (As a matter of fact, I promised very conscientiously that I would see to it there was no change in the basic health delivery system because so far as the AMA and Congress were concerned, this was sacred.)[90]

That Medicare ultimately proved exceedingly beneficial to most physi-cians (the *New Republic* characterized the program as a "Doctors' Bonanza" in 1967)[91] has led some critics to conclude that the medical fraternity bought and paid for this outcome. Allen Matusow, for example, has described Medi-care as "ruinous accommodation between reformers and vested interests, in this case the organized doctors." Matusow notes that "in the climactic final days of congressional debate," the AMA "paid twenty-three lobbyists a total of $5,000 a day to prevent passage. Though the doctors were no longer strong enough to defeat Medicare, they nevertheless extracted their pound of flesh." The result, in Matusow's view, was a federal program that "guaranteed galloping medical price inflation" (and thus rising physician incomes) over subsequent years.[92]

[88] 79 Stat. 296, Sec. 1814 (b); 79 Stat. 322, Sec. 1861 (v).
[89] Social Security Amendments of 1965, P.L. 89–97, July 30, 1965 [H.R. 6675], Sections 1814 (b), 1833 (a) (1), 1861 (v), 1801, and 1802.
[90] Wilbur Cohen, "From Medicare to National Health Insurance," in David C. Warner, ed., *Toward New Human Rights: The Social Policies of the Kennedy and Johnson Administrations* (Austin: University of Texas at Austin, 1977), 146–47.
[91] E. T. Chase, "The Doctors' Bonanza," *The New Republic* (1967), 15–16.
[92] Allen J. Matusow, *The Unraveling of America: A History of Liberalism in the 1960s* (New York: Harper Torchbooks, 1984), 228.

Although this is perhaps the most intriguing of the various capture arguments, it too suffers from a number of problems. Even if the AMA had been instrumental in obtaining the "reasonable cost" provision, the organization and its political action committee nevertheless vigorously *opposed* the final legislation – and lost. The most trusted accounts of the process, moreover, suggest that the AMA was *not* an important player in influencing the specific language of the bill. According to Marmor,

It should not be assumed that American medical organizations cleverly pressured the Johnson Administration for these provisions. The A.M.A. was not fully consulted during the writing of the Medicare law in the Ways and Means Committee. The A.M.A.'s diehard opposition to Medicare led men like committee chairman Wilbur Mills to bar A.M.A. officials from the hearings, where their frantic objections had been of little help in the writing of detailed legislation. And when the Social Security Administration turned to writing up the regulations on the basis of the committee's vague set of guidelines, its intermittent consultations with representatives from the A.M.A. did not produce substantial changes in the payments arrangements.[93]

Significantly, congressional proponents of Medicare seemed most troubled not by the AMA's lobbying operations, but rather by the threat of a physicians' boycott, which had the support of many doctors (including the Association of American Physicians and Surgeons). The AMA flirted with this idea but never officially endorsed it.[94] Marmor subsequently observed that "the provisions for paying doctors under Part B of Medicare reflected the legislators' fears that the doctors would act on their repeated threats of non-cooperation in implementing Medicare." In characterizing these developments, Marmor was also careful to highlight "congressional sympathy with the doctors' distaste for government control," suggesting that members of Congress may not have needed a whole lot of pushing on this issue.[95]

That lawmakers were apparently influenced by the threat of a doctors' boycott reflects a dynamic different than that typically suggested by the economic theory of legislation. If true, it implies that doctors may have been more influential as producers of medical services than as political

---

[93] Theodore R. Marmor, "Why Medicare Helped Raise Doctors' Fees," *Trans-Action* (September 1968), 17.

[94] Austin C. Wehrwein, "Doctors Pressed to Defy Medicare," *New York Times*, June 19, 1965, 30; Austin C. Wehrwein, "A.M.A. Split on Proposals for a Boycott of Medicare," *New York Times*, June 22, 1965, 1.

[95] Marmor, *Politics of Medicare*, 80. See also Meyers, "Mr. Mills's Elder-medi-bettercare," 166 ("[Mills] sought to preserve the independence of the medical profession; he had no wish to set in motion any forces that might lead, along whatever path of good intentions, to government control of doctors or hospitals").

lobbyists. Members of Congress, it seemed, genuinely wanted Medicare to work. Certainly they would look bad if it collapsed in the face of passive resistance from the medical community. For this reason, physician participation was essential. Consider the traditional exit-voice-loyalty framework, for example.[96] The economic theory of legislation emphasizes "voice" – the power to influence through lobbying. In the case of Medicare, however, the historical record suggests that physician influence, although admittedly limited, was exercised most effectively through the threat of "exit" – the power to undermine the program through nonparticipation.

Although one can read the story of Medicare in many different ways, in the end the most straightforward interpretation is the strongest. Medicare succeeded because a clear majority of the public wanted it and viewed it unambiguously as a political priority. After the bid for national health insurance collapsed in the middle of Truman's second term, social reformers saw federal health insurance for the elderly as a reasonable (and potentially far more popular) alternative. Their campaign finally captured the public's attention about a decade later, when they began to confront the electorate with tragic tales of elderly Americans facing financial ruin and humiliating dependency through no fault of their own as a result of illness. Although the AMA put up a powerful fight (and may have influenced the shape of the legislation on the margins), the tide of public opinion rapidly turned against such opponents. The Democrats' landslide victory in 1964 broke down the floodgates altogether, leading to Medicare's enactment the following year.

Although it might be tempting to conclude that because the doctors ultimately benefited so much from Medicare they must have bought the legislation, the facts show otherwise. The leaders of the AMA – apparently guided more by ideology than by an accurate assessment of their constituents' material interests – did their best to defeat the legislation, but failed, overwhelmed by massive public support for the program. In this case, once again, the preferences of the majority proved very relevant indeed.

Superfund, 1980

In December 1980, Congress passed the Comprehensive Environmental Response, Compensation, and Liability Act (CERCLA) to facilitate the costly clean-up of hazardous substances that threatened environmental and public health. Nicknamed "Superfund," CERCLA enabled the federal government

---

[96] Albert O. Hirschman, *Exit, Voice, and Loyalty: Responses to Decline in Firms, Organizations, and States* (Cambridge, Mass.: Harvard University Press, 1970).

to hold involved parties responsible for cleaning up toxic spills and waste sites, regardless of fault. In addition, CERCLA established a $1.6 billion trust fund – financed mostly by taxes on the chemical and petroleum industries – to pay for the clean-up of old or abandoned dumps for which no responsible party could be found.

The chemical industry and its trade organization, the Chemical Manufacturers Association (CMA), emerged as Superfund's most vocal and aggressive opponent.[97] Although there were other interest groups on both sides – including the insurance industry, which generally opposed the Superfund proposals, and environmental groups, many of which pushed for more far-reaching reforms – by most accounts the chemical industry was the most active. In addition, the chemical industry also appeared to be the most well organized and funded. But although the CMA fought like "stormtroopers" to stop the legislation, with emphatic lobbying and public relations campaigns, Congress passed the bill 78 to 9 in the Senate and 274 to 94 in the House.[98] On December 11, outgoing President Jimmy Carter signed CERCLA into law, no doubt pleased that the final bill closely resembled his original proposal to Congress eighteen months earlier.

In many respects, the final outcome may seem surprising given the CMA's staunch opposition and the range of proposals Congress considered along

---

[97] By comparison, the oil industry, which also opposed Superfund, does not appear to have used public relations and advertising as aggressively. Spokesmen from various oil companies and industry groups (e.g., Shell Oil and Standard Oil of California for the American Petroleum Institute (API) and the Rocky Mountain Oil & Gas Association) did appear at congressional hearings and firmly opposed the combination of oil and hazardous substances with hazardous wastes under one law. Like the chemical industry, API went on record stating that any cleanup fund for abandoned waste sites "will have to be from the general fund" (Statement of Claude S. Brinegar, chairman of API's task force on clean air and water, in *Hearing by the Senate Subcommittees on Environmental Pollution and Resource Protection and the Committee on Environment and Public Works* on S. 1341, S. 1480, and S. 1325, "Hazardous and Toxic Waste Disposal, Part 4," 96th Cong., 1st sess., July 19, 1979, 482). However, API did not oppose – and in fact "widely accepted" – the proposal for a $200 million compensation and liability fund for water-borne spills financed by fees on crude oil: "This bill [H.R. 85 (see n. 108, 141)] could and should be enacted quickly. To postpone action encourages multiple approaches by the states, none of which can be as efficient or as equitable as this overall federal approach" (Brinegar in "Hazardous and Toxic Waste Disposal, Part 4," 480–81).

[98] "Staff members of congressional committees and the EPA [Environmental Protection Agency] noted that during the battle over Superfund, they [Dow Chemical and Allied Chemical, two of the larger member firms in the CMA] were the 'stormtroopers of the industry'" [John F. Mahon and James E. Post, "The Evolution of Political Strategies During the 1980 Superfund Debate" in Alfred A. Marcus, Allen M. Kaufman, and David R. Beam, ed., *Business Strategy and Public Policy: Perspectives from Industry and Academia* (New York: Quorum Books, 1987), 66].

the way. Nearly everyone, including the CMA, agreed that leaking dump sites constituted a problem. The disagreement revolved around who should pay to fix it. Although the CMA's preferred outcome – that clean-up should be funded solely out of general government revenues – was never seriously considered on Capitol Hill, Congress did take up a range of proposals, which differed with respect to fund size (from several hundred million dollars to $4.1 billion), scale of industry contributions (from 50 to 87.5 percent of total fund size), liability rules for responsible parties (reaching all the way to "joint, strict, and several liability"), and the scope of coverage (from material losses and clean-up only, to much broader coverage including third-party compensation).

In the end, Congress passed a moderately tough version of the legislation. It did so for many reasons, but perhaps the most powerful motivator was a broadly informed and mobilized public, galvanized on the toxic-waste issue by intense media coverage of leaking dump sites in the Love Canal neighborhood of Niagara Falls, New York. Press reports on the tragic and disturbing story of the Love Canal disaster transformed the political climate, leaving key special interests, including the CMA, directly in the path of a political hurricane.

CONTEXT: GROWING ENVIRONMENTAL AWARENESS AND A RISING FEDERAL ROLE

Interest in the problem of hazardous chemical contamination developed in earnest during the 1960s and set the stage for the following "environmental decade." Rachel Carson's *Silent Spring* (which documented the deadly effects of pesticides on birds) reached a broad audience, while "killer" smogs in New York City and various oil and chemical disasters drew further public attention, dramatically increasing Americans' sensitivity to the dangers of chemical pollution. Indeed, widely covered environmental disasters continued with what appeared to be alarming frequency into the 1970s.

In step with rising public awareness, Congress responded with a "wave of environmental legislation," including the Environmental Protection Act (1970), the Endangered Species Act (1973), and the Safe Drinking Water Act (1974). Federal lawmakers also strengthened existing clean air and water laws.[99] With respect to hazardous and toxic substances, Congress passed no

---

[99] Peter S. Menell, "The Limitations of Legal Institutions for Addressing Environmental Risks," *Journal of Economic Perspectives*, vol. 5 (Summer 1991), 96. The Clean Air Act was passed in 1963, extended in 1970, and amended in 1977. The first Federal Water Pollution

fewer than twenty-four pieces of legislation in the 1970s. Among these were the 1976 Resource Conservation and Recovery Act (RCRA) and the 1976 Toxic Substances Control Act (TSCA), which regulated the introduction, movement, and disposal of hazardous chemicals.[100]

Beyond RCRA and TSCA, Congress also passed remedial laws to address the problem of pollution clean-up and the associated costs. Before the Federal Water Pollution Control Act (FWPCA) of 1972, the federal government could not automatically recover clean-up costs for spills of oil and hazardous substances unless the polluter was "grossly negligent" or had made the spill "willful[ly]."[101] The FWPCA established strict liability for clean-up, meaning the federal government no longer had to prove fault to collect.[102]

In 1976, large oil spills off the coasts of Spain and Nantucket Island highlighted the narrow focus of the FWPCA, which was "intended... as an additional remedy, not as the federal government's only source of compensation."[103] The following year, Congress introduced various bills to establish a "comprehensive oil pollution liability and compensation" law.[104] Most proposed tougher liability provisions to make it possible to hold one identified polluter fully responsible for a site polluted by several parties (i.e., via joint-and-several liability). Moreover, a proposed trust fund, financed through a new industry fee, was included to cover emergency clean-up costs and "otherwise uncompensated losses."[105]

Following two more disastrous spills – but this time of toxic chemicals – in late 1977 and early 1978, Congress considered similar bills that added

Control Act was passed in 1948, extended numerous times, and amended significantly in 1961, 1966, 1970, 1972, and in 1977, when the act was renamed the Clean Water Act.

[100] Walter A. Rosenbaum, *Environmental Politics and Policy* (Washington, D.C.: CQ Press, 1985), 200; P.L. 94-580; P.L. 94-469.

[101] P.L. 89-753 as quoted in "Oil Spills and Cleanup Bills: Federal Recovery of Oil Spill Cleanup Costs," *Harvard Law Review*, vol. 93 (June 1980), 1763.

[102] 33 U.S.C. §1321 as quoted in "Oil Spills and Cleanup Bills," 1766.

[103] "Oil Spills and Cleanup Bills," 1762. The *Urquiola* oil tanker crashed on a shoal off the northwestern coast of Spain on May 12, 1976, spilling about 513,000 barrels and affecting about 200 km of coast; the *Argo Merchant* ran aground southeast of Nantucket Island on December 15, 1976, spilling about 183,000 barrels and leaving an oil slick 160 km long and 97 km wide (Centre de documentation de recherche et d'expérimentations sur les pollutions accidentelles des eaux, "Urquiola" [text online], accessed October 2007, available at http://www.cedre.fr/uk/spill/urquiola/urquiola.htm; Friends of the Earth, "A Chronology of Oil Spills: 1967–2002" [text online], accessed October 2007, available at http://www.foe.org/new/releases/oilchron.pdf).

[104] See, e.g., 95 S. 2083 (and H.R. 6803), S. 121, S. 687, H.R. 3711, S. 1187 (and H.R. 6213), S. 2900. Similar bills were also introduced in the 94th Congress (e.g., 94 H.R. 9294, H.R. 10969, S. 2162, H.R. 10363, H.R. 10756, H.R. 14862).

[105] See, e.g., 95 S. 2083.

hazardous substances to the liability regime.[106] During hearings in May 1978, representatives from the chemical industry argued against combining oil and hazardous substances in one law.[107] Although the Senate Committee on the Environment and Public Works favorably reported a bill that included both oil and hazardous substances, the ninety-fifth Congress ultimately dropped not only the two-in-one approach but also the broader idea of a comprehensive pollution liability and compensation law.[108]

POLITICAL TRANSFORMATION: LOVE CANAL
AND THE POWER OF THE PRESS

Whatever political firewall the chemical industry might have helped to build over the preceding months was suddenly and irreparably breached on August 2, 1978. On that day the story of Love Canal, a small middle-class community in Niagara Falls, New York, which had been built on a toxic waste dump, appeared on the front page of the *New York Times*. The *Times* reported "large numbers of miscarriages and birth defects among the residents of the homes along the [dump] site," which had leaked "suspected carcinogens... into the backyards and basements of... homes and a public school..." Readers learned that "children and dogs... received chemical burns... playing in the fields" and that the city had long been "uncooperative with neighborhood requests for help." The story also quoted an official from the Environmental Protection Agency (EPA), who described

---

[106] On December 8, 1977, a chemical explosion and fire killed at least two persons in Bridgeport, New Jersey. On March 10, 1978, heavy rains caused a portion of a California dam to collapse and necessitated the release of toxic waters from the Stringfellow acid waste pits into the Santa Ana River. 95 S. 2900, e.g., introduced April 12, 1978, covered spills of hazardous substances and of oil.

[107] *Hearing held by the Senate Committee on the Environment and Public Works* on S. 2900, S. 1187, and S. 2083, "To Establish a Comprehensive Oil Pollution Liability and Compensation Law," 95th Cong., 2nd sess., May 24, 1978, 485.

[108] 95 S. 2083, "a bill to establish a uniform and comprehensive legal regime governing liability and compensation for damages and cleanup costs caused by oil pollution" (i.e., covering oil only), was introduced by senator Warren Magnuson (D-WA) on September 12, 1977. In August 1978, the Committee on Environment and Public Works amended S. 2083 to include hazardous substances and sent the bill to the full Senate. In October 1978, the Senate passed H.R. 6803, which covered oil only under joint, strict, and several liability. The House incorporated parts of H.R. 6803 into a different bill "to establish a policy for the management of oil and natural gas in the Outer Continental Shelf" and this was the bill that was passed by the ninety-fifth Congress and that was signed into law in September 1978 (P.L. 95-372). However, in the very first days of the ninety-sixth Congress (January 15, 1979), New York representative Mario Biaggi (D) introduced H.R. 85, "a bill to provide a comprehensive system of liability and compensation for oil spill damage and removal costs, and for other purposes" (see n. 97).

the *thousands* of similar toxic dumpsites all around the country as "ticking time bombs." The dumper in the Love Canal case, Hooker Chemical Company (which had used the site from 1947 to 1953), was characterized as a thoroughly unscrupulous business that supposedly had sold the toxic landfill in 1953 to the city's unwitting Board of Education for $1, knowing that the city intended to build an elementary school on the site.[109]

The same day the initial *Times* story appeared, the state health commissioner declared a health emergency at Love Canal, announcing that there was a "great and imminent peril to the health of the general public at or near the said site." The commissioner also recommended that families with pregnant women or children under two years of age leave the area.[110]

The *New York Times* put the Love Canal story on the front page again the next day, reporting that most families were unable to follow the commissioner's recommendation because they "could not afford to move."[111] Faced with a street gathering of 150 irate residents who had resolved to stop paying their mortgage and tax bills, Governor Hugh Carey asked President Carter for federal aid to help clean up the dumpsite and relocate some thirty-five families in its immediate vicinity.[112] In Washington, New York representative John LaFalce (D) began searching for untapped appropriations in existing pollution control laws to help pay relocation expenses, and New York senators Daniel Patrick Moynihan (D) and Jacob Javits (R) proposed contributing $4 million in federal aid to support state and local efforts.[113]

Before President Carter approved emergency federal aid on August 7, numerous other newspapers, including the *Chicago Tribune, Los Angeles Times*, and *Washington Post*, had picked up the story.[114] All focused on

---

[109] Donald G. McNeil, Jr., "Upstate Waste Site May Endanger Lives," *New York Times*, August 2, 1978, A1. Regarding the allegations against Hooker, the company did sell the land for $1, but after the Board of Education threatened to claim it under eminent domain despite repeated disclosure that the site was a toxic waste dump. See "Love Canal Warnings," *Wall Street Journal*, June 19, 1980, 22.

[110] Donald G. McNeil, Jr., "Health Chief Calls Waste Site A 'Peril,'" *New York Times*, August 3, 1978, A1; "Residents Told of Landfill's Chemical Peril," *Chicago Tribune*, August 3, 1978, 5.

[111] McNeil, Jr., "Health Chief Calls Waste Site A 'Peril,'" A1.

[112] Donald G. McNeil, Jr., "Upstate Waste Site: Carey Seeks U.S. Aid," *New York Times*, August 4, 1978, B14.

[113] Donald G. McNeil, Jr., "Toxic Waste Fund Sought In Congress," *New York Times*, June 10, 1979, 51; McNeil, Jr., "Upstate Waste Site: Carey Seeks U.S. Aid," B14; Donald G. McNeil, Jr., "First Families Leaving Upstate Contamination Site," *New York Times*, August 5, 1978, 20.

[114] "Residents Told of Landfill's Chemical Peril," 5; "Long-Buried Poisons Ooze Out of the Ground," *Washington Post*, August 5, 1978, A1; "Rains Let Up in Texas; Victims Sought," *Los Angeles Times*, August 6, 1978, OC2.

the mortal dangers of chemical waste exposure and highlighted the tragic health records – high incidence of cancer, miscarriages, birth defects, and other chronic ailments – of the Love Canal residents. Over the next two weeks, more than three dozen nonlocal news agencies covered the story, including the Associated Press, the three major television networks (ABC, CBS, and NBC), the MacNeil-Lehrer Report on PBS, the nation's two dominant news magazines, *Time* and *Newsweek*, and foreign media from seven countries.[115] Residents of Love Canal received invitations to appear on television and radio talk shows in New York City, Denver, and Chicago, turning "canal housewives... [into] media stars" and the name Love Canal into a powerful symbol of "our sick environment."[116]

By early 1979, the problem of hazardous chemical pollution and clean-up had become, in the eyes of a key Senate staffer, "certainly the number one environmental issue" in Washington.[117] Not surprisingly, in light of the public attention, EPA, Congress, and the White House all promised to develop meaningful proposals, despite the expectation that such legislation would be "extremely controversial" and "vigorous[ly]" fought by the chemical industry.[118]

In fact, the industry had already had some success stalling earlier clean-up ideas before Love Canal. Prior to 1978, officials at EPA had been exploring the idea of a national trust fund to pay for emergency clean-up of hazardous waste sites, financed on the basis of per-ton fees levied on dumped waste. But the chemical industry staunchly objected, arguing that it would unjustly impose taxes on currently compliant waste generators for "the environmental sins of others in the past."[119] As one industry spokesperson complained, "It's not fair, and more important, it probably isn't legal."[120]

The chemical industry continued with this approach with some success through the early months of 1979, as policymakers from various parts of

[115] Mark Francis, "Reporters flock to canal crisis," *Niagara Gazette*, August 20, 1978 (available online from the Love Canal Collection of the University at Buffalo Libraries at http://ublib.buffalo.edu/libraries/projects/lovecanal/ newspapers/nia_gazette/index.html, accessed November 2007).

[116] Francis, "Reporters flock to canal crisis." See also Donald G. McNeil, Jr., "Reporter's Notebook: Niagara Olfactory Impact," *New York Times*, August 9, 1978, D19; Casey Bukro, "Is environment mortally ill?" *Chicago Tribune*, April 20, 1980, A1.

[117] Senate Public Works and Environment Committee counsel Philip Cummings as quoted in "Kentucky Hunts Cleanup Funds for Valley of Drums," *Washington Post*, February 4, 1979, A1.

[118] "Kentucky Hunts Cleanup Funds for Valley of Drums," A1; Bill Richards, "U.S. to Seek Hazard Fund In Industry," *Washington Post*, April 30, 1979, A1; George Estep, "EPA proposes industry fund for waste spills," *Chicago Tribune*, May 11, 1979, A6.

[119] Bill Richards, "Oozing Earth," *Washington Post*, September 4, 1978, A3.

[120] Industry official as quoted in Richards, "Oozing Earth," A3.

the government – "spurred by Love Canal" – considered potential avenues for new legislation.[121] In mid-June, the *Washington Post* reported that after months of deliberation (and contrary to EPA recommendations), the Carter Administration had prepared a proposal for a "totally government-paid hazardous waste fund because of industry opposition to the fees."[122]

In the end, however, public pressure (presumably stemming from the Love Canal coverage) proved more powerful than industry opposition.[123] In the final week of deliberation, the administration reversed course on the funding issue. When President Carter publicly announced his proposal for financing emergency clean-up of hazardous spills and abandoned toxic dumps on June 13, 1979, he asked Congress to create a $1.6 billion trust fund and to impose 80 percent of the cost on industry.[124]

The CMA: From Offense to Defense

Not surprisingly, the CMA responded fiercely to the Carter plan, denouncing the proposed legislation as "defective" and "unfair" for "singl[ing] out" the chemical industry to pay a "disproportionate burden of cleanup costs."[125] Robert A. Roland, chief executive of the CMA, declared that the bill "fail[ed] to adequately reflect society's responsibility for resolving a problem which everyone has helped to create and for whose solution everyone should help pay."[126] Chemical waste was a by-product of advancing

---

[121] Maryann Bird, "Battle of Toxic Dumps: Who Pays for Cleanup?" *New York Times*, July 11, 1980, B4. Philip Shabecoff, "Waste Cleanup Bill Approved By House," *New York Times*, September 24, 1980, A16.

[122] Edward Walsh, "Carter Asks $1.6 Billion to Clean Up Chemical, Oil Hazards," *Washington Post*, June 14, 1979, A2.

[123] In the years immediately after Love Canal, opinion polls indicated that the vast majority of Americans thought cleaning up toxic waste sites and stricter regulations for hazardous substances should be a high federal priority. See Ronald T. Libby, *Eco-Wars: Political Campaigns and Social Movements* (New York: Columbia University Press, 1998), 22; Ed Magnuson, "The Poisoning of America," *Time*, September 22, 1980. On the timing of the administration's reversal regarding industry funding, see Walsh, "Carter Asks $1.6 Billion to Clean Up Chemical, Oil Hazards," A2.

[124] Carter's proposal, the "Oil, Hazardous Substances, and Hazardous Waste Response, Liability, and Compensation Act of 1979," was introduced in the Senate as S. 1341 on June 14, 1979, and in the House as H.R. 4566 and H.R. 4571 on June 21, 1979.

[125] Robert A. Roland, chief executive of CMA, as quoted in Walsh, "Carter Asks $1.6 Billion to Clean Up Chemical, Oil Hazards," A2 and in "Carter Proposes $1.6 Billion Fund To Fight Chemical Waste Hazards," *New York Times*, June 14, 1979, A1.

[126] Roland as quoted in "Carter Proposes $1.6 Billion Fund To Fight Chemical Waste Hazards," A1.

technology, industrialization, and of an "increasingly complex lifestyle," Roland insisted, and everyone who benefited from electronics or plastics, for example, was partly responsible.[127]

During congressional hearings by the Senate Committee on Environment and Public Works in July 1979, the CMA and other industry representatives voiced objections to additional regulations on hazardous substance disposal and to the idea of an industry-financed trust fund, calling it "unfair, unsound, and probably unconstitutional."[128] They testified that state and federal tax dollars should pay for clean-up of orphan dumps and that the existing regulations on hazardous substances under RCRA and the Clean Water Act were adequate.[129]

Vowing to "fight this until the last dog is dead," the CMA simultaneously pursued a "multimillion-dollar advertising effort to counter 'growing evidence that the public image of the chemical industry is unfavorable.'"[130] In the same month that Carter announced his plan, Roland increased the association's dues-based revenue from $4 million to $7.5 million and doubled its staff, increasing manpower "particularly in the technical and legal departments."[131]

Led by "hardliners" Dow Chemical and Allied Chemical (as well as Union Carbide and DuPont), the CMA made sure that congressional candidates and the country at-large learned about its position.[132] Collectively, the chemical industry spent more than $2.5 million on 1980 campaign contributions and donated heavily to industry-sympathetic think tanks, scholars, and probusiness philanthropic foundations.[133] It further worked to convince charitable foundations with a record of supporting environmental public interest groups (such as the Environmental Defense Fund, which favored strong Superfund legislation) to stop funding these organizations.[134]

In short, the industry remained on the political offensive. Roland frequently spoke to the press, calling the Superfund proposals "kinky," "truly

[127] Robert A. Roland, "Toxic Scapegoats," *Washington Post*, April 21, 1979, A15.
[128] "Chemical Industry Attacks Carter Cleanup Proposal," *Washington Post*, July 13, 1979, A3.
[129] "Hazardous and Toxic Waste Disposal, Part 4," 421–24.
[130] William M. Stover, vice president of CMA, as quoted in Bryce Nelson, "Getting Rid of Toxic Wastes: Cost Is High," *Los Angeles Times*, September 30, 1979, 14. Internal industry document as quoted in John H. Cushman, Jr., "After 'Silent Spring,' Industry Put Spin on All It Brewed," *New York Times*, March 26, 2001, A14.
[131] Mahon and Post, 66.
[132] *Chemical and Engineering News* (January 5, 1981) as quoted in Mahon and Post, 66.
[133] "18 Finance Panel Members Got $300,000 From Chemical Industry," *Washington Post*, November 17, 1980, A1; Richard J. Lazarus, *The Making of Environmental Law* (Chicago: University of Chicago Press, 2004), 95–96.
[134] Lazarus, 95–96.

radical," "overkill," and "unconstitutional," and repeated insistently that
clean-up costs be financed solely out of general government revenues.[135] At
the same time, the CMA also tried to shift public perceptions about the
extent of the toxic waste problem.[136] In early 1980, it issued a report that
disputed EPA data on the number of toxic dumpsites nationwide and the
proportion that posed "current threats" to public health, suggesting that
the government had grossly overestimated both figures.[137]

Only in mid-September of 1980, as the Senate Finance Committee
announced that there was "a consensus on the committee that we want some
kind of legislation this year," did the CMA try a different approach.[138] Fearing the worst, the association announced its support for the weakest bill in
the mix, which proposed a $600 million fund financed equally by indus-
try and taxpayers.[139] Technically, however, the CMA supported only half
of the bill, the half that provided $300 million from general government
revenues.[140]

---

[135] See Joanne Omang, "Warfare Brewing on Hill Over Chemical Clean-Up 'Superfund,'"
Washington Post, January 3, 1980, A5; Joanne Omang, "U.S. Lawyers Argue Both Sides
of a Deadly Issue," *Washington Post*, May 3, 1980, B8; Ward Sinclair, "Subtle Spray From
Chemical Firms May Stifle Hill Cleanup," *Washington Post*, August 30, 1980, A5; Robert
A. Roland, "Hazardous Wastes and the Law," *Washington Post*, September 23, 1980, A14;
"Chemical Industry Attacks Carter Cleanup Proposal," A3; Nelson, "Getting Rid of Toxic
Wastes," 14; Philip Shabecoff, "Congress Set to Debate 'Superfund' to Clean Up Hazardous
Wastes," *New York Times*, September 18, 1980, A24.

[136] "'The issue ... has been blown out of proportion,' Mr. Roland said. 'The public health
risk is not nearly as great as the perception by the press and by Government'" (Roland as
quoted in Shabecoff, "Congress Set to Debate 'Superfund' to Clean Up Hazardous Wastes,"
A24).

[137] November 1978 EPA report as quoted in Richards, "U.S. to Seek Hazard Fund In Industry,"
A2. Whereas the EPA estimated as many as 50,000 hazardous sites nationwide, 1,200 to
2,000 of which had "potentially significant problems," the CMA offered its own study
in March 1980 identifying just 4,196 sites, 431 of which were "potentially hazardous."
See EPA study as quoted in Nelson, "Getting Rid of Toxic Wastes," p. A1; CMA study,
released in March 1980 (Mahon and Post, 67), as quoted in Bill Stall, "Congress Treads
Legal Minefield With Chemical Cleanup 'Superfund,'" *Los Angeles Times*, May 18, 1980,
G4.

[138] Senate Finance Committee member William V. Roth, Jr. (R-DE) as quoted in Irvin Molot-
sky, "Senate Panel Nears Approval of Waste Cleanup Bill," *New York Times*, September 14,
1980, 54.

[139] 96 H.R. 7020.

[140] "Mr. Roland said that the chemical industry agreed that there was a need for a cleanup
fund *but that the fund should be ... financed by the Government*. The industry favors the bill
originally drafted by the House Commerce Committee, which would set up a $600 million
fund, half of which would be financed from general revenues and half from industry
fees. The Ways and Means Committee later increased the proposed fund to $1.2 billion"
(Shabecoff, "Congress Set to Debate 'Superfund,'" A24), emphasis added.

Finding Consensus in Congress

Between August 1978, when the *New York Times* first reported the Love Canal story, and the passage of CERCLA in December 1980, leaders of the chemical industry repeatedly found that no matter how hard they pushed, the political headwinds ultimately proved stronger. During that time, Congress, in its typical committee-based approach, explored a range of options for dealing with toxic waste – nearly all of which the industry viewed unfavorably.

After Carter introduced his proposal in June 1979, members of Congress continued to search for a clean-up solution, concerned by certain aspects of the Carter plan – particularly, the relatively low limits it set on federal aid to states, its failure to compensate third-party damages, and its attempt to cover oil, hazardous substances, and hazardous wastes all under one system (especially since an oil-only liability and compensation bill, introduced in January, was already under consideration in the House).[141] In mid-July 1979, a bipartisan group of twenty-five senators introduced a new proposal that, unlike the Carter approach, focused solely on hazardous-substance spills and waste sites and included a degree of compensation for third-party damages.[142] Like the Carter bill, the Senate proposal would establish an industry-financed trust fund to clean up orphan dumpsites.

On the House side, Congressman James Florio (D-NJ) introduced the Hazardous Waste Containment Act on April 2, 1980, "to respond to releases of hazardous waste from inactive hazardous waste sites which endanger public health and the environment."[143] The proposal included a $600 million clean-up trust fund financed largely by industry fees and also promised compensation for at least some third-party damages.[144]

---

[141] According to New Jersey senator Bill Bradley (D), the Carter bill provided inadequate federal aid to states, limiting relief, for example, to a low $300,000-per-incident for "emergency assistance" ("A 'Superfund' For Toxic Waste," *New York Times*, July 8, 1978, NJ1). Others found the bill lacking for not covering third-party damages, which had already been proposed as a separate issue in at least twelve different bills between 1977 and 1979. See e.g., 95 H.R. 4524, H.R. 9616, H.R. 9947, H.R. 12633, H.R. 14282, H.R. 14301, S. 899, S. 1531 and 96 H.R. 3797, H.R. 3798, and S. 1046. No hearings were held on any of these bills and none made it out of committee. See n. 97, 108 on H.R. 85, the "Oil Pollution Liability and Compensation Act."

[142] Frank P. Grad, "A Legislative History of the Comprehensive Environmental Response, Compensation and Liability ("Superfund") Act of 1980," *Columbia Journal of Environmental Law*, vol. 8 (1982), 1. Senator John Culver of Iowa (D) and twenty-four cosponsors introduced S. 1480, the Environmental Emergency Response Act, on July 11, 1979.

[143] 96 H.R. 7020.

[144] "Dump Cleanup Funds Are Voted By a House Panel," *Wall Street Journal*, May 14, 1980, 7.

Although the CMA initially convinced the House Committee on Interstate and Foreign Commerce to reduce the proposed industry contribution to 50 percent and to eliminate third-party damages, this victory proved short-lived.[145] The Committee on Ways and Means, which received the bill next, held hearings in early June and ultimately reported a bill that doubled the fund size to $1.2 billion and increased the proposed industry contribution from 50 to 75 percent.[146] The committee did not restore provisions for third-party damages, however. The full House passed the Ways and Means bill by a vote of 351 to 23 on September 23, 1980, after repeatedly defeating proposed amendments to weaken the legislation.[147]

Meanwhile, the Senate Committee on Environment and Public Works had dramatically expanded the July 1979 Senate bill, creating the most ambitious and far-reaching of all the Superfund proposals. Recalling "the three major pre-Love Canal incidents that came to national attention . . . [and] also pay[ing] particular attention to Love Canal," the committee recommended a $4.1 billion fund, of which 87.5 percent would be financed by industry contributions. It also expanded third-party compensation to cover medical costs and lost wages (including backdated compensation for the Love Canal victims); extended liability from owners and operators of hazardous substances and wastes to third parties such as transporters; and explicitly imposed strict, joint-and-several liability, which could not be evaded through contractual waivers.[148]

Despite a Republican landslide on November 4, 1980 – which some observers thought would strengthen the industry's position – and the fact that time was running out for the ninety-sixth Congress, the news seemed to get only worse for the CMA. On November 17, the *Washington Post* reported on its front page that eighteen members of the Senate Finance Committee

---

[145] Omang, "U.S. Lawyers Argue Both Sides," B8; "Dump Cleanup Funds Are Voted By a House Panel," 7.

[146] Mahon and Post, 69.

[147] See Grad, 14–18.

[148] Grad, 7, 12, 10, 9; "Congress Clears 'Superfund' Legislation," *Congressional Quarterly Almanac*, vol. 50 (1980), 587–88. The three major pre-Love Canal incidents were: "the kepone contamination of the James River, the PCB (polychlorinated biphenyl) contamination of the Hudson River, and the contamination of Michigan livestock by the ingestion of PBBs (polybrominated biphenyls)" (Grad, 7). Regarding the CMA proposal that cleanup costs be funded out of general revenues, the committee declared: "The concept of a fund financed largely by appropriations was not adopted. A largely appropriated fund establishes a precedent adverse to the public interest – it tells polluters that the longer it takes for problems to appear, the less responsible they are for paying the consequences of their actions, regardless of the severity of the impacts." See Senate Report No. 848, 96th Cong., 2d Sess. (1980), 72.

had received $300,000 in 1980 campaign contributions from chemical polit-
ical action committees.[149] The Finance Committee, which had been working on a compromise measure ostensibly to improve the chances of passage,
responded immediately by "wash[ing] its hands of the controversy" and
voting unanimously to report the bill as received from the Environment
and Public Works Committee to the full Senate without comment.[150]

Between November 18 and 24, under considerable time pressure and
apparently convinced that the Environment Committee's controversial bill
would not survive, Senate Majority Leader Robert Byrd (D-WV) and Minority Leader Howard Baker (R-TN) worked out a compromise that they
believed was a "feasible solution."[151] The compromise reduced the fund
from $4.1 billion to $1.6 billion (but maintained the 87.5 percent industry contribution) and eliminated compensation for third-party damages.
It also struck much of the language explicitly defining the scope and standard of liability for responsible parties. Nevertheless, the final bill effectively
retained strict liability by reference to section 311 of the Clean Water Act and
implied joint-and-several liability – "with no allowance for apportionment
of damages among multiple contributors to a hazardous waste site."[152]

When the compromise was finally presented to the full Senate on
November 24, Sen. Jennings Randolph, the chairman of the Environment
and Public Works Committee, stated that although he thought his committee's bill had been "reasonable," he supported the compromise and "ask[ed]
for a chance to show we care."[153] The Senate passed the compromise that
day 78 to 9.

With time quickly running out, the House took up the Senate bill
several days later without amendment.[154] As in the Senate, many House

---

[149] "18 Finance Panel Members Got $300,000 From Chemical Industry," A1.

[150] Joanne Omang, "Senate Committee Sends 'Superfund' Bill to Floor," *Washington Post*,
November 19, 1980, A5; "Superfund Superrush," *Wall Street Journal*, November 20, 1980,
26.

[151] Senator Robert Byrd as quoted in the 126 Cong. Rec. S14,929 (daily ed. November 24,
1980).

[152] Brett Dalton, David Riggs, and Bruce Yandle, "The political production of Superfund: Some
financial market results," *Eastern Economic Journal*, vol. 22 (Winter 1996), 77. Subsequent
court decisions confirmed this interpretation of joint-and-several liability.

[153] Senator Jennings Randolph as quoted in the 126 Cong. Rec. S14,964 and S14,966 (daily
ed. November 24, 1980).

[154] "On December 3, 1980, Congressman Florio moved to suspend the rules and concur
in the Senate amendments to H.R. 7020. [The Senate had passed its compromise under
the House bill title to ensure that Superfund, which included new revenue-generating
provisions, originated in the House, as required by the Constitution.] The suspension of
the rules was agreed to. Under a suspension of the rules, bills must be passed as they are
received and no amendments are possible" (Grad, 29–30).

members expressed their earlier hope for a more comprehensive solution that included, among other things, compensation for third-party damages. Despite this, as well as the unpalatable take-it-or-leave-it condition, the House voted for the bill 274 to 94 and sent it on to the President one week later. Upon signing the Superfund bill into law on December 11, 1980, President Carter declared that the federal government had

responded directly and quickly to some of the highly publicized problems with toxic wastes that are just representative of many similar challenges and problems throughout the country. Love Canal and Valley of the Drums come to my memory right this moment.... [H]ere is a bill that substantially meets the criteria that I set out in the original proposal that I made to the Congress a year and a half ago. Most important, it enables the Government to recover from responsible parties the costs of their actions in the disposal of toxic wastes.... [T]his superfund bill represents a fine achievement for the Congress and for my own administration and for the whole Nation.[155]

THE LEGACY OF LOVE CANAL

The enactment of Superfund in the waning days of the Carter Administration seems, once again, to illustrate the power of a horror story – and, by extension, that of the press – to transform the political landscape. Of course, there is no way of knowing if Superfund would have become law had the story of Love Canal never surfaced. Perhaps it was a coincidence that the legislative effort took on new life in the wake of the story from upstate New York or that President Carter cited Love Canal by name in his signing statement. Perhaps congressional committees would have held hearings in any case and ignored the protests of the chemical industry. Perhaps, but it seems doubtful.

Some skeptics might argue that industry lobbyists succeeded in this case – that they should be credited with capturing the legislative effort, because Congress did not adopt the most extreme proposal under consideration. To be sure, the law established a trust fund of $1.6 billion, not $4.1 billion, and excluded compensation of third-party losses. But this argument would be difficult to sustain, not least because the CMA staunchly opposed the president's original proposal of June 1979, which closely resembled the final legislation in key respects.

---

[155] Jimmy Carter, "Comprehensive Environmental Response, Compensation, and Liability Act of 1980. Remarks on Signing H.R. 7020 Into Law. December 11, 1980," *Weekly Compilation of Presidential Documents*, vol. 16, no. 50 (Monday, December 15, 1980), 2798.

Others might also argue that the Superfund legislation was captured, but by environmental interest groups rather than by the chemical
industry.[156] Still others might insist that the legislative outcome simply
reflected the balance of competing interest groups, with little or no input
from the broader citizenry. Of the two, the second argument is more plausible than the first, since the chemical industry was widely viewed as the
dominant interest involved in the debate and because many environmentalists at the time viewed the final compromise measure more as a defeat
than a victory.[157] Regardless, our core point still holds: The entire political
configuration changed after the press exposed the horrors of Love Canal in
the late summer of 1978. Interest groups, both for and (especially) against
a Superfund-style proposal, existed before Love Canal. But it was only after
the public was informed and mobilized as a result of the ensuing press coverage that Congress finally enacted legislation pushing the costs of clean-up
onto industry.

Indeed, by almost all accounts, the revelations from upstate New York
proved pivotal, seizing public attention and giving new urgency to an otherwise sleepy set of proposals regarding the clean-up of hazardous substances.

[156] A related argument highlights the hazardous waste management industry as a big winner
from Superfund. This industry, however, was still in its infancy in the late 1970s. "As a new
and developing business, the hazardous waste disposal industry is currently composed
of many smaller companies operating in different regions of the country.... All have revenues of less than $40 million with only a portion of this from the disposal of hazardous
wastes" (Barbara Bry, "Industry Fueled by Environmental Regulations: Hazardous Waste
Collectors Piling Up," *Los Angeles Times*, July 9, 1979, G1). Such a group would not appear
to have a particularly low cost of political action.

[157] Although the news media generally hailed (and historians since have hailed) Superfund as
a triumph for environmentalists, many environmentalists at the time felt they had failed
to secure the kind of Superfund they wanted. "The past year [1980] has seen some sad
losses for those who are championing the cause of ecological awareness. Some of them
euphemistically refer to the following defeats as 'compromises' [including] the defeat by
Congress of the $4.1 billion 'superfund' to clean up chemical and oil spills and make
compensation for victims more attainable. The proposal was scratched, at the behest of
powerful chemical concerns ... in favor of what some are calling the $1.6 billion 'minifund'
(Leo H. Carney, "For Environmentalists, The Battle Goes On," *New York Times*, January
4, 1981, 22). In addition, after Congress passed the bill, but before President Carter signed
it into law, Maine Senator George J. Mitchell (D), who was also a member of the Senate
Committee on Environment and Public Works, published a piece in the *New York Times*
in which he wrote: "While I voted, reluctantly, for the compromise, the people of the
United States should understand that it does not deal with the most serious part of the
problem.... Our failure to provide compensation from the fund for persons who are
injured is even less defensible when we recall that the original Senate bill provided liability
only for out-of-pocket medical expenses" (George J. Mitchell, "Not a Super Fund," *New
York Times*, December 8, 1980, A27).

In all of this, it was the media – beginning with the *New York Times* on August 2, 1978 – that seem to have catalyzed the political reaction by bringing the horrors of Love Canal and the broader issue of toxic waste directly into America's kitchens and living rooms, which in turn generated widespread demands for action. After that, lawmakers appear by and large to have been more responsive to what they interpreted as the concerns of the general public, than to the lobbying of the special interests, in crafting Superfund.

INTERESTS, INFORMATION, AND DEMOCRACY

The three cases reviewed – the Voting Rights Act of 1965, the creation of Medicare that same year, and the passage of Superfund in 1980 – suggest that one cannot always predict policy outcomes in a democracy simply (or primarily) by identifying the relevant interest groups and assessing their respective costs and benefits of organized political activity. Apparently, majority opinion may sometimes matter after all (a possibility that Donald Wittman also explores from a theoretical perspective elsewhere in this volume).

George Stigler observed in his seminal article back in 1971 that the political system "is calculated to implement all strongly felt preferences of majorities and many strongly felt preferences of minorities but to disregard the lesser preferences of majorities and minorities."[158] Since then, attention in the political-economy literature has been largely focused on explaining, modeling, and cataloging the triumph of strongly held minority preferences (i.e., the power of special interests). Relatively little attention has been devoted to the question of when – and how – majority preferences become "strongly felt" and ultimately prevail. One possible answer is that majorities develop strong preferences when policy issues or proposals achieve a high profile, thereby becoming highly visible to the electorate. Of course, this only begs the question of how an issue or policy proposal becomes highly visible.

A vital project in political economy, therefore, is to identify the conditions under which majority preferences become "strongly felt" and, as a result, triumph over both weakly and strongly felt minority preferences. To make progress on this project, social scientists need to look closely not only at cases in which special interests defeat the general interest (as has been the tendency in the literature), but also at cases in which the general interest

[158] Stigler, "Theory of Economic Regulation," 12.

prevails (as we have done here). In particular, we should seek to identify what these general-interest cases have in common.

Although the three cases surveyed here represent just a start, already they suggest an intriguing possibility: namely, that "horror stories" of various kinds may play an important role in empowering the majority in a democracy. Stigler posited that the precision of the political process in reflecting majority interests would be increased "by any reduction in the cost to the citizen of acquiring information and expressing desires...."[159] When a public policy issue intersects with a horror story – or, perhaps more generally, with a story that the press determines to be newsworthy or otherwise likely to sell papers – the cost to citizens of acquiring information about the policy issue naturally falls (and may even turn negative, if the story is sufficiently appealing). As a result, stories of this sort that intersect with policy issues, either by accident (e.g., Love Canal) or by design (e.g., Selma, Medicare hearings), may create a sufficient condition for the general interest to prevail over special interests.[160]

Many other cases undoubtedly also merit study, which may prove equally or more revealing than the three considered here. One recent paper, for example, observes that antigouging legislation seems, almost by definition, to violate the economic theory of regulation. After all, the "affected firms lose money, and the 'winners' (namely the consumers that end up paying lower prices) are quite scattered. Indeed, it is difficult to know [in advance] which consumer will win by paying a low price and which consumer will lose by being rationed."[161]

More than logic is required, however. If we want to understand the politics of antigouging laws or of any other public policy, we need to start by closely examining the historical record. The prevailing economic theory of regulation provides an enormously powerful tool. But it may have proved too powerful, focusing scholarly attention on the triumph of special interests almost to the exclusion of other outcomes. Although a cynical perspective on the political process is often hard to resist (especially when the alternative feels naïve, even Panglossian), we must resist when this view conflicts with the facts, no matter how compelling is the theory that lies behind it.

---

[159] Stigler, "Theory of Economic Regulation," 12.

[160] For further elaboration, modeling, and empirical testing of this idea, see Alexander Dyck, David Moss, and Luigi Zingales, "Media versus Special Interests," NBER Working Paper Series, No. 14360 (September 2008).

[161] Julio J. Rotemberg, "Behavior Aspects of Price Setting, and Their Policy Implications," unpublished draft paper, July 19, 2007, 25.

As Sherlock Holmes instructed Dr. Watson, "It is a capital mistake to theorize before you have all the evidence. It biases the judgment."[162]

---

[162] Arthur Conan Doyle, "A Study in Scarlet" in *The Complete Sherlock Holmes* (Garden City, New York: Doubleday & Company, Inc., 1988), 27. Holmes repeats himself in "A Scandal in Bohemia," 163: "It is a capital mistake to theorize before one has data. Insensibly one begins to twist facts to suit theories, instead of theories to suit facts."

NINE

Law, Policy, and Cooperation

Yochai Benkler

INTRODUCTION

The marginal productivity of *homo economicus* is declining. The thin view of the rational actor, whose preferences are well ordered and transitive, who readily calculates many steps forward and single-mindedly pursues the optimization of his own welfare, has been a productive model across many fields. It has formed the basis of mainstream economics, much of contemporary political science, as well as law and economics. It has informed business organization and engineering models. But it has always operated under significant pressure. Some criticism was internal to economics,[1] as Jessica Leight discusses in her essay on the intellectual history of public choice. Mostly, the weight of the other social sciences, literature, critical theory, and philosophy were arrayed against it. The defense of *homo economicus* has usually been some version of Milton Friedman's argument: The model is justified by the quality of the predictions it offers, not the plausibility of its assumptions.[2]

A large body of empirical work has put *homo economicus* to controlled tests and field studies. It has shown that simple behavioral model to be less predictive of observable behavior than previously thought. Famous in the legal literature has been observational work on social norms and trust,[3] common property regimes,[4] and, later, experimental behavioral law

---

[1] Herbert Simon, *A Behavioral Model of Rational Choice, in* Models of Man, Social and Rational: Mathematical Essays on Rational Human Behavior in a Social Setting (1957); Amartya Sen, *Rational Fools: A Critique of the Behavioral Foundations of Economic Theory*, Phil & Pub Aff (1977).

[2] Milton Friedman, Essays in Positive Economics (1953).

[3] Robert Ellickson, Order Without Law: How Neighbors Settle Disputes (1991).

[4] Ostrom, Governing the Commons (1991).

and economics.[5] The better known aspect of the experimental work has been divergence from the predictions of rationality itself, as Joseph Stiglitz emphasizes in this volume. Less well known is work that does not take aim at cognitive failures of rationality, but undermines two core simplifications, neither entailed by rationality, that made *homo economicus* user-friendly: (a) individuals are similarly motivated, and (b) they are all selfish. Instead, we find that human beings have diverse motivational–behavioral profiles. In experiments, almost one-third indeed behave as predicted by selfish *homo economicus*. But more than half act cooperatively. Many are active reciprocators – respond kindly and cooperatively to cooperating others, and punish, even at a cost to themselves, those who behave uncooperatively. Others cooperate unconditionally, whether because they are true altruists or solidarists, or because they simply prefer to cooperate and do not measure what others are doing. The overarching finding, however, is clear: In no human society studied under controlled experimental conditions have people on average behaved as predicted by the standard economic model. Given that the assumptions of *homo economicus* are so inconsistent with intuition, experience, and the pervasive cultural practices of inculcating sharing and prosocial behavior in children, the fact that they now have also been seen to be systematically poor predictors of observable human behavior under controlled conditions requires significant attention.

Consider three puzzles for different models of human motivation and interaction.

(a) In firms, some experienced workers have acquired significant know-how. The firm wishes these agents to transfer as much of their know-how as possible to newer employees, to make them more productive. The traditional economic view of human motivation would assume that employees will wish to retain their own value and relative productivity, and so will withhold know-how. That view would therefore recommend that firms create incentives for experienced employees to transfer knowledge by compensating employees for teaching, and then monitoring their performance. It would predict that a relatively unsupervised environment, where employees work in teams without well-monitored interactions and without compensation tied to knowledge transfer, would result in experienced employees keeping as

---

[5] Christine Jolls, Cass R. Sunstein, and Richard Thaler, *A Behavioral Appoach to Law and Economics*, 50 Stan L. Rev. 1551 (1998).

much of their know-how as possible to themselves to maximize their nonfungible value to the firm and hence their bargaining power to extract a larger share of the firm's value. Analysis based on a large emerging literature on cooperation, which I will address in this chapter, would, to the contrary, predict that at least half of the employees prefer to cooperate. Given the opportunity to engage in more loosely supervised teamwork, many employees would be predicted freely to share information with coworkers through a social system of mutual aid. This view would recommend a radically different organization for the workplace. Empirical and theoretical work suggests that the the looser cooperative approach yields better organizational design to implement knowledge sharing.[6] Moreover, Toyota's legendary innovations in teamwork, rather than fine-grained incentives pay and monitoring, are usually thought of in organization science precisely in terms of organizing the workplace as a better platform for experimentation and knowledge sharing.[7]

(b) *Homo economicus* predicts that Wikipedia cannot exist. Tens of thousands of volunteers, none paid, acting effectively without crisp lines of authority, would simply be impossible. In a world populated exclusively by self-interested actors, an institutional designer of an online encyclopedia would have focused on ways to monitor and reward contributions, or to identify and sanction deviations. *E pur si muove.* Wikipedia is based on a model of self-selection, communication, human interaction, community norms, and mutual peer-based review and discipline.[8] Whether it is imperfect, or of lower quality than Britannica, is beside the point. The fact that contemporary debates focus on comparisons to Britannica is the strongest evidence of success. These design characteristics are common in peer-production projects

---

[6] Bruno Frey and Margit Osterloh, MANAGEMENT BY MOTIVATION: BALANCING INTRINSIC AND EXTRINSIC MOTIVATIONS (2002); Charles F. Sabel, *Ungoverned Production, in* CONVERGENCE AND PERSISTENCE IN CORPORATE GOVERNANCE, Jeffrey N. Gordon and Mark J. Roe, eds. 310–27 (2004); THE FIRM AS A COLLABORATIVE COMMUNITY, Charles Heckscher and Paul Adler, eds. (2006); John Hagel and John Seeley Brown, THE ONLY SUSTAINABLE EDGE: WHY BUSINESS STRATEGY DEPENDS ON PRODUCTIVE FRICTION AND DYNAMIC SPECIALIZATION (2005).

[7] Sabel, *Ungoverned Production.*; John Seeley Brown and Paul Duguid, *Knowledge and Organization: A Social-Practice Perspective.*

[8] Yochai Benkler, *Coase's Penguin or Linux and the Nature of the Firm,* 112 YALE LJ 369 (2002); Andrea Forte and Amy Bruckman, *Scaling Consensus: Increasing Decentralization in Wikipedia Governance,* PROC. 41ST HAWAII INT'L CONFERENCE ON SYSTEMS SCIENCES (2008).

generally, and more closely follow the design characteristics predicted by the cooperation literature than those predicted by selfishness.

(c) Consider two approaches to crime reduction. The first assumes that criminals, as rational actors, are deterred by the size of the penalties discounted by the probability of detection.[9] This theory calls for tougher penalties and/or more vigorous enforcement efforts. The second approach characterizes high crime rates as a failure of community – a failure to create a cooperative environment in which most people do not commit crimes, and members actively work together to control, report, and prevent crime when possible. That diagnosis would see high crime rates not in terms of penalties or probabilities of detection that are too low, but of insufficiently rich cooperation. For proponents of the cooperative perspective, sensible interventions would seek to facilitate a cooperative dynamic in the neighborhood, as exhibited in the dramatic rise and popularity of community policing.[10] It is the foundation of a substantial policy shift toward community policing in many communities in the United States.

The three stories are intended to render intuitive the critical points that will drive my analysis in this chapter. People are diversely motivated with regard to cooperation. Policymakers and organizational entrepreneurs can design institutions and social systems to foster cooperation by shaping social and psychological dynamics, rather than by focusing on individual incentives. The question then becomes, what aspects of the design of an institution or system – be it technical platform, legal rule, business process, or policy intervention – are likely to lead to a stable cooperative social dynamic?

The immediate "policy" or "business" reason to pursue this approach to design is the increasing recognition of the necessity of loosely coupled systems design. In many different domains, loosely coupled systems are replacing tightly bound systems: from Taylorism and Fordism to Toyotism, from the Bell System to the Internet, from IBM's massive patent portfolio and structured hierarchical model to its new services-based model built around a mixture of proprietary and open source software, from hierarchical command structures in the military to network-centric warfare, and from

---

[9] Gary S. Becker, *Crime and Punishment, an Economic Approach*, 76 J. Pol. Econ. 169–217 (1968).

[10] Dan M. Kahan and Tracey L. Meares, *The Coming Crisis of Criminal Procedure*, 86 Geo. L.J. 1153 (1998); for the current state of federal and state investment in community policing see http://www.cops.usdoj.gov/Default.asp?Item=34.

the Hollywood studio system to do-it-yourself media on the Web.[11] As the scale of global interactions increases, as the complexity of operating environments intensifies, and as the rate of economic, social, and cultural change escalates, the large, centralized, monitored, and carefully managed systems that dominated the twentieth century are fraying at the edges. In the face of all these transformations, human creativity, insight, wisdom, and learning capability become core imperatives for all systems design. And as these difficult-to-observe aspects of system performance increase in salience, the capacity of that system fully to characterize, monetize, monitor, and reward all desirable action declines. Instead, what all these systems need is intrinsically motivated human action. The goals of organizational strategies increasingly have turned away from such traditional tasks of organizing action and structuring motivation. The newer objectives call for shaping social and psychological dynamics so that people, acting autonomously in an environment where command is ineffective and pricing inefficient, can assess, experiment, learn, adapt, communicate, and adopt better practices dynamically over time. In short, the operating premises of economic life have become substantially more cooperative than *homo economicus* could have predicted. We now need a modeling framework whose ambition is to become broadly applicable and flexible, but which will build on new insights into human cooperation. That is the goal of studying cooperation and human systems design.

A. An Emerging Literature on Cooperation

Deciding which body of literature to use in constructing an approach to design for cooperation is not trivial. From poems, novels, or folk tales, through history, religion, and social theory, to mathematical game theory, we have many ways of talking about foundational questions of human motivations: When do we respect others and care about them? When do we look out for ourselves? Are we by nature generous or selfish? No approach can be fully comprehensive. No approach can be generalizable and usable without being to a significant extent reductionist – taking highly complex problems and reducing them to some manageable number of salient variables, leaving

---

[11] See Sabel, *supra*; Heckescher and Paul, *supra*; David Isenberg, *Rise of the Stupid Network*, 1997, http://isen.com/stupid.html; Jerome Saltzer, David P. Reed, and David Clark, End-to-End Arguments in System Design, 2 ACM Transactions in Computer Systems 277 (1984); *Henry Jenkins, Convergence Culture: Where Old and New Media Collide* (2006) David S. Alberts, John J. Garstka, and Fredrick Stein, *Network Centric Warfare: Developing and Leveraging Information Superiority* (2d ed. 1999).

residual uncertainty that is at a minimum comprehensible and sufferable. Using this reducibility to the tractable as my guide, I focus on six intellectual strains from which to synthesize the new approach to cooperative human systems design. These fields are: (a) experimental economics, with related cooperative game theory; (b) evolutionary biology and a strand of anthropology dealing with gene-culture co-evolution; (c) psychology of motivation and social psychology of solidarity; (d) organizational sociology and management science work focused on cooperative business processes; (e) observational work on successful common property regimes; and (f) the study of online collaboration and social software design. The fields vary in the degree of reductionism they impose and tractability they enable. My hope is that by maintaining all of them within our peripheral vision we can develop a framework both simple enough to be as generalizable and tractable as mechanism design and law and economics while providing a richer and more humanly grounded characterization of how human beings are motivated, how they interact with each other, and how they are likely to respond to various system manipulations we can propose – be they in the form of legal–institutional reform, or broader technical, business process, or social interventions.

Contemporary economic studies of cooperation are anchored in experiments.[12] These studies use well-understood games that have predictable theoretical outcomes and observe people under controlled and manipulated conditions, comparing actual behavior to the behavior predicted by the selfish rational actor model. Most of these are social dilemma games: Investigators structure available behaviors and payoffs such that cooperation will lead to higher payoffs for all participants, and lack of cooperation will lead some or all players to have a lower payoff, but may lead to higher payoffs to noncooperators if others do act cooperatively. The Prisoner's Dilemma is the most famous social dilemma game. Other games more closely approximate contributions to public goods or elicit the presence or absence of reciprocity under varying conditions. Some games, like the Dictator Game, are designed to detect the presence of "pure altruism" with no gains from cooperation. Social scientists have developed, critiqued,

---

[12] Three excellent reviews are Ernst Fehr and Herbert Gintis, *Human Motivation and Social Cooperation: Experimental and Analytical Foundations*, 33 ANNU. REV. SOCIOL. 43, 50 (2007); Colin F. Camerer & Ernst Fehr, *Measuring Social Norms and Preferences Using Experimental Games: A Guide for Social Scientists, in* FOUNDATIONS OF HUMAN SOCIALITY: ECONOMIC EXPERIMENTS AND ETHNOGRAPHIC EVIDENCE FROM FIFTEEN SMALL-SCALE SOCIETIES, Joseph Henrich *et al.,* eds., 2004) 55–95; Elinor Ostrom, *A Behavioral Approach to the Rational Choice Theory of Collective Action*, 92 AM. POL. SCI. REV. 1, 1–22 (1998).

and refined these games for over two decades, observing the behavior of students in many different developed cultures; workers and ethnic groups in various societies;[13] individuals within several small-scale, relatively isolated, societies,[14] and across industrialized countries with diverse degrees of rule-of-law and social capital indicators.[15] Throughout this period, participants in this field have also developed increasingly sophisticated mathematical models to include other-regarding preferences into the utility function of agents.[16]

We have seen a parallel trajectory in the study of cooperation in evolutionary biology. The first rise and fall of sociobiology begins with the nineteenth-century rise of Social Darwinism and eugenics, the emergence of anthropology and Frans Boas's critique, and the resolution of the battle in the revulsion caused by Nazi eugenics and scientific racism.[17] The desire to read the Book of Nature to understand God – to ground our moral self-understandings in our understanding of nature, remained. By the late 1960s to mid-1970s the horrors of the first interaction with biological explanations of human social behavior had subsided, and could be categorized as "bad science." This created room for a second rise of sociobiology.[18] Though subject to extensive critique,[19] biological inquiry into human sociality and morality has not subsided since. Some of it, particularly evolutionary psychology, followed the heavily criticized adaptationist model, complete with the idea that human moral drives were both instantiated in physically localized modules in the mind and had evolved to stability 50 million years ago.[20] Other strands, however, began to focus more heavily on evolutionary dynamics as an alternative approach to the optimality analysis common in economics. Evolutionary stability did not mean optimality; it merely meant feasibility of arising from a random

---

[13] Camerer & Fehr.

[14] Henrich *et al.*, Foundations; The findings were introduced and subject to insightful critique in Henrich *et al.*, *"Economic Man" in Cross-Cultural Perspective: Behavioral Experiments in 15 Small-Scale Societies*, 28 Behavioral and Brain Sciences 795–855 (2005).

[15] Benedikt Herrman, Christian Thonni, and Simon Gaechter, *Antisocial Punishment Across Societies*, 316 Science 1362 (2008).

[16] Matthew Rabin, *Incorporating Fairness into Game Theory and Economics*, 83 Am. Econ. Rev. 1281 (1993).

[17] Elazar Barkan, The Retreat of Scientific Racism: Changing Concepts of Race in Britain and the United States between the World Wars (1993).

[18] E. O. Wilson, Sociobiology (1976); Richard Dawkins, The Selfish Gene (1976).

[19] Stephen J. Gould and Richard C. Lewontin, *The Spandrels of San Marco and the Panglossian Paradigm: A Critique of the Adaptationist Model*, 205 Proc. Royal Soc. 581–98 (1979).

[20] See *e.g.*, David Buss, Evolutionary Psychology: The New Science of the Mind (3rd ed. 2008).

assortment of possible behaviors or proclivities, and relative survivability and stability by comparison to other possible behaviors and proclivities. Work on the evolution of cooperation in particular has changed over time. Its roots in the 1960s and 1970s focused purely on individual benefits from cooperation, and narrowed the range of possible cooperation to genetic kin[21] or directly reciprocal exchanges of benefits.[22] More recently, both the strict individualism and the need to achieve direct benefits in exchange for "generous" behavior have been superseded. The notion of reciprocal altruism grew, a quarter of a century later, into the concept of indirect reciprocity – that is, agents cooperate in a society when they can process enough information about who did what to whom so as to reciprocate indirectly.[23] Indeed, in the last two years the leading scientific journals have published a number of papers suggesting that the need to track cooperation and defection served as the driving force behind the evolution of human intelligence.[24] The strict necessity of individualism has been relaxed by the restatement of old views on group selection as a new approach, multilevel selection, which allows forces to operate as vectors, sometimes in competing directions, at the individual or group level, and thereby create a dynamic that allows for stability even for genuinely self-sacrificial strategies.[25] Most significantly from the perspective of contemporary studies of cooperative human systems design, there has been substantial work to mesh evolutionary dynamics with cultural practice. We now see economists, like Bowles and Gintis,[26] and anthropologists, like Boyd and Richerson,[27] using evolutionary dynamics to explain and explore the stability of cultural practices as salient sources of successful cooperation. Because of its formality, this approach adds theoretical tractability to the analysis of cooperation, applicable at

[21] W. D. Hamilton, *The Evolution of Altruistic Behavior*, 97 AMERICAN NATURALIST 354, 354–56 (1963); John Maynard Smith, *Group Selection and Kin Selection*, 201 NATURE 1145, 1145–46 (1964).

[22] Robert L. Trivers, *The Evolution of Reciprocal Altruism*, 46 Q. REV. OF BIOLOGY 35, 35–57 (1971).

[23] Richard Alexander, THE BIOLOGY OF MORAL SYSTEMS (1987); Martin Nowak and Karl Sigmund, *Evolution of indirect reciprocity* 437 NATURE 1291–98 (2005).

[24] Martin Nowak, *Five Rules for the Evolution of Cooperation* 314 SCIENCE 1560–63 (2006).

[25] Elliot Sober and David Sloan Wilson, UNTO OTHERS: THE EVOLUTION AND PSYCHOLOGY OF UNSELFISH BEHAVIOR (1998).

[26] Samuel Bowles and Herbert Gintis, *The Evolution of Strong Reciprocity: Cooperation in Heterogeneous Populations*, 65 THEORETICAL POPULATION BIOLOGY 17, 17–28 (2004); Sober & Wilson, *supra*.

[27] See Robert Boyd and Peter J. Richerson, CULTURE AND THE EVOLUTIONARY PROCESS (1986); Peter J. Richerson and Robert Boyd, NOT BY GENES ALONE: HOW CULTURE TRANSFORMED HUMAN EVOLUTION (2004).

the level of social institutions on historical time frames, rather than stating biological facts that have to be considered as hard limits on institutional design.

The last of the three lines of literature that seem particularly promising on the tractability side of the cooperation synthesis are lines of work within social psychology that go to human motivation and social solidarity. Much of the experimental work on psychology, certainly work that has made its way into economics and law, has been focused on predictable cognitive failures. The work of Kahneman and Tversky and their followers is particularly influential. But there is substantial work on cognitive failure and its application to law and institutional design beyond the behavioral economics frame.[28] Although work on designing cooperative human systems will have to consider cognitive failures, it is primarily oriented toward nailing down motivational and social–dynamic effects. To this end, two lines of work within social psychology provide more direct benefits. The largest influence on the framework offered here is work on the difference between intrinsic and extrinsic motivations, and concerns with the risks of crowding out internal reasons for action through imposition of control and explicit incentive systems, in particular the work of Edward Deci and Richard Ryan.[29] In much of the observational literature, the emphasis on the importance of intrinsic motivations – reasons and desires for action that come from within – plays a significant role. Deci and Ryan developed over the past two or three decades an approach based on characterizing human needs for competence, autonomy, and relatedness, which offers a convenient framework for mapping design interventions based on the extent to which they go to intrinsic or extrinsic motivations, and offers a reasonably tractable way of considering potential negative effects between the various levers and in the relationship between cooperative and noncooperative levers. Crowding out, or the nonseparability of social preferences from the introduction of explicit extrinsic motivation, poses a systemic challenge to using traditional, incentives-based mechanisms, both private and public, for eliciting desirable behavior.[30] Another line of literature within social psychology goes in particular to one important

---

[28] Dan Simon, *A Third View of the Black Box: Cognitive Coherence in Legal Decision Making*, 71 CHICAGO LAW REVIEW 511 (2004); Jon Hanson & David Yosifon, *The Situational Character: A Critical Realist Perspective on the Human Animal*, 93 GEO. L.J. 33 (2004).

[29] Edward L. Deci and Richard M. Ryan, *The "What" and "Why" of Goal Pursuits: Human Needs and Self-Determination of Behavior* 11 PSYCH. INQUIRY 227 (2000).

[30] Samuel Bowles, *Policies Designed for Self-Interested Citizens May Undermine "The Moral Sentiments": Evidence from Economic Experiments* 320 SCIENCE 1605–09 (20 June 2008).

element in cooperation, and that is the construction and functioning of social solidarity.[31]

The remaining three lines of literature are observational. They each take a class of phenomena where cooperation is salient and describe and analyze it in rich retail. In each case, the observations lead to some form of abstraction and systematization. In the approach I outline here, however, the role of these classes of literature is to ground the more abstract and reductionist approaches in a richer, thicker set of descriptions. It recognizes that practical reason and problem solving involve application of tacit knowledge as much as explicit knowledge, and tacit knowledge is evoked and applied more through narrative and heuristics than abstraction. Abstraction then allows us to discipline, structure, generalize, and critically examine intuition and experience. The trick, ultimately, of a successful synthesis will be to match up plausible abstractions of the observational work to plausible synthetic generalizations of the experimental and theoretical work to mobilize both tacit and explicit knowledge to the design of human systems.

The first of these has emerged within organizational sociology and management science. Growing from the work on post-Fordism, trust, and increasing knowledge intensity in firms, sociologists had observed increasing adoption of networked organization models emerging within firms, and in some cases across firms in supply relationships.[32] Globalization and rapid technological change put organizations under increasing pressure to innovate in their processes, adapt to changes, learn about a rapidly changing environment and increasingly complex processes, and implement learning continuously. Under a variety of monikers, such as TQM, team production, and quality circles, business processes have emerged that depend heavily on communication, on locating responsibility in the hands of employees, or on the emergence of what Sabel has called new routines for trust-based collaboration, replacing the traditional models of market and hierarchies to govern internal relations within firms and between firms.[33] A second line of literature in the observational vein is the extensive, and in law well known, political science work on common property regimes, led and epitomized

---

[31] Toshio Yamagishi, Nobuhito Jin, and Toko Kiyonari, *Bounded Generalized Reciprocity, Ingroup Boasting and Ingroup Favoritism*, 16 ADVANCES IN GROUP PROCESSES 161, 161–97 (1999).

[32] Charles Heckscher and Paul Adler, THE FIRM AS A COLLABORATIVE COMMUNITY: RECONSTRUCTING TRUST IN THE KNOWLEDGE ECONOMY (2006); Walter W. Powell, *Neither Market Nor Hierarchy: Network Forms of Organization*, 12 RESEARCH IN ORGANIZATIONAL BEHAV. 295 (1990).

[33] Charles F. Sabel, *A Real Time Revolution in Routines*, in Heckescher and Adler.

by the work of Elinor Ostrom.[34] A third distinct line of work examines online cooperation and peer production generally, and the design of "social software" in particular.[35] The creators of social software design platforms with the group in mind – they seek to structure opportunities and constraints that make the group work better, rather than ease the lot of any given individual. Such programs might gradually increase authority and opportunities for individual users as they act over time in ways that show trustworthiness or diligence. The work is largely observational and heuristic at this stage, but because of the explosion of collaboration online as a global practice, there is enormous variety and intellectual effort directed at these design problems, which in turn are also explicitly rendered because they have to be embedded in the software or communicated among far-flung communities. This makes online cooperation a particularly rich space for observation and field experimentation.

Several rough regularities emerge from these diverse lines of literature. First, people on average do not behave as predicted by the standard economic model. Second, people appear to have diverse motivational–behavioral profiles. In most experiments about one-third behave much as *homo economicus* predicts. About half cooperate.[36] Of these cooperators, more than half reciprocate kindness or trust with kindness or trust, and meanness and defection with like meanness and defection, even at material cost to themselves. Others are unconditional cooperators. Not everyone falls neatly, however, into one or the other of these categories. The distribution of behaviors is not smooth, but has modes around what a selfish actor would do and what a cooperator or reciprocator would do. This pattern lends some support to the idea that discrete personality types are deeply ingrained, culturally, biologically, or both, within human societies. Neuroscientific studies support the proposition that different people's brains light up differently in fMRI studies, in similar situations, suggesting a distribution of types whose brain "lights up" differently, and that the differences are consistent with different behavioral patterns.[37] On the other hand, cross-country comparisons within industrialized countries show substantial differences in the ways in which people do, or do not, punish defectors in social dilemma games and

---

[34] Elinor Ostrom, GOVERNING THE COMMONS: THE EVOLUTION OF INSTITUTIONS FOR COLLECTIVE ACTION (1990).

[35] Benkler, *Coase's Penguin*; Clay Shirky, *Social Software and the Politics of Groups*, March 9, 2003 (published online, http://shirky.com/writings/group_enemy.html).

[36] Ernst Fehr and Herbert Gintis, *Human Motivation and Social Cooperation: Experimental and Analytical Foundations*, 33 ANNU. REV. SOCIOL. 43, 50 (2007).

[37] See Fehr et al., *Neuroeconomic Foundations*.

in how their punishing behavior correlates with their own levels of contribution. These differences appear to be associated with measures of rule of
law in the country, suggesting substantial cultural and learning effects as
well.[38] Experiments in small-scale societies exhibited even wider variation,
which increases the more a society is removed from markets, and to some
extent is correlated to cultural practices of giving aimed to establish status
and dependence relations, or the degree of cooperation practiced in hunt-
ing and gathering or other day-to-day activities.[39] Evolutionary arguments,
both genetic and cultural, provide plausible stories about how a population
of selfish actors could invade a population of cooperators, whereas over time
a population with a high level of cooperators would drive out groups with
too many free riders, stabilizing the average prevalence of each type. In other
words, it provides an analytic frame through which to explain the rise of
diverse equilibria for any given moment, from cooperative to selfish, in different societies. The stability of types, at least in a known target population
in a given time frame, limits the range of predicted behaviors and responses
to design constraints and affordances to a manageable set. Understanding
whether that distribution at a given time is itself subject to intervention –
that is, whether human beings are perfectible along the dimension of their
motivation and proclivity to cooperate – will have a large effect on what
the feasible and proper targets for human systems design can be.[40] But the
present literature cannot yet tell us with sufficient confidence whether there
is such as thing as an individual proclivity to cooperate independent of the
situational condition, whether arising from genetics or education, and if
so whether this proclivity is stable over a lifetime or itself susceptible to
education and perfection over time.

   Whether we ultimately come to believe that differences among human
beings in terms of proclivity to cooperate are innate, acquired, or mixed, the
experimental and observational work certainly supports the proposition
that these behavioral patterns are also situational. That is to say, certain

---

[38] Herrman et al., *supra.*
[39] For variations in quality and focus of punishing responses between Western European and
      some post-Communist societies see Simon Gaechter, Benedikt Herrman, and Christian
      Thoni, *Cross Cultural Differences in Norm Enforcement*, 28 BEHAVIORAL AND BRAIN SCI-
      ENCES 822 (2005). The big difference was represented in the studies of small-scale societies,
      where deviations were much larger and correlated to cultural mapping of the games onto
      group-specific practices, some of which called for supergenerosity or none at all where
      market-integrated societies would have had a focal point of equal division of windfall
      gains. See Henrich et al., FOUNDATIONS.
[40] Yochai Benkler & Helen Nissenbaum, *Commons-based Peer Production and Virtue*, 14 J.
      POL. PHIL. 394 (2006).

characteristics of the situation or context, of the system of interaction, will more likely lead people to cooperate stably, and others will likely lead to deterioration into behavior more consistent with the Hobbesian view of the state of nature. This structured context should preoccupy architects of institutions or social systems aiming for productive cooperation. The following discussion therefore assumes that human beings are diverse; that the diversity of human types is not infinite, that types are stable in the short term, and that each type can be predicted to have a typical behavior under specified conditions of interaction, which will change the social conditions and hence payoffs to all of them.

To render the broad and diverse kinds of relevant scholarly literature usable for policymakers and institutional entrepreneurs alike, I have identified an initial set of thirteen considerations, or focal points, that designers of such systems should consider. I call these "design levers," because they are elements or focal points in the system design intended to affect the dynamics of the social system to which they apply. Addressing these areas of concern properly increases the likelihood that participants will be motivated to behave cooperatively, by setting the social context so that it facilitates cooperation among cooperators and allows selfish actors to be policed and incentivized in ways that do not undermine the intrinsic motivation of the more cooperative participants. These design levers are intended to be a midlevel abstraction: abstract enough to capture a wide range of experimental and field observations, and concrete enough to be tied to particular types of feasible interventions that could be causally tied to achieving one or another of the design levers.

By cooperation in a given interaction or system I mean behavior that contributes to the attainment of goals by others in that system. The behavior can reflect one of a range of attitudinal and intentional states: (a) *altruism*: action aimed to contribute to success of an other, irrespective of success of self; (b) *committed mutualism*: action aimed to contribute to success of an other, consistent with success of self; (c) *collective efficacy*: action aimed toward the success of a common goal that transcends the agent's specifiable individual success; (d) *heuristic reciprocity*: action aimed at benefiting one's own goal pursuit, guided by an implicit sense that "what goes around comes around" (less sensitive to explicit payoff structures than to social and psychological structures that trigger a judgment that the context is one where reciprocal benefits may arise); (e) *strategic mutualism*: action aimed at attaining one's own goal, which advances the goal of another as a by-product. This latter is the behavior that game theoretical mechanism design seeks to elicit, and in animal studies would be thought of as by-product mutualism.[41] To dispel misinterpretations: "cooperation" does not mean "behaving nicely." It means acting in ways that advance the goals of others, including in contexts where even a selfish and solipsistic person would do so, but most importantly beyond what a selfish and self-centered person would be predicted to do. Gang members are often highly cooperative. Suicide bombers exhibit high degrees of self-sacrifice for collective efficacy. Learning the dynamics of cooperation can help disrupt successful cooperation that we judge normatively harmful no less than allowing us to construct successful cooperation whose outcomes and processes we normatively affirm.

The design considerations, or levers, are not strictly necessary or sufficient to achieve cooperation. Some, particularly those that aim to manage selfish actors, may present trade-offs with other levers – as we will see with discipline and trust. But they characterize loci and types of intervention, or questions presented for the designer of a system, which would predictably affect the likelihood that participants will cooperate.

B. Design Levers for Cooperative Dynamics

Communication

Communication plays a robust role in the scholarly literature on social cooperation. It has a large effect in experimental work,[42] and its routinization is one of the core design principles of the organizational shift to collaborative models.[43] The salience of communication partly locates the work on cooperation in the tradition of dialogic theories of the self: The self comes to know its interests, desires, and meaning through communication with others, rather than through solipsistic or egocentric reflection. This makes the relationship stand apart as an object of design, rather than making the individual, fully formed before the interaction, the object of monitoring, reward, punishment, and similar manipulation to achieve the desired behavior. It also suggests the possibility of perfectibility: that the distribution of cooperative proclivities is stable and given, and cannot itself be the object of longer-term design.

---

[41] Lee A. Dugatkin, Cooperation Among Animals: An Evolutionary Perspective (1997).

[42] David Sally, *Conversation and Cooperation in Social Dilemmas*, VII Rationality and Society 57, 57–92 (1995).

[43] Sabel, *Ungoverned Production, supra.*

FACTORS AFFECTING INTRINSIC MOTIVATION

A significant focus of organizational sociology, a major line of the work in psychology, and a heavy focus of the management studies, is on intrinsic motivation – that is, motivation to act that comes from within, rather than in response to external efforts to affect the behavior through reward and punishment. The definition of cooperation as I use it here emphasizes the degree to which an agent whose actions we are assessing intends to do something beyond merely advance his or her own goals – be they a commitment to advance the success of a partner to a mutual exchange, the success of a group in its collective effort, or the flourishing of an other in a context that suggests pure altruism. The next four factors, or design levers, focus on the degree to which large portions of the population adopt cooperation as an internally desired activity.

Solidarity and Humanization/Empathy

Two important levers that have been experimentally and observationally shown to improve the degree of cooperation in a group are solidarity and empathy, or humanization. The fact that people are more generous toward, and cooperate more with, others who are perceived to be within even a very minimally specified group is long established experimentally,[44] and team-building activities and solidarity-constructing rituals are widely reported in observational work.[45] A rich literature in psychology has worked to define social identity and the relationship between the formation of social identity and the quality of collaboration on a team.[46] Psychologists tend to view social identity as a condition through which an individual develops a sense of self, a "knowledge that he belongs to certain groups together with some emotional and value significance to him of the group membership."[47] Individuals who so define themselves generally work especially hard to create and sustain

---

[44] Henri Tajfel & John Turner, *An Integrative Theory of Intergroup Conflict, in* THE SOCIAL PSYCHOLOGY OF INTERGROUP RELATIONS (W. G. Austin and S. Worchel, eds. 1979); Toshio Yamagishi, Nobuhito Jin, and Toko Kiyonari, *Bounded Generalized Reciprocity, Ingroup Boasting and Ingroup Favoritism*, 16 ADVANCES IN GROUP PROCESSES 161, 161–97 (1999).
[45] FIRM AS COLLABORATIVE COMMUNITY, *supra.*
[46] See S. Alexander Haslam, PSYCHOLOGY IN ORGANIZATIONS: THE SOCIAL IDENTITY APPROACH (2001);
[47] Henri Tajfel, quoted in S. Alexander Haslam, Rachel A. Eggins, and Katherine J. Reynolds, *The ASPIRe Model: Actualizing Social and Personal Identity Resources to Enhance Organizational Outcomes*, 76 J. OCCUPATIONAL AND ORGANIZATIONAL PSYCH. 83, 84 (2003).

positive distinctions between their group and other groups.[48] Empirical
work over the last two decades has tied this change in identity or self-
perception to organizational citizenship, the willingness to contribute to
collective goals and behave cooperatively in collective action settings, and
increasing group productivity.[49] This work is consistent with work in evolutionary biology on the relative success of groups. Boyd and Richerson
make the evolved psychological proclivity to identify with large, symboli-
cally marked groups as calling for cooperation beyond kin the core of their
explanation of the successful rise of human societies of the scope and scale
we see, in contradistinction to other primates.[50] Bowles and Gintis, although
recognizing the power of group identity, emphasize its double-edge. The
identification of "in" the group is usually associated with a characterization
of other, and can (as it so often has in history) breed xenophobia, or simply
moral indifference.[51] In work I have done with collaborators, we have shown
that identifying individuals who respond with high activation to a strong
solidarity signal (in our case, knowing that they are in a team of Democrats
or Republicans) and putting them in groups of similar individuals allows
them to sustain very high levels of cooperation in public goods games over
long periods, without need for reputation, communication, or punishment
mechanisms. And yet, in a study about behavior of supporters of competing
contenders in the Democratic primary in 2008, we found that this effect had
particularly large effects in mobilizing men to be more generous to other
members of their group during perceived conflict with a distinct outgroup –
consistent with the double-edge warning.[52]

Tribalism is not, however, the only way we have of avoiding solipsism.
Empathy toward another human being *qua* human being is another. In several experimental contexts, humanization – mechanisms to assure that participants know and recognize the humanity of their counterpart – improves
the number of cooperators and the degree of "generosity" they are willing to show others.[53] Simply seeing the face of the human being involved
in the experiment, without any change in the game design or possibility
of communication or reputation effect, significantly affects the degree of

[48] Tajfel & Turner, *supra*.
[49] Haslam, *et al.* at 84–86.
[50] Boyd and Richerson, NOT BY GENES ALONE, *supra*, Chapter 6.
[51] Samuel Bowles and Herbert Gintis, *Persistent Parochialism: Trust and Exclusion in Ethnic Networks* 55 J. ECON BEHAVIOR & ORG. 1 (2004); Samuel Bowles and Herbert Gintis, *Social Capital and Community Governance* 112 ECON J. F419–36 (2002).
[52] D. Rand *et al.*, (in progress); D. Rand *et al. From Friend to Foe* (submitted).
[53] Bohnet & Frey, *supra*.

cooperation and generosity that both average and even mostly selfish players exhibit. Adding more personal information, such as hobby or undergraduate major, further improves cooperation and generosity. The distinct effects of interacting with another human being as such, by comparison to a computer, for example, have also been documented in neuroscience studies.[54]

Trust and Fairness

The importance of trust is central to organizational sociology, but is also strongly present in experimental work. "Trust" has attracted its own immense literature, with a variety of purposes and implications. Often scholars deploy it to characterize the success of a system that removes the possibility of human defection or error. When used in this sense, "trust" does not act as a design lever at all, but rather as a description of the outcome that signifies confidence in the *system's* performance, not the other person. To characterize trust as an element subject to design intervention, I use it to refer to an attitude that agents in the interaction possess toward each other: It is a belief that others in a given system will act in ways that are cooperative toward the trusting agent or the common goal when they do in fact have an effective choice to act in ways harmful or helpful to the trusting agent. Risk is therefore a precondition to trust. To facilitate trust, the architects of social systems should break down cooperative actions into observable chunks, where participants can lower their exposure to each other while observing the proclivities of others to cooperate or defect, for example. I treat trust in this sense as one of the mechanisms of intrinsic motivation, because it is an internal belief about others, by definition not under conditions where the other's action can be controlled (including, presumably, under conditions where threatened retaliation would underenforce cooperative behavior), and because this internal belief triggers for many an intrinsic will to reciprocate the anticipated cooperative behavior with like cooperation. Trust as intrinsic motivation plays the role of anticipatory cooperation, in anticipation of which others can open an interaction cooperatively even before actual cooperative action has been taken by the other toward them.

Another consistent finding of the experimental literature is that perceptions of fairness are endogenous to the cooperative dynamic. Selfish

---

[54] Rilling et al. (2002), *supra*; Rilling et al., (2004) *supra*. See also Tania Singer et al., *Empathetic neural responses are modulated by perceived fairness of others*, 439 NATURE 466 (2006) (describing changes in empathy level based on counterparty's play in a prisoner's dilemma game).

rationality puts fairness of outcomes aside, focusing on whether the individual is made better or worse off by an interaction as the sole predictor of that agent's behavior. Consistent with this approach, scholars engaging in policy analysis often separate considerations of fairness from claims about predicted efficiency, turning to the former only after egocentrically defined incentives have induced the desired level of activity. The experimental literature consistently shows that this approach fails to take account of the extent to which people care about the fair distribution of outcomes, the perceived fairness of the intentions of others in the interactions, and probably the fairness of the process of the interaction.[55] What is socially and psychologically experienced as fair is, however, cross-culturally contingent and diverse, subject to framing, ideology, and manipulation. The goal of pursuing fairness as a design principle, then, is not to create one universal norm of fairness (e.g., equal division of the gains from interaction); instead, systems designers should seek to build in mechanisms to achieve widely held perceptions of fairness with regard to outcomes and intentions. Fairness in the particular interaction will often be a central target of norm development for the community.

Norms: Intrinsic and Extrinsic

Another relevant and substantial literature explores social norms, probing the workings of longstanding, usually tightly knit communities.[56] These communities have typically integrated many of the design levers I try to separate into discrete building blocks, thereby fashioning ongoing, stable, social relations. When thinking of design for systems that may be as new as a collaborative wiki launched yesterday, or a new system for getting local citizens to offer solutions to local problems, social norms must refer to something more primitive than longstanding internalized norms. Norms in this minimal sense must be instances of more-or-less clearly understood behavioral expectations about what counts as "cooperative" in a given system. Once participants know what counts as cooperation, and what is defection, they can adjust their own actions, as well as judge the actions of others. At the simplest levels, these could be Schelling coordination norms: that is, norms that have no claim to apply other than that they are convenient focal

---

[55] Fehr and Schmidt, *Fairness and Reciprocity, supra.*
[56] Robert Ellickson, ORDER WITHOUT LAW: HOW NEIGHBORS SETTLE DISPUTES (1991).

points for coordination (e.g., if two New Yorkers decide to meet at 1 p.m., they will disproportionately choose to meet next to the clock in Grand Central). Beyond that, they can be explicitly stated expectations about behavior, like those that anchored Wikipedia and made it unique among cooperation models in its early days in being purely norms-based. Finally, they can be evocations of existing background norms that are internalized and long-standing in a given applicable community, applied metaphorically or by analogy to the new context.

Norms can be either extrinsically or intrinsically motivating, depending on the history of their adoption and the degree to which they reflect internalized discipline. Some work suggests that norms that are explicitly adopted by a group after deliberation achieve high adherence.[57] This is consistent with the idea, central to the psychology of crowding out, that what makes for intrinsic motivation is self-determination. Here, at the collective or public level, norms chosen through a process of self-governance can be internalized as belonging to the agent who lives by them (an actual, psychologically felt consent of the governed, rather than the notional one of social contract). These norms, although "extrinsic" in their form as external constraints on behavior, really are a species of internal reasons for action, what Deci and Ryan called "integrated regulation."[58] This is the kind of effect observed by Edward Balleisen, in this volume, as a common argument in favor of self-determination in the construction of norms for self-regulation. On the other hand, norms can be externally given, or largely random in their selection (such as driving on the right-hand or left-hand side), in which case they will improve cooperation, but through external processes of compliance and comprehension of what is cooperative, not through internal adaptation of desired behavior.

Efficacy

Coming out of the psychological work on motivation, people seem to work on projects that make them feel effective or competent. A cooperation system is improved to the extent that people see their actions individually, as well as their collective effort, as being effective. We see this in studies of fundraising, where reports of success and exhortations of how close we are to the goal are common, as well as in the shape of online peer production efforts, whose

---

[57] Ostrom, Walker, Gardner, 1994, *supra.*
[58] Deci and Ryan, *supra.*

adoption and takeoff suggests that as the prospect of successful cooperation becomes clearer over time, it draws increasing numbers of contributors.

FACTORS AFFECTING EXTRINSIC MOTIVATION

Punishment and Reward

Of all the findings in the experimental literature, most consistent with the selfish rational actor model is the importance of punishment and reward. In many studies, the presence of mechanisms for punishing defectors and/or rewarding cooperators improves cooperation. Given that roughly one-third of agents generally behave selfishly, and that in many contexts enduring cooperation depends on effective deterrence of their free riding, this result should come as no surprise. The "surprising" or "altruistic" aspect of this research rather involves the existence of a sizable segment of participants in experiments who will undertake actions to punish defectors, and thereby police them, even when these actions have a net negative private return to them personally in the game design. This punishment represents a second-order public goods problem, because those who mete out punishment bear the full cost, while the benefits are shared by all participants in some game designs or reaped by entirely other participants in other game designs. The experimental literature finds, however, that with the right design, reciproca-tors can solve the second-order public goods problem of punishment with-out intervention from an external body, such as the state or management.[59]

This finding is complemented by many field studies, which show that mutual monitoring and graduated sanctions on defectors play an important role in sustaining, for example, commons-based resource systems. Ostrom's studies of irrigation districts and the role played by local "riders" checking that participants do not take too much water from the common irrigation district accompanied by a system of sanctions enforced locally offer the clas-sic example.[60] Experimental work suggests, however, that poorly designed punishment mechanisms can also backfire, leading to punitive rounds of misfired retaliation and deterioration of cooperation. Fehr and Rockenbach, for example, ran a trust game with punishment. In a trust game, experi-menters give principals a sum. Principals can transfer as much or as little of

---

[59] Bowles and Gintis, *Homo Reciprocans*; Fehr & Gachter, *Altruistic Punishment*.
[60] Ostrom, GOVERNING THE COMMONS; Ostrom, *Behavioral Approaches*; see also Henry E. Smith, *Semicommon Property Rights and Scattering of in the Open Fields*, 29 J. LEGAL STUD 131 (2000).

the endowment to a trustee agent. The experimenter then multiplies whatever was transferred to the trustee and gives the new large endowment to the trustee. The trustee can then go home with the entire multiplied endowment, or transfer as much or as little of it as she wishes back to the principal. The selfish rational actor model predicts that the trustee will transfer back nothing, and therefore principal will entrust nothing and go home with the original endowment. Many experiments have shown that trustees do transfer back substantial amounts, and that these amounts increase in the degree of trust exhibited – that is, the proportion of the initial endowment transferred. In this particular series of experiments, however, principals were allowed to specify in advance that they would impose a penalty on trustees who did not transfer back, or were given the option affirmatively to abjure the power to punish. Inverting the prediction of the selfish rational actor model, trustees transfer back the smallest portion of the entrusted amount when punishment is threatened, a middling amount when punishment is not possible, and the most when principals, though they have the option to punish, disclaim it in advance.[61] This is an example of another design consideration that I discuss later: crowding out. Here, it suggests that punishment, introduced as a threat before action in a two-person game, has a very different valence than punishment available as a background power, without affirmative threat, and in group settings where the imposition of punishment itself is an act of cooperation in the second-order public goods game. Calibrating the negative and positive effects of punishment in repeat games is likely to continue to be a substantial focus of research. One study suggested that negative reciprocity can be triggered even in parties who "deserved" the punishment because they were first to defect,[62] and another study suggests that the extent to which retaliation and spiteful punishments devolve into feuds is cross-culturally diverse.[63] On the other hand, a recent study suggests that the potential negative effects of punishment disappear in longer games.[64]

Transparency/Reputation

Another important design element, the transparency of a system, bears powerfully on the issues of both trust and punishment. Critically, many of the

---

[61] Fehr and Rockenbach, *Detrimental Effects*; Falk et al., *Driving Forces*.
[62] Dreber et al., *supra*.
[63] Hermann et al., *supra*.
[64] Simon Gaechter, Elke Renner, and Martin Sefton, The Long-run Benefits of Punishment (unpublished).

other design features depend on participants knowing who did what, to and with whom, to what effect, by which mechanism. Recognition of this dependence lies behind the argument that biologists Nowak and Sigmund make about the evolutionary impact of moral accounting (although they did not call it that) – such accounting, they suggest, was necessary to sustain indirect reciprocity, which in turn may have been the driving force behind the evolution of human intelligence.[65] Whether or not they are correct, studies in experimental economics typically show that reputation-rich games lead to cooperation more quickly and robustly than anonymous games.[66] Similarly, reputation systems play a significant role in social software platforms, ranging from commercial systems like eBay and Amazon, to the wide range of commons-based peer production projects that deploy the possibility of creating a stable locus for reputation, and observable behavior and opinion, as a major design element.

Transparency can affect both intrinsic and extrinsic motivations. Intrinsically, participants can observe that others are cooperating and be driven to reciprocate. Participants can also gauge the payoffs and processes and determine the fairness of the interaction. Extrinsically, it facilitates monitoring, punishment, and reward. Transparency requires a system that truthfully reflects actions, outcomes, and intentions, and hence must be designed to weed out deception. This is an observation that is, of course, quite central to regulation. In the public regulatory framework, Joseph Stiglitz in his essay here identifies disclosure as the first modality of formal public regulation, whereas Balleisen's essay emphasizes the centrality of transparency to the design of self-regulation as well.

Cost

Cost is an additional consideration. People will cooperate more when the cost of doing so is lower, such as when the opportunity cost of cooperating in a prisoner's dilemma is lower because of payoff structure[67] or because cooperative tasks are structured in fine-grained modules so that the cost of useful incremental contribution becomes smaller for any given individual participating in peer production.[68]

---

[65] Nowak and Sigmund, *supra*.
[66] Ernst Fehr and Simon Gaechter, *Cooperation and Punishment in Public Goods Experiments*, 90 Am. Econ. Rev. 980, 980–94 (2000).
[67] Fehr and Camerer, in Foundations.
[68] Benkler, *Coase's Penguin*.

Crowding Out

An important design constraint already introduced in the discussion of punishment and norms is crowding out. Intrasystem crowding out refers to situations when use of one design lever would reduce the efficacy of another. The effect of threatened punishment in a two-person trust game I described above is one example, but the crowding out of trust by punishment has older roots in the literature.[69] Intersystem crowding out can occur when one tries to mix-and-match elements from cooperative systems with elements from other systems, such as market mechanisms or bureaucratic control systems. In economics, the literature is anchored in the old Titmuss–Arrow debate over blood donations and sales. Since then, a large literature has demonstrated that introducing money into a relationship can crowd out nonmonetary motivations and undermine otherwise cooperation-based interactions.[70] The most widely used psychological explanation for crowding out is self-determination theory. Arising from the work of Edward Deci, beginning around the same time, but in apparent mutual ignorance of the Titmuss–Arrow debate, self-determination theory posits that individuals have innate needs for competence, autonomy, and relatedness.[71] Certain kinds of extrinsic rewards and controls tend to make individuals feel that all or some aspects of these needs are rejected by the person offering the reward or punishment, leading to a decline in motivation. Other possible explanations may have more to do with the social dynamic more consistent with a reciprocity model of cooperation – the fact that social capital, for example, can only be built within activities not fully fungible with monetized relationships.[72] Given that we observe many mixed systems, such as open source software innovation and certainly the introduction of cooperative models into firms, mixing is not impossible. Indeed, the psychological literature itself sees the tenor and framing of rewards as important, as well as the type of tasks involved. But introduction of money in particular, and similar tangible rewards, as well as formal bureaucratic control, requires attention to the interactions between the motivational and organizational

---

[69] Toshio Yamagishi, *The Provision of a Sanctioning System as a Public Good*, 51 J. Personality Social Psychology 110–16 (1986).

[70] Bruno S. Frey and Reto Jege, *Motivation Crowding Theory: A Survey of Empirical Evidence*, 15(5) J. Econ. Surveys 589 (2001).

[71] Deci and Ryan, *supra*.

[72] Yochai Benkler, *Sharing Nicely: On Shareable Goods and the Emergence of Sharing as a Modality of Economic Production*, 114 Yale LJ. (2004).

forms rather than a simple assumption of additive effect.[73] This creates a particular problem for policy, where a policymaker will, by definition, be external to the social interaction and act upon it from the outside. Monica Prasad's discussion of carbon taxes in this volume is an excellent example of the tension. Managing crowding out then becomes a central problem that others, for example technical platform designers, have less of a need to address as long as use of their platform is not mandatory or users are not conscious of the constraints the system imposes on their interaction.

Exit and Entry

First, the ease of exit and entry into a cooperation platform is an important design element. At baseline, where exit is not itself a form of defection, and where participation does not easily permit expropriation of collectively created value, easy exit and entry will usually draw cooperators and repel selfish actors. Cooperators will tend to select into a cooperative framework, and would perceive its cooperative characteristics and absence of defection opportunities as affirmative benefits. Selfish actors, by contrast, will select themselves out unless there are opportunities for gainful abuse.[74] In other contexts, such as employment, easy exit tends to leave firms with easier recourse to market-based mechanisms to structure their relationship, which undermines trust.[75] Here, longer-term, enforceable commitments, and even asymmetric ease of entry and exit, may be preferable. Ironically, in many states, at-will employment combined with enforceable noncompete agreements achieves exactly the inverse of the desired asymmetry.[76] More generally, expensive entry and exit will deter defectors, who will only undertake entry when the potential gains from defection outweigh the cost. As another of the design levers suggests, however, high cost may also decrease the demand for participation among cooperators.

Leadership/Asymmetric Contribution

Another significant element in the design of cooperation dynamics involves leadership, asymmetric contribution, and influence. This observation is

---

[73] Samuel Bowles, *Policies Designed for Self-Interested Citizens May Undermine "The Moral Sentiments": Evidence from Economic Experiments* 320 SCIENCE 1605–09 (20 June 2008).

[74] Ostrom, *Behavioral Approaches*.

[75] John Paul MacDuffie and Susan Helper, *Collaboration in Supply Chains with and without Trust*, in FIRM AS COLLABORATIVE COMMUNITY.

[76] Matt Marx, Deborah Strumsky, and Lee Fleming, *Mobility, Skills, and the Michigan Noncompete Experiment* (working paper 2008).

anchored in organizational sociology[77] and examinations of open source software[78] and online cooperation. It is important to recognize, however, that "leadership" does not necessarily imply "hierarchy." What is required of leadership, how asymmetric contribution leads to leadership and motivates it, are important areas of research into cooperation platforms, currently less well worked out than other areas. In the domain of online cooperation and social software, systems frequently allow some participants to take on heavier workloads, thereby earning a claim on their cooperators to exert greater influence over the process. This dynamic certainly characterizes Wikipedia and the larger free and open source software projects. Some scholars have argued that this tendency implies the reemergence of hierarchical organization, but this position overstates the degree of control exerted by "leaders" and understates the degree of communication, persuasion, and agreement.

As a whole, the design levers (summarized in Table 9.1) provide an initial checklist, a framework for focusing those engaged in cooperative human systems design on a set of likely intervention points that are likely to improve the level of cooperation engaged in through the system considered.

C. Law and Policy: Examples of Cooperative Systems Design

Law and various other policy mechanisms are systems. They interact with other systems – technical, organizational, and social, most often – to allow people to act in the world: say, drive a car, or make an investment. Like these other systems, which have at times formed various observational grounds for the cooperation literature, law and policy are systems of affordance and constraint that can be (even if they often are not) susceptible to conscious design through purposeful human action. How might legal and policy design look if it were subject to analysis as a cooperation system? Although no one has yet begun to apply the full range of the literature on cooperation to questions of law and policy, there are enough efforts to apply the insights of some of the work in experimental economics, and separately the work in organizational sociology, to offer us a glimpse at how applying this approach may facilitate the design of interventions in the future.

The rise of cooperation as an alternative approach to markets and hierarchies has placed the most direct and politically mobilized pressure on law and policy in the areas of copyrights and patents, particularly, but not

---

[77] Michael Maccoby and Charles Heckscher, *A Note on Leadership for Collaborative Community, in* FIRM AS COLLABORATIVE COMMUNITY, *supra*, at 469–78.
[78] Steve Weber, THE SUCCESS OF OPEN SOURCE (2005).

Table 9.1. *Design considerations for cooperation*

Design element	Description
Communication	Allowing participants to communicate, even without any enforceable commitment, increases cooperation.[a]
Empathy/Humanization	Participants who identify with the counterparty to a game increase cooperation in social dilemma games and altruistic giving in Dictator Games.[b]
Solidarity	Participants who see themselves as part of a common identity group increase cooperation.[c]
Fairness	Participants consistently appear to care about the fairness of the outcomes, the intentions of other participants, and the processes.[d]
Norms	The presence of even minimal coordination focal points, or Schelling norms, can improve cooperation by clarifying what is expected from whom and what counts as defection or cooperation. Self-chosen norms appear to improve cooperation, as will, likely, background norms already encoded by participants as "values."[e]
Trust	Trust as a design lever refers to an attitudinal stance participants can have toward each other. As a design lever it is narrower than the term is usually applied, and characterizes a belief agents have about the likely actions of others when unconstrained by other system elements. When it functions, it acts as a form of anticipatory cooperation, which agents can "reciprocate" by themselves cooperating in their first move.[f]
Efficacy	Individuals are internally driven to act with competence and efficacy. Providing a sense of efficacy in the cooperation likely improves intrinsic commitment to the cooperative project.[g]
Punishment/Reward	There is consistent evidence that introduction of a possibility of punishment into social dilemma games increases cooperation by keeping selfish actors in check. Punishment is a complex social and psychological phenomenon, is cross-culturally contingent, may decrease overall value of the cooperative activity, and may crowd out trust and fairness.[h]
Crowding Out	Systems can crowd each other out, and elements within a given system can crowd each other out. The introduction of money into an interaction can limit participation motivated by intrinsic motivations. There is also evidence that introducing punishment can crowd out trust. Crowding out complicates cooperative systems design: not all potential interventions interact positively.[i]
Transparency (Reputation)	Transparency of cooperation platforms enables agents to observe what others are doing, characterize actions, intentions, and outcomes, and identify cooperation for positive reciprocity and defection for negative reciprocity. Reputation is a core instance of transparency.[j]
Cost	The level of cooperation is sensitive to, but not dominated by, the cost of cooperation.[k]

Design element	Description
Exit/Entry	Whether a system is easy or hard to enter will affect the mix of types that participate and the level of trust participants will have. The direction of the effect will depend on whether exit itself is a form of defection and whether there are opportunities for appropriation within the interaction.[l]
Leadership/Asymmetric Contribution	Leadership is important in creating and sustaining cooperation.[m] Leadership is not hierarchy, but the flexibility of a system to allow asymmetric contributions and levels of capabilities and powers within a system without upsetting the cooperative dynamic.

[a] Sally, *supra.*

[b] Iris Bohnet & Bruno Frey, *The sound of silence in prisoner's dilemma and dictator games*, 38 J. OF ECON. BEHAVIOR & ORG. 43–57 (1999); James K. Rilling et al., A Neural Basis for Social Cooperation, 35(2) *Neuron* 395–405 (2002); James K. Rilling et al., Opposing Bold Responses to Reciprocated and Unreciprocated Altruism in Putative Reward Pathways, 15(6) *Neuroreport*, 2539–43 (2004).

[c] Toshio Yamagishi, Nobuhito Jin, and Toko Kiyonari, *Bounded Generalized Reciprocity, Ingroup Boasting and Ingroup Favoritism*, 16 ADVANCES IN GROUP PROCESSES 161, 161–97 (1999); L. Zucker, *Production of Trust: institutional sources of economic structure*, 1840–1920 8 RESEARCH IN ORGANIZATION BEHAVIOR 53 (1986); Miller McPherson, Lynn Smith-Lovin, and James M. Cook, *Birds of a Feather: Homophily in Social Networks*, 27 ANNUAL REVIEW OF SOCIOLOGY 415 (August 2001); S. Alexander Haslam, *Psychology in Organizations: The Social Identity Approach.* (Sage Publications 2001).

[d] Ernst Fehr and K. Schmidt, *Theories of Fairness and Reciprocity, Evidence and Economic Applications, in Advances in Economics and Econometrics* – 8th World Congress, Econometric Society (M. Dwatripont et al., eds. 2001).

[e] Elinor Ostrom, Roy Gardner, and James Walker, RULES, GAMES, AND COMMON POOL RESOURCES (1994).

[f] Diego Gambetta (ed.), TRUST, MAKING AND BREAKING COOPERATIVE RELATIONS (Blackwell, Oxford 1988).

[g] Deci and Ryan, *supra.*

[h] Samuel Bowles and Herbert Gintis, *Homo Reciprocans: Altruistic Punishment of Free Riders*, 415 NATURE 125 (2002); Ernst Fehr & Simon Gachter, *Altruistic Punishment in Humans*, 415 NATURE 137 (2002); Ernst Fehr and Bettina Rockenbach, *Detrimental effects of sanctions on human altruism*, 422 NATURE 137 (2002); Armin Falk *et al.*, *Driving Forces Behind Informal Sanctions*, 73 ECONOMETRICA 2017 (2005). Punishment is a double-edged sword and may undermine cooperation, see Anna Dreber *et al.*, *Winners Don't Punish*, 452 NATURE 348, 348–51 (2008); effects are cross-culturally varied Benedikt Herrman *et al.*, *Antisocial Punishment Across Societies*, 319 SCIENCE 1362, 1362–67 (2008).

[i] Bruno S. Frey and Reto Jege, *Motivation Crowding Theory: A Survey of Empirical Evidence*, 15(5) J. ECONOMIC SURVEYS 589 (2001); Fehr and Rockenbach, *supra.*; Bowles (2008) *supra.*

[j] Ernst Fehr and Simon Gaechter, *Cooperation and Punishment in Public Goods Experiments*, 90 AM. ECON. REV. 980–94 (2000) (explaining that partner treatment with reputation yields higher levels of cooperation).

[k] Camerer & Fehr, *supra*; Benkler, *Coase's Penguin, supra.*

[l] Elinor Ostrom, *A Behavioral Approach to the Rational Choice Theory of Collective Action*, 92 AM. POL. SCI. REV. 1, 1–22 (1998).

[m] Michael Maccoby and Charles Heckscher, *A Note on Leadership for Collaborative Community, in* FIRM AS COLLABORATIVE COMMUNITY, *supra*, at 469–78; Weber, *supra.*

solely, as they relate to software and Internet-based cultural production and communication. The rise of peer production, first as free or open source software and then more generally throughout the digitally networked environment, has offered not only strong proof of enormously creative and innovative alternative models of production, but also widespread practices that are negatively affected by excessively strong exclusivity regimes.[79] It joined with the more general critique aimed at the position that strong patents and copyrights are justified by the need for powerful monetary incentives to motivate individuals and firms to undertake the costs and risks associated with research and development or mass-scale cultural production. Although some of the arguments made against excessively strong exclusive rights rested on the public goods nature of information goods from the consumption perspective, much of it focused on the role of intrinsically and socially driven innovation and creative expression to defend the importance of the public domain and the commons.[80] Reflecting a deep recognition of the constitutive role of law in markets, similar to claims in Marc Eisner's essay in this volume, the strong emphasis on enhancing copyrights and patents was seen as putting the thumb on the scales in favor of incumbents at the expense of new modalities of social production.

Nowhere have the proponents of this alternative economic culture been more politically effective than in fighting to a standstill the efforts of the copyright industries to push for stronger exclusivity regimes in this decade. The year 1998 was the last great successful legislative year for the copyright industries in the United States: the passage of the Digital Millennium Copyright Act, the No Electronic Theft Act, and the Sonny Bono Copyright Term Extension Act marked what appeared to be an unstoppable coalition for expanding rights. But a loose coalition of free and open source software developers, civil society activists, and a small number of large companies dedicated to building free-software-based services and computing equipment business models, and whose business model did not depend on, and was harmed by, exclusivity rules, successfully fought the Hollywood-based coalition to a standstill around new paracopyright regulations like "trusted systems," a proposed database protection law, and an exclusivity-expanding

---

[79] Benkler, *Coase's Penguin*; Benkler, *Sharing Nicely*.

[80] See, among many other works, Jessica Litman, DIGITAL COPYRIGHT (2001); Siva Vaidhyanathan, COPYRIGHTS AND COPYWRONGS: THE RISE OF INTELLECTUAL PROPERTY AND HOW IT THREATENS CREATIVITY (2001); Lawrence Lessig, FREE CULTURE: HOW BIG MEDIA USES TECHNOLOGY AND THE LAW TO LOCK DOWN CULTURE AND CONTROL CREATIVITY (2004); Eric Von Hippel, DEMOCRATIZING INNOVATION (2006); Yochai Benkler, THE WEALTH OF NETWORKS, HOW SOCIAL PRODUCTION TRANSFORMS MARKETS AND FREEDOM (2006).

reform of the Uniform Commercial Code. In Europe, a similar coalition successfully blocked the adoption of a particularly contentious expansion of software patents by the European Union.

The case of the commons, and peer production, as the basis for resisting regulation of information production through expanded patents or copyrights offers one example of a broader implication of the study of cooperation. It suggests the possibility that, to some extent, the provisioning of public goods can be achieved through voluntary cooperation rather than through regulation or markets. In this regard, it points in similar directions as does the study of social norms. I certainly have made similar claims about the possible use of user-owned wireless networks to provision last-mile Internet connectivity, in place of spectrum auctions or regulation.[81] Christine Jolls has claimed that the fairness dynamic documented in experimental economics may suggest why minimum wage protection is unnecessary for domestic workers: They function in a work relationship that requires employers to pay fair (i.e., above market-clearing) wages, without legal constraint.[82] Robert Scott has made similar claims on behalf of the argument that courts should refuse to enforce incomplete contracts, rather than filling in missing details with commercially reasonable terms, thereby creating a regulation-free zone in which parties can explicitly be vulnerable to each other to occupy a trust and reciprocity dynamic, rather than a court-regulated one. Neither argument is clearly supported by the cooperation literature. Jolls's argument does not incorporate the cultural contingency of what is perceived as fair and its manipulability. Cultural "out group" status and local economic dynamics can make the baseline conditions for a class of workers – in this case domestic help – so abusive that even otherwise quite shabby treatment (by comparison to wages or terms in other sectors) can seem generous and generate a reciprocity dynamic by comparison to the treatment of others in the "out" group. In that case, application of minimum wage laws could effectively set a minimal level, without impeding the capacity of the fairness dynamic in places where fairness would drive wages above that level. Scott understates the significance of the third-party status of courts, and the trappings of "fairness" attached to their decisions, that actually offer discipline, or punishment and reward, services to the parties to enforce their own understanding of what is cooperative, or at least can do so

---

[81] Yochai Benkler, *Overcoming Agoraphobia: Building the Commons of the Digitally Networked Environment* 11 Harv. J. L. & Tech 287 (1998); Yochai Benkler, *Some Economics of Wireless Communications*, 16 Harv. J. L. & Tech. 25 (2002).

[82] Christine Jolls, *Fairness, Minimum Wage Law, and Employee Benefits*, 77 NYU L. Rev. 47 (2002).

if done properly. But the point is not to adopt any given particular presently available interpretation of cooperation to law. The point is to emphasize that a focus on cooperation can have the implication that people can run their own affairs cooperatively without state intervention.

Moreover, the crowding out effect between discipline systems and trust also suggests not only that regulation may be unnecessary, but that it can be counterproductive. Taiwanese irrigation associations are one prominent case. Created and run by farmers, these voluntary associations achieved considerable success in managing common irrigation systems. For local political reasons, in 1993 the Taiwanese government sought to look "pro farmer" by replacing association fees that farmers paid out of their own pockets with government grants. In later studies, that benign intervention seems to have shifted the associations from highly participatory associations of farmers who knew their system well and volunteered to run the association and manage it, to a system that "one gets from the government." The study does not account for the details and framing of displacement, but it is not implausible that loss of a personal sense of being part of a collective responsibility in a self-managed and provisioned system seems to have been associated with the breakdown. The introduction of "the state" *as system* crowded out the community as system.[83]

Although the dynamics of social cooperation, on the one hand, and corrupt political economy, on the other hand, caution us in adopting government-run policy interventions, the study of cooperation would be only mildly interesting if all it did was replace the mantra that "the market will take care of it all" with a similarly lethargic "social cooperation will take care of it all." The fact that cooperation includes a significant component of group identity and member/nonmember distinction, and harbors the potential for intergroup conflict, and the fact that groups can have all sorts of goals, not all of them laudable or defensible from the perspective of a society at large, suggests that an important role of applying cooperation to institutional design is to achieve greater efficacy in the pursuit of democratically adopted public goals, as well as offering "services," like legal dispute resolution, that can be relied upon by parties in a cooperative dynamic as an aspect of the discipline elements of social interaction.

One important line of implementation in this vein has been the work of Dan Kahan and Tracy Meares on policing and criminal law

---

[83] See Elinor Ostrom, *Policies that Crowd Out Reciprocity and Collective Action, in* MORAL SENTIMENTS AND MATERIAL INTERESTS: THE FOUNDATIONS OF COOPERATION IN ECONOMIC LIFE, (Herbert Gintis, Samuel Bowles, Robert Boyd, and Ernst Fehr, eds., 2005) 253, 261–63.

enforcement.[84] At root, their approach has been to emphasize interventions aimed at treating the community in which there is a high crime rate, in contradistinction to the Becker-inspired rational maximizer focus on adjusting payoffs to the individual criminal. Such interventions may prove uncomfortable to a wide range of political views. Liberals would oppose low-threshold stops and temporary arrests intended to disrupt gangs and allow community members to congregate on the streets instead, fostering stronger local community and commitment, or the idea that the police should engage with African-American churches to mobilize local communities. Conservatives would likely oppose the argument that the ubiquity and length of incarceration do more harm than good by breaking up communities and in particular excluding families of convicts from the communities.[85] My point here is not to support these particular interventions, but to show an instance of policy intervention aimed to address a certain public goods problem – local security – through treating the local social dynamics of cooperation in the community, rather than through adjusting the incentives of the individual criminal conceived as a selfish utility maximizer.

Another important area that lends itself to design based on the insights of cooperation is labor and employment law. Much of the sociological literature on cooperation examines the workings of business organizations. Stone's work on the new psychological contract offers an especially fruitful example, drawing on this literature to suggest a wide range of adaptations in labor, employment, trade secret, and antidiscrimination law.[86] Stone argues that business processes have changed, with leading firms seeking a more fluid relationship aimed at engaging employees' affective commitment but moving away from lifetime employment. This strategy requires a new level of training and general knowledge acquisition by employees, at the employers' expense, which employees are then free to take with them as they move from one job to the next. The relative stability of union-defined jobs and job ladders as well as nonunion white collar positions that married excellent benefits with an expectation of career-long service, has thus been replaced by, among other features, flatter structures and less formal task definitions and structures of promotion. As a result, many older legal arrangements have fallen out of step, suggesting the importance of

---

[84] Dan M. Kahan and Tracey L. Meares, *The Coming Crisis of Criminal Procedure*, 86 Geo. L.J. 1153 (1998).

[85] Donald Braman, Doing Time on the Outside: Incarceration and Family Life in Urban America (2004).

[86] Katherine Stone, *The New Psychological Contract: Implications of the Changing Workplace for Labor and Employment Law*, 48 UCLA L. Rev. 519 (2001).

adjusting them to fit the more cooperative dynamic observed in these kinds of workplaces.

More generally, the scholarly emphasis on social cooperation has prompted numerous proposals for reform of tax policy and tax enforcement.[87] Furthermore, Bowles and Gintis have written about how our understandings of the demands of reciprocity should shape the design of our welfare system. In particular, they emphasized that the demands of reciprocity justify reducing or limiting welfare payments made to those whom the state can properly identify as free riders, making those payments available only to reciprocators and cooperators.[88] Amy Wax later developed a more worked out version of this argument, applied specifically to the 1996 Personal Responsibility and Work Opportunity Act.[89]

One of the more detailed studies of interventions is Ann Carlson's review of literature on recycling norms, suggesting which interventions seem to have resulted in higher utilization and compliance rates.[90] Consistent with some of the design levers outlined here, lowering costs of recycling (by curb pickup) was an important element, but, consistent with a crowding-out dynamic, high prices had a more ambiguous impact. Face-to-face group meetings and feedback, and appeals from boy/girl scout visitors were effective, consistent with the importance of humanization, communication, and norm-setting. Feedback on household performance tended to be more effective in increasing low contributors' contributions when given in a group meeting as opposed to writing individually, but slightly lowered participation by those households contributing more than their fair share – consistent with the fairness lever. Group feedback, delivered in face-to-face meetings, resulted in a higher compliance level after the intervention ended than when observed in groups with individual written feedback. Whether this more persistent efficacy resulted from the creation of a mechanism for social sanctions in the community, from a sense of humanization of the participants and local solidarity, or from an adaptation of personal principles and goals through communication is not clear from any of these studies. The efficacy of meeting face-to-face, talking, and providing feedback in the context of a community, which clearly enables any and all of these forms, was clear.

---

[87] Dan Kahan, *The Logic of Reciprocity: Trust, Collective Action, and Law*, 102 MICH L. REV 71 (2003); Leandra Lederman, *The Interplay Between Norms and Enforcement in Tax Compliance*, 64 OHIO L.J. 1453 (2003).

[88] Samuel Bowles and Herbert Gintis, *Is Equality Passe?* 22 BOSTON REVIEW. no. 3–4 (Summer 1997).

[89] Amy Wax, *A Reciprocal Welfare Program*, 8 VA. J. SOC. POL'Y 477 (2001).

[90] Ann Carlson, *Recycling Norms* 89 CAL. L. REV 1231 (2001).

CONCLUSION

Application of extensive work on cooperation to law and policy interventions remains in its infancy. Present translational work of the kind I
described on minimum wage law, contract law, or recycling has mostly
focused on one or two of the design levers, using them as a springboard
from some particular reform proposal, or some defense of an existing doctrine in the face of critique. An important part of the reason to outline
the design levers or focal points and map their interaction is to develop a
framework that would allow us to organize and discipline our use of this
literature as we come to apply it to questions of law and policy design.

Design for cooperation begins with a different model of human beings
than the selfish rational actor model. It emphasizes the diversity of human
motivational profiles and the importance of the interaction to determining
actual behavior. To the extent that the literature probing cooperation better
predicts human behavior under differently designed systems, it holds the
promise of improvement in the design of systems for human action. Just
as theorists and policymakers applied the selfish rational actor model in
very different contexts, so too can scholars and officials apply cooperation
to very different systems. Technical systems, such as online collaboration
forums, business processes and organizational strategies, legal and regulatory regimes, and constructed social contexts are all systems of affordance
and constraint for human action. They can all utilize cooperation-based
design approaches.

One may wish to analyze which of the various types of free and open
source software licenses in use, like the GPL or BSD licenses, is best for
facilitating contributions to free and open source software development
projects, or whether trade secret law should or should not include the
inevitable disclosure doctrine given a shift to knowledge-based, more cooperative business processes. The questions one would ask would be different
under the cooperative or the selfish model. Similarly, if one is trying to
decide whether it is important to include a profile page on a collaborative
wiki site, or whether to allow anonymity, introduce tiered privileges based
on length of time that a user has been part of a cooperative effort, or introduce explicit pricing into one's technical platform, these are all amenable to
cooperation-based analysis. My point is merely to emphasize that refining
design based on the large and diverse empirical and theoretical literature on
cooperation holds the promise of significant improvement in our ability to
design human systems for cooperation.

We have seen a long-term trend in "scientific policymaking" to push
back on foundational cultural norms and educational practices that are, if

not universal, certainly broadly shared across cultures. The hours spent by parents teaching their children to share toys, to play with a child who is perhaps unpopular, to be polite, to tell the truth because it is the truth, not because it is expedient, etc.; the religious teachings of love thy neighbor; and the long tradition of argument from principle and the demands of ethical behavior all fall by the wayside when "scientific policymakers" brush off their game theoretic models and translate the myriad emotions, relations, commitments, and beliefs that make up human action into a question of mechanism design. In the past twenty years or so in academic literature, in the past decade and a half in some of the business literature, and in the past decade in explicit writing about our core technical systems of communication and computation, we have seen a series of efforts to reassert the human and the social. The drive in some cases has been intellectual – in the case of evolutionary theory, for example, too many observations refused to fit pure selfishness and were better explained by expanded models of reciprocity or group selection. In other cases, the drive has been practical – in the case of management studies and the businesses studied in organizational sociology, rapid rates of change and the imperative to optimize learning and adaptation, rather than necessarily efficiency for more-or-less known conditions. In all events, the inputs into scientific policymaking – theoretical, experimental, and observational – are increasingly pushing against holding on to universal selfishness as a core design assumption, and toward learning how to improve the cooperative social dynamics of human beings who will interact through the system under contemplation. We need to develop a field of cooperative human systems design to fill that need.

SECTION THREE

BEYOND COMMAND AND CONTROL

## TEN

What Opportunity Is Knocking? Regulating Corporate Governance in the United States[1]

Mary A. O'Sullivan

I. Introduction

A series of major corporate scandals around the turn of the millennium prompted a burst of regulatory changes that together represented the most significant development in corporate regulation since the New Deal. The most prominent reform was the Sarbanes-Oxley Act of 2002 (SOX), but the Securities and Exchange Commission (SEC) also implemented a host of important rule changes, and stock exchanges made significant alterations to their listing requirements. The new regulations elicited considerable controversy, with business elites and their political allies vehemently complaining about the burdens that they imposed on firms and managers. As the corporate scandals retreated from the front pages of newspapers, the impetus for reform waned. However, the recent change in the political leadership of the United States and, crucially, the context of a worsening financial crisis in which it occurred, seem certain to renew the momentum for further reform of the corporate economy.

The various proposals for increased regulation of America's corporations find intellectual support in academic research, where there is a lively debate about the villain of the piece in recent American corporate and financial scandals. Different diagnoses abound: Some scholars emphasize the failure of gatekeepers – especially auditors, analysts, and rating agencies – to protect investors; others stress the inadequacies of corporate boards as internal oversight mechanisms; still others focus on an alleged cause of weak corporate boards and other flaws in the governance of American corporations – insufficient rights for shareholders. Although, on the surface, these alternative perspectives have generated a wide range of heterogeneous ideas for

[1] I would like to gratefully acknowledge the excellent advice and suggestions of Ed Balleisen in the process of writing this article.

reform, on closer scrutiny there is a striking unanimity in the fundamental goal of reform at the root of these ideas – to make the reality of corporate governance in the United States more closely approximate the shareholder theory of the firm.

Understanding how shareholder value came to be the pervasive ideology for corporate governance in the United States, and the particular way in which shareholder value was put into practice, goes a long way toward explaining how the debate on corporate governance ended up where it is today. In thinking about the possible role of academics and other intellectuals in this debate, there is considerable work to be done to advance governance reforms, even if one remains committed to the logic of shareholder value. However, there is good reason to challenge that logic in an effort to reorient the basic terms of the debate on corporate governance in the United States by considering alternative perspectives to shareholder value as the benchmark for good corporate governance. Scholars have already invested considerable effort in developing such perspectives and have taken a renewed interest in doing so in recent years. The leading approaches are often grouped as "stakeholder theories of governance," but this is a loose grouping, representing a motley collection of theories. Indeed, their heterogeneity has weakened the influence of stakeholder theories but it is also true that their impact has been muted by their need to grapple with some fundamental issues central to a persuasive theory of corporate governance.

A broader range of theoretical options would certainly create a more meaningful debate about improving the U.S. system of corporate governance. Yet, it is also important to recognize that the challenges of, and opportunities for, corporate governance will never be fully understood using general theories of corporate governance that ostensibly hold for all societies in all eras. Everything we know from comparative–historical research on the institutions of corporate governance, and on capitalism more generally, suggests that countries do not choose their system of corporate governance by selecting from a menu of general options. Instead, these institutions emerge through the messiness of history and are inextricably linked to broader economic, political, and cultural contexts. Therefore, the scope for fundamental change in corporate governance systems is profoundly conditioned by much broader societal dynamics. Only by understanding this process of conditioning, such as how the political system creates opportunities for, and constraints on, systems of corporate governance, can we appreciate what types of regulatory initiatives might forge novel directions in corporate governance, and thereby determine what opportunity is knocking for reform of American corporate governance.

II. The Momentum behind Regulatory Reform

During the late 1990s, many observers argued that the U.S. system of corporate governance, which fostered a fervent commitment by corporations to the maximization of shareholder value, was a crucial contributor to the country's economic dynamism. This interpretation was not confined to Americans; prominent academics and policymakers in other countries around the world often expressed this view and, in some cases, worked hard to change their institutions to emulate the U.S. system of corporate governance. Then, at the beginning of the new millennium, the United States was rocked by a wave of scandals involving some of the leading corporate lights of the 1990s. In December 2001, Enron, an aggressive energy company and a darling of Wall Street and the business press, filed for bankruptcy, the largest in U.S. history until that time. Shortly afterward, the scale of its failure was surpassed by the demise of WorldCom. Moreover, the accounting and other improprieties that brought these companies down reverberated throughout the corporate sector in a large number of cases, including Sunbeam, Waste Management, Tyco, and Global Crossing.

These scandals brought major problems in U.S. corporate governance to the surface and generated a debate about what needed to be done to remedy them. A flurry of regulatory activity ensued as legislators, the SEC, and the leading stock exchanges introduced reforms to bolster the effectiveness and legitimacy of the U.S. system of corporate governance. The first and most dramatic response was the Public Company Accounting Reform and Investor Protection Act, which Congress enacted on July 30, 2002, less than a year after the Enron scandal broke. The legislation, described as Sarbanes–Oxley, Sarbox or SOX after its sponsors, Senator Paul S. Sarbanes (D-Md.) and Michael G. Oxley (R-Ohio),[2] primarily sought to restore the integrity of corporate disclosure. As such, its objectives mirrored the central aspirations of New Deal era securities regulation: The goal was not just to furnish a means of fixing some market failures, but to buttress the public confidence that underpins market activity – to create public institutions that constitute and sustain markets.[3]

In part, Sarbanes–Oxley sought to achieve this outcome by strengthening the oversight of the accounting profession and the relationship of auditors to firms. To that end, it created the Public Company Accounting Oversight Board (PCAOB) and made it responsible to the SEC, charging it with

---

[2] Oxley was the chairman of the House Financial Services Committee at the time.
[3] For an analogous purpose for pharmaceutical regulation, see Carpenter, this volume.

oversight of the auditing of public companies and bringing the tradition of self-regulation of the accounting profession to an abrupt end ("SOX at 5: the profession reflects on a milestone," *Accounting Today*, August 20, 2007). The Act also made it illegal for a public accounting firm that audits a company to provide it with nonaudit services, much as New Deal banking legislation partitioned commercial and investment banking. SOX also limited membership of corporate audit committees to independent directors and mandated that at least one of them had to be a financial expert. In parallel, it expanded the responsibilities of this committee, notably assigning it direct responsibility for the appointment, compensation, and oversight of the work of the company's accountants.

The Sarbanes–Oxley Act introduced additional measures to remedy perceived failures in corporations' internal controls. It required CEOs and CFOs to certify, on pain of criminal penalties, the accuracy of their firms' periodic financial reports, as well as the effectiveness of their companies' internal controls. It introduced a "clawback" provision that requires CEOs and CFOs to return incentive pay awarded to them based on fraudulent accounting. Section 404 of the Act also contained a notorious requirement for corporations to produce annual reports on their internal controls that must be vetted by outside accountants.

The Act's various provisions sought to increase the transparency of America's corporations to investors not only through the disclosure of more information but also by improving its quality. In this sense, it fit with the general emphasis of federal securities regulation since the New Deal on transparency and information. Important regulatory changes were also proposed and introduced by the SEC, the primary body responsible for the regulation of the country's financial markets. Most of these new rules also embodied additional disclosure requirements, notably with respect to proxy voting policies and records by mutual funds and other investment companies; the operating procedures of board nominating committees and the mechanisms, if they exist, for security holders to communicate with board members; as well as executive pay. The move to require information about the governance of U.S. corporations, and not just their business operations, was controversial and the SEC moved further in that direction with the enactment of a rule on board independence for investment companies. Perhaps most dramatically, the SEC acted to reduce conflicts of interest in investment banking that were deemed to have corrupted the recommendations issued by its research analysts. In 2003, acting in concert with state regulators, notably the former attorney general for the state of

New York, Eliot Spitzer, the SEC reached an agreement with the world's leading investment banks to sever reporting and compensation links between their research and investment banking businesses.

In addition to these public initiatives, a number of private bodies changed their norms and practices in ways that have implications for the governance of the corporate economy. Both the New York Stock Exchange and NASDAQ revised their listing requirements, mandating new standards for the composition of boards of directors and shareholder voting on equity-based compensation plans. For companies listed on the NYSE, for example, a majority of directors must now be independent. Listed firms must have wholly independent audit, compensation, and nominating committees, while at least one member of the audit committee must have accounting or related financial management expertise. In addition, NYSE required shareholder approval for a company's overall equity-based compensation plan.

These reforms proved highly controversial and almost certainly would not have been successful without the media scrutiny and public attention stimulated by the wave of corporate scandals. The Sarbanes–Oxley Act was the brainchild of the Democrats and the Republicans initially refused to support it, preferring their own, less restrictive legislation. However, the WorldCom scandal brought them on board and, in the end, the bill was passed with the unanimous approval of the Senate and the overwhelming approval of the House, where it garnered 423 votes in favor and only 3 against. However, immediately after its passage, it attracted an avalanche of criticism, much of it remarkably vitriolic, with one noted legal commentator, Roberta Romano, going so far as to describe it as "quack corporate governance" (Romano, 2005, for a general discussion of academic critiques of Sarbanes–Oxley, see Brown 2006). In the policy realm, some detractors suggested that the Act profoundly damaged America's position as a global financial center (McKinsey & Co., 2006, p. ii).

Much of the criticism of SOX focused on the increased costs to public companies of strengthening their internal controls to comply with Section 404 of the Act. However, the Act itself, and several SEC rules adopted subsequent to its passage, granted several compliance extensions to smaller companies, the focus of greatest concern. Moreover, the PCAOB approved the adoption of a new auditing standard that gave auditors more scope to tailor their audits to the scale of the company being audited as well as to exercise more discretion in interpreting the provisions of the Act. Most knowledgeable observers regarded these technical adjustments as having considerably reduced the costs of implementation of Sarbanes–Oxley, an

assessment supported by the increasing capacity of companies and auditors to meet its provisions. As accumulated experience lessened the costs
of implementation of the Act, the steam subsided from challenges to its
survival.

SOX may have weathered the storm of criticism it faced, but visceral
attacks stymied the progress of other regulatory proposals to overhaul the
governance of the country's corporations. Of particular note were proposed
changes to the rules that determine the rights of shareholders to participate
in the nomination and election of corporate directors. These changes proved
to be a lightning rod for debate on corporate governance. In the fall of 2007,
after a lengthy process drawn out over several years, SEC commissioners
voted down the proposed change to the status quo by a 3–1 vote. In doing so,
they restated their support for the existing rules, which prohibit shareholders from accessing the company proxy to nominate directors to corporate
boards ("Corporate voting rights package fails," *Daily Deal*, November 29,
2007).

Investor groups had feared this outcome from the moment that President
Bush appointed Christopher Cox as chairman of the SEC in 2005. When
he took office, Cox initially defused these concerns by promising to prove
vigilant in upholding the SEC's mission of protecting investor rights. He
encouraged a greater attention to enforcement at the SEC, sponsoring an
important effort to enforce the clawback provision of the Sarbanes–Oxley
Act by initiating an investigation of option-backdating practices.[4] He also
sought to build consensus, looking to forge agreement among the SEC
commissioners, who tended to divide along partisan lines on contentious
issues ("New head of SEC defies sceptics," *International Herald Tribune*,
November 8, 2006, p. 16).

However, the debate on changes to the SEC rules on shareholder rights to
nominate and elect directors brought an end to such accommodation. Faced
with starkly opposing views among his commissioners, Cox eventually sided
with the other two Republican commissioners against the lone Democratic

---

[4] "Backdating" refers to the practice of retroactively setting the date of issue of stock option
grants. The practice is not illegal in the United States but the practice must be disclosed. In
the process, it investigated more than 150 American corporations and initiated proceedings
against large numbers of them ("New head of SEC defies sceptics," *International Herald
Tribune*, November 8, 2006, 16). The settlements were delayed as SEC commissioners
reportedly argued over the details of how large the penalties should be ("The Slow Pace
of Justice on Options Backdating," *New York Times*, February 23, 2007, 2) but agreement
was finally reached on a method for penalty assessment and the first settlements were
announced in 2007.

commissioner.[5] As the *Washington Post* put it: "Chairman Chris Cox gave up on his effort to find a compromise between shareholder activists who want a way to allow investors to nominate candidates for corporate directorships and his Republican colleagues, who believe deeply that investors aren't mature enough to vote on such weighty matters. Unable to find a middle ground, Cox sided with the corporate Putinists to kill any shareholder access to the corporate proxy ("Regulatory Pushback," *Washington Post*, Dec. 2, 2007, p. F03)." Earlier in 2007, Cox also proposed two other rule changes for consideration that many regulatory experts viewed as diminishing investor rights. As a result, he faced increasing criticisms of his chairmanship of the SEC, standing accused of hijacking the SEC's mission by pandering to the interests of business at the expense of investors' concerns (*New York Times*, Feb. 13, 2007).

Reflecting on the more general political climate for corporate reform, observers issued gloomy prognoses. They pointed out that the moment of bipartisanship that had allowed the passage of SOX had given way to a much more partisan and contentious debate as Republicans and Democrats settled into anti- and pro-regulation camps with respect to corporate governance. By 2004, that trend, and the Republican majorities in both houses, led observers to predict an end to corporate governance reform (see, e.g., Cioffi 2006).

However, only a couple of years of later, the outlook for corporate reform looked a lot better. The midterm elections of November 2006 brought Democratic majorities in the House and the Senate and an important change in personnel with Barney Frank (D-Mass.) replacing Oxley as chairman of the House Financial Services Committee. Frank, who had long railed against growing income inequality in the United States, quickly made executive compensation a target of his reform efforts and promised more action on shareholder rights. He introduced a bill to give shareholders an advisory vote on executive compensation, which passed easily through the House.[6] When the sponsor of that bill in the Senate, Barack Obama, swept to a historic victory in the 2008 presidential election, the advocates of corporate reform became more bullish still.

---

[5] She was Annette Nazareth. Roel Campos, the other Democratic commissioner, resigned in 2007 to go into private practice. Cox could have delayed the vote until another Democratic commissioner was appointed but he refused to do so on the grounds that the issue needed to be resolved before the 2008 proxy season began. In any case, this would not have changed the outcome since Cox would still have had the deciding vote.

[6] There was a bigger split on this bill in the Republican camp with as many as 55 "Ayes" to 129 "Noes."

It was not just the political change that seemed promising but the fact that it occurred in the context of the most serious financial crisis since the 1930s. Although nobody would say that the U.S. system of corporate governance possesses primary responsibility for the credit crisis, some of its flaws, especially the structure of executive compensation packages, have been cited as important contributing factors (see Eichengreen, this volume). Such logic led to the inclusion of a provision against executive incentives for "unnecessary and excessive risks" in the American government's $700 billion Emergency Economic Stabilization Act of 2008. Even as analysts expressed doubts that the provision would have any significant effect, they suggested that it might change the broader discussion of executive pay in America. As the *Wall Street Journal* put it: "Pay experts say the provision is sparking debates on the link between pay and risk, and how to tweak incentives to limit risky bets. Some of those ideas run counter to long-held tenets of good compensation plans, such as tying pay closely to financial results or stock price" (*Wall Street Journal*, October 6, 2008, p. B5). Moreover, debates on other issues fostered by the financial crisis, such as the behavior and role of ratings agencies, as well as the vigilance and resources of the SEC, will surely spill over into more general debates on corporate governance.

III. The Leading Diagnoses of the Problems of U.S. Corporate Governance

Immediately after the corporate scandals of the new millennium broke, some policymakers, scholars, and pundits attributed them to the egregious behavior of a few bad apples. However, as the number of scandals increased and patterns of behavior emerged across cases, most commentators came to the conclusion that the U.S. system of corporate governance was beset by systemic shortcomings. But exactly what shortcomings? Here scholars can be classified into a number of categories.

Perhaps the most influential diagnosis of the problems afflicting American corporate governance shined the spotlight on the financial markets' gatekeepers, the "independent professionals who pledge their reputational capital to protect the interests of dispersed investors who cannot easily take collective action" (Coffee 2004, p. 302). These include, *inter alia*, the auditors who sign off on a company's accounts, the financial analysts who assess the quality of its stock, and the rating agencies who evaluate its creditworthiness. Protagonists of this view argued that, in the 1990s, far from protecting the interests of dispersed investors, these gatekeepers "acquiesced in managerial fraud – not in all cases, to be sure, but at a markedly higher rate than during the immediately preceding period" (Coffee 2004). One important piece of evidence to support this view was the growing number of earnings restatements during the 1990s. A variety of sources also suggested a substantial breakdown in the quality of analysts' reports over the course of the 1990s (see, e.g., Attorney General of the State of New York 2002; Hong and Kubik 2003) and recent analyses confirm suspicions of serious conflicts of interest at the ratings agencies (SEC 2008).

As we have seen, crucial elements of the Sarbanes–Oxley Act followed the logic of the gatekeeper diagnosis. As the legal scholar John Coffee has noted with approval: "The Sarbanes–Oxley Act of 2002 understandably focused on gatekeepers and contained provisions regulating auditors, securities analysts and credit-rating agencies" (Coffee 2005, p. 11). Regulators' efforts to build Chinese walls between securities analysts and investment bankers reflect the same spirit. The regulatory impact of the gatekeeper analysis can also be seen in the recent rules for rating agencies introduced by the SEC to reduce conflicts of interest in, and increase disclosure of information about, the ratings process (*Wall Street Journal*, "Crisis on Wall Street: SEC Tightens Rules for Ratings Firms," December 4, 2008, p. C3).

A second diagnosis of the problems of U.S. corporate governance looks to the machinery of corporate governance within the corporation and, in particular, points to the shortcomings of corporate boards. In principle, the board of directors performs a variety of roles in the governance of the U.S. corporation, including selecting the CEO and other senior executives, monitoring their strategies and performance, and shaping their incentives through the design of executive compensation. Scholars, along with policymakers and pundits, have issued stern criticism of how the boards of U.S. corporations acquitted all of these roles in the late 1990s, but their performance on executive compensation has struck many commentators as particularly egregious (see, e.g., Bebchuk and Fried 2003; idem. 2004). Major structural changes in the compensation of U.S. corporate executives have occurred since the mid-1970s, leading to a massive increase in levels of executive pay, whether measured in real terms or relative to average workers' pay. These increases, which were especially pronounced in the 1980s and 1990s, were driven not only by the growing use of stock options in executive pay packages, but also by the fact that salaries and bonuses increased dramatically as well (for statistics on these trends, see Frydman and Saks 2007).

Executive pay in the United States has attracted criticism on the grounds that its link to corporate performance is weak, even though the rationale for more lavish compensation has always rested on its presumed positive impact on productivity. Critics point to several aspects of U.S. executive pay packages as especially problematic: the prevalence of rewards after the fact (mostly in the form of golden parachutes); rewards for absolute rather than relative performance (stock option packages that do not take the performance of comparable companies into account); rewards for manipulable performance measures (such as earnings statements that reflect questionable accounting assumptions, or options backdating); as well as rewards for short-term stock price movements rather than improvements in underlying long-term corporate performance (Murphy 1999; Grinstein and Hribar 2004; Bebchuk and Fried 2005; Bolton et al. 2006). Besides the waste of corporate resources that poorly structured pay packages entail, scholars have pointed out that there may be additional economic costs associated with the exorbitant pay of American corporate elites. In an era in which an emphasis on teamwork is pervasive, at least in corporate rhetoric, gargantuan compensation packages for top-level corporate managers, as the pay of other employees stagnates, may demotivate employees and undermine productivity growth.[7] Moreover, the structure of compensation plans, notably their reliance on stock option awards and severance packages, may induce executives to engage in excessive risk-bearing with company assets. This dynamic has become a central focus of the critiques of banks' behavior leading up to the financial crisis.

In looking for an explanation of the problems with U.S. executive compensation, many commentators have placed the blame on boards of directors, with the most common argument being that they are too dependent on management. Therefore, reform efforts have tended to focus on ensuring there are substantial numbers of "independent" directors on corporate boards and, in particular, the compensation and nomination committees. This type of diagnosis lay behind the stock exchanges' efforts to reform their listing standards to specify standards for board composition.

A third diagnosis of the ills besetting American corporate governance steps back from the internal and external mechanisms of corporate governance to focus on the overall representation of shareholder interests in the operation of the corporation (see, e.g., Bebchuk 2005, 2007). It emphasizes the lack of formal rights that shareholders have in the governance of the American corporation, with their limited role in the nomination and election of the boards of directors of public companies stimulating particular concern. In principle, the American corporation is a representative democracy in which boards of directors act as the elected representatives

[7] For the importance of fairness in inducing cooperation, see Benkler, this volume, 13–14.

of shareholders. In practice, the owners of most large, publicly held American enterprises have little or no influence over the election and removal of directors. The nomination process for directors is typically controlled by incumbent directors and, in some cases, even by senior corporate executives. Under SEC Rule 14a-8, shareholders do not have access to the proxy to nominate candidates for the board. And, because most companies had plurality (rather than majority) voting for director elections until recently, only one favorable vote was required to elect a director. For all of these reasons, any effort by shareholders to propose alternative slates of directors faces substantial barriers of cost and collective organization. This interpretation of the problems of U.S. corporate governance has influenced the recent debates within the SEC over reforming the proxy process and, in particular, giving shareholders more of a practical say in the nomination and election of the board of directors.

In 2003, the SEC finally responded to pressure to increase shareholder rights by proposing a new rule to permit them to nominate one to three directors, depending on the size of the board, in opposition to the incumbent board's proposed slate. The proposal would permit shareholders to nominate directors only after one of the following two, rather restrictive, conditions were met. Either the shareholder body would have to register its disapproval of the directors to be opposed by withholding 35 percent or more of the votes cast at a meeting to elect them. Or a shareholder proposal to nominate a shareholder candidate would have to be passed before the nomination process could proceed. Moreover, the proposal would only allow shareholders with at least 1 percent of the company's voting equity to nominate their own candidates for director.

The proposed rule change proved to be a lightning rod for debate on the reform of corporate governance. It elicited 12,000 letters to the SEC, the highest number of comments on record for any proposed rule change by the SEC until then. Many public pension funds, union funds, and individual investors expressed support for the rule's basic thrust; an investment officer at one leading institutional investor was quoted as saying that the proposal was "perhaps the most important rule the SEC has put forth for the investing public in decades." Nevertheless, the strings attached to the specific proposed rule led some of them to question its value.

Even so, the constraints on shareholder action embodied in the proposed rule were not enough to assuage the concerns of its most vociferous critics. Representatives of corporate elites, such as the Business Roundtable, railed against the proposal, arguing that the proposed rules "exceed the commission's authority, would initiate sweeping and harmful changes in corporate governance and fail to achieve the commission's objective of improving the proxy process at unresponsive companies" ("Record response to SEC proposal," *Financial Times*, December 23, 2003, p. 20). The SEC commissioners themselves were reportedly divided over the proposal and, in the end, it was never put to a formal vote.

However, the issue refused to go away, reappearing in 2006 with a legal challenge to the SEC's rule on shareholder participation in director elections. Unable to reach consensus on board nominations by shareholders, the SEC issued two conflicting proposals for comment in July 2007. One would reiterate and, therefore, reinforce the existing situation, which excluded shareholders from using the proxy to nominate directors; the other would permit them some access to it but subject to greater restrictions than the rule that the SEC proposed in 2003; now it was suggested that only shareholders who could garner 5 percent or more of a company's voting equity would participate in director elections. Once again the proposed rule changes attracted enormous interest, breaking new records with 20,000 submitted comments. Most of them were from shareholders, many protesting both proposals. One public pension fund executive was quoted as saying "[o]ne proposal is bad and the other is worse... One is a repudiation of the concept of shareholder access to the proxy and the second is so onerous that it creates an illusion of access but, practically, it is useless. The thing to do is stop and start over" ("The owners who can't hire or fire," *New York Times*, October 14, 2007). As I noted earlier, the SEC commissioners eventually voted down to the rule change, leaving the *status quo* intact, but the academic and political support for advancing shareholder rights will ensure that it will find a place on the SEC's agenda again.

All of these disagreements – about how seriously one should view the problems afflicting corporate governance in the United States; about where one should locate the sources of those problems; and, about the appropriate remedies to redress them – are substantial and divisive. Yet for all of the debate about what is wrong and how to fix things, most of the discussion takes place within a relatively narrow intellectual frame. Specifically, the leading commentators maintain a commitment to the view that corporations ought to be run in the interests of shareholders. An appreciation of how the ideology of shareholder governance came to predominate in the United States, and the particular way in which policymakers and corporate leaders put it into practice, takes us a long way toward understanding the preoccupations and limitations of the contemporary debate.

IV. Shareholder Value as the Dominant Ideology of Corporate Governance

That companies should be run to advance the interests of shareholders is certainly not a new idea in the history of American corporate governance. In the late nineteenth century and the early twentieth centuries, corporate executives in U.S. corporations typically contended that their control over corporate resources was based on property rights and that their primary responsibility was to run corporations in the interests of shareholders. The ideology that corporations were run in the interests of shareholders lived on through the Great Depression and after the Second World War. The theme of "People's Capitalism" – the idea that U.S. corporate enterprises were owned and controlled in the interests of masses of small stockholders – was frequently expounded by organizations like the New York Stock Exchange and many corporate managers were inclined to employ a similar rhetoric (Ott 2004).

However, the growing separation of ownership and control in many of the nation's leading corporations made managers' characterization of themselves as shareholder-designates seem coy. As Bayless Manning, the dean of Stanford Law School, put it in 1958: "People's Capitalism and Corporate Democracy are slogans with an inverse relationship. Each expansion of the first undermines the second. Every sale of common stock to a new small investor adds to the fractionation of share-ownership which lies at the root of the impotence of shareholder voting as a check on management" (Manning, 1965, p. 113). Faced with growing skepticism about the reality and legitimacy of the shareholder-oriented corporation, U.S. corporate managers sought other grounds for justifying the control that they exercised over the allocation of corporate resources. As early as the 1920s, senior executives at General Electric challenged the view that corporate managers were "the paid attorneys of capital." As corporate shareholding became more diffuse, their views resonated more broadly with corporate managers who increasingly represented themselves as trustees who acted in the interests of a variety of stakeholders.

This view of corporate management was by no means confined to the self-descriptions of executives. It was already apparent in the view expressed by Berle and Means in the early 1930s that corporate management could develop into a "purely neutral technocracy." A similar view of management is found among many journalists, writers, and leading scholars of the postwar period and was captured well by the editors of *Fortune* in 1951 when they declared that "[t]he manager is becoming a professional in the sense

that like all professional men he has a responsibility to society as a whole"
(Fortune 1951; see also Drucker 1949, pp. 35, 99, 102, 340, 342; Kaysen
1959; Sutton et al. 1956, pp. 57–58, 65, 86–87, 155, 163, 165, 359; *Fortune*,
1956).

Proponents of the "managerialist" thesis of the corporation assumed that
professionalism would ensure that the broader objectives that corporate
managers espoused would be achieved. These social responsibilities were
certainly not enshrined in corporate law. Although the burst of federal
securities regulation in the 1930s, as well as later regulatory initiatives such
as industrial safety and accident laws, created new legal requirements that
corporate managers had to take into account in their allocation of corporate
resources, they did not interfere with the internal governance of the corporation in a way that would directly challenge managerial control. With the
development of the "business judgment rule," the courts became more and
more reluctant to challenge corporate management on decisions that were
deemed to be part of the normal process of running a business (Kaufman
et al. 1995, p. 51). The one exception to this pattern was bankruptcy law,
where the Chandler Act of 1938 transformed existing practice in large-scale
reorganizations by insisting that the firm's management and reorganization be entrusted, not to incumbent managers and the firm's investment
bankers, as had been common since the late nineteenth century, but to a dis-
interested trustee. However, as David Skeel notes, the effect of the Chandler
Act was to reduce the number of large-scale corporate reorganizations and
to motivate a search for loopholes that allowed firms to escape its exacting
provisions. Eventually the Bankruptcy Code of 1978 and, in particular, its
Chapter 11, reintroduced "an explicitly manager-friendly approach to corporate reorganization" by obliterating the mandatory trustee requirement
of the Chandler Act (Skeel 2001, Chapters 4, 6, and 8; quoted at p. 216).

Even though the governance of corporations remained firmly in the
hands of managers, the acquiescence of corporate law and the courts to
unilateral managerial control remained implicit. As the legal historian James
Willard Hurst observed, with the exception of laws authorizing the use of
corporate funds for philanthropic purposes, "the law added no definition
of standards or rules to spell out for what purposes or by what means
management might properly make decisions other than in the interests of
shareholders" (Hurst 1970, p. 107). As Erber put it, "[T]he managers have
not succeeded, either through legislation or adjudication, to resolve their
ambivalent, contradictory status of power without property" (Erber 1986,
p. 202). This left the legitimacy of managerial control vulnerable to challenge
and, ultimately to a concerted attack from scholars and other pundits who

were intent on reviving the philosophy that corporations should be run for the sole benefit of their shareholders.

The opening for that attack came as U.S. corporations confronted a combination of major productive and financial challenges beginning in the 1970s. U.S. corporations faced an intensification of international competition in a wide range of industries in which they had been dominant in the postwar period (for a detailed discussion, see O'Sullivan 2000, pp. 146–54). These competitive challenges demanded a response, but as U.S. enterprises struggled with what was going on in the productive sphere, as they attempted first to define the competitive problem and then to react to it, they discovered that the financial ground had shifted in ways that had important implications for the recalibration of industrial strategies.

Structural changes in U.S. financial institutions, and a related transformation of the way Americans saved, fostered their growing reliance on corporate securities, especially corporate stocks, to augment personal income and wealth. By 2001, 51.9 percent of U.S. households had direct or indirect stock holdings, up from 40.4 percent in 1995 and 31.6 percent in 1989 (U.S. Department of Commerce). Unlike the days when stockholding was fragmented among thousands of individual investors, households increasingly held stocks indirectly through pension and mutual funds and other institutional investors. By the late 1990s, more than 50 percent of American-owned equities were held by these aggregators of financial portfolios (O'Sullivan 2000, pp. 155–56).

This transformation in how American households saved greatly intensified the pressures on U.S. corporations to deliver higher returns on their corporate stocks. These pressures initially manifested themselves in a dramatic way in the 1980s, with the rise of a market for corporate control. In historical perspective, the "Deal Decade" was distinctive for the emergence of hostile transactions, the large size of the average target, and the unprecedented reliance on aggressive financial techniques to conclude transfers of corporate control.

Financial economists like Michael Jensen and legal scholars such as Henry Manne provided important intellectual support for this movement. They articulated a new theory of corporate governance, based on agency theory, casting shareholders as the principals in whose interests managerial agents should run corporations. However, the most important impetus for the Deal Decade came from members of the financial community, including investment bankers, private equity executives, and institutional investors, who showed how theory could be put into practice in ways that generated enormous financial returns.

Crucial to the success of these transactions was the capacity of key players to rapidly raise huge amounts of capital to finance them, chiefly through borrowing. The new mechanisms of finance did not emerge automatically but depended in their early stages on the forging of an important network of relationships among bankers, private equity executives, and institutional investors and, subsequently, on the development of the junk bond market. As financial historians of the era have observed, Michael Milken and Drexel Burnham Lambert played crucial roles in developing the networks to make these markets hum.

By the end of the 1980s, of course, the Deal Decade came to an abrupt conclusion. In the wake of the 1987 stock market crash, investors became increasingly concerned about the risk that they were bearing on junk bonds. Other factors that contributed to the decline included the crisis in the savings and loan industry, which had played a critical role in the junk bond market, the criminal prosecution and conviction of several players in the market for corporate control, including Michael Milken, and the general slowdown of the U.S. economy. The enactment by most states of antitakeover statutes that permitted corporations to adopt mechanisms to fend off hostile bids, along with the adoption of a range of antitakeover defenses by a large number of public corporations, also helped in sharply curtailing mergers and acquisitions.

While the culture of the big deal lasted, institutional investors reaped huge profits in the market for corporate control, not only through their holdings of junk bonds and investments in leveraged buyout funds, but also as sellers of corporate stock in mergers and acquisitions (Useem 1996, pp. 25–26). With the demise of that new financial market, institutional investors turned to different means to enforce their demands for higher returns, an impulse only heightened by the dramatic decline in interest rates during the 1990s. In particular, from the mid-1980s and especially the late-1980s, a number of major institutional investors began to take a more aggressive stance vis-à-vis corporate managers in the proxy process.

Initially, this newfound activism by institutional investor activism sought to knock down barriers to the market for corporate control by sponsoring shareholder resolutions to reduce poison pills, greenmail, and golden parachutes, as well as by pressuring corporations to opt out of states' antitakeover statutes. Notwithstanding some success in these efforts, the nation's largest pension fund, the California State Public Employees Retirement System (CalPERS), and other institutional investor activists soon recognized that, by focusing narrowly on antitakeover provisions, they left corporate managers considerable latitude to fight back. Therefore, they widened the scope of their activism from antitakeover provisions in particular to the structure of the shareholder–management relationship in general.

Ultimately, these developments fostered a fundamental transformation in the relationship between the corporate economy and the stock market. Deregulation played an important role in this story, though in spheres such as finance, pension, and tax policy rather than in the rules aimed primarily at the corporate sector.[8] In fact, corporate regulation continued to operate much as it had since the 1930s. If we focus, for example, on the proxy process, we find that it continued to operate through the 1990s, as it had since at least the 1950s, to protect managerial discretion from shareholder interference. Shareholders usually submitted their proposals under SEC Rule 14a-8 since, if the proposal was accepted, the shareholder then had the right to have it included, together with a 500-word supporting statement, in the proxy statement distributed by the corporation to its shareholders in advance of the annual shareholder meeting. There is an obvious cost advantage of this approach, but its primary disadvantage is that Rule 14a-8 restricts the subjects that can be raised by shareholders. The prevailing regulatory rules excluded (and still exclude) all shareholder proposals from a corporation's proxy materials if they dealt "with a matter relating to the conduct of the ordinary business operations" of the company. The "ordinary business rule" was adopted by the SEC in the early 1950s "to confine the solution of ordinary business problems to the board of directors and place such problems beyond the competence and direction of the shareholders," as the then-SEC chairman explained. He considered that "it is manifestly impracticable in most cases for stockholders to decide management problems at corporate meetings." (Statement of J. Sinclair Armstrong to the Subcommittee on Banking and Currency, 1957, quoted in Whitman 1997).

In the 1990s activist institutional investors put pressure on the SEC to reform the proxy process in ways that made it easier for them to press their concerns with U.S. corporations. Despite some successes, none of the changes that navigated the administrative rule making gauntlet constituted a major transformation in the regulation of corporate governance. Most of the efforts by activist shareholders to press for reform of the proxy process failed, in large measure because of strong resistance from powerful lobbying groups for corporate managers, especially the Business Roundtable. These corporate elites raised questions about the competence of

[8] For a discussion of the general trends toward deregulation in the United States from the 1970s, see Eisner, this volume, Section 1.

institutional investor activists to play an important role in the governance
of multibillion-dollar corporations (see, e.g., Wohlstetter 1993, p. 78). And,
with public pension funds and unions as the most visible faces of pension
fund activism, corporate managers also questioned the motivations behind
these special interest groups' governance initiatives.

This same ideology of the sanctity of managerial discretion had initially
led many corporate executives to resist the logic of shareholder value when
it burst on the scene in the 1980s on the back of hostile takeovers. However,
in the 1990s, executive resistance to shareholder value as the benchmark for
corporate governance abated as upper management pay packages became
more and more dependent upon equity compensation. Yet even as corporate
managers embraced the rhetoric of shareholder value, they continued to
brook little interference with their "right to manage."

These attitudes of corporate managers, and their success in clinging to
them, generated a great irony in the system of U.S. corporate governance by
the late 1990s. This system promoted a veritable obsession with shareholder
value as the most important benchmark for corporate performance. It
provided fantastic rewards for corporate executives who maintained that
they were responsible for generating that value. But, the system actually
provided very limited governance rights for shareholders themselves, and
an increasingly wealthy managerial elite remained largely hostile to any
reforms that might extend those rights.

V. The Intellectual Challenges of Corporate Governance Reform

Even this brief description of the historical evolution of corporate governance in the United States helps us understand why there is such a preoccupation with shareholder value here today. It simultaneously explains
the widespread dissatisfaction with the way shareholder value has been put
into practice in U.S. corporate governance and why, as a result, there is so
much momentum behind reforms that would make the American system
more closely accord with the theory of shareholder governance. Yet, even
to deliver on the promise that momentum holds out, there are important
intellectual challenges to be overcome by advocates of all three of the leading
diagnoses of the failures of shareholder governance in the United States.

For those who call for reforms to address the shortcomings of gatekeepers, the primary task is to show that generating higher-quality information
will make a substantial difference to the behavior of corporate shareholders. From the dawn of federal securities regulation, and even earlier by
some accounts, Americans have placed primary emphasis on the virtue of

disclosure and the transparency it supposedly fosters, in regulating their corporate sector. Yet the evidence that investors actively take advantage of public information at their disposal and put it to useful purpose in their investment decisions is remarkably thin on the ground.

For scholars who identify the behavior of corporate boards as the critical problem of American corporate governance, their primary challenge is to show that the widespread emphasis on board composition and, in particular, the role of independent directors, will truly make a difference. Even leaving aside concerns about whether independence, as conventionally interpreted, actually delivers what it implies, one might well doubt whether the presence of independent directors fosters a significant improvement in the behavior of boards. There is little encouraging evidence on this issue, with studies repeatedly failing to find any robust association between the role of independent directors and any kind of performance outcome. Absent such evidence, the widespread advocacy of an increased role for independent directors seems like a "political correctness" of board composition. And, indeed, some scholars have argued for greater attention to the way in which boards operate, rather than their structural characteristics, as a more likely means of improving their governance role.

Finally, for scholars who call for an increase in shareholder rights to participate in the governance of the American corporation, the major challenge is to show that shareholders have the incentives and abilities to exercise these rights. There is, in fact, good reason to be skeptical of the incentives of American shareholders to play an important role in corporate governance. The problem of collective action in this regard is well understood: The costs of intervening to improve corporate governance are substantial and borne only by the active shareholder, whereas the benefits of activism are spread across all investors. It is hardly surprising, therefore, that the vast majority of individual and institutional investors have displayed little interest in exercising the governance rights they already have. When it comes to voting on shareholder proposals, moreover, most institutional investors historically voted their proxies in support of management. These days, with greater public scrutiny of their proxy voting behavior, institutional investors are less inclined to such blatant passivity but they have opted for another, subtler form of it in their growing reliance on "proxy firms," which provide boilerplate voting advice on various issues.

The abilities of investors to intervene effectively in the governance of U.S. corporations must also be addressed. Since the middle of the 1970s, there has been a dramatic rise in the rate at which stockholders in America's corporations churn their shares. As a result, investors' ability to understand anything meaningful about the companies whose shares they own is limited. Corporate executives' critiques of investors' capacities to intervene in U.S. corporate governance are blatantly self-serving but they also are not entirely without foundation.

For all the substantial intellectual challenges associated with reforming corporate governance from within the confines of the shareholder theory, even greater ones await if we break loose of its intellectual strictures to consider fundamental alternatives to shareholder value. Yet there is good reason to make that intellectual leap. In recent years, scholarly critics have chipped away at the shareholder theory of corporate governance with increasing force making it increasingly implausible as the intelligent person's guide to corporate governance.

One key critique examines the theory of the firm on which arguments for shareholder governance build. A basic claim in this regard is that, as equity investors, shareholders are the only participants in the corporation for whom returns to their productive contributions are "residual." In contrast, the returns to all other groups who provide resources to the firm, whether employees, suppliers, or creditors, are characterized as deriving solely from contractual claims. As "residual claimants," shareholders supposedly bear the risk of the corporation's making a profit or loss and thus have an interest in allocating corporate resources to their best alternative uses to make the residual as large as possible. This assumption is essential to the shareholder theory's claim that the maximization of shareholder value will result in superior economic performance for corporations and the economy as a whole but it has been roundly criticized on several different grounds.

First there is the claim that other stakeholders in the corporation, besides shareholders, also take substantial risks for the benefit of corporations. Insofar as the investments that these stakeholders make are "firm-specific," we cannot assume that they are adequately rewarded by the market mechanism. Instead, that outcome is assured only by stakeholders' participating to some extent in the success or failure of the firm (Blair 1995). Second is a challenge to arguments that advance the claims of shareholders to enterprise residuals without providing an adequate explanation of how these residuals are generated. The way firms divide the returns from their activities affects their ongoing capacity to generate them, and focusing only on the distribution of returns without an analysis of the process through which value is generated by firms, as the shareholder theory does, may endanger the long-term value-creating potential of corporations. Instead, the relationship between productivity and reward in a firm should be guided by an analysis of the process through which firms develop and use resources to generate their so-called residuals (O'Sullivan 2000; Lazonick and O'Sullivan 2000, 2002). Third, there are critiques of the shareholder perspective that emphasize the limits of the agency theory it employs for understanding the crucial organizational interactions among economic agents that make firms tick. Concerns have been expressed even by advocates of agency theory about its relevance to the real world, with leading microeconomist Canice Prendergast admitting that "[t]he available evidence suggests that incentives do matter, for better or worse. It is much less clear, however, whether the theoretical models based on this premise have been validated in the data" (Prendergast 1999, p. 56). The criticism from outsiders has been even more scathing, with Herbert Simon, for example, contending that "[t]he attempts of the new institutional economics to explain organizational behaviour solely in terms of agency, asymmetric information, transaction costs, opportunism, and other concepts drawn from neoclassical economics ignore key organizational mechanisms like authority, identification, and coordination, and hence are seriously incomplete" (Simon 1991, p. 42; see also Perrow 1986).

Certainly there are good reasons for the considerable and growing skepticism about the theory of the firm on which the shareholder theory of corporate governance is built. In addition, the other crucial element of the shareholder theory of corporate governance, its perspective on the mechanisms that encourage or constrain corporate managers to maximize shareholder value, is also on increasingly shaky ground. Whether we are talking about pay for performance in executive compensation or the market for corporate control, all of these mechanisms depend for their efficacy on the process through which the stock market assigns prices to corporate securities. If that pricing process does not work effectively and, in particular, if it is subject to fads and bubbles, then these mechanisms may lead the corporate economy away from value creation rather than toward it. One of the intellectual forefathers of the shareholder theory of corporate governance, Michael Jensen, once remarked that the efficient markets hypothesis was one of the best-proven facts in the social sciences. Today he is a wiser man, urging managers to "just say no" to Wall Street and its fads and bubbles. More generally, the efficient markets hypothesis has taken a substantial beating, especially as behavioralists have gained influence in financial economics. Were the efficient market hypothesis a stock, it certainly would have been delisted in the current financial crisis.

In addition to identifying the weaknesses associated with the shareholder theory of governance, scholars have invested considerable energy in developing alternatives to it. In her book, *Ownership and Control: Rethinking Corporate Governance for the Twenty-First Century*, for example, Margaret

Blair has called for an analysis of corporate governance based on "a broader range of assumptions [than in the shareholder theory] about how wealth is created, captured, and distributed in a business enterprise" (Blair 1995, p. 15). Blair argues that the firm-specific investments made by employees and suppliers create significant claims as economic stakeholders, alongside shareholders. In a different approach, this author and William Lazonick have made the case for a theory of the firm that emphasizes the cumulative and collective nature of innovation as a crucial foundation for thinking about corporate governance (O'Sullivan 2000; Lazonick and O'Sullivan 2000, 2002). Blair, with a coauthor, Lynn Stout, has also emphasized the organizational foundations of firm performance in arguing for a theory of team production as a basis for thinking about corporate governance (Blair and Stout 1999; see also Kaufman and Englander 2005). Although in the 1990s in the United States these types of "stakeholder" theories of governance were given short shrift by most economists, they have attracted more attention in recent years (see, e.g., Gelter 2008; Allen, Carletti, and Marquez 2007; Goergen 2007). Distinct from these economic arguments described above is an older and still vigorous strand of stakeholder theory that appeals to philosophical arguments and moral justifications. Typically, this approach leads to a broader conception of stakeholders than the more instrumental logic of economic theories of stakeholding suggests. To paraphrase Donaldson and Preston (1995), stakeholders are those with a legitimate interest in the corporation regardless of whether the corporation has an interest in them (for a recent review and discussion, see Agle et al. 2008). That framework would certainly encompass the communities that host corporate facilities (and that often "invest" in them through tax breaks) as well as unskilled workers with little hope of economic reward.

Clearly, stakeholder theories of governance are a heterogeneous bunch and the differences and disagreements among them have undermined their impact, compared to the rather unitary shareholder theory. However, there are also important conceptual shortcomings of stakeholder theories of governance that require attention if they are to gain greater purchase on political debate and policymaking. For dealing with the firm, the greatest weakness of this perspective relates to the treatment of managerial behavior. Stakeholder theories have failed to explain exactly how a structure of corporate governance might systematically induce corporate managers to act as responsible stewards of the resources of firms, or to promote the development of their innovative capabilities, or to ensure that firms act as upstanding corporate citizens. It is precisely this failure that has made, and will continue to make, stakeholder theories vulnerable to attack from shareholder advocates who place so much emphasis on incentives.

Another shortcoming of stakeholder theories is their failure to specify the mechanisms of governance that would induce or require desirable behavior from corporations. In an edited volume on *Employees and Corporate Governance*, Margaret Blair and Mark Roe took a significant step in this direction with their specification of a number of mechanisms to give a voice to employees in corporate governance. The contributing authors explored several possibilities, including employee ownership and employee representation on boards of directors, but they wrestled with problems in the logic of these mechanisms. In general, the theoretical analysis of how stakeholder governance might actually work well in practice remains woefully underdeveloped.

Clearly, the intellectual challenges of developing a rigorous alternative to the shareholder theory of corporate governance are substantial. Yet it would be a mistake to invest all of our intellectual energy in resolving them to the neglect of an even more fundamental and provocative question about the relevance of stakeholder and shareholder and, indeed, all general theories of corporate governance. The assumption behind these theories, like many theories generated by social scientists, is that they have relevance across time and place. For dealing with corporate governance, there is good reason to subject that assumption to some critical scrutiny.

A society's system of corporate governance, which is essentially preoccupied with the distribution and exercise of power in the corporate economy, is inextricably linked to the broader socioeconomic characteristics and dynamics of that society. How that governance system operates depends, to an important degree, on the particular characteristics of time and place in which it operates. How it changes is conditioned by the history of the society in which it is instituted. To take an example, how stakeholder capitalism worked in postwar Germany was, in part, a function of the influence, interests, and ideas of German industrial workers at that time. We should not expect that codetermination, as a practice, can be airlifted by ambitious policymakers from this context and instituted in another and still operate in the same way.

Taken to an extreme, an emphasis on the importance of time and place for structuring systems of corporate governance would lead to an abandonment of any theoretical project for understanding how governance works and for guiding improvements to it. Yet, such an extreme position hardly seems justified. In corporate governance, as in capitalism more generally, there is, as Sewell puts it, "a recurrent logic at the centre of the flux that generates a continuous, monotonously repetitive pattern" (Sewell 2008, p. 521). This logic lends itself to generalization. Therefore, in seeking to better understand corporate governance the challenge is not to opt for either general theory or detailed contextualization. Instead, the generalizations that our theories make about corporate governance need to be made explicitly contingent on particular institutional characteristics and changes.

There are a variety of different questions that such an approach might address. One area deserving attention is the role of social attitudes in conditioning particular approaches to corporate governance. Another issue is the way that prevailing economic conditions, whether for particular firms, industries, or nations, create barriers against, inducements to, and possibilities for alternative forms of governance. Perhaps the most salient concern in thinking about the prospects for regulatory reform in the United States today is the role of politics in conditioning the prospects for, and path of, corporate governance reform.

This topic has begun to be explored in recent years with contributions from scholars such as Mark Roe (2003), John Cioffi and Martin Höpner (2006), and Gourevitch and Shinn (2005). Some of this work challenges intuitive ideas about partisan interests with respect to particular characteristics of corporate governance. Cioffi and Höpner highlight what they cast as a "striking paradox" – "[c]ontrary to common understandings of corporate governance reform," they note, "political conservatives were seldom enthusiastic reformers and often resisted pro-shareholder laws, while the center-left has tended to champion the cause of shareholders, and thus finance capital, in opposition to managers" (2006, p. 464). This point certainly echoes the historical experience of the United States, since the origins of the SEC and federal securities legislation are clearly rooted in a moment in which the "center-left" of American politics reigned. Casting the Democratic Party as an advocate of investor rights suggests that the recent shift in political power in the United States augurs well for the future of shareholder rights. However, closer scrutiny reveals that partisan lines on issues of corporate governance may no longer be drawn as they were in the past. Before the United States found itself mired in corporate scandals and financial crisis, important elements of the Democratic coalition articulated positions that paralleled those taken by leading Republicans; these conservative forces may reassert their influence over the Democratic Party as scandal and crisis wane. To be fair, Cioffi/Höpner recognize this possibility themselves, noting that the Democrats' commitment to corporate reform is "tempered by their evolution into a purely centrist and largely pro-business party" (Cioffi and Höpner 2006, p. 484; see also Cioffi 2006).

If understanding the interests and ideas of America's new political leadership is important for understanding where the likely opportunities for reform of corporate governance, there is also the question of how extraordinary are these political times. There are historical examples of critical junctures that have allowed for systemic change in corporate governance, both in the United States and elsewhere.[9] Indeed, the most celebrated forms of stakeholder capitalism in Germany and Japan were forged in the economic and social chaos that followed World War II. But is the current economic crisis likely to prompt similar developments in corporate governance? An analysis of the conditions under which historical crises have allowed for the transformation of a system of corporate governance, from a system oriented toward one set of interests to one that favors another, would certainly give some sense of the plausible scope of the possible new futures for corporate governance in America.

VI. Conclusion

Given the continued support for shareholder value in the United States today, it seems almost certain that corporate reform in the near term will be about strengthening the regulatory foundations of shareholder capitalism. Even within that narrow frame, as I have emphasized in this article, there are substantial intellectual challenges to be met for the specific reforms that have been proposed to be compelling. Yet, there is also good reason to broaden the basic terms of the debate on corporate governance in the United States to consider alternatives to shareholder value as a benchmark for corporate governance, even if it demands greater intellectual effort and creativity. Social scientists especially need to address the central weaknesses bedeviling existing stakeholder theories of governance, which remain the most promising alternatives to the shareholder perspective.

It is also imperative that we do more to understand how the broader socioeconomic context, especially the political context, constrains and encourages variety and change in systems of corporate governance. Certainly it would help us to better assess the prospects for substantial reform in corporate governance while the financial crisis is ongoing. Comparative–historical research on systems of corporate governance would also furnish an excellent laboratory for thinking about the potential influence of regulation in bringing about these futures. Intriguingly, and perhaps not surprisingly,

---

[9] For the role of crises in facilitating policy change by stimulating public outrage and blunting the blocking power of special interests, see Moss–Oey chapter, this volume.

many of the critical junctures that drove major changes in corporate governance were characterized by much broader political change, raising the issue of whether the transformative role of corporate regulation depends on broader contexts of political crisis and reconstruction. As policymakers contemplate new regulations for corporate governance, they could surely use the findings of such research, which should offer pointers about whether reform should seek to identify and reflect broader political changes, or to pursue directions that are somewhat at variance with the existing political trajectory.

References

Agle, Bradley, Donaldson, Thomas, Freeman, R. Edward, Jensen, Michael, Mitchell, Ronald, and Wood, Donna. 2008. "Dialogue: Toward Superior Stakeholder Theory." *Business Ethics Quarterly* **18** (2): 153–90.

Allen, Franklin, Carletti, Elena, and Marquez, Robert. 2007. "Stakeholder Capitalism, Corporate Governance and Firm Value." European Corporate Governance Institute, Finance Working Paper, No. 190/October 2007.

Attorney General of the State of New York. 2002. Affidavit in Support of Application for an Order pursuant to General Business Law Section 354, with regard to the acts and practices of Merrill Lynch & Co., Inc., etc., available at http://www.oag.state .ny.us/media_center/2002/apr/MerrillL.pdf.

Bebchuk, Lucian, and Fried, Jesse. 2003. "Executive Compensation as an Agency Problem." *Journal of Economic Perspectives*, Summer **17** (3).

Bebchuk, Lucian, and Fried, Jesse. 2004. *Pay Without Performance*. Cambridge, Mass.: Harvard University Press.

Bebchuk, Lucian, and Fried, Jesse. 2005. "Pay without Performance." *Journal of Corporation Law*, Summer **30** (4).

Bebchuk, Lucian. 2005. "The Case for Increasing Shareholder Power." *Harvard Law Review* **118** (3): 833–914.

Bebchuk, Lucian. 2007. "The Myth of the Shareholder Franchise." *Harvard Law School Discussion Papers*, No. 567, March.

Blair, M. 1995. Ownership and Control: Rethinking Corporate Governance for the Twenty-First Century. Washington, D.C.: Brookings Institution.

Blair, M., and Roe, M. 1999. eds. *Employees and Corporate Governance*. Washington, D.C.: Brookings Institution.

Bolton, Patrick et al. 2006. "Pay for Short-Term Performance." *NBER Working Papers*, No. 12107, March.

Brown, J. Robert. 2006. "Criticizing the Critics: Sarbanes-Oxley and Quack Corporate Governance." *Marquette Law Review* **90**: 309–35.

Cioffi, John. 2006. "Expansive Retrenchment: The Regulatory Politics of Corporate Governance Reform and the Foundations of Finance Capitalism in the United States and Germany," in *The State After Statism: New State Activities in the Age of Globalization and Liberalization*, ed. Jonah Levy (Cambridge, Mass.: Harvard University Press).

Cioffi, John, and Martin Höpner. 2006. "The Political Paradox of Finance Capitalism: Interests, Preferences, and Center-Left Party Politics in Corporate Governance Reform." *Politics and Society* **34** (4): 463–502.

Coffee, John. 2004. "Gatekeeper Failure and Reform: The Challenge of Fashioning Relevant Reforms." *Boston University Law Review* **84**: 301–80.

Donaldson, T., and Preston, L. 1995. "The Stakeholder Theory of the Corporation: Concepts, Evidence, and Implications." *Academy of Management Review* **20** (1): 65–91.

Drucker, P. 1949. *The New Society: The Anatomy of the Industrial Order.* New York: Harper Bros.

Frydman, Carola, and Saks, Raven. 2007. "Executive Compensation: A New View from a Long-Term Perspective, 1936–2005." Finance and Economics Discussion Series, Federal Reserve Board, Washington, D.C., No. 2007–35.

Gelter, Martin. 2008. "The Dark Side of Shareholder Influence: Toward a Holdup Theory of Stakeholders in Comparative Corporate Governance." John M. Olin Center for Law, Economics, and Business, Fellows' Discussion Paper Series, No. 17, July.

Goergen, Marc. 2007. "What Do We Know about Different Systems of Corporate Governance?" European Corporate Governance Institute, Finance Working Paper, No. 163/April 2007.

Gourevitch, Peter, and Shinn, James. 2005. *Political Power and Corporate Control: The New Global Politics of Corporate Governance.* Princeton, N.J.: Princeton University Press.

Grinstein, Yaniv, and Hribar, Paul. 2004. "CEO Compensation and Incentives." *Journal of Financial Economics,* **73**.

Hong, Harrison, and Jeffrey D. Kubik. 2003. "Analyzing the Analysts: Career Concerns and Biased Earnings Forecasts." *Journal of Finance* **58**: 313–51.

Hurst, J. W. 1970. *The Legitimacy of the Business Corporation in the Law of the United States, 1780–1970.* Charlottesville: University Press of Virginia.

Kaufman, A., Zacharias, L., and Karson, M. 1995. *Managers vs. Owners: The Struggle for Corporate Control in American Democracy.* New York: Oxford University Press.

Kaufman, Alan, and Englander, Ernie. 2005. "A Team Production Model of Corporate Governance." *Academy of Management Review* **19** (3): 1–14.

Kaysen, C. 1959. "The Corporation: How Much Power? What Scope?" in *The Corporation in Modern Society,* ed. E. Mason (New York: Atheneum), 85–105.

Lazonick, William, and O'Sullivan, Mary. 2000. "Maximising Shareholder Value: A New Ideology for Corporate Governance." *Economy & Society* **29** (1): February.

Lazonick, William, and O'Sullivan, Mary. 2002. eds. *Corporate Governance and Sustainable Prosperity.* Basingstoke: Palgrave.

Manning, B. 1958. "Review of Joseph Livingston: The American Stockholder." *Yale Law Journal* **67** (8): 1477–1496.

McKinsey & Co., Inc. 2006. *Sustaining New York's and the US' Global Financial Services Leadership.* New York.

Murphy, Kevin. 1999. "Executive Compensation," in *Handbook of Labor Economics,* vol. 3B, eds. Orley Ashenfelter and David Card (Amsterdam: Elsevier).

O'Sullivan, M. 2000. *Contests for Corporate Control: Corporate Governance and Economic Performance in the United States and Germany.* Cambridge: Oxford University Press.

Ott, Julia. 2004. "The 'Free and Open' 'People's Market': Public Relations at the New York Stock Exchange, 1913–1929." *Business and Economic History On-Line*, vol. 2.

Perrow, C. 1986. "Economic Theories of Organization." *Theory and Society* **15**: 11–45.

Prendergast, C. 1999. "The Provision of Incentives in Firms." *Journal of Economic Literature* **37** (1): 7–63.

Securities and Exchange Commission. 2008. "Summary Report of Issues Identified in the Commission Staff's Examinations of Select Credit Rating Agencies." United States Securities and Exchange Commission, July.

Sewell, William. 2008. "The Temporalities of Capitalism." *Socio-Economic Review* **6**: 517–37.

Simon, H. 1991. "Organizations and Markets." *Journal of Economic Perspectives* **5** (2): 25–44.

Skeel, David A., Jr. 2001. *Debt's Dominion: A History of Bankruptcy Law in America.* Princeton, N.J.: Princeton University Press.

Sutton, F., Harris, S., Kaysen, C., and Tobin, J. 1956. *The American Business Creed.* Cambridge, Mass.: Harvard University Press.

Useem, M. 1996. *Investor Capitalism: How Money Managers Are Changing the Face of Corporate America.* New York: Basic Books.

Whitman, R. 1997. "Including Employment Practice Data in Proxy Statements." *New York Law Journal*, November 6.

Wohlstetter, C. 1993. "The Fight for Good Governance." *Harvard Business Review*, January–February.

## ELEVEN

Taxation as a Regulatory Tool: Lessons from Environmental Taxes in Europe

Monica Prasad

I. Introduction

Governments have always used taxation to regulate their citizens' behavior, from the Babylonian divorce tax of 2350 B.C. (Burg, 2004) to the latest child tax credits. The regulatory tax receiving the most attention from scholars, activists, and policymakers these days is a tax on pollution. Ever since A.C. Pigou argued that some market exchanges produce externalities that are not captured in the exchange itself, pollution has been the classic example of a market externality, and recently a carbon tax has been proposed as an alternative to the more popular cap-and-trade method of controlling pollution. Cap and trade, critics argue, causes excessive price volatility, cannot adjust for swings in the business cycle, and too easily captured by special interests. Taxation, on the other hand, is more flexible and less bureaucratic. Environmental taxes seem to be a benefit for all: They would reduce the negative outcome of bad pollution; they would generate revenue that could be used to reduce other taxes (a "double dividend"), or to offset the regressivity of the tax; and they would contribute to energy independence. Although at the national level American policymakers seem more interested in cap-and-trade, interest in green taxes is intense in many countries, and several American states have adopted them.

But do green taxes work? Environmental taxes have been in place in several countries since the early 1990s, but the experience is mixed. For example, although carbon taxes have been implemented in every Scandinavian country, no country other than Denmark has seen large declines in CO_2 emissions. All countries have seen decreases in energy intensity (CO_2 emissions per unit of per capita GDP), but Norway is perhaps the worst performer, with increases in per capita CO_2 emissions and limited declines

Table 11.1. *Growth in CO_2 emissions and energy intensity, 1990–2006*

	Growth in CO_2 emissions per capita (tons)	Growth in energy intensity (tons of CO_2 emissions per unit of per capita GDP)
Denmark	−.1497	−62.99
Finland	.051	−45.99
Netherlands	.1639	−39.8
Norway	.1295	−7.36
Sweden	−.0262	−55.78
United States	.0232	−1374.83

Source: Energy Information Administration, International Energy Annual. Columns present the slope of the regression line through all points from 1990 to 2006. An earlier version of this chapter had presented the simple year on year change between 1990 and 2005. I am grateful to Charles Komanoff for pointing out that the slope of the regression gives a fuller picture by using all data points. This does not change the comparative picture or affect the conclusions.

in energy intensity (Table 11.1).[1] Case studies accounting for factors such as changes in the sectoral composition of the economy and attempting to compare current emissions against the counterfactual of what would have been the case in the absence of the tax likewise suggest greater success in Denmark than in Norway or Finland (Enevoldsen 2005 on Denmark; Bruvoll and Larsen 2004 on Norway; Vehmas 2004 on Finland; and see especially Enevoldsen, Ryelund, and Andersen 2007 on Denmark, Norway, and Sweden). Speck et al. (2006) summarize studies that show that in all countries emissions are lower than they would have been without the tax, but that emissions reductions are much more significant in Denmark.

Of course, an environmental tax may be "working" even if it is not leading to declines in pollution: An economist might argue that if taxes are not leading to lower emissions, this must mean that the costs of emissions are outweighed by the benefits of higher economic growth or increases in general social welfare that come along with those higher emissions. But political coalitions in favor of environmental tax are not likely to last if these taxes do not reduce pollution. Proponents of environmental taxes have sold them as a way to address climate change, and in the end, that is the metric by which they will be measured, for better or worse. This suggests that the only politically durable environmental tax is one that can substitute for cap and trade or for command and control as a regulatory tool.

[1] The figures in this chapter were the latest comparative figures available at the time of writing.

Taxes can only work as a regulatory tool if they discourage the behavior being taxed – but do they? This chapter first develops a framework for analyzing when taxes discourage the behavior being taxed, and when and why they might not, applies this framework to analyze the experience of green taxes in Scandinavia – particularly, why Denmark's taxes have worked better than other countries' – and finally, draws lessons from the Scandinavian experience for how the United States might implement green taxes. Many of the arguments that I make in this chapter are compatible with the logic of public choice. The irony of this case is that a public choice analysis of how tax revenues would be used shows the need for regulatory constraints on those revenues.

II. Do Taxes Discourage Behavior?

It makes intuitive sense that taxes should discourage the behavior being taxed – as in Figure 11.1, a diagram of the ideal Pigovian tax – but the empirical evidence is mixed. The question has been most intensively examined in the case of the Reagan tax reforms of 1982 (passed in 1981) and 1986 – the famous "Laffer curve" tax cut, and the response to it four years later. The research on the effects of regulatory taxation is much less sophisticated than that on the effects of income tax cuts,[2] so I begin with a brief survey of what we know on the question of whether income tax cuts increase work effort. Although the case of income tax cuts is different from the situation of regulatory taxation that we are concerned with in this chapter, economic theory does not distinguish between taxation for different purposes: In theory, all taxes discourage the behavior being taxed (see e.g., Yandle and Barnett, 2004) so any example should demonstrate the general principles.

The 1982 tax reform reduced marginal rates on high income earners from 70 percent to 50 percent, and the 1986 reform further reduced them to 28 percent, allowing economists to examine whether the labor supply of high income earners was thereby encouraged. The first estimations were positive. Lawrence Lindsey (1987) noted that income reported by high wage earners increased after the 1982 tax cut, and Feenberg and Poterba (1993) and Feldstein (1995) concluded that there was a high effect of the marginal tax rate changes for high-income individuals. However, researchers quickly cast those findings into doubt. They noted first that the early researchers were

---

[2] The handful of studies that have been done reach conflicting conclusions (e.g., Johnson and Meier 1990; Meier and Licari 1997); I will discuss below related studies on the price elasticity of products that are often the subject of regulatory taxation.

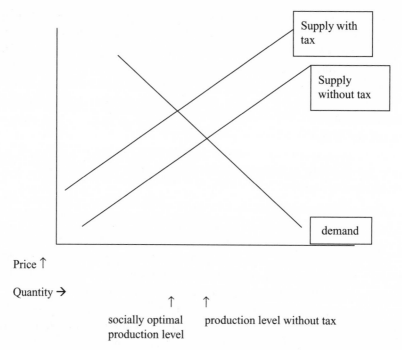

Price ↑

Quantity →

                       ↑   ↑

               socially optimal   production level without tax
               production level

Figure 11.1. Ideal Pigovian tax: tax adds to price, which lowers quantity demanded.

assuming that increases in income represented increases in labor supply. Research by Auten and Carroll (1999) showed that increases in income were largely due to a difference in the way that income was claimed (income that would otherwise have been claimed as corporate income and taxed at corporate tax rates was now being claimed as personal income and taxed at the lower personal income tax rates). Slemrod (1995) pointed out that income shifting was another reason: When income is taxed highly, some of it may be taken in the form of stock options, which could be classified and taxed as capital gains; when tax rates are lowered, stock options become less attractive, and high earners may prefer to receive those benefits as income instead. Goolsbee (1999) criticized the methodology of the earlier studies[3] and found almost no actual response to the tax cuts.

Slemrod concludes about labor supply elasticity in general: "With some exceptions, the profession has settled on a value for this elasticity close to

---

[3] The earlier studies had used lower income groups (who did not experience tax reductions) as a control group against which to measure the behavior of the upper income groups who did experience tax reduction, but Goolsbee argued that the elasticity of behavior with regard to tax may be different for these two groups.

zero (i.e., no response at all of aggregate labor supply to the after-tax wage rate) for prime-age males, although for married women the responsiveness of labor force participation appears to be significant. Overall, though, the compensated elasticity of labor appears to be fairly small" (Slemrod 2006, 77). Similar trends in the analysis of consumption and investment are observed (Bosworth and Burtless 1992; Skinner and Feenberg 1990; Auerbach and Slemrod 1997). That such central elements of the economy as labor supply, consumption, and investment show lack of sensitivity to taxation suggests that the question of the behavioral implications of taxation may be more complicated than generally thought.

III. *When* Do Taxes Discourage Behavior? A Framework for Decision Making

If absolute statements about the behavioral implications of taxes are not empirically supported, the research agenda must be to investigate when taxes discourage behavior, and when and why they might not. Although this question has not been specifically posed in economics or sociology, several traditions of research in both disciplines have circled around related questions, and can be brought together into a framework that sheds some light: organizational sociology, the sociology of the state, and social psychology and behavioral economics.

(1) Regulatory Taxes and the Firm

From the point of view of a firm, there is no particular reason to respond to a tax hike by buying less of the taxed product: it may also respond by shedding unnecessary labor; reducing benefits and other voluntary costs; increasing surveillance of workers to reduce shirking behavior; passing on the price increase to consumers if demand is inelastic; evading the tax or shifting accounting practices to avoid it; shifting production or consumption to a country with lower tax on the product, etc. Because organizations are composed of factions, some may use the price shock to push through an unrelated change that they favor for other reasons. Changing its reliance on the tax is only one of a set of options, even if the firm wants to maximize profit. But Leibeinstein (1966) famously argued that firms do not always (or even usually) operate with profit maximization in mind, citing as evidence, for example, the long lag in uptake of cost-improving technological improvements. Living with lower profits is an option if the firm's competitive environment allows it. And of course, the firm may decide that its best option is to lobby politicians for a tax exemption, with the chance of success quite high on the American political scene (Clawson, Neustadtl, and Weller 1998). For all of these reasons, the assumption that a firm will avoid the tax by engaging in product or process innovations that minimize its dependence on the taxed product may be unrealistic.

What is needed is a theory of firm behavior that predicts when a firm will be sensitive to the increased tax. Neil Fligstein (2001) has proposed a theory that the general behavior of firms may be described not as profit-maximization, but as seeking to generate a stable source of profit, whether or not that profit is at an optimal level. Fligstein notes that with some exceptions (such as restaurants), intense price competition between firms is not the usual state; rather, Fligstein argues that we gain greater analytical leverage if we examine firm behavior as attempts to *avoid* the emergence of price competition between firms. He observes that the actual determination of which actions will lead to profit maximization is beyond the cognitive, computational, and informational resources present to any actor or group of actors within a firm; in this situation, the most successful are those organizations that are able to establish a "stable world" within which complicated relationships between suppliers, workers, competitors, consumers, and the state can be resolved into a source of profit. Thus, firms will on balance prefer to continue transacting with a trusted supplier rather than risk forming a new relationship with an unknown supplier, firms will change the content of their products only rarely, for fear of jeopardizing brand loyalty, and firms will not necessarily move to expand even if they are capable of doing so. Once established, actors are reluctant to threaten the elements of this stable world, as the interdependencies between its various elements make repercussions difficult to predict and control.

In one of the few sociological studies of sensitivity of demand to price, Lutzenhiser et al. investigate why building designers do not take advantage of the large cost savings to be gained from installing more energy-efficient technologies, and agree with Fligstein that risk is managed, and costs are controlled, through stable social ties. As Lutzenhiser et al. conclude: "Since innovation represents a deviation from approaches that work, it introduces risk, the market may not like it, and it could threaten project income" (52). As one of their interviewees notes: "There's a reason what's being built in the market is being built in the market. It's because it's what the market's buying. And, to the extent that you vary from that and become a pioneer, you may find out that there's a reason no one was building that. Because people don't want it. And there's always a risk in being a pioneer that you've made a value judgment that people want this and you're entirely wrong."

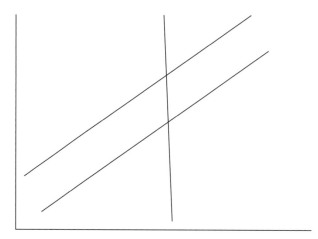

Figure 11.2. Relatively inelastic demand: Firms do not respond for Fligstein's reasons: Quantity demanded does not drop to optimal levels even though price including tax is higher.

In the case of taxation, another major source of uncertainty involves the possibility of a future government repealing or reducing the tax. A firm that makes the costly decision to switch to a lower carbon content fuel, only to see a new government cut tax rates to the point where the higher carbon content fuel would have been cheaper, is courting unnecessary costs at both ends.

If the "stable worlds" hypothesis is correct – if price competition between firms and the innovation that it leads to is not the norm – then Figure 11.1 is a special case that is only true under certain conditions. Specifically, behavioral response to taxation is a subset of the larger question of price elasticity: As Figure 11.2 shows, the ideal Pigovian tax depends on a degree of price elasticity for the product that may not exist, for the reasons Fligstein specifies. We know that the price elasticity of products varies enormously. A recent metastudy analyzing 1,851 price elasticities from eighty-one published studies conducted between 1961 and 2004 concluded that the average price elasticity was −2.22, with a standard deviation of 2.21: that is, price elasticities of close to zero fall well within one standard deviation (Bijmolt, van Heerde, and Pieters 2005).[4] Similarly, although we do not have a strong tradition of research on the behavioral effects of regulatory taxation, there are many studies analyzing price elasticity of products that are usually the objects of regulatory taxation, such as tobacco and alcohol, and these have

---

[4] The true number of elasticities close to zero may be higher: Tellis (1988) speculates that studies that find unusual price elasticities or positive price elasticities do not get published.

produced mixed results, with some studies finding inelastic demand (Gallet 2007; Gallet and List 2003).

Unfortunately the reasons for variation in elasticity are not well understood. Economists who study demand have concentrated on the measurement questions, which are very difficult to resolve and have produced a bottleneck in the research tradition. Within sociology, apart from a handful of extremely interesting investigations (e.g., Lutzenhiser and Hackett 1993; Lutzenhiser, Biggart, Kunkle, Beamish, and Burr), the research probing sensitivity of consumption to price is thin on the ground. One often cited argument is that elasticity depends on substitutability. Although this suggestion has not been tested for the economy as a whole, in the case of regulatory taxes, we do have evidence that they are most effective not at reducing behavior, but at shifting it to a better alternative – in the case of unleaded petrol, low-tar cigarettes, and low-alcohol drinks, for example (Ogus 1999, 255). If such an alternative does not exist, organizations may forgo the cost advantages, substitute into equally undesirable but untaxed products or ways of behaving, or "substitute" into tax evasion. Thus, this discussion leads to the suggestion that environmental taxes will be most successful when the product being taxed has an easily available substitute.

(2) Regulatory Taxes and the State

Firms may not respond to the set tax rates in ways that reduce the taxed activity. However, a prior question is whether the state will set the tax rates at levels designed to reduce the taxed activity.

A tax is a curious thing, because although it is an exercise of coercion, it makes the state dependent upon the object of its coercion. Martin, Mehrotra, and Prasad (2009) tell a story originally told by Gabriel Ardant about Genghis Khan: "Having conquered China, the Khan was advised by one of his generals to slaughter the Chinese peasants and take their land for pasture; a perspicacious local advisor named Yelü Chucai persuaded him that he could instead generate more hay for his horses by letting Chinese cultivators live and imposing an annual tax. This policy was good for the Khan and good for the peasants." (4). As the authors note, a tax gives the state an interest in seeing the continual reproduction of the taxed activity.

But if states have an interest in the continuation of the taxed activity, then a regulatory tax has an inherent ambiguity: It can be unclear whether the goal of such a tax is to discourage behavior or to raise revenue, leading to confusion in both analysis and actual implementation of the taxes. Even when the initial impetus behind a tax is a desire to reduce some externality, fiscal pressures can change priorities, leading officials to stress revenue production as they periodically adjust tax policy.

This confusion is echoed in much of the scholarly analysis of regulatory taxes, where a vibrant theme is the possibility of a "double dividend" from the tax, in that taxing the behavior to be discouraged generates "free" revenue that can be used to lower taxes on other activities. This issue has generated an outpouring of analysis, focusing on questions such as which distortionary taxes should be reduced, how the higher environmental taxes will interact with other taxes, etc. (Goulder 1995, provides an overview of the early literature).

The problem with this approach is that the revenue from a regulatory tax arises only if some firms are not changing behavior – indeed, only those who are not reducing their reliance on the taxed product are paying the revenue. At the extreme, where all taxpayers change their behavior, there is no revenue. At the other extreme, all taxpayers may decide to pay the tax rather than change their behavior.[5] The hope is that some set of firms will be able to make pollution-reducing changes so great that they will counterbalance the decisions of other firms to pay the tax, but this depends on the existence of a precise level of inequality in the technological capabilities of firms: The tax itself has no means of ensuring this. Thus, unlike command and control regulation, a tax may fail to achieve the regulatory aim even when it works as intended.

This feature of taxes can be exploited to advantage in areas of uncertainty, where prior prevention is more difficult than restorative action after the fact. But it is not clear that taxes on pollution can work in this way, because it may not be possible to "reverse" the effects of climate change after the fact. This means that if the tax does not discourage behavior, it will have failed in comparison to command and control legislation. If a tax is to achieve the same effect as a regulation, the revenue it generates (a signal that it has failed to change the behavior) should be used to achieve the regulatory aim in some other way.

As Ogus observes, "Realisation of the regulatory function of a fiscal instrument will necessarily involve a sacrifice of some of the revenue yield and for that reason may not be popular with civil servants or politicians. On similar grounds, it can be predicted that the revenue yielding function of a

---

[5] It would be possible to set the tax rate at levels *higher* than would be necessary to achieve equivalent gains as from command and control legislation, on the assumption that the extra revenue would come on top of the regulatory gains, but this would lose the main benefit of taxes, their transparent and accurate internalization of externalities.

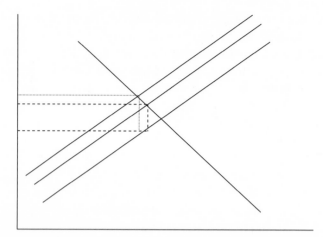

Figure 11.3. State does not set tax rates at levels that would be socially optimal, because it wants to maximize revenue: dotted box represents revenue from tax at the socially optimal level, dashed box represents revenue from tax at actual tax level. If area of dotted box < area of dashed box, revenue is not maximized at socially optimal level.

tax will be more assiduously enforced than its regulatory function" (1999, 258). The prediction here is that if the state becomes too dependent on the tax, it will cease to set rates high enough to discourage behavior – it will set rates where they maximize revenue, but these may be different from rates that minimize pollution. Figure 11.3 shows this point in schematic form: The dotted box in that figure represents the revenue the state would receive from a green tax set at the rate that minimizes pollution, while the dashed box represents the revenue the state receives from the tax set at its actual rate. If the area of the dotted box is smaller than the area of the dashed box – that is, if revenue for the state is greater at a lower tax rate – then the state has a choice between maximizing revenue and minimizing pollution.

The evidence on regulatory taxes to date is that the state often ends up using them to raise revenue, rather than to discourage behavior. There is circumstantial evidence as well as historical evidence on this point. First, as Yandle and Barnett point out, taxes that have been introduced for regulatory reasons in fact tend to fall mostly on goods for which the demand is highly inelastic, such as cigarettes, alcohol, and tobacco (see also Gallett and List 2003). The discussion above showed that taxes discourage behavior when the demand is elastic, suggesting that something other than a wish to discourage behavior is involved here – a point that would not surprise scholars holding a public choice view of politics.

Second, historical research on alcohol taxes suggests that although discouraging consumption is a leading rationale for their imposition and continuation, over time governments come to rely on them as revenue sources (Mosher and Beauchamp 1983; Hu 1950). Yelvington (1997), for example, argues that although various American states introduced alcohol taxes to discourage consumption, by the late nineteenth century they were no longer "justified solely as ways of protecting the country's health and morals. Rather, excise taxes were rationalized as patriotic ways of raising additional revenues during wartime emergencies" (37; cited in Yandle and Barnett, 2004). Similarly, Gifford (1997) shows that by the late eighteenth century, taxes on alcohol introduced in Britain for regulatory purposes had become revenue-raising measures (cited in Yandle and Barnett, 2004). Indeed, Lee (1973) notes that in the United States the Supreme Court routinely overturned taxes that did *not* raise revenue, on the grounds that Congress was not entitled to interfere with economic activity for any reason other than revenue raising.

There are some exceptions to this generalization: Licari and Meier (1994) suggest that since the rise of the "health scare" associated with tobacco, cigarette taxes have been concerned with regulation rather than revenue generation, although the opposite was true before this point; Moss (1994) gives the history of a regulatory tax that achieved elimination of the taxed object (phosphorous matches), and notes that taxes have been used for regulatory purposes in other cases as well (269, 274), with perhaps the most well-known case being the nineteenth-century taxation of state bank notes. Thus, it is not inevitable that regulatory taxes will be used for revenue raising, but this been the case for some major kinds of regulatory taxes and remains a possible impediment to their use as an alternative to command and control.

The one sure way to turn the tax into a revenue-raiser is to treat it as a situation of a "double dividend," in which the revenue generated is used for other purposes that have their own defenders for other reasons. If the state uses the revenue from the regulatory tax for some other purpose, and if the need for revenue for that other purpose rises, it may come to adopt rates that maximize revenue rather than discourage behavior. One way of preventing this from happening is to ensure that the revenue generated is *not* used for any function other than environmental goals – that it is used either to reach the targeted goal in some other way, or to rectify the environmental damage from the behavior being taxed. In short, if the revenue from a regulatory tax is a measure of the extent to which the tax has failed to discourage the behavior, then the revenue should be used to reach the goal in some other way.

(3) Regulatory Taxes and Ethical Motivation

Finally, taxes may have effects on the motivations of taxpayers, because a tax prices things – in this case, polluting behavior – that otherwise do not have a price, and some who had previously been restraining themselves from polluting for moral reasons may decide that they are willing to pay the price for polluting.

Titmuss (1970) famously suggested that paying donors to donate blood would lessen the blood supply, because it would crowd out the ethical motivation to donate. In the intervening decades, considerable evidence from laboratory experiments, and a trickle of evidence from surveys and field experiments, has supported the proposition that the implementation of monetary incentives changes behavior in curious ways. To cite just a few examples, Frey and Oberholzer-Gee (1997) found that 50.8 percent of Swiss survey respondents were willing to have a nuclear waste site located in their neighborhood, but that if offered compensation (between $2,175 and $6,525) the percentage willing dropped to 24.6 percent. Gneezy and Rustichini (2000a) in a famous experiment showed that the introduction of a fine for late arrival at a daycare *increased* the likelihood of late arrival: Instead of serving as a disincentive to late arrival, the introduction of the fine turned the right to arrive late into a commodity, which could then be purchased as needed. Brekke, Kverndokk, and Nyborg (2003) report that 15 percent of survey respondents would prefer to reduce their recycling efforts and pay a fee. Bowles (1998) reports similar findings from several parallel research traditions.

As Yochai Benkler notes in this volume, the study of intrinsic versus extrinsic motivation is extremely well advanced, and several decades' worth of studies have shown that external rewards for an act reduce intrinsic motivation for it, at least for tasks that are seen to be intrinsically rewarding at the outset (see Deci, Koestner, and Ryan, 1999, for a meta-analysis). Deci has argued that the decision to complete a task contributes to a sense of self-determination that, he suggests, is an intrinsic human motivation; external reinforcements take away this sense of self-determination. Fehr and Falk (1999, 717) suggest that the introduction of the payment changes behavior because it shows that the payer is willing to pay; but in fact other studies have already shown that the phenomenon is far stronger than that: People are also *willing to pay* to complete a task a second time if asked to pay the first time (see Loewenstein 2001). The signal, not the incentive, is key.

Bowles (1998) suggests that command and control should also have these effects, because it is an extrinsic punishment. However, research shows that the very *mention* of money has behavioral effects: Vohs, Meade, and Good (2006) found that extremely subtle cues that primed participants to think about money (such as having a stack of Monopoly money on the edge of the desk, or having a screensaver of dollar bills flashing on a computer while the subject worked on an unrelated task) makes people feel and behave in more self-sufficient and independent and less altruistic ways even when they do not actually *receive* any money. One thing price mechanisms do that command and control does not is "commensurate" – turn qualities into quantities – allowing comparisons that were not possible before (Espeland and Sauder 2007). The introduction of market incentives creates an endogeneity problem, in that it changes the ideals, preferences, and information on which people act. As Carruthers and Babb (1996) write, money is a "self-fulfilling collective prophecy."

A study by William Upton (1974) offers useful qualification: Although offers of financial compensation did reduce intrinsic motivation to donate blood among those who were already motivated to do so, they increased motivation to donate blood among those who were not already motivated to do so. Frey and Goette (1999) and Gneezy and Rustichini (2000b) find that the worst of all possible worlds is a small monetary reward: It monetizes the issue, leading to some loss of participation because of the crowding out of ethical motivation, but does not give enough monetary reward to lead to increased participation based on utilitarian motivation. As Gneezy and Rustichini (2000b) put it, "pay enough or don't pay at all." Paternoster and Simpson (1996) find that incentives work in the expected directions only when moral inhibitions are weak. The evidence seems to be consistent with Loewenstein's description of decision making: People "first attempt to figure out what kind of situation they are in and then adopt choice rules that seem appropriate for that situation" (2001, 503). Monetization first tells people that they have entered a domain of monetary incentives, and then (and only then) they behave in accordance with those incentives.

These various studies indicate that markets can reduce the motivation to behave altruistically. Moreover, once a market has been introduced, removing it does not reinstate altruistic behavior (Gneezy and Rustichini 2000a). Rather, norms seem to be fragile: Once a practice or good becomes commodified, it is difficult to de-commodify it. (However, see Healy 2006, for

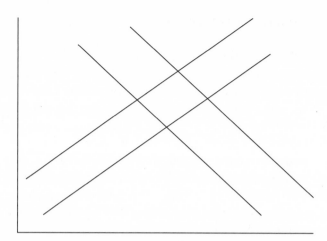

Figure 11.4. Ethical motivations are crowded out, and demand actually *increases* when pollution is priced – shifts the demand curve to the right.

the important caution that individual motivation may not be as relevant to behavior as the social organization of altruism.)

The discussion is summarized in pictorial form in Figure 11.4, which shows that if ethical motivation is "crowded out," then shifting the supply curve to the left shifts the demand curve to the right, resulting in stability of demand. The implication of this research is that green taxes should not be levied on those who are restraining themselves from environmentally polluting activities for ethical reasons. Although the fine-grained distinctions among taxpayers that this calls for are unrealistic, it is possible to distinguish between two broad categories of taxpayers: firms and households. Whereas firms may not be behaving in profit-maximizing ways for the reasons discussed above (and the ethical motivations of their leaders may be an important factor in their compliance with environmental issues), it seems clear that households are even less likely to be behaving rationally, and are more likely to be constrained by ethical norms, because households are not guided by the social processes that *attempt* to engineer rationality in firms (Beckert, 2003).

This discussion suggests that the ideal Pigovian tax is a special case that depends on certain conditions holding: First, it is dependent on price elasticity of the product being high; second, it is dependent on the state setting the rate at the socially optimal rather than the revenue-maximizing level; and third, it depends on ethical motivation not being "crowded out."

Drawing on the solutions to these problems discussed above, the framework that arises is that green taxes will work best when (1) the product being taxed is easily substitutable (which should increase price elasticity), (2) the revenue from the tax is earmarked for environmental purposes (which should prevent the state seeking to keep revenue at maximum levels), and (3) the tax is levied on firms rather than households (which should limit the crowding out of ethical behavior).

IV. Denmark's Green Taxes

Taxes on energy were first implemented in the Scandinavian countries in the wake of the oil crisis as a means of promoting energy independence. Concerns over pollution in the 1970s and 1980s, particularly over acid rain, led to increasing environmental consciousness. Finland became the first country in the world to tax pollutants, but this was intended as a revenue-raising measure. The real push toward green taxation for environmental reasons began with the 1987 report "Our Common Future" by the Brundtland Commission. In 1991 Norway and Sweden implemented green taxes, and Denmark followed in 1992. Although a pure carbon tax has been part of the package in some years in some countries, the general model is of differentiated taxes on different products and different categories of taxpayers.

However, as Table 11.1 shows, these taxes did not lead to stable declines in carbon emissions – except in Denmark. Denmark is the only country to have seen a large decline in CO_2 emissions between 1990 and 2006, nearly .15 tons fewer CO_2 emissions per capita per year.[6] Interestingly, Finland, the Netherlands, and Norway actually did worse at controlling CO_2 than the United States. The most careful comparative study of the effect of energy taxes in the Scandinavian countries is by Martin Enevoldsen, Anders Ryelund, and Michael Skou Andersen (2007), and concludes that Denmark has been much more successful at "decoupling" energy and carbon intensity from economic growth than Norway or Sweden.

Did Denmark sacrifice economic growth to achieve its environmental objectives? It is possible that growth would have been even higher without the tax, but Denmark has posted a remarkably strong economic record since 1993, to the point that some speak of a "Danish miracle." Campbell and Pedersen (2007) compare Danish economic performance in the 1990s to German, American, and Swedish economic performance: They find that in

---

[6] In addition, the United Kingdom saw a decline because of the (politically motivated) decline of its coal industry, and Germany saw a decline because of the closing of factories in the east.

Table 11.2. *Danish energy profile, 1990 and 2007*

	1990	2006
Share of Coal in Energy Production (%)	33.86	22.61
Per Capita Energy Consumption, PJ	.113	.122

Source: Danish Energy Authority, Copenhagen, 2007.

terms of GDP per capita, unemployment, and inflation, Denmark, Sweden, and the United States perform similarly and much better than Germany, whereas in terms of reducing inequality Denmark and Sweden perform much better than the United States. They note that "the World Economic Forum ... ranked Denmark, Sweden, and the United States among the top-five most competitive economies in the world in 2004" (315).

The decline in total CO_2 emissions in Denmark has been driven by a decline in CO_2 emissions from coal (Table 11.2, Figure 11.5) – petroleum emissions are basically stable, having returned to 1990 levels from a mid-90s peak, and natural gas emissions have risen steadily. Because 90 percent of coal products are consumed in the manufacturing sector in Denmark, the decline of coal – and thus the decline of CO_2 emissions in Denmark, the only country to have seen CO_2 emission decline on this scale – is largely a story of Danish manufacturing reducing its use of coal and coal products. Denmark has traditionally had a very small nationalized sector, and over 99 percent of manufacturing firms are privately owned (Christoffersen and Paldam 2003), so the decline cannot be explained by the actions of state-owned enterprises. It is private firms that have been making the decision to move away from coal. Table 11.3 shows that this is entirely a result of substitution away from coal rather than decline in energy consumption. The coal intensity of the economy has declined, even as total per capita consumption of energy has risen. The decline of coal was unexpected: Since 1974 oil has become relatively more expensive in relation to coal, and as Denmark is an importer of both oil and coal, the preference should have been for coal (Lin 1984). Furthermore, Denmark managed this without relying on nuclear power.

The question, then, is how and why the Danish manufacturing sector substituted away from coal in the 1990s, and what role energy taxes played in this. The best way to answer this would be through an analysis at the micro level of data on coal consumption in firms in Denmark as well as other countries before and after the introduction of green taxes. In the absence of such detailed data, the framework suggested above allows us to make a

Table 11.3. *Coal and alternative energy in Scandinavian countries*

	CO_2 Emissions from coal, 1990 (million metric tons)	% of Energy from renewable sources, 1995	% of Energy from renewable sources, 2001
Denmark	24.41	5.5	16.4
Finland	16.00	30.9	29.1
Netherlands	40.71	1.6	3.5
Norway	3.49		
Sweden	9.61	47.6	51.3

Sources: Energy Information Administration, International Energy Annual; del Río and Gual (2004: 228).

circumstantial case by giving clear predictions of what to look for in case studies of successful versus unsuccessful regulatory taxes. First, we would expect that firms had an easily available substitute for coal in Denmark, to a greater degree than in other countries. Second, we would predict that the revenue from the tax is being used for environmental purposes in Denmark, to a greater degree than in other countries, or is otherwise not available for general use. And third, we would predict that the tax hits firms rather than households to a greater degree than in other countries.

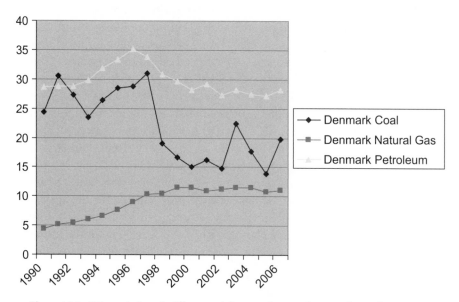

Figure 11.5. CO_2 emissions (million tons) from coal, natural gas, and petroleum. *Source:* Energy Information Administration, International Energy Annual.

The case study gives some evidence for each of these propositions, although strongest for the first and weakest for the third. There is good evidence that Denmark (unlike the other Scandinavian countries) had much greater scope of substitutability, both because of the large starting role of coal in its economy (leading to an easy substitution toward natural gas), because of the low role of renewable energy sources in its energy profile at the time of introduction of the tax, and because unlike the other countries it coupled high energy taxes on coal with low taxes on natural gas, which emits less CO_2. Second, uniquely in Denmark, the revenue was recycled back to industry, up to 40 percent of it in the form of earmarking for specific environmental measures. This was not the case in any other country. The Danish case gives only mixed support for the prediction of motivation crowding out, however: Denmark, like all the other countries, in fact taxed households more than firms. But in the 1990s, Denmark taxed households at lower rates than other countries tax households, and Denmark taxed firms at higher rates than other countries tax firms.

Environmental Taxes and Danish Firms

The prediction from Fligstein's "stable worlds" theory is that firms will avoid the tax only when a substitute source of energy is easily available. Denmark had greater substitutability than the other countries in three ways. First, it was much more dependent on coal at the beginning of this period than Sweden, Norway, or Finland (Table 11.4). This means that the shift away from coal was easier in Denmark than in the other countries, because Danish firms could simply switch to other, cleaner sources, particularly natural gas. Second, Denmark, like other European countries, has invested heavily in alternative energy sources: in Denmark's case, wind turbines, and "combined heat and power" (CHP) plants, which recycle energy that is lost through the production process. Today some 20 percent of electricity is generated from wind power, and the expectations are that that will rise to 50 percent by 2010. Part of the story is, again, that Denmark was not already heavily invested in renewable energy sources, particularly hydroenergy, when carbon tax was introduced.[7] Third, Denmark engineered an artificial "substitutability" by placing high energy taxes on natural gas (a cleaner-burning fuel) than on coal; while this approach loses the feature

[7] The Netherlands' energy profile was similar to Denmark's – heavy reliance on coal, low reliance on renewable energy. But the Netherlands largely exempted industry from the carbon tax, relying on voluntary agreements alone. In Denmark voluntary agreements were a supplementary mechanism.

Table 11.4. *Reimbursement and earmarking of CO_2 tax*

	Reimbursement of tax to industry	Earmarking of tax revenue for specific purposes
Denmark	Duty on CO_2: "Registered businesses can obtain a partial reimbursement of 13/18 of the tax on products used in energy intensive processing, and additionally a reimbursement of 11/45 of the tax if an energy savings agreement is made with the Ministry of Transportation and Energy." Duty on CO_2: "Taxes paid on LPG, natural gas, low sulphur and sulphur free diesel and electricity used in public transportation are reimbursed."	40% of revenue earmarked for subsidies to firms adopting environmental measures
Norway	CO_2 tax on mineral products: "A proportionate refund is given according to the content of biodiesel in the mineral oils."	None
Sweden	Energy and CO_2 tax on fuels except petrol: "Refunds are given to ambassadors, diplomats and the like." Energy and CO_2 tax on fuels except petrol: "Refunds are given for the whole energy tax and 70% of the carbon dioxide tax when heat produced from fuels is delivered for use in manufacturing industries and agriculture, incl. commercial greenhouse cultivation." Energy and CO_2 tax on fuels except petrol: "Refunds are given for the whole energy tax and 70% of the carbon dioxide tax when fuels are used in manufacturing industries and agriculture, incl. commercial greenhouse cultivation."	None, but tax relief or exemptions for research in developing environmentally friendly products
Netherlands	None	NA
Finland	"Strict demands for granting tax refunds effectively mean that only a very limited number of industrial facilities can, in fact, claim a tax refund. Basically, tax exemptions are restricted to around 10–12 companies, primarily in the paper and pulp sector" (Speck et al., 2006: 101)	NA

Source: Reimbursement: OECD Environmentally Related Taxes Database; Speck et al. 2006; *Earmarking:* Daugbjerg and Pedersen 2004, from Speck, "Database of Environmental Taxes and Charges."

of taxing all fuels equivalently according to carbon content, it generates a strong incentive to shift to natural gas.

In short, Denmark's environmental taxes were successful because the shift from coal was easy for firms. This is bad news for the hope of applying such taxes elsewhere, of course: It suggests that these taxes work best during the early phases of a search for alternative energy sources, or for the countries that are the most dependent on coal, and that the shift to natural gas was a one-time windfall for Denmark (although the scope for energy from renewable sources is larger). But the general principle to be taken away here is that the behavioral response to tax was sensitive to substitutability.

In addition, the ease of substitution was brought to the attention of firms through a unique process that tied voluntary industry-wide agreements to reduce pollution to lower tax rates. Voluntary agreements have been tried in other countries, but Denmark is the only one that gave lower tax rates to industries that had reached a voluntary agreement. Shopley and Brasseur (1996) interviewed firms to assess the effectiveness of the scheme, and wrote: "The majority of interviewees indicated that the Scheme enabled or accelerated their investment in energy-efficient technologies. Some reported that without the subsidy they would not have proceeded with the investment because the payback period was too long. Others would have postponed replacement of current technologies until absolutely necessary" (156). The Danish Energy Agency (1999) found that voluntary agreements worked by calling attention to the issue.

Environmental Taxes and the Danish State

The prediction from the discussion about ambiguous goals is that Denmark devotes the revenue from the taxes to environmental measures, and this allows it to keep tax rates on industry high. This is partially supported. When the carbon tax was first introduced in Denmark, 100 percent of it was recycled back to industry outright; as of 1996, firms had to enter into the "voluntary agreements" described above to take advantage of these tax refunds (Speck et al. 2006), and in more recent years 60 percent has been returned outright, with 40 percent earmarked to environmental goals (Daugbjerg and Pedersen 2004). Although the refund to industry helps to explain how Denmark has avoided losing economic competitiveness, and also helps to explain why the state might resist setting tax rates at revenue-maximizing rather than socially optimal levels, it is not clear why this should have any effect on environmental quality – a firm that knows it will get back in tax revenue what it pays in environmental tax has no incentive to change behavior. Some have suggested that the tax has a signaling effect beyond its effect on incentives. However, the 40 percent of the returned revenue earmarked for environmental measures seems clearly related to environmental success: This revenue is earmarked to be returned to industry in the form of investment subsidies for environmental initiatives. Although the full revenue is not earmarked to environmental programs, Denmark is the only country with earmarking to this degree; Table 11.4 gives details.

Moreover, the nonearmarked revenue has not been politically popular: A survey in the Scandinavian countries found that lack of trust that government would use the revenues for environmental purposes was a major reason for lack of popularity of the tax (Dresner, Dunne, Clinch, and Beuermann 2006). But the main point here is that revenues from Denmark's green taxes are not included as part of the general budget, and thus are not available to policymakers for other purposes. If the theoretical discussion above – that looking for a double dividend gives state actors incentives to set tax rates at revenue-maximizing levels rather than socially optimal levels – is correct, then the complete reimbursement of revenue may be a factor in the Danish green tax's success, as the state has no incentive to set tax rates at other than socially optimal levels. Indeed, Denmark maintains comparatively high tax rates on Danish industry, discussed further below.

Environmental Taxes and Ethical Motivation

Finally, the literature on motivation crowding would predict that firms are more responsive to tax rates than households, and that therefore successful taxes will be taxes levied on firms, while unsuccessful ones will be those levied on households.

In all of the Scandinavian countries, energy taxes, including on carbon, are levied according to a more differentiated model than purists would want, with exemptions for different categories of taxpayers, for example: "The Danish energy taxation framework for industry is probably the most complex, because the effective CO_2 tax burden depends on the specific energy use, differentiated between space-heating, light and heavy processes. In addition, the tax burden can be further reduced if companies complete an agreement to improve energy efficiency. In addition, the industrial sector as a whole is completely exempt from the basic energy tax payment" (Speck et al. 2006, 42). This means that effective comparison of tax rates requires differentiation among different energy uses.

Figures 11.6 and 11.7 show total tax rates (for pure carbon tax as well as energy taxes) on nonindustrial and industrial fuel uses for the late 1990s.

Non-Industrial Use Fuel Tax Rates ($PPP/ton CO2)

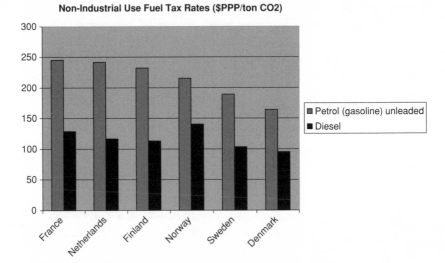

Figure 11.6. Baranzini, Goldemberg, Speck, 2000: 398.

In fact the Danish state does not tax firms more than households: In all the countries, households pay higher tax rates than firms. Indeed, all of the countries have implemented green taxes in a manner that is remarkably friendly to industry – following the general European mode of regulatory policymaking (Prasad 2006). The Danish green tax was part of a neoliberal

Industrial Use Fuel Tax Rates ($PPP/ton CO2)

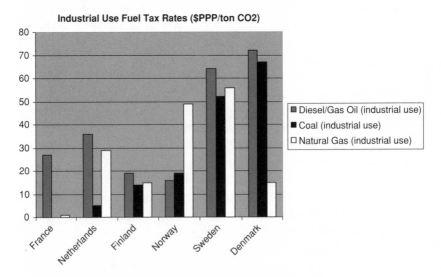

Figure 11.7. Baranzini, Goldemberg, Speck, 2000: 398.

tax reform that reduced marginal tax rates and corporate tax rates and financed this by increasing the number of taxpayers and by lowering the exemptions on the green taxes. This was part of an overall turn to the right in Danish politics that included some privatizations and a welfare reform that has been called a "reconsideration of the social rights of citizenship" (Cox 2001, 464; see also Campbell and Pedersen 2007). The refund of tax revenue to industry seems to have been necessary to get the measures passed while meeting concerns about competitiveness. But Denmark has no indigenous coal industry, and has been able to levy high tax rates on coal.

However, although households are taxed at higher rates than firms Denmark taxes firms more than other Scandinavian countries tax firms (rates on industrial use of diesel/gas, coal, and natural gas are higher in Denmark than elsewhere), and Denmark taxes households less than other countries tax households (rates on nonindustrial use of petrol and diesel are lower in Denmark than elsewhere) (Figures 11.6 and 11.7).

Also telling in Figure 11.7, in light of the discussion on substitutability above, is Denmark's differential effective tax rates for coal and natural gas, providing clear incentives for a switch away from one and into the other.

V. Lessons for the United States

The lessons from the case study of Scandinavian green taxes cannot literally be applied to the United States. The gains from wind power, for example, may be relatively greater for Denmark because of its climate and geography. But it is possible to apply the general principles of providing *substitutes*, *targeting* the revenue to environmental aims, and taxing *firms* rather than households. These three principles identifying the conditions under which taxation can be used as a regulatory tool are extensions to Benkler's list of "design levers."

It was the first of these three principles that received the strongest support from the Danish case, suggesting that the clearest lesson of this study is that green taxes should be levied on products that have substitutes (or coupled with policies to provide substitutes, such as lower taxes on a cleaner alternative or investment into alternative energy sources). Some social process of coordination, such as industry-wide agreements, can prod firms to make the substitution. In addition, the case study suggests that policymakers should avoid the trap of looking for a "double dividend." Actual revenue collected is a signal that the tax has failed in its regulatory aims, indicating that the state should use those revenues to reach the aims in some other way (such as funding research into alternative energy sources or subsidies for firms that undertake projects to improve energy efficiency). This will also avoid giving incentives to state actors to use the tax for revenue-raising purposes. And finally, although the evidence is less clear here, governments should perhaps tread cautiously during this moment of worldwide norm creation, avoiding the imposition of taxes on those who are behaving in altruistic ways to protect the environment for fear of permanently crowding out their ethical motivations. Because households may be more likely to be altruistically motivated than firms, firms are a better target when deciding *whom* to tax.

Is there a policy that would meet all these guidelines? These arguments suggest that, although gasoline taxes make up 90 percent of environmental tax revenue in the OECD countries, it is not clear that extending gasoline taxes will be productive in the United States in the absence of major investments in public transportation – a gas tax taxes households that do not have substitutes. Although the measurement of price elasticity is complicated, a consensus is forming that gasoline demand is less sensitive to price today than it was in the 1970s and 1980s, even in the long run. Short run elasticities are close to zero (e.g., Hughes, Knittel, and Sperling 2006) and it is unclear that high rates on such a common and unpopular tax could remain in place long enough to see the long-run effects (indeed, the uncertainty of the long-run outlook of the tax may itself prevent people from changing behavior). In addition, a gasoline tax will directly hurt the poor.

Instead, this discussion suggests that the correct policy is to tax the industrial production and consumption of coal and other high carbon content fuels in conjunction with stable or lower tax rates on lower carbon content fuels and provide the revenue back to the affected industries in the form of tax exemptions or subsidies for investments in alternative energy sources, cleaner-burning technologies, carbon capture and sequestration technologies, or energy capture and recycling programs.

Environmental taxes have seemed in some ways to be a panacea: just pop in the economic incentives and watch them work their magic. But the experience of the European countries suggests that a certain surrounding infrastructure, including substitutability and carrots as well as sticks, is necessary to make these taxes work. In particular, this examination leads to the prediction that environmental taxes will fail in the absence of investments into alternative energy sources. In the presence of alternative and cleaner-burning fuels, currently developing norms may well lead households to behave in environmentally friendly ways even without taxes. The role of environmental taxes should be to nudge firms to take up the substitute fuels and technologies once they are present and to invest in their creation until they are.

References

Auerbach, Alan J., and Joel Slemrod. 1997. "The Economic Effects of the Tax Reform Act of 1986." *Journal of Economic Literature* 35: 589–632.

Auten, Gerald, and Robert Carroll. 1999. "The Effect of Income Taxes on Household Income." *Review of Economics and Statistics* 81 (4): 681–93.

Baranzini, Andrea, José Goldemberg, and Stefan Speck. 2000. "A Future for Carbon Taxes." *Ecological Economics* 32: 395–412.

Bijmolt, Tammo H. A., Harald J. van Heerde, and Rik G. M., Pieters 2005. "New Empirical Generalizations on the Determinants of Price Elasticity." *Journal of Marketing Research* 42 (2): 141–56.

Bosworth, Bary, and Gary Burtless. 1992. "Effects of Tax Reform on Labor Supply, Investment, and Saving." *Journal of Economic Perspectives* 6 (1): 3–25.

Bowles, Samuel. 1998. "Endogenous Preferences: The Cultural Consequences of Markets and Other Economic Institutions." *Journal of Economic Literature* 36: 75–111.

Brekke, Kjell Arne, Snorre Kverndokk, and Karine Nyborg. 2003. "An Economic Model of Moral Motivation." *Journal of Public Economics* 87: 1967–83.

Bruvoll, Annegrette, and Bodil Merethe Larsen. 2004. "Greenhouse Gas Emissions in Norway: Do Carbon Taxes Work?" *Energy Policy* 32: 493–505.

Burg, David. 2003. *A World History of Tax Rebellions.* Routledge.

Campbell, John L., and Ove K. Pedersen. 2007. "The Varieties of Capitalism and Hybrid Success." *Comparative Political Studies* 40 (3): 307–32.

Carruthers, Bruce, and Sarah Babb. 1996. "The Color of Money and the Nature of Value: Greenbacks and Gold in Postbellum America." *American Journal of Sociology* 101 (6): 1556–91.

Chaloupka, Frank J., and Kenneth Warner. 2000. "The Economics of Smoking," in *Handbook of Health Economics*, eds. Anthony Culyer and Joseph Newhouse, 1539–628. Elsevier.

Chaloupka, Frank J., Michael Grossman, and Henry Saffer. 2002. "The Effects of Price on Alcohol Consumption and Alcohol-Related Problems." *Alcohol Research & Health*, Winter, 2002.

Christoffersen, Henrik, and Martin Paldam. 2003. "Privatization in Denmark, 1980–2002." http://www.cesifo-group.de.

Cox, Robert Henry. 2001. "The Social Construction of an Imperative." *World Politics* 53: 463–98.

Daugbjerg, Carsten, and Anders Branth Pedersen. 2004. "New Policy Ideas and Old Policy Networks: Implementing Green Taxation in Scandinavia." *Journal of Public Policy* 24 (2): 219–49.

Deci, Edward L., Richard Koestner, and Richard M. Ryan. 1999. "A Meta-Analytic Review of Experiments Examining the Effects of Extrinsic Rewards on Intrinsic Motivation." *Psychological Bulletin* 125 (6): 627–68.

Del Río, Pablo, and Miguel Gual. 2004. "The Promotion of Green Electricity in Europe: Present and Future." *European Environment* 14: 219–34.

Dresner, Simon, Louise Dunne, Peter Clinch, and Christiane Beuermann. 2006. "Social and Political Responses to Ecological Tax Reform in Europe: An Introduction to the Special Issue." *Energy Policy* **34** (8): 895–904.

Enevoldsen, Martin. 2005. *The Theory of Environmental Agreements and Taxes.* London: Edward Elgar.

Enevoldsen, Martin K., Anders V. Ryelund, and Michael Skou Andersen. 2007. "Decoupling of Industrial Energy Consumption and CO2-Emissions in Energy-Intensive Industries in Scandinavia." *Energy Economics* **29**: 665–92.

Espeland, Wendy, and Michael Sauder. 2007. "Rankings and Reactivity: How Public Measures Recreate Social Worlds." *American Journal of Sociology* **113** (1): 1–40.

Feenberg, Daniel R., and James M. Poterba. 1993. "Income Inequality and the Incomes of Very High Income Taxpayers: Evidence from Tax Returns." NBER Working Paper Series. Working Paper W4229. Available at SSRN: http://ssrn.com/abstract=270367.

Fehr, Ernst, and Armin Falk. 1999. "Psychological Foundations of Incentives." *European Economic Review* **46**: 687–724.

Feldstein, Martin. 1995. "The Effect of Marginal Tax Rate on Taxable Income: A Panel Study of the 1986 Tax Reform Act." *Journal of Political Economy* **103** (3): 551–72.

Fligstein, Neil. 2001. *The Architecture of Markets: An Economic Sociology of Twenty-First Century Capitalist Societies.* Princeton, N.J.: Princeton University Press.

Frey, Bruno S., and Lorenz Götte. 1999. "Does Pay Motivate Volunteers?" Working Paper No. 9. Zurich, Switzerland: Institute for Empirical Research in Economics, University of Zurich.

Frey, Bruno S., and Felix Oberholzer-Gee. 1997. "The Cost of Price Incentives: An Empirical Analysis of Motivation Crowding-Out." *American Economic Review* **87** (4): 746–55.

Gallet, Craig A. 2007. "The Demand For Alcohol: A Meta-Analysis of Elasticities." *The Australian Journal of Agricultural and Resource Economics* **51** (2): 121–35.

Gallet, C. A., and List, J. A. 2003. "Cigarette Demand: A Meta-Analysis of Elasticities." *Health Economics* **12**, 821–35.

Gifford, Adam, Jr. 1997. "Whiskey, Margarine, and Newspapers: A Tale of Three Taxes," in *Taxing Choice: The Predatory Politics of Fiscal Discrimination,* ed. William F. Shughart II (New Brunswick, N.J.: Transaction Press), 57–77.

Gneezy, Uri, and Aldo Rustichini. 2000a. "A Fine is a Price." *Journal of Legal Studies* **29**: 1–17.

Gneezy, Uri, and Aldo Rustichini. 2000b. "Pay Enough or Don't Pay at All." *Quarterly Journal of Economics.* **115** (3): 791–810.

Goolsbee, Austan. 1999. "Evidence on the High-Income Laffer Curve from Six Decades of Tax Reform." *Brookings Papers on Economic Activity* **2**: 1–64.

Goulder, Lawrence H. 1995. "Environmental Taxation and the Double Dividend: A Reader's Guide." *International Tax and Public Finance* **2** (2): 157–83.

Healy, Kieran. 2006. *Last Best Gifts: Altruism and the Market for Human Blood and Organs.* Chicago: University of Chicago Press.

Hu, Tun Yuan. 1950. *The Liquor Tax in the United States: 1791–1947.* New York: Columbia University Press.

Hughes, Jonathan E., Christopher R. Knittel, and Daniel Sperling. 2006. "Evidence of a Shift in the Short-Run Price Elasticity of Gasoline Demand." NBER Working Paper Series. Working Paper 12530. http://www.nber.org/papers/w12530.

Johnson, Cathy M., and Kenneth J. Meier. 1990. "The Wages of Sin: Taxing America's Legal Vices." *The Western Political Quarterly* **43** (3): 577–95.

Leibenstein, Harvey. 1966. "Allocative Efficiency vs. 'X-Efficiency.'" *American Economic Review* **56** (3): 392–415.

Lee, R. Alton. 1973. *A History of Regulatory Taxation.* Lexington: University Press of Kentucky.

Licari, Michael J., and Kenneth J. Meier. 1997. "Regulatory Policy When Behavior is Addictive: Smoking, Cigarette Taxes and Bootlegging." *Political Research Quarterly* **50** (1): 5–24.

Lin, Ching-yuan. 1984. "Global Pattern of Energy Consumption Before and After the 1974 Oil Crisis." *Economic Development and Cultural Change* **32** (4): 781–802.

Lindsey, Lawrence B. 1987. "Individual Taxpayer Response to Tax Cuts: 1982–1984, With Implications for the Revenue Maximizing Tax Rate." *Journal of Public Economics* **33** (2): 173–206.

Loewenstein, George. 2001. "The Creative Destruction of Decision Research." *The Journal of Consumer Research* **28** (3): 499–505.

Lutzenhiser, Loren, and Bruce Hackett. 1993. "Social Stratification and Environmental Degradation: Understanding Household CO_2 Production." *Social Problems* **40**: 50–73.

Lutzenhiser, Loren, Nicole Woolsey Biggart, Richard Kunkle, Thomas D. Beamish, and Thomas Burr. "Market Structure and Energy Efficiency: The Case of New Commercial Buildings." Report to the California Institute for Energy Efficiency.

Martin, Isaac, Ajay Mehrotra, and Monica Prasad. 2009. "Introduction," in *The New Fiscal Sociology: Comparative and Historical Perspectives on Taxation*, eds. Isaac Martin, Ajay Mehrotra, and Monica Prasad. Cambridge University Press.

Meier, K. J., and M. J., Licari 1997. "The Effect of Cigarette Taxes on Cigarette Consumption, 1955 through 1994." *American Journal of Public Health* **87** (7): 1126–30.

Mosher, James F., and Dan E. Beauchamp. 1983. "Justifying Alochol Taxes to Public Officials." *Journal of Public Health Policy* **4** (4): 422–39.

Moss, David. 1994. "Kindling a Flame under Federalism: Progressive Reformers, Corporate Elites, and the Phosphorous Match Campaign of 1909–12." *Business History Review* **68** (2): 244–75.

Ogus, Anthony. 1999. "Nudging and Rectifying: The Use of Fiscal Instruments for Regulatory Purposes." *Legal Studies* 245–66.

Paternoster, Raymond, and Sally Simpson. 1996. "Sanction Threats and Appeals to Morality: Testing a Rational Choice Model of Corporate Crime." *Law and Society Review* **30** (3): 549–84.

Phelps, Orme W. 1941. "The Supreme Court and Regulatory Taxation." *The Journal of Business of the University of Chicago* **14** (2): 99–126.

Prasad, Monica. 2006. *The Politics of Free Markets: The Rise of Neoliberal Economic Policies in Britain, France, Germany, and the United States.* Chicago: University of Chicago Press.

Skinner, Jonathan, and Daniel Feenberg. 1990. "The Impact of the 1986 Tax Reform Act on Personal Saving." NBER Working Paper Series. *Working Paper No.* 3257.

Slemrod, Joel. 1995. "Income Creation or Income Shifting? Behavioral Responses to the Tax Reform Act of 1986." *American Economic Review* **85** (2): 175–80.

Slemrod, Joel. 2006. "The Consequences of Taxation." 73–87. *Social Philosophy and Policy* **23** (2): 73–87.

Speck, Stefan, Mikael Skou Andersen, Helle Ørsted Nielsen, Anders Ryelund, and Carey Smith. 2006. "The Use of Economic Instruments in Nordic and Baltic Environmental Policy 2001–2005." National Environmental Research Institute, Denmark.

Tellis, Gerard J. 1988. "The Price Elasticity of Selective Demand: A Meta-Analysis of Econometric Models of Sales." *Journal of Marketing Research* **35**: 331–41.

Titmuss, Richard M. 1970. *The Gift Relationship: From Human Blood to Social Policy.* New York: Pantheon.

Upton, William Edward III. 1973. "Altruism, Attribution, and Intrinsic Motivation in the Recruitment of Blood Donors." Doctoral dissertation, Cornell University.

Vehmas, Jarmo. 2004. "Energy-Related Taxation as an Environmental Policy Tool – the Finnish Experience 1990–2003." *Energy Policy* **33**: 2175–82.

Vohs, Kathleen D., Nicole L. Meade, and Miranda R. Goode. 2006. "The Psychological Consequences of Money." *Science* **314** (5802): 1154–56.

Yandle, Andy H., and Bruce Barnett. 2004. "Regulation by Taxation." *Handbook of Public Finance.*

Yelvington, Brenda. 1997. "Excise Taxes in Historical Perspective." In William F. Shughart II (Ed.), *Taxing Choice: The Predatory Politics of Fiscal Discrimination.* New Brunswick, N.J.: Transaction Press.

TWELVE

Redesigning Regulation: A Case Study from the Consumer Credit Market[1]

Elizabeth Warren

The consumer credit market is broken. Businesses have learned to exploit customers' systematic cognitive errors, selling complex credit products that are loaded with tricks and traps. Because customers cannot see or understand complete credit terms until it is too late, the market no longer operates to achieve competitive efficiency. Instead, creditors engage in a race to the bottom, boosting profits by offering ever-riskier products that families are poorly equipped to handle. The consequences are serious: Americans are sinking deeper in debt each year, and defaults, foreclosures and bankruptcies are on the rise.

The regulatory framework that once controlled consumer credit is now in tatters. From colonial times until 1979, state-based usury laws were the central feature of consumer protection. In 1979, a Supreme Court interpretation of ambiguous language in a national banking law effectively ended state usury laws. Congress could easily have reversed the opinion by clarifying the language, but it turned away while this critical consumer protection vanished. By the 1990s, product innovation from payday lending to universal default to creative mortgage financing took root largely outside the purview of any regulatory body. Truth-in-Lending laws, which were designed to supplement usury protection, failed to keep pace with market changes. The

[1] The idea for a Financial Product Safety Commission was introduced by Elizabeth Warren at a Tobin Project working group meeting in May 2007, and published in Elizabeth Warren, Unsafe at Any Rate, Democracy: A Journal of Ideas (Summer 2007) http://www .democracyjournal.org/article.php?ID=6528. By July 2009, bills to create a Financial Product Safety Commission had been introduced in both chambers of Congress, and the Obama administration had put forth a similar proposal for a Consumer Financial Protection Agency.

The paper benefited from the thoughtful comments of Ed Balleisen. I also appreciate the excellent research assistance of Abbye Atkinson, Harvard Law School Class of 2009, in the preparation of this chapter.

Federal Reserve, the Office of the Controller of the Currency, the Office of Thrift Supervision, and other federal and state agencies regulate various financial institutions, but the mission of these regulators is aimed squarely at protecting the banks and the stability of the overall financial system, with scant attention to consumer protection.

This combination of outdated regulation, misdirected regulation, deregulation, and no regulation has produced a stew of state and federal rules that increased lender costs decreasing effective consumer protection. Gaps in regulation created opportunities for regulatory arbitrage and often left even the most conscientious regulators frustrated. With no single agency or set of laws to provide a meaningful regulatory foundation, a new approach to consumer financial regulation is in order: a single, new commission aimed at regulating consumer financial products. Such an agency could develop expertise and make regulatory changes to respond to market innovations. Like its counterpart, the Consumer Product Safety Commission, the Financial Product Safety Commission would have the authority to cover all relevant products – all home mortgages, all credit cards, all payday loans, etc. – thereby ending the spotty regulation that depends on whether the product was issued by a state bank, federal bank, a thrift, a credit union, or a group of private investors. Safety standards would be product based, in place to protect all consumers.

The demonstrated failure of the existing fractured regulatory regime presents the case for a unitary regulatory authority with respect to financial products – and a counterpoint to Professor Stiglitz's call for multiple oversight authorities as a counter to regulatory capture. Instead of empowering one agency to fill in regulatory gaps when another agency fails to act, the fractured oversight in consumer financial products has advanced a form of regulatory arbitrage, so that financial institutions that do not like the regulations imposed by one agency can reincorporate under a new charter – and a new regulator. An unhappy thrift, for example, may reincorporate as a bank if it finds the Office of the Controller of the Currency more hospitable than the Office of Thrift Supervision. With regulators' revenues, budgets, and prestige following the number and size of the institutions they govern, the consequence has been to keep regulators timid, firmly under the thumb of those they regulate. The example does not prove that divided authority never works, but it suggests that division of power among regulators along certain fault lines can have substantial downsides.

The consumer credit market presents a case study to explore the impact of ineffective regulation and to identify the systemic problems in the regulatory design that led to these failures. Much of what is discussed here would be applicable with only slight variation in other financial product areas such as pensions, insurance, banking, and investments. Applicability to other arenas such as environmental law, health care policy, and immigration, I leave to others.

THE PROBLEM WITH GOING IT ALONE

Americans are choking on debt. One in four families say they are worried about how they will pay their credit card bills this month.[2] Nearly half of all credit card holders missed at least one payment last year,[3] and an additional 2.1 million families missed one or more mortgage payments.[4] In 2006, 1.2 million families lost their homes in foreclosure,[5] and an estimated 2 million more families were headed into mortgage foreclosure by 2009.[6] The net effect of subprime mortgage lending is that 1 million fewer families now own homes than did a decade ago.[7]

The credit card industry offers a glimpse at the wealth transfer that takes place each year in credit markets. In 2006, for example, Americans turned over $89 billion in fees, interest payments, added costs on purchases, and other charges associated with their credit cards.[8] That is $89 billion out of the pockets of ordinary middle-class families, people with jobs, kids in

---

[2] Holiday Spending Survey, Consumer Federation of America (November 2007) (40 percent of families are either "very concerned" (18 percent) or "somewhat concerned" (22 percent) about how they will pay their monthly bills).

[3] Walechia Konrad, *How Americans Really Feel About Credit Card Debt*, Bankrate.com (Survey 2006).

[4] Sandra Block, *Foreclosure Hurts Long after Home's Gone, So Cut a Deal While You Can*, USA Today quoting Mortgage Bankers Assn (March 23, 2007).

[5] Amy Hoak, *Marketwatch, Foreclosed Properties Abound, and So Do the Risks*, Washington Post (March 3, 2007) (quoting RealtyTrac).

[6] Report and Recommendations by the Majority Staff of the Joint Economic Committee of the United States Congress, The Subprime Lending Crisis (October 2007), available at www.jec.senate.gov/Documents/Reports/10.25.07OctoberSubprimeReport.pdf.

[7] *Subprime Lending: A Net Drain on Home Ownership*, Center for Responsible Lending, CRL Issue Paper No. 14, p. 2 (March 27, 2007), available online at http://www .responsiblelending.org/page.jsp?itemID=32032031.

[8] Currently, credit card companies earn revenues from six sources:

Interest	$71.13 billion
Interchange fees	20.62 billion
Penalty Fees	7.88 billion
Cash-Advance Fees	5.26 billion
Annual Fees	3.26 billion
Enhancements	0.85 billion
Total	$109.00 billion

Source: *Cards & Payments*, reproduced in *Bank Card Profitability, 2005–2004*, Card Web (2006).

school, and groceries to buy. That is also $89 billion that was not used to purchase new cars, new shoes, or any other goods or services in the American economy. Today the typical family with credit card debt spends only slightly less on fees and interest each year than it does on shirts, skirts, dresses, pants, underwear, socks, shoes, boots, coats, gloves, scarves, laundry, and dry-cleaning for the whole family.[9] To be sure, the money kept plenty of bank employees working full time, and it helped make "debt collector" one of the fastest-growing occupations in the economy.[10] But debt repayment has become a growing part of the American family budget. Household debt service is at an all-time high.[11]

Nor are all costs associated with debt measured in dollars; not surprisingly, the impact on family life is considerable. Anxiety and shame have become constant companions for Americans struggling with debt. Since 2000, nearly 10 million families have filed petitions for bankruptcy.[12] Today about one in every seven families in America is dealing with a debt collector.[13] Mortgage foreclosures and credit defaults sweep in millions more families.[14] How do they feel about their inability to pay their bills? A 2005 survey by the National Opinion Research Council, which asked families about negative life events, on a ranking of one through one hundred, offers some instructive evidence on that question. Respondents ranked the death of a child (94.3) and being forced to live on the street or in a shelter (86.7) as the most devastating possibilities, but filing for bankruptcy ranked close behind (83.5), more serious than death of a close friend (80.8), or separating from a spouse (82.1).[15] More than half of Americans won't tell a friend their

---

[9] A family carrying credit card debt spends, on average, about $1600–1700 per year on interest and fees. The average family spends about $1,889 on clothing, etc. http://www.bls .gov/news.release/cesan.nr0.htm.

[10] The Bureau of Labor Statistics estimates that the number of people employed as bill or account collectors has grown markedly from 288,190 individuals in 1998 to 423,090 in 2006. http://www.bls.gov/oes/1998/oesnat98.htm (data for 1998); http://www.bls.gov/oes/ oes_data.htm (data for 2006).

[11] Federal Reserve Board, Merrill Lynch Analysis, Economic Commentary, *Household Net Worth Hits a Record High*, Chart 5: Household Debt Burden at Record Levels (January 2008) (explaining why debt service rather than net worth shows the true measure of the economic health of the American family).

[12] Yearly data reported by the Administrative Office of the United States Courts.

[13] Tom W. Smith, *Troubles in America: A Study of Negative Life Events*, National Opinion Research Council (December 2005); Lucy Lazarony, *Denying Our Debt*, Bankrate.com (July 2006 (11 percent in collection on credit cards).

[14] Mortgage foreclosures are in the introduction. Credit card default rates are just under 4 percent of all accounts.

[15] TOM W. SMITH, NAT'L OPINION RES. CTR., TROUBLES IN AMERICA: A STUDY OF NEGATIVE LIFE EVENTS ACROSS TIME AND SUBGROUPS 10 (2005), available at http://www-news.uchicago.edu/releases/05/051228.troubles.pdf.

credit card balances,[16] and 85 percent of those who file for bankruptcy are struggling to hide that fact from families, friends, or neighbors.[17]

For Americans steeped in a tradition of rugged individualism and a belief that hard work will yield decent rewards, the pill of economic failure is especially bitter. For 90 percent of families, job losses, medical problems, or family breakups preceded their collapse into bankruptcy.[18] But the credit industry saw that it could trim its costs if fewer people had access to bankruptcy, so it wrote anticonsumer bankruptcy legislation, initiated a well-financed public relations campaign, and lobbied Congress hard to adopt its bill. After nine years and millions in campaign donations, Congress complied by adopting the Bankruptcy Reform Act of 2005.[19] In the move to assist the credit industry, the devastation of millions of families was not a national priority.

Rational choice scholarship has long emphasized the disproportionate power that concentrated interest groups bring to bear on the legislative process. The 2005 bankruptcy laws present a paradigmatic example of the impact that such groups can have on the regulatory process.

Despite the constant focus on the individual, the pain of bad credit decisions is not borne by the debtor alone. From 2000 to 2007, when lenders flooded the housing market with loan offers, housing prices skyrocketed. When lenders started foreclosing on hundreds of thousands of mortgages, the effects were not evenly distributed across the country. Instead, places that had been targeted by predatory lenders suffered much higher foreclosure rates. Entire neighborhoods have been devastated. The Center for Responsible Lending estimates that the spillover from subprime lending will cost neighbors an estimated $223 billion in value on their own homes.[20] Nearly 45 million families that stayed away from predatory lenders will nonetheless be hit by the financial fallout of subprime lending as their property values sink, their local governments lose the tax revenues needed to provide basic services, and their neighborhoods are dotted with badly maintained, boarded-up buildings. Bad credit policies can have powerful third-party effects.

---

[16] Lucy Lazorony, *Denying Our Debt, Financial Literacy in America*, Bankrate.com (July 2006).

[17] Two-Income Trap, supra note___, at 213 n. 13, 74–75.

[18] Two-Income Trap, supra note___, at xx.

[19] Lobbying costs and campaign contributions for the first few years of the effort are documented in Elizabeth Warren, *The Phantom $400*, 13 JOURNAL OF BANKRUPTCY LAW AND PRACTICE 77 (2004).

[20] Center for Responsible Lending, *Subprime Spillover: Foreclosures Cost Neighbors $223 Billion* (November 17, 2007). http://www.responsiblelending.org/pdfs/subprime-spillover .pdf.

PERSONAL RESPONSIBILITY AND REGULATION

Why do people get into debt trouble in the first place? People know that credit cards are dangerous, all the more so if the customer carries a balance. Mortgage financing is a serious undertaking, with reams of documents and papers; any consumer who signed papers without reading carefully or seeking legal assistance should not be surprised if terms come to light later that are unfavorable to the consumer. Payday lenders have a bad reputation for taking advantage of people; no one should expect to be well treated by them. Car lenders, check-cashing outlets, overdraft protection – the point can be repeated again and again: Financial products are dangerous and any consumer who is not careful is inviting trouble. And yet, dangerous or not, millions of Americans engage in billions of credit transactions, adding up to trillions of dollars every year.[21]

Some commentators claim that Americans face crushing debt loads because they have been heedless of risk or because they are so consumed by their appetites to purchase, so driven to sustain their lifestyle, that they willingly ignore the potential consequences. For example, Fifth Circuit Court of Appeals Judge Edit Jones (long mentioned as a possible nominee to the Supreme Court) and Professor Todd Zywicki (a frequent guest at congressional hearings) have been unrelenting in their criticism of families overwhelmed by debt.[22] "Because the current bankruptcy system rewards short-term and irresponsible behavior while penalizing those who live within their means, it is not surprising that an increasing number of Americans choose the short-term chance to walk away from their debts rather than the long-term challenges of living within their means and paying off their responsibilities."[23] They argue, for example, that bankruptcy no longer carries any stigma, and that the very process of taking on debt is taking advantage of their creditors.[24]

The repeated insistence that American policymakers should stick by Dickensian, market discipline for consumers reflects more than just ideological cant. Some portion of the credit crisis in America is the result of

---

[21] Government Accountability Office, *Increased Complexity in Rates and Fees Heightens Need for More Effective Disclosures to Consumers* (September 2006), http://www.gao.gov/new.items/d06929.pdf.

[22] Edith H. Jones and Todd J. Zywicki, *It's Time for Means-Testing*, 1999 BYU L. Rev. 177; Todd J. Zywicki, *Institutions, Incentives, and Consumer Bankruptcy Reform*, 62 Wash. & Lee L. Rev. 1071, 1097 (2005).

[23] Todd Zywicki, Bankruptcy Law as Social Legislation, 5 *Texas Law & Policy Review* 397, 408 (2001).

[24] See Jones & Zywicki, supra note___.

consumer foolishness and profligacy. Some people are in trouble with credit because they simply use too much of it. Others confront a steady stream of phone calls from debt collectors because they have been willing to tap an ever more accessible stream of credit for speculation, most recently in the housing market. In the debates over the bankruptcy laws, rational choice advocates focused almost exclusively on the hypothetical debtor who was, in all cases, the perfect rational maximizer – selfish, scheming, and ready to exploit any advantage. This approach justified an institutional design that privileges harsh consequences as part of an powerful incentive structure.So, for example, Judge Jones and Professor Zywicki argued that if bankruptcy laws were harsh enough, foolish people would mend their ways, avoiding debt and embracing the virtues of thrift.[25] If the bankruptcy debates had been driven instead by the approach Professor Yochai Benkler outlines in this volume, placing a priority on explicit rewards and punishments as a way to trigger "extrinsic motivations," a very different law would have emerged.

Focusing on the decision making of presumptively rational, individual debtors misses crucial dimensions of the story. Lenders have deliberately built tricks and traps into some credit products so they can ensnare families in a cycle of high-cost debt. It is this specific risk – the danger designed into the product that can ensnare even the careful consumer – that only regulation can protect against.

Professor Stiglitz argues forcefully that repeated transactions based on asymmetric information or cognitive errors justify regulatory intervention. The consumer credit area offers a multitude of examples to illustrate his point. So, for example, a customer today might carefully calculate the cost of a washing machine and dryer, including the cost of charging it on a credit card at 12 percent interest. But that customer is unlikely to account for the possibility that a dispute with the used car lot that sold her vehicle could ratchet up the interest rate on her credit card to 33 percent – and double her monthly payment. But a universal default clause, hidden in the fine print, gives the credit card company the opportunity to do just that – raise rates on a customer who makes payments in full according to the contract terms – because another creditor reports a problem.

Similarly, a customer might limit her charges and pay off her bill in full each month, but when she protested a $500 charge that she had not made, she could discover the impact of an arbitration clause. Such clauses can require customers to travel to distant locations, pay fees, and ultimately face an arbitrator who rules in favor of the credit card company 96 percent of the

---

[25] Id.

time.[26] Because of the fine print in her contract, she would have no recourse to the court system, no access to consumer protection laws, and no record of the decision making that cost her hundreds of dollars. The fine print contained in credit contracts can be devastating for even the most careful customer.

For some, Shakespeare's injunction that "neither a borrower nor a lender be" seems to be good policy. Just stay away from all debt and avoid the trouble. But this position simply ignores the central role that consumer credit has played in the basic functioning of modern, capitalist economies, especially since the 1920s. If every American heeded the call for total personal avoidance of debt, the macroeconomic consequences would be fearful.

Tellingly, hardly anyone suggests that Americans should adopt an analogous position with regard to tangible consumer goods. No one advocates that people who do not want their homes burned down should stay away from toasters, or that those who do not want their fingers and toes cut off should give up on mowing the lawn. Instead, product safety standards set the floor for all consumer products, and an active, competitive market revolves around the features consumers can see, such as price or convenience or, in some cases, even greater safety. To say that credit markets should follow a *caveat emptor* model is to ignore the success of the consumer goods market – and the pain inflicted by dangerous credit products.

Indeed, the pain imposed by a dangerous credit product is even more insidious than that inflicted by a malfunctioning kitchen appliance. If toasters are dangerous, they may burn down the homes of rich people or poor people, college graduates, or high school dropouts. But credit products are not nearly so egalitarian. Wealthy families can ignore the tricks and traps associated with credit card debt, secure in the knowledge that they will not need to turn to credit to see themselves through a rough patch. Their savings will protect them from medical expenses that exceed their insurance coverage or the effects of an unexpected car repair; credit cards are little more than a matter of convenience. If they are cheated by a credit card company, a well-placed phone call or a letter to a consumer advocate in the state attorney's general office will likely settle the matter. But working and middle-class families are far less insulated. For the family that lives closer to the economic margin, a credit card with an interest rate that unexpectedly escalates to 29.99 percent or misplaced trust in a broker who recommends a high-priced mortgage can push a family into a downward economic spiral from which it may never recover.

---

[26] Simone Baribeau, *Consumer Advocates Slam Arbitration*, Christian Science Monitor, (July 16, 2007) http://www.csmonitor.com/2007/0716/p13s01-wmgn.htm.

To be sure, creating safer marketplaces is not about protecting consumers from all possible bad decisions. Instead, it is about making certain that the products themselves do not become the source of the trouble. This means that terms hidden in the fine print or obscured with incomprehensible language, unexpected terms, reservation of all power to the seller with nothing left for the buyer, and similar tricks and traps have no place in a well-functioning market.

SOLUTIONS THAT MADE THE PROBLEM WORSE

Credit products are marked by the fact that they are typically complex, that they pit a one-time player against a million-time player, and that innovation is relatively quick and cheap. Because of these factors, private solutions to rate products or warn of dangers, such as *Consumer Reports* or *Car & Driver*, which effectively redress asymmetries of information for consumers of manufactured goods, confront serious difficulties. By the time any rating agency can work through a complex financial contract and rate it, the lender can shift to new terms. Customers using rating agencies, moreover, typically struggle to identify which rated products correspond to the loan products they are considering. In effect, the consumers choose between products with terms and conditions that they are unlikely to understand from sellers who know precisely how to exploit this lack of understanding.[27]

The deregulated credit market has produced two innovations that would seem to correct for these market imperfections – new financial intermediaries, including mortgage brokers and debt counselors, and policies that purport to "disclose" the key terms of loan products. Many observers within the financial industry confidently predicted that these innovations would solve the informational challenges posed by loan complexity. Rather than address the structural problems that have come to bedevil the consumer credit market in the decades since deregulation, however, both innovations have only made those problems worse.

THE DANGEROUS HELPER

According to economic theory, a complex market will soon develop experts who will sell their services to unsophisticated players to help them navigate the complexity. Real estate agents, for example, not only market houses, but also help consumers learn about the additional services, such as title

---

[27] Examples of this exploitation are discussed in greater detail at *infra* note __ and accompanying text.

insurance and flood insurance. At its libertarian extreme, the argument posits that government need not furnish any market regulations for even the most complicated markets. Thus there would be no need for food safety or drug regulations because buyers would insist on third-party certifiers to validate the safety of any purchase of food or drugs. In the consumer credit arena, the theory of expert helpers has been tested. Here market complexity has yielded faithless agents – and another chance to fleece the consumer.

Recognizing their limited ability to understand complex financial documents, some consumers understandably have looked for outside help. In the mortgage market, for example, many consumers responded to the pitches from mortgage brokers, whose advertisements promise "a friend to help you find the best possible mortgage," "someone on your side," who has "access to thousands of mortgages with a single phone call." When prospective homeowners or current owners who wish to refinance do call a mortgage broker, they may find a responsible, reputable intermediary who will guide them through a dangerous thicket. But consumers are just as likely to encounter an unscrupulous agent with no sense of professional ethics, who pursues only short-term economic advantage, taking what amounts to bribes from mortgage companies to steer clients into unnecessarily high-priced mortgages, all the while assuring them that the offerings represent the best possible deal. For example, a family that might qualify for a 6.5 percent fixed-rate, 30-year mortgage could easily end up with an 8.5 percent mortgage because their broker has pocketed a fee (what the industry calls a "yield service premium," or YSP) from the mortgage company to place the higher-priced loan.

Despite the characterization of YSPs by one Fannie Mae vice president as "lender kickbacks,"[28] the practice of taking these fees is legal. Congress has refused to regulate mortgage brokers. Proposals to ban bribe-taking, to establish minimum responsible practices, or to register all brokers have been met with an outcry from brokers and have died quiet deaths. It is no surprise then that mortgage brokers originate more than half of all mortgage loans, particularly at the low end of the credit market.[29] YSPs are present in 85 percent to 90 percent of subprime mortgages, which implies that brokers are needlessly pushing tens of thousands of clients into more expensive products. The costs are staggering: Fannie Mae estimates that fully 50 percent of those who were sold ruinous subprime mortgages would have qualified

---

[28] James Carr and Lopa Koluri, *Predatory Lending: An Overview*, at 13 Fannie Mae Foundation (2001).

[29] James Carr and Lopa Koluri, *Predatory Lending: An Overview*, at 13 Fannie Mae Foundation (2001).

for prime-rate loans.[30] A study by the Department of Housing and Urban Development revealed that one in nine middle-income families (and one in fourteen upper-income families) who refinanced a home mortgage ended up with a high-fee, high-interest subprime mortgage.[31] Of course, YSPs are not confined to subprime mortgages. Pushing a family that qualifies for a 6.5 percent loan into an 8.5 percent loan and pocketing the difference will cost the family tens of thousands of dollars, but it will not show up in anyone's statistics on subprime lending. Legal scholar Howell Jackson has demonstrated that across a wide range of loan products, transactions involving mortgage brokers resulted in substantially higher costs to consumers.[32]

The lack of transparency and the strategies of deception fit neatly into Professor Stiglitz's typology of regulation, once again underlining the need for effective regulation in the consumer credit area. The incentive structure within mortgage brokerages constitutes a badly designed institutional system. In Professor Benkler's conceptualization, the regulatory – or deregulatory – system encouraged short-term commissions at the expense of lenders, borrowers, and even the long-term reputations of mortgage brokers. The damage continues to ricochet through the housing market and the national economy, as it threatens to bring down financial institutions around the world.

In addition to mortgage brokers, consumer credit counselors have also positioned themselves as helpers in the financial markets. These experts, who circle families in financial trouble, have also been beset by scandal. Numerous ostensibly nonprofit agencies that advertise "Christian Counseling" or "Family Services" have been unmasked by the IRS as predators, enriching themselves at the expense of the consumers who turn to them for help.[33] Disreputable counselors have squeezed the last remaining assets from families. Some suggest they take second or third mortgages on their homes to pay credit card debts – a move that later costs them their homes. Others suggest debt consolidation loans secured by their homes, a move that increases total credit costs and again often costs families their homes. Those without homes are often encouraged to pay certain credit card companies – the

---

[30] James Carr and Lopa Koluri, *Predatory Lending: An Overview*, at 7 Fannie Mae Foundation (2001).

[31] HUD, *Unequal Burden*. To be sure, subprime lenders have focused more of their efforts among poorer homeowners; 26 percent of low-income homeowners end up with predatory refinancing, more than twice the rate of moderate-income families.

[32] Howell Jackson and Laurie Burlingame, *Kickbacks or Compensation: The Case of Yield Spread Premiums*, 12 Stanford J. Law, Bus. & Fin. 289 (2007).

[33] See, *e.g.*, *IRS Ends Exempt Status for Some Credit Counselors*, New York Times (May 16, 2006), available at http://www.nytimes.com/2006/05/16/business/16debt.html.

companies that pay the credit counseling agencies. With the rise in mortgage foreclosures, the currently popular scam involves tricking people into
conveying away their homes and stripping the little equity that may remain,
costing consumers their last opportunity to save their homes.[34] The impact
of counseling scams has not spread as far as the impact of mortgage brokerage deception, but the structural problems are parallel.

The unregulated market was supposed to produce independent experts to
guide one-time players and those with less sophistication. Instead, antireg-
ulatory zeal has added new barkers to the financial services carnival, new
forms of bait and switch, new strategies for preying on consumers.

THE DISCLOSURE HOAX

Many policy analysts and politicians who acknowledge the evidence of
fundamental asymmetries of information in the consumer credit markets
have a ready solution for this market failure: disclosure. If people truly
know about the risks, tricks, traps, and so on, these observers argue, then
they legitimately must accept the consequences if their expectations end up
not getting met. Further regulation is unnecessary, and the free market can
proceed without regulation.

Truth-in-Lending laws from the early 1970s were based on this principle: get good, comparative information into the hands of consumers and
consumers will generally make wise choices. The principle here is similar
to that animating a good deal of securities regulation – put the focus of
the government on policing flows of commercial information. Mandating
disclosure to consumers represents a fairly unobjectionable regulatory goal.
Requiring lenders to price all similar loans on the same terms – for example,
an Annual Percentage Rate, or APR – surely makes comparison shopping
easier. But relying exclusively on the disclosure option has significant, structural drawbacks.

Within the contemporary consumer credit markets, a great deal of disclosure is simply ineffective. Mortgage-loan documents, payday-loan papers,
car-loan, and credit card terms – all these and other lending products have
become long and jargon-filled, often proving entirely incomprehensible to
those with law degrees – much less to those whose specialty is not reading legal documents. This generalization does not represent a subjective

---

[34] Gretchen Morgenson and Vijaj, *New Scheme Preys on Desperate Homeowners*, New
York Times (July 3, 2007), available at ⟨http://www.nytimes.com/2007/07/03/business/
03home.html.

claim of the consumer advocacy movement. In a recent memo aimed at bank executives, the vice president of the business consulting firm Booz Allen Hamilton observed that most bank products are "too complex for the average consumer to understand."[35] The Federal Trade Commission (FTC) reiterated this point in a recent study of the mortgage market, concluding that "[b]oth prime and subprime borrowers failed to understand key loan terms when viewing current disclosures."[36] The General Accounting Office (GAO) reached a similar conclusion about credit card holders, noting that card issuers "buried important information in text, failed to group and label related materials, and used small print." "As a result," said the GAO, many credit card holders "failed to understand key aspects of their cards."[37]

For consumers willing to wade through paragraph after paragraph replete with obscure terms like "LIBOR" and "Cash Equivalent Transactions," lenders have built in enough surprises to frustrate even the most dogged readers. So, for example, after forty-seven lines of text explaining how interest rates will be calculated, one prominent credit card company concludes, "We reserve the right to change the terms at any time for any reason."[38] Evidently, all the earlier convoluted language was in the agreement only to obscure the bottom line: The company will charge whatever it wants whenever it wants. In effect, such text is an effort for lenders to have it both ways. Lenders won't be bound by any term or price that becomes inconvenient for them, but they will expect their customers to be bound by whatever terms the lenders want to enforce – and to have the courts back them up in case of any dispute.

Other creditors have their own techniques for disclosing without disclosing. Payday lenders offer consumers a friendly hand when they are short of cash. But hidden in the tangle of disclosures is a staggering interest rate. For example, buried back in a page of disclosures for one lender (rather than on the fee page, where the customer might expect to see it) was the note that the interest rate on the offered loan was 485.45 percent.[39] For some

---

[35] Booz Allen Hamilton, Inc., *Innovating Customer Service: Retail Banking's New Frontier,* Strategy + Business, Knowledge@Wharton (December 22, 2006) (quoting Alex Kandybin, Vice President, Booz Allen Hamilton, Inc.).

[36] *Improving Consumer Mortgage Disclosures: An Empirical Assessment of Current and Prototype Disclosure Forms,* Federal Trade Commission Bureau of Economics Staff Report ES-1 (June 2007).

[37] United States General Accounting Office, *Credit Cards Increased Complexity in Rates and Fees Heightens Need for More Effective Disclosures to Consumers* 1 (September 2006).

[38] First BankCard offer. Copy on file.

[39] *Report on Predatory Lending Practices Directed at Members of the Armed Forces and Their Dependents,* Department of Defense, August 10, 2006.

families, the rates run even higher. In transactions recently documented by the Center on Responsible Lending, a $300 loan cost one family $2,700, while another borrowed $400, paid back $3,000, and was being hounded by the payday lender for $1,200 per month when the family gave up and filed for bankruptcy.[40] In total, the cost to American families of payday lending is estimated to be $4.2 billion dollars a year[41] – all from contracts that carry the full panoply of legally required disclosures.[42]

The disclosure paradigm also assumes that the term under consideration can be explained in a comprehensible manner. Double-cycle billing and trailing-cycle billing are tricking forms of billing that increase yield for the lenders by forcing customers to pay interest on amounts they have not borrowed. They are so complex that even senior bank loan officers sometimes struggle to convey how they are calculated. Describing them to a consumer – particularly to a consumer who has no experience with any other mathematical formula for calculating interest payments – is unlikely to produce much reasoned understanding.

Even clauses that are comprehensible on their face carry hidden meanings that many consumers would never grasp. Arbitration clauses, for example, may look benign to the customer, but their point is often to permit the lender to escape the reach of class-action lawsuits. This exemption allows lenders to skirt the disciplinary impact of tort liability by imposing a collective action problem. If a given lender repeatedly breaks the law, but the amounts at stake for any given customer are small – say, generally under $500 – few customers would ever bother to sue. Moreover, recent data about arbitration suggests pervasive conflicts of interest. Arbitrators, who are keenly aware that credit card issuers keep track of how they rule, and that systematically avoid assessors adjudged too customer-friendly, rule in favor of the lenders in 96 percent of the cases.[43] A state Supreme Court judge who trained as an arbitrator after his retirement was appalled by what he discovered, denouncing arbitration as "collection agencies to extract the last drop of

---

[40] *Pentagon Finds Predatory Lending Harming Troops*, Center for Responsible Lending (August 11, 2006).

[41] http://www.responsiblelending.org/issues/payday/.

[42] The Department of Defense identified payday lending as such a serious problem for those in military service that it noted that the industry "impaired military readiness." Report on Predatory Lending Practices Directed at Members of the Armed Forces and Their Dependents, Department of Defense, August 10, 2006. In fact, the practices were so outrageous that Congress banned all companies from charging military people more than 36 percent interest. This change in the law will protect military families from payday lenders, but it will leave all other families subject to the same predatory practices.

[43] Simone Baribeau, *Consumer Advocates Slam Arbitration*, Christian Science Monitor, (July 16, 2007) http://www.csmonitor.com/2007/0716/p13s01-wmgn.htm.

blood from desperate debtors."[44] But a five-word "take our disputes to arbitration" clause conveys none of this to the typical borrower.

Finally, it is worth pausing to observe that the consumer's time is not free. People have jobs and families, homework to check, and laundry to fold. A consumer with three credit cards, a car loan, a mortgage, an insurance contract, a checking account, a 401(k) and a passbook savings account cannot master the details of each account – and the details of its close competitors – without investing hours and hours of scarce time. Lenders, by contrast, can hire a team of lawyers to draft the terms that most favor the lender, and then spread the costs of such legerdemain across millions of transactions. In the midst of busy lives, few consumers will read complex disclosures – a fact that permits lenders to impose their own terms on consumers with no loss of business or other punishment in the marketplace.

Credit card contracts display much of what is wrong with the theory of disclosure in an unregulated market. According to the *Wall Street Journal*, in the early 1980s the typical credit card contract was a page long; by the early 2000s, that contract had grown to more than thirty pages of tricks, traps, and unreadable prose.[45] The contracts scrupulously follow Truth-in-Lending requirements, but the larding in of pages and pages of incomprehensible text have turned disclosure into a weapon to be used against consumers.

Can disclosure be made better? Of course it can. But disclosure has limits in its capacity to balance badly unbalanced borrower–lender negotiations.

DESIGNING BETTER REGULATION: LESSONS FROM CONSUMER CREDIT

By using consumer credit as a case study, it is possible to identify some of the critical system errors in the mix of outdated regulation, weak regulation, and deregulation.

SCATTERED FENCE POSTS DON'T MAKE A FENCE

Traditionally states bore the primary responsibility for protecting their citizens from unscrupulous lenders by imposing usury caps and other credit regulations on all companies doing business locally. Although states still play some role, particularly in the regulation of real-estate transactions

---

[44] Richard Neely, *Arbitration and the Godless Bloodsuckers*, The West Virginia Lawyer 12 (September/October 2006).

[45] Mitchell Pacelle, *Putting Pinch on Credit Card Users*, Wall Street Journal (July 12, 2004) (citing industry consultant Duncan MacDonald, formerly a lawyer for the credit card division of Citigroup Inc.).

and payday lending, their primary tool – interest rate regulation – has been effectively destroyed for any national credit card issuer. Today, under federal law, any lender that gets a national bank charter can locate its operations in a state with high usury rates (e.g., South Dakota or Delaware), then export that state's interest rate caps (or no caps at all) to customers located all over the country. Numerous interest rate caps remain on the statute books of the various states, but making an end run around local usury law is now as easy as running around a single fencepost.[46]

Dividing power among various state and federal regulators not only creates enormous loopholes; it also triggers regulatory arbitrage. Regulators are acutely aware that if they push financial institutions too hard, those institutions will simply reincorporate in another guise under the umbrella of a different regulatory agency – or no regulatory agency at all. In recent years, for example, a number of credit unions have dissolved and reincorporated as state or national banks, precisely to employ a regulatory charter that would permit them more options to develop and market financial products. If regulated companies have the option to choose the regulators they want, many will invariably seek to game the system. Although speaking strictly off the record, the head of one federal agency publicly declared that she agreed with several consumer protection ideas, but that she could not adopt them or the banks she regulated would simply reincorporate under different federal or state charters.[47]

The current regulatory jumble creates another problem: Financial products are regulated based mainly on the identity of the issuer, rather than the nature of the product. As a result, any serious regulator can never throw a net over the whole problem. The subprime mortgage market provides a stunning example of the resulting fractured oversight. In 2006, for example, 23 percent of subprime mortgages were issued by regulated thrifts and banks. Another 25 percent were issued by bank holding companies, which were subject to different regulatory oversight through the federal system. But more than half – 52 percent, to be exact – of all subprime mortgages originated with companies with no federal supervision at all, primarily stand-alone mortgage brokers and finance companies.[48]

---

[46] In 2007, the Supreme Court took another step in the same direction in *Watters v. Wachovia*, 127 S. Ct. 1559 (2007), giving federal regulators the power to shut down state efforts to regulate mortgage lenders without providing effective federal regulation.

[47] The conversation, described as "off the record," took place in front of about a hundred people following a speech I had given.

[48] Greg Ip and Damian Paletta, *Regulators Scrutinized in Mortgage Meltdown*, Wall Street Journal A1 (March 22, 2007).

Regulation needs to match the consumer credit market, rather than the type of commercial institution that participates in that market. As lenders have consolidated and credit markets have expanded to assume truly continental proportions, the option to play off various state and federal regulators gives credit issuers multiple opportunities to probe every weakness in the regulatory fence. In a competitive credit market, exploiting the gaps in the regulatory system is just one more way to succeed.

EVERY TRIP TO THE LEGISLATURE IS COSTLY

In the nearly three decades since the effective deregulation of interest rates, almost any proposal to reform statutory regulation of financial products has been met by a torrent of industry lobbying that has swamped the best efforts of the consumer. As a result, even the most minimal reforms are blocked from becoming law. A few hearty souls have repeatedly introduced legislation to halt such practices, but with no well-financed groups supporting them, those bills rarely make it out of committee. For example, before the subprime mortgage crisis was full blown, Representatives Miller and Watt proposed modest limits on the mortgage market to rein in the most dangerous practices.[49] The bill attracted fifteen cosponsors, but it never made it out of committee. Over time, the consequences of this lopsided legislative situation have been stark. A decade ago mortgage-lender abuses were rare. Today, experts estimate that fraud and deception has stripped $9.1 billion in equity from homeowners,[50] particularly from elderly and working-class families.

Asymmetric political clout has also left important imprints on state usury laws. Although state usury laws have been largely overridden by credit card issuers through the use of nationally chartered financial institutions, such laws still govern the state-based payday loan industry. As a result, the financial industry has quietly and successfully encouraged state legislatures to rewrite their usury laws with two goals in mind. The first has been to raise usury limits to the point that even the most aggressive payday lenders face few limits on what rates they can charge. Mean usury caps rose from 36 percent APR in 1965 to 398 percent in 2007.[51] The second objective

---

[49] *HR 3974: The Prohibit Predatory Lending Act*, Miller (D-NC) & Watt (D-NC), fifteen cosponsors. Introduced 3/16/2004. *HR 1182: The Prohibit Predatory Lending Act*, Miller (D-NC), Watt (D-NC), Frank (D-MA) Introduced 3/9/2005. See links to the 108th & 109th on this page: http://www.responsiblelending.org/policy/congress/.

[50] http://www.responsiblelending.org/issues/mortgage/reports/page.jsp?itemID=31217189.

[51] Christopher Peterson, The Mythology of American Usury Law, at 27 (manuscript 2007).

was to redraft the usury statutes to obscure the increase in usury caps, primarily by allowing lenders to disclose their rates through convoluted, technical language that hides the actual rate.[52] So, for example, the Montana legislature amended its usury law so that, on first reading, it appears to cap finance charges at 25 percent, but it allowed complicated calculations mechanisms that created an effective cap of 652 percent APR, more than thirty times more.[53] The only explanation for this systematic distortion is that the industry, working through its legislative agents, hopes to fool voters into believing that the legislature has acted to protect them, whereas in fact it has eviscerated any meaningful protection.

The financial-services industry has cemented its stranglehold over credit regulation through assiduous cultivation of both political parties. Routinely one of the top three contributors to national political campaigns, the credit industry collectively gave $133 million over the past five years. Absent a dramatic reconfiguration of the country's political economy, the likelihood of statutory changes to develop meaningful oversight is vanishingly slim.[54]

MARKETS INNOVATE, BUT STATUTES REMAIN FROZEN IN TIME

During the late 1960s and 1970s, Congress moved the regulation of some aspects of consumer credit from the state to the federal level through a series of landmark bills that included Truth-in-Lending (TIL), Fair Credit Reporting, and antidiscrimination regulations. They helpfully instituted uniform application to large categories of consumer transactions, correcting some of the partial-fence problem. Unfortunately, these statutes, drafted forty years ago, tended to be highly specific about precisely what behavior is required or prohibited, so that they quickly became antiquated in a rapidly changing marketplace.

The specificity of these laws works against their effectiveness, trapping the regulations like flies in amber. For example, TIL specifies the information that must be revealed in a credit transaction, including the size of the typeface that lenders must use and how they must state interest rates. Such statutes inhibit some beneficial innovations (e.g., new ways of informing consumers) while failing to regulate dangerous innovations (e.g., the laws do not mandate explanations of negative amortization or disclosure of default rates on loans with low teaser rates that then adjust to much higher payments).

---

[52] id. at 22, Figure 1.
[53] Id. at 27.
[54] PoliticalMoneyLine (aggregating FEC data, run by Congressional Quarterly) http://www.fecinfo.com/cgi-win/x_sic.exe?DoFn=&all=1.

Worse yet, these generation-old regulations do not take any note of a slew of new loan features, such as universal default,[55] double-cycle billing,[56] or the capacity of lenders to change their terms with minimal notice.[57] Because financial products are subject to high levels of innovation, any new legislative constraints may well lead to similar regulatory disconnects.

LEGISLATORS ARE NOT EXPERTS

Because they are generalists, covering a multitude of criminal and civil matters, neither state nor federal legislators have time to develop much expertise in commercial products. They are like consumers: Credit is just one of many issues they need to think about. By contrast, people within the industry spend a career on a single kind of financial product – pension plans, mortgages, credit cards – and often in a single kind of institution – a thrift, a bank, a mortgage company.

The impediments to effective regulation are much like the impediment to fair contracts: The issues are complex, and a one-time player is up against a repeat player with highly specialized knowledge and substantial resources. As a result, industry innovations typically far outpace legislative attention, much less legislative control.

WITHOUT REGULATION, CONSUMERS HAVE LITTLE STRUCTURAL PROTECTION

Ironically, consumers are protected from dangerous physical products by a range of legal tools – tools that are not mirrored in the financial services industry. Long before the Consumer Product Safety Commission came into place, courts and legislators had expanded manufacturers' liability for consumer injuries. A movement that took hold in the early twentieth century made manufacturers of food, cars, and a host of other consumer goods liable if someone was injured by a defective product. The tort system was vigorous and innovative. As liability expanded, so did insurance. Ultimately, insurers took on the role of assuring that manufacturers and sellers followed best practices. The insurers' risk-management work left Americans with safer products.

---

[55] Universal default involves declaring a default against a customer who has made all payments on time because the customer defaulted or got into a dispute in another credit transaction.

[56] Double-cycle billing occurs when a lender charges retroactive interest on a balance that originally qualified for an interest-free grace period.

[57] Many credit cards reserve the right to change terms at any time for any reason – or for no reason at all.

By contrast, financial products are governed by contract law. Based on an early nineteenth century model of two fully informed parties with equal bargaining power who each work out terms of their agreement, contract law leaves little room for protection against terms in documents that the borrower has signed. Contract law explicitly makes disclaimers of liability for personal injury from defective products unenforceable,[58] thus leaving tort liability firmly in place regardless of what paper the consumer signed. But for purchasers of financial products, no such protection exists. With only the smallest exceptions, whatever the consumer signs will bind her into the future.

DIVIDED GOALS LEAVE CONSUMERS IN SECOND PLACE

At present, any new national regulation of financial products occurs through the indirect mechanism of the Federal Reserve, the Office of the Comptroller of the Currency (OCC), and the Office of Thrift Supervision. Each agency has some power to control certain forms of predatory lending. But their main mission is to protect the financial stability of banks and other financial institutions, not to protect consumers. As a result, they focus intently on bank profitability and the maintenance of sufficient capital reserves relative to outstanding loans, and far less on the financial impact that many of the products sold by the banks will have on consumers.

In fact, federal agencies face an inherent conflict. Each product that boosts profits for a financial institution helps the regulator meet its primary goal of assuring the safety and soundness of the financial institutions. Products that involve sharp business practices or are misleading to consumers may be very profitable to the banks, and hence may satisfy a regulator's prime directive.

Alan Greenspan faced this problem – and resolved it in favor of bank profitability. For several years while interest rates were falling, Chairman Greenspan had no advice for homeowners about the kinds of home mortgages they should carry. In a falling-rate environment, fixed-rate instruments were costly to consumers but profitable for the banks. Greenspan's silence might be excused if he had embraced the theory that individual families should not take on the risk of rate resets. But any such concerns Chairman Greenspan may have felt evidently dried up once interest rates were at their lowest possible point. In 2004, Chairman Greenspan urged American families to switch to variable-rate mortgages – just in time to

[58] UCC 2-719(3).

take on the costs of the inevitable rise in mortgage rates.[59] Once again, he advocated the action that was profitable for banks and costly to consumers. Chairman Greenspan protected – indeed, promoted – bank profitability at a cost of billions to consumers.

WHAT'S BAD FOR CONSUMERS CAN BE BAD FOR BUSINESS AS WELL

Both Professor Carpenter and Professor Stiglitz point out that regulation plays a crucial role in buttressing public confidence in markets. The converse helps illustrate their point. Without effective regulation, competitive pressures in the financial services industry have encouraged a race to the bottom. Ironically, this race harms consumers and prudent lenders alike, shaking public confidence as it threatens the very foundations of the financial system. The informal names that subprime mortgage industry insiders gave to exotic mortgage instruments signaled their risks: Liar's Loans (loans in which the borrower could claim an income, but never needed to document it); Teasers (also called 2-28s and 3-27s, reflecting two or three years of below-market payments that escalate wildly when the teaser period is over); and NegAms (low introductory payments that left the borrower owing more – not less – money after a couple of years of payments). All lenders knew the basic risks, but prudent lenders compete against imprudent lenders for capital and market share. High risk lenders could return staggeringly high profits, at least over the short run, and by the late 1990s and into the early years of the new millennium, investors seemed to have only a short-run mentality. Regulated lenders, such as banks and thrifts, found themselves competing for capital with unregulated or lightly regulated mortgage originators that were thinly capitalized and willing to bet heavily on a rising market. From the vantage point of a postcrisis world, the smart lenders were obviously those that shied away from risky lending, even at the cost of lost market share. But for otherwise prudent lenders who confronted impatient shareholders and an industry culture predicated on aggressiveness and quarterly returns, the impulse to join the fray was powerful indeed. Developments in the secondary and tertiary credit markets

---

[59] Remarks by Chairman Alan Greenspan, Understanding Household Debt Obligations, at the Credit Union National Association 2004 Governmental Affairs Conference, Washington, D.C. (February 23, 2004) ("American consumers might benefit if lenders provided greater mortgage product alternatives to the traditional fixed-rate mortgage . . . the traditional fixed-rate mortgage may be an expensive method of financing a home.") http://www.federalreserve.gov/boarddocs/speeches/2004/20040223/default.htm.

only intensified this tendency. With bond ratings agencies willing to anoint collateralized debt instruments with AAA assessments, even when the underlying loans reflected minimal due diligence and considerable risk, banks found themselves able to make it someone else's problem to worry about whether borrowers could actually repay those loans.

After the riskiest lenders had become the driving force behind the American consumer credit market, regulators finally began to worry about safety and soundness. By the fall of 2007, unprecedented profits for the nation's financial institutions ran into a wave of defaults and an associated credit crunch of historic proportions. The nation's regulators accordingly found themselves belatedly grappling with a series of interlocked, exceedingly complex financial crises that potentially threaten the solvency of numerous financial institutions. If lenders could conduct business without competing with companies whose business model is to mislead the customer, then the companies offering safer products would be more likely to flourish. Effective consumer regulations would level the playing field between responsible lenders and predatory, and innovation would be less likely to turn toward "Liar's Loans" and similar products.

The point has ample precedent. The Truth in Advertising Movement in the early twentieth century was led by reputable business firms.[60] Of course, they preferred the disciplinary action of self-regulation rather than governmental bureaucracy, but the idea took hold that reputable companies wanted insulation from competing with cheaters. This is also very much the argument that led meatpackers to support federal inspection of meat[61] and food producers to support the Food and Drug Act.[62] Clean business practices can be good for clean businesses.

A NEW APPROACH: FINANCIAL PRODUCTS SAFETY COMMISSION

The United States needs a refashioned regulatory system that corrects the flaws of the current system, a system that will help the market function well for borrowers and lenders. As the events of late 2007 suggest, when economic actors lose confidence in the financial markets, flows of credit can seize up. If financial products were subjected to the same routine safety

---

[60] Ed Balleisen, *Private Cops on the Fraud Beat: American Business Self-Regulation and Its Discontents, 1895–1932* (in submission 2008).

[61] E.g., Gabriel Kolko, *The Triumph of Conservatism* (1965); Morton Keller, *Affairs of State* (1977).

[62] Donna J. Wood, The Strategic Use of Public Policy: Business Support for the 1906 Food and Drug Act, *59 Business History Review 403*, 403–32 (Autumn 1985); Jack High and Clayton A. Coppin, Wiley and the Whiskey Industry: Strategic Behavior in the Passage of the Pure Food Act; *62 Business History Review* 286–309 (Summer 1988).

screening that now governs the sale of every toaster, washing machine, and child's car seat sold on the American market, innovation and competition would work for consumers, not against them.

The model for such safety regulation is the U.S. Consumer Product Safety Commission (CPSC), an independent health and safety regulatory agency founded in 1972 by the Nixon Administration. The CPSC's mission is to protect the American public from risks of injury and death from products used in the home, school, and in recreation.[63] The agency has the authority to develop uniform safety standards, order the recall of unsafe products, and ban products that pose unreasonable risks. In establishing the commission, Congress recognized that "the complexities of consumer products and the diverse nature and abilities of consumers using them frequently result in an inability of users to anticipate risks and to safeguard themselves adequately."[64]

The evidence clearly shows that CPSC is a cost-effective agency. Since it was established, product-related death and injury rates in the United States have decreased substantially. The CPSC estimates that just three safety standards for three products alone – cigarette lighters, cribs, and baby walkers – save more than $2 billion annually. The annual estimated savings is more than CPSC's total cumulative budget since its inception.

Like its counterparts for ordinary consumer products, a Financial Product Safety Commission (FPSC) would be charged with responsibility:

- To establish guidelines for consumer disclosure
- To collect and report data about the uses of different financial products
- To review new financial products for safety
- To require modification of dangerous products before they can be marketed to the public

The agency could review mortgages, credit cards, car loans, and a number of other financial products. It could also exercise jurisdiction over other financial products, such as life insurance and annuity contracts. In effect, the FPSC would evaluate these products to eliminate the hidden tricks and traps that make some of them far more dangerous than others. It could provide a regulatory floor that all companies would be required to comply with if they wanted to issue financial products.

The FPSC would promote the benefits of free markets by assuring that consumers can enter credit markets with confidence that the products they

---

[63] "Saving Lives and Keeping Families Safe," U.S. Consumer Product Safety Commission 2002 Performance Plan, April 2001.

[64] "Just Be More Careful?" by Gail Javitt and Susan DeFrancesco, *Legal Times* (June 18, 2001).

purchase meet minimum safety standards. No one expects every customer
to become an engineer to buy a toaster that does not burst into flames, or
analyze complex diagrams to buy an infant car seat that doesn't collapse on
impact. By the same reasoning, no customer should be forced to read the
fine print in thirty-plus-page credit card contracts to determine whether
the company claims it can seize property paid for with the credit card or
raise the interest rate by more than twenty points if a credit card customer
gets into a dispute with the car lender.

Instead, an FPSC would develop precisely such expertise in consumer
financial products. A commission would be able to collect data about which
financial products are least understood, what kinds of disclosures are most
effective, and which products are most likely to result in consumer default.
The investigatory dimension of an FPSC could facilitate monitoring of the
industry by nongovernmental organizations. With uniform reporting and
limitations on a lender's ability to change product terms every few weeks,
groups such as Consumers Union could offer meaningful comparisons that
could help drive greater market efficiency. An agency might open up the
possibility of private enforcement through the judicial process. Professor
Freyer's explanation of the iterative process between antitrust regulation
and private market enforcement could be replicated in the financial services
field, with regulation facilitating its private-enforcement alternative.

With better information and greater institutional expertise, an FPSC
could develop nuanced regulatory responses; some terms might be banned
altogether, whereas others might be permitted only with clearer disclosure.
A commission might promote uniform disclosures that make it easier to
compare products from one issuer to another and to discover conflicts of
interest on the part of a mortgage broker or seller of a currently loosely
regulated financial product.

With every agency, the fear of regulatory capture is ever-present. As Professors Moss and Oye observed, regulatory capture has been the constant
complaint about current regulatory efforts and a key device for undermining confidence in any form of regulation. No one's confidence in regulation
is boosted by the current Consumer Product Safety Commission, which is
badly weakened by years of budget cutting and staff attrition, and by the
leadership of a chairwoman constantly on the lookout for ways the commission can do less.[65] When examples of regulatory capture and outright failure
abound, it may seem aggressively optimistic to propose a new regulatory
agency.

[65] http://www.nytimes.com/2007/10/30/washington/30consumer.html.
http://www.nytimes.com/2007/11/04/opinion/04sun1.html.

But in a marketplace with little coherent, consumer-oriented regulation of any kind, a commission with power to act is far more valuable than any of the available alternatives. Whether it is housed in a current agency or stands alone, the opportunity to concentrate the review of financial products in a single location, with a focus on the safety of the products as consumers use them, creates a structure for beneficial regulation. Instead of asking whether regulation might fail, the far better question is to ask how it might succeed. Professor Stiglitz hypothesizes that divided regulatory authority and multiple regulators might prevent capture, a theory that is not supported by evidence from the consumer credit field. But his central insight about the benefits of multiplicity might work along another dimension. A regulatory commission that regulates a single group with convergent interests may have great difficulty withstanding the constant pressure to bend regulations to the benefit of the group rather than the public. In the area of financial services, however, many different kinds of lenders specialize in different lending products – mortgages, car loans, credit cards, payday lending, title loans, student loans, etc. To some degree, they are cross-product competitors who recognize that a dollar used to pay off the mortgage is a dollar not available to pay the car loan – and that aggressive payday loans undermine the ability of the borrower to pay anyone. With different groups to regulate, the agency may be under enough competing pressures that no one group will be able to control the agency's agenda.

THE NEXT STEP: A RESEARCH AGENDA

As Moss and Oey point out, for decades, the academic literature on regulation has focused almost exclusively on the failure of various agencies to accomplish all that they might have. The criticisms of agency action are so well known that questions about how to design effective agencies have been squeezed out of the discourse. If a Financial Product Safety Commission moves from an academic idea to a serious legislative proposal, a new set of scholarly investigations could be critical to the design and implementation of such an agency.

- Confront regulatory capture head-on. What can we surmise about the conditions for capture that make it more or less likely? Can we improve on the Stiglitz model? If, for example, the regulations are likely to vary across industry groups and the industries to be regulated have hostile interests, can the energy of the regulated industries themselves be harnessed to avoid regulatory capture by any single group?

- How might a Financial Product Safety Commission intersect with self-regulation? Regulatory oversight is expensive and requires detailed expertise. Could industry groups offer meaningful self-regulation that would exempt them from specific government rules? How could such self-regulation be promoted and monitored? Study of the National Association of Securities Dealers (now the Financial Industry Regulatory Authority) or similar groups might provide some clues.
- What are the design levers, as Benkler describes them, that could be used to align the interests of lenders with the borrowers' needs for safe products? How can the emerging literature on behavioural economics best be used in the design of minimally invasive and maximally productive regulatory schemes?
- What role can consumer groups play in shaping a regulatory agenda? Consumer advocacy groups currently have extensive expertise both about the industry operations and their impact on families, raising the question of how their expertise might be brought into formal consideration for an agency. To what extent can such groups be used to counter the much-discussed regulatory capture?
- How can the current overlapping and inconsistent issuer-based regulatory scheme best be resolved? Should an FPSC be the exclusive source of product regulation, or can other forms of regulatory authority sensibly coexist? Should FPSC set only a regulatory floor, leaving the states, for example, to impose more extensive regulations to protect their own citizens, or should the federal rules be exclusive?
- Historical studies of the Consumer Product Safety Commission and other consumer-oriented commissions, such as the Food and Drug Administration, the Food Safety and Inspection Service of the Department of Agriculture, and the Occupational Health and Safety Administration of the Department of Labor can offer powerful guidance. What can be learned from their greatest successes and from their worst failures?
- Comparative studies of financial product regulation in other industrialized countries can expand our vision. If we think of such exercises as experiments, what regulatory decisions offered the best consumer protection while advancing credit markets?

For a generation, discussion of regulation has centered on how to cut, trim, eliminate, obliterate, or otherwise reduce its impact. It is time to ask the next generation of questions about how best to regulate in areas that require more regulation.

CONCLUSION

The consumer credit market illustrates the terrible consequences of a failure to develop meaningful regulations. Families are harmed. Neighborhoods are damaged. Responsible lenders are pushed into risky practices or driven out of the marketplace altogether. No amount of competition is likely to push the market toward easier-to-understand, simpler, safer products. Perhaps of greatest concern, given the stakes, is that the absence of a sensible regulatory policy has placed the structural stability of the financial system under serious strain.

Market imperfections in the consumer financial services industry call for a classic regulatory reliance on empowered government employees. Regulation can make up for market defects, leveling the playing field between borrower and lender. It can move product innovation away from tricks and traps and toward features that would increase consumer value.

Each instance of regulation is embedded in its own facts. The case study from consumer credit offers ideas, some of which may generalize to other areas and some of which may not. But whether this chapter stands for larger points about regulation or not, it should make clear that in this important market, a growing number of consumers have fallen victim to the worst predators. Consumer credit is now the poster child to explain the need for revitalized regulation.

Product safety standards will not fix every problem associated with consumer credit. It is possible to stuff a toaster with dirty socks and start a fire, and, even with safety standards, it will remain possible to get burned by credit products. Some people will not even have to try very hard. But safety standards can make a critical difference for millions of families. Families who were steered into higher-priced mortgages solely because the broker wanted a higher fee would have a greater chance of buying – and keeping – a home. A student who wanted a credit card with a firm credit limit – not an approval for thousands of dollars more of credit and higher fees and interest – could stay out of trouble. An older person who needed a little cash to make it until her Social Security check arrived would have a manageable loan, not one that would quickly escalate into thousands of dollars in fees.

Personal responsibility will always play a critical role in dealing with credit, just as personal responsibility remains a central feature in the safe use of any other product. But a Financial Product Safety Commission could eliminate some of the most egregious tricks and traps in the credit industry. And for every family that avoids a trap or does not get caught by a trick, that would be regulation that works.

Would Congress ever set up such an agency? The financial product industry has demonstrated its political muscle – buying the 2005 bankruptcy amendments, rewriting state interest rate legislation to allow for massive increases in allowable effective rates and support for a growing payday lending industry, and persuading its own regulatory agency to intervene on behalf of lenders when they are sued by consumers for deceptive practices. The consumer credit industry stands as a powerful example of special interest influence. Any change opposed by the lending industry would seem to have no prospect for survival.

But as Professors Moss and Oey so eloquently remind us, the political landscape of the past three decades has suddenly altered. The scope of the financial crisis engulfing the country is precisely the kind of environment in which aroused public attention can overcome the concentrated opposition of the financial industry. In effect, this may be the regulatory moment for consumer credit. If so, it is important to use the moment wisely. A commission requires only one trip to the legislature to become law. Once the commission is set up, it continues to innovate as needed. In effect, unlike many financial product laws that become useless in the face of product innovation and changing consumer practices, the commission can adapt to new information and can develop new tools. A fight for a Financial Product Safety Commission might be a fight worth having.

THIRTEEN

Origins and Regulatory Consequences
of the Subprime Crisis

Barry Eichengreen

James Tobin would have been saddened by the subprime crisis, but he would not have been surprised.[1] He would have been saddened by the human consequences, not so much for investment strategists forced to forgo their bonuses as families unable to keep their homes. He would have been further saddened that economic analysis had not done more to warn of financial risks so that policymakers could have avoided those social costs. But he would not have been surprised that financial markets, left to their own devices, produced unforeseen and socially suboptimal outcomes.

At the same time, Tobin would have been reluctant to move too far in the direction of re-regulation. He appreciated the role of financial markets in resource allocation and in enhancing the productive efficiency of the economy. He emphasized the role of finance, and financial innovation, in mobilizing resources for the investment that undergirds economic growth and rising living standards. He understood the limits of our knowledge about how markets work and that interventions could have unintended consequences. He would have urged regulators to proceed cautiously. He would have cautioned against killing the golden goose.[2]

He also studied these problems for the better part of fifty years. We by comparison have had considerably less time to assess the causes and consequences of the current crisis. Not only do we lack the perspective that time and distance create, but there is the fact that the crisis continues

[1] Prepared for a conference of the Tobin Project, "Toward a New Theory of Financial Regulation," White Oak Conference and Residency Center, Yulee, Florida, February 1–3, 2008. Financial support was provided by the Coleman Fung Risk Management Center at the University of California, Berkeley.
[2] Recall that, in the context of international financial markets, Tobin advocated taxing, not regulating, much less prohibiting, international capital flows. His proposal was for a small tax to slow down international capital flows, thereby balancing the private benefits with what he saw as both private and social costs, not for draconian regulation to stop them.

to unfold. Since the Tobin Project held its conference in January 2008, there has been the government-brokered acquisition of Bear Stearns by J. P. Morgan in March, the failure of the IndyMac Bank in July, the extension of an emergency credit line to Freddie Mac and Fannie Mae by the Federal Reserve System and the U.S. Treasury in August, and the bankruptcy of Lehman Brothers, bailout of AIG and failure of Washington Mutual in September – to name only selected "highlights." What was known in January as the "subprime crisis," reflecting the perception that problems were centered in the market for securities backed by subprime mortgages, is now referred to as the "credit crisis," indicating the extent to which problems have spilled over to credit markets and the economy generally. Nor is there any question that the crisis will continue to evolve in the interregnum between when this chapter is completed and the volume containing it appears.

Hitting such a rapidly moving target can be an all-but-impossible task. I attempt to make that task tractable in this chapter by focusing on the origins of the crisis in the market for mortgage-backed securities and on its implications for regulatory reform. Other issues like the mechanisms through which the crisis spread to the markets in asset-backed commercial paper, credit card receivables, and student loans and the efforts of monetary and fiscal policymakers to limit the macroeconomic damage are left for another day.[3]

I. Roots of the Crisis: The Originate and Distribute Model

Over the past twenty years, large banks have refined strategies of securitizing credit – that is, they originate loans or purchase them from specialized brokers and transfer them to a special purpose vehicle, which then packages them into collateralized debt obligations (CDOs) for sale to other investors.[4] Some commentators have argued that it was this business model that set the stage for the crisis. Securitization, they argue, weakens the incentive for the originator to assess the credit quality of those loans, relative to the once-upon-a-time world in which banks held their loans on their balance sheets.[5] As a result, the stability of the credit markets has come to hinge on the acumen of investors, who lack the specialized expertise needed to

---

[3] I take a first stab at these other issues in Eichengreen (2008).

[4] For more on mortgage brokers see Section 2 below.

[5] Special-purpose vehicles then signaled credit quality by dividing the streams of income from the underlying mortgages into tranches (senior, mezzanine, and junior) that absorb default losses on the entire mortgage pool in lexicographic order and using quantitative models to predict default probabilities. These procedures made it possible to market the senior tranches to regulated investors and those with strict covenants.

undertake such scrutiny of creditworthiness. Thus, although securitizaton spreads risk, it also has a tendency to raise it (creating more risk to be spread and ultimately borne by someone).

In principle, even banks that transfer loans off balance sheet will pay a price in reputational damage if they fail to adequately monitor those loans or systematically overstate their quality. Those who buy the nonperforming CDOs will blame the bank that set up the special purpose vehicle. But it is evident that this reputational mechanism is insufficient to ensure adequate monitoring.[6] Some would say that this situation reflects problems of incentive alignment within financial institutions: The employment relationship creates incentives for decision makers to gamble with the firm's reputation. Investment analysts and financial engineers change jobs and employers. They thus have an incentive to take risks with the firm's reputation, since a good outcome means larger bonuses while a bad outcome tarnishes the reputation of an institution with whom they will no longer have a relationship. One can make similar arguments about the incentives provided by the structure of compensation within corporate America. A CEO who encourages risky behavior will be paid handsomely if the bet pays off and will be paid less than zero if it does not (in other words, the distribution of returns is asymmetric).[7]

Observations like these have led some observers to recommend that originators should be required to hold a specific minimum share of the securities on their own balance sheets. Banks might be required to hold, say, 20 percent of each CDO (or 20 percent of each CDO tranche). This proposal would, at least in part, restore the traditional financial incentive of a bank that held the loans it originated to carefully scrutinize their credit quality.

By design, such a reform would be a step back in the direction of good old-fashioned banking, in which institutions making loans would have less scope for diversifying their risks.[8] One should recall, therefore, that the old model had limitations. It left banks vulnerable to housing-market downturns, in turn rendering them more cautious about extending housing finance and raising the price of the latter. Reforms along these lines would thus solve problems in securities markets at the cost of heightening risk in the banking system and raising costs to consumers.

One can also question whether regulation of this form would be effective. In particular, one would expect banks to seek ways of hedging the additional

---

[6] As acknowledged by Bernanke (2007a).

[7] Indeed, recent severance packages suggest that CEOs are handsomely compensated even when the bet doesn't pay off.

[8] The "good-old-fashioned banking" line is from Alastair Darling (see below).

exposure that regulators were attempting to force them to hold. They could take offsetting short positions in other assets whose returns were correlated with their own CDOs, use credit derivatives markets, or have their own financial engineers design and sell instruments tailored to offset the associated risks. To the extent they succeeded, incentives would not differ very much from the current situation.

The counterargument is that hedging is not free; to the extent that such offsetting operations are costly, there would still be changes in behavior. But those large investment and commercial banks, which did in fact retain substantial fractions of the CDOs and other residential-mortgage-backed securities that they issued, did not obviously behave more prudently in 2006–2007. A number of financial institutions, from Citibank to Merrill Lynch, ended up holding a large fraction of those securities themselves, either because they found them hard to sell or because in order to do so they were obliged to provide liquidity insurance – effectively, to buy them back in the event of difficulties.[9] The fact of these actual and contingent holdings does not appear to have sufficed to induce more conservative behavior.[10]

II. Agency Problems in the Mortgage Broking Industry

A second change in the structure of the home loan market, in addition to the fact that banks funding loans do not hold mortgages, is that many banks do not deal with the homeowner. Instead, banks outsource dealings with homeowners to independent mortgage brokers who receive fee income from both the borrower and lender. Because the broker does not look forward to a thirty-year relationship with the borrower, his incentive to provide the best possible information and advice may be less than in the case of an old-fashioned bank that brokers, services, and holds the loan. Outsourcing the broking function also creates principal–agent problems for the banks, which may find it more difficult to maintain loan documentation standards when the assessment of loan applications does not rest in the hands of their own employees. The result has been an explosion of inadequately documented and ultimately unsustainable subprime loans that have left in their wake defaulted mortgages, foreclosed houses, disappointed families, and nonperforming securities.[11]

---

[9] Interestingly, they often had better success in selling the high-risk and mezzanine tranches of CDO issues, for which there was a strong demand from hedge funds, than the relatively low-risk tranche.
[10] See also Section 4 below.
[11] Industry sources suggest that nearly two-thirds of subprime mortgages in 2006 were originated by brokers (Joint Economic Committee 2007).

Mortgage companies specializing in such brokerage have been a feature of the American financial landscape for more than a century.[12] In other words, it is not likely that policymakers can put this genie back in the bottle. Officials are therefore left to contemplate strengthened regulation and tougher legal liability. The argument for better regulating mortgage broking is mainly an argument for regulation on consumer-protection grounds – that the state must hold brokers to minimum standards when communicating and explaining mortgage provisions and alternatives to their clients. A modest first step would be self-regulation by the mortgage-broking industry, along the lines of the initiatives discussed by Balleisen's chapter in this volume. More ambitiously, Congress could adopt legislation that subjects brokers to agency obligations – thus giving them a fiduciary responsibility to their clients – and that requires them to disclose their fees so that their clients can help enforce those obligations.[13] In a similar vein, the Joint Economic Committee has suggested that the federal government subject brokers to the provisions of the Truth-in-Lending Act, which would establish their fiduciary responsibility for their customers and make them subject to federal penalties.[14]

The issue for systemic stability, namely that brokers who originate loans should furnish enough documentation to enable banks and other entities providing funding to know what they are purchasing, relates to the banks' basic business practices. Concerns about these practices are appropriately addressed by strengthening supervision and regulation of the banks that fund the loans originated by mortgage companies and brokers.

III. Capital Inadequacy

By applying minimum capital requirements to bank balance sheets and requiring more capital protection of riskier assets, the 1988 Basel Accord encouraged banks to shift risky activities off-balance sheet. The growth of structured investment vehicles (SIVs) and conduits was no coincidence, in other words.

---

[12] Snowden (1995) provides a very interesting account of the agricultural mortgage boom and bust of the 1880s and 1890s that emphasizes principal-agent problems between the Western mortgage agents and companies identifying potential borrowers and broking the loans and the Eastern insurance companies ultimately holding the mortgage-backed securities. The more things change...

[13] Currently, independent mortgage companies are state chartered and subject to state law and oversight, whose provisions and enforcement are variable. Under most state laws, brokers are not fiduciaries with a legal responsibility to put the borrower's interest first.

[14] Going further and making loan purchasers and investors responsible for the malfeasance of brokers would probably have the effect of destroying significant parts of the mortgage market.

By design, the creation of these off-balance sheet entities allowed banks to reduce the capital associated with a given risk profile.[15] It reduced the transparency of risky activities and hid them from regulatory scrutiny. Unsurprisingly, these innovations encouraged excessive risk taking, inadequate transparency, and weak regulatory scrutiny.

Basel II, which international banking authorities have designed to correct some of these deficiencies, came into operation at the beginning of this year. Under Basel II, regulators take into account the riskiness of a bank's overall portfolio, including contingencies, when establishing capital requirements. The new approach requires banks to use portfolio models, in the spirit of Tobin, to assess the riskiness of the portfolio. Banks will be permitted to use their own internal models in making these assessments. Where circumstances do not allow such modeling, banks must calculate their capital requirements from the credit ratings assigned to the bond portfolio.[16] This accounting regime should reduce the incentive for shifting risky activities to a special purpose vehicle or conduit, insofar as the probability that the position will come back onto the bank's balance sheet is part of the modeling exercise.

One can question the incentive of those undertaking these procedures to give proper weight to downside risks.[17] Even state-of-the-art models have a tendency of underestimating the probability of extreme outcomes. (Of late, once-in-a-thousand-year events have a habit of happening every ten years in financial markets.) They underestimate the correlation of returns on different assets in periods of high volatility. Financial engineers are familiar with distributions with fat tails, but the tails may be even fatter than they think.

Banks will also retain the same incentives to make convenient assumptions about when the loans they originate and distribute will come back onto the balance sheet, and it is not clear that supervisors will be in a position to correct them. Typically banks can assume that a loan, once sold, is gone for good.[18] In practice, however, originators may feel compelled to repurchase securities that they previously sold for reputational reasons.[19] David

---

[15] This profile included the risks that banks would face if off-balance sheet activities were forced back onto the balance sheet by funding problems or contractual provisions.

[16] On the rating agencies, see below.

[17] Ratings from the major rating agencies will be used by banks that do not have their own internal models.

[18] An exception, presumably, is when the sales contract includes a provision that explicitly provides for repurchase in the event of specified contingencies.

[19] Note the tension with the previous subsection, where I discuss Reserve Board Chairman Bernanke's suggestion that reputational factors may not be enough to induce responsible behavior by originators. The tension dissolves in cases like that of Citigroup, which inserted

Dodge, the now former governor of the Bank of Canada, has argued that bank capital requirements should be raised across the board to compensate for the tendency to make convenient assumptions about when loans they originate and distribute will come back onto the balance sheet.[20]

Raising questions about Basel II is easy – not so identifying effective reforms. One option would be to go back to something resembling Basel I, under which regulators require banks to hold a fixed minimum amount of capital against their assets (after perhaps again placing assets into buckets by credit-risk type). This would relieve regulators of having to rely on credit ratings and internal models, neither of which have emerged from the subprime crisis with burnished reputations. But here it is important to recall that the authorities launched the mammoth effort culminating in Basel II because of flaws in this then-existing procedure, notably the relatively arbitrary categorization of assets by risk class and the failure to account for correlations among their returns.

At the other extreme, regulators might acknowledge the impossibility of fixing the capital adequacy regime and jettison capital requirements for market discipline. They could require banks to issue subordinated debt in the hope that debt holders would exercise strong oversight of banks' investment and management decisions.[21] But proposals for proceeding in this way assume more confidence to the effectiveness of market discipline than is likely to be comfortable for many observers.

A compromise would be to stick with Basel II and its reliance on credit ratings and internal models but to address problems of regulatory arbitrage and procyclicality.[22] Regulators would have to adopt more rigorous treatment of contingent and off-balance sheet assets and liabilities – they would have to insist that the portfolios of structured investment vehicles (SIVs) and conduits (see below) be brought back onto bank balance sheets and that adequate capital be held against them.[23] In other words, the so-called

put options into many of the CDOs backed by subprime mortgages that it sold to customers. Those puts allowed buyers who ran into financing problems to sell them back to the originator at original value – something that was not accounted for on the bank's balance sheet. See Wray (2007) and the references therein.

[20] See Dodge (2007).

[21] This is the recommendation of Calomiris (2007).

[22] This alternative would, however, place an even greater premium on dealing with another set of problems associated with the credit ratings that provide the basis for weighted capital requirements for small banks (those without internal models). On the rating agency problem, see Section 6 below.

[23] An interesting article by Tett (2008) asks why there have been no major bank failures or related problems in Spain despite that country's overheated and now declining housing market. The explanation appears to be that the Bank of Spain signaled Spanish banks that

shadow banking system would have to be brought into the light. This could be part of a more general effort to require banks to hold more capital as a cushion against complex and opaque securities that can suddenly become illiquid – and against the new risks of twenty-first century banking generally. Banks could be similarly required to hold a portion of any derivative securities they originate and distribute on their own balance sheets. Such reforms will only be attractive to national regulators concerned with the competitive position of the institutions they regulate if they are coordinated internationally. Of course, that is precisely why we have the Basel Capital Accord in the first place.

A reformed Basel II should also deal with the backward-looking nature of ratings and other traditional determinants of capital requirements. Goodhart and Presaud (2008) have argued that capital requirements should be made forward looking by indexing them not just to bank lending but to the rate of growth of bank lending and not just to the value of residential mortgage collateral but to the rate of growth of residential mortgage collateral. Thus, capital requirements would rise in good times instead of falling as the rating agencies respond by upgrading the constituents of bank portfolios. Simple reforms along these lines could go a long way toward containing the unsustainable credit booms that have a history of leaving financial wreckage in their wake.

A final option is to combine all of the above. Benink and Kaufman (2008) suggest that banks should be required to supplement the risk-weighted capital requirement they calculate under Basel II with a Basel I-style non–risk-weighted leverage requirement to ensure an adequate capital cushion under all circumstances. The Basel I-style component might usefully be adjusted procyclically with the credit cycle. They recommend complementing capital requirements with a requirement to issue subordinated debt. Discussion thus seems to be moving not in the direction choosing between the alternatives but combining them.

IV. Problems with Stress Testing

Financial institutions and their supervisors do extensive stress testing of portfolios. Regulators similarly use simulation exercises to test the adequacy of crisis-management systems. The question is whether the scenarios they

---

they would be required to hold capital against the assets of any SIVs they established, in contrast to regulatory practice in, inter alia, the United States and Germany. The result was that Spanish banks chose not to rely on SIVs but held their residential mortgage exposure on balance sheet – and therefore held capital against it.

simulate are extreme enough. These are based on estimates derived from finance–theoretic models of the distribution of returns and on how returns on different assets covary in more and less volatile periods. The experience of the last decade suggests that these models may systematically underestimate the likelihood of extreme returns and the increase in covariances when volatility spikes.

Thus, stress tests based on these estimates produce a maximum loss in portfolio value that is only a fraction of actual losses when things go bad.[24] In the same sense, supervisors and regulators simulating a market event to test the adequacy of their management systems may be too conservative in their assumptions about the violence of the shock and scope of the market reaction.[25]

Better models of financial market dynamics may eventually allow for more effective stress testing and systems simulation. But if the shortcomings of existing models are severe and mainly work in one direction, one can reasonably ask whether supervisory and regulatory practice should be based on such flawed frameworks.

V. Illusive Liquidity

The distinguishing features of CDOs and other made-to-measure mortgage-backed securities are their complexity, opacity, and specialized clientele. These characteristics meant that when doubts arose in the summer of 2007 about the performance of these securities, market liquidity dried up. Investors all lined up on one side of the market, as the imperfectly informed attempted to infer underlying conditions from the actions of others. Potential buyers of last resort were unable to fund their operations by borrowing from banks reluctant to lend against uncertain collateral. There was a spike in interbank rates and worries about gridlock in the interbank market as banks reluctant to lend to other banks were forced to take complex structures bank onto their balance sheets.

In light of these events, some economists have argued that banks and other financial entities should be subject to liquidity requirements so that when some institutions are forced by deteriorating market conditions to

---

[24] A case in point is Northern Rock, the British building and loan society that has become a prominent casualty of the crisis. This bank reportedly passed all the stress-testing exercises to which it and the U.K. Financial Services Authority agreed in the first half of 2007. Evidently, the possibility that of the bank's funding sources all could dry up at the same time was not one of these scenarios.

[25] As Buiter (2007a) puts it, their "war games" lack imagination.

sell CDOs, others are in a position to buy, obviating liquidity problems. They similarly suggest that regulation should be used to prevent banks like Northern Rock, which possessed liquid liabilities and illiquid assets, from pursuing such a risky business model; in short, the state should require such banks to keep a proportion of their investments in liquid assets, where that portion is a function of their funding strategy.[26] Champions of the Basel Accord defend its lack of specified liquidity requirements on the grounds that the accord is concerned with capital adequacy, not liquidity. But this argument, critics insist, ignores the extent to which the accord's approach encouraged regulators to neglect the importance of liquidity in their supervisory activities.

By definition, liquidity requirements raise the cost of doing business and the price of housing finance, as well as other forms of lending. Banks have always been in the liquidity transformation business, and the more that the regulatory framework requires them to hold liquid assets, the more expensive their liquidity transformation services will become. And even if banks and other institutional investors had more liquidity on hand, it by no means follows that they would wish to deploy it under the conditions anticipated by the advocates of more restrictive reserve policies. The problem in 2007 was not that the banks as a group had no liquidity to deploy but that they had no wish to deploy it, given the pervasive lack of information about the underlying economic condition of potential counterparties. The liquidity problem is thus intimately connected to the information problem, in other words. And it is to that information problem that I now turn.

VI. Reforming the Rating Agencies

The role of credit rating agencies is to provide specialized intelligence, in the form of publicly available ratings, for use by investors seeking to price securities. The subprime crisis suggests that the rating agencies' execution of this function was subpar. They failed adequately to distinguish between the riskiness of different securities. They were too generous in providing AAA ratings. They failed to downgrade mortgage-backed securities as the housing market and hence the value of the underlying mortgage obligations deteriorated. They then aggravated the crisis by reacting with wholesale downgrades once the market collapsed.

---

[26] This proposal assumes that supervisors can reliably determine what assets are liquid. Given that some normally liquid assets can become illiquid abruptly, as the subprime crisis reminds us and numerous past financial crises demonstrate, one would presumably want a narrow definition of the category.

One explanation for this dismal performance lies with the imperfect models used by the rating agencies to value residential-mortgage-backed securities and the associated derivatives. Their methods emanate from long experience (in two cases, more than a century's worth) of rating corporate bonds. Mason and Rosner (2007) point to a number of reasons why the application of valuation models for corporate bonds to securities backed by claims on the residential mortgage market may be misleading. For example, the performance of a corporate bond depends on both the condition of the issuing firm and the condition of the macroeconomy. By comparison, debt securities backed by baskets of mortgage loans depend more heavily on the macroeconomic cycle and therefore are more highly correlated.[27] Similarly, in building their estimates of default probabilities on historical evidence, the rating agencies used data from both good and bad times for corporate bonds but only data from good times for newer assets (since these novel products had never previously experienced serious market turbulence).

A second set of problems, cited by Calomiris (2007) stems from the use of ratings by bank regulators. Basel II directs regulators to use bond ratings to determine the range of permissible bank investments and, for (smaller) banks lacking their own internal models, weighted capital requirements. Unsurprisingly, banks have responded to this delegation of public authority by applying subtle pressure on the rating agencies to elevate the entire spectrum of bonds a couple of notches, without necessarily disguising information about relative risks, in order to widen their investment choices and lower their capital costs. This dynamic works to heighten banking-sector risk and subverts the intent of regulators' use of bond ratings.[28]

A related source of problems concerns the agencies' conflicts of interest. Rating agencies first earn fees from advising on how to structure bonds and derivatives so that these receive the desired rating. They then have a not-so-subtle incentive to rate those issues in the promised manner.[29] These

---

[27] It is worth observing that this problem is not simply Monday-morning quarterbacking. Well before the crisis erupted (back in May 2007), *The Economist* wrote how "the models misread the level of correlation between different types of assets – a crucial variable – and ignored signs that risks were greater than historical data suggested." See *Economist* (2007).

[28] Evidence of the extent of this problem is conflicting. Dittrich (2007), for example, questions the significance of this "grade-inflation" problem.

[29] I am not alone in this critique. Something similar was argued by the International Organization of Securities Commissions, the umbrella organization of the world's securities watchdogs, last September. As it put it, the agencies may have traded quality for "getting the business." The one systematic empirical analysis of the issue of which I am aware is Covitz and Harrison (2003), who looked at rating downgrades of corporate bonds and asked whether there were significantly longer delays when the rating agency in question

patterns were apparent in earlier emerging market crises. But now that the problem has hit home – now that it has hit the United States, in other words – perhaps policymakers will take the question of how to constrain the ratings process more seriously.

The rating agencies' conflicts could be addressed by Glass-Steagall-style legislation that prevents them from both acting as advisors and issuing ratings.[30] Since the problem of uniformly optimistic ratings has probably been exacerbated by the oligopolistic nature of the rating industry, Congress might also seek to foster more competition, since the better rating agencies will presumably outcompete the bad ones over time. The Credit Agency Reform Act of 2006 (implemented by the Securities and Exchange Commission [SEC] in 2007) has the goal of increasing competition by making it easier for potential entrants to obtain preferred status from SEC staff, so that regulators and banks can use their ratings in setting capital requirements (and so that they can thus get business). But to date there has been little real progress in this direction. Finally, on December 21, 2007, the SEC agreed to confer Nationally-Recognized-Statistical-Rating-Organization status on Egan-Jones, a narrow rating agency (one that does not also advise on the structuring of bond issues), but only after eleven years of trying on the part of the firm. Potential entrants continue to complain about insurmountable regulatory hurdles. Until entry and real competition are possible and, as a result, rating agencies incur the standard market penalty for being wrong – namely, loss of business or even franchise – significant improvements in their performance are unlikely.

VII. The Role of Hedge Funds

The hedge fund industry is more than half a century old, but it has never been as prominent and well capitalized as at present. Criticism of hedge funds as opaque, unregulated, and unaccountable is a by-product of every

---

had other business with the issuer. They find no evidence of significant conflicts of interest, at least insofar as these influence the speed of rating downgrades. There is anecdotal evidence pointing the other way – the rating agencies did not downgrade Northern Rock until after the market reacted on September 14 – but as yet no systematic study. As noted above, Mason and Rosner (2007) provide a range of arguments for why evidence from the corporate bond market may in any case be inapplicable to residential mortgage-backed securities.

[30] Some argue that the problem runs deeper: It will be impossible to eliminate conflicts of interest, they insist, so long as the issuer (the seller) rather than the investor (the buyer) pays for the rating. Schemes for placing a model tax on all transactions in the relevant securities ("Tobin tax 2") as a way of funding the process of acquiring a rating are not obviously practicable but worth contemplating.

financial crisis. That two prominent hedge funds run by Bear Stearns and a number of stand-alone funds were casualties of the subprime crisis has resuscitated those complaints and renewed the question of whether hedge fund regulation should be part of the next round of regulatory reform.

Another reading of the crisis is that all this attention to hedge funds is misplaced. Although some hedge funds took significant losses and even went out of business, others profited. Hedge funds as a class posed no special threat to financial stability. Moreover, hedge funds played no special role in the crisis. Everything they did, from risk taking to the use of credit and procyclical portfolio adjustments, a variety of other investment vehicles from SIVs to conduits to investment and commercial banks similarly did.

Even if hedge funds posed a special problem, it is by no means clear what regulators can do about them. Requiring hedge funds to periodically release more information about their investments would make little difference for market transparency, since these firms can turn their portfolios upside down in a single trading day.[31] Requiring them to hold more capital, use less leverage, or divulge more information runs the risk of simply facilitating physical and virtual relocation, whether to London or a post office box in the Cayman Islands.

Regulators generally agree that the main way of addressing the risks posed by hedge funds is by encouraging more effective counterparty risk management. Banks providing credit to hedge funds should be encouraged to monitor the positions of their hedge fund clients, to demand adequate collateral from those counterparties, and to hold adequate capital as a buffer against counterparty risks.[32] Credit is as essential as oxygen for the managers of highly leveraged hedge funds, and banks, as its suppliers, have the leverage to demand to see the books – unlike even many hedge fund investors. This should enable the banks to adjust their lending decisions to limit their exposure to hedge fund-propagated risks. Those same banks,

---

[31] The requirement of additional information disclosure from hedge funds might also encourage herd behavior by investors, insofar as other actors regard hedge fund managers as the smart money.

[32] Truth in advertising requires acknowledging that this is a case where the present author has a dog in the race, as lead author of the IMF report that reached many of these same conclusions almost ten years ago (there is nothing unique about hedge fund position taking or funding; calls for greater hedge fund transparency are problematic; attempts at tighter regulation are limited by the high mobility of these entities; and the main way of any threat to systemic stability is by tighter oversight of bank lending). See Eichengreen and Mathieson et al. (1998). A recent analysis that reaches broadly similar conclusions is Ferguson et al. (2007).

which are at the center of the financial system and, historically, the weak link in the financial chain, can be insulated from hedge fund-propagated financial shocks by adequate collateral and capital buffers. For their part, highly leveraged hedge funds that might otherwise take on large exposures using borrowed funds – positions that could destabilize financial markets if a sudden price movement forced them to be unwound – will be restrained from using excessive leverage by the suppliers of bank credit. Such is the magic of counterparty risk management.

In practice, matters are more complicated. What constitutes adequate collateral for credit exposures is unclear when a hedge fund is large relative to the market or asset class in which it invests. In this case, sales of an asset by a hedge fund faced with investor redemptions can trigger a drop in asset prices that reduces the value of the collateral; not only does the hedge fund end up unable to repay its bank borrowings, but the collateral it put up in return for that line turns out not to be worth the paper it was written on.

More generally, one can imagine a number of reasons why counterparty risk management might be ineffective or lax.[33] The key problem that arose in the subprime market – banks and brokers earn fees from originating and distributing securities now but leave for someone else the problem of cleaning up the mess later – operates in this context as well. Some hedge funds are willing to pay handsomely for bank credit lines, and if that creates a large contingent liability for the bank in the future, that will be future management's problem.

Similarly, hedge funds and the proprietary trading desks of commercial and investment banks may have many of the same positions.[34] Then when an asset-price shock forces a hedge fund to sell into a falling market, eroding the value of the collateral held by the bank, that bank's own proprietary trading desk will suffer additional losses. The existence of firewalls between the trading and credit departments may mean that this risk is not adequately taken into account.

In addition, large hedge funds often deal with more than one prime broker and negotiate credit lines from several banks, which means that no one counterparty automatically sees the fund's total leverage. Even in this situation, prime brokers and credit providers can still presumably insist on seeing the books as a condition of providing their services. Insofar as one function of a credit supplier is to monitor whether its hedge fund counterparty is taking on excessive risk, there may be a temptation not to

---

[33] A good summary of the central points is Kambhu, Schuermann, and Stiroh (2007).

[34] As was the case, in some instances, during the Asian crisis in 1997.

invest in due diligence, insofar as other banks also known to be supplying credit to the same outfit are assumed to have done their due diligence. The result at the end of the day may be that the oversight function is undersupplied.

These three market failures have familiar names: agency problems, externalities, and the tragedy of the commons, respectively. (They are discussed at more length in Stiglitz's chapter in this volume.) They are the reasons why the stability of the financial system cannot be blindly entrusted to banks and their risk management officers. They are among the most basic reasons why banks are supervised and regulated. Supervisors are supposed to sanction banks that fail to do their due diligence and in extreme cases to revoke their licenses. They are supposed to force bankers to worry about how distress experienced by one of their large counterparties can erode the value of its collateral or cause the bank itself to suffer proprietary trading losses. Regulators are supposed to be in the business of forcing banks to hold adequate capital and to demand adequate collateral to protect against these contingencies. The appropriate response to the real-world limitations to counterparty risk management is not to imagine that effective regulation can somehow be imposed on footloose hedge funds but rather to strengthen the supervision and regulation of the banks that are the providers of credit to the hedge fund industry.

VIII. SIVs and Conduits

Structured investment vehicles and other mechanisms for using short-term bank funding to invest in long-term derivative securities pose some of the most striking dilemmas of the current crisis. Few market participants had even heard of SIVs and conduits before the summer of 2007. At that point they abruptly discovered that their own financial prospects and the stability of the U.S. financial system turned on their condition.

The best way of understanding the role of these programs is by distinguishing those with and without a formal commercial bank connection. Consider self-standing SIVs. These investment funds issue asset-backed commercial paper, typically of three months maturity, to fund investments in CDOs and other long-term securities. When a CDO portfolio comprises senior or super senior- (AAA) rated securities, its managers fund as much as 90 percent of the vehicle by issuing asset-backed commercial paper.[35] In practice, commercial banks are among the main purchasers of that paper,

---

[35] The other 10 percent being the conduit's own equity (Calomiris 2007).

but typically on an arm's-length basis – that is, they have no ongoing business relationship with the SIV issuing the paper.[36]

These SIVs are essentially hedge funds by another name. They invest in risky and sometimes illiquid assets; they use significant amounts of leverage and credit in their operations; and they are not transparent. If their investment practices require significant regulatory responses, then those responses should be broadly similar to those applied to hedge funds as a class (see above). Investors in such funds are well capitalized, savvy individuals, firms, and mutual funds; it is not at all obvious that state intervention into their affairs is required on consumer-protection grounds. These funds remain outside the financial safety net; in the event of difficulties, their principals can choose to restructure them or close them down.

The banks extending credit to SIVs, by contrast, do not reside outside the financial safety net and frequently are too big to fail. Regulators therefore need to be sure that the banks extending back-up credit lines engage in realistic assessments of the likelihood that associated SIVs will draw on those lines; banks, in other words, must not simply assume that, because SIVs had no need to draw on credit lines in the past, they will not do so in the future. As the events in the latter half of 2007 make clear, stress testing by banks and supervisors should include the possibility of wholesale disruption of the asset-backed commercial paper market.[37]

Some SIVs are wholly owned and operated by a commercial or investment bank, with bank employees running the portfolio and the same bank providing the credit line.[38] In such cases, financial engineers simply disguise and repackage traditional banking, and the distinction between the bank protected by the safety net and the SIV left to its fate becomes artificial. Among other things, banks are in the business of maturity transformation (they use short-term funding to make long-lived, long-term investments). Here the maturity transformation by which banks use short-term funding to make long-lived term investments occurs through the off-balance sheet arm, outside the purview of regulators.

It follows that banks that own and operate SIVs should bring them onto their balance sheets, and those SIVs should be subject to regulatory scrutiny. To the extent that regulatory and tax arbitrage explain the creation of many of these bank-sponsored SIVs, then Congress and regulatory agencies need to tighten the relevant provisions.

---

[36] In addition, an SIV may contract for a back-up line of credit with a bank or syndicate as a precaution against disruptions in accessing the commercial paper market.

[37] As it presumably will after that seizure of the market for commercial paper.

[38] This was essentially the case of Rhineland Funding, the conduit operated by the German Bank IKB, whose difficulties ignited the crisis in August.

IX. Transparency

Numerous commentators maintain that the subprime crisis was aggravated by the opacity of mortgage-related derivative securities. With one layer of derivatives built on another built on another, even specialists incompletely grasped the risks of the structured products they had bought. Because holders rarely traded these securities, their market value was elusive at best; often holders relied on their own complex economic models, with all of their limitations, to assign a value.

Thus, when the market for mortgage-backed derivatives soured and some investors headed for the exits, other investors concluded that their holdings were riskier than previously thought, leading to panicked attempts to liquidate. Financial institutions worldwide recalibrated their valuation models, which in turn generated alarming balance-sheet revisions. Liquidity problems spilled over to other markets as investors refused to accept residential-mortgage-backed securities as collateral for issuing asset-backed commercial paper. This latter-day version of a cascading crisis of economic confidence suggests how a sharp shock to a limited segment of the U.S. housing market could ultimately come to threaten the entire financial system.[39]

Concocting ever more complex derivatives is the bread and butter of financial engineers. There is a market for their products because they allow economic agents to efficiently identify, isolate, and resell risks during periods of low volatility. (What happens in periods of high volatility is another matter.) Thus, to the extent that regulators are inclined to push for greater simplicity and transparency in the design of financial securities, they will be swimming against a powerful tide.

One way to tackle the financial rip currents would be to apply higher capital requirements to more complex derivative securities. This approach would involve going back to something resembling Basel I, in which accountants placed different kinds of securities in different risk buckets, with banks then adjusting capital requirements accordingly. Unfortunately, such a tack would obviate a key feature insight of Basel II – that regulators and banks should take into account the correlation of returns on different kinds of assets when assessing risk.[40]

Another strategy would be for central banks to announce that they were prepared to accept relatively simple, transparent instruments when providing collateral, but not complex ones. This reform would in turn reduce

---

[39] The disproportion between the underlying real shock and the financial consequences has been noted by inter alia Bernanke (2007b).

[40] Whether these costs would dominate the benefits of this simpler approach is an open question, as I explain above.

the attractiveness of holding relatively complex securities. The problem is that this policy might ultimately come into conflict with the authorities' responsibility for financial stability, limiting their capacity to act as liquidity provider of last resort to the markets most in need.

X. Exchange-Based versus Over-the-Counter Trading

Another explanation for the severity of the current crisis stresses that brokers trade CDOs and residential mortgage backed securities (MBSs) over the counter (traditionally by telephone but now electronically) rather than through an organized exchange. An exchange would require participants to hold margin in order to maintain positions. It would subject nonbank participants to the equivalent of capital requirements. It would encourage instrument standardization, enhancing transparency and the liquidity of the market for distress sales.

As evidence that exchange-based trading would function more smoothly, Cecchetti (2007) cites the contrasting reactions to news of the difficulties of Long-Term Capital Management (LTCM) in 1998 and of Amaranth Advisors in 2006. LTCM dealt mainly in swaps traded over the counter, while Amaranth dealt in natural gas futures contracts through an organized exchange. Because the exchange required Amaranth to put up margin, it could stretch its distress sales over time rather than having to make them in bunches. And because the existence of exchange-based trading encouraged the standardization of futures contracts, the relevant parties had a much clearer sense of the situation than was the case with LTCM. The argument for an exchange follows directly.

What then explains the continuing domination of over-the-counter trading? Cecchetti has speculated that there might be tax or regulatory incentives that encourage over-the-counter trading, but without specifying them. This situation may be a case of path dependency, where history matters. It may be equally efficient to organize trading of a security on a centralized exchange or over the counter, but whichever venue starts first attracts the bulk of the business and thus offers superior liquidity and lower transaction costs. The initial disinclination to rely on exchanges may have partly reflected fee-seeking behavior by banks, since as originators of the relevant securities they also receive fees when they trade them over the counter, but are less likely to receive fee income from trading on an exchange. If it is the case that trading can be organized as efficiently over the counter or on an exchange, and that the latter has external social benefits, then regulations requiring exchange-based trading would have few if any costs to market participants, aside from the changeover costs – and, by the preceding arguments, significant social benefits. A few years ago Peru exempted the income on exchange-traded fixed-income securities from interest income tax in an effort to move over-the-counter trading onto an organized exchange.[41] This might not be a bad example for other countries, including the United States, to follow.

XI. Is There a Case for Consolidated Supervision?

The credit crisis of 2007, and specifically the response of the Bank of England to the liquidity squeeze at Northern Rock, raises several questions about consolidated bank supervision. Throughout the industrialized world, financial regulators are increasingly separating bank supervision from monetary policy and delegating the former to an agency independent from the central bank – preferably a single agency, to facilitate the centralization of that information about different financial institutions linked together through the interbank market. This model has been adopted not only by the United Kingdom, where since 1997 prudential supervision has been the responsibility of the Financial Services Authority (FSA), but also by a growing number of other countries.

The question is whether this structure actually impeded the flow of information about the condition of at a financial institution to the central bank, causing it not to appreciate the gravity of the unfolding problem and thus delaying its response. If so, and if such problems are commonplace, then there is an argument for either returning supervisory responsibility to the central bank or giving the financial supervisor an unlimited credit line at the central bank so that it can provide lender-of-last-resort services when needed.

At this juncture, the severity of this problem remains unclear. Mervyn King, the governor of the Bank of England, has described how deputies from the Bank, the FSA, and the Treasury met on August 14, 2007, when the FSA relayed to the two other institutions its judgment that Northern Rock had serious problems. The key question is whether the FSA already had a glimmering of those problems some days earlier but did not communicate them.[42]

---

[41] As described in IMF (2004), 136.
[42] See Telegraph (2007). FSA officials' testimony to the Treasury Select Committee suggests that they had already developed serious concerns about Northern Rock's funding practices earlier in the year and placed them under special supervision (Parliament 2007).

In principle, nothing prevents a country's financial supervisor from picking up the phone and sharing its latest information about the condition of the banking system with central bankers. In theory, information can flow as freely between two agencies as between two departments of the same agency. But one suspects that different bureaucratic incentives lead to different behavior in the two circumstances. When two agencies have different objectives or when they are simply jockeying for influence, they may have an incentive to strategically withhold information. But when the same individual oversees the two entities (when the central bank governor appoints and can demand the resignation of key supervisory staff as well as sitting on the monetary policy committee), the scope for strategic behavior by underlings surely diminishes – since the sanctions in the event that it occurs are greater.

An American recommending that countries avoid separating the lender-of-last-resort function from the financial-supervision function will likely encounter accusations of parochialism. But advocates of such regulatory separation should encounter accusations that they are courting excessive risk.[43]

XII. Implications for Regulatory Reform

The subprime crisis is the first crisis of the age of mass securitization.[44] Some conclude on the basis of this experience that the costs of securitization, in the form of risks to financial stability, exceed the benefits. The implication is that we should return to the simpler days of "good old-fashioned banking" in which commercial banks originate loans to households and firms and hold them on their balance sheets, rather than slicing them, dicing them, and selling them off.[45]

This back-to-the-1960s formula ignores – that there is no turning back the clock on financial technology and, more fundamentally, on advances in information and communications. Securitization is bound up with the

---

[43] In early January 2008, the chancellor of the exchequer proposed changes in the organization of bank supervision in the United Kingdom designed to eliminate ambiguity in the allocation of responsibilities between the Treasury, the FSA, and the Bank of England. See Parker (2008). Whether the changes he proposed come to pass only time will tell. But this would seem to represent an acknowledgment of the problems alluded to in the text.

[44] Champions (as it were) of the Long-Term Capital Management crisis in 1998 may argue that it deserves this mantle, since LTCM's problems centered on its positions in interest-rate swaps.

[45] To quote Alastair Darling in a speech from mid-September (BBC 2007).

broader deregulation of financial markets and with the information-technology revolution. Policymakers cannot eliminate it short of reimposing the kind of restrictive regulation to which banking and financial systems were subject half a century ago. Even then, regulatory agencies may well fail to suppress securitization, given the ease with which financial institutions can move their activities offshore in the age of broadband and low-cost communication.

In any case, turning back the clock would not be desirable because the constellation of financial innovations referred to as securitization has real benefits. Those innovations have allowed the financial system to repackage and spread risk. They have reduced the amount of equity capital that this system requires to absorb that risk.[46] The result has been to lower funding costs for both firms and homeowners as a class.[47]

Regulatory dilemmas not uncommonly arise in the course of the diffusion of a technology or financial innovation, a pattern to which financial securitization offers no exception. Some early adopters lack the training and capacity to safely operate new machinery. Like a novice driver given the keys to a more powerful car, they have a troubling tendency to run off the road or to collide with other vehicles. This problem was compounded, in the case of the automobile, by the mismatch between the design of the roads and traffic regulations and the capabilities of the new generation of engines.

In the aftermath of the subprime crisis, financial regulators will similarly set out to repave, regrade, and rethink speed limits and rules of the road more generally. But specifying desirable changes is not easy. In my view, policymakers should focus on the banking system. The rise of securitization notwithstanding, banks still play a unique role in the economy. They are at the center of the information-impacted segments of the financial system. They are critical suppliers of credit to hedge funds, SIVs, monoline bond insurers, and all the other entities active in the financial system. Historically, the only times when financial volatility has resulted in a sharp drop in economic activity is when it is allowed to destabilize the banking system. This is why banks receive official protection via the financial safety net. It is also why they need to be vigorously supervised and regulated.

Thus, focusing on the banking system means focusing on bank regulation, including but not limited to the Basel Accord. Banks should be required to

---

[46] To be sure, regulators may have allowed the amount of capital to fall too far, but this point is analytically distinct.

[47] This conclusion parallels that of Eisner in his analysis of deregulation of the transportation and energy sectors elsewhere in this volume.

hold more capital as a cushion against shocks and an incentive to avoid excessive risk. This could be accomplished by subjecting banks not just to a Basel II-style requirement, based on a model-based assessment of credit risk, but also an old-fashioned Basel I-style requirement where capital is a multiple of bank investments. The latter should be related not just to the level of bank investments but the rate of growth of those investments, and not just to the value of the collateral pledged against bank loans but the rate of growth of the value of that collateral. The former, meanwhile, can function as part of a larger effort to reduce the scope for regulatory arbitrage and to bring back onto bank balance sheets the shadow banking system of SIVs and conduits. Banks could also be usefully required to hold on their own balance sheets a portion of any security issues they originate and distribute. Adding a subordinated debt requirement would not hurt, although it would be no panacea.

This panoply of regulations will also have to be extended from commercial to investment banks. The need for this already should have been evident before the crisis. Requiring commercial banks to hold minimum level of capital and indexing that minimum to the riskiness of their assets all but guaranteed that risky activities would shift to investment banks free of analogous capital requirements, which could undertake them at lower cost. Where commercial bank assets were roughly ten times their capital on the eve of the crisis, investment bank assets were twenty-four times capital, which left no margin for error. And when the existence of errors was discovered at Bear Stearns, the Fed felt obliged to step in, taking $30 billion of the bank's assets onto its own balance sheet, on the grounds that the Bear was too connected to the rest of the financial system to be allowed to fail. Regulation of the investment banking sector, including but not limited to regulation of capital adequacy, is essential now that there is no question that these banks do their trapeze act over a federally provided safety net. It is thus reassuring, if unseemly, that we see the Fed and the SEC jostling for this responsibility.

There is much more to do beyond tightening up regulation of the banking system. In addition, there is the need for regulations to more effectively protect consumers against deceptive practices of banks and mortgage brokers where these exist, considering changes in the tax treatment of executive compensation in the financial sector in order to better align the incentives of managers, shareholders, and other stakeholders, introducing more competition in the rating industry, and encouraging the development of organized derivatives exchanges to replace over-the-counter trading. But it is with addressing recently revealed problems in the banking system that work should start.

References

Benink, Harald, and George Kaufman. 2008. "Turmoil Reveals the Inadequacy of Basel II," *Financial Times* (February): 11.

Bernanke, Ben. 2007a. "Housing, Housing Finance and Monetary Policy," Speech to the Jackson Hole Symposium of the Federal Reserve Bank of Kansas City (August 31).

Bernanke, Ben. 2007b. "The Recent Financial Turmoil and its Economic and Policy Consequences," Speech to the Economic Club of New York (October 15).

Buiter, Willem. 2007a. "The Lessons from Northern Rock," www.ft.com (November).

Buiter, Willem. 2007b. "How Bad Can a US Downturn Possibly Get?" www.ft.com (November).

Calomiris, Charles. 2007. "Not (Yet) a Minsky Moment." Unpublished manuscript, Graduate School of Business, Columbia University.

Cecchetti, Stephen. 2007. "A Better Way to Organize Securities Markets," *Financial Times*, www.ft.com (4 October).

Covitz, Daniel M., and Paul Harrison. 2003. "Testing Conflicts of Interest at Bond Rating Agencies with Market Anticipation: Evidence that Reputation Incentives Dominate." Unpublished manuscript, Federal Reserve Board.

DiMartino, Danielle, and Jon Duca. 2007. "The Rise and Fall of Subprime Mortgages," *Economic Letter* 2, Dallas: Federal Reserve Bank of Dallas.

Dittrich, Fabian. 2007. "The Credit Rating Industry: Competition and Regulation." Unpublished Ph.D. dissertation, University of Cologne.

Dodge, David. 2007. "Turbulence in Credit Markets: Causes, Effects, and Lessons to be Learned," Speech to the Vancouver Board of Trade (September 23).

Eichengreen, Barry, and Donald Mathieson et al. 1998. "Hedge Funds and Financial Market Dynamics." Occasional Paper no. 166, Washington, D.C.: International Monetary Fund.

Eichengreen, Barry. 2008. "Thoughts on the Subprime Crisis." *Economic Politica* 2: 265–82.

Economist. 2007. "Rating Agencies: Measuring the Measurers." www.economist.com (May 31).

Ferguson, Roger, Phillip Hartmann, Fabio Panetta, and Richard Portes. 2007. *International Financial Stability*. Geneva Reports on the World Economy, London: CEPR.

Goodhart, Charles, and Avinash Presaud. 2008. "How to Avoid the Next Crash." *Financial Times* (January 30): 14.

International Business Times. 2007. "Darling Calls for 'Old Fashioned Banking,'" www.ibtimes.com (September 13).

International Monetary Fund. 2004. "Development of Corporate Bond Markets in Emerging Market Countries." *Global Financial Stability Report*: 103–41.

Joint Economic Committee, U.S. Senate. 2007. *The Subprime Lending Crisis*. Washington, D.C.: Joint Economic Committee.

Kambhu, John, Til Schuermann, and Kevin Stiroh. 2007. "Hedge Funds, Financial Intermediation, and Systemic Risk," *Economic Policy Review of the Federal Reserve Bank of New York* 13: 1–18 (December).

King, Mervyn. 2007. "Turmoil in Financial Markets: What Can Central Banks Do?" Paper submitted to the Treasury Select Committee, House of Commons (September 12).

Leamer, Edward. 2007. "Housing IS the Business Cycle." NBER Working Paper no. 13428.

Mason, Joseph, and Joshua Rosner. 2007. "Where Did the Risk Go? How Misapplied Bond Ratings Cause Mortgage Backed Securities and Collateralized Debt Obligation Disruptions." Unpublished manuscript, Drexel University and Graham Fisher.

Mishkin, Frederic. 2007. "Housing and the Monetary Transmission Mechanism." NBER Working Paper no. 13518.

Parker, Geoffrey. 2008. "MPs Skeptical as Bankers Support Darling's Plan." www.ft.com (April 4).

Parliament. 2007. "Uncorrected Transcript of Oral Evidence: Financial Stability and Transparency." www.parliament.publications.uk (October 25).

Snowden, Kenneth. 1995. "The Evolution of Interregional Mortgage Lending Channels, 1870–1914: The Life Insurance-Mortgage Company Connection," in *Coordination and Information: Historical Perspectives on the Organization of Enterprise*, eds. Naomi R. Lamoreaux and Daniel M. G. Raff (Chicago: University of Chicago Press), 209–56.

Telegraph. 2007. "Transcript of Mervyn King's BBC Interview." www.telegraph.co.uk (November 7).

Tett, Gillian. 2008. "Spain's Banks Weather Credit Crisis." *Financial Times* (January 31): B12.

Wray, L. Randall. 2007. "Lessons from the Subprime Meltdown." Levy Economics Institute Working Paper no. 522, Annandale-on-Hudson: Levy Economics Institute (December).

FOURTEEN

The Prospects for Effective Coregulation in the United States: A Historian's View from the Early Twenty-First Century

Edward J. Balleisen[1]

As just about any observer of the American political scene over the past thirty years can attest, traditional modes of economic regulation by administrative agencies fell sharply out of favor in the United States in the quarter century after 1975. In areas as various as transportation, workplace safety, the environment, banking, and labor standards, skepticism about regulatory agencies became a dominant premise of policy debates. The assumptions and precepts of public choice scholarship, so carefully laid out by Jessica Leight in her contribution to this volume, filtered into the conceptual assumptions of elected officials and leading political commentators alike. Politicians and governmental officials increasingly worried about the "capture" of public agencies by private interests, leading to the latter's unjust enrichment; they grew ever more disquieted by the possibility that regulatory action would produce unanticipated outcomes that would harm economic growth; they feared that the enduring shortcomings of government – venal officialdom and tangled bureaucracy – would hamstring regulatory responses to even substantial socioeconomic problems. Although the critiques of the regulatory state emanated most consistently from political conservatives and libertarians, as well as business groups that viewed particular regulatory regimes as antithetical to their interests, they significantly shaped the worldview of many moderates and liberals as well.

The most prominent consequence of the intellectual and political onslaught against the administrative state has been deregulation – the selective dismantling of legal restrictions, mechanisms of governmental price/rate/fare setting, and systems of administrative monitoring that had

[1] The author would like to thank David Moss, Mitchell Weiss, Daniel Carpenter, Jodi Freeman, and Karin Shapiro for comments on drafts of the essay.

previously structured market activity. As Marc Eisner traces in his essay, the most important examples within America's federal government included the airline, trucking, and energy industries, along with the financial and communications sectors. But deregulation has occurred in a great many other federal settings, as well as in statehouses and city halls across the country, and in most other industrialized countries.[2]

Skepticism about regulation also powerfully shaped budgetary policy for those agencies of the United States government that retained regulatory missions. Beginning with Presidents Nixon and Carter, executive orders compelled regulatory agencies and the Office of Management and Budget (OMB) to analyze the economic impact of proposed regulations. Presidents Reagan, George Herbert Walker Bush, and Clinton extended this procedural requirement. Reagan instituted the requirement that OMB officials produce formal cost–benefit analyses of all proposed regulatory changes. Bush I created the Competitiveness Council, headed by Vice President Dan Quayle, to scrutinize federal regulations with the goal of removing those rules that imposed excessively high costs on the business community. Clinton, as part of his more general effort to "reinvent government," similarly called on all executive agencies to identify obsolete regulations for either modification or repeal, and to construct new regulatory initiatives with the goal of "maximiz[ing] voluntary compliance by business."[3] Particularly under Republican Presidents Reagan, George Herbert Walker Bush, and George W. Bush, the federal government additionally pared enforcement budgets for regulatory agencies such as the Federal Trade Commission, the Securities and Exchange Commission (SEC), the Occupational Health and Safety Commission (OSHA), and the Consumer Products Safety Commission.

---

[2] Richard Vietor, *Contrived Competition: Regulation and Deregulation in America* (Cambridge, Mass., 1996); Charles Calomaris, *U.S. Banking Deregulation in Historical Perspective* (New York, 1998); Michael Bernstein, "Regulatory Economics and Its Discontents: Some Theoretical and Historical Observations," *Info: the Journal of Policy, Regulation and Strategy for Telecommunications, Information and Media* 9 (2007): 28–43; Severin Borenstein, "The Trouble with Electricity Markets: Understanding California's Restructuring Disaster," *Journal of Economic Perspectives* 16 (2002): 191–211; Dipendra Sinha, *Deregulation and Liberalisation of the Airline Industry: Asia, Europe, North America and Oceania* (Aldershot, 2001); Jörg Vollbrecht et al., eds., *Insurance Regulation Liberalisation and Financial Convergence* (Paris, 2001); Giampaolo Galli and Jacques Pelkmans, eds., *Regulatory Reform and Competitiveness in Europe* (Cheltenham, 2000); Mitsuhiro Kagami and Masatsugu Tsuji, eds., Privatization, Deregulation and Economic Efficiency: a Comparative Analysis of Asia, Europe and the Americas (Cheltenham, 2000).

[3] Robert W. Hahn, "State and Federal Regulatory Reform: A Comparative Analysis," *Journal of Legal Studies* 29 (2000): 873–912; Christine Parker, *The Open Corporation: Effective Self-Government and Democracy* (New York, 2002), 14.

The resulting cutbacks in manpower significantly compromised the government's ability to investigate and prosecute firms that did not comply with federal law.[4]

Full-fledged deregulation and pinched regulatory enforcement budgets have garnered considerable attention from both academics and the mainstream press. The same goes for the related practice of contracting out governmental functions to private companies, in contexts that range from prison management and garbage collection to tax collection, the provision of disaster relief, and the supplying of America's military forces.[5] Another extremely important policy trend associated with deregulation, however, has received far less sustained notice and analysis, particularly in the nation's most heated political debates. From the mid-1970s onward, antagonism toward New Deal-style governmental regulation encouraged many businesses and policymakers to experiment with forms of private governance, often called "self-regulation."

This essay offers an analytical framework for evaluating the growing reliance on nongovernmental rule making and oversight as a basic tool of regulatory policy. Offering a composite view, based primarily on assessments by economists, sociologists, legal scholars, academics focusing on organizational management, and political scientists, it has several goals:

- to clarify what makes this approach a distinctive category of regulatory oversight;
- to place its recent appeal in historical context;
- to review the primary intellectual justifications offered by its proponents, and the contexts where it seems to work well;
- to consider the shortcomings of nongovernmental regulation identified by its critics, and the contexts in where it falls short of furthering fundamental regulatory purposes;
- to identify a series of general best practices for governmental monitoring of private regulation when American policymakers choose to rely on it; and

---

[4] Ross Petty, "FTC Advertising Regulation: Survivor or Casualty of the Reagan Revolution?" *American Business Law Journal* 30 (1992): 1–34; John B. Judis, "It's the EPA and OSHA, Stupid," *The American Prospect* 21 (Sept. 25–Oct. 9, 2000), 12–13; Carrie Johnson, "SEC Enforcement Cases Decline 9% Staff Reduced Because of Budget Crunch," *Washington Post*, Nov. 3, 2006, D3; E. Marla Flecher, "Product Recalls: Gaping Holes in the Nation's Product Safety Net," *Journal of Consumer Affairs* 37 (2003): 170–79; Stephen Labaton, "Safety Chief Is Opposing More Money," *New York Times*, Oct. 30, 2007, C1.

[5] Martha Minow and Jody Freeman, eds., Government by Contract: Outsourcing and American Democracy (Harvard University Press, 2009).

- to sketch a research agenda that might deepen understandings of this increasingly significant regulatory strategy, by scholars and policymakers alike.

I pursue these various issues through a historical lens, a vantage point that can claim some comparative advantage. This perspective indicates how frequently American policymakers have created regulatory roles for non-state actors over the past hundred years, and how often they have connected those actors within larger regulatory frameworks. It further helps to identify enduring patterns with quasi-public and private regulation – their tendency to go in and out of fashion with the oscillating degree of popular faith in government; their capacity to foster innovative and preventive regulatory policies and effective compliance regimes; and the very real danger that their primary impact can be to forestall more substantial public regulation rather than to achieve regulatory goals. The historical record suggests that in the right political context and with the right safeguards, private regulatory governance can be an effective strategy, though not necessarily a cheaper or less complicated one. But without such safeguards, it can rather allow serious social and economic problems to fester, with potentially grave consequences.

CONCEPTUALIZING PRIVATE REGULATION

Nongovernmental regulation comes in many guises. In the last thirty years, it has frequently revolved around the creation of an "ethics and compliance" department within corporations, which sought to guide corporate behavior away from illegal or socially undesirable practices. Within firms committed to this kind of self-regulation, internal corporate regulators created detailed plans to address some social ill, such as environmental degradation, unacceptably high rates of food contamination, or endemic overcharging on government contracts; their departments then took on responsibility for showing that their firms were carrying out the plans, and for monitoring their impact. Some scholars refer to this variant of private regulatory activity as "management regulation."[6] Especially in the domain of environmental policy, corporations pursuing such strategies have increasingly sought certification from the International Organization for Standardization that they meet its norms for best practice in a given area, with over 66,000 firms gaining

---

[6] Cory Coglianese and David Lazer, "Management-Based Regulation: Prescribing Private Management to Achieve Public Goals," *Law and Society* 37 (2003): 691–730.

ISO 14001 certification, which relates to environmental management practices, by 2002.[7]

Internal compliance departments, however, are not always the key actors
within a nongovernmental self-regulatory scheme. Frequently, private governance involves oversight by a nonprofit organization with close links to the
business community, such as a trade association. These entities, frequently
called "self-regulatory organizations," or SROs, typically set standards for
commercial practices in a given industry or sector and disseminate information about "best practices" throughout that sector; they also usually monitor
commercial behavior with respect to those standards and sometimes impose
penalties on companies that violate them. In many instances such efforts
emerge without any explicit governmental sanction; but often they enjoy
the formal blessing of the state, as when the government vests a private organization with the power to certify that businesses meet the eligibility criteria
for receiving government reimbursements for a particular program, or to
license and police the members of a particular profession. Private regulation can also involve less integrated approaches, in which nongovernmental
actors play a role in rule making but not enforcement, or vice versa.

When industry self-regulation reflects purely voluntary actions by firms,
through an industry association or some other similar intermediary, available sanctions tend to be limited, at least in the United States, by antitrust
constraints.[8] In contexts of such voluntary self-regulation, the individuals
charged with overseeing regulatory initiatives usually rely either on publicity, such as "naming and shaming" firms that do not live up to their
broader responsibilities, or on forms of ostracism, such as formally expelling
perceived violators from industry associations or securities exchanges. By
contrast, when legislation clothes self-regulatory bodies with quasi-public
authority, the range of available penalties almost always widens, often
encompassing fines, the possibility of losing licenses to do business, or
even, in some cases, criminal prosecution. Figure 14.1 depicts these various
approaches to private regulatory governance.

The embrace of private forms of regulation has occurred not just in the
United States, but in other industrialized nations, especially in English-
speaking common-law countries such as Canada, Britain, New Zealand,
and Australia, and in a range of emerging economies such as Brazil and
India. Especially in the last generation, it has shaped nongovernmental

---

[7] Todd Steelman and Jorge Rivera, "Voluntary Environmental Programs in the United States:
Whose Interests Are Served," *Organization & Environment* 19 (2006): 507.

[8] David Garvin, "Can Industry Self-Regulation Work?" *California Management Review* 25
(1983): 46.

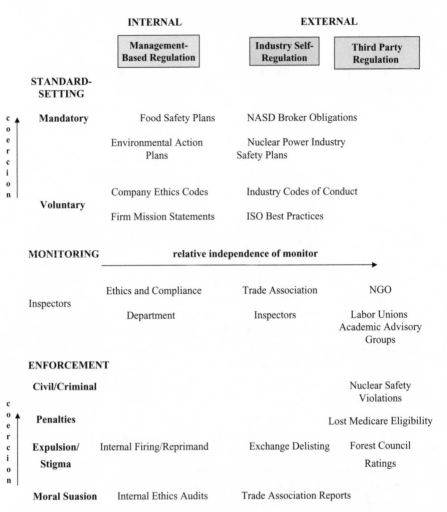

Figure 14.1. A schematic overview of private regulatory governance.

oversight of the global economy in areas as diverse as forest management, transoceanic shipping, the safe handling of toxic chemicals, and the labor standards for suppliers of multinational clothing companies. Reliance on mechanisms of private governance has become a major regulatory strategy pursued by policymakers all over the globe, at every level of governance, from municipalities to organizations affiliated with the United Nations.[9]

[9] For indications of the enormous range of efforts across the globe that fall under the broad category of self-regulation, see: Gurjeet Singh, "Business Self-Regulation and Consumer Protection in India: A Critique," *Journal of Consumer Policy* 16 (1993): 1–33; Sergio

The regulatory experience of the past two generations reinforces the longstanding reality that regulatory options exist on a continuum between intensive governmental oversight and the inclination to maintain a much more hands-off approach. If elected officials and governmental bureaucrats who confront particular regulatory dilemmas are to adopt techniques of private and quasi-public regulation sensibly, or reject them sensibly, they need to have an appreciation for its distinctiveness and what it can accomplish, as well as where its vulnerabilities lie, in both the short and the long term. Such understanding requires, in the first instance, a sense of history.

THE TURN TO PRIVATE GOVERNANCE

Business self-regulation was by no means uncommon before the attack on governmental regulation gathered steam in the 1970s. Stock and commodity exchanges, the Better Business Bureaus, the Motion Picture Ratings Board, the Underwriters Laboratory, the Joint Commission on the Accreditation of Healthcare Organizations (JCAHO – formerly the Joint Commission on the Accreditation of Hospitals), and the Financial Industry Regulatory Authority (FINRA) – all of these American self-regulatory bodies have a decades-long history. They set far-reaching standards of commercial practice for particular corners of the American marketplace that explicitly claimed to safeguard the public good, generally policed those standards through monitoring of various kinds, and imposed meaningful sanctions against wayward enterprises.[10]

In many cases, business leaders founded these institutions of private governance in the hopes of improving their industry's reputation, thereby increasing demand for its products. The goal, as with the various institutions associated with America's early twentieth-century campaign for "Truth in Advertising," was either to foster public confidence in goods and services where none had previously existed, or to shore up public confidence in goods

Lazzarini and Pedro Carvalho de Mello, "Governmental Versus Self-Regulation of Derivative Markets: Examining the U.S. and Brazilian Experience," *Journal of Ecnomics & Business* 53 (2001): 185–207; Michael Urminsky, ed., "Self-Regulation in the Workplace: Codes of Conduct, Social Labeling and Socially Responsible Investment," *International Labor Organization Working Paper* (2002); Marian Garcia Martinez, Andrew Fearne, Julie Caswell, and Spencer Henson, "Co-regulation as a Possible Model for Food Safety Governance: Opportunities for Public-Private Partnerships," *Food Policy* 32 (2007): 299–314; Helen Sampson and Michael Bloor, "When Jack Gets out of the Box: The Problems of Regulating a Global Industry," *Sociology* 41 (2007): 551–69.

[10] Jody Freeman makes a similar point. "The Private Role in Public Governance," *New York University Law Review* 75 (2000): 551–55, 640–47.

or services that had been damaged by the unscrupulous commercial practices or the shoddy performance of some firms within the industry. In other contexts, as with the insurance industry's move to create Underwriters' Laboratory (UL), firms in a given economic sector turned to structures of private governance as a way to reduce transaction costs and economic uncertainty through the creation of new commercial standards, thereby improving access to crucial information. Underwriters' Laboratory achieved this goal, first for fire insurance companies and then for a broader segment of the industry. The organization developed clear safety standards for businesses wishing to insure their factories and headquarters against fire, and then created the technical infrastructure to test and rate the safety of buildings. UL eventually expanded into the related area of consumer product safety.[11]

Equally important, the move to create or extend the jurisdiction of such nongovernmental regulators was usually prompted by a credible threat of impending state regulation. Thus in 1914, the New York Stock Exchange broadened its demands of listed corporations, requiring that they "promptly" inform investors of "any action in respect to dividends on shares or interest on bonds," so as to limit the opportunities for insider trading, and thereby shore up the investing public's confidence in the stock market. It did so, however, only after the Senate Pujo Committee had issued withering criticism of prevailing corporate practices and had signaled that without reform from the New York Stock Exchange (NYSE), Congress would pass legislation compelling such reform. A decision by the relatively new Better Business Bureaus to vet unlisted securities offerings in the 1920s and then warn the public about allegedly fraudulent stocks similarly sought to forestall regulatory action by the state. Recipients of substantial funding from Wall Street, the bureaus moved into this area partly to bolster confidence in the securities markets as a whole, and partly to ward off prevailing proposals for much more substantial government oversight of all new issues of stocks and bonds. In a similar vein, the growing significance of JCAHO as a private regulator of quality in American health care was directly correlated with regulatory pressures associated with public health care funding. During the 1950s, representatives of the health care industry created JCAH (JCAHO's predecessor) and its accreditation program as a way to forestall governmental inspections for state licensing, which had become the path to eligibility for federal hospital construction grants; in the mid-1960s, the American

---

[11] Edward Balleisen, "Private Cops on the Fraud Beat: American Business Self-Regulation and Its Discontents, 1895–1932," *Business History Review* 83 (2009): 113–60. Scott Knowles, "Inventing Safety: Fire, Technology, and Trust in Modern America," Ph.D. dissertation, Johns Hopkins University (2003), 184–259.

Hospital Association convinced the Johnson Administration that the only way to launch Medicare quickly would be to rely on JCAH as a means of certifying that providers would qualify for the program.[12]

An analogous dynamic has driven much of the expansion of self-regulation since the Carter Administration. Consider four especially significant examples, all initiated in the last thirty years – the Institute of Nuclear Power Operators, launched in 1979 to monitor performance and safety procedures at nuclear power plants; the Defense Industry Initiative on Business Ethics and Conduct, charged in 1985 with overseeing the efforts of defense firms to clamp down on fraudulent billing; the chemical industry's Responsible Care Program, started in 1988 with the goal of improving manufacturers' record of environmental protection and safety in the production and transportation of its products; and the move to establish extensive ethics and compliance programs at major health care providers in the mid-1990s, with the primary goal of eliminating excessive charges to government health care programs. In each case, industry action was triggered by highly publicized accidents or scandals, which generated substantial political and administrative pressure for heightened regulatory measures. For the nuclear power industry, the precipitating event was the reactor meltdown at Three Mile Island; for the defense and health care industries, it was a protracted series of contracting fraud scandals; for the chemical industry, it was the disaster at Union Carbide's plant in Bhopal, India.[13]

In the case of several already highly regulated businesses, such as food processing plants and manufacturers subject to pollution controls, the path to management regulation ran through thickets of previously extensive administrative regulation, as well as around the threat of additional regulatory action. During the 1980s and 1990s, firms in these industries drew on

---

[12] Howard C. Westwood and Edward G. Howard, "Self-Government in the Securities Business," *Law and Contemporary Problems* 17 (1952): 523–24; Balleisen, "Private Cops on the Fraud Beat"; Timothy Jost, "The Joint Commission on Accreditation of Hospitals: Private Regulation of Health Care and the Public Interest," *Boston College Law Review* 24 (1983): 850–52; Eleanor Kinney, "Private Accreditation as a Substitute for Direct Government Regulation in Public Health Insurance Programs: When Is It Appropriate?" *Law and Contemporary Problems* 57 (1994): 52–53. For still other examples, see Garvin, "Can Self-Regulation Work?" 42–43.

[13] Joseph Rees, *Hostages of Each Other: The Transformation of Nuclear Safety since Three Mile Island* (Chicago, 1994); Nancy Kurland, "The Defense Industry Initiative: Ethics, Self-Regulation, and Accountability," *Journal of Business Ethics* 12 (1993): 137–46; Edward Balleisen, *Scenes from a Corporate Makeover: Columbia/HCA and Healthcare Fraud, 1992–2001* (Durham, 2003); Andrew King and Michael Lenox, "Industry Self-Regulation without Sanctions: The Chemical Industry's Responsible Care Program," *Academy of Management Journal* 43 (2000): 698–716.

the work of sociologists, political scientists, and legal scholars to propose the replacement of administrative rule setting and inspection with new strategies of risk analysis and prevention. They convinced federal policymakers that these strategies would bring about better outcomes than traditional regulatory approaches. As a result, the government loosened the regulatory regime that governed their production practices. (In the case of food safety, this regulatory outcome emerged even though consumer groups strenuously lobbied for more stringent governmental inspections after a spate of *e. coli* outbreaks during the early 1990s.) Firms developed their own plans for meeting regulatory objectives, which were reviewed and approved by governmental officials. They then carried out their internal regulatory blueprints, which ostensibly included mechanisms for ensuring compliance and evaluating the plans' impact.[14]

The United States Sentencing Commission gave corporations a powerful incentive to consider these and other strategies of self-regulation in 1991, when it passed new sentencing guidelines for corporations and other organizations convicted of criminal wrongdoing. An independent agency within the federal judicial branch, the Sentencing Commission owes its existence to the 1984 Comprehensive Crime Control Act, which sought to reduce disparities in punishments meted out by the federal courts and to incorporate the most recent scholarly understandings of crime and law enforcement strategies into judicial sentencing. The commission's guidelines both dramatically increased fines for organizations convicted of white-collar crimes and specified that judges should reduce such penalties by as much as 95 percent if a given organization had a system in place to investigate and prevent criminal wrongdoing by its employees. This policy was prompted by the Reagan Administration's response to the defense contracting scandals of the 1980s, which called for a new system of industry self-policing as a cost-effective means of preventing overbilling to the federal government.[15]

Within a matter of months, the sentencing guidelines received close attention in corporate headquarters throughout the country, spawning a host

---

[14] Coglianese and Lazer, "Management Based Regulation"; John M. Antle, "Efficient Food Safety Regulation in the Food Manufacturing Sector," *American Journal of Agricultural Economics* 78 (1996): 1243; Steelman and Rivera, "Voluntary Environmental Programs in the United States"; Marc Eisner, "Corporate Environmentalism, Regulatory Reform, and Industry Self-Regulation: Toward Genuine Regulatory Reinvention in the United States," *Governance* 17 (2004): 146–67.

[15] Barbara Ettore, "Crime and Punishment: A Hard Look at White-Collar Crime," *Management Review* 83 (May 1994): 10–16; O. C. Ferrell, Debbie Thorne LeClair, and Linda Ferrell, "The Federal Sentencing Guidelines for Organizations: A Framework for Ethical Compliance," *Journal of Business Ethics* 17 (1998): 353–64.

of ethics and compliance departments. As late as 1990, the organizational charts of American corporations mostly lacked boxes for such units, though a few firms who had run afoul of the 1977 Foreign Corrupt Practices Act had created them, as had a handful of other companies who had been beset by scandal. Within the next decade, the number of ethics and compliance units mushroomed, becoming commonplace among large companies. Just a year after the adoption of the new sentencing guidelines, the heads of these units had created a professional organization, the Ethics and Compliance Officers Association, which by 2006 boasted membership of well over a thousand companies, including a majority of the Fortune 100. The brief of these corporate officers has grown to encompass periodic risk assessments of their employers' business practices, largely as a result of 2004 amendments to the federal sentencing guidelines, which required companies to carry out such ethics and compliance audits in order to qualify for reductions in criminal sentencing.[16]

Heightened pressures from activist organizations and broader public opinion represent an additional explanation for this explosion of corporate ethics and compliance programs. By the early 1990s, many groups in the consumer, labor, and environmental movements concluded that the political will to pursue coercive regulatory measures had all but disappeared in America and many other industrialized countries, and that globalization had severely diminished the regulatory effectiveness of nation–states. As a result, these organizations strenuously encouraged corporations to adopt forms of self-regulation in domains like labor and environmental standards for their foreign suppliers, often in the shape of voluntary codes. Activists further offered to assist in the creation of such private forms of governance. Their efforts were amplified by waxing public concern about these same issues, particularly in the aftermath of major crises or scandals, a key consideration for many business leaders who chose to pursue forms of self-regulation.[17]

Adoption of substantial regimes of private regulation in the United States, then, has generally emerged in the shadow of feared or already developed

---

[16] Megan Barry, "Why Ethics Programs Can Fail," *Journal of Business Strategy* 23 (Nov./Dec. 2002): 37–40; "Ethics & Compliance Officer Association Launches 2006 ECOA Compensation Survey," ECOA Press Release, CSR Newswire, May 16, 2006 [http://www.csrwire .com/News/5610.html], accessed Nov. 30, 2007; Sarah Johnson, "Another Increase in Compliance Costs," *CFO.Com*, Sept. 21, 2006 [http://www.cfo.com/article.cfm/7956569], accessed Nov. 30, 2007; John M. Spinnato, Debra Sabatini Hennelly, and Steven A. Lauer, "A General Counsel And His Experts Tackle Risk Assessments," *The Metropolitan Corporate Counsel*, Oct. 2006, 50.

[17] Aaron Chatterji and Siona Listokin, "Corporate Social Irresponsibility," *Democracy Journal* (Winter 2007): 52–56; Parker, *Open Corporation*, 56.

regulatory action by the state. The same pattern obtains in other parts of the world.[18] Although one can point to instances in which industry leaders spearheaded initiatives in the absence of pressure from government and the broader public, American business elites have tended to pursue strategies of self-regulation when the prospect of new or heightened governmental regulation stared them in the face, or when they already confronted significant regulatory oversight and wished to diminish it. And although initiatives in private regulatory rule making and enforcement have occurred throughout the past century and a half, they have emerged most frequently during eras in which the prevailing political discourse has evinced especially strong skepticism toward the effectiveness of governmental bureaucracy, and especially deep confidence in the capacity and public-spiritedness of private institutions associated with the business community. The Hooverian associationalism of the 1920s and the thirty-year era of deregulation initiated by the Carter and Reagan Administrations stand out in this regard.

THE THEORETICAL UNDERPINNINGS OF NONGOVERNMENTAL REGULATION

Over the past century, proponents of self-regulation have consistently portrayed this strategy as possessing a series of strengths that correspond neatly to the weaknesses of traditional regulation by public bureaucracies, a line of argument that has received sophisticated elaboration in the last few decades. As an army of "public choice" and "law and economics" scholars have explored the shortcomings of the regulatory state, a battalion of social scientists positively disposed toward private governance have adumbrated its corresponding advantages. In other words, the increasingly familiar indictment of "command and control" regulation provides a quite useful guide to the leading arguments for relying on private regulatory structures.[19]

---

[18] Singh, "Business Regulation and Consumer Protection in India," 16–28; Neil Gunningham and Joseph Rees, "Industry Self-Regulation: An Institutional Perspective," *Law and Policy* 19 (1997): 400–2.

[19] For especially trenchant overviews of the weaknesses of "command and control regulation," paired with the corresponding theoretical advantages of self-regulation, see John Braithwaite, "Enforced Self-Regulation: A New Strategy for Corporate Crime Control," *Michigan Law Review* 80 (1982): 1466–507; Douglas C. Michael, "Federal Agency Use of Audited Self-Regulation as a Regulatory Technique," *Administrative Law Review* 47 (1995): 171–253; Gunningham and Rees, "Industry Self-Regulation," 364–414; Freeman, "Private Role in Public Governance"; Coglianese and Lazer, "Management-Based Regulation"; Parker, *Open Corporation*, 8–16.

Adaptability and Precision

Government agencies ostensibly craft rigid regulatory regimes that ignore the diversity of businesses in a given part of the economy, become ever more detailed and complex with time, and respond slowly to technological innovations or other economic transformations that reshape the relevant economic context, except in the aftermath of crisis. Private regulators, their champions insist, are far more likely to act prospectively and to adopt flexible standards and approaches to enforcement. With considerably more knowledge about the peculiarities of a given business or sector, nongovernmental regulators can more effectively tailor a regulatory plan that makes sense for that firm, in the case of management regulation, or industry, in the case of regulation by a trade association. They also can more readily adjust rules to changing circumstances. And they have far more leeway and capacity to think through the systemic implications of plural and sometimes competing regulatory objectives. This last point has particular salience in the realm of environmental regulation, since solutions to environmental problems often give rise to new dilemmas (i.e., smokestack scrubbers that limit airborne pollutants at the cost of creating new forms of solid waste), and manufacturers frequently confront a wide array of environmental prescriptions that all impinge on production processes.[20]

Coverage

Perennially faced with insufficient budgets, government regulators all too often become victims of overload, unable to cope with the demands of monitoring the firms that fall under their jurisdiction. Between 1996 and 1998, for example, the Environmental Protection Agency was able to inspect fewer than 1 percent of the more than 100,000 large-scale corporate facilities subject to the Clean Air, the Clean Water, and the Resource Conservation and Recovery Act. The task of inspecting imported consumer goods has proved even more daunting for the Consumer Product Safety Commission (CPSC), which in 2007 relied on a single inspector to monitor over 15 million containers annually entering the United States through Los Angeles ports. Faced with such an impossible situation, the CPSC has become almost entirely dependent on the adoption of voluntary standards by manufacturers

---

[20] Braithwaite, "Enforced Self-Regulation," 1474–77; David Weimer, "The Puzzle of Private Rulemaking: Expertise, Flexibility, and Blame Avoidance in U.S. Regulation," *Public Administration Review* 66 (2006): 574–75; Eisner, "Corporate Environmentalism, Regulatory Reform, and Industry Self-Regulation," 146.

and distributors, and on the issuance of recalls after safety issues emerge.[21] As a result of such constrained enforcement capacities, regulators often take the easy option, focusing on tasks that seem doable, even if they may not result in the greatest return for the expenditure of regulatory time and effort. By contrast, private regulators can often inspect a much larger percentage of an industry's firms, do so with greater frequency and intensity, and at lower cost, freeing up state regulators to focus on those businesses that prove "genuinely recalcitrant."[22] This more substantial capacity of private regulators, for example, largely accounts for the SEC's initial and ongoing willingness to delegate considerable regulatory authority to the National Association of Security Dealers (NASD – the forerunner of FINRA).[23]

The challenges of operating in an international business environment provide additional force to this line of argument. Corporations with far-flung production facilities confront a bewildering array of jurisdictions, with widely varying regulatory rules and enforcement cultures. In light of this reality, the advocates of private governance structures stress that they offer a way to impose at least some meaningful constraints on the foreign subsidiaries of multinationals that might otherwise take even fuller advantage of permissive offshore legal environments and the impulse to engage in regulatory arbitrage.[24]

Focus on Problem Solving

Administrative regulatory regimes overseen by governments frequently become rule-bound, focusing more on retrospective enforcement of exceedingly detailed prohibitions rather than on potential strategies for preventing

---

[21] Matthew Potoski; Aseem Prakash, "The Regulation Dilemma: Cooperation and Conflict in Environmental Governance," *Public Administration Review* 64 (Mar/Apr 2004): 154; Eric Lipton, "Safety Agency Faces Scrutiny amid Changes," *New York Times*, Sept. 2, 2007, A1.

[22] Neil Gunningham, Martin Phillipson, Peter Grabosky, "Harnessing Third Parties as Surrogate Regulators: Achieving Environmental Outcomes by Alternative Means," *Business Strategy and the Environment* 8 (1999): 221–23; Braithwaite, "Enforced Self-Regulation," 1468–69. As Braithwaite notes, the inspectors of self-regulatory organizations, whether internal or external to firms, often are more knowledgeable about a given industry and particular firms than government inspectors, allowing them to achieve more substantial investigative "depth."

[23] Thomas K. McCraw, "With Consent of the Governed: SEC's Formative Years," *Journal of Policy Analysis and Management* 1 (1982): 346–70; Joel Seligman, *The Transformation of Wall Street: A History of the Securities and Exchange Commission and Modern Corporate Finance* (Boston, 1995), 184–89, 323–34.

[24] John Braithwaite and Peter Drahos, *Global Business Regulation* (Cambridge, 2000), 253–54, 605; Eisner, "Corporate Environmentalism, Regulatory Reform, and Industry Self-Regulation," 147.

the emergence of problematic business practices in the first place. This outcome, especially common in the twentieth-century United States, partly reflects the institutional logic of bureaucracy. As Marc Eisner has argued, "by mandating specific technologies or performance standards" and "'one size fits all' solutions," regulatory administrators greatly ease the task of monitoring the business community. As Eisner also notes, over the past forty years, many American policymakers have harbored considerable fears of regulatory "capture," an outcome made more difficult by the adoption of relatively unambiguous rules.[25]

Defenders of private regulation argue that nongovernmental regulators, by contrast, tend to be more willing to seek innovative, cooperative solutions to market failures. They are far better placed to facilitate internal reengineering processes or business practices so as to meet, or even exceed, regulatory targets through technological or organizational innovation, giving life to "principles" and realizing "goals" precisely because they do not confront unbending commands. Compliance officers who work within private firms have a particular advantage in this regard, especially if they have mastered the art of balancing the commercial imperatives of their firms with regulatory constraints.[26]

Facilitation of Cooperation

Relations between public regulators and regulated industries have often become intensely adversarial. This pattern is especially evident in the United States, where legal culture has long emphasized attention to procedural niceties and the importance of furnishing regulated entities the ability to challenge regulatory outcomes in the courts, twin impulses codified by the 1946 Administrative Procedures Act. Such endemic conflict often generates wasteful expenditure of time and money on legal controversies, as well as an organizational sensibility of treating regulatory prosecutions and fines as just another cost of doing business. Especially in the decades since World War II, the Federal Trade Commission (FTC)'s oversight of deceptive advertising has stood out as an especially problematic example, with many of its enforcement actions taking years to wind their way through administrative and then legal processes. Regulatory action in a host of areas has confronted similar barriers to expeditious policy implementation.[27]

---

[25] Eisner, "Corporate Environmentalism," 147–49.
[26] Parker, *Open Corporation*, 117–29; Freeman, "Private Role in Public Governance," 650–52.
[27] For typical complaints about regulatory process at the FTC, see: "Trade Rules and Trade Conferences: The FTC and Business Attack Deceptive Practices, Unfair Competition,

Advocates of business self-regulation argue that private regulators generally maintain much better relationships with the firms they oversee, since the latter view them as insiders to the industrial community, or in the case of company-based ethics and compliance programs, insiders to the corporation, rather than as snooping interlopers. As a result, the oversight activities of nongovernmental institutions are far less likely to provoke outright defiance from regulated firms, and can rely more effectively on techniques of persuasion and informal social sanctions, including public disclosure/shaming, to address problematic behavior. A New York City department store executive adroitly articulated this position in the 1930s, when he sought to explain the advantages of advertising self-regulation by the Better Business Bureau, rather than by intrusive agents of the state. The bureau, he proclaimed, "is not a police organization. It is not an organization run by somebody trying to interfere with our business. It is an organization designed and financed by New York stores and investment houses. Our membership is costing us several thousands dollars a year. We are members of this Bureau because we want an outside check upon our activities."[28]

Buy-in

Under ideal circumstances, the proponents of self-regulation maintain, private regulators can help to recast corporate norms, balancing short-term pressures for profitability against broader time horizons and a wider set of social and economic concerns. By explicitly defining a company's or industry's "public commitment to moral restraint and aspiration," private regulators can help to forge organizational cultures that redirect employees away from transgressing legal boundaries or widely held social values. The prospects for such "remoralization" of the commercial realm are especially bright when representatives of businesses throughout a particular industry take the time to hammer out aspirational principles and codes of conduct to guide corporate decision making, and when corporate leaders evince real dedication to the implementation of those guidelines. According to the

and Antitrust Violations," *Yale Law Journal* 62 (1953): 913–16; "'Corrective Advertising' Orders of the Federal Trade Commission." *Harvard Law Review* 85 (1971): 482–84. On other arenas, see Eugene Bardach and Robert Kagan, *Going by the Book: The Problem of Regulatory Unreasonableness* (Philadelphia, 1982); Jack Barkenbus, "Is Self-Regulation Possible," *Journal of Policy Analysis and Management* (1983): 576–88; Weimer, "Puzzle of Private Rulemaking."
28 "Department Store Has Accuracy Meeting," *Accuracy* 1 (Sept. 1925): 1. For a similar description of internal compliance staff at an international pharmaceutical company as "family," see Braithwaite, "Enforced Self-Regulation," 1469.

supporters of private mechanisms of oversight, this kind of participation can produce ethical principles that set higher standards than legal restraints; it can further generate far deeper internal commitment than external rule setting by government, commitment that can have more long-lasting impact than mere fear of running afoul of the law.[29]

In the 1920s, spokespersons for the business community consistently characterized the prevailing regulatory associationalism of the time as "business home rule." This formulation encapsulates much of the enduring appeal of business self-regulation. Taken as a package, the leading arguments for this regulatory strategy appeal to the power of decentralized self-government. These arguments imply a powerful analogy between decentralized modern corporations, with their semiautonomous divisions, and decentralized modern regulatory institutions. In each case, the allocation of decision rights to the individuals most familiar with the relevant context presumably generates good decision making. Whether corporate managers or private regulatory officials, the men and women "on the spot" ostensibly possess the knowledge and experience to craft the most sensible and effective approaches to particular regulatory challenges and opportunities, as well as the capacity to implement them efficiently.

By the same token, proponents of self-regulation either implicitly or explicitly invoke the transformative dimensions of civic participation. A given industry's or enterprise's engagement in policy formulation and enforcement, this line of thinking suggests, will generate not only innovative problem solving but also a powerful form of consent – an acceptance of the standards that emerge from debate, an embrace of a social identity bound up with the larger aspirations underlying the standards, and an accompanying commitment to uphold those norms against firms that ignore or contravene them.[30] Throughout the last century, proponents of self-regulation have thus embraced the logic of civic republicanism.[31] They assume that engagement in the deliberative search for a common good will encourage economic actors to temper their impulses toward narrow self-interest, to expand their analytical time horizons, and to forge communitarian identities that constrain both destructive individualism and corrosive corporate amoralism.

---

[29] Braithwaite, "Enforced Self-Regulation," 1478–79; Gunningham and Rees, "Industry Self-Regulation," 376.

[30] Gunningham and Rees, "Industry Self-Regulation," 376–80; Freeman, "Private Role in Public Governance," 656–57.

[31] For a helpful framing of the recent advocacy of self-regulation in these terms, see William Scheurman, "Is Republican Regulatory Law the Answer to Globalization?" *University of Toronto Law Journal* 52 (2002): 301–11.

SELF-REGULATION AS SMOKESCREEN

If the proponents of self-regulation tout it as a form of "home rule" suffused with the virtues of small-town participatory democracy, its detractors implicitly view it rather as akin to the "home rule" of late nineteenth- and early twentieth-century Southern segregationists – an oligarchic means by which an economic elite avoids meaningful accountability to the values and concerns of a larger democratic majority. To most skeptics of regulatory self-governance by the business community, the case developed by the strategy's champions bears only minimal relation to economic, social, and political realities. For a broad group of consumer groups, environmental activists, unions, and safety organizations, along with a substantial number of like-minded academic critics, the vision of self-regulation as a preeminently effective means of achieving fundamental regulatory aspirations has never been anything more than a pipe dream.

Harboring considerable distrust of corporations, these critics fear that left to their own devices, business leaders and corporate bureaucracies will inevitably craft Potemkin regulation – programs with pious-sounding principles and goals that do not actually change corporate behavior. One 1999 study of ethics and compliance programs at America's largest corporations gives credence to this worry, concluding on the basis of extensive survey data that such initiatives typically had "a largely symbolic organizational role."[32] In the absence of clearly identified public rules and sufficiently well-funded regulatory agencies to police those rules, critics of private regulation predict that corporate decision makers inevitably will focus on short-term economic advantage. Without a credible deterrent, without the fear of significant legal consequences, the most ambitious standards and codes of conduct will have minimal practical import. Indeed, the efforts to build internal mechanisms of oversight frequently displace more vigorous governmental action, leaving serious socioeconomic ills unaddressed.[33]

Perhaps no recent episode has more forcefully elicited this particular criticism than the SEC's Consolidated Supervised Entities (CSE) program, created in 2004 as a part of a regulatory initiative meant to shield America's largest investment banks from potentially "hostile" oversight by European financial authorities. That initiative extended the SEC's regulatory

---

[32] "Gary R Weaver, Linda K. Trevino, and Philip L Cochran, "Corporate Ethics Policies of the Mid 1990s: An Empirical Study of the Fortune 1000," *Journal of Business Ethics* 18 (Feb. 1999): 283–94.

[33] See the studies cited by Steelman and Rivera, "Voluntary Environmental Programs," 510, 512.

jurisdiction to these investment banks, but also vested the primary authority for setting their capital requirements with internal risk managers, who would adjust overall exposure to debt in line with periodic risk assessments. CSE risk evaluations, based on the banks' own complex computer models, constituted a form of management self-regulation. Voluntary, and minimally overseen by just a handful of SEC officials, the CSE program proved entirely inadequate as a means of limiting debt-related vulnerabilities, a reality that became painfully obvious in the aftermath of the multiyear global financial crisis that began to unfold in late summer 2007. Derided by observers and members of Congress as "toothless and largely ineffectual," and eventually characterized by SEC Chair Christopher Cox as a "failure," this experiment in financial self-governance badly miscalculated the capacity and willingness of broker–dealers such as Bear Stearns, Merrill Lynch, and Lehman Brothers to recognize and manage risk, and thus contributed to their downfalls. The SEC accordingly terminated the program in September 2008.[34]

The doubters of self-regulatory schemes, whether deployed in the financial world, like the CSE program, or elsewhere, implicitly appropriate key assumptions that public choice scholars make about human motivation and the omnipresent dangers of regulatory failure; they then apply those assumptions to the likely behavior of private regulators whose careers and social identities are bound up with the profit-making entities that they supposedly will regulate. In other words, for many skeptics of self-regulation, the motives and sensibilities of any self-regulatory bodies closely affiliated with the business community are inherently suspect. Alternatively, critics assume that however well intentioned, self-regulation will inevitably founder because of structural imperatives within the corporate world. A prominent political blogger recently exemplified this pessimism in a commentary on the torrent of product safety fiascoes that bedeviled American importers of consumer goods in 2007. Entitling his post, "Self-Regulation Fails Once Again," this commentator characterized the prevailing efforts by American importers to police Chinese supply chains as essentially worthless.

---

[34] Letter from Representative Edward J. Markey to Christopher Cox, Chairman of the Securities & Exchange Commission, Oct. 1, 2008, http://markey.house.gov/docs/finance/letter_sec_risk_assessment.pdf, accessed Dec. 31, 2008; "Chairman Cox Announces End of Consolidated Supervised Entities Program," Press Release, Securities & Exchange Commission, Sept. 26, 2008, http://www.sec.gov/news/press/2008/2008–230.htm, accessed Dec. 31, 2008; Office of Inspector General, U.S. Securities and Exchange Commission, *SEC's Oversight of Bear Stearns and Related Entities: The Consolidated Supervised Entity Program* (Washington, D.C., 2008); Stephen Labaton, "Agency's '04 Rule Let Banks Pile up New Debt," *New York Times*, Oct. 3, 2008, p. A1.

The American corporations refused to adopt substantial systems of quality control, he surmised, because doing so "might have added a few pennies to the cost" of their goods.[35]

A smaller cluster of critics shares the suspicion of the motives behind private regulation, but not the assumption that the strategy has little chance of disciplining unruly marketplaces. Comprised primarily of marginal business owners whose commercial practices have run afoul of the rules set by some private or quasi-public regulatory regime, along with some economists, this second group has attacked self-regulation for being all too effective. To these detractors, the efforts of Better Business Bureaus to monitor advertising, or of the American Chemistry Council's Responsible Care Program to oversee the safe handling of chemicals, share much in common with unjustifiably restrictive occupational licensing regimes. Whatever their pretensions, such regimes impose anticompetitive rules that create barriers to entry and economic rents for well-entrenched firms.[36]

The practical insulation of private governance structures from democratic influence compounds these various concerns, raising a host of procedural worries. Citizens, whether acting as individuals or through organizations, generally have far less capacity to engage with or challenge the decision-making process of private regulators than the agencies of government. The public often has minimal access to information about how private regulators function, and little or no ability to participate in their deliberations. And in the United States, if individuals or groups wish to challenge a hospital's accreditation or the safety ranking of a nuclear facility, they frequently lack the legal standing to do so.[37]

To its opponents, then, business self-regulation represents at best a misguided attempt to achieve fundamental public goals on the cheap. At worst, it constitutes a cynical, antidemocratic strategy to deflect more substantial governmental oversight, assuaging political pressure to come to grips with some significant social or economic problem without actually addressing it, or even a mechanism of protecting entrenched businesses against potential competitors. This critique largely parallels the growing dissatisfaction with the movement for Corporate Social Responsibility (CSR), which strikes an increasing number of observers as little more than a distraction from much

---

[35] "Chris in Paris," "Self-Regulation Fails Again, Consumer Products Safety Commission Requests Funding," Americablog, Sept. 20, 2007 [http://www.americablog.com/2007/09/self-regulation-fails-again-consumer.html, accessed Nov. 25, 2007].

[36] Anthony Ogus, "Rethinking Self-Regulation," *Oxford Journal of Legal Studies* 15 (1995): 97–108; Garvin, "Can Self-Regulation Work?" 38–39, 43.

[37] Freeman, "Private Role in Public Governance," 612–16, 619–21.

more fundamental debates over the appropriate role of the state in shaping political economy.[38]

PRIVATE REGULATORY GOVERNANCE IN ACTION: LESSONS FOR POLICYMAKERS

Social scientists have offered detailed appraisals of business self-regulation since the early twentieth century. Until recently, though, such engagement was mostly piecemeal – an overview of self-regulation in one arena or another, without much in the way of explicit theoretical conceptualization, comparison between different varieties of private governance in a given society, or comparison of approaches and outcomes across societies. Over the past two decades, though, social scientists have paid increasing attention to private regulation as a policy tool, examining its impact in both the United States and a number of other countries, and, in a growing number of studies, fitting the particularities of individual cases into larger patterns. This analysis has been especially rich in Australia, where sociologists and legal scholars interested in self-regulation, such as John Braithwaite, have had significant input over the development of regulatory policy. Collectively, this research suggests an emerging scholarly consensus about the circumstances that lend themselves to reliance on private governance to achieve public goals, and on the preconditions for successful attempts at self-regulation.

Fertile and Barren Ground for Nongovernmental Regulation

Strategies of private governance by trade associations tend to work best when firms in a given industry possess shared interests in reducing economic uncertainties, generating network efficiencies through commercial or product standards, or diffusing fundamental challenges to the industry's collective reputation. These various contexts align regulatory goals with corporate profitability over the medium to long term, giving business elites incentives to reshape industry norms, disseminate best practices, and invest sufficient resources to police firms that do not measure up to the new standards. The theme of building or shoring up reputation looms especially large in many case studies of effective sector-wide self-regulation, such as the American securities industry's oversight of stock exchanges and brokerages

---

[38] See for example David Vogel, *The Market for Virtue: The Potential and Limits of Corporate Responsibility* (Washington, 2005); Chatterji and Listokin, "Corporate Social Irresponsibility," 61–63; Simon Enoch, "A Greener Potemkin Village? Corporate Responsibility and the Limits of Growth," *Capitalism, Nature, Socialism* 18 (June, 2007): 79–82.

in the aftermath of the Great Depression, and the monitoring and develop-ment of safety policies by the American nuclear power industry in the wake of Three Mile Island. Here one sees an instructive parallel to the political dynamics of crisis that David Moss and Mary Oey discuss in their contri-bution to this collection. The experience of crisis can open eyes within the business community as well as outside of it.[39]

Private governance through management regulation also appears to offer comparative advantages when relevant firms differ greatly in their organi-zational cultures and business practices, and the relevant regulatory issues defy easy mechanisms of oversight or universal standards. Coglianese and Lazer identify the maintenance of food safety by large-scale processors and the safe handling of chemicals as two arenas that share these characteristics. In the case of food safety, the growing threat of microbial contamination has rendered longstanding "poke and sniff" inspection methods far less effec-tive, while the requirements of chemical safety vary so enormously from one industrial context to the next that they greatly complicate attempts to frame comprehensive regulatory rules. Numerous scholars make a similar argument for a large swath of environmental regulation, given the extraor-dinary range of issues confronted by thousands of firms and the significance of rapid technological change in altering the regulatory landscape. In the realm of occupational safety, there is the further possibility of jointly dele-gating authority to management and workers in particular workplaces, espe-cially where these two groups are predisposed toward collaborative effort. This approach significantly cut the incidence of construction accidents in California during the 1980s.[40]

The dilemmas of pursuing regulatory objectives across national bound-aries led many scholars to still another context in which policymakers have good reason to draw on mechanisms of self-policing. Whatever the limita-tions associated with private regulation, it sometimes offers the only practi-cal means of constraining the behavior of multinational corporations whose production facilities and distribution networks span the globe. This argu-ment parallels the view that in light of strong political headwinds against vigorous regulatory rules and substantial enforcement budgets, domestic governments may well do best by relying wherever possible on business firms to monitor themselves as a means of stretching scarce regulatory capacity.

[39] McCraw, "With Consent of the Governed;" Rees, *Hostages of Each Other.*
[40] Coglianese and Lazer, "Management-Based Regulation," 698–700; Eisner, "Corporate Environmentalism"; Gunningham, Phillipson, and Grabosky, "Harnessing Third Parties as Surrogate Regulators;" Joseph Rees, *Reforming the Workplace: A Study of Self-Regulation in Occupational Safety* (Philadelphia, 1988).

Some economic contexts have also proved to be inhospitable to effective self-regulation. One key scholarly conclusion involves the unsuitability of compulsory management regulation for small and medium-sized enterprises. Assessments of self-regulation almost universally observe that such firms lack the resources and administrative capacity to set up their own internal regulatory plans or monitoring structures. Fairman's and Yapp's study of British self-regulation pertaining to food safety during the 1990s nicely illustrates this point. Consumed by the challenges of keeping relatively capital-poor restaurants or catering businesses afloat, the owners and managers of these firms had little interest in or patience with new legal requirements to develop an integrated plan to prevent food-borne illnesses. Instead, they tended to pester government regulators for unambiguous rules and guidelines to follow.[41]

The Centrality of Transparency and Accountability

In addition to identifying the kinds of regulatory terrain that are comparatively well-suited to self-regulation, scholars have spent considerable effort assessing best practices within the realm of private governance. These studies invariably point to the absolutely pivotal importance of **transparency** and **accountability,** reinforcing the stress that Yochai Benkler's essay places on these pivotal institutional "design levers." Regulatory standards and responsibilities must be clear and well communicated throughout a particular corporation, and where relevant, throughout an entire industry. Firms must set up mechanisms to collect relevant data about their adherence to the standards, and must report that data, not only up the chain of corporate command, but also publicly, so that interested parties can assess the outcomes of self-policing. In addition, the regulatory infrastructure must be able to analyze the reports on performance, so that firms can grade employees on their compliance efforts, and industry-wide regulatory bodies can do the same for firms. In the absence of such data analysis, mechanisms of enforcement are severely compromised, whether they concentrate on persuading laggards to improve their efforts, on shaming backsliders initially resistant to persuasion, or on creating deterrence through more formal penalties such as expulsion from a trade association.[42]

---

[41] Robin Fairman and Charlotte Yapp, "Enforced Self-Regulation, Prescription, and Conceptions of Compliance with Small Businesses: The Impact of Enforcement," *Law and Policy* 27 (2005): 491–519.

[42] Gunningham and Rees, "Industry Self-Regulation," 382–89.

Self-regulation in the American defense industry and in British rail transport underscores these conclusions. The Defense Industry Initiative (DII) on ethical contracting ostensibly put in place far-reaching industry controls to constrain billing practices. But the new standards were far from transparent, especially to anyone outside individual firms. The agreement to set up the DII subjected signatory companies to only minimal auditing and reporting requirements, making assessments of their various programs all but impossible. British Rail found itself compelled to adopt wide-ranging self-regulation as a consequence of the 1974 Health and Safety at Work Act. That legislation delegated considerable authority for occupational health and safety policy to employers, who were supposed to assess risks and craft safety practices in conjunction with union representatives, and then jointly monitor work settings through workplace safety committees. Even before the privatization of British Rail in 1993, the internal regulatory performance of the national railroad manifested significant shortcomings. Although British Rail formally met the procedural requirements of the 1974 Act, communication about safety issues often proved spotty, leaving many employees uncertain of their obligations. In addition, managers and workers both shied away from serving in unpopular regulatory roles that demanded considerable time and subjected participants to complaints, and British Rail failed to develop a systematic capacity to assess risks through compilations of company-wide accident statistics, an omission that compromised the organization's policymaking. All of these problems intensified after rail privatization.[43]

Accountability in systems of private regulation, moreover, generally depends on independent monitoring and evaluation of regulatory performance, both to guard against the possibility of false reporting and to ensure that businesses actually incorporate regulatory goals into their most basic practices. That independence depends in the first instance on the provision of adequate resources and standing for those individuals responsible for overseeing self-regulation. As Christine Parker has argued, if internal regulators do not have sufficient budgets to communicate effectively with key workers and assess everyday business operations, if they lack direct relationships with the highest levels of corporate leadership, and if their assessments do not count in performance reviews, compliance departments will lack the "clout" to do their jobs well. Parker further stresses the importance of professionalization, centered on the forging of a private "regulatory community"

---

[43] Bridget Hutter, "Is Enforced Self-Regulation a Form of Risk Taking?: The Case of Railway Health and Safety," *International Journal of Sociology of Law* 29 (2001): 379–400.

that fosters shared commitments to integrity and long-term social responsibilities, alongside the imperative of corporate profitability. Similar considerations apply to private regulators working for trade associations.[44]

Scholars of nongovernmental regulation have also increasingly pointed to third-party interest groups as an additional means of holding the business community to its regulatory professions and responsibilities. In some contexts, as with the Sustainable Forests Initiative and the Forest Stewardship Council since the mid-1990s, public interest groups have stepped in as auditors of business self-regulation. These groups rely on independent scientists to certify that lumber and paper companies are abiding by industry codes that constrain clear-cutting and limit logging in slow growth forests, a process that has enabled large-scale purchasers of these products to differentiate between potential suppliers. In this example, self-regulation combines standard-setting by an industry in conjunction with public interest groups, monitoring by those nonprofit organizations, and practical enforcement by other enterprises that possess countervailing economic power. In a similar vein, a growing number of powerful multinational manufacturers, from Volvo to Dow Chemicals to the Tesco supermarket chain, have begun to impose far-reaching environmental and safety requirements on their suppliers. Such pressure can prove far more effective than governmental mandates in reshaping the priorities of relatively small enterprises, especially when they are located across national boundaries.[45]

Within the United States, social scientists have tended to hold up the safety initiatives of the nuclear power industry in the 1980s and early 1990s as a model of especially effective self-regulation, largely because its practices were predicated on clear rules, public dissemination of performance reviews, at least within the industry, and tangible modes of accountability. After Three Mile Island, nuclear power executives gave the newly created Institute of Nuclear Power Operators (INPO) the mandate and resources to craft detailed regulations for the prevention of nuclear accidents. INPO's efforts included detailed risk analyses as a basis for rule making, regular conferences to share information on effective management practices, and rigorous inspections of nuclear plants. It developed extensive measures of plant safety performance and publicized its findings, both within and outside the industry. Perhaps no INPO tactic proved more effective than

---

[44] Parker, *The Open Corporation*, 179–92; Braithwaite, "Enforced Self-Regulation," 1497–1500.

[45] Gunningham and Rees, "Industry Self-Regulation," 385; Gunningham, Phillipson, and Grabosky, "Harnessing Third Parties as Surrogate Regulators," 214–16; Tetty Havinga, "Private Regulation of Food Safety by Supermarkets," *Law and Policy* 28 (2006): 515–33.

its annual meeting of nuclear plant CEOs, during which the organization announced its safety ratings for all of its members, an action that played to the competitive impulse of business executives to match the performance of industry pacesetters.[46]

The Promise of Coregulation

As with most examples of especially effective private regulation, the activities of INPO occurred within a larger fabric of governmental oversight, in this case by the Nuclear Regulatory Commission. The scholarship on private regulation suggests that such oversight by the state usually constitutes an essential dimension of any well-crafted regulatory design that intends to rely substantially on nonstate actors. Even in the most favorable circumstances – amenable corporate elites, intraindustry relations that permit extensive cooperation, scrutiny from public interest organizations and the broader public – effective private governance is likely to depend heavily on forms of "coregulation" by government, also referred to as "enforced self-regulation," or "audited self-regulation."[47]

Without meaningful governmental oversight, voluntary standards frequently descend into the realm of platitude and private enforcement mechanisms tend to lack bite, as occurred with the CSE program for major investment banks. The Climate Voluntary Innovative Sectors Initiative: Opportunities Now (Climate VISION), pushed by the administration of George W. Bush, also exemplifies this pattern. Begun in 2003, Climate VISION relies on utilities to develop voluntary plans to curb greenhouse gas emissions. Although a few utilities have reported substantial reductions, most participants, in the judgment of one recent study, engaged in "free riding on the reputation of the responsible businesses while cloaking themselves in the appearance of action."[48]

Another key issue concerns the monitoring and reporting of internal regulatory efforts. As we have seen, in some cases, third-party auditing by other nongovernmental actors, such as the scrutiny that conservation groups have brought to global forestry, seems to have worked well. But as the attempts of several NGOs to check up on the implementation of fair labor standards by foreign clothing suppliers suggests, third-party monitoring often cannot be

---

[46] Rees, *Hostages of Each Other.*
[47] Braithwaite, "Enforced Self-Regulation"; Michael, "Federal Agency Use of Audited Self-Regulation."
[48] Steelman and Rivera, Voluntary Environmental Programs in the United States," 506–10.

assured of access to sufficient information from corporations.[49] In addition, supposedly independent evaluations of corporate behavior sometimes turn out to be corrupted by troubling conflicts of interest – a concern made all too evident by the scandals involving accounting firms and stock analysts in the technology boom of the late 1990s, and the bond ratings agencies in the more recent implosion of collateralized debt securities.[50]

Purely voluntary self-regulatory initiatives further raise questions about the viability of private enforcement mechanisms. Even when corporations have powerful reputational incentives to enforce private regulations, as in the case of supermarkets and food safety, the pressures of a competitive marketplace can compromise enforcement efforts. European grocery chains, for example, generally boast of their commitment to safety standards for their suppliers; but cognizant of the consumer's continuing attachment to affordability, those chains often find ways to cut their suppliers some self-regulatory slack, particularly if doing so will result in favorable prices.[51] And even in industries that build robust cultures of communal responsibility and legal compliance, some companies are still likely to flout the rules. Indeed, some voluntary programs of environmental self-regulation in the United States appear to attract firms that disproportionately pollute, especially if those programs lack significant enforcement mechanisms. Most likely, these firms hope to gain public relations points for signing on to an industry code, and perhaps even qualify for insurance discounts, without actually reforming their methods of operation.[52] For the corporate miscreants who emulate Oliver Wendell Holmes's "bad man of the law," credible recourse to legal sanctions is essential; perhaps of even greater importance, recourse against malevolent enterprises is often necessary to convince many other companies that their competitors will abide by the rules.[53]

But what does "meaningful" coregulation entail; what does it look like in practice? Scholars who study self-regulation have developed increasingly

[49] Parker, *Open Corporation*, 142–43.

[50] Joseph Stiglitz, *The Roaring Nineties: A New History of the World's Most Prosperous Decade* (New York, 2003); Roben Farzad, "Let the Blame Begin: Everyone Played Some Role," *Business Week* Aug. 6, 2007, 32; "Testimony of Robert Kuttner," Hearing on Systemic Risks in the Financial System, Financial Services Committee, United States House of Representatives, Oct. 4, 2007, *Political Transcript Wire* [Proquest.] Dec. 2, 2007. See also Havinga, "Private Regulation of Food Safety," 526, for concerns about conflicts of interest with third-party certifiers of food safety practices.

[51] Havinga, "Private Regulation of Food Safety by Supermarkets," 528–29.

[52] Michael Lenox and Jennifer Nash, "Industry Self-Regulation and Adverse Selection: a Comparison across Four Trade Association Programs," *Business Strategy and the Environment* 12 (2003): 343–56.

[53] Gunningham and Rees, "Industry Self-Regulation," 393–94.

detailed assessments of such a multilayered approach to attaining regulatory objectives. Governmental regulators, their research suggests, must take on numerous roles to make mechanisms of private governance work over the long term, developing an integrated strategy of "metaregulation."[54] These administrative functions include:

1. *Mandating appropriate reporting requirements for internal regulatory plans, including substantive assessments of regulatory performance.* Such mandates take on particular importance in contexts where the state enacts compulsory management regulation, such as food safety, occupational heath and safety, and environmental management systems. Without good information, firms cannot embed regulatory goals into their managerial decision making, nor can outside watchdogs, whether from government, industry associations, or public interest groups, even plausibly attempt to assess the effectiveness of internal regulation. Toward this end, governments might prescribe third-party auditing of information provision as a means of guarding its integrity.

   When primary oversight responsibilities rest with nonstate actors, moreover, the state has particularly strong reasons to prescribe reporting that addresses substance rather than form. As the Australian sociologist Andrew Hopkins has noted, the tendency in many regulatory contexts is to require reporting of "tick-in-the-box" kinds of information – whether or not firms have engaged in hazards analysis, furnished training, or followed their own procedures – rather than truly probing evaluations of regulatory quality.[55]

2. *Publicizing the regulatory performance of firms.* If governmental regulators can identify the right kind of performance measures, public rankings of those indicators can serve as powerful motivations for corporate managers to make vigorous internal regulation a priority. Information disclosure of this kind will intensify public criticism of regulatory laggards and burnish the public standing of enterprises that meet or exceed their regulatory obligations. Such reporting can also then feed into standards for insurance coverage, access to credit, eligibility for government contracting, and tort liability, much as accreditation or ratings by private agencies sometimes function. This form of regulatory policy promises to leverage the disciplinary force inherent

---

[54] On the use of this term, see Peter Grabosky, "Using Non-Governmental Resources to Foster Regulatory Compliance," *Governance* 8 (1995): 527–50.

[55] Andrew Hopkins, "Beyond Compliance Monitoring: New Strategies for Safety Regulators," *Law and Policy* 29 (2007): 210–12.

in countervailing economic power, and seems to be particularly promising in the environmental domain, as insurance companies and banks are increasingly inclined to demand that commercial borrowers disclose their potential liability as a result of their environmental impact.[56]

3. *Facilitating and sustaining the professionalization of private regulatory officers.* Business self-policing will not work in any context without competent and committed internal regulators. American regulators would do well to consider the approach of the Australian Competition and Consumer Commission. Heavily influenced by Australian social scientists who study business self-regulation, such as John Braithwaite, Peter Grabosky, and Christine Parker, the ACCC has expended considerable resources on encouraging such professionalization, in part by forging close links to the country's professional association for ethics and compliance officers, which it helped to set up. The idea here is to foster institutional supports for the "intrinsic" motivations for cooperation identified by Yochai Benkler in his chapter on social cooperation.[57]

4. *Developing the analytical capacity to evaluate the impact of private governance.* Expertise in this area is crucial, both to identify best practices in particular regulatory domains and to distinguish areas suitable for self-regulation from those that require alternative approaches, both of which may shift over time. Once a government agency has developed this analytical infrastructure, it will be able to refine reporting requirements, disseminate best practices within and, where appropriate, across industries, and serve as an information clearinghouse for the business community, interest groups, and the public more generally.

5. *Undertaking periodic inspections of self-regulated firms, and maintaining the capacity for more intrusive investigations in cases of corporate recalcitrance.* Regulatory regimes that rely heavily on corporate self-regulation still require the capacity to carry out formal monitoring as a check on backsliding. The appropriate degree of inspection will surely vary from one regulatory context to the next. But corporate management must know that the state can and will enforce legal requirements, both to ensure managerial commitment to meeting regulatory objectives, and to furnish compliance officers with leverage against

[56] Gunningham and Rees, 403; Gunningham, Phillipson, and Grabosky, 216–17; Eisner, 150–52.
[57] Christine Parker, "Compliance Professionalism and Regulatory Community: The Australian Trade Practices Regime," *Journal of Law and Society* 26 (1999): 215–39.

other actors within their firms, and the representatives of industry watchdog groups with leverage against the members of their associations. The current situation with oversight of food safety in American seafood plants or the safety of imported consumer goods from China, for example, provides so little monitoring by government inspectors that internal regulators have little reason to look over their shoulders. A similar dynamic obtained with the CSE program, as the SEC gave a mere twenty people the responsibility of furnishing regulatory oversight for investment banks that collectively controlled assets exceeding $4 trillion. By contrast, a recent study of voluntary self-policing of environmental standards in the United States has found that firms under close scrutiny by the EPA proved far more likely to report significant violations of regulatory rules.[58]

6. *Maintaining regulatory floors for firms or industries that do not opt for self-regulation, and adjusting corporate penalties for regulatory breeches along an enforcement pyramid.* These policies have several goals. Regulatory floors create incentives for the development of robust structures of internal regulation, since firms can thereby gain exemption from more burdensome oversight; they also offer a means of constraining firms that do not opt to police themselves.[59] Graduated "sticks" for violators of regulatory standards seek to foster "restorative justice." As elucidated by John Braithwaite and Ian Ayres, this approach to enforcement ranges from consultation, to warnings, to required adjustments of internal regulatory policies, to fines and eventually criminal prosecution. Regulators have the ability to escalate penalties, but they seek wherever possible to use threatened sanctions to encourage firms to address problems, thereby deepening their internal commitment to regulatory objectives.[60] A similar objective lies behind the imposition of variable corporate and managerial liability for regulatory breeches, depending on the extent to which firms can show that they have effective systems of internal regulatory policymaking

---

[58] Braithwaite, "Enforced Self-Regulation," 1488; Coglianese and Lazer, "Management-Based Regulation," 717; Deborah Silver, "Government Report Rebukes FDA for Lax Regulation of Shellfish Safety," *Restaurants and Institutions* 111 (Sept. 1, 2001): 60; Geoff Dyer, "A Big Crisis of Confidence," *Financial Times*, Oct. 9, 2007, 6; Office of Inspector General, *SEC's Oversight of Bear Stearns*, 2; Labaton, "Agency's '04 Rule"; Jodi Short and Michael Toffel, "Coerced Confessions: Self-Policing in the Shadow of the Regulator," *Journal of Law, Economics, & Organization*, forthcoming.

[59] Eisner, "Corporate Environmentalism," 158–62.

[60] Ian Ayres and John Braithwaite, *Responsive Regulation: Transcending the Regulation Debate* (New York, 1992).

and self-policing. The maintenance of clear legal standards for tort liability further encourages insurance companies and banks to take on supplementary roles as private regulators.[61]

7. *Empowering supplemental nongovernmental watchdogs.* Where appropriate, policymakers can formally incorporate third parties, such as labor unions, community associations, consumer groups, or environmental organizations, into the mix of self-regulation, either through participation in the formulation of rules and standards or the work of monitoring and enforcement. Examples include requiring representation of such groups within the policymaking structures of self-regulation, as in the case of workplace safety councils, or giving such organizations standing to initiate enforcement proceedings, a now common provision in environmental legislation. Such efforts to draw on countervailing power by nongovernmental groups can bring additional expertise and creativity to bear on regulatory problems while "multiplying the eyes and ears" on both private regulators and the public officials charged with overseeing them.[62]

8. *Retaining the authority, and the credible capacity, to impose more far-reaching regulatory obligations should self-regulatory schemes prove to be ineffective.* Scholars who study private regulation use a variety of metaphors to describe this point, but the most common is the one William O. Douglas used to describe the relationship between the SEC and the various institutions of self-regulation in the securities markets – that of a "well-oiled" regulatory "shotgun," kept at the ready "behind the door."[63] Business self-regulation works best when those responsible for it know not only that their actions will be visible to their peers and public officials, and not only that poor performance will trigger sanctions, but also that if business institutions systematically fail to achieve regulatory objectives, a more vigorous regulatory shotgun waits in the wings. That expectation in turn depends on the

[61] Gunningham and Rees, "Industry Self-Regulation," 403; Eisner, "Corporate Environmentalism," 151. Some scholars and many industry groups have advocated that governmental regulators create a zone of confidentiality around self-reported regulatory violations as a further means of encouraging more vigorous compliance. But unlike reductions in formal penalties, the creation of an "audit privilege" does not appear to improve regulatory compliance. Short and Toffel, "Coerced Confessions," 18–20; James Cox, "The Case against a Judicially Created, Common Law Self-Audit or Self-Evaluation Privilege Applicable to Environmental Cases," *Fordham Environmental Law Journal* 51 (2004): 1–30.

[62] Ayres and Braithwaite, "Tripartism," 435–44, 480–86; Freeman, "Private Role in Public Governance," 662–64.

[63] Seligman, *Transformation of Wall Street*, 184–86.

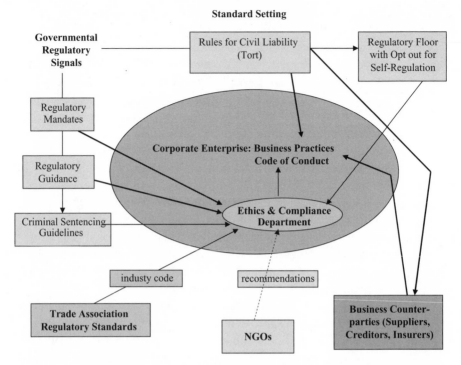

Figure 14.2. Schematic of "coregulation" standard setting.

perception that governmental leaders, and public opinion, are willing to pursue regulatory techniques of command and control as part of the arsenal of governance.

Together, the varied approaches described above amount to a system of "hybrid" regulation, or "regulatory pluralism," with societies depending on a multitude of policymaking structures and oversight mechanisms inside and outside the state.[64] The resulting array of public regulatory roles would challenge the most gifted political entrepreneurs, as suggested by the complex interrelationships sketched in Figures 14.2–14.4. In addition to sustained bureaucratic leadership, the creation and maintenance of sufficient administrative capacity to oversee such a complicated regulatory environment will surely depend on significant investment of resources. Most obviously, regulatory agencies will need to develop the human capital and

---

[64] I take these conceptualizations from Eisner, "Corporate Environmentalism," 161; and Gunningham, Phillipson, and Grabosky, "Harnessing Third Parties as Surrogate Regulators," 221.

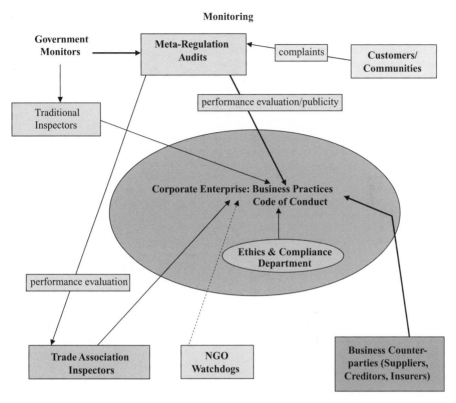

Figure 14.3. Schematic of "coregulation" monitoring.

information systems to perform the numerous functions associated with "metaregulation."[65] A governmental strategy predicated on enforced self-regulation, then, may well offer the possibility of smarter regulation. But it is unlikely to achieve that lofty goal, especially once the particular crises that prompted action by both the state and business fades from political view, without significant public expenditure on administrative oversight.

Herein lies a potential irony in the case for self-regulation as a leading approach of American, and indeed, global, political economy. One of the supposed virtues of business self-regulation touted by its advocates is its

---

[65] Michael W. Toffel and Jodi L. Short, for example, have observed that although many federal agencies have adopted "self-policing" mechanisms, in which firms that have systems in place to identify and voluntarily disclose violations of regulatory standards often receive penalty waivers, most bureaucracies currently lack the capacity to assess the impact of these programs. Toffel and Short, "Coming Clean and Cleaning up: Voluntary Disclosure As a Signal of Effective Self-Policing," unpublished working paper, March 2008.

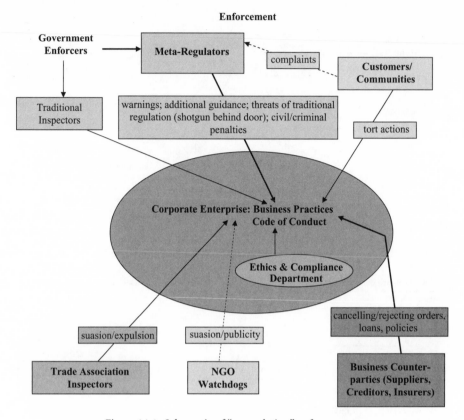

Figure 14.4. Schematic of "coregulation" enforcement.

public costs, which they assume to fall considerably below those of command and control regulation. As a March 2007 Treasury Department report typically proclaimed in this regard, "self-regulation meant cost-effective regulation," since "the industry directly bears the costs, . . . which results in a significant savings to taxpayers."[66] In light of the complex public institutions necessary to support, direct, and constrain private regulation, so that it is effective – and in light of the disastrous consequences that can follow from failed self-regulation, as occurred with the CSE program – one might well evince skepticism about that central presupposition.

---

[66] Department of the Treasury, _Blueprint for a Modernized Financial Regulatory Structure_ (Washington, D.C., 2008), 123.

AN AGENDA FOR FUTURE RESEARCH

Three decades of scholarship, then, have produced a rich set of guidelines for designing mechanisms of coregulation that accentuate the virtues of decentralized policymaking and oversight while forestalling ineffective or even dangerous regulatory charades. And yet, a host of crucial issues remain largely unanswered, questions that call out for attention from across the social sciences. Most obviously, the fundamental economic transformations of the last decade have generated a slew of socioeconomic problems that might lend themselves to coregulation. The threats that an online world poses to privacy; the dangers that highly leveraged hedge funds pose to overall global financial stability; the emergence of financial instruments so complex that even "the smartest guys in the room" struggle to make sense of their full implications; the democratization of credit through securitization of subprime loans, and the resulting collapse of trust in the credit markets – all of these developments have produced new regulatory debates. How might scholars assess the strengths and weaknesses of relying on strategies of private governance as at least a component of regulatory reform in these emerging policy contexts?

Other potential avenues of research entail revisiting current and past instances of regulatory self-governance to refine understandings of this strategy's more general dynamics. We now know, for example, that the adoption of serious initiatives in business self-regulation typically depends on the fear of far-reaching governmental action. But what degree of perceived threat is necessary to concentrate the minds of business elites? And what happens to the institutions of self-regulation, either within firms or across industries, when the prevailing political climate becomes hostile to regulatory action by the state?

The administration of George W. Bush beckons to researchers with respect to both questions. The first six years of the Bush Administration brought extraordinarily cozy relationships between corporations and federal regulatory bodies, with the latter possessing perhaps unparalleled capacity to craft regulatory policy. How has the closeness of that relationship impinged on the trajectory of enforced self-regulation in particular contexts? Analyses of the EPA's handling of environmental management programs, OSHA's engagement with workplace safety initiatives, and the Food and Drug Administration's interaction with food processors who have implemented risk assessment and prevention systems stand out as obvious examples here.

These same regulatory arenas, along with the Nuclear Regulatory Commission, constitute promising avenues of more carefully specifying the economic costs associated with "metaregulation" of private regulatory schemes. What does internal regulation actually cost firms and the governmental agencies charged simultaneously with assisting and policing those efforts? And how might one assess the budgetary implications of a more substantial governmental investment in "metaregulation," either within or across particular agencies? At what point, if any, might the complexities of truly effective regulatory pluralism suggest the advisability of a return to command-and-control regulatory approaches?

A related question would be to consider a few self-regulatory canines that intriguingly did not bark. The accounting scandals of the late 1990s and the new millennium elicited wide-ranging calls for heightened regulation, eventually resulting in much tighter public regulation of corporate disclosure through the Sarbanes–Oxley Act. The current debacle in the mortgage market is similarly stoking demands for revamped regulation of both consumer credit and secondary debt markets, as well as much tighter oversight of the nonbank, "shadow" financial system. In none of these contexts, however, have the affected economic constituencies mounted a concerted effort to head off legislative imposition of new regulatory regimes by organizing self-regulatory alternatives. That absence deserves explanation, which might deepen our understanding of how broader political and cultural contexts shape the emergence of efforts at self-policing in particular economic sectors.

The implications of coregulation for the handling of enduring regulatory conflicts raises still other issues deserving of attention. For the most part, the scholarship on private mechanisms of regulation assumes relatively unambiguous, agreed-upon regulatory objectives – redressing information asymmetries in order to build confidence in markets; maintaining public health; preventing workplace injuries; constraining pollution. Most research into private governance takes such ends as given and focuses on questions of means, on the strategies and regulatory tools that might more effectively and efficiently bring about those ends. But what if regulatory objectives conflict with one another, as when the maintenance of competition conflicts with the policing of commercial speech, or the impulse to reduce greenhouse gas emissions bumps up against concerns over nuclear safety? Will reliance on institutions of self-regulation facilitate the resolution of such fundamental political dilemmas, or complicate them?

Two additional areas seem ripe for investigation – one by sociologists and anthropologists, and the other by historians. The case for increased reliance on self-regulation as a fundamental governmental strategy rests on assumptions about culture within particular areas of economic life – or "organizational fields," as sociologists sometimes refer to them. Business culture, advocates of private governance explicitly assume, is almost always antagonistic to inflexible command and control regulation, unless firms see such regulation as consolidating their market advantages, while the world of governmental regulators tends to be hamstrung by bureaucratic turf battles. The culture of private regulation, they similarly presuppose, is inherently fragile, requiring careful nurturing to sustain itself against the relentless forces of corporate politics and market competition. Nonetheless, appeals for private regulation generally remain confident that in the right circumstances, it can redirect economic morality, reshaping the bases of legitimacy within business.

These assumptions may well encapsulate organizational culture in modern, industrial societies. But we could use a more substantial evidentiary demonstration of such bedrock premises. That goal calls for many case studies of the specific values and habits of minds displayed by corporate agents in heavily regulated industries, or by ethics and compliance officials in the corporate world, or by the private regulators who work for industry associations or other nonprofit organizations. We could similarly benefit from careful consideration of the complex interactions and negotiations among these various regulatory actors, as well as their experiences with representatives of the state or of public interest groups. Economic and legal sociologists have pursued some research along these lines; legal and economic anthropologists have largely ignored nongovernmental regulatory bureaucracies as potential subjects for study. We need much more "thick description" of private governance, and the interplay between private regulators and their public overseers.

Finally, there remains a very important role for historians, who, with a few exceptions that mostly involve governance of the financial markets or the professions, have largely ignored the increasingly important realm of business self-regulation.[67] Numerous questions suggest themselves about the operation of particular self-regulatory initiatives and the evolution of private governance more generally. Do the institutions of self-regulation manifest a life cycle similar to that characteristic of many public regulatory

---

[67] For an exception in the arena of international labor standards, see John D. French, *Globalizing Protest and Policy: Neoliberalism, Worker Rights, and the Rise of Alt-Global Politics* (Durham, North Carolina, forthcoming).

agencies, evolving from a relatively innovative culture to a more hide-bound one? What are the prospects for creating some degree of enduring bureaucratic autonomy within such institutions, whether they are embed-ded within corporations as ethics and compliance departments or operating within industry organizations? What happens to self-regulatory zeal once the crisis and intense public scrutiny that triggered it diminishes? To what extent does self-regulation ebb and flow with the prevailing regulatory prac-tices of government, or the dominant predilections of political discourse, or the ups and downs of the business cycle? Answering such questions will require close examination of self-regulatory institutions over time.

Within the United States, the National Association of Securities Dealers (now part of FINRA) and the Better Business Bureaus stand out as two organizations that merit this kind of intensive historical study. Both have now been part of the American regulatory fabric for the better part of a century, adapting to shifting technological and commercial landscapes and responding to fundamental changes in governmental policy, whether in the realm of securities brokerage or advertising. Historical assessments of their evolution will surely offer scholars helpful perspectives on a host of questions related to issues of regulatory design. There is some indication, for example, that the seriousness of NASD enforcement activities has varied directly with the degree to which the SEC has made a priority of holding the financial markets to regulatory standards, diminishing during the 1950s, and becoming reinvigorated in the 1960s. And the Better Business Bureaus appear to have gone through a difficult period of transition in that same decade, as a generation of organizational leaders who came of age during the 1920s and 1930s, when the business community vigorously pursued self-regulation, retired in the midst of waxing assertion of governmental responsibility for consumer protection.[68]

Policymakers could greatly benefit from historical investigation of a much wider array of efforts to address regulatory dilemmas through private mech-anisms. This point, moreover, holds not just within the United States, but also in regions of the world with different regulatory traditions, like Europe, and with regard to the global activities of multinational corpora-tions. Indeed, this last arena offers historians to engage with an ever more significant domain of transnational experience in the past half-century, opening up new frontiers in the discipline's embrace of global history.

---

[68] Seligman, *Transformation of Wall Street*, 298–300; Edward J. Balleisen, "Business Self-Regulation over the Long Haul: The Better Business Bureaus and the Policing of Deceptive Marketing, 1933–1975," unpublished paper.

The recent failures of some prominent experiments in self-regulation, the CSE program perhaps foremost among them, have significantly tarnished the appeal of private governance. Voluntary self-regulation has particularly, and appropriately, come in for withering criticism. But in light of the dominant role of corporations in structuring contemporary economic life, the jurisdictional conundrums posed by global economic networks, and the constrained capacities of governments at all levels, policymakers will likely continue to turn to varieties of nongovernmental regulatory governance in some contexts. The challenge for those elected representatives and governmental officials will surely involve identifying *which* contexts best lend themselves to private governance, and even more importantly, fashioning structures of coregulation that keep nongovernmental regulators committed to public purpose. When faced with such vexing questions of regulatory design, policymakers would greatly benefit from as rich an evidentiary and analytical foundation as possible. Scholars of the modern regulatory state accordingly have every reason to deepen their already growing engagement with the world of private governance, from every potentially useful disciplinary perspective.

FIFTEEN

Deregulation Theories in a Litigious Society: American Antitrust and Tort

Tony Freyer

For much of the twentieth century, conceptions of market efficiency in American antitrust and tort law combined understandings of market incentives with moralistic concerns and social values. The relative institutional autonomy of these judicial-centered fields contrasted with the public choice school of thought that, Jessica Leight demonstrates, has dominated American policy analysis in recent decades. The two fields of law challenge public-choice assumptions that government's "self-centered behavior" succumbs to "private capture" and inevitably undermines legitimate economic policies. Similarly, though these legal fields are not expressly addressed in Daniel Carpenter's constitutive theory of regulation, they provide evidence that the adversarial judicial process can, employing his vocabulary, "constitute" certain market practices as "approval regulation," and through discovery "overcome information asymmetries," which in turn "credence good markets" defined as "improved social welfare." In addition, large damage awards won though antitrust and tort litigation suggest how the adversarial judicial process could be applied – by strengthening private actions within the securities field – to ameliorate what Mary O'Sullivan calls the "hegemony" of "maximizing shareholder value" that has prevailed for decades in American corporate governance.[1]

[1] Compare essays by Jessica Leight, "Public Choice: A Critical Reassessment," Daniel Carpenter, "Confidence Games: How Does Regulation Constitute Markets?" Mary O'Sullivan, "Regulating Corporate Governance in the United States: Energized Government,

For support the author thanks Law School Dean Kenneth C. Randall, University of Alabama Law School Foundation, and the Edward Brett Randolph Fund; he also recognizes University of Alabama Office of Academic Affairs for funding from the University Research Professorship he holds in the History Department and Law School. At the University of Alabama School of Law he thanks his secretary, Mrs. Caroline Barge, and for indispensable research assistance in the Law Library, Paul Pruitt, Penny Gibson, Creighton Miller, and Robert Marshall.

Since the 1970s a global deregulation movement has sought to orient market relations, political systems, and legal institutions around a particular conception of economic rationality, which stressed reliance on monetary incentives and the pursuit of economic efficiency, narrowly construed. American antitrust and tort law were consistent with this movement's effort to adjust incentives for individual and group action. Still, as the economic historian and theorist Douglass C. North has recognized imperfect information, transaction costs, and other factors often frustrate attempts to improve social welfare through such manipulation of the rules of the game. Within antitrust and tort law, the effort to reconfigure economic incentives resulted in a mix of productive and adverse outcomes. Examining a handful of revealing cases as representative of broader trends, this chapter contends that the *adversarial process* itself can have more impact than the substantive rules being litigated. This is so because vital policy issues involving business conduct are channeled into a judicial process pitting weaker individuals or stronger groups against corporate interests on relatively fairer terms than usually exist in legislative and executive politics or administrative agencies.[2]

The practical outcomes of deregulation, as Steven Vogel shows, have been paradoxical. A theory aimed at reducing regulation often actually fostered it; a theory driven by internationalized markets facilitated national regulatory distinctiveness; and a theory based upon limiting governmental control of private business conduct depended upon the government itself. Even so, wrote Pietro S. Nivola in a 1996 *Wall Street Journal* article, the American economy was "singularly unfettered." Nevertheless, "American entrepreneurs face a profusion of legal fine points and perils different from, but not necessarily less exacting than, the regulatory perils in other places." Moreover, because "private litigants do much of the enforcing in

Attenuated Politics," Marc Eisner, "Markets in the Shadow of the State: An Appraisal of Deregulation and the Implications for Future Research," and Edward Balleisen, "Prospects for Economic 'Self-Regulation' in the United States: An Historians' View from the Early Twenty-First Century," in this volume – including quoted phrases – and to Richard Hofstadter, "What Happened to the Antitrust Movement? Notes on the evolution of an American Creed," in Earl Frank Cheit, ed., *The Business Establishment*, (Wiley, New York, 1964), 150, 151; and, for tort liability to Robert W. Gordon, "The American Legal Profession, 1870–2000," and Lawrence Friedman, "The Litigation Revolution," in Michael Grossberg and Christopher Tomlins, *The Cambridge History Of Law In America Volume III The Twentieth Century and After (1920–)* (Cambridge University Press, New York, 2008), 98–99, 118–120, 171, 182–86, 190–91.

2 Douglass C. North, *Institutions, Institutional Change and Economic Performance* (Cambridge University Press, Cambridge, U.K., 1993); Tony A. Freyer, "Business Law and American Legal History," Stanley L. Engerman and Robert E. Gallman, eds., *The Cambridge Economic History Of The United States Volume II The Long Nineteenth Century* (Cambridge University Press, Cambridge, U.K., 2000), 435–82.

the U.S.... we wind up with smaller government but millions of civil suits. Swapping a somewhat lower level of public control for a high degree of privatized legal wrangling is not always an advantage." More skeptically, Reza R. Dibadj and others contend, many "private actors" basically oppose competition and regulatory regimes promoting distributional, social welfare goals. Alternatively, the judicial process could stimulate, as Edward Balleisen suggests, reconstituting business self-regulation into a more effective system as a key dimension of deregulation.[3]

This chapter argues that American antitrust and mass tort litigation reflect market failure in various business sectors governed by deregulation theories. Although my choice of cases to illustrate the adversarial process in operation is selective, I hope to demonstrate that class actions offer real advantages, especially imposing checks and balances by drawing upon the energies and creativity of private enforcers including business and other groups. Section I describes a relatively autonomous adversarial judicial process promoting antitrust and mass tort private actions, and places that process within the context of postoil crisis deregulation. The second section considers the scope of this autonomy in the *Relafen* antitrust class action; it also examines a California class action and foreign litigation arising from the U.S. government's *Microsoft* case. The third section considers mass tort litigation, including the ironic consequences of tort reform suggested by *BMW* v. *Gore*. Section IV provides an outcomes assessment indicating that the adversarial process in antitrust and mass tort private actions has enforced multiple-policy goals compared to deregulation theories that emphasize primarily consumer prices. The conclusion urges further research on the adversarial judicial process employing the work of those noted above and Marc Eisner's typology of regulatory purpose: constituting markets, facilitating economic activity, and constraining it so as to avoid negative externalities.[4]

---

[3] Steven K. Vogel, *Free Markets, More Rules: Regulatory Reform in Advanced Industrial Countries* (Cornell University Press, Ithaca, N.Y., 1996); Pietro S. Nivola, "When It Comes to Regulations, U.S. Shouldn't Cast the First Stone," *Wall Street Journal,* Wednesday May 15, 1996, at A15; Reza R. Dibadj, *Rescuing Regulation* (State University of New York Press, Albany, 2006), at 61; all compared to Edward Balleisen's essay in this volume.

[4] Compare Marc Eisner's typology developed in this volume to Herbert Hovenkamp, *The Antitrust Enterprise Principle and Execution* (Harvard University Press, Cambridge, Mass., 2005); Peter H. Schuck, "Mass Torts an Institutional Evolutionist Perspective," in *The Limits of Law Essays On Democratic Governance* (West View Press, Boulder, Colo., 2000), 345–91; Eleanor M. Fox, "Remedies and the Courage of Convictions in a Globalized World, How Globalization Corrupts Relief," Thomas, B. Leary, "The Bipartisan Legacy," J. Douglas Richards, "What Makes an Antitrust Class Action Remedy Successful? A Tale of Two Settlements," 80 *Tulane Law Review* No. 2 (December 2005), 571–94, 605–20, 621–60. Full case style cited below.

I. Adversarial Judicial Process in Antitrust and Mass Tort Private Actions

The two energy crises of the 1970s engendered throughout the world an accelerating public concern about allocative efficiencies. The response was the global deregulation movement. Particularly in America, increased commercial and regulatory uses of computer technology enabled business and government increasingly to achieve such efficiencies. Among industrialized economies, the American deregulation movement nonetheless remained distinctive regarding the significance of private litigation. Although the civil codes of industrialized economies as diverse as Japan or the European Community's member states in principle permitted private actions, strict limitations on remedies impeded their practical use in antitrust and tort cases. Private actions in the United States thus presented a stark contrast to other industrial economies, even after the 1990s, when regulatory bureaucrats themselves altered civil code provisions in order to encourage private actions. Notwithstanding this recent development, America remained the clear leader in private actions as a means to achieve regulatory aspirations. The deregulation movement partially limited private actions. Yet the unintentional result was to increase reliance upon private actions for enforcement of regulatory goals in business sectors where administrative or political oversight of business self-regulation was ineffective.[5]

U.S. antitrust private actions suggested an ongoing evolution. The Sherman Antitrust Act of 1890 relied upon judicial enforcement; its framers intended, moreover, that the provision for treble damages would encourage private actions as a complement to government enforcement. The Clayton Antirust Act of 1914 broadened the incentives for private actions. And though Congress intended the Federal Trade Commission enacted the same year to provide an administrative alternative to litigation through publicity derived from official reports and enforcement through cease and desist orders, private litigation continued to complement government action. The most dramatic expansion of American antitrust occurred under Thurman Arnold, head of the Justice Department's Antitrust Division, 1938–43. Although Arnold resisted private litigation, his model of enforcement activism paved the way for expanded private actions. Between 1960

---

[5] Gordon, "American Legal Profession," and Friedman, "Litigation Revolution," full cite note 1; Schuck, "Mass Torts," 364; Clifford A. Jones, "Trilateralism in Private Antitrust Enforcement: Japan, the USA, and the European Union," in Clifford A. Jones and Mitsuo Matsushita, eds., *Competition Policy in the Global Trading System Perspectives from the EU, Japan and the USA* (Kluwer Law International, The Hague, 2002), 211–24.

and 1978 the number of private antitrust suits filed jumped from 228 to 1,611. Until 1986 the number did not fall below 1,052, before dropping to 654 two years later. In 2003, despite decades of the deregulation movement, the total number of antitrust private actions filed in federal court remained 729, or 95.6 percent of all antitrust actions.[6]

The tort system evolved along a somewhat different course. Since their emergence in the early nineteenth century, modern tort doctrines of negligence, fault, duty, and risk varied among and even within states, as well as between federal and state courts. While business defendants initially held an advantage in outcomes, by the end of the century the tort system facilitated sufficiently diverse results that a plaintiff's market for legal services emerged, in which personal injury lawyers relying on contingent fees succeeded more often than they failed against corporate defendants. Following the turn of the century, New York judge Benjamin Cardozo's warranty rule weakened the fault principle underlying the negligence system. As courts extended the liability of manufacturers for harm caused third parties throughout the twentieth century, they moved toward rules favoring strict liability for torts. The weakening of negligence doctrines by the principle of worker compensation represented the growth of bureaucratically managed limitations of negligence doctrines through insurance. By the end of the twentieth century, this principle had extended to a broad swath of tort contexts. In the legal domain of personal injuries caused by automobile accidents, for example, courts routinely handled over 500,000 cases annually by the 1990s, with a systematized process usually avoiding jury trials.[7]

By the 1980s, moreover, courts increasingly broadened procedures granting standing to sue (known as certification) to groups of plaintiffs pursuing class-action suits. A burgeoning number of mass tort class actions followed,

---

[6] Donald I. Baker, "Revisiting History – What Have We Learned About Private Antitrust Enforcement We Would Recommend To Others?" Clifford A. Jones, "Exporting Antitrust Court Rooms to the World: Private Enforcement in a Global Market," 16 *Loyola Consumer Law Review* No. 4 (2004), 379–408, 409–30; Tony A. Freyer, *Antitrust and Global Capitalism, 1930–2004* (Cambridge University Press, Cambridge, U.K., 2006), 24–59; Tony Freyer, *Regulating Big Business Antitrust in Great Britain and America 1880–1990* (Cambridge University Press, Cambridge, U.K., 1992), 282; Hovenkamp, *Antitrust Enterprise*, 57–76. For 95.6 percent figure see Joseph P. Bauer, "Reflections on the Manifold Means of Enforcing the Antitrust Laws: Too Much, Too Little, or Just Right?" 16 *Loyola Consumer Law Review*, No. 4 (2004), at 308.

[7] Freyer, "Business law and American Economic History," 479, 480; Edward A. Purcell, Jr., *Litigation and Inequality: Federal Diversity Jurisdiction in Industrial America, 1870–1958* (Oxford University Press, New York, 1992), 13–137; John C. Coffee, Jr., "Class Wars: The Dilemma of the Mass Tort Class Action," 95 *Columbia Law Review* No. 6 (October 1995), 1351.

the most publicly covered of which targeted companies that produced substances that caused health problems over the long term, such as asbestos, diethylstilbestrol (DES), a drug doctors once routinely prescribed to prevent miscarriages, the purportedly "safe and effective contraceptive" Dalkon Shield, silicone breast implants, or Agent Orange, a supposedly benign defoliant. Mass torts involved new organizations of plaintiffs' lawyers to represent classes of harmed individuals numbering in the thousands. Regarding private antitrust actions, a major issue concerned the extent to which such class actions could or even should compensate plaintiffs identified as "indirect purchasers." The *Relafen* case of 2004 suggested the financial stakes involved in the courts' designation of class-action plaintiffs as either direct or indirect purchasers: the first of these designations meant that claims against the drug company would amount to $175 million, whereas the latter reduced liability to $70 million. In both antitrust and mass tort class actions, plaintiff groups and their lawyers sometimes won enormous settlements. A widely publicized example was the $4.23 billion settlement in *Silicone Gel*; a less well-known case, discussed below, was the $1.1 billion payout Microsoft made to consumers in a California private action. To stem such victories, the losing defendant corporations mounted a political campaign designated "tort reform." Essentially, this campaign applied the larger premises of deregulation – business desiring liberation from as many regulatory restraints as possible – to limit the autonomy of the adversarial process in private actions.[8]

The growth of antitrust and tort class actions reveals a pivotal market failure. Since the early twentieth century, business corporations have possessed a legal "multiple personality." A collection of corporate units formally chartered in a host state but doing business as a "foreign" legal entity in other domestic and international states, the large-scale firm has maintained a unified strategy common to its distinct operating units. These units do business within and are bound by the local laws and regulations of separate states. Cash flow demands within such operating units, in conjunction with a variety of local rules and regulations, frequently created conflicting incentives for legal obedience or disobedience within an enterprise. One common conflict has pitted foreign subsidiaries, who must compete in a lax regulatory environment, against the parent company, which confronts a very different political and legal set of constraints. As the evidence produced by numerous

---

[8]   Richards, "What Makes an Antitrust Class Action Remedy Settlement Successful?" 622–26; *In re* Relafen Antitrust Litig., 231 F.R.D.52 (D Mass. 2005). Schuck, "Mass Torts," 347; Alex Berenson, "Analysts See Merck Victory In Vioxx Deal," *The New York Times National* Saturday, November 10, 2007, Front page, A12.

antitrust and mass tort class actions suggests, repeated business misconduct in multistate operating firms has become commonplace. Pharmaceutical and computer firms discussed below are leading examples. The extent of such illegal conduct suggested that it amounted to a calculation of market risk. Put another way, deregulation privatized conflicting incentives within diverse legal forums, often engendering a business judgment that illegal conduct was rational.[9]

The evidence of such business conduct revealed through the adversarial judicial process offers a considerable challenge to prevailing theories of deregulation. Executive and legislative branches, as well as many bureaucratic agencies, are of course subject to dynamic, partisan, interest-group political pressures. As Jessica Leight shows in her intellectual history of public choice, deregulation theories give much weight to images of motivation and conduct grounded on rationally self-interested choices freely competing for dominance in political markets. Moreover, most scholars and policymakers conceive of deregulation as limiting or removing altogether the regulators' authority over private conduct, relying upon rational market incentives to shape and maintain the accountability of business behavior.[10] Antitrust and mass tort class actions, by contrast, channel sociomarket and political interests into a judicial process characterized by a more autonomous adversarial professional culture, due process rules, legal damage systems, claims of private litigants, and appellate review. As legal scholars have shown since the 1930s, external politics may impinge upon the judiciary's autonomy. Nevertheless, in antitrust and mass tort class actions, that autonomy usually engenders outcomes shaped by an adversarial process in which procedure can be more significant than the formal substance of law and policy.[11]

This conception of judicial autonomy is distinguishable from the dichotomy between a command–control regulatory regime and deregulation. Under the command–control regime the legislature proscribes certain

---

[9] Tony A. Freyer, "Managerial Capitalism Contested Government Policy, Culture, and Corporate Investment," in Mark C. Carnes, ed., *The Columbia History Of Post-World War II America* (Columbia University Press, New York, 2007), 448–449, 450; Tony A. Freyer, "Regulatory Distinctiveness and Extraterritorial Competition Policy in Japanese-US Trade," 21 *World Competition Law and Economics Review*, No. 5 (September 1998), 9–10.

[10] Compare Jessica Leight's essay cited in full note 1 to Ian Ayres and John Braithwaite, *Responsive Regulation Transcending the Deregulation Debate* (Oxford University Press, New York, 1992).

[11] See Gordon, "American Legal Profession," and Friedman, "Litigation Revolution," cited in full note 1; and citations, note 4.

conduct and empowers a regulatory agency to monitor and enforce compliance, ultimately relying upon litigation or the threat of litigation. By contrast, although deregulation theories recognize the role of courts as enforcers, they may underestimate the degree to which institutional autonomy grounded upon adversarial process and procedure shape outcomes in antitrust and mass tort class actions. Moreover, antitrust and mass tort class actions suggest that the dichotomy between command–control and deregulation obscures the degree to which no preexisting market entity or relationship exists outside state authority. Accordingly, deregulation does not establish a regulatory vacuum. Rather, government policies legitimate particular private incentives for conduct while lacking the means of directing that conduct toward wider compliance goals sought in antitrust and mass tort class actions. Thus, class actions can be part of the multiple regulatory purposes Marc Eisner discusses elsewhere in this volume. Coercion imposed through command–control, however, often has a narrow impact, at most compelling corrective behavior in an immediate set of circumstances. Leading examples were the administrated price regimes government agencies instituted in airline, telephone, and railroad sectors before the triumph of deregulation. Government and private antitrust price-fixing litigation is a further example that remains important because, as many deregulation proponents advocate, it employs *per se* rules to address proven criminal conduct.[12]

Michael Porter places this point in a global context. Employing a comparative, firm-centered research base, Porter popularized during the 1990s the view that competitiveness in the domestic market is a precondition for international competitiveness. By imposing effective "product standards regulation," Porter argued, governments had a vital role in fostering competitiveness. "Stringent standards for product performance, product safety, and environmental impact," he pointed out, "contribute to creating and upgrading competitive advantage." Moreover, "[t]hey pressure firms to improve quality, upgrade technology, and provide features in areas of important customer (and social) concern." Porter favored a regulatory policy mix that rejected the "short-term cost of dealing with tough standards" in favor of one that promotes the "longer-term benefits in terms of innovation." Such a policy mix thus should recognize that "[s]elling poorly performing, unsafe, or environmentally damaging products is not a rout to real competitive

---

[12] Ibid.; notes 2, 9; and John Braithwaite, *Regulatory Capitalism How it works, ideas for making it work better,*" (Edward Elgar, Cheltenham, U.K., (2008).

advantage in sophisticated industries and industry segments, especially in
a world where environmental sensitivity and concern for social welfare are
rising in all advanced nations."[13]

Since deregulation became a governing ideal in the United States, however, corporate elites frequently have ignored Porter's advice. Antitrust and
mass tort class actions indicate that corporate pursuit of short over long-
term gains has become commonplace. As one-time Federal Reserve Chairman Alan Greenspan noted, the tightened links between a firm's asset base
and the stock market imposed upon corporate executives an overriding
demand for short-term profitability. Large corporate failures, such as Enron
and WorldCom at the turn of the millennium, powerfully demonstrated this
tendency. The creation of a global capital market during the 1980s, eventually spreading risk through complex methods of securitization, tied the
firm's strategic management decisions to short-term profitability, a dynamic
that incorporated assessments of complying with a given regulatory regime.
Thus, regarding antitrust and mass tort litigation, we might restate the
American deregulation paradox accordingly: Antitrust private actions continued to have market significance despite the vacillation of government
enforcement from the 1970s through the 1990s, while over the same period
mass tort class actions steadily increased as a result of weakened government regulation in many product markets.[14] Deregulation, in other words,
often did not so much end regulatory action as shift its institutional setting,
moving it from administrative agencies to the courts, and placing much
greater initiative in the hands of nongovernmental plaintiffs.

II. Antitrust: Private and Government Actions

Enforcement of antitrust law in the United States has gone through several
incarnations. Between the 1890s and the 1920s, antitrust possessed a largely
ideological content identified with small business, farmers, and labor, all
struggling against the dominance of managerial capitalism. Although private litigation was sporadically noteworthy in this first era of the Sherman Act, it was clearly subordinate to government litigation.[15] Between
1938 and 1943 Thurman Arnold reconstituted antitrust activism; he shifted

---

[13] Michael E. Porter, *The Competitive Advantage of Nations* (MacMillan, New York, 1990),
       647,648–49.
[14] Freyer, *Antitrust and Global Capitalism*, 142, 143; "Will the credit crisis trigger a downturn?"
       and "Securitisation: When it goes wrong," *The Economist* September 22, 2007, 15, 85–87.
[15] Freyer, *Regulating Big Business*, 43–120, 133–35; and Gordon, "American Legal Profession,"
       and Friedman, "Litigation Revolution," full cite note 1.

government enforcement priorities from promoting narrow social welfare to imposing accountability upon market groups through the wide-ranging efficiency goals that the *Alcoa* case symbolized. A federal court's 1945 decision in this case linked economically oriented efficiency concerns that emphasize corporate competition to the social benefits resulting from attacking bigness. Arnold distrusted private litigation. Indeed, private litigation did not become the leading mode of antitrust enforcement until the electrical equipment cases of the 1960s, which probed endemic price fixing in the industry. Private actions reached a high point in the late 1970s, and from that juncture they have remained the leading form of antitrust enforcement, a trend greatly facilitated by the new techniques of class-action litigation, which overcame longstanding collective action problems.[16] As the Microsoft litigation shows, successful class actions employing complex computer databases to define harm to consumers could emerge in the aftermath of weak government enforcement; nevertheless, in other cases lacking such data class actions failed.[17]

The Nixon Administration began the shift in government enforcement. Early in his first term, Richard Nixon maintained a policy of antitrust activism traceable to Arnold, expanded to include the government's aggressive prosecutions of conglomerate mergers. Nixon's original embrace of activism resulted from some Republican elite's dislike of newcomers who ran certain conglomerates, as well as the president's own distrust of low-level managers who neglected consumers' interests. This strong enforcement policy initially persisted despite vigorous criticism from Robert Bork and others influenced by the Chicago School's approach to economic theory. Beginning with Nixon's second term and accelerating under Jimmy Carter, that approach gradually gained ground, achieving dominance during Ronald Reagan's Administration. In 1986, Stanford University law professor and Antitrust Division head William Baxter did win a major victory under long-standing monopoly doctrines, breaking up AT&T. In the merger and cartel

---

[16] Ibid., 282; Freyer, *Antitrust and Global Capitalism*, 24–59; Hovenkamp, *Antitrust Enterprise*, 57–76.

[17] *In re* Relafen Litig., 231 F.R.D. 52 (D.Mass. 2005); *United States* v. *Microsoft Corp.*, 97 F. Supp. 2d 59 (D.D.C. 2000), *aff'd in part, rev'd in part, remanded in part*, 253 F.3d 34 (D.C. Cir.), *cert denied*, 534 U.S. 952 (2001); *United States* v. *Microsoft Corp.*, 2002–2(CCH Trade Cases) ¶ 73,860 at 95 (D.D.C. 2002); compare: *Microsoft* I-V *Cases* Case No. J.C.C.P. NO. 4106 Class Action Superior Court Of The State Of California For The City And County Of San Francisco (August 24, 2004); "Townsend and Townsend and Crew Announces Microsoft and California Plaintiffs Settle California Class Action Lawsuits; Settlement to Benefit Consumers and California Schools," Look Smart Business Wire Jan. 10, 2003; Hovenkamp, *Antitrust Enterprise*, 292–305.

field, however, Baxter significantly altered the budgeted allocation of cases. Following policy priorities reaching back decades, the Carter Justice Department had brought 67.5 cases annually – 30 civil, and 37.5 criminal. Baxter and his successors, by contrast, initiated 94 cases annually, 80 criminal and 14 civil, almost all against relatively small firms operating in local markets. Reagan antitrust authorities generally declined to prosecute price or non-price vertical restraints by large-scale corporations with a national or international footprint, a policy federal courts increasingly sanctioned. Reagan antitrust officials also manifested considerable leniency toward most mergers and toward companies who allegedly took part in international cartels.[18]

The ascendancy of Chicago economics engendered a reaction, both within and outside the government. The Federal Trade Commission, for example, acquiesced less than Reagan's Justice Department to a lax policy toward mergers. Under the elder George Bush's Administration, even many Republican antitrust authorities embraced an American Bar Association Task Force report arguing that Reagan antitrust officials had too easily assumed that most mergers created "efficiency," because the dictates of Chicago price theory adjudged market entry barriers to be generally unimportant. In such cases the Chicago mantra was not to protect "competitors" but rather "competition" achieved through economies of scale. During the early 1990s, self-described Chicago economist Donald Dewey concluded that price theory could not sustain antitrust policy. Meanwhile, critics Harry First, Eleanor Fox, and Robert Pitofsky sought to "revitalize" antitrust. The outcomes of this reaction were mixed. Overall, the substantive issues decided by the Supreme Court concerning predatory pricing, vertical restraints, mergers, patent policies, and joint ventures applied a more restrictive "Harvard School approach." As Herbert Hovenkamp has explained, "While the Chicago School emphasized the way firms would continue to compete notwithstanding imperfect structures, the Harvard School emphasized the ways that firms could avoid competing."[19]

In the same period, private antitrust actions took on a greater significance, even though their incidence decreased substantially. As government antitrust enforcement declined under Reagan, private actions also dropped noticeably, from 1,052 in 1986 to 654 in 1988.[20] Still, by the turn of the millennium, private actions constituted about 95 percent of all antitrust

[18] Freyer, *Antitrust and Global Capitalism*, 147; and Freyer, *Regulating Big Business*," note 15.
[19] Freyer, *Antitrust and Global Capitalism*, 148; Hovenkamp, *Antitrust Enterprise*, 35–38, quoted at 35; Bert Foer, President American Antitrust Institute, Interviewed in "The Competition Counterweight," 10 *Global Competition Review* Issue 8 (August/September 2007), 24–26.
[20] Freyer, *Regulating Big Business*, 282.

actions annually. In addition, notwithstanding the much fewer government cases, their findings of law and fact often fostered numerous private suits in federal and state courts. Moreover, lawyers in private actions might eventually win cases that reshaped theories which the Department of Justice had rejected in earlier cases.[21]

There were important limitations to private actions, especially concerning the rights of "indirect purchasers." Thus in *Illinois Brick Co.* (1977) a Supreme Court 6–3 majority basically foreclosed compensation to "indirect purchaser" plaintiffs through antitrust class actions, because of logistical difficulties in defining such purchasers as a class for remedial purposes. Over the years, state laws and plaintiffs' lawyers nonetheless managed to narrow this constraint, employing a legal theory first articulated by Justice William J. Brennan argued in an *Illinois Brick* dissent. "Since that time," attorney J. Douglas Richards has observed, "the ubiquitous growth of computers, data base software, scanning technologies, and the like have vastly reduced the costs of collecting and using data identifying specific purchase transactions to particular consumers."[22]

Relafen was a case in point. This antitrust class-action litigation arose in 2004 from the prescription drug industry. "We Americans spend $200,000,000,000.00 on prescription drugs per year," federal judge William G. Young has noted. "As a result, courts are seeing a rise in cases challenging the pharmaceutical industry's practices in the pricing, development, and mass marketing of pharmaceuticals." In *Relafen*, SmithKline Beecham Corporation (SmithKline) procured in 1983 a patent on Nabumetone (brand name Relafen), a drug health care professionals prescribed primarily for arthritis pain and related rheumatoid inflammation. The proven facts showed that SmithKline's patent was "invalid or unenforceable" under U.S. Patent Office regulations. Yet the company employed the patent in an attempt to establish a monopoly through "sham litigation" involving Copley Pharmaceutical, Inc., Teva Pharmaceutical Industries, Ltd., and Teva Pharmaceuticals USA, and Eon Laboratories, Inc. Plaintiffs' lawyers used this evidence to represent numerous direct and indirect purchasers of Relafen in Massachusetts and other states. An eventual settlement compensated the indirect purchasers, relying on computer databases to identify 900,000 purchases of Relafen.[23]

---

[21] Note 4.

[22] Richards, "What Makes an Antitrust Class Action Remedy Successful?" 623–24, quote at 624. *Illinois Brick* Co. v. *Illinois* 431 U.S. 722, 749–65 (1977) (Brennan, J., dissenting).

[23] *In re* Relafen Litig., 231 F.R.D. 52 (D. Mass. 2005); Richards, "What Makes an Antitrust Class action Remedy Successful?," 624–27, 631–33, 640–43, 647–48. *J.E. Pierce Apothecary*,

The distinct phases of the *Relafen* litigation were representative of other private actions. The initial phase raised complex factual issues about scientific research – especially whether the original patent was "invalid" for purposes of competitors seeking from the U.S. Patent Office new drug approvals (ANDAs). Once the discovery process proved that the patent was unenforceable, the central issue involved the setting of compensation to Eon and other competitors of SmithKline, as well as the companies' various customers and consumers. The court sanctioned three certifiable classes of purchasers. "Direct purchasers" were pharmaceutical wholesalers to whom Smith-Kline directly sold Relafen; "end payors" purchased nabumetone not from SmithKline but "other sources" for nonretail purposes;and "drug store" plaintiffs "indirectly purchased Relafen and the generic drug nabumetone for resale." Under Judge Young's steady intervention, the parties negotiated a "settlement fund" through which SmithKline paid out to these class groups and the plaintiffs' lawyers. Allocation of the settlement among the classes paralleled the lengthy negotiation of class certification, including the use of the computer database to establish numerous consumers nationwide as indirect purchasers.[24]

The process engendered quantifiable outcomes. "Caught out committing fraud on" the Patent Office, judge Young observed, SmithKline avoided still more "serious consequences," being "able to buy peace nationwide without any admission of liability for an aggregate payment of $175,000,000 to wholesale pharmaceutical firms and $75,000,000 to consumers and their insurers." More particularly, "268,648 consumers . . . receive[d] a minimum of $10 (a total of at least $2,686,480) without any need for the filing of daunting and cumbersome claim forms." Three thousand five hundred and eighty-one other consumer claimants divided $1,320,225.44 and 1,980 "third party payors" tentatively divided $50,212,378.85. The judge also ordered that attorney fees could not exceed 33.3 percent, allocated as $58,333,333 for the pharmaceutical wholesalers' lawyers and $25,000,000 for lawyers representing "consumers and their insurers." In addition, Maryland enacted legislation repealing the *Illinois Brick* restrictions against indirect purchasers, "better to empower its consumers in future similar situations." Finally, these results were attained "at a transaction cost (other than attorney fees) of $1,799,023 to the wholesale pharmaceutical firms . . . and $1,284,657.91 to consumers and their insurers."[25]

Inc. v. *Harvard Pilgrim Health Care, Inc.,* 365 F. Supp. 2d 119 (D. Mass. 2005), Judge Young quote at 124.

[24] *In re* Relafen Litig. 231 F.R.D. 52, 59–83 (D. Mass. 2005).

[25] Ibid., 83–84.

Thus, *Relafen* was indicative of a drug company operating within a national and global market risking illegal conduct until other firms within the industry joined with "indirect purchasers" to challenge such conduct through private actions.

The U.S. *Microsoft* case also facilitated private antitrust litigation. The Clinton Administration prosecuted Microsoft for misconduct under the Sherman Act's monopolization provision. New York, Massachusetts, and other states joined the U.S. government's suit. Extensive discovery involving expert analysis of computer technology established Microsoft's abusive conduct. As a result, the trial judge ordered Microsoft to separate its operating systems from its program applications. In the U.S. Court of Appeals for the District of Columbia, however, Microsoft won important changes in the lower court's order. Though the Appeals Court upheld the evidence proving abusive conduct, it vacated the break-up remedy for reasons concerning the lower court's problematic public notifications during the trial. In addition, the Appeals Court was most critical of the economic analysis the trial judge employed to order the separation of the operating systems from the program applications. Basically, the Appeals Court rejected a theory that the record of extensive abuse justified break-up, instead favoring Microsoft's economic theory that the fundamental technological efficiencies should be preserved because, ultimately, they benefited consumers.[26]

On remand to the federal district court in Washington, D.C., Judge Colleen Kollar-Kotelly ordered settlement proceedings. The terms of the settlement had to accommodate both the factual findings of Microsoft's abusive conduct and the Appeals Court's rejection of the break-up remedy and endorsement of the economic efficiency theory. In 2002 Microsoft offered a "proposed decree" to Judge Kollar-Kotelly that the U.S. Justice Department, now under the George W. Bush Administration, as well as nine plaintiff states, largely accepted. Following public interest hearings resulting in minor changes, the judge based her final judgment on this decree. The District of Columbia and nine states rejected the settlement, seeking stronger remedies through further litigation. A federal trial on the nonsettling states' suits led to a final judgment adopting most of the remedies in Judge Kollar-Kotelly's decree in the U.S. government's case. There were some differences nonetheless concerning the terms of compliance and

---

[26] Note 17 for citation to *Microsoft* case. The text follows closely Fox, "Remedies and the Courage of Convictions in a Globalized World: How Globalization Corrupts Relief," 587–90. See also, Hovenkamp, *Antitrust Enterprise*, 292–305; William H. Page and John E. Lopatka, *The Microsoft Case Antitrust, High Technology, and Consumer Welfare* (University of Chicago Press, Chicago, IL, 2007).

means of enforcement that established the grounds for further litigation on behalf and states and private plaintiffs. Only Massachusetts appealed the final order; in particular it sought "open source licensing for Internet Explorer." The Court of Appeals, however, rejected the claim.[27]

Ongoing litigation in the United States and abroad suggested that the consent decree constituted, declared Herbert Hovenkamp, a major "debacle." The federal district court's endorsement of the decree shaped by Microsoft itself reflected the Court of Appeals' assertion that functionally bundling software benefited consumers. Thus, the decree incorporated the Court of Appeals' reversal of the district court's original holding based on factual findings that the tie between the browser and operating system was "illegal per se." Accordingly, the remedies the decree proposed for the proven violations were merely "prophylactic," imposing upon Microsoft a duty "to disclose certain interoperability information, including disclosure of information necessary for workgroup server software rivals to interoperate with Microsoft's operating system." Recognizing the limitations of the Court of Appeals' economic efficiency theories, Hovenkamp has concluded that "there is little reason to believe that the consent decree that the government negotiated with Microsoft will achieve any of these goals." Even so, the factual findings of proven anticompetitive violations facilitated a proliferation of domestic and international litigation that Microsoft has consistently lost.[28]

Microsoft's most important defeat came before the European Commission and the Court of First Instance. Antitrust authorities in Europe, South Korea, and elsewhere scrutinized the findings of fact proving misconduct in the federal district court of the District of Columbia. Although the Court of Appeals basically affirmed these findings of fact, its application of economic efficiency theory resulted in a remedy that to a considerable extent depended upon Microsoft's good-faith compliance. By contrast, the European Commission, and upon appeal the Court of First Instance, examined the proven evidence of Microsoft's misconduct under the Treaty of Rome's Article 82 abuse of dominance provision. Applying this standard, the commission and the court found the company's media player and operating system tie-in to be violations of European competition standards. Also illegal were Microsoft's rejection of sharing "interface information" with competitor "workgroup server operating systems," which would enable the rivals to

---

[27] Ibid.; and *Massachusetts* v. *Microsoft Corp.*, 373 F. 3d 1199, 1227–31 (D.C. Cir. 2004).

[28] Hovenkamp, *Antitrust Enterprise*, 298; Fox, "Remedies and the Courage of Convictions in a Globalized World: How Globalization Corrupts Relief," 587–90.

work harmoniously with the company's operating system and workgroup server. Ultimately, the EU authorities declared unlawful the conduct outcomes that their American counterparts had approved.[29]

Unlike the United States government's consent decree, EU and South Korean authorities imposed more stringent remedies somewhat like that rejected by the U.S. Court of Appeals' *Microsoft* opinion. The European Commission required the company to sell within the European Union's common market a type of operating system that did not include Windows Media Player. The commission's order also compelled the company to share full interface information with "workgroup server" competitors' software and "Microsoft's operating system and workgroup servers," instituting "seamless interoperability." In addition, Microsoft paid a fine of € 497 million. Following this defeat, Microsoft faced a stiff order from South Korea's Fair Trade Commission. After finding that Microsoft had abused its dominant market position, the commission impelled the company to sell one version of Windows without Windows Media Player and Windows Messenger, and another version "carrying links to Web pages that allow consumers to download competing versions of such software." Microsoft also paid a fine of 32.5 billion Korean ($35.4 million). In October, 2007, Microsoft dropped its appeal to the Seoul High Court.[30]

Class-action litigation against Microsoft in California indicated an alternative approach to these remedies. During the U.S. government's Microsoft case in 1999, two classes of indirect purchasers sued the company for violating California's antitrust laws. Plaintiffs alleged that since 1988 Microsoft's global monopoly over "Intel X86 compatible operating system, word processing and spreadsheet markets with its MS-DOS, Windows, Word, and Excel products" resulted in unlawful conduct "to overcharge its reseller customers, who in turn passed on Microsoft's monopoly overcharge" to the plaintiffs. A similar attempt failed to develop a nationwide class-action case against Microsoft in Maryland's federal district court. California's class action representing indirect purchasers nonetheless went forward in San Francisco Superior Court. During almost four years of litigation, court-appointed plaintiff's counsel presented the court numerous motions,

---

[29] Fox, "Remedies and the Courage of Convictions in a Globalized World: How Globalization Corrupts Relief," 589; Freyer, *Antitrust and Global Capitalism*, 306–07; Steve Lohr and Kevin J. O'Brien, "Microsoft Is Yielding In European Antitrust Fight," *The New York Times* [nytimes.com], October 23, 2007; Shin Jung-Won, "Microsoft to Drop Appeal In South Korea Antitrust Case," The Wall Street Journal On Line [WSJ.com] Tuesday, October 16, 2007. Comm'n Decision Case COMP/C3/37.792, Microsoft, 2005.

[30] Ibid.

including "over 20 motions to compel discovery." As a result Microsoft gave up "over four million pages of documents." Massive materials from other cases against the company, as well as 160 depositions were also part of the extensive pretrial proceedings.[31]

During 2001–02, the failed efforts to craft a settlement in the nationwide class action encouraged negotiations in the California case. Although a first mediator did not succeed, a second attempt at mediation resulted in a settlement agreement that the court ordered approved on July 18, 2003. Four basic points comprised the settlement. The second mediation expert on notification programs certified that "at least 80% of the estimated 14.7 million class members" would receive formal notice of their right to receive payments. Second, the total amount of the settlement was $1.1 billion; thirdly, a distribution program stipulated payouts. Finally, the settlement covered costs of program administration, class notification, and "attorney's fees and costs." A claims administrator sent vouchers to qualified claimants; individual consumers could receive up to $100, while "businesses may recover substantially more, with some large businesses conceivably recovering hundreds of thousands of dollars or even millions of dollars." In addition, given that only about one-third of the $1.1 billion settlement was likely to be claimed by individual consumers, as much as $733 million (two-thirds) would go to "California's public schools serving students from low income households."[32]

The $1.1 billion payout in the California case suggested the stakes in the shifting patterns of private and government antitrust enforcement amid public choice as the dominant theory of individual behavior. By the millennium, private actions remained the primary form of antitrust enforcement largely because the adversarial process – including extensive discovery procedures – instituted a market for legal services that drew upon established patterns of corporate misconduct. Plaintiffs' firms developed organizational efficiencies that funded large class actions; the resulting investigations and discovery processes exposed pervasive willingness among corporate managers to countenance illegal conduct as "rational," given short-term demands imposed by conflicting national and transnational enforcement regimes and capital markets. College and university undergraduate and graduate economics and business school curriculums – as well as corporate culture – impressed upon students the public choice theory of "rational" individual behavior. Nevertheless, in the adversarial process lawyers, judges,

---

[31] Note 17, for cite to California class action, quotes at 3, 4, 5; and commentary.
[32] Ibid., quotes at 13, 14.

and juries usually encountered difficulty in balancing claims of corporate allocative efficiency against proven misconduct. This process in turn usually resulted in complicated settlement negotiations, facilitated by third-party mediation experts. The vacillation of government antitrust enforcement, moreover, encouraged plaintiffs' firms in the role of "private attorneys general." These institutional imperatives reinforced the stronger antitrust remedies that American private plaintiffs often won and state and foreign antitrust authorities repeatedly imposed.[33]

Antitrust experts like Herbert Hovenkamp emphasize the significance of private actions in part because "follow-on" litigation, especially in "big cases" has been fairly common. Law professor Joseph P. Bauer noted that in 2004 there were 249 antitrust class actions pending, over half of which arose in the federal court of the Southern District of New York and the Eastern District of Pennsylvania. He then notes a number of major "follow-on" cases reported in the *New York Times* or other national media during 2003–04, including Visa/Mastermoney ($3 billion settlement), 35,000 ranchers winning against Tyson beef packers a $1.28 billion jury award, the $1.1 billion settlement in the California Microsoft litigation, three cigarette makers paying tobacco growers a $188 million settlement, and Microsoft's payment of $750 million settlement to AOL Time Warner. In each of these cases government investigation was crucial to revealing evidence plaintiffs and their lawyers used as "private attorneys general." Bauer notes, too, the unusual case where the government initiates suit *after* a private action has begun, such as the *U.S. v. Visa U.S.A.* (2001). Fundamentally, such cases revealed how important discovery procedures and the adversarial process generally are to imposing checks and balances upon business in the deregulation context.[34]

III. Mass Tort Litigation

The American tort system traditionally balanced costs and risks on the basis of a reasonable-person standard. The usual litigants were an individual harmed by another individual or business enterprise. In such cases, the emergence of a personal injury bar funding litigation through contingency

---

[33] Notes 15, 16, 18, 22, 26, 28, 29. Erby Johnson Fischer II Interview, Monday, October 8, 2007, Birmingham, Alabama; Jay Aughtman, Montgomery, Alabama Phone Interview, Friday October 12, 2007. On business education see Rakesh Khurana, *From Higher Aims to Hired Hands: The Social Transformation of America's Business Schools and the Unfulfilled Promise of Management as a Profession* (Princeton University Press, Princeton, N.J., 2007); and "Roundtable on Business Education," 82 *Business History Review*, No. 2 (Summer 2008), 329–58.

[34] Hovenkamp, *Antitrust Enterprise*, 57–63; Bauer, "Reflections," 311–12.

fees was a distinctive institutional innovation compared to other common law nations and their civil law counterparts. Outside the United States,
courts generally have not permitted the contingency fee system. Up through
the 1960s, the vast majority of tort cases were brought by individual plaintiffs. After 1969, however, mass tort cases became increasingly conspicuous
in the media, reflecting the key institutional innovation of class actions. A
system based on individual liability thus shifted toward duties owed large
groups of plaintiffs that courts "certified" as having suffered harm. These
class-action groups required escalating compensation. "Once courts began
to realize that they were confronting a new quite different phenomenon,"
wrote Yale law professor Peter H. Schuck in 1995, "they entered a period
of desperate improvisation that has only recently congealed into a system."
Although "some . . . innovations in mass tort law occurred with lightening
speed. . . . courts have viewed most of these innovations – including some of
the most controversial ones – as incremental, not radical departures from
past practices."[35]

Over the past four decades, the process of legal innovation has resulted in
two tort systems. The clear majority of civil actions involving tortuous liability – including the roughly half-million automobile cases that American
courts hear annually – were comparatively simple disputes often seeking
damages of $10,000 or less. Through the 1980s such cases often resulted
in jury trials, with juries awarding damages to the plaintiffs. But legislative
intervention such as tort reform, requiring binding arbitration in certain
cases, reduced the incentives for plaintiffs' lawyers to represent many small
claimants. Still, in many automobile accident cases, where police reports or
other evidence clearly establish fault and either or both parties had insurance, court procedure is now formalized, awarding judgments without a jury
trial. The amount of compensation nonetheless remains fairly modest.[36] At
the end of the 1980s, by contrast, mass tort litigation reached, according
to expert Francis McGovern, a level whereby "litigation matures after there
has been full and complete discovery, multiple jury verdicts, and persistent
vitality in the plaintiffs' contentions." When this point is reached, "a large
number of similar but discrete, high cost disputes [can] be consolidated
into groups of similar cases to facilitate settlement *en mass.*"[37]

By the 1990s lawyers evolved and courts affirmed increasingly complex methods of identifying and certifying classes of mass tort litigants.

[35] Schuck, "Mass Torts," 34; notes 5–8.
[36] Erby Johnson Fischer II Interview, Monday, October 8, 2007, Birmingham, Alabama; Jay
Aughtman, Montgomery, Alabama Phone Interview, Friday October 12, 2007.
[37] Schuck, "Mass Tort," quote at 349; Francis E. McGovern, "Resolving Mature Mass Tort
Litigation, 69 *Boston University Law Review* (1989), 659–94.

Costs and benefits – as well as issues of fundamental fairness – nonetheless seemed elusive. Leading corporate law authority and Columbia law professor John C. Coffee has observed that the judicial-centered process provided incentives comporting with the parties' "mutual self-interest" to "grossly underestimate the [future] claims likely to be filed." Coffee offered persuasive evidence that settlements reached in certain prominent cases reflected plaintiff lawyers' ineffectual challenge to defense attorneys' "underestimate by defendants of likely future claims." A glaring example was the *Georgine* class action settlement, part of the ubiquitous *Asbestos* case, that "fail[ed] to deal responsibly with the issue of inflation." Coffee offered the *Silicone Gel* class action as the "almost unique case in which there was no hint of impropriety surrounding the settlement process." Yet even here, the plaintiff's lawyers endorsed an allocation from a total settlement of $4.23 billion, dividing $1 billion for fees and expenses "among a core group of 21 lawyers and thousands of referring attorneys." Even so, defense lawyers learned "to define the class to include only future claimants (who predictably will not seek to opt out during a brief initial opt out period ending well before their symptoms manifest themselves)," a maneuver that greatly facilitated the willingness of defendants to sign off on settlements.[38]

Compared to other common law nations and their civil law counterparts, Schuck noted, the U.S. phenomenon of mass tort litigations was distinctive. Foreign jurisdictions handled such problems through the legislative and bureaucratic process, often providing small groups of individuals with limited compensation. Such actions had little or no deterrent impact on the harm-causing enterprise. In the United States, by contrast, entrenched faith in the jury system and engrained distrust of bureaucracies established a fundamental presumption favoring courts. In some contexts, as with the pervasive incidence of black lung disease among American coal miners, the federal government has opted for a bureaucratic means of redress. Yet the cost of the administrative system Congress created to compensate black lung sufferers has worked against more widespread reliance upon such an approach. Similarly, on the state level (as discussed below), tort reform has had unintended consequences, encouraging a shift from smaller "simple" cases to more complex and costly "mature" mass tort-type litigation. Thus, "despite the mass tort system's many problems," Schuck has concluded, "it compares rather favorably to competing models."[39]

Schuck helpfully identifies three elements constituting the mass tort system that had emerged by the 1990s. First, as common law courts increasingly

[38] Coffee, "Class Wars," quotes at 1399, 1417, as quoted 1418.
[39] Schuck, "Mass Torts," 367; and note 35 above.

litigated mass torts, they employed class actions to safeguard large numbers of claimants through innovative settlements. Thus, courts guaranteed meaningful notice; they also alleviated intraclass tensions concerning claimants and their own lawyers, clearing away collective action barriers to legal means of redress. In particular, courts policed attorneys' fees and expenses. Courts also evolved various devices for "damage schedules," which were "in effect, insurance-fund judgments for future claims." Through such settlement devices, courts used procedure as best they could, "shifting ... class action costs and contingency fee awards, as well as through agreements by defendants to bear the costs of claims processing and plaintiffs counsel fees." Second, Schuck points out that "courts do not currently auction the right to represent the class, despite the enormous economic value of that right both to the lawyers and to the class members." The legislature could through "fiat" and effective regulation promote "efficient trading of claims." Finally, amid Americans' engrained resistance to bureaucracy, the court's fashioning of settlements through these and other devices turned the process of negotiating settlements into a judiciary-centered administrative system.[40]

Meanwhile, tort reform facilitated an organizational transformation among plaintiffs' law firms. By the 1980s, a limited number of national firms specialized in mass torts and class actions, employing economies of scale to win and manage multibillion-dollar damage awards, accrued over many years, in high-profile suits such as the asbestos litigation. Since 2000 the complex procedures established in these conspicuous cases proved adaptable to smaller plaintiffs' firms in Alabama, Mississippi, Texas, and other states, as a result of various elements of state-based tort reform. Pushed by business groups and the Republican Party, these provisions established binding arbitration and caps on damage awards. Previously, these smaller firms handled the simple disputes before juries, usually winning relatively modest damage awards. Tort reform, however, led these same plaintiffs firms increasingly to shift their contingency fee system to mass tort and class actions. This change in the market for legal services enabled plaintiffs firms to avoid binding arbitration or damage caps in favor of voluntary mediation as a means of reaching settlements. Ironically, although tort reform limited recovery in cases involving individuals, it channeled plaintiffs' litigation into much more costly mass tort and class actions.[41]

BMW v. *Gore* was at the nexus of these changes. Beginning in 1990, an Alabama plaintiffs' firm representing various individual purchasers of BMW

---

[40] Schuck, "Mass Torts," 367–72, quotes at 368, 372.
[41] Ibid.; and notes 5, 7, 8, 35, 36 above.

cars initiated thirty-five different cases in Alabama's and Georgia's courts. In two separate trials before different juries, Dr. Thomas Yates and Dr. Ira Gore, Jr. proved that the German company's affiliated distributor knowingly sold vehicles designated as new that had been repainted in spots owing to minor damage from acid rain. The evidence demonstrated that in Alabama and other states, BMW followed an intentional policy of nondisclosure when the spot-refinishing did not – according to the industry standards – diminish the value of luxury automobiles. Following state damage guidelines, a jury in the *Yates* case awarded compensatory damages of $4,600 and no punitive damages; in *Gore* the compensatory damages were $4,000, but the punitive damages awarded were $4 million. On appeal in 1993 the Alabama Supreme Court reduced Gore's award to $2 million. Claiming that $2 million in punitive damages was unreasonably excessive, BMW appealed to the United States Supreme Court. In 1995 the Court's 5 to 4 majority decided in favor of the company; the case then went back to the Alabama Supreme Court.[42]

The Alabama Supreme Court decided *Gore* in 1997. By that year the tort reform campaign resulted in the election of a court majority belonging to the Republican Party for the first time since Reconstruction. With one justice recusing himself because he directly targeted the *Gore* case during his election campaign, the court upheld an award of punitive damages totaling $50,000. The one justice who recused himself had portrayed *Gore* during the election as symptomatic of the whole tort process gone awry. Put simply, Republicans and their business supporters claimed that this entire process – reaching from the trial courts up to the Alabama Supreme Court – was too influenced by plaintiffs' lawyers who manipulated jurors' emotions in order to achieve economically inefficient ends.[43]

Still, the U.S. Supreme Court's alignment in the area of tort damages had been unpredictable amid conflicting pressures, cutting across the usual divide of the post-Clinton Rehnquist Court. The majority tended to include Justices John Paul Stevens, Sandra Day O'Connor, Anthony Kennedy, Stephen Breyer, and David Souter. The dissenting opinions generally came from Justice Antonin Scalia, joined by Justice Clarence Thomas, and Justice Ruth Bader Ginsberg joined by Chief Justice William Rehnquist. In *Gore*, the majority held that the $2 million punitive damage award violated

---

[42] *Yates v. BMW of North America, Inc.* 642 So.2d 937 (Ala.Civ.App. 1993); *BMW of North America, Inc. v. Ira Gore, Jr. Bayerische Motoren Mwerke, A. G. v. Ira Gore, Jr.* Supreme Court of Alabama 1993 Ala. Lexis 1146; *BMW of North America, Inc. v. Gore* 646 So.2d 619 (Ala. 1994); *BMW of North America, Inc. v. Gore* 517 U.S. 559 (1996); *BMW of North America, Inc. v. Gore* 701 So.2d 507 (Ala. 1997).

[43] *BMW of North America, Inc. v. Gore* 701 So.2d. 507 (Ala. 1997); and note 36.

the Fourteenth Amendment's due process clause because there was only modest "economic harm" and the award was unreasonable in relation to compensatory damages. The dissenters, however, asserted that the state's authorization of wide jury discretion was consistent with state authority within American federalism. A brief submitted by a group of law and economics scholars buttressed the dissenters' reasoning. Briefs from state and national trial lawyers organizations supported Gore; those favoring BMW unsurprisingly included the American Automobile Manufacturers Association, several national insurance corporations, the American Tort Reform Association, the Alabama Business Council, the Pharmaceutical Research and Manufacturers of America, the Product Liability Advisory Council, and the Washington Legal Foundation.[44]

The Court's requirement that plaintiffs show a sufficient degree of harm in order to justify punitive damages still permitted juries to make large awards. The prospect of such damages surely helps to explain Merck's decision in 2004 to cease marketing the painkiller Vioxx after a clinical trial demonstrated that its use increased stroke and heart attack risk. This incident has spawned much litigation. A Texas jury in one case awarded Carol Ernst $254 million in punitive damages, based on evidence that her husband's taking of the drug for under one year resulted in his death. Applying state law, an appeals court reduced the verdict to $26.1 million. Although Merck lost only two out of ten such cases that reached a jury, the firm's lawyers privately joined plaintiffs' attorneys to negotiate a settlement under pressure from judges in Louisiana, New Jersey, and California, who presided over the large majority of 27,000 state and federal Vioxx cases. On November 9, 2007, Merck and the plaintiffs announced a $4.85 billion settlement. In 2005, by contrast, certain experts had projected a possible $25 billion payout. Still, as Schuck suggested, judicial settlements had become sufficiently predictable to constitute a viable administrative process.[45]

IV. Outcomes Assessment

Since the 1970s, U.S. regulators generally eschewed command-and-control regulatory regimes. Instead, deregulation theories and practice displayed

[44] *BMW of North America, Inc.* v. *Gore* 517 U.S. 559–62, 562–597, 598–606, 607–14.

[45] Merck Agreement to Resolve U.S. Vioxx ® Product Liability Lawsuits, http://www .merck.com/newsroom/press_releases/corporate/2007_1109.html [11/15/2007]; Settlement Agreement Between Merck & Co., Inc. and Counsel on the signature Pages Hereto Dated As Of November 9, 2007 (960026907_47.DOCi); Alex Berenson, "Analysts See Merck Victory In Vioxx Deal," *The New York Times National,* Saturday, November 10, 2007, Front page, A12; Schuck, "Mass Torts," 345–91.

degrees of creativity that matched the aggressive technological, financial, and organizational innovation that has enabled American business to maintain global leadership against challenges from Europe and Asia. Deregulation, moreover, has often relied upon governmental supervision of various industry self-regulation programs, epitomized by the U.S. government's consent decree in the *Microsoft* case. Yet comparisons of global product standards enforcement indicates that in major U.S. consumer industries like drugs or computers, deregulation facilitated a burgeoning market for legal services in antitrust and mass tort private actions, all predicated on factual demonstration of corporate harm-causing conduct. Thus, a more effective policy of "self-regulation" would conform to Balleisen's schematics of "co-regulation" embracing standards setting, monitoring, and enforcement. Since the millennium, the administrative character of the more durable settlements in antitrust and tort class actions incorporate these three elements.[46]

Americans' faith in the adversarial process transcended their dismay regarding electoral politics and distrust of bureaucrats. Consistent with the economic historian Douglass North's recognition that ideology as much as institutions engendered contested legal rights was consistent with contemporary trial lawyers' routine appeals to community values before juries as a means of imposing accountability upon big business. Thus from the 1970s on, the incremental growth of procedural innovations opened state and federal courts to increasing numbers of groups whom judges certified as antitrust and mass tort class-action plaintiffs. "Tort Reform" imposed some limits on jury discretion in these private actions. Ironically, these limitations also strengthened the procedural incentives to pursue discovery until sufficient evidence of actionable misconduct emerged so that courts would encourage plaintiffs and defendants to reach settlements without a jury trial. Moreover, a divergence among states embracing and rejecting tort reform – as well as the Supreme Court's linking of punitive damages to economic and noneconomic harm – imposed new cost imperatives upon American business, not unlike those multinational corporations faced in global product markets. An example was the Archer Daniels Midland (ADM) litigations of the mid-1990s. Although within the U.S. domestic market ADM projected a "good corporate citizen" image, a federal court convicted it and foreign parties of an international criminal conspiracy to fix the worldwide price of lysine, an amino acid essential to the nutrition of animals and humans.

---

[46] Notes 8–13.

The whole litigation resulted in corporate executives from various nations being imprisoned, and fines totaling approximately $1 billion.[47]

The degree to which this adversarial process shaped antitrust outcomes reflected multiple contingencies. The Chicago inspired "new learning" that gained prominence during the 1970s and dominated under the Reagan Administration, focused primarily upon price competition. By the new millennium, however, reaction against assumptions that regulators could nearly always count on effective price competition over the long term achieved sufficient influence that a Republican appointee to the Federal Trade Commission "suggest[ed] that current antitrust doctrine needs to take larger account of nonprice competition, which ever way it cuts." Concerning mergers, he declared that "intangible efficiencies like quality of management or the compatibility of different corporate cultures may be more important than anything else, but we do not take formal account of them in our *Merger Guidelines*." This commissioner also recalled that a convicted business conspirator bound for jail could look upon anticompetitive conduct with cold detachment, acknowledging that "I learned never to talk prices with more than one other guy in the room." Thus, the commissioner observed, "many people in business still think antitrust offenses are more like speeding than stealing."[48]

The Federal Trade Commission (FTC) commissioner's recognition that certain business leaders risked antitrust violations as a cost of doing business resonated with Herbert Hovenkamp's conclusion that the government's problematic consent decree in *Microsoft* ultimately facilitated inefficiencies. After 2001, federal authorities rejected a structural or "break-up" remedy for proven antitrust violations, preferring a "conduct" remedy that purportedly did not hinder innovation, thereby supposedly ensuring lower consumer prices in the short term. Hovenkamp and other critics disputed such reasoning, favoring long-term gains achieved through adoption of "open-source software as an alternative to Microsoft products." Writing in 2005, he correctly predicted that foreign authorities such as the European Commission or South Korean Fair Trade Commission would order more stringent remedies "promoting increased use of open-source software code. If the United States is a laggard we may witness the emergence of competitive platform markets in foreign countries while we remain shackled to an

---

[47] Notes 4–8, 36, 37.
[48] Leary, "Bipartisan Legacy," 611, 613, quoted, and as quoted, 615. See also, Jon Leibowitz, "Building on the Muris and Pitofsky Years: Evolving Remedies from 'Time-Outs' to Civil Penalties (Not the Third Rail of Antitrust,)" 80 *Tulane Law Review*, No. 2 (December 2005), 595–604.

expensive, innovation-stifling monopoly. That could threaten the position of the United States as a leader in personal computer technology."[49]

Microsoft's victory also increased costs by fostering U.S. private actions and foreign litigation. The findings of fact provided a public record proving Microsoft's abusive conduct. Defense lawyers effectively overturned the break-up remedy based on those facts; with the change in party administration it also won the federal government's embrace of a conduct remedy upheld in federal as well as state court. None of these victories, however, immunized Microsoft from private actions initiated in California and other states. Indeed, the massive public record Microsoft accumulated in achieving its victories facilitated the California plaintiffs' numerous discovery motions, revealing a record of harmed direct and indirect consumers constituting violations under state law. This evidence was sufficiently strong, in turn, to convince plaintiff and defense counsel and the presiding judge that negotiating a mediated settlement was necessary to avoid a jury trial. A second attempt at mediation resulted in the record $1.1 billion settlement. Moreover, U.S. companies like Sun Microsystems used much the same evidence to initiate cases before foreign antitrust authorities; this evidence was part of the larger record those authorities used to decide against Microsoft.[50]

Antitrust and mass tort class actions increasingly have incorporated diverse values and policy concerns, especially through the settlement process. Even though tort reform circumscribed jury discretion to a certain extent, Americans' fundamental trust in the jury remained quite durable. Indeed, as the U.S. Supreme Court's dissenters in the *Gore* case affirmed, juries continue to reflect deeply held values of local autonomy, corporate accountability, and human worth transcending a single measure of economic harm. Of course, courts have formalized the process of reaching antitrust and mass tort settlements in class actions partially as a means of avoiding jury discretion. Negotiation of settlements nonetheless usually has proceeded under the expectation of what would be a likely damage award *if* the case reached the jury. The multiple values inherent in jury discretion thus either directly or indirectly shaped the settlement process in these private actions.[51]

Judge Young's assessment in *Relafen* case reflected the wider dispute over whether judicial intervention was "worth it." He listed the costs of the general litigation and the settlement's allocation of damages to direct and

---

[49] Hovenkamp, *Antitrust Enterprise*, 302, quotes at 303.
[50] Notes 17, 26, 27, 28, 29.
[51] Notes 23, 24, 40, 42.

indirect consumers. Young then addressed the critics' point that too often settlements were deeply flawed because defense and plaintiff's lawyers "rushed to settlement" without sufficiently calculating losses to future claimants. Notwithstanding certain "wrong" examples, Young declared, class-action litigation had matured sufficiently so that judges could address such criticisms if they chose to do so. The starting assumption was that given the absence of regulation, "viable claimants will recover nothing absent class action treatment." The fundamental question was then: "What percentage need be achieved for those deserving recovery to make the enormous transaction costs of class-action litigation worthwhile?" Even so, that calculus required determining contingency litigation costs of the plaintiffs' lawyers, which in turn depended on the complex process of identifying numerous direct and indirect consumers.[52]

In his opinions, Judge Young straightforwardly explained the relationship between attorneys' fees and his active role in shaping the settlement. The court set an early trial date, compelling both parties to fashion the issues and findings that could result in a motion for summary judgment concerning whether the evidence of SmithKline's wrongdoing was sufficient to continue. At the same time, a "brilliant voluntary mediation . . . not only brought the litigants to the table but ably framed the settlement agenda, all without slowing the march to trial." When after due consideration the judge dismissed the motion for summary judgment, the parties pursued mediation to settlement: "32.5% of viable consumer claims have been (or will be) paid and 12,790 consumers in states where no recovery is afforded due to the pro-business stance of their state legislatures will get something to warrant SmithKline receiving its nationwide litigation ban." The settlement further set aside funds to support nonprofit groups' consumer education programs and campaigns regarding "generic medicines." Young then explained the underlying force of attorneys' fees. The "plaintiffs' attorneys, while . . . assuming great risks, in the end achieved satisfactory recompense" in effect because "the corporate interests have paid for and achieved a nationwide litigation bar" rather than eschew the risk of misconduct.[53] In this instance, then, judicial enforcement of civil torts achieved multiple public policy goals.

---

[52] *In re* Relafen Antitrust Litigation 231 F.R.D. 52, 83, 84, 85, 86 (D. Mass. 2005).

[53] Ibid., 82–83, 84, 85. The judge's allocation of the award to fund nonprofit institutions' public service programs, like that apportioned to poorer California public schools, follows the *cy pres* equity doctrine whereby courts distribute unclaimed portions of a class-action judgment or settlement funds to a charity that will advance the interests of the class.

Taken by itself, the federal court's *Microsoft* decree took a very different and much narrower path, implementing the Chicago economics "mantra that antitrust is about protecting competition, not competitors." But Hovenkamp's "Harvard school" theory hypothesized a remedial order promoting broader computer network efficiencies, and transnational antitrust authorities enforced such efficiencies to foster several competitors over monopolist behavior. Similarly, judicial supervision of the adversarial settlement process in antitrust and mass tort class actions facilitated negotiated remedies that, in many cases, have compelled corporate managers to adjust their assessment of the costs of misconduct, focusing less on short-term advantage and more on long-term economic and noneconomic goals. In California's *Microsoft* case, for example, as much as two-thirds of the $1.1 billion settlement funded giving computers to materially poorer public schools. The *Relafen* settlement designated reasonable compensation for larger direct and smaller indirect purchasers; it also funded nonprofit organizations undertaking various consumer drug education programs. Although the Vioxx case was not a class-action settlement it employed those procedures to reduce liability while providing reasonable compensation to thousands of individuals.[54]

CONCLUSION

Although deregulation theories rejected command-and-control bureaucratic oversight, those theories diverged regarding the appropriate scope of government enforcement. Ironically, Chicago economics, public choice theories, and the "tort reform" movement reflected policy presumptions favoring government supervision of business self-regulation. Faith in self-regulation was evident in the government's endorsement of the consent decree essentially crafted by Microsoft or Merck's voluntary withdrawal from the market of Vioxx – knowing massive litigation would undoubtedly follow – after a clinical trial demonstrated its use increased risk of stroke and heart attack. On this view, antitrust or mass tort private actions were appropriate only to address exceptional market failure. By the 1990s the proliferation of private actions suggested that business self-regulation was not adequately addressing the complex incentives fostering misconduct, incentives rooted in global capital markets, and the multinational corporation's "multiple legal personality." The commentary discussed previously offers policy prescriptions derived from relative judicial autonomy that underscores

[54] Ibid.; Foer, "The Competition Counterweight," "Mantra" quote at 25; and note 49 above.

Eisner's variety of constitutive, promotional, and constraining regulatory tools available to policymakers including tort liability and antitrust instituting direct government oversight, monitoring, and enforcement actions.

This chapter suggests further research challenging the deregulation–public choice impulse Leight so well describes. Deregulation channeled aggrieved parties into private antitrust and tort litigation. Notwithstanding tort reform, these mass class actions confirmed Americans' durable faith in the adversarial process. The principle of "private attorneys general" driving many private actions, as Judge Young's careful accounting of cost and benefits in *Relafen* demonstrated, combines recognition of financial efficiencies and incentives with implementation of social-welfare programs and the need to preserve checks and balances. For these purposes, the plaintiffs' bar and contingency fee system are agents of constitutional legitimacy. Further research might determine whether American private actions could facilitate these public uses of market conduct (or misconduct). Indeed, consistent with O'Sullivan's discussion of corporate governance, in 2008 a federal appeals court upheld a shareholders' suit including thousands of plaintiffs against Merck for hiding the dangers of Vioxx. Such suits amid the growing international credit crisis may lead certain market interests themselves to advocate stronger constitutive "approval" regulation along lines Daniel Carpenter suggested. Further research targeting such private actions as complementary to Eisner's multiple regulatory regimes could fashion litigation strategies promoting financial efficiencies as well as social welfare goals.[55]

This proposed research should proceed within the wider Tobin Project agenda Balleisen develops. He reconstitutes "self-regulation" policies in terms of "regulatory pluralism" embracing standard setting, monitoring, and enforcement. Such a system, he warns, is costly. Research could examine whether the systemization of mature class-action litigation Judge Young profiles – which possesses key elements of Balleisen's schematics – may be less costly. Indeed, the 2008 Court of Appeals decision upholding shareholders' litigation against Merck suggests how the adversarial judicial process may be turned to significant fields of deregulation as fraudulent lending practices, securitization practices, or the importing of dangerous products. Another area worthy of research involves merger policies, including those the FTC is currently pursuing as well as conglomerate mergers that have not been examined sine the 1970s in the United States but are the subject of considerable activity now in Europe. These may be particularly useful fields of

---

[55] Notes 1, 4, 10; Anonymous Editor, "Court Reinstates Merck Vioxx Shareholder Lawsuit," *The Jere Beasley Report*, (Montgomery, Ala., October 2008), 1.8

research not only because harm to weaker consumer groups is an issue, but also because business groups often are arrayed against each other, thereby providing incentives for "coregulation" strategies that combine financial efficiencies with social welfare measures and checks and balances. Even so, such a research program undoubtedly would test the value of private actions and the relative judicial autonomy upon which they depend.[56]

---

[56] Ibid.; Edward Balleisen, "Prospects for Economic 'Self-Regulation' in the United States: An Historian's View from the early Twenty-First Century" in this volume; William E. Kovacic, "The Modern Evolution of U.S. Competition Policy Enforcement Norms," 71 *Antitrust Law Journal* No. 2 (2003), 377–478; William E. Kovacic, "Competition Policy in the European Union and the United States: Convergence or Divergence?" Barcelona, November 19–20, 2007 (unpublished, cited with author's permission); William E. Kovacic, "The Intellectual DNA of Modern U.S. Competition Law For Dominant Firm Conduct: The Chicago/Harvard Double Helix," 2007 No. 1 *Columbia Business Law Review* (2007), 1–81; and generally, David Skeel, *Icarus in the Boardroom The Fundamental Flaws in Corporate America* (Oxford University Press, New York, 2005), Lawrence E. Mitchell, *The Speculation Economy How Finance Triumphed Over Industry* (Berrett-Koehler Publishers, Inc. San Francisco, 2007); and Kara Scannell and Sudeep Reddy, "Greenspan Admits Errors To Hostile House Panel," *The Wall Street Journal*, Friday, October 24, 2008, front page and A16; Edmund L. Andrews, "Greenspan Concedes Flaws In Deregulatory Approach," *The New York Times*, Friday, October 24, 1008, B1 and B6.

## SIXTEEN

Markets in the Shadow of the State: An Appraisal of Deregulation and Implications for Future Research[1]

Marc Allen Eisner

From the late nineteenth century through the post-World War II era, the case for "economic" regulation – that is, policies that govern entry and exit, competitive practices, the size of economic units, or the prices that firms could charge – rested on a combination of two claims. First, concentrations of economic power enabled large corporations to impose monopoly prices on consumers, citizens, and potential competitors. As a result, governments had to fashion some means to hold corporations accountable and preserve competitive markets or, if this proved impossible for technical reasons, to guarantee results that would be sufficiently market-like. A second claim, most salient during the Great Depression, was that "ruinous" market competition could be the source of great instability. Left to their own devices, corporations would engage in price wars, creating destabilizing price fluctuations and bankruptcies. Regulations could inject stability by managing the conditions of competition. Regardless of the claim in question – claims that were, in practice, difficult to reconcile – policymakers asserted that regulations provided the only means of forcing higher levels of political accountability and thereby promoting the public interest.

Quite naturally, regulation became an issue of abiding interest to political scientists from the first legislative adoption of regulatory strategies to constrain the economic power of businesses. Research ranged across a host of issues including bureaucratic politics, the power of organizational life cycles, the challenges of exercising political control over regulatory bureaucracies, the relative power of competing principals, the representation of interests in the regulatory process, the dynamics of regulatory capture, the vagaries of regulatory federalism, and the quality of regulatory policies more generally.

---

[1] The author would like to thank Edward J. Balleisen and James A. Wooten for valuable comments on earlier versions of this paper.

From the 1950s onward, as shown in Jessica Leight's reassessment of public choice, much of this research portrayed prevailing regulatory techniques as inefficient or even counterproductive, helping to create the intellectual foundation for wide-ranging moves to deregulate markets in the 1970s, 1980s, and 1990s.

Although the politics surrounding the process of deregulation received a great deal of attention,[2] there has been something of a paucity of political science research on the impacts of deregulation. It was as if deregulation – commonly understood as the diminution of state control over the economy or the substitution of the market for the state – justified a transfer of analytical responsibilities to economics, the discipline best equipped to scrutinize markets. In many respects, deregulation has been a success. As predicted by advocates, it brought higher levels of competition and incentives for cost-saving innovations. Consumers were rewarded with lower prices and expanded opportunities for choice. Although deregulation imposed costs, it would be difficult to argue, on balance, that a wholesale return to the previous regime would be desirable. One might surmise – incorrectly – that although there remains some demand for research quantifying the magnitude of the benefits, three decades after the initiation of deregulation the time has come for another transfer of custody, this time from economists to historians.

Custody battles are always complicated and disputants are rarely satisfied with the results. The goal of this chapter is not to propose a simple solution. Indeed, it is a core argument of this chapter that the rather simple state–market dichotomy that has framed much of our thinking about deregulation has come at a high intellectual cost. The binary concepts of the state versus the market obscure the complex array of governance mechanisms that are often subsumed by the term "the market." One may, mistakenly, attribute market-like outcomes to interorganizational relations that have little in common with the stylized textbook portrayal of the market. More importantly, it has diverted attention from the role of public policy in constituting markets and shaping economic activity more generally. Law and public policy are as foundational in a deregulated setting as they were under regulation, even if the effects are different. If one frames deregulation in terms of the transfer of control from the government to the market, one may conclude that citizens can no longer reasonably entertain expectations of public accountability. Yet, if regulation *and* the collection of governance mechanisms that are employed as means of industrial self-regulation are

---

[2] See, for example, Martha Derthick and Paul J. Quirk, *The Politics of Deregulation* (Washington, D.C.: Brookings Institution, 1985).

both expressions of public policies and public institutions, it is not at all clear that the public sector can be absolved of its responsibility for ensuring that all significant economic actors remain accountable to wider political processes and broader social values.

This chapter proceeds in three steps. First, it briefly explores the empirical record regarding the performance of deregulation. Second, the chapter turns to the question of governance and argues that a broader appreciation of the role of law and the variety of governance mechanisms normally subsumed by the concept of the market can provide a richer understanding of the dynamics of deregulation. Third, it considers some of the implications for research. Once we unpack the concept of deregulation and place it in a larger institutional context, it becomes clear that much of the most important research on deregulation has yet to be done and this work cannot be delegated to any single discipline.

I. Bringing the Market Back In

The late 1960s and early 1970s brought mounting evidence that many of the agencies and policies inherited from the Progressive Era and the New Deal had failed to promote enduring regulatory aspirations. They were more often the causes of, rather than the solutions to, market failure. Critics may have offered different explanations, ascribing regulatory failure to poor institutional design, organizational life cycles, or mutually beneficial exchanges between profit-maximizing firms, vote-maximizing congressmen, and budget-maximizing bureaucrats. But consumer advocates, economists, and policy analysts arrived at something of a consensus that cut across ideological lines. When the stagflation of the 1970s opened a window of opportunity, deregulation moved rapidly forward in a host of industries – particularly within transportation, communications, the classic utilities of gas and electricity, and financial services. As a generalization, the federal government, and to a lesser extent the states, eliminated regulatory barriers to entry and exit, as well as administratively determined pricing, allowing for a greater play of competitive forces. In some cases, Congress eliminated well-established regulatory agencies altogether (e.g., the Interstate Commerce Commission, the Civil Aeronautics Board). Initially, deregulation elicited considerable skepticism. Critics anticipated numerous costs that would be associated with change, including sharp dislocations to local economies, declining wages in formerly regulated industries, and the reemergence of oligopoly and monopoly. After three decades of deregulation, it is no longer necessary to speculate.

Consider the case of commercial aviation. It provides the paradigmatic story of deregulation in which the removal of state controls unleashed market forces, enabling consumers to reap the benefits of expanded opportunities and lower prices. Under regulation, the Civil Aeronautics Board (CAB) managed the industry as a government-sponsored cartel. The CAB governed entry into the industry, assigned route authority, and regulated fares, all of which stymied price competition. When airlines competed, they did so on the basis of service, purchasing new aircraft and operating them at low load factors. The Airline Deregulation Act of 1978 eliminated regulatory barriers to entry and the administrative control of airfares, thereby introducing competition into an industry that had been regulated since its inception. Much as expected, the number of competitors per market increased and between 1978 and 2005, total passenger miles more than tripled from 188 billion to 584 billion. The elimination of administrative controls had the anticipated effects on rates: between 1980 and 2005, inflation-adjusted fares fell by almost 40 percent.[3]

The transition to a deregulated environment imposed some costs. Airlines discarded a number of unprofitable small markets. And although the entry of new carriers brought dramatic increases in employment, it also led to appreciable reductions in union membership.[4] Earnings – which were high under regulation – remained relatively stable in the immediate aftermath of deregulation, but fell significantly beginning in the latter 1980s. Of even greater concern, as the volume of air travel increased, the failure to expand the nation's major airports and upgrade the air traffic control system created problems of congestion while legacy carriers' control of gates in the hub-and-spoke system created barriers to entry and opportunities for predation. Nonetheless, with annual net benefits to travelers exceeding $20 billion, few would argue that a return to the old regulatory regime – even if possible – would be in the public interest.

The benefits of deregulation were not limited to airlines. As a generalization, deregulation brought greater efficiencies and cost reductions that were passed on to consumers in the form of lower prices. In the case of trucking – an inherently competitive industry with few natural barriers to

---

[3] U.S. Government Accountability Office, *Airline Deregulation: Reregulating the Airline Industry Would Likely Reverse Consumer Benefits and Not Save Airline Pensions.* (Washington, D.C.: Government Accountability Office, 2006) GAO 06–630, p. 11.

[4] James Peoples, "Deregulation and the Labor Market." *The Journal of Economic Perspectives* 12, 3 (1998): 116. Barry T. Hirsch and David A. Macpherson, "Earnings, Rents, and Competition in the Airline Labor Market." *Journal of Labor Economics* 18, 1 (January 2000): 125–55.

entry – deregulation allowed for relatively free entry and rate flexibility. In the first five years of deregulation, the number of motor carriers almost doubled. Even with growing safety regulations, competitive pressures led to substantial reductions in operating costs per vehicle mile and significant rate reductions both in the less-than-truckload and truckload trucking, along with single-digit rates of return. Shippers mostly passed along the resulting savings to consumers.[5] In the railroad industry, the government discontinued rigid rate structures and granted lines the freedom to customize rates and provide shippers with incentives to combine long-distance shipments. Deregulation also provided firms with the ability to consolidate and abandon or divest unprofitable lines, streamline the workforce and rail lines, introduce new technologies, and shift some costs to shippers (e.g., railcar ownership). Railroads realized significant productivity gains and increases in annual profits. At the same time, inflation-adjusted rates remain well below regulatory levels (although the magnitude of the reductions varies by commodity).[6]

Although the benefits of deregulation were clear, the instability induced by rapid policy change also imposed costs. New entrants, waves of consolidation, the introduction of new products and services, and the intensification of price competition had negative consequences for those who had benefited from regulations. The ramifications for labor in formerly regulated industries raised serious concerns.[7] Regulation generated rents for the

---

[5] John S. Ying and Theodore E. Keeler, "Pricing in a Deregulated Environment: The Motor Carrier Experience." *The RAND Journal of Economics* 22, 2. (Summer, 1991): 264–73. Clifford Winston, "U.S. Industry Adjustment to Economic Deregulation." *The Journal of Economic Perspectives* 12, 3. (Summer 1998): 89–110.

[6] John S. Ying, "The Inefficiency of Regulating a Competitive Industry: Productivity Gains in Trucking Following Reform." *The Review of Economics and Statistics* 72, 2 (May 1990): 191–201; U.S. Government Accountability Office, *Freight Railroads: Updated Information on Rates and Competition Issues.* (Washington, D.C.: Government Accountability Office, 2007). GAO-07–1245T. David E. Davis and Wesley W. Wilson, "Wages in Rail Markets: Deregulation, Mergers, and Changing Networks Characteristics." *Southern Economic Journal* 69, 4 (2003): 867.

[7] Peoples, "Deregulation and the Labor Market," 111–30. Some argue that deregulation provided a natural experiment for testing Gary Becker's thesis that firms in noncompetitive industries have the latitude to discriminate in employment decisions and that competition would provide the best remedy. Certainly, one might argue that some reductions in discrimination were a product of the Civil Rights Act and the enforcement efforts of the Equal Employment Opportunity Commission. Yet, the period in question would be difficult to characterize as one of vigorous enforcement. Although it might be impossible to fully disentangle the effects of employment regulations and deregulation, industries with higher levels of competition postderegulation witnessed improvements in wage equity and the racial composition of the workforce. See Gary Becker, *The Economics of Discrimination.* (Chicago: University of Chicago Press, 1957); James Peoples and Lisa Saunders, "Trucking

regulated firms. Because cost increases could be passed on to customers, unions in the regulated industries were able to secure wages that exceeded those received in other industries by some 14 percent.[8] In industries where deregulation brought waves of new entrants – trucking being the best example of an industry that moved toward full competition – unionization rates, the union premium, and wages more generally fell,[9] although weekly earnings (2006) remain 24 percent above industry averages.[10] In contrast, consider the railroads. Despite massive consolidation of lines (the number of firms fell from forty-one to twelve in the period 1978 to 1994) and a 60 percent reduction in industry employment, railroad labor remained highly unionized (74 percent) and realized real increases in compensation.[11] In telecommunications, pronounced declines in unionization rates (from 56 percent to 22 percent) occurred in the decades following the 1984 breakup of AT&T and the deregulation of long-distance services.[12] Yet, by 2006, the average weekly earnings of nonsupervisory workers in the industry were 66 percent above industry averages.[13]

The instability associated with deregulation was most evident in finance. A series of regulatory statutes enacted in the late 1920s and 1930s created a stable financial system through prohibitions on interstate banking and

Deregulation and the Black/White Wage Gap." *Industrial and Labor Relations Review* 47, 1 (October 1993): 23–35, Jacqueline Agesa and Anita Brown, "Regulation, Unionization, and Racial Wage Discrimination: An Analysis of the Trucking Industry." *American Journal of Economics and Sociology* 57, 3 (July 1998): 285–305, Sandra E. Black and Philip E. Strahan, "The Division of Spoils: Rent-Sharing and Discrimination in a Regulated Industry." *The American Economic Review* 91, 4 (September 2001): 814–31; and Jacqueline Agesa, "Deregulation and the Racial Composition of Airlines." *Journal of Policy Analysis and Management* 20, 2 (Spring 2001): 223–37.

[8] Wallace Hendricks, "Deregulation and Labor Earnings." *Journal of Labor Research* 15 (1994): 209–34.

[9] Dale L. Belman and Kristen A. Monaco, "The Effects of Deregulation, De-Unionization, Technology, and Human Capital on the Work and Work Lives of Truck Drivers." *Industrial and Labor Relations Review* 54, 2A (March 2001): 502–24. James M. MacDonald and Linda C. Cavalluzzo, "Railroad Deregulation: Pricing Reforms, Shipper Responses, and the Effects on Labor." *Industrial and Labor Relation Review 50, 1* (1996): 80–91.

[10] Bureau of Labor Statistics, U.S. Department of Labor, Career Guide to Industries, 2008–09 Edition, Truck Transportation and Warehousing, on the Internet at http://www.bls.gov/oco/cg/cgs021.htm (visited January 02, 2008).

[11] David E. Davis and Wesley W. Wilson, "Deregulation, Mergers, and Employment in the Railroad Industry." *Journal of Regulatory Economics* 15 (1999): 5–22. David E. Davis and Wesley W. Wilson, "Wages in Rail Markets: Deregulation, Mergers, and Changing Networks Characteristics." *Southern Economic Journal* 69, 4 (2003): 866.

[12] Peoples, "Deregulation and the Labor Market," 116.

[13] Bureau of Labor Statistics, U.S. Department of Labor, Career Guide to Industries, 2008–09 Edition, Telecommunications, on the Internet at http://www.bls.gov/oco/cg/cgs020.htm (visited January 02, 2008).

branching, the separation of commercial and investment banking, and via
Regulation Q, the imposition of interest rate caps and prohibitions on the
payment of interest on demand deposits. As inflation and interest rates
increased beginning in the mid-1960s, the rising costs of funds threatened
the industry. Congress responded by seeking to develop secondary markets for mortgages, with the partial privatization of the Federal National
Mortgage Association (Fannie Mae) in 1968, and the creation of the Federal Home Loan Mortgage Corporation (Freddie Mac) in 1970. In the late
1970s, as inflationary pressures mounted and nonbanks circumvented Regulation Q through the creation of money market funds, the pressure for
deregulation mounted. Over the course of the next several years, Regulation
Q was phased out and a series of deregulatory statutes eliminated key features of the New Deal regulatory regime. An industry once characterized by
heavy regulation and conservative practices quickly became, arguably, the
most dynamic sector of the economy, generating innovations that defied
the barriers imposed by public policy and geography.

Consider the instability in the market for mortgage finance. During the
1980s, many savings and loans sought to profit in the new regulatory environment by aggressively competing for funds and making unsound real
estate loans – a potent combination that ended in waves of thrift failures
and mounting public liabilities through federal deposit insurance. The S&L
crisis did little to stem deregulation, and financial institutions continued to
introduce a bewildering array of innovative debt instruments and derivatives. By the mid-1990s, as Elizabeth Warren's essay chronicles, lenders
began to provide loans to borrowers with weak credit histories, charging
higher interest rates but making the loans attractive through various means
(e.g., with low initial interest rates that convert to a higher adjustable rate
after two years). Such practices were arguably sustainable when there was a
real estate bubble and borrowers had the ability to refinance. However, with
the collapse of the housing market in 2007, the promise of an "ownership
society" was replaced by the reality of record foreclosures and new waves
of insolvencies. Indeed, as the bourgeoning subprime crisis evolved into a
general credit crisis, the failure of investment houses, commercial banks,
Fannie Mae and Freddie Mac, and the costs of the Emergency Economic Stabilization Act of 2008, may lead many lenders, borrowers, and policymakers
to look back longingly to a stable regulatory regime that no longer exists.[14]

---

[14] See Marc Allen Eisner, Jeff Worsham, and Evan J. Ringquist, *Contemporary Regulatory
Policy,* 2nd ed. (Boulder, Colo.: Lynne Rienner, 2006), Chapter 5, and Kristopher Gerardi,
Harvey S. Rosen, and Paul Willen, "Do Households Benefit from Financial Deregulation
and Innovation? The Case of the Mortgage Market." Federal Reserve Bank of Boston Public
Policy Discussion Paper 06–6, June 2006.

Despite the instability associated with deregulation and the financial collapse of 2008, many analysts would nonetheless characterize deregulation, on balance, as a success. Many would draw a simple lesson from the events of the past three decades: Policymakers decided to trust the market and the market acted much as predicted. Indeed, some would look to other policy areas – social welfare reform, the liberalization of trade policy, the introduction of pollution trading under the provisions of the Clean Air At of 1990 – and draw some broad overarching conclusions. Perhaps the rise of neoliberalism – much decried in some circles – was grounded less in ideology than in an empirically based appreciation of the marvels of the market relative to the heavy hand of the state. Perhaps future research should search out new areas where the market could be employed in lieu of the state. Before accepting this conclusion, it might be useful to determine whether the dominant story is, in fact, the most accurate portrayal of deregulation.

II. Placing "the Market" in Context

In a perceptive 1982 essay entitled "The Market as Prison," Charles E. Lindblom argued that the market "as an institution and as an intellectual concept ... seems to have imprisoned our thinking about politics and economics." Rather than seeing the market as a variable, analysts tend to "treat it as the fixed element around which policy must be fashioned."[15] Indeed, policy debates – particularly within political science and economics – are often grounded, explicitly or implicitly, within the conceptual confines of the state–market dichotomy. They are replete with discussions of the state's *intervention* in the market, and deregulation is portrayed as the cessation of such intervention. This conceptual bifurcation contributes to a failure to explore the variety of institutions subsumed by "the market" and the role that the state plays in creating the institutional foundations of economic activity. Although one can identify some exceptions – e.g., the black market, the trade in illicit drugs – as a generalization there are no markets without the state. Rather than existing as a self-constituting and self-regulating realm of human action, markets are in a real sense an expression – both intended and unintended – of public policies and institutions.

It may be useful to clarify the role of the state in economic activity by considering the various roles played by the law. Following Lauren B. Edelman and Mark C. Suchman, one can argue that the law creates a *constitutive* environment, a *facilitative* environment, and a *regulatory*

---

[15] Charles E. Lindblom, "The Market as Prison." *Journal of Politics* 44, 2 (May 1982): 332, 333.

environment within which economic organizations function.[16] In the constitutive environment, law "constructs and empowers various classes or organizational actors and delineates the relationships between them."[17] Law is an organic and inseparable part of corporations, financial institutions, trade associations, and labor unions – the basic building blocks of the economy. It defines pivotal elements of these entities (permanence beyond the life of individuals, members, or directors, limited liability, rules for governance) and sets parameters for the formal relationships among them – a point reinforced by Mary O'Sullivan's examination of American law relating to corporate governance.[18] In its facilitative capacity, the law provides a set of tools that organizations can draw on to accomplish their goals (e.g., litigation, alternative dispute resolution), in many cases creating legal procedures for changing the terms of competition. The state may also use law to shape economic activity through subsidies of various kinds (infrastructure provision, differential tax rates, preferential access to the public domain). As Monica Prasad reminds us in her analysis of taxes as a regulatory instrument, carbon taxes – if correctly designed – can simultaneously create incentives to move toward more environmentally acceptable substitutes and provide a stream of revenue to stimulate investments in alternative energy sources. In the regulatory environment, the law imposes rules that govern acceptable modes of competition and coordination (e.g., antitrust, regulatory rate-setting, information disclosure, and constraints on deception) and imposes penalties and incentives to shape corporate decision making and investment decisions (e.g., environmental and occupational safety and health regulations, debt and tort law). Moreover, regulation may stimulate corporate efforts to preempt further regulatory action through corporate or associational self-regulation. Environmental regulations, for example, have created powerful incentives for corporate adoption of environmental management systems and participation in trade association-based self-regulatory programs (e.g., Responsible Care in the chemical industry).[19]

Law and public policies define property rights, the organization of firms and economic organizations more generally, legally permissible transactions, and forms of competition and cooperation. The market, then, is not the absence of the state but in a real sense, a particular expression of public

[16] See Lauren B. Edelman and Mark C. Suchman, "The Legal Environments of Organizations." *Annual Review of Sociology* 23 (1997): 479–515.
[17] Ibid., 483.
[18] Richard Swedberg, "The Case for an Economic Sociology of Law." *Theory and Society* 32, 1 (February 2003): 4.
[19] See, for example, Marc Allen Eisner, *Governing the Environment: The Transformation of Environmental Regulation.* (Boulder, Colo.: Lynne Rienner, 2007), chapters 8–10.

authority. Any references to state *intervention* in the market ignore the basic fact that the market itself is constituted by public policy. Granted, the boundaries between the constitutive, facilitative, and regulatory environments may be somewhat porous, but the key point is unavoidable: Whether one is speaking of markets, government regulation or various forms of self-regulation, the institutional foundations are created by the state. And as Edward Balleisen demonstrates in his essay for this volume, even a single category like "self-regulation" can describe a great variety of institutional forms with very different consequences for performance.

Governance and the Market

Rather than considering "the market" in its broadest sense (i.e., as being synonymous with anything short of a command economy), much of the research in institutional political economy and economic sociology has been devoted to unpacking the complicated combination of governance mechanisms that are often subsumed by the term "the market" and understanding the ways in which laws shape the evolution of institutions that coordinate the behavior of economic actors in different industries and societies.[20] In this research, social scientists tend to see a "market" as one of many potential governance mechanisms available to economic actors. As governance mechanisms, markets are best understood as decentralized systems of exchange linking formally autonomous actors. The terms of exchange are not affected by the identity of the parties. Because each transaction is self-liquidating, markets do not provide a context for the long-term coordination of specific buyers and sellers. Markets tend to function most effectively when used to exchange standardized goods or commodities that involve little asset specificity.[21] Transaction-cost economics commonly suspends conditions of complete information, assuming that firms function in an uncertain environment under conditions of bounded rationality. When enterprises seek to make transactions in the market, the potential for slippage or opportunist

---

[20] See, for example, John L. Campbell, J. Rogers Hollingsworth, and Leon N. Lindberg, eds., *Governance of the American Economy.* (Cambridge: Cambridge University Press, 1991), J. Rogers Hollingsworth, Phillipe C. Schmitter, and Wolfgang Streeck, *Governing Capitalist Economies: Performance and Control of Economic Sectors.* (New York: Oxford University Press, 1994), J. Rogers Hollingsworth and Robert Boyer, *Contemporary Capitalism: The Embeddedness of Institutions.* (Cambridge: Cambridge University Press, 1997), and Neil Fligstein, *The Architecture of Markets: An Economic Sociology of Twenty-First Century Capitalist Societies.* (Princeton, N.J.: Princeton University Press, 2001).

[21] See Oliver E. Williamson, "The Economics of Organization: The Transaction Cost Approach." *The American Journal of Sociology* 87, 3 (1981): 558, and more generally, Oliver E. Williamson, *The Economic Institutions of Capitalism.* (New York: Free Press, 1985).

behavior may force the adoption of nonmarket governance mechanisms, particularly if the costs of executing and monitoring transactions become prohibitively high. As the complexity of the transaction increases or involves higher levels of asset specificity, for example, corporations will seek to reduce transaction costs by employing alternative governance mechanisms such as long-term contracting, joint ventures, or, at the extreme, integration.

One can challenge transaction cost economics on a number of grounds. By viewing various governance structures as a response to market failure, theorists assign the "market" a privileged status both as the starting point in the analysis of the evolution of governance and as something of a benchmark. After all, transaction cost economists often frame the search for nonmarket mechanisms as a response to market failure rather than as part of a larger dynamic of governance failure.[22] More important, for current purposes, is the fact that transaction-cost accounts focus primarily on issues of efficiency. Governance theorists recognize that the selection of governance mechanisms is imbued with power and involves important strategic considerations.[23] Economic actors seek to control the terms of exchange, thereby reducing their uncertainty and bringing greater stability to their environment.

Governance also extends beyond the relationships between the individual parties to a transaction. As we move from bilateral to multilateral settings, for example, actors can adopt a range of mechanisms including corporate interlocks, research and development alliances, trade associations, and standard-setting organizations. Given that institutions necessarily entail a distribution of power among economic actors that shapes the terms of economic exchange, one should not be surprised that the asymmetrical distributions of power in an industry may well find an expression in governance regimes that reinforce and reproduce the power of key economic actors. In the postderegulation airline industry, for example, industry governance was grounded in the control of gates at key airports – itself a legacy of route assignments under regulation (see the following).

Regulation and Governance

Although governance regimes can combine myriad mechanisms, I wish to concentrate here on the role of regulation and the state. Regulations can serve as one of many governance mechanisms, insofar as they provide institutional

---

[22] Greta R. Krippner, "The Elusive Market: Embeddedness and the Paradigm of Economic Sociology." *Theory and Society* 30, 6 (December 2001): 786.

[23] Campbell, Hollingsworth, and Lindberg, *Governance of the American Economy*, pp. 9–10.

means of coordinating corporate behavior over a range of activities. The classic example would be traditional economic regulation as exercised by the Civil Aeronautics Board or the Interstate Commerce Commission. Regulatory bureaucracies coordinated corporate pricing and investment decisions. They imposed a rigid process for determining rates, assigning markets, and dictating the products or services that could be offered by regulated firms. Firms did not have to develop their own mechanisms for allocating markets or coordinating pricing and investment because the state fulfilled this role. They did not have to respond to the challenge of new entrants because, in each case, regulatory barriers to entry allowed the industries to function as *de facto* cartels. Moreover, trade associations within the regulated industries remained relatively underdeveloped because government regulators largely preempted the need for industry-wide coordination.

Regulations can have a significant impact on the patterns and trajectories of industrial evolution, although the effects vary depending on the nature of the regulations in question. As one might suspect, classical economic regulation tended to promote isomorphism within an industry. As regulatory institutions controlled pricing and investment decisions, prevented new entry, and muted the impact of exogenous forces, regulated firms exhibited similar organizational forms and practices. Environmental regulations can also promote isomorphism to the extent that they dictate pollution control technologies. Yet, innovative regulatory designs such as cap-and-trade systems can provide firms with the flexibility to experiment and thus stimulate innovations. Similarly, active antitrust enforcement can promote divergent change, particularly if it constrains the role of trade associations in coordinating corporate decisions.[24]

Moving beyond the specific role of regulations, the state must occupy a privileged theoretical position in any discussion of political economy. As noted previously, law is constitutive for economic organizations and the market more generally. Public policies and institutions shape the organization of the firm, demarcate acceptable forms of competition and cooperation, and constrain managerial discretion over products and services, pricing, marketing, entry and exit, and technology. In so doing, the state creates the larger institutional structure that defines property rights and social relations, thereby shaping the distribution of power among economic actors.[25]

---

[24] Thomas D'Aunno, Melissa Succi, and Jeffrey A. Alexander, "The Role of Institutional and Market Forces in Divergent Organizational Change." *Administrative Science Quarterly* 45, 4. (December 2000): 679–703.

[25] See John L. Campbell and Leon N. Lindberg, "Property Rights and the Organization of Economic Activity by the State." *American Sociological Review* 55, 5 (October 1990): 634–47.

For any given temporal period, it usually creates a stable environment that can provide a cognitive lens through which economic actors can interpret and anticipate the behavior of others.[26] The state, in short, not only provides regulatory institutions that serve as governance mechanisms in their own right, but it defines the conditions under which enterprises, unions, and nonprofit organizations can select other governance mechanisms, and under which larger governance regimes can evolve.

Although governance regimes create greater stability and predictability, they are nonetheless subject to change. Such transformation may reflect endogenous pressures (e.g., evolving technologies, changing competitive pressures induced by new entrants). In other contexts, it emerges primarily in response to exogenous forces (e.g., rising foreign competition, changes in the supply chain, rising prices in global commodity markets). And yet, the options for change are not boundless. The existing governance regime and the distributions of power it represents create a situation of path dependency, constraining the magnitude, direction, and rapidity of change. In the context of governance transformation, the importance of deregulation becomes clear. Deregulation – and changes in public policies more generally – will necessarily force the transformation of governance regimes. The precise character of property rights shifts. New forms of competition and cooperation become available; others may disappear from the opportunity set. Changes in – or the elimination of – regulatory governance structures necessarily create new sources of uncertainty. New competitors may enter the industry; some will survive, some will fail, others will be acquired by established firms. Freed from regulatory restrictions, corporations may experiment with new products and services, or seek to package prevailing products and services in new bundles. Decisions over pricing, technology, and investment – once defined by policy or negotiated within the confines of public bureaucracies – now occur against a backdrop of assumptions that may not be entirely clear to industry actors attempting to make sense of a complex environment. Over time, economic actors will forge new governance mechanisms to coordinate behavior and manage uncertainty, thereby lending a new, if temporary, sense of stability to an industry. In sum, deregulation will become both an exogenous force in the story of industrial change and, along with the larger network of public policies and institutions, it will define the conditions under which industrial governance evolves.

[26] Neil Fligstein, "Markets as Politics: A Political-Cultural Approach to Market Institutions." *American Sociological Review* 61, 4 (August 1996): 664–65.

Airline Deregulation and Governance Transformation

Earlier in the chapter, I presented the now standard story of airline deregulation in skeletal form. Its key components were rather simple: Congress lifted public controls, engaging market forces, and, much as predicted, consumers, on the whole, enjoyed greater consumption options and lower prices. Let us return to the case of airlines and consider an alternative story through the lens of governance. Under deregulation, major carriers moved from point-to-point routes to hub-and-spoke systems. Hub-and-spoke systems offered a number of cost-based benefits. Smaller planes could be filled close to capacity to transport travelers to hubs; travel between hubs could occur in larger planes, now functioning close to capacity. Moreover, maintenance and other activities could be centralized in the hubs, thereby allowing for additional economies. Although efficiency was an important part of the story, hub airports were dominated by one or two airlines, thereby allowing airlines to control travel between locations. The allocation of hubs among legacy carriers was largely the inheritance of earlier route assignments under regulation. Moreover, under regulation, legacy carriers acquired exclusive-use gate leases and voice in the approval of subsequent expansions in return for their financing of airport revenue bonds. While the control over gates may have been relatively immaterial in a regulated setting, it created distinct barriers to entry in deregulated era.[27]

The state is partially responsible for determining the capacity of the industry and the terms of competition through its investment in airport expansion and its operation of the air traffic control system. Both have been cited by industry analysts as critical bottlenecks that have impacted industry performance.[28] Hypothetically, there is no reason that hubs could not be open to high levels of competition. Public financing of airport and gate expansion could address this critical bottleneck and make new gates available to entrants. Although the Federal Aviation Administration (FAA) directly funds some 21 percent of airport expansion through grants, the adequacy of the Airport and Airways Trust Fund – generated through a 7 percent tax on airline tickets – constitutes a major fiscal constraint. The

[27] Steven A. Morrison and Clifford Winston, "The Remaining Role for Government Policy in the Deregulated Airline Industry," in Sam Peltzman and Clifford Winston, eds., *Deregulation of Network Industries: What's Next?* (Washington, D.C.: AEI-Brookings Joint Center for Regulatory Studies, 2000): 4, 22.

[28] Robert W. Poole Jr., and Viggo Butler, "Airline Deregulation: The Unfinished Revolution." *Regulation* 22, 1 (1999): 44–51.

constraint was exacerbated by deregulation. Reduced fares – a product of deregulation – translated into a reduction in revenues. More importantly, the pressure on the fund was a product of the decision during the past decade to use it as a revenue source to cover the majority of the FAA's activities. To fund airport modernization and gate expansion, many large airport authorities continue to rely on their major airline tenants for finance, thereby extending earlier patterns of control. As Elizabeth Bailey observes: "Instead of using regulation to open competition, airport policy has locked in monopoly elements."[29]

Deregulation created powerful incentives for new entry into the industry, but price competition and the difficulties of negotiating long-term leases over gates quickly took their toll. Between the passage of the Airline Deregulation Act in 1978 and 1990, fifty-eight carriers started operation. By 2000, only one of the carriers – American West – was still in operation, and it merged with US Airways in 2005. Indeed, many of the new carriers merged with legacy carriers, particularly during the 1985–87 merger wave. In 1986, Continental merged with Eastern and People Express, Northwest merged with Republic, TWA merged with Ozark, and Delta merged with Western Airlines. The next year brought merges between American and Air Cal, and US Air purchased Pacific Southwest and Piedmont. As a result of the heavy merger activity and airline control of gates at hubs, by the late 1990s, a dominant carrier controlled between 70 and 91 percent of the market share at fifteen major airports, and between 50 and 70 percent at another six airports, leading attorneys general from twenty-five states to file comments in support of an antipredation rule at the Department of Transportation.[30]

As the airline industry has become more concentrated via consolidations, airlines have formed a variety of international and domestic alliances to coordinate their behavior and extend their networks. In international travel, alliances such as Star Alliance, Sky Team, and One World allow airlines to engage in joint marketing through reciprocal frequent flyer programs and the coordination of flight schedules. A domestic carrier can offer relatively seamless service to destinations that are outside of its network and do so at lower fares (e.g., through the elimination of double marginalization). Code-sharing alliances have been used with increasing frequency as a means of

---

[29] Elizabeth E. Bailey, "Aviation Policy: Past and Present." *Southern Economic Journal* 69, 1 (July 2002):17; U.S. Government Accountability Office, *Airline Deregulation*, p. 9.

[30] Mark A. Cooper, "Mergers Between Major Airlines: The Anti-competitive and Anti-consumer Effects of the Creation of a Private Cartel." Statement before the Subcommittee on Commerce, Trade and Consumer Protection, Committee on Energy and Commerce, United States House of Representatives, March 21, 2001, p. 3, appendix 1.

expanding airline networks without adding new planes or acquiring rights to gates. Under code sharing, a carrier (e.g., US Airways) forms an alliance with another carrier (e.g., United Airlines) and allows it to market and sell seats on some of its flights using its unique two-letter identification code. In the decade before deregulation, code sharing was largely used to link commuter airlines to the major carriers they serviced. Even if commuter lines did not become the formal subsidiaries of larger lines, they acted as parts of a vertically integrated organization. In the decades since deregulation, code sharing has proliferated even among major airlines.

Code sharing can serve some important functions when linking commuter and lines and major carriers (e.g., coordination of scheduling, baggage, and ticketing). By contrast, code sharing among major lines appears to provide a means by which alliance partners can augment their schedule frequency, thereby allowing them to collectively capture a larger share of the traffic from a given city. Moreover, since the same itinerary will appear for each alliance member, they can effectively crowd out the itineraries of nonalliance members (e.g., on computer screens). Where the networks of alliance members are complementary, code sharing may increase consumer opportunities. Where networks are overlapping, however, they may provide a means of exerting control and limiting competition. There are ongoing concerns, moreover, that commuter lines and some nonlegacy entrants may be at a competitive disadvantage if they are not integrated into an alliance.[31] Yet, the success of some low-fare, point-to-point providers (most notably, Southwest) and regional jet services suggest that the alliances and major airline dominance of slot allocations at major hubs have not fully stabilized the industry. In fact, one is witnessing the competition between firms that have adopted very different approaches to governance.

Thus far, our discussion has focused on changes in governance that affect the coordination of air carriers. Yet, public policy and institutions have also played a significant role in reshaping the relationship between legacy carriers and organized labor. Under regulation, stability in industrial relations was maintained through the collective action of the regulated carriers. Although the Air Transport Association was relatively weak – any coordinative functions it might have served were either legally prohibited or assumed by the

[31] See Committee for a Study of Competition in the U.S. Airline Industry, Transportation Research Board, National Research Council, *Entry and Competition in the U.S. Airline Industry: Issues and Opportunities.* (Washington, D.C.: National Academy Press, 1999), Chapter 4, and Harumito Ito and Darin Lee, "Domestic Code Sharing, Alliances, and Airfares in the U.S. Airline Industry." *Journal of Law and Economics* 50, 2 (May 2007): 355–80.

Civil Aeronautics Board (CAB) – the industry's Mutual Aid Pact created a mechanism by which carriers would make windfall payments to any struck carrier equal to the revenue increases attributable to a strike.[32] More importantly, airlines realized that the costs of wage and pension agreements could be passed on to consumers through the CAB's rate-setting formula and, thus, there were few incentives to engage in protracted labor conflicts. Following deregulation, legacy carriers, burdened by costly labor contracts and pension plans, found themselves at a disadvantage relative to new entrants. In the wake of the terrorist attacks of 2001, Congress decided to subsidize the burdened carriers through the creation of the Air Transportation Stabilization Board, which had the authority to issue $10 billion in loan guarantees.

The majority of the legacy carriers used the favorable political climate and economic leverage created by 9/11 and the recession to eliminate the defined-benefit pension liabilities that were a product of earlier patterns of industrial relations. Trans World Airlines (2001), US Airways (2002), United Airlines (2002), Northwest Airlines (2005), and Delta Air Lines (2005) sought bankruptcy protection to restructure their debt. In 2005, for example, United and US Airways canceled pensions that were underfunded by $12.3 billion. The Pension Benefit Guarantee Corporation (PBGC) – a government corporation – assumed a significant portion of these liabilities (some $8.9 billion) by guaranteeing payments that fell within the statutorily guaranteed maximum pension limit set by Congress. The costs of uninsured pensions – valued in the billions of dollars – were borne by workers.[33] The financial rescues carried a significant *quid pro quo*. As the PBGC provided a de facto subsidy worth billions of dollars, it acquired a major equity stake in the airline industry. For example, the Federal Bankruptcy Court in Chicago awarded the PBGC a 23.4 percent stake in United Airlines, making it the single largest investor in the airline.[34] It had previously been awarded a 7 percent stake in US Airways. Under regulation, the federal government served as a gatekeeper into the industry and oversaw rate-setting; control

---

[32] See Vernon M. Briggs, Jr., "The Mutual Aid Pact of the Airline Industry." *Industrial and Labor Relations Review* 19 (1965): 3–20.

[33] In the case of United, significantly higher levels of pension benefits were promised in 2002 (from $60 per month per week of service to $87 per month per week of service). After bankruptcy, the PBGC provided a level of support above the pension as it existed before 2002. Indeed, United's claim that it had to terminate the plan was grounded, in part, on its inability to meet its contribution obligations at the higher level of support. See James A. Wooten, "A Historical Perspective on the "Crisis" of Private Pensions." Presentation to the Industrial Relations Research Association 57th Annual Meeting, Allied Social Science Association Annual Convention, January 7, 2005.

[34] U.S. Government Accountability Office, *Airline Deregulation*, p. 4.

did not extend to the *direct* ownership of industry actors.[35] Ironically, under deregulation the state has assumed an ownership stake that few would have imagined to be one of the consequences of market-based reforms.

The story of deregulation as movement from the state to the market simply cannot capture the fascinating array of governance mechanisms that have evolved to coordinate behavior and manage uncertainties. The emergence of the hub-and-spoke system to reduce costs and limit competition, the *de facto* integration of commuter lines and major carriers, and the formation of international and domestic code-sharing alliances reveal an institutional structure that has little in common with the features of classical markets. The account of deregulation as the withdrawal of government controls, moreover, may veil the important role played by the state even in an era of deregulation. Decisions about levels of public investment, as well as the financing mechanisms for and distribution of those investments, can erode or extend the advantages of major carriers. Decisions about the status of existing contractual obligations between airlines and labor can have profound consequences for the evolution of industrial relations and the terms of competition. Although deregulation is the dominant story with respect to public policies addressing aviation, it has coincided with the introduction and progressive expansion of new environmental and, in the wake of September 11, safety regulations. As Eldad Ben-Yosef notes: "If economic regulation was pushed out one door, social regulation was invited welcomed in at another; one form of regulation has been substituted for another."[36]

We have, then, two competing stories of deregulation. One story pits the market – broadly conceived – against the state. In this narrative, the state dismantled regulatory barriers and eliminated regulatory rents; the mighty market then generated rapid growth in the industry, new entry, and significant reduction in the costs borne by consumers. In this account, analysts generally ascribe any remaining problems to a failure to extend the market to critical bottlenecks (e.g., air traffic control and airport capacity). The second story alternatively recounts how the elimination of regulatory governance mechanisms gave rise to a complicated set of responses on

---

[35] Aircraft manufacturers were also beneficiaries of regulation. It promoted the creation of overcapacity by forcing airlines to compete via service and creating a mechanism for recouping capital costs through the rate structure. Regulation served as an indirect industrial policy by subsidizing the large fixed investments and research expenses of manufacturers. See Eldad Ben-Yosef, *The Evolution of the US Airline Industry: Theory, Strategy and Policy.* (Dordrecht: Springer, 2005), 132.

[36] Ben-Yosef, *Evolution of the US Airline Industry*, 18–19.

the part of industry actors, including control over key resources, vertical integration, the forging of vertical and horizontal alliances – all of which emerged as a result of public policy decisions. Ultimately, forms of public financial support through which the state altered the terms of industrial relations led it to assume a major ownership stake in the very airlines that it used to regulate.

Although the case of airline deregulation is in many ways distinctive, deregulation in other industries has been similarly accompanied by fundamental changes in governance. In trucking – usually identified as the best example of a competitive industry – deregulation did, indeed, bring substantial increases in entry. But common carriage (spot markets for trucking) has been replaced increasingly by contract carriage (long-term contracting). Between 1987 and 1992, some $25 billion worth of transactions moved from sport markets to long-term contracts – an amount equivalent to the entire amount of transactions within the rail industry.[37] The trend away from markets and toward long-term contracts and vertical integration (via private carriage) has continued to this day. Unlike trucking, where entry was relatively easy, the railroads underwent a period of substantial consolidation in the wake of partial deregulation. The continuation of some regulatory oversight by the Surface Transportation Board (including some residual rate regulation) has led railroads to make decisions in the hope of avoiding maximum rate cases. This strategy, in turn, has slowed the pace of industry innovation.[38]

The technological stability in the railroad industry finds no greater contrast than in telecommunications. After antitrust policy partially deregulated the industry, waves of corporate consolidations combined with rapid technological innovation to transform the economic terrain. As a result, the compromises in the 1996 Telecommunications Act, which were struck by regional Bell companies seeking relief from the provisions of the AT&T decree and long-distance companies seeking access to existing networks, now seem antiquated. Heavy investments and new technological innovations – broadband, wireless communications, and Voice-over-Internet Protocol – blurred established regulatory distinctions and created a situation that, to date, seems to frustrate the search for a new governance regime.[39]

---

[37] Thomas N. Hubbard, "Governance Structure in the Deregulated Trucking Industry." Working Paper, October 1998.

[38] See Curtis Grimm and Clifford Winston, "Competition in the Deregulated Railroad Industry: Sources, Effects, and Policy Issues." In *Deregulation of Network Industries: What's Next?*, ed., Sam Peltzman and Clifford Winston (Washington, D.C.: AEI-Brookings Joint Center for Regulatory Studies, 2000).

[39] See Robert W. Crandall and Jerry A. Hausman, "Competition in U.S. Telecommunications Services: Effects of the 1996 Legislation." In *Deregulation of Network Industries: What's*

Here we have a clear contrast between an almost wholly deregulated industry that moved rapidly toward long-term contracting and vertical integration (trucking), a partially deregulated industry that consolidated and evolved within the confines of policies that impede technological innovation (railroads), and a partially deregulated industry in which innovations have proceeded so rapidly as to raise questions as to the viability of existing regulatory categories (telecommunications). Detailed analyses of events in each industry would reveal much about the dynamics of deregulation, particularly if grounded in a careful consideration of the ways in which the law in its constitutive, facilitative, and regulatory dimensions, constrained and directed the transformation of governance.

III. The Implications for Future Research

The overarching goal of this conference is to think critically and expansively about the future of research on regulation. It is only appropriate that this essay conclude with several implications for the study of deregulation. The implications and some compelling questions for future research are developed under five subheadings.

1. The Role of Regulation in the Evolution of Industrial Governance

The role of regulation in the evolution of industrial governance – a role that will depend largely on the kind of regulations in question – is an area ripe for future research. Economic regulations imposed bureaucratic procedures for the coordination of decisions involving pricing, investment, products and services, and the allocation of markets. One can hypothesize that because regulated firms had little discretion over organizational forms and practices, economic regulation promoted a convergence in organizational evolution. In contrast, regulatory policies that forced heightened competition (e.g., antitrust regulation) should have the opposite effect, promoting divergent organizational evolution. This divergence, when combined with legal prohibitions on various forms of cooperation and coordination, necessarily limit the role of trade associations, alliances, and corporate interlocks, frustrating the search for stable governance regimes.[40]

By virtue of the subject matter, this chapter has focused on economic regulation. Fascinating research is being conducted on social regulatory design

---

Next, ed., Sam Peltzman and Clifford Winston (Washington, D.C.: AEI-Brookings Joint Center for Regulatory Studies, 2000), and Eisner, Worsham, and Ringquist, *Contemporary Regulatory Policy*, Chapter 6.

[40] See D'Aunno, Succi, and Alexander, "The Role of Institutional and Market Forces in Divergent Organizational Change."

in environmental protection policy and the implications for self-regulation. Research has examined the development of corporate capacities for managing externalities (e.g., through the creation of environmental management systems), the impact of regulatory concerns on product design decisions (e.g., through life cycle analysis and design for environment), and the coordination of corporate behavior via supply-chain pressures (e.g., environmental conditions imposed through contracting), association-based self-regulation (e.g., trade association environmental codes and systems of certification), and international standards (e.g., the International Organization for Standardization's ISO 14000 series). The research has explored variations across industries, cross-nationally, and over time, and remains concerned with the extent to which regulatory design and enforcement patterns empower and constrain corporate environmental governance and self-regulation more generally.[41] Scholars interested in exploring self-regulation, moreover, would be well advised to explore the research agenda presented in the essay by Edward Balleisen. There is much work to be done to understand the general dynamics of self-regulation as a form of governance and whether the institutions of self-regulation exhibit life cycles comparable to those found in many public regulatory agencies.

2. The Role of Deregulation in Governance Transformation

If economic regulation constitutes a cornerstone of governance regimes, one should expect deregulation to create significant pressures for governance transformation. One should expect, moreover, that the resulting process of institutional reordering should be facilitated by regulation-induced convergent organizational evolution (i.e., firms that have adopted common organizational forms and practices should encounter fewer difficulties in coordinating pricing, production, and investment decisions). Several interesting research questions arise from this supposition. To the extent that regulation creates a situation of path dependency, will deregulated industries develop governance regimes that essentially replicate key features of those that were imposed in a regulatory setting? Insofar as this is the case,

---

[41] Impressive examples of current research on environmental governance include Cary Coglianese and Jennifer Nash, eds., *Regulating from the Inside: Can Environmental Management Systems Achieve Policy Goals?* (Washington, D.C.: Resources for the Future, 2001), Neil Gunningham, Robert A. Kagan, and Dorothy Thornton, *Shades of Green: Business, Regulation, and Environment* (Stanford: Stanford University Press, 2003), and Aseem Prakash and Matthew Potoski, *The Voluntary Environmentalists: Green Clubs, ISO 14001, and Voluntary Environmental Regulations* (Cambridge: Cambridge University Press, 2006).

will the industrial adjustment to deregulation subvert some of the goals or justifications for deregulation? If deregulation, for example, was promoted in the belief that government controls would be replaced by open market competition, will successful attempts to coordinate behavior undermine these expectations?

There is no reason to assume that a single governance regime will emerge to coordinate activities within an entire industry. In airlines, trucking, and telecommunications, deregulation did eliminate regulatory barriers, thereby permitting new entry into the industries. As suggested earlier, it would appear that in the airline industry, many legacy carriers constructed a governance regime that was grounded in route allocations inherited from regulation. New entrants, in contrast, have had to work outside of the hub-and-spoke system, offering point-to-point service. Outside of airlines, did the governance mechanisms adopted by new entrants differ in systematic ways from those adopted by firms that had evolved within a regulatory environment? How, if at all, did different decisions regarding governance result in different economic outcomes? Were new entrants more likely to employ new technologies or novel strategies? Were they more capable of adapting to change? Are governance decisions systematically related to firm survival or success in a deregulatory context? Drawing on Tony Freyer's essay in this volume, how have trends in antitrust and tort law shaped deregulatory outcomes and the success of new entrants relative to established industry actors?

Although virtually every deregulated industry would provide a useful context for exploring many of these issues, finance and telecommunications could prove particularly fruitful. In both industries, deregulation has been accompanied by, and shaped by, technological change and rapid and significant innovations. Old regulatory distinctions (e.g., various classes of financial intermediaries and products, computers vs. telephony) were quickly overwhelmed by the changes in question. Whereas large established firms made the transition to a deregulated environment, the combination of deregulation and technological dynamism created myriad opportunities for new entrants. In each case, one could explore whether there are differences in the governance decisions made by incumbents and new entrants and the extent to which these decisions affected technological dynamism and economic success or survival. Both industries underwent waves of consolidation; some firms prevailed in the new competitive environment, others failed. In the case of finance, the credit crisis was so profound as to lead proponents of deregulation to support various forms of reregulation and nationalization.

3. Placing Deregulation in a Regulatory Context

Political scientists and policy analysts routinely draw a sharp distinction between economic regulations and the new social regulations in the environment and occupational safety and health. Research on these two areas has been largely segregated such that studies of deregulation seldom take account of the growing impact of social regulations during the past several decades. As deregulation has moved forward, there has been something of a regulatory double movement via the introduction of new environmental, health, and safety regulations. Future research on deregulation could explore the ways in which social regulations have impinged on the process of deregulation.

Several questions automatically arise. Have the demands of complying with environmental regulations and the differential treatment of existing firms and new entrants (e.g., new source performance standards) created new regulatory barriers to entry to replace those eliminated under deregulation? Electricity deregulation would provide an interesting context for such an analysis. Thanks to the vagaries of New Source Review Process, well-established providers have been able to make piecemeal changes in their facilities without being forced to comply with the same environmental requirements applied to newly constructed plants. Several states have been experimenting with renewable portfolio standards requiring that some portion of a load-bearing entity's electricity be generated by renewable sources. To what extent have these requirements shaped competitive performance? Have various forms of association-based and standard-based self-regulation in the area of the environment[42] provided opportunities for firms to coordinate other activities? Several industries (e.g., chemicals, petroleum, and wood and paper industries) have developed systems of self-regulation employing various combinations of association codes, environmental management systems, peer review, reporting protocols, and external certification.[43] These self-regulatory activities will necessarily contribute to the coordination of decisions regarding technology, production processes, and product design.

---

[42] See Marc Allen Eisner, "Corporate Environmentalism, Regulatory Reform, and Self-Regulation: Toward Genuine Regulatory Reinvention in the United States." *Governance* 17, 2 (April 2004): 145–6.

[43] See, for example, Prakash and Potoski, *The Voluntary Environmentalists.*

4. The Costs of Deregulation and Governance Transformation

Although analyses of deregulation commonly focus on the benefits afforded consumers, governance transformation necessarily imposes costs. In some contexts, the costs may emerge through the competitive process. Formerly regulated firms may coordinate behavior to limit the success of new entrants, thereby causing increased rates of failure, higher prices, and lower levels of innovation than might otherwise be the case. In other instances, costs may be a direct inheritance from decisions made under regulation. In these cases, policymakers must consider whether to subsidize these costs and how otherwise to manage the social costs of adjustment. In electric utility deregulation, for example, utilities were permitted to pass on stranded costs from uncompleted nuclear plants through surcharges, creating a *de facto* subsidy that may have made it more difficult for alternative energy providers to offer energy at competitive prices. In the case of the airlines, bankruptcy provided the opportunity to eliminate fixed-benefit pension obligations. The costs of change were borne by the Pension Benefit Guarantee Corporation and, more importantly, by organized labor.

Nothing compelled this assignment of costs: they were a product of public policy decisions made by Congress (and in the case of airlines, the courts). Social scientists should explore the magnitude and nature of the costs of governance transformation in the aftermath of deregulation, as well as determine the extent to which these costs are directly attributable to deregulation or path-dependent governance decisions on the part of industry actors. Research should also examine the importance of public policy in mitigating adjustment costs and determining their distribution. To what extent did these decisions impact on the relative performance of new entrants and incumbent firms? To what extent did they alter established patterns of labor relations? What role did formerly regulated interests play in shaping these decisions?

The need to explore the costs of deregulation has never been greater. The partial deregulation of finance in general – and securitization, in particular – brought real benefits for the economy. Yet, rapid financial innovation, informational asymmetries, gaps in regulatory oversight, and general problems of moral hazard created a highly unstable environment prone to abuse. As the housing bubble burst, the subprime crisis rapidly evolved into a general financial crisis the reverberated around the globe. The financial collapse involved a complex combination of market failure and government failure. As Barry Eichengreen argues in his essay in this volume, policymakers and regulatory analysts face a number of important regulatory design questions that evade simple solutions. The precise features of a new financial regulatory regime are uncertain at this point. However, it is clear that the costs of managing the crisis will be unprecedented. The costs of this crisis – the bankruptcies and foreclosures, the liquidation of lifetime savings and retirement funds, the increases in unemployment and the slowing of growth, the mounting tax liabilities – will not be borne primarily by the firms that reaped the greatest benefits from deregulation.

5. The Issue of Political Accountability

There is a strong normative component to deregulation that has received scant attention. From the Progressive Era through the apogee of the New Deal state, regulation in the United States rested partly on the claim that public authority could compel heightened corporate accountability. Political scientists could usefully reevaluate regulation by exploring the way in which various interests were represented in the regulatory process, whether agencies were, in fact, responsive to the demands of political principles, and whether regulatory outcomes could be judged as being in the public interest. With the advent of deregulation and the enhanced role for "the market," scholarly attention turned resolutely to efficiency-based criteria, as academics developed a near obsessive focus on the impact that deregulation had on prices. If deregulation is understood as the movement from the state to the market, the privileged status of efficiency is defensible. If one adopts a richer conceptualization – as suggested previously – and recognizes the role that public policies and institutions play in making available various forms of coordination and cooperation and assigning the costs of adjustment, then the primacy of efficiency may be difficult to justify relative to competing political values. If one appreciates the role of the state in shaping the evolution of governance regimes, one must conclude that regulation and the responses to deregulation are both expressions of public authority. Expectations of political accountability – while certainly less pronounced than under traditional models of regulation – remain a central concern. Future research on deregulation should seek to develop the language and the evaluative criteria necessary to assess deregulation not as a single event but as an ongoing process that has been shaped by public policy and institutions.

In the last thirty years, then, there has been something of a transfer of custody in the study of deregulation. Political scientists, rather than assuming that they have discharged their professional duties once they have explained the political variables that produced deregulatory outcomes, have much work to do to understand the impact of the dense network of public policies and institutions and their role in economic evolution. Much of this work will take the form of fine-grained case studies of specific industries. Other research will call for comparisons across industries and on a cross-national basis. This investigation cannot be the sole province of any discipline but will demand interdisciplinary work. The considerable body of research in economic sociology and economic history is particularly important for understanding the institutional foundations and evolution of capitalism, a task that requires engagement with the broad historical context. The challenge, in the end, is to understand deregulation not solely as a historical event, but as part of a larger dynamic that continues to develop.

Conclusion

Toward a New Theory of Regulation:
A Research Agenda for the Future

Edward J. Balleisen and David A. Moss

As the global economy confronts its worst downturn since the Great Depression, and America begins to undertake some of the most ambitious policy initiatives since the New Deal, the country is urgently in need of fresh ideas about economic regulation. The financial crisis has shaken many core assumptions of the prevailing academic view of regulation, while popular attitudes toward government are shifting as well. Abundant evidence from polling data and the discussions surrounding the 2008 election suggest that a great many Americans want to see new approaches for addressing the nation's most pressing challenges. The deregulatory mindset that most influenced American policymakers over the last three decades seems to have given way to a new openness about the role of government in the market. What we need now are compelling conceptual frameworks for fashioning public policy that can encourage innovation while maintaining long-term financial stability, optimize both economic growth and shared prosperity, and strike sensible and cooperative balances between public and private governance.

The necessity for such innovative thinking motivated the conference that in turn gave rise to the essays in this volume. In February of 2008, as the true significance of the emerging global financial crisis was just becoming visible, more than fifty scholars and policymakers met for several days to begin the work of fashioning a new research agenda on regulation and the economic role of the state. Participants considered how to craft a more complete intellectual framework for regulatory design and decision making, one that recognizes the explanatory power of rational self-interest as a determinant of economic and political behavior while acknowledging the limits of the prevailing rational actor model.

Cognizant that intensifying critiques of the conventional wisdom had yet to solidify into a coherent alternative, we structured the conference to encourage debate about the most important open questions regarding regulatory policymaking. We additionally sought to prompt cross-fertilization between academic disciplines, bringing a variety of perspectives to bear on the most constructive roles of government and markets.

Our focus on identifying key questions that deserve attention was also motivated by a larger conviction – the belief that raising the right questions is central to scientific progress. In this vein, we borrowed from an institutional strategy developed by the medical pioneer Dr. Judah Folkman. In the main conference room of his Harvard laboratory, Dr. Folkman kept a special whiteboard on which he recorded the most important unanswered questions in the fields of vascular biology and cancer research. These were the questions that, if answered, had the potential to transform the practice of medicine and the lives of literally millions of patients. At weekly lab meetings, Dr. Folkman always encouraged – and sometimes implored – the dozens of scientists who worked with him to take up these big questions and to try to answer them, rather than focus solely on smaller questions that were safer but far less significant. Dr. Folkman's original question about whether (and how) tumors stimulated blood vessel growth ended up transforming scientific understanding of cancer and vascular biology, leading to new treatments (such as the cancer drug Avastin) and the promise of many more in the years ahead. Over the years, questions on the Folkman whiteboard launched wide-ranging research that eventually generated new treatments and potential treatments for diseases ranging from cancer to macular degeneration (which causes blindness) and even heart disease.

Although our focus is on social rather than medical conditions, we have adopted the research whiteboard as a strategy for identifying and disseminating fundamental – and potentially transformative – questions in our fields of study. In the months after the 2008 conference, and with additional input from participants, we developed a "whiteboard" of twenty-four questions that capture (and condense) the wide-ranging issues raised at the conference. Our "whiteboard" questions do not yet reflect the specificity of those on Dr. Folkman's whiteboard, but they nonetheless point in important directions. They are as follows:

I. Models of Economic and Political Behavior

Behavioral Research

1. How accurately does the standard rational actor model characterize economic and political behavior, both by individuals and by institutions?

2. What findings from behavioral economics, psychology, and cognitive science have the greatest relevance/implications for the study and practice of regulation?

General Interest vs. Particular Interests

3. What are the conditions under which regulatory policy serves the general interest ("common good") rather than narrow but influential special interests?
4. How influential is "capture theory" in the social sciences today, and where is it most/least influential?

II. Assessing Regulatory Outcomes

Patterns of Success and Failure

5. What characteristics or dynamics, if any, cut across cases of "successful" or "unsuccessful" regulation, either domestically or internationally?
6. What conditions enable effective regulatory institutions – whether public, quasi-public, or private – to remain so over time, warding off the tendency to become complacent or inflexible in the face of changing circumstances?
7. What relationships exist between types/modes/strategies of regulation, on the one hand, and broader distributional outcomes on the other?

Public Opinion

8. Is it true that Americans tend to hate the idea of regulation but greatly value specific regulatory policies and agencies (FDA, SEC, EPA, etc.)? If so, how do we explain this tension?
9. What types of regulatory purposes do Americans regard as most/least important? How do these views compare with other countries' experiences, and why?
10. What factors most determine the public credibility of a regulatory agency or strategy?

Techniques of Assessment

11. How can we best ascertain the effectiveness of particular regulatory policies, agencies, or broader regulatory strategies? To what extent

can sophisticated cost–benefit analysis lead to fair assessments of the impact of regulatory policies by public agencies, in the short, medium, and long terms?

12. In light of the growing reliance on mechanisms of private government, how can governments and other parties, such as NGOs, effectively monitor and evaluate self-regulation?

III. Information Flows and Regulatory Politics

Patterns of Regulatory Decision Making

13. How do individual lawmakers and regulators make decisions? Specifically: What motivates them, where do they get their information, how do they process it, and how do they decide which problems most require regulatory action? [Could ethnographic research be fruitfully employed to help address these questions?]

Role of Media, Crises/Scandals, and Social Movements

14. How does media coverage – and the networked public sphere – shape regulatory political decision making? How, if at all, does the current dynamic in America differ from that in previous generations, or from the situation in other countries?

15. What is/has been the role of crisis/scandal in prompting regulatory action or influencing regulatory choices?

16. How important have social movements been in creating political environments conducive to the adoption of major regulatory initiatives and in shaping the details of particular regulatory reforms?

Political Processes

17. What do we know, and what do we most need to know, about the role of political processes (veto points, formal and informal information flows, etc.) in aiding, forestalling, or channeling regulation?

18. How have prevailing rhetorical narratives about the broadest purposes of government, in different eras and societies, facilitated, blocked, or otherwise shaped regulatory policy?

Regulatory Arbitrage and Competition

19. Under what conditions do competitive dynamics across jurisdictions drive a regulatory "race to the bottom," or conversely, a "race to the top?"
20. How big of a problem is regulatory arbitrage? To what extent does it limit, or even eliminate, regulatory discretion?

IV. Regulatory Strategy and Design

21. What would a full taxonomy of regulatory strategies/methods (e.g., information disclosure, regulatory taxation, command and control, self-regulation) look like? In what contexts do these various approaches typically work well or poorly?
22. What is known, from within and outside the American context, about how best to improve or rebuild the capabilities of a regulatory agency?
23. What characteristics of a regulatory agency, either in the United States or elsewhere, render it most/least vulnerable to "capture" by narrow interest groups, both at its inception and over time?
24. How can the architects of regulatory institutions take advantage of inclinations toward social cooperation as well as more individualistic incentive structures?

Our hope is that this volume will spark sustained academic engagement with these questions and with the broad agenda of new research on regulation and regulatory decision making that inform them. Many of the questions suggest new directions and new opportunities for existing fields. Increased engagement with the regulatory state in the field of anthropology, for example, would greatly illuminate central questions of group behavior and institutional culture, within industries and even regulatory agencies. Similarly, behavioral researchers in economics and psychology could continue to deepen our understanding of individual decision making in a regulatory setting, in part by considering the significance of organizational culture as a context for individual action. For their part, historians can bring their skills to bear on the evolution of the modern regulatory state, at once drawing on the conceptual insights of other disciplines, and testing the salience of social science models against the historical record. Within every social science discipline, more attention to instances of regulatory success, rather than just failure, should yield a clearer understanding of best practices in regulatory design, offering means of improving the very legal and political structures in which regulatory decision making occurs. Mainstream economics, which has perhaps provided the most influential perspectives on regulation, could seek to synthesize budding research across all of these domains into new models of regulation and regulatory formation.

Our focus on big questions, we realize, cuts against some powerful trends within academic life. Though the movement toward increased specialization within the academy has ushered in an era of unprecedented refinement and rigor, the phenomenon has been a double-edged sword. Career advancement in the academy has increasingly required that scholars delve deeply into confined topics so that they can demonstrate full command of a particular domain of knowledge. Too often, scholars choose research topics based not so much on how important they might be, but on how tractable they are and how likely they are to provide a foundation for a successful academic career. Such pressures also lead scholars to shy away from producing synthetic overviews that reframe a field's core contributions and make those contributions more visible and accessible to nonspecialists. As a result, scholarly endeavors at times falter into narrowness, with conceptual sophistication trailing off into jargon and rigorous modeling descending into idealized worldviews.

We contend that a new boldness in the scope of social scientific engagement is both possible and more necessary than ever. Decades of research on global climate change have led to a powerful consensus on the urgency of the problem, moving policy reform from the margins to the mainstream. Earlier in the century, the "scientific" work on the hierarchical intelligence of the races, so long buttressing policies of segregation and eugenics, was systematically dismantled by Franz Boas and a small but highly influential cohort in the social sciences – work that furnished one pillar of the landmark *Brown v. Board* decision. Ultimately, first-rate academic research has the potential to shape the intellectual climate in which policymaking occurs, in many ways redrawing the very boundaries of the politically possible.

The unraveling of America's financial system, and the long process of reconstruction ahead, will require sacrifice and newfound exertion in a great many walks of American life. It is a critical moment for academics, and particularly social scientists, to rededicate themselves to the foundational purposes of scholarly work – the dual commitments to the scientific spirit of inquiry and the principle of framing research with a concern for the public good. It is a time when economists, sociologists, political scientists, historians, anthropologists, and legal scholars should strive to touch upon common grounds of their disciplines and forge new collaborations. It is a time to reach outward, toward audiences beyond traditional scholarly boundaries. These include the public, which is so urgently awaiting answers, and the legislators and government officials who must grapple with our many complicated and vexing socioeconomic dilemmas.

The current financial crisis presents an opportunity to rethink old assumptions about economic and governmental institutions, to pursue the implications of new insights about economic behavior and social motivation, and to pay far greater attention to the contexts and strategies that have generated both governmental success and failure. We may well stand at a unique historical moment with regard not only to regulatory policy, but to America's place in the world, to the structuring of economic systems, and to the relationships between the nation–state and international mechanisms of governance.

We are convinced that developing a more comprehensive view of the economic role of the state, a view equal to the many challenges we confront, will require scholars – especially younger scholars – to continue pushing disciplinary boundaries and creating connections between seemingly disparate perspectives or approaches. Questions of regulatory policy are now central to our future economic health, and the answers from various methods and disciplines will be equally critical in forging new approaches to political economy. The essays that comprise this volume and the research questions – or "whiteboard" – to which they gave rise are meant ultimately as guideposts, pointing researchers in a host of promising new directions. Amid such turbulent times, and with the stakes so high, American social scientists can make an important contribution and a real difference.

Index

Abrams, Burton A., 219, 227
accountability, research need on, 50
Adams, Henry C., 98–100, 100n11, 101n11, 112, 116, 125, 137
administered prices, 116–117
Administrative Procedures Act (1946), 457
advertising, deceptive, 457
agricultural program payments, 197, 197*t*, 198
agriculture mortgage boom, 423n12
aircraft manufacturers, 529n35
airline deregulation, 514–515
  code sharing alliances, 526–527
  governance transformation and, 525–531, 533
  mergers, 526
  move to hub-and-spoke systems, 525–531
  organized labor and, 527–529
Airline Deregulation Act of 1978, 515
Airport and Airways Trust Fund, 525–526
air traffic controllers union, 133
Air Transport Association, 527–528
Air Transportation Stabilization Board, 528
Akerlof, George A., 176–178
alcohol tax, 372–373
altruism, 311
  reciprocal, 306
Amaranth Advisors, 436–437
American Association for Labor Legislation, 121
American Association of Retired Persons (AARP), 275n77, 276n77
American Chemistry Council, 462
American Federation of Labor, 109

American Federation of Labor and Congress of Industrial Organizations (AFL-CIO), 274–275, 276–277
American Medical Association (AMA), opposition to Medicare, 267–269
American Medical Political Action Committee (AMPAC), 273
American Petroleum Industry (API), 282n97
American Medical Association (AMA), opposition to Medicare, 267–269
Anderson-King bill, 269, 270–272
Angrist, 54n3
anti-gouging legislation, 297
antitrust and tort
  adversarial judicial process, 485–490
  Alcoa case, 490–491
  antitrust government actions, 490–492
  antitrust private actions, 492–493
  behavioral incentives affect on, 28
  Chicago School approach to, 492, 506, 508–509
  cy pres equity doctrine, 508n53
  direct purchasers, 487
  fault principle, 486
  follow-on cases, 499
  foreign subsidiaries, 487–488
  Harvard School approach to, 492, 509
  Illinois Brick Co. v. Illinois, 487, 494
  indirect purchasers, 487, 493, 494
  judicial autonomy *vs.* command-control regulation and deregulation, 488–489
  mass tort litigation, 499–504
    Asbestos case, 501
    black lung sufferers, 501

545